This book provides a thorough introduction to African languages and linguistics, covering typology, structure and sociolinguistics. The twelve chapters are written by a team of eminent Africanists, and the topics presented include the four major language groupings (Niger-Congo, Nilo-Saharan, Afroasiatic and Khoisan), the core areas of modern theoretical linguistics (phonology, morphology, syntax), typology, sociolinguistics, comparative linguistics, and language, history and society. Basic concepts and terminology are explained for under-graduates and non-specialist readers, but each chapter also provides an overview of the state of the art in its field, and as such will also be referred to by more advanced students and general linguists. This is the first book to bring this range of material together in accessible form for anyone wishing to learn more about this challenging and fascinating field.

BERND HEINE is Professor of African Studies at the University of Cologne, and President of the Permanent Committee of World Congresses of African Linguistics. His publications include *Status and Use of African Lingua Francas* (1971), *A Typology of African Languages Based on the Order of Meaningful Elements* (1976), *Sprache, Gesellschaft und Kommunikation in Afrika* (1977), *Possession* (1997) and, as co-editor, *Die Sprachen Africas* (1981).

DEREK NURSE is Professor of Linguistics at the Memorial University of Newfoundland, Canada and works on comparative Bantu, historical linguistics, language contact, and tense and aspect systems. His book publications include *Language and History on Kilimanjaro, the Taita Hills, and the Pare Mountains* (1979), and *The Swahili* (with T. Spear, 1985), *Swahili and Sabaki: A Linguistic History* (with T. J. Hinnebusch, 1993), and *Inheritance, Contact, and Change in Two East African Languages* (1999).

African Languages
An Introduction

EDITED BY
BERND HEINE
Universität zu Köln

AND
DEREK NURSE
Memorial University of Newfoundland

PUBLISHED BY THE PRESS SYNDICATE OF THE UNIVERSITY OF CAMBRIDGE
The Pitt Building, Trumpington Street, Cambridge, United Kingdom

CAMBRIDGE UNIVERSITY PRESS
The Edinburgh Building, Cambridge CB2 2RU, UK   www.cup.cam.ac.uk
40 West 20th Street, New York, NY 10011–4211, USA   www.cup.org
10 Stamford Road, Oakleigh, Melbourne 3166, Australia
Ruiz de Alarcón 13, 28014 Madrid, Spain

First published 2000

Printed in the United Kingdom at the University Press, Cambridge

Typeface Times 9/13   [GC]

A catalogue record for this book is available from the British Library

Library of Congress Cataloguing in Publication data

African languages:an introduction / edited by Bernd Heine (Universität zu Köhn) and
Derek Nurse (Memorial University of Newfoundland).
     p.   cm.
Includes bibliographical references and index.
ISBN 0 521 66178 1 (hardback)
1. African languages.   I. Heine, Bernd, 1939–   II. Nurse, Derek.
PL8005 .A24 2000
496 – dc21   99-056881

ISBN 0 521 66178 1 hardback
ISBN 0 521 66629 5 paperback

CONTENTS

List of maps   *page* vi

Notes on contributors   vii

1   Introduction, BERND HEINE and DEREK NURSE   1

2   Niger-Congo, KAY WILLIAMSON and ROGER BLENCH   11

3   Nilo-Saharan, LIONEL M. BENDER   43

4   Afroasiatic, RICHARD J. HAYWARD   74

5   Khoisan, TOM GÜLDEMANN and RAINER VOSSEN   99

6   Phonology, G. N. CLEMENTS   123

7   Morphology, GERRIT J. DIMMENDAAL   161

8   Syntax, JOHN R. WATTERS   194

9   Typology, DENIS CREISSELS   231

10   Comparative linguistics, PAUL NEWMAN   259

11   Language and history, CHRISTOPHER EHRET   272

12   Language and society, H. EKKEHARD WOLFF   298

References   348

Index of authors   374

Index of languages   379

Index of subjects   389

MAPS

1.1	African phyla and major languages	*page* 2
2.2	Niger-Congo	12
3.3	Nilo-Saharan	44
4.4	Afroasiatic	75
5.5	South African Khoisan (pre-colonial situation)	100
9.6	Basic word order types (according to Heine 1976a)	251
12.7	The main African language-based linguae francae	325
12.8	Pidgins and creoles (based on Crystal 1997)	328
12.9	Dominant non-African languages	343

CONTRIBUTORS

LIONEL BENDER is Professor Emeritus at Southern Illinois University, USA. His main research interests are language classification and history in Africa, especially the Nilo-Saharan and Afroasiatic phyla and the Omotic family. His recent publications include *The Nilo-Saharan Languages: A Comparative Essay* (1996) and *Comparative Morphology of the Omotic Languages* (2000).

ROGER BLENCH is based at the Overseas Development Institute, London, England. He works on Benue-Congo languages, historical languages, language and prehistory and ethnoscience. His recent publications include R. M. Blench and M. Spriggs (eds.), *Archaeology and Language*, volumes I–IV (1997–9), and R. M. Blench and K. MacDonald (eds.), *Origin and Development of African Livestock* (1999).

G. N. CLEMENTS is *Directeur de Recherche* at the CNRS, Institut de Phonétique, Paris, France, and teaches regularly at several universities in Paris. He has previously held positions at Harvard University (1979–82) and Cornell University (1982–92), as well as a number of visiting professorships in the US, Europe and Africa. His specialisms are phonetics, and the phonology of African languages. His publications include *Problem Book in Phonology* (with Morris Hallé, 1983) and *Autosegmental Studies in Bantu Tone* (with John Goldsmith, 1984).

DENIS CREISSELS is Professor at the Université Lumière, Lyon, France, working on the typology of African languages and on Tswana. He is the author of *Les constructions dites 'possessives', étude de linguistique générale et de typologie linguistique* (1979).

GERRIT DIMMENDAAL is Professor at the Universität zu Köln, Germany. He specialises in the area of Nilotic and Surmic languages and comparative African linguistics and has published *The Turkana Language* (1983) and *Aspects du basaa* (1988).

CHRISTOPHER EHRET is Professor of History at the University of California, Los Angeles, USA, working on African history, and historical linguistics in Africa. His numerous publications include *Reconstructing Proto-Afroasiatic (Proto-Afrasian): Vowels, Tone, Consonants, and Vocabulary* (1995) and *An African Classical Age: Eastern and Southern Africa in World History from 1000 BC to AD 400* (1998).

TOM GÜLDEMANN teaches at the Universität Leipzig, Germany. He specialises in Bantu, Khoisan linguistics, grammaticalisation and language typology. His publications include *Verbalmorphologie und Nebenprädikationen im Bantu* (1996) and *San Languages for Education* (1998).

RICHARD HAYWARD is Professor at the School of Oriental and African Studies, University of London, England, and is best known for his work on the languages of the Horn of Africa, including *The Arbore Language: A First Investigation* (1984) and, as editor, *Omotic Language Studies* (1990).

BERND HEINE is Professor at the Universität zu Köln, Germany, and works on comparative African linguistics, grammaticalisation theory and Khoisan languages. His recent books include *Possession: Cognitive Sources, Forces, and Grammaticalization* (1997) and *Cognitive Foundations of Grammar* (1997).

PAUL NEWMAN is Professor of Linguistics at Indiana University, USA, where he is also Director of the West African Languages Institute. He is a specialist in Hausa, Chadic linguistics, ideophones and field methods and has published books including *Nominal and Verbal Plurality in Chadic* (1990) and *The Hausa Language: An Encyclopedic Reference Grammar* (2000).

DEREK NURSE is Professor at the Memorial University of Newfoundland, Canada, and works on comparative Bantu, historical linguistics, language contact, and tense and aspect systems. His book publications include *Swahili and Sabaki: A Linguistic History* (with T. J. Hinnebusch, 1993) and *Inheritance, Contact, and Change in Two East African Languages* (1999).

RAINER VOSSEN is Professor at the Universität Frankfurt, Germany. He has published widely on Khoisan languages and comparative Nilotic linguistics and is the author of *Die Khoe-Sprachen: Ein Beitrag zur Erforschung der Sprachgeschichte Afrikas* (1997). He is also the editor of the series *Quellen zur Khoisan-Forschung*.

JOHN WATTERS works at the Summer Institute of Linguistics, Nairobi, Kenya and has been the Africa Area Director of SIL since 1989, having previously taught linguistics at UCLA and directed the SIL linguistics programme based at the University of Oregon. His specialism is the description of African languages, and he is the author of several journal articles and of the Bantoid overview in J. Bendor-Samuel's *Niger-Congo* (1989).

KAY WILLIAMSON is Professor of Linguistics at the University of Port Harcourt, Nigeria, and a specialist in Nigerian languages and comparative Niger-Congo. She has published articles in a number of journals, and also wrote the Niger-Congo overview in J. Bendor-Samuel's *Niger-Congo* (1989).

H. EKKEHARD WOLFF is Professor at the Universität Leipzig, Germany, working in the field of Chadic linguistics, Hausa and sociolinguistics. He is the author of *A Grammar of the Lamang Language* (1983) and of *Referenzgrammatik des Hausa* (1993).

1

Introduction

BERND HEINE AND DEREK NURSE

1.1   **How many African languages are there?**

We are sometimes asked 'Do you speak African?', as if there were but a single African language. A recent authority (Grimes (ed.) 1996) puts the number of African languages at 2,035: this number is not fixed, as some languages are still being 'discovered', while others with few speakers are being eliminated. Excluding languages introduced over the past two millennia or so, such as Arabic, Malagasy, Afrikaans, English, French, Spanish, and Portuguese, this figure of just over 2,000 breaks down into four large phyla: Niger-Congo 1,436 languages (including the Bantu family, which itself is often said to have 500 members), Afroasiatic 371, Nilo-Saharan 196 and Khoisan 35. A few Afroasiatic languages are spoken exclusively outside Africa, in the Middle East, which would reduce the figure for Africa somewhat. If we believe this figure of 2,000, then it represents nearly one-third of the world's languages.

But in fact it is an estimate which should be treated with caution, because it depends crucially on where one draws the line between language and dialect. A language is often defined by some combination of: having national status; being written; being the standard form of a range of speech varieties; not being intelligible to speakers of other 'languages'; and having a relatively large number of native speakers. By contrast, dialects are said to be local, not written, not the standard form, be mutually intelligible, and to have fewer speakers. In Africa, and also often outside Africa, such definitions frequently fail. There are of course many cases where what are generally considered 'languages' or even two or more varieties of what is usually considered the same language are not mutually intelligible, especially across language families. In many cases some agreed standard form is used as a national or official language, is the only officially condoned written

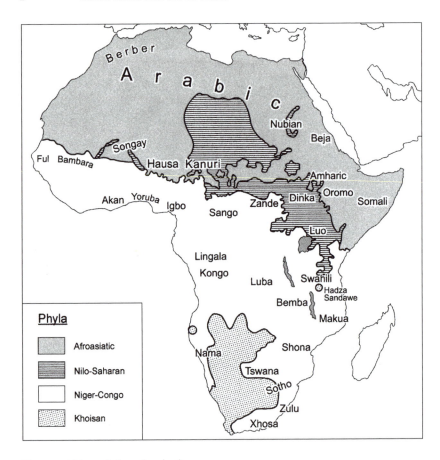

Map 1.1. African phyla and major languages.

form, and is used by millions of people, either as first or second language. In what follows, we sometimes use 'variety' to avoid confusion between language and dialect.

These conditions are not met in many other places in Africa. A common situation is a string of similar varieties, in which the speakers of variety A understand those of adjacent B, who in turn understand those of C, and so on, but the speakers of A do not understand speakers of the variety at the other end of the continuum, or even those part way along. Even if we can define 'understand', where is the divide between language and dialect in this situation? While some African countries, such as those in North Africa, or Somalia, harbour few languages, many others have many language communities within their boundaries: Nigeria is said to have nearly 500, Cameroon nearly 300, and three other countries over 100. This proliferation introduces the practical problem of how to communicate across the nation, often solved by using an ex-colonial language, or Arabic, as the national language, which then reduces all other languages, some spoken by millions of people, often with a rich written literature, to the status of local 'dialects'. In other cases, no variety, or several varieties, are written. In yet other cases, speakers are not agreed on a standard variety, or on what ought to be a or the national language.

Linguists who try to deal with this welter of languages are often referred to as 'splitters' or 'lumpers'. Splitters tend to regard 'varieties' as distinct languages, thus boosting the 2,000, while lumpers treat varieties as just dialects, reducing the number.

1.2   The intended audience of this book

Anyone producing a book about this mass of languages has inevitably to make certain choices. There are older introductions to African languages in English (Berry and Greenberg 1971, Welmers 1973, Gregersen 1977), there are volumes that deal with some but not all African languages (Bender 1997, Bendor-Samuel 1989, Ehret 1995, Heine 1970, 1976a), there are books about African languages in languages other than English (Alexandre 1967, Heine *et al.* 1981). But there is no up-to-date, reasonably comprehensive, basic introduction to African languages in English. It is a gap we have heard mentioned by many, both colleagues and students, and it is the gap which this book aims to fill. We want to produce a book that will above all be accessible to undergraduates worldwide, and especially in Africa, but also elsewhere in the world. At the same time we hope it will be of interest to other audiences, such as general linguists or cognitivists who know little of the African situation, and to Africans or Africanists who are not linguists, but are knowledgeable in the history, culture or anthropology of Africa.

Our primary target, 'undergraduates worldwide', is an amorphous bunch of readers. African students are relatively easy to characterise as they acquire one or more African languages well as they grow up, and come to linguistics later, during their university studies. Outside Africa, undergraduates learn African languages as adults but while some learn an African language before studying linguistics, for others it is the other way round. So 'undergraduates' approach this book with different mixes of languages and linguistics. They will also come with differing linguistic approaches. Some will come with 'traditional' theoretical assumptions, others will come with older versions of 'modern' linguistics (often reflecting the unavailability of up-to-date texts in much of Africa), and others again will come equipped with different versions of contemporary theory.

1.3   **Contents of the volume**

To deal with this range of background and interest, we have in practice divided the book in three. The first four chapters deal with the four African phyla, Niger-Congo (Williamson and Blench), Nilo-Saharan (Bender), Afroasiatic (Hayward), and Khoisan (Güldemann and Vossen). Readers should understand that space limitations mean that no language receives more than a few words of coverage, and many are not mentioned at all (for a complete list, see Grimes (ed.) 1996). Our aim is the general, not the specific. A further four chapters (chs. 6–9) examine certain linguistic components of African languages. Our aim is to produce a text that is linguistically informed but not about linguistic theory. After discussion, we narrowed our range of topics to: phonology (including phonetics; Clements), morphology (Dimmendaal), syntax (Watters), and typology (Creissels). A third part consists of two chapters (chs. 10 and 11), on comparative linguistics (Newman) and language and history (Ehret). These are included because, while the proportion of professional linguists interested in this topic has diminished over the past quarter-century, we felt our audience would certainly be interested in it, and also because linguistic findings have contributed significantly to our understanding of recent African history. Finally, no book of this type would be complete without reference to language in its social setting, hence the chapter 'Language and Society'. While we recognise the limitations of this range of topics, we feel it best corresponds to the likely knowledge and interests of our audience. Some of the more important omissions are covered briefly at the end of this introduction. All the chapters are written by scholars who are specialists in their areas. With a couple of exceptions, the authors have been in their fields for at least twenty years, and in some cases, for thirty or more.

The first four chapters share certain design features. Each contains: a survey of the main branches and languages of the phylum; a statement of the current evidence for, and status of, the phylum; a brief history of work on the phylum; and reconstruction of some features of the language assumed to be ancestral to the members of the phylum. These features are above all lexical and morphological, and only in some cases phonological. We use the term 'phylum' to refer to a language grouping larger, less well defined, and less widely accepted than a 'family', and which typically contains several families. Readers should note that while this distinction of phylum versus family is common usage today, it is not necessarily followed by all the authors in the current volume. The presentation of the kinds of evidence used to support each phylum has been sharpened by Dixon (1997), which casts doubt on the genetic validity of African phyla in general.

Readers will also note differences among these four chapters, differences which reflect partly the different genetic statuses of the phyla, partly the quantity of scholarship that has gone into them, and partly the authors' personal choices in what they consider the essential characteristic features of the phylum. The least secure of the four is Khoisan. Is Khoisan a language phylum, or is it a collection of languages that have grown together over tens of thousands of years, and thus share certain typological features? The great age of Khoisan has led to a massive loss of shared material, if you believe in the genetic unity of Khoisan, or a massive convergence, if you do not. Nilo-Saharan, in more or less its present shape, was first proposed by Greenberg forty years ago, using evidence which many considered provisional. In the meantime a dedicated group of scientists have worked hard at collecting the kinds of evidence needed to substantiate or modify Greenberg's proposals. Although a grouping akin to Niger-Congo has been acknowledged for longer, since the nineteenth century, and although most Africanists recognise the validity of Niger-Congo, work here has been beset by the same problems as affect the other phyla, and especially by its having more members than any other phylum in the world. Of the four, Afroasiatic is the most widely recognised, the best analysed, and has the longest history of scholarship carried out by the largest number of scholars. However, most of this activity has gone into a few large languages in the Middle East, while the majority, that is, its African members, have suffered from relative neglect.

The search for the truth in all four phyla is slowed down by the same factors. These are: the small size of the group of scholars who worked on them; the many languages involved; the poor documentation for most; the long-standing interaction between adjacent languages; and, in the second half of the twentieth century, the disappearance of some languages. We will not presume to estimate the numbers of scholars involved in work on the various African phyla or even families because discussion suggests that there are too many variables and much disagreement.

The quality and quantity of the documentation for African languages ranges from fairly high to nil. We say 'fairly high' because no African language has been documented or analysed to the extent of the better researched European or Asian languages. If we define 'fairly high' as having a reasonably accurate and comprehensive reference grammar available, then less than a hundred African languages are in this category. For most, the documention consists of an inadequate grammar, an analysis of part of the language, an article or two. For yet others, all we have is a reliable word list, or less than that.

A particular problem that affects work on comparative linguistics, that is not always acknowledged, results from having many languages adjacent over a long period of time. We now know that most linguistic features, not vocabulary alone, can be transferred from one language to another, or to several. Unique sounds such as the clicks of southern Bantu, word order in some Ethiopian languages, predominantly suffixing morphology becoming predominantly prefixing, these and many other features can all be diffused across language and phylum boundaries. Areas are recognised elsewhere in the world, where long-standing interaction between settled communities has led to such an areal mixing of features that it is often difficult to distinguish their point of origin. Outside Africa, the Balkans are one such *Sprachbund*, the Indian subcontinent another. In Africa, such areas exist in Ethiopia, where speakers of different branches of Afroasiatic came together, in highland parts of East Africa, where speakers of all four phyla interacted historically, in southern Africa, where Bantu and Khoisan met and mixed, apparently in two discrete areas and times, and the broad region south of Lake Chad, where Central Sudanic, Chadic, and Adamawa-Ubangian speakers mixed. In fact, the vast number of African languages combined with the small size of many and the fact that many current languages, or rather their ancestors, have been in place for millennia means there has been interaction in many other places, too, and much transfer of inherited features. It is often hard to know where some of the features started. Readers will note that in some places in the first four chapters, authors will say that such and such a feature defines a language phylum or family but is also found in some neighbouring group(s).

A final phenomenon that has not affected comparative work much yet but is likely to do so in the twenty-first century is language death. Social, political and economic pressures are already conspiring to eliminate the languages of smaller communities, and the pressures will increase. In Africa and elsewhere these languages are being eliminated because they have lost their function and it is in no one's interest to maintain them. Almost no one's interest, that is, because for comparative and historical linguists, data from Friesian, on the north-west coast of Europe, may be just as valuable for language family work as is data from its much larger and better-known sibling, English. In the same way, data from Dahalo, a dying Cushitic language with clicks in north-east Kenya, from the isolated and small West African languages mentioned in chapter 2, or from Kwadi, a Khoisan language of south-western Angola mentioned in chapter 5, are of great importance to some linguists. Worldwide, there is a growing awareness of the need to document endangered languages. In Africa alone, more than a hundred languages are seriously endangered (see Brenzinger ed. 1992, 1998). We hope that this book will also contribute to stimulate interest in the study of these languages, some of which will no longer be there in a few decades.

Despite all that has just been said, at the start of the twenty-first century, we are very much further ahead than we were a century ago, both in terms of African language data and in terms of the syntheses made from it. The linguistic progress made in the twentieth century can be better seen in the second part of the book, in the chapters dealing with specific linguistic topics. A century ago such overview chapters would have been impossible since all we had was analyses of a few African languages, mainly done by missionaries, mainly using Latin-based models. We have moved from missionary work through analyses meant to provide teaching materials to sophisticated analyses done by professional linguists. Some of the latter are so technical that it is part of the job of the authors in our second part to explain it to the worldwide undergraduate. At the same time, theory has changed. From the growing recognition in the first half of the twentieth century that the world was full of languages whose design features were not those of Latin or Western European languages, emerged new linguistic theories and insights that transformed the linguistic landscape in the second half.

Each of the authors of the four chapters on phonology, morphology, syntax and typology was faced with an unenviable task: how to reduce to twenty or thirty pages the significant features of two thousand languages and express them in terms which are at once professional, yet easily understood by the worldwide undergraduate? That was perhaps easiest for Clements. As he himself says, most contemporary phonology emerged from the research perspective of generative grammar, and many of the theoretical advances of the last thirty years have been made by phonologists who were also Africanists. For them, theory and African languages are inseparably connected. This was less true of syntax and typology. Chapters 8 and 9 have two roots. On the one hand they owe much to the perspectives of generative grammar, on the other hand they also partly rest on the typological impetus provided by Greenberg in the 1960s. Language typology arose in the nineteenth century and was originally based on the notion that languages could be reduced to a small set of morphologically based types. This was increasingly replaced by Greenberg's (1963b) approach, which was based on the study of word order and syntactic patterns. Syntactic patterns came to subsume much of morphology, and this in turn fitted well with generative perceptions: both the chapters in this book have to do with morphosyntax, how syntax and morphology meld to produce sentences and express meaning.

Despite this relegation of morphology to being a subcomponent of morphosyntax (and of phonology), we think it important to include a separate chapter on morphology. One reason is that the undergraduate audience will be regularly faced with words that make better sense if segmented morphologically. Another is that there are clearly recognised links between phonology and morphology and between syntax and morphology. A third is that African languages show a great range of morphological patterns. They are rich in noun-class and verbal tense-aspect systems. Undergraduates need insight into grammatical categories and how they are expressed.

We also feel it important to include the chapters on historical and comparative linguistics. The tools for building African history are different from those for Europe. African history has no long written tradition and thus resources such as archaeology and linguistics become more important. Linguistics has provided new insights into the history of, especially, the last three millennia in Africa, and Ehret has been associated with many of these. At the same time we feel it is proper procedure to have the methods of historical and comparative linguistics evaluated separately from their results, hence Newman's chapter. These methods are also not always clear to non-linguists and non-Africanists.

The author of the last chapter has to try to deal with the daily interaction of 750 million people speaking some 2,000 languages. Some things do not much change. Thus Africa has, and had long had, many bi- or multi-linguals. It has older koinés, pidgins, and creoles, all used to facilitate communication among different linguistic populations. It has communities giving up their traditional form of speech for others. At the same time the language situation in Africa is changing rapidly. Some languages themselves are changing, some are disappearing, new languages are arising. People are flocking into cities. Countries and leaders are struggling to formulate new language strategies, in situations where languages are often not viewed just as languages but as an integral part of people's culture, which they vigorously defend. This all makes for an exciting situation, but one which is hard to encapsulate adequately.

1.4   Further issues

One of the most difficult tasks we have to face is how to reduce the multitude of important topics that have been raised in the history of African linguistics to a manageable set. The various authors in this volume have tried to take care of many of them, and have provided suggestions for readers who want to know more about a particular topic. In some cases these suggestions take the form of a suggested further reading list at the end of the chapter, but more often there are references liberally scattered through the text, which are up-to-date or standard works, which in turn mention older works. Inevitably there remain some subjects that could only be mentioned in passing or could not be covered at all.

We would have liked, for example, to expose the reader to the whole gamut of scholarly discussion on the description and classification of African languages. In a volume that aims at presenting what is widely or commonly accepted, this is possible only within limits. Nevertheless, not infrequently authors express contrasting views on the same subject and this is reflected in this volume. It is perhaps most obvious in the reconstruction of Nilo-Saharan, the subject of controversy ever since Greenberg first proposed it as a genetic grouping. The reader may participate in this discussion in chapters 3 (Bender) and 11 (Ehret), where the two main alternative hypotheses are presented, each with considerable implications for our understanding of Africa's prehistory.

Work on classifying African languages has focused mainly on problems of genetic relationship. Accordingly, the classification most widely accepted is genetic, as is apparent in the present volume, where chapters 2 to 5 each treat one of the four African phyla proposed by Greenberg (1963a). Compared to that work, other approaches to language classification have received much less scholarly treatment. Areal, that is, contact-induced linguistic relationship in particular, has been out of vogue for a long time and has only very recently started to receive the kind of detailed attention it deserves. Conceivably, some of the classifications proposed could be more profitably analysed with reference to areal rather than genetic relationship. Earlier we drew attention to the problems in establishing Khoisan, the subject of chapter 5, as a phylum. It may well turn out that Khoisan could be more appropriately defined as a convergence area rather than as a genetic unit.

While the study of African-language structures can be divided fairly well into the four domains highlighted in this volume, namely phonology, morphology, syntax and typology, we have not been able to treat other topics in the way they merit. Thus, for instance, some colleagues wanted us to devote space to linguistic aspects of the diaspora, to African languages in the Americas. We settled for asking John McWhorter to write a brief overview for us, as follows, and we are indebted to him for this.

> The principal fate of African languages in the New World has been to serve as primary sources for the creoles which slaves developed in plantation colonies. Often speaking closely related languages while having minimal contact with whites, early slaves' transfer-laden approximations of a given European language conventionalised into new languages, African-derived as much as European. The most extreme manifestations are Surinam creoles, whose syntaxes are broad reproductions of Kwa ones: the Saramaccan *di nákináki dágu bi wáka gó a wósu báka* 'the beaten dog walked behind the house' superimposes English lexicon on Kwa features such as a reduplicated attributive adjective, verb serialisation, and a postposed nominal as spatial deictic. Other creoles include Gullah, Haitian, Papiamentu and the extinct Negerhollands.
>
> Lighter African influence can be seen in the speech of many Afro-Hispanics, whose speech diverges slightly from local Spanish varieties in features such as a double negator pattern (*no lo tengo no* 'I don't

have it') found in Kongo. Popular Brazilian Portuguese is similar, in idiom calques such as *o dia ta limpo* 'The day is clean' for 'It's dawn', an expression found also in Yoruba. These New World Iberian varieties, as well as creoles in general, also preserve many West African lexical borrowings.

Evidence suggests that African slaves did not usually transmit their native languages to following generations. A notable exception is in Brazil, where Fon, Kongo, and Yoruba were maintained by communities of blacks, the latter into the twentieth century. More typically, African languages were preserved in fossilised ritual registers often kept today, such as Twi and Gbe in Jamaica; these two and Kongo in Surinam, and Mende in the Sea Islands of South Carolina.

The editors would also have wished to include a separate treatment of semantics. Most of what determines how African languages are used and structured relates to how meanings are expressed. The study of meaning has been approached in different ways, using contrasting theoretical frameworks, and quite a number of semantic characteristics of African languages have been identified. But we lack a more cohesive view of how the different scholarly traditions dealing with meaning and the many details we have on the semantic characteristics of individual African languages can be presented as a book chapter.

A related matter covers discourse structure, text analysis and forms of creative language use. African narrative discourse and conversation structure are fascinating fields of research and they have been approached variously by syntacticians, anthropologists, translators, literary scholars and others.

A final issue concerns new directions in linguistic research paradigms. Grammaticalisation theory, for instance, has yielded fresh insights on how grammatical forms arise and develop, how the boundary between the grammar and the lexicon should be studied, and how to explain why grammar is structured as it is. African languages have figured prominently in formulating principles of grammatical evolution and in proposing new parameters of linguistic explanation (see Heine and Reh 1984, and Heine, Claudi, and Hünnemeyer 1991 for details).

It is hardly possible to name all those who have contributed to this volume in some way or another. To you all we say: thank you. Our immediate gratitude is to Erhard Voeltz, for taking the time and trouble to make valuable comments on various chapters, to Monika Feinen for her work on the maps, and to Yvonne Treis for assisting in the editorial work.

2

Niger-Congo

KAY WILLIAMSON AND ROGER BLENCH

2.1   **Introduction**[1]

The Niger-Congo language phylum has 1,436 languages according to the most recent estimates (Grimes 1996). This makes it the largest phylum in the world; its nearest rival, Austronesian, has 1,236. It occupies a greater area than any other African phylum. Some of the languages in Africa with the greatest number of speakers belong to Niger-Congo: Wolof, the largest language of Senegal; Fulfulde, which has spread over much of West and Central Africa; Manding, varieties of which are spoken in several West African countries under various names, including Bambara, the national language of Mali, and Dyula, a widespread trade language; Akan, the largest language of Ghana; Yoruba and Igbo, major languages of Nigeria; Sango, the lingua franca of the Central African Republic, and a number of Bantu languages, of which some of the best known are Ganda, Gikuyu, Kongo, Lingala, Luba-Kasai, Luyia, Mbundu (Luanda), Northern Sotho, Nyanja, Rundi, Rwanda, Shona, Southern Sotho, Sukuma, Swahili, Tsonga, Tswana, Umbundu, Xhosa and Zulu.

On the basis of the figures available in Grimes (1996), at least 360 million Africans speak Niger-Congo languages. Since the figures in Grimes are not always up to date, it is possible they are higher, and thus that one could round them up to 400 million.

2.2   **The Niger-Congo languages: typological or genetic unity?**

No comprehensive reconstruction has yet been done for the phylum as a whole, and it is sometimes suggested that Niger-Congo is merely a typological and not a genetic unity. This view is not held by any specialists in the phylum, and reasons for thinking Niger-Congo is a true genetic unity will be given

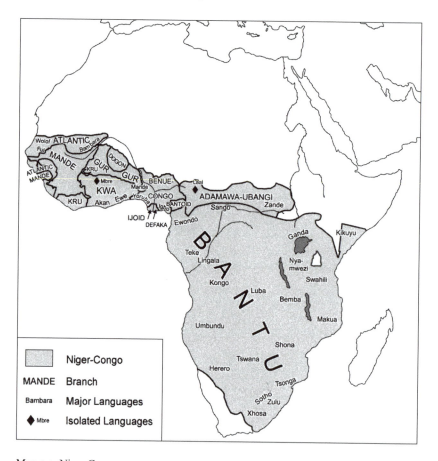

Map 2.2. Niger-Congo.

in this chapter.[2] It is, however, true that the subclassification of the phylum has been continuously modified in recent years and cannot be presented as an agreed scheme. The factors which have delayed reconstruction are the large number of languages, the inaccessibility of much of the data, and the paucity of able researchers committed to this field. Emphasis will be placed on three characteristics of Niger-Congo: noun class systems, verbal extensions and basic lexicon.

Niger-Congo is remarkable for an elaborate system of noun classification which marks singular/plural alternations with affixes (most commonly prefixes, sometimes suffixes, and occasionally infixes), and often requires concord of other elements in the sentence with their governing noun. In some families or branches the system has been remodelled, or indeed lost with virtually no trace; but in others, of which the best-known case is Bantu, it is retained in considerable detail. Unlike a typical sex-gender system, where male/female oppositions are extended to inanimates, Niger-Congo semantic classification involves multilateral oppositions: humans, animals, plants, paired body parts, mass nouns and liquids, abstracts, and others which are less transparent. The affixes which mark these oppositions appear throughout Niger-Congo; apart from those for singular and plural person classes, which often resemble the third person pronouns, they have no discernible etymology. The system was clearly grammaticalised, blurring its original semantic basis, as far back as it can be traced. Approximately twenty noun classes occur in conservative languages, with singular-plural pairing of classes for count nouns contrasting with single, unpaired classes for mass nouns and abstracts. Other elements in the sentence, typically modifiers of the noun and sometimes the verb of which the noun is the subject, show concordial affixes in full systems.

The notion that these noun classes are 'typological' and typical of African languages is erroneous. African languages have in common the fact that they do not generally use numeral classifiers, but the systems of noun categorisation differ considerably. Afroasiatic has sex-gender systems. North Khoisan has a small number of noun classes marked by agreement but not on the noun, while Central Khoisan has sex-gender systems (distinguishing masculine, feminine and common) (Bernd Heine, p.c.). Some families of Nilo-Saharan do have systems which recall simplified noun-class systems of Niger-Congo; this may be due to common genetic origin (see section 2.3.5). Noun class systems are reported from other parts of the world: notably the Caucasian, non-Pama-Nyungan Australian, Papuan languages and most strikingly, Yeniseian (Werner 1994).

Verbs commonly end in suffixes that modify their meaning and often their valency, creating causatives, reciprocals, and the like. Some of these suffixes can be reconstructed to Niger-Congo level, and thus constitute evidence for its genetic unity (Voeltz 1977). Newman (1990) has drawn attention to 'pluractional' verbs in Chadic, that is verbs which require plurality in their subject or object, or which refer to multiple action. Such verbs are also widespread in Niger-Congo, either as part of the verbal extension system or as different lexical items.

Given the extensive similarity of sound and meaning in particular grammatical elements as well as in basic vocabulary, and the complex changes they have undergone, it is inconceivable that this could be due to chance and extremely unlikely that it is due to borrowing. Moreover, there are many words of basic vocabulary which recur throughout Niger-Congo, often in modified form after undergoing sound changes.

It is sometimes claimed that genetic relationship cannot be considered proved until much of the proto-language has been reconstructed. It is, however, not possible to initiate the process of reconstruction until large numbers of probably cognate grammatical and lexical items are available to compare, and until a subgrouping hypothesis exists to ensure that all parts of the phylum are properly represented. This is the stage at which Niger-Congo studies are at present. Reconstructions have been made for some families and groups of Niger-Congo, and the way is now open for a full-scale reconstruction of Proto-Niger-Congo.

The section on each family presents a summary stating whether it has a full, reduced or remnant noun class system; what type of affixes are used; and what traces remain of earlier systems where they have been lost. Each family is presented in a 'tree' format, usually combining a published classification with recent material, and simultaneously presenting the main languages and groups. Such trees should be treated with due caution; they represent working hypotheses and have been derived in a variety of ways, most prominently lexicostatistics and lexical and grammatical innovation.

2.3   History of Niger-Congo classification

2.3.1   *Early views*

One of the largest and best-known groups of Niger-Congo is the Bantu languages. They occupy an enormous area and are closely related; their well-preserved noun class systems attracted the attention of European scholars in the nineteenth century. Their relationship was recognised early, and Meinhof carried out a reconstruction of Proto-Bantu. Koelle and Bleek noted that many languages of West Africa also showed noun classes marked by prefixes, and Bleek went so far as to include a West African division in the family he named Bantu. A different tradition culminated in Meinhof's work; he saw languages without noun classes (typically Ewe, but including many Nilo-Saharan languages) as a type he named 'Sudanic'. He regarded languages that were obviously lexically related but had noun classes as being influenced by Bantu and therefore 'Semi-Bantu'. The result of such views was a typological rather than a truly genetic classification.

2.3.2   *Westermann*

Westermann was a student of Meinhof who undertook to do a reconstruction of 'Sudanic' corresponding to Meinhof's work on Bantu. His first comparative book (1911) established a basic division between 'East' and 'West' Sudanic; his second (1927) was devoted to West Sudanic, which he divided into six families: Kwa, Benue-Cross, Togo *Restsprachen* (now the Central Togo languages), Gur, West Atlantic and Mandingo. He proposed a large number of Proto-West Sudanic (PWS) reconstructions, often of CV structure, and compared them with Meinhof's Proto-Bantu reconstructions, which were generally of CVCV shape. Perhaps out of respect for his teacher Meinhof, he did not explicitly state the obvious conclusion, that West Sudanic and Bantu belonged to the same phylum, until much later in his career.

2.3.3 *Greenberg*

Greenberg, unencumbered by such considerations, took a fresh look at the classification of African languages in a series of articles published between 1949 and 1954 which were later collected in final book form in 1963. He combined West Sudanic and Bantu into a phylum he named Niger-Congo, while he treated East Sudanic as a different phylum, renamed Nilo-Saharan. Within Niger-Congo he largely retained Westermann's subgrouping, with the following differences:

(a) Mandingo was renamed Mande

(b) Central Togo was incorporated into Kwa

(c) Benue-Cross was renamed Benue-Congo

(d) Bantu was placed as a subgroup of a subgroup of Benue-Congo

(e) Fulfulde was added to the group of West Atlantic which contained Serer and Wolof

(f) a new family, Adamawa-Eastern, was added to the phylum

(g) finally, in 1963, Kordofanian, previously treated as a small separate phylum, was combined as a subphylum co-ordinate with Niger-Congo as a whole, and consequently the phylum was renamed Niger-Kordofanian (or Congo-Kordofanian)

Greenberg criticised the use of typological and non-linguistic criteria for language classification. He compared not general features such as the presence of a noun class system, but sound meaning correspondences in particular noun class affixes: for example, he noted that Kordofanian *ŋ-* corresponds to Niger-Congo *m-* in noun class prefixes, and that this correspondence recurs in pronouns and basic vocabulary items such as 'tongue'.

2.3.4 *Post-Greenberg*

Greenberg's work was initially controversial but was gradually accepted by most scholars. The only researcher since Greenberg to present an overview of the phylum and to support his conclusions with extensive lexical evidence was Mukarovsky, a student of Westermann. Mukarovsky (1976–7) accepted the position of Bantu within Niger-Congo but did not use evidence from Kordofanian, Mande, the Wolof-Serer-Fulfulde group, Ijoid and Adamawa-Eastern for unstated reasons.[3] He compiled data to illustrate the relationship of the remaining parts, which he named Western Nigritic; and his work remains a very useful compendium despite the missing families and the exclusion of roots for which he could not cite a Bantu cognate.

Bennett and Sterk (1977) proposed a major reclassification of Niger-Congo, mainly based on lexicostatistics and lexical innovations. They argued that Kordofanian, with relatively few lexical cognates, and Mande, with its complete loss of the noun class system, should be treated as the first families to break off from the rest; this yielded a three-way initial split. The remaining families were sampled lexicostatistically. The results led to a family tree in which the next family to separate was West Atlantic; the remaining families were treated as Central Niger-Congo, splitting into North and South. North Central Niger-Congo comprised Gur and Adamawa-Eastern, possibly with Kru; South Central Niger-Congo comprised Western and Eastern, possibly with Ịjọ. Alternatively, both Kru and Ịjọ were placed as co-ordinate branches of Central Niger-Congo. Their article concentrated on South Central Niger-Congo, where they split Greenberg's Kwa, not only by removing and promoting Kru and Ịjọ, but by renaming his group (b) (often known as Western Kwa) as 'Western South Central Niger-Congo', while combining the remaining groups with his Benue-Congo as 'Eastern South Central Niger-Congo'.

This branching structure, suggesting hypotheses about the prehistory of speakers of Proto-Niger-Congo that could not be envisaged under Westermann's or Greenberg's flat arrays, gave rise to intense discussion over the next decade, and culminated in the publication of *The Niger-Congo Languages* (Bendor-Samuel 1989), in which a modification of Bennett and Sterk's proposal was presented as a working hypothesis (Williamson 1989b). 'Niger-Congo' replaced 'Niger-Kordofanian' as the overall name for the phylum. The initial three-way branching was retained, as was the next branching between Atlantic (a simplification of 'West Atlantic') and Volta-Congo ('Central Niger-Congo'), with Ijoid tentatively forming a third branch. Volta-Congo was presented with a more conservative flat array comprising Kru, New Kwa ('Western South Central Niger-Congo'), New Benue-Congo ('Eastern South Central Niger-Congo'), North Volta-Congo ('North Central Niger-Congo') and, tentatively, Dogon, which had been removed from Gur. A system of nomenclature proposed by Stewart was adopted, in which the direct ancestors of Bantu, from Niger-Congo to Benue-Congo, all had compound names ending in '-Congo', while lower nodes naming relatively closely related groups ended in '-oid'. More detailed revisions of classification are treated under the separate families.

2.3.5   ***The Nilo-Saharan connection***

Westermann (1911) had combined Niger-Congo and Nilo-Saharan as 'Sudanic' in his first synthesis of lexical data. Gregersen (1972) put forward both morphological and lexical similarities as evidence for a macrophylum conjoining Niger-Congo and Nilo-Saharan, for which he proposed the name 'Kongo-Saharan'. Creissels (1981) listed the many morphological and lexical similarities between Mande and Songhay, which are too striking and numerous to be due to chance convergence, and questioned the division between Niger-Congo and Nilo-Saharan. Blench (1995; in press a) has presented substantial further lexical and phonological evidence to support this macrophylum, for which he proposes the name 'Niger-Saharan'. He suggests that Niger-Congo, rather than being united with Nilo-Saharan at the highest level, is related most closely to Central Sudanic and Kadu within Nilo-Saharan – a realignment that recalls Greenberg's demotion of Bantu in relation to Niger-Congo.

2.4   Current family tree

Figure 2.1 presents the tree of the phylum as currently understood. Lexical evidence for uniting Kordofanian with Niger-Congo is more scanty than for any other family, and therefore it is presented as the first branch to split. We do not have clear evidence for either Mande or Atlantic as the next division, and therefore have presented them as equal splits from the remainder. The divisions of Volta-Congo are shown with doubled lines, following a convention established by Ross (1988) to indicate the diversification of a dialect continuum. In the case of Gur and Adamawa-Ubangi (Bennett 1983), it has been argued that these form such a continuum and a similar situation seems to occur with Kwa and Benue-Congo.

2.5   Linguistic survey by families

2.5.1   *Kordofanian*

The Kordofanian languages are all small, and were spoken in the Nuba Mountains in the Republic of the Sudan. In recent years, many have been displaced through political insecurity and their status is now uncertain. Greenberg assigned five groups of languages, grouped together as Kordofanian, to Niger-Congo. Schadeberg (1981c) suggested the removal of one of these groups, Kadugli-Krongo or Kadu (Greenberg's Tumtum), from Kordofanian, and assigned it to Nilo-Saharan, a proposal that has met with general acceptance. The classification of the remaining four groups is shown in figure 2.2, following Schadeberg (1989).

Table 2.1 summarises the linguistic features of Kordofanian.

Greenberg and, in more detail, Schadeberg (1989: 72) showed that the noun class affixes correspond in a regular way to those of the rest of Niger-Congo. Kordofanian languages remain the most poorly documented languages within Niger-Congo; no complete descriptive grammar exists of even one language. Further research is essential to any convincing reconstruction of Niger-Congo.

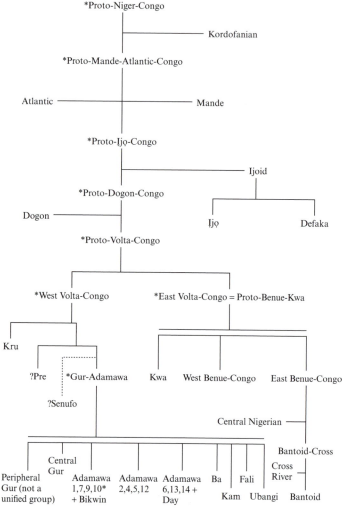

* numbers refer to Greenberg's Adamawa groups, amended by Boyd (1989).

Fig. 2.1. The internal structure of Niger-Congo.

2.5.2   *Mande*

The Mande languages extend over the greater part of the western half of West Africa. Mande speakers form a large proportion of the population of Mali, Côte d'Ivoire, Guinea, Sierra Leone and Liberia; they are also found in substantial numbers in Burkina Faso, Senegal, Gambia and Guinea Bissau, with outlying groups in Mauretania, Benin, Ghana, Togo, and Nigeria (Dwyer 1989; Kastenholz 1991/2). They have between 10 and 12 million speakers, of whom over

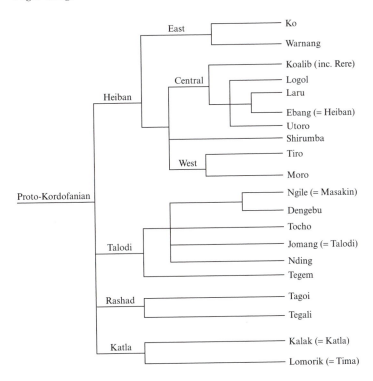

Fig. 2.2. Classification of Kordofanian languages.

Table 2.1. *Linguistic features of Kordofanian*

Noun classes	Full/reduced/absent; incorporated old prefixes; new prefixes
Verbal extensions	Widespread
Pronouns	Inclusive/exclusive
Sentence order	SVO (Tegem SOV); Prepositions
Noun phrase	N + Gen; N + Poss (Tegem Poss + N); N + Adj; N + Num; N + Dem

half speak forms of Manding. Koelle (1854) first used the name 'Mandén.ga' for the family, a name which is indigenous. It is now normal practice to use 'Mande' for the family and 'Manding' for the widespread and prominent dialect cluster known under different names in different parts of West Africa.

Most modern internal classifications of Mande have been based on lexicostatistics. Kastenholz (1991/2, 1996) points out various problems of these classifications: inaccurate data, incomplete coverage and difficulties in interpreting the results. After surveying previous attempts to apply comparative reconstruction methods, he studies lexical innovations to reach an improved classification before applying the

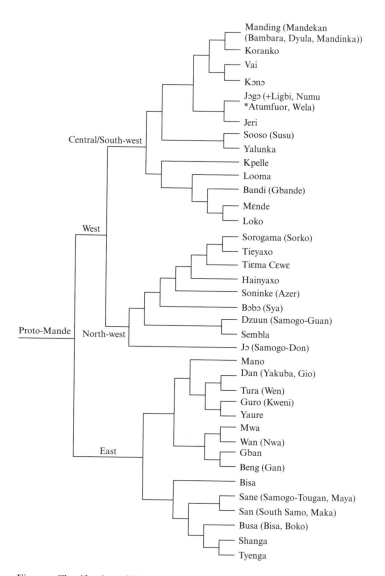

Fig. 2.3. Classification of Mande languages.

comparative method to West Mande. Figure 2.3 shows Kastenholz's (1996) classification, supplemented for the details of East Mande by Dwyer (1989) and (1996).

Table 2.2 summarises the linguistic features of Mande languages.

2.5.3   ***Atlantic***

        The Atlantic languages are, as their name suggests, spoken along the
Atlantic coastline of West Africa, from the mouth of the Senegal River as far as

Table 2.2. *Linguistic features of Mande*

Noun classes	Remnant; remodelled by suffixes; initial consonant mutation unconditioned; tone alternation marks singular/plural (e.g. Sembla)
Verbal extensions	Not generally, but Bɔbɔ has causative, intransitive
Pronouns	Alienable/inalienable, inclusive/exclusive common. Jɔ has a separate feminine
Sentence order	SMOVA; Prepositions/Postpositions
Noun phrase	Gen + N; Poss + N; N + Adj; Dem + N, N + Dem; N + Plural

Liberia. The largest ones are Fulfulde, spoken by several million people scattered over much of West Central Africa; Wolof, with nearly 2 million speakers in Senegambia; the Diola cluster, with nearly 400,000 speakers in the Casamance province of Senegal; Serer, with 600,000 speakers near Kaolack in Senegal; and Temne, with over 600,000 speakers in Sierra Leone (Wilson 1989). Doneux (1975) shortened the name 'West Atlantic' used by Westermann to 'Atlantic'.

The present internal classification of Atlantic was provided by Sapir (1971) and reproduced by Wilson (1989). Sapir, using a rather strict lexicostatistic method, made a basic three-way division into Bijago, Northern and Southern (figure 2.4).

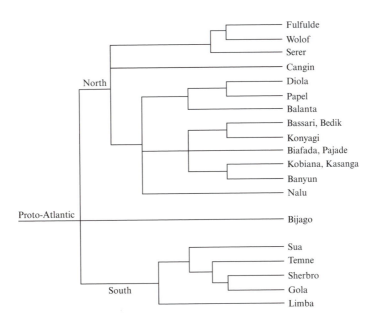

Fig. 2.4. Classification of Atlantic languages.

Table 2.3 summarises the linguistic features of Atlantic languages, drawn from Doneux (1975) and Wilson (1989).

Table 2.3. *Linguistic features of Atlantic*

Noun classes	Full; original prefixes; weakened, renewed by suffixes, or augments; initial consonant mutation grammatically conditioned
Verbal extensions	Widespread
Pronouns	Inclusive/exclusive common
Sentence order	SVOA; Prepositions
Noun phrase	N + Gen (Gen + N in Sua); N + Num; N + Dem

2.5.4   ***Ijoid***

Ijoid is a small family spoken only in the Niger Delta in Nigeria consisting of Defaka, a tiny endangered language, and Ịjọ, a language cluster, with over a million speakers. The largest language is Ịzọn. Although Ijoid is closely related internally, it is very distinct from all other Niger-Congo families. Figure 2.5 shows a classification derived from Jenewari (1989) and Williamson (in prep.).

Table 2.4 summarises linguistic features of Ijoid (Jenewari 1989 and Williamson (in prep.)).

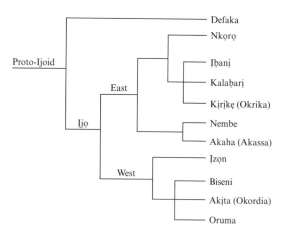

Fig. 2.5. Classification of Ijoid languages.

Table 2.4. *Linguistic features of Ijoid*

Noun classes	Remnant; *a-* marks plural nouns preceded by modifier, some initial vowels; new human suffixes
Verbal extensions	Few, mostly new formations
Pronouns	Inalienable/alienable traces. New gender system, always distinguishing feminine human from masculine, sometimes masculine from neuter, in singular, reflected in determiners
Sentence order	SAOVM; Postpositions
Noun phrase	Gen + N; Poss + N; Adj + N; Num + N; Dem + N; N + Definite

2.5.5 **Dogon**

Dogon has about half a million speakers in Mali and Burkina Faso. The name is an indigenous one accepted by the speakers. Dogon is frequently referred to as a single language. Bertho (1953), however, showed that there is considerable diversity, and proposed that at least four languages should be recognised. Calame-Griaule (1978) lists five groups of dialects, plus some small ungrouped ones, as shown in figure 2.6.

Table 2.5 lists linguistic features of the Dogon languages (Bendor-Samuel *et al.* 1989).

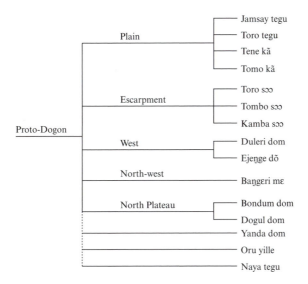

Fig. 2.6. Classification of Dogon languages.

Table 2.5. *Linguistic features of Dogon*

Noun classes	Remnant; no prefixes; human nouns take distinct plural suffix
Verbal extensions	Few, mostly new formations
Pronouns	One basic set, with object, possessive and 'embedded' sets derived
Sentence order	SAOVM, ASOVM
Noun phrase	N + Poss; N + Adj; N + plural; N + Num; N + Dem; N + Definite

2.5.6   *North Volta-Congo*

North Volta-Congo comprises the three families of Kru, Gur and Adamawa-Ubangi, which were first grouped together by Bennett and Sterk (1977). The membership of Kru is less certain than that of Gur and Adamawa-Ubangi. The implication of this grouping is that the languages are presumed to have once spread continuously across much of the savannah of West Africa before Kru moved south and west and Gur and Adamawa-Ubangi were broken apart by the expansion and incursion of Chadic and Benue-Congo.

2.5.6.1   *Kru*

The Kru languages are spoken in the south-west quadrant of Côte d'Ivoire and the greater part of Liberia, extending inland from the Atlantic coast, by between 1 and 2 million speakers (Marchese 1989). Westermann (1927: 52) claims that the name 'Kru' is based on a European confusion of the indigenous name 'Klao' with English 'crew', and prior to the twentieth century 'Kroomen' frequently worked as sailors on European ships. Westermann (1927) and Greenberg (1963a) classified Kru within Kwa. Bennett and Sterk (1977) removed it from Kwa and suggested that it was a part of North Volta-Congo or, alternatively, an independent family within Volta-Congo; the first view is tentatively accepted here, but the question should be re-examined.

Westermann observed that the main body of Kru languages are quite closely related; this is consistent with a relatively late settlement within the dense rainforest near the coast. Marchese (1989) notes that in addition to the main body there are three Kru isolates: Kuwaa, to the north-west of the main body; Tiegba and Abrako, two of the group known as Aizi, to the east of the main body; and finally Seme, far to the north in Burkina Faso, which is much more distantly related. The major subdivision within the main body of Kru is between East and West. The classification in figure 2.7 follows Marchese (1989).

Table 2.6 summarises the linguistic features of the Kru languages (Marchese 1983; 1989).

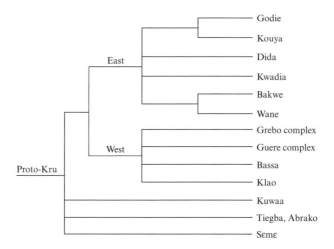

Fig. 2.7. Classification of Kru languages.

Table 2.6. *Linguistic features of Kru*

Noun classes	Remnant; suffixes or final vowel change in the plural; some concord in the noun phrase
Verbal extensions	Causative, benefactive, inchoative, instrumental, dative, locative, passive
Pronouns	Human/non-human common, feminine in 2nd and 3rd singular in Niaboua and Wobé
Sentence order	SVOA, SMOVA; Postpositions
Noun phrase	Gen + N; Poss + N; N + Adj; N + Dem; N + Num; N + Definite

2.5.6.2   *Gur (Voltaic)*

Gur is a very large family spoken in a belt of the savannah extending through the south of Mali, the northern parts of Côte d'Ivoire, Ghana, Togo, Benin, the greater part of Burkina Faso, and just into Nigeria. Manessy (1978) estimates some 5,500,000 speakers, of whom at least 1,700,000 speak Mõõre. The name Gur, proposed by Krause (1895), is taken from language names like Gurma and Gurunsi. The name Voltaic is based on the River Volta and is generally used in French (*voltaïque*).

There is a clear body of Central Gur languages whose relationship has never been doubted, surrounded by others whose affiliation is less clear or highly doubtful. Dogon is no longer considered Gur and the membership of the Senufo group is doubtful; it has therefore been placed as a branching immediately before

Gur. Within Gur, the relationships within Central Gur have been worked out by Manessy (1975; 1979), whereas 'Peripheral Gur' is essentially ungrouped (figure 2.8).

Table 2.7 shows the linguistic features of Gur, excluding Senufo (Manessy 1975, Prost 1964, Voeltz 1977, Naden 1989).

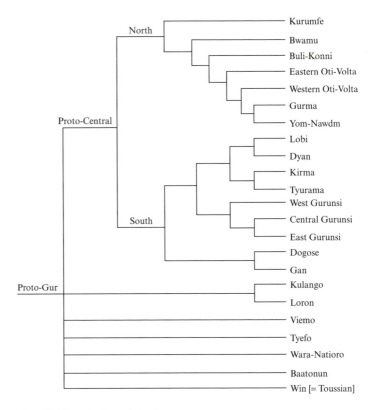

Fig. 2.8. Classification of Gur languages.

Table 2.7. *Linguistic features of Gur*

Noun classes	Full/reduced; normally suffixes; Eastern Grusi (Tem) has survivals of older prefixes in some common nouns
Verbal extensions	Widespread
Pronouns	Reconstructed with consonant plus varying vowels
Sentence order	SVO, SMOV; Postpositions (one preposition 'with')
Noun phrase	Gen + N; Poss + N; N + Adj; N + Num; N + Dem

2.5.6.3   *Adamawa-Ubangi*

The Adamawa-Ubangi languages extend from north-west Nigeria through northern Cameroon, southern Chad, Central African Republic (CAR), northern Gabon, Congo (Brazzaville) and the Democratic Republic of the Congo (DRC) and south-west Sudan. Greenberg (1963a) first grouped them as part of Niger-Congo under the name Adamawa-Eastern, which Samarin (1971) changed to Adamawa-Ubangi. Delafosse (1924) had previously used the name Ubangi (French *oubangien*) for the eastern part of the family.

No previous author suggests a total number of speakers, but summing the figures of speakers for the various languages given for Nigeria by Crozier and Blench (1992), and for Cameroon, Chad, and the CAR by Grimes (1996), gives a total of about one and a half million for Adamawa speakers. Similarly, summing the various groups given by Barreteau and Moñino (1978) gives a total of 2,300,000 for the Ubangi languages. The total number of first language speakers of Adamawa-Ubangi languages is thus about 3,800,000. This figure does not include all the speakers of Sango, which has become the national language of the Central African Republic as well as a lingua franca in neighbouring countries.

Greenberg (1963a) originally divided Adamawa into fourteen numbered groups, and 'Eastern' into eight. Bennett (1983) suggested that group 3, containing Daka, belonged to Benue-Congo rather than Adamawa, and this is now widely accepted. Figure 2.9 represents a synthesis of Boyd (1989) and Kleinewillinghöfer (1996).

Table 2.8 gives some linguistic features of Adamawa-Ubangi languages (Boyd 1989).

2.5.7   **South Volta-Congo**

This term is a revision of Bennett and Sterk's (1977) 'South-Central Niger-Congo'. Greenberg (1963a: 39) had pointed out that 'Kwa and Benue-Congo are particularly close to each other and . . . legitimate doubts arise concerning the validity of the division between them'. The name 'Benue-Kwa' came into informal use in the 1970s for this grouping. While our discussion follows the Bennett and Sterk (1977) rearrangement of Kwa and Benue-Congo, placing their major subgroups along the same line in the overall tree, figure 2.1 expresses a doubt about the division between the Kwa languages, including Gbe, and the westernmost 'Benue-Congo' languages, such as Yoruboid.

2.5.7.1   *Kwa*

The languages currently known as Kwa are spoken along the Atlantic coast of West Africa from the south-eastern quadrant of Côte d'Ivoire to the extreme south-western corner of Nigeria. By summing the figures for

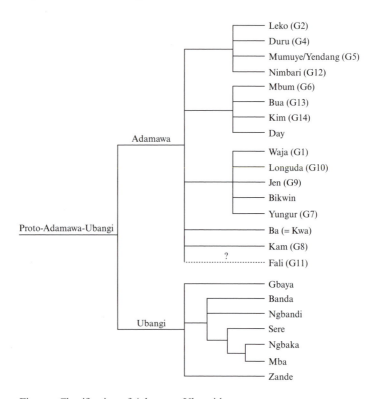

Fig. 2.9. Classification of Adamawa-Ubangi languages.

Table 2.8. *Linguistic features of Adamawa-Ubangi*

Noun classes	Reduced/remnant; suffixes in some groups; if concord markers, prefixed to postposed modifiers
Verbal extensions	A few, including iterative, intensive, benefactive, and causative
Pronouns	Sometimes inclusive/exclusive. 2nd singular often #mo (as in Kru, Senufo, and Kasem (Gur), contrasting with normal 1st singular #mi.
Sentence order	SVO, SMOV; Prepositions
Noun phrase	N + Gen (Duru Gen + N); N + Adj (often Adj + N in Ubangi); N + Num; N + Dem

speakers given by Grimes (1996), a total number of about 20 million speakers is obtained. The name 'Kwa' was introduced by Krause (1895).

Greenberg (1963a) divided Kwa into eight groups and integrated the Central Togo languages into his group (b). Bennett and Sterk (1977) reduced Greenberg's Kwa by promoting Ijoid and Kru and by reassigning his groups (c–g) to Benue-

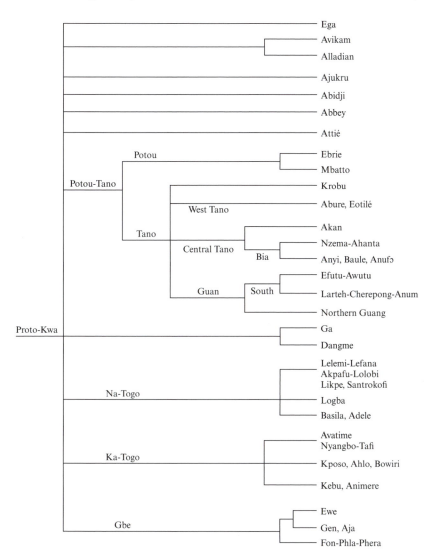

Fig. 2.10. Classification of Kwa languages.

Congo. 'New Kwa' therefore corresponds to Greenberg's group (b), 'Western Kwa'. Figure 2.10 gives Stewart's current classification of this New Kwa (p.c., revised from Stewart 1989), retaining only subgroupings for which he is satisfied there is really good evidence. Greenberg's grouping of Avikam and Alladian has been confirmed by Bole-Richard and Lafage (1983); Stewart has reconstructed Potou-Tano in depth; Ga and Dangme are uncontroversially grouped; Na-Togo and Ka-Togo correspond to the two major divisions of Central Togo (cf. Heine 1968a), which correspond to Bennett and Sterk's Tu and Mo groups; Gbe follows Capo (Stewart 1994); the remaining languages are conservatively left ungrouped, although Bole-Richard and Lafage suggest a loose grouping of Abbey–Abidji–Adioukrou.

Table 2.9 summarises some of the linguistic features of Kwa (Hérault 1983b).

Table 2.9. *Linguistic features of Kwa*

Noun classes	Full (Ega)/reduced/remnant; prefixes; some plural suffixes; initial consonant mutation, often phonologically conditioned
Verbal extensions	At least causative and reflexive/reciprocal
Pronouns	Independent, subject, object, possessive. Animate/non-animate common in 3rd person
Sentence order	SMVOA; Postpositions
Noun phrase	Gen + N; Poss + N; N + Adj; N + Num; N + Dem; N + Definite

2.5.7.2   *Benue-Congo*

2.5.7.2.1   *The definition of Benue-Congo*   The Benue-Congo languages, as currently conceived, occupy a vast area; roughly, the southern two-thirds of Nigeria and Cameroon, the southern part of the Central African Republic and Congo (Brazzaville), and the greater part of the DRC, Tanzania, Uganda, Kenya, the Comoros Islands, Mozambique, Angola, Rwanda, Burundi, Namibia, Zambia, Malawi, Zimbabwe, Botswana, Swaziland, South Africa, Lesotho, Equatorial Guinea and Gabon, with an outlier in Somalia. The vast number of languages makes it impractical to obtain the total number of speakers by adding the totals for individual languages.

The name 'Benue-Congo' was introduced by Greenberg (1963a). He divided the family into four branches: Platoid, Jukunoid, Cross River and Bantoid. Following Shimizu (1975) and Gerhardt (1989), Jukunoid was subsumed under Platoid. Bennett and Sterk (1977) expanded Benue-Congo by adding the eastern branches (c–g) of Greenberg's Kwa; these branches were grouped together as 'West Benue-Congo' by Blench (1989), and Greenberg's original Benue-Congo was therefore renamed 'East Benue-Congo'. Ohiri-Aniche (1999) suggests that the small language group Ukaan (perhaps with Akpes) forms a bridge between West and East Benue-Congo. Data on the Ukaan languages is exiguous and Connell (1998) has proposed a link with Cross River languages. As a compromise, Ukaan is placed as an independent branch of East Benue-Congo. Figure 2.11 draws on the model in Blench (1989) but incorporates these additional proposals.

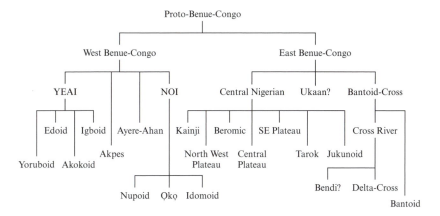

Fig. 2.11. Classification of Benue-Congo languages.

2.5.7.2.2   *West Benue-Congo*   West Benue-Congo, corresponding to the former 'Eastern Kwa', is spoken over the greater part of southern Nigeria, extending further north in the west than the east, and overlapping into Benin. The largest languages are Yoruba, with some 20 million speakers, and Igbo, with some 15 million (Grimes 1996). Table 2.10 summarises the linguistic features of West Benue-Congo.

Table 2.10. *Linguistic features of West Benue-Congo*

Noun classes	Full (Gade)/reduced (Edoid)/remnant (Yoruba); prefixes
Verbal extensions	Edoid has a number (often indicating plurality) and Igboid many, most of which are new developments
Pronouns	Independent, subject, object, possessive
Sentence order	SMVOA, SVMOA; Prepositions
Noun phrase	N + Gen; N + Poss; N + Adj; N + Num; N + Dem; N + Definite

2.5.7.2.3   *East Benue-Congo*   East Benue-Congo corresponds to Greenberg's original Benue-Congo, and will be discussed under its three major branches.

2.5.7.2.3.1   Central Nigerian (= Platoid)   Platoid was devised as a cover term for two of Greenberg's original branches of Benue-Congo, Plateau, which he divided into seven numbered groups, and Jukunoid. Gerhardt (1989) made the primary break not between Plateau and Jukunoid, but between Kainji, corresponding to Greenberg's Plateau 1, and the rest. Blench (in press b) has recently argued that these sharp divisions do not well represent the lexical overlap between individual branches and that they would be better represented as a dialect chain. He proposes the name 'Central Nigerian' to cover these languages, which, spreading from the far north-west of Nigeria to Cameroon, are no longer closely identified with the Jos Plateau. Figure 2.12 summarises this classification.

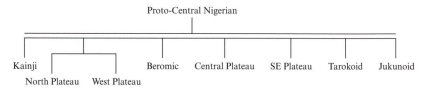

Fig. 2.12. A proposal for the classification of Central Nigerian languages.

This ensemble includes as many as 150 languages, many of which are barely documented, and membership of many of these groupings remains impressionistic. One group that has been studied in some detail is the West Kainji languages and figure 2.13 summarises their classification, derived from Blench (1988).

Table 2.11 summarises the linguistic features of Central Nigerian (Gerhardt 1989).

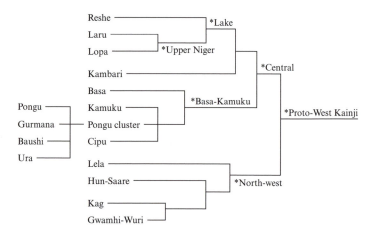

Fig. 2.13. Classification of West Kainji languages.

Table 2.11. *Linguistic features of Central Nigerian*

Noun classes	Full/reduced; prefixes, occasional infixes
Verbal extensions	Widespread, including pluractionals
Pronouns	Intransitive copy pronouns (pronominal elements in slot where object pronouns would follow transitive verbs)
Sentence order	SMVOA, SVMOA; Prepositions
Noun phrase	N + Gen; N + Poss; N + Adj; N + Num; N + Dem; N + Definite

2.5.7.2.3.2   Cross River   Cross River is a group which has survived from Green-berg's classification with only internal rearrangement. Greenberg subdivided it into Cross River 1, 2 and 3. Following a suggestion by Crabb (1969), the original Cross River 1 is now known as Bendi. Tom Cook (p.c.) joined the remaining languages as Delta-Cross, and then divided them into four groups: Upper Cross (basically the same as 'Cross River 3'), Lower Cross, Kegboid (Ogoni), and Central Delta. Connell (1998) has reviewed the classification of Cross River; a summary of his conclusions is given in figure 2.14. He reiterates doubts previously raised about the affiliation of Bendi, hence the use of broken lines to link it to Delta-Cross.

Table 2.12 summarises the linguistic features of Cross River (Faraclas 1989, Connell 1994b).

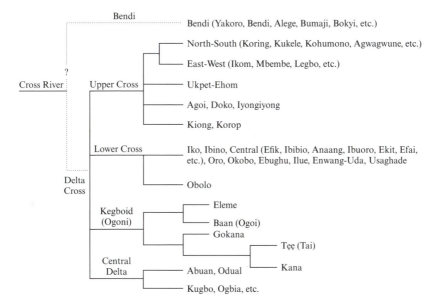

Fig. 2.14. Classification of Cross River languages.

Table 2.12. *Linguistic features of Cross River*

Noun classes	Full (some Upper Cross)/reduced (Abuan)/none (Gokana)
Verbal extensions	Various, often coalescing with verb root; often indicate plurality
Pronouns	Independent, subject, object, possessive
Sentence order	SMVOA, SVMOA; Prepositions
Noun phrase	N + Gen; N + Poss; Adj + N, N + Adj; N + Num; N + Dem; N + Definite

2.5.7.2.3.3   Bantoid   The term Bantoid was first used by Krause in 1895, for languages that showed resemblances in vocabulary to Bantu. Guthrie (1948) used it for languages with noun class systems resembling Bantu, but without regular sound correspondences to Bantu. Greenberg gave it its present meaning, the group to which Bantu belongs together with its closest relatives, first known collectively by the clumsy name 'non-Bantu Bantoid'. In the 1970s and 1980s, a loosely constituted group of scholars, the Benue-Congo Working Group, and a related, overlapping Grassfields Working Group, whose members carried out extensive fieldwork in Cameroon on previously little-known languages, worked on Bantoid. They attempted to find criteria first to distinguish Bantu from non-Bantu languages, and secondly to distinguish a subgroup within this 'Wide Bantu' which would correspond to 'Narrow Bantu', the languages recognised by Guthrie (1948) as Bantu. He had provided a geographical classification into zones labelled A–T, subdivided into numbered groups: thus A is a zone, A.70 is a group, A.71 is a language (consisting of a dialect cluster), A.71a is a dialect of A.71 (see also Guthrie 1967–71). Although this scheme is in standard referential use, most of the zones are not genetic groups. The working groups were not successful in providing watertight definitions of 'Wide' and 'Narrow' Bantu, although the internal membership of various groups within Wide Bantu was greatly clarified.

Blench and Williamson (1988), popularised in Bendor-Samuel (1989), proposed that the basic division within Bantoid is between North Bantoid, corresponding to the old 'non-Bantu Bantoid' without Tivoid, and South Bantoid, consisting of all remaining Bantoid languages. In this view, North Bantoid consists basically of Mambiloid and Dakoid. Dakoid is a group including Chamba Daka, classified by Greenberg as Adamawa; Bennett (1983) pointed out that it was rather Benue-Congo, and Blench (n.d.) assigned it specifically to North Bantoid together with Tikar. This view is disputed by Boyd (1994), Piron (1998), and Connell (in press), although each author makes a different proposal. In this chapter, we have adopted a conservative view whereby the components of North Bantoid are treated as separate branches from the main stem rather than as a coherent group (see figure 2.15).

Nurse (1996) shows that all major modern attempts to classify Narrow Bantu have been based on lexicostatistics, but have not produced an agreed overall scheme. The most widespread agreement is that there is a North-west Bantu, corresponding to zones A, B, C and parts of D; these languages are both more distinct from the rest and from one another, suggesting more ancient splits. After this many authors see a division between East and West Bantu, but the boundaries differ from one scholar to another, with some suggesting an intermediate Central Bantu.

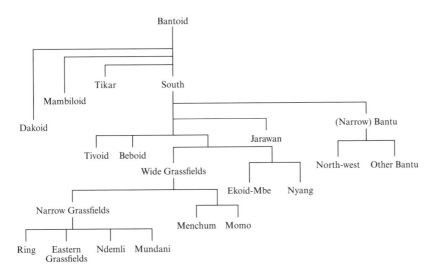

Fig. 2.15. Classification of Bantoid languages.

These classifications all have the defect that they accept the somewhat arbitrary boundaries to Bantu set by Guthrie. The next logical step has been taken by Piron (1998), who presents a classification which extends the most recent lexicostatistic classification of Bantu (Bastin, Coupez, and Mann, forthcoming) to include samples of all Bantoid groups. In spite of problems caused by inadequate or unrepresentative data from some groups, and defective lists in others, which are known to cause distortion of results, her work suggests various levels of relationship between the Bantoid groups. South Bantoid appears as a coherent group, but the next division is problematical; only the Furthest Neighbour method of calculation shows a clear break between (Narrow) Bantu and the rest of Bantoid, while the Branch Average method separates East plus South Bantu from all the rest. Clearly further work with better data is needed to resolve this contradiction, and work with other methods (shared innovations, reconstruction) is also required to confirm or modify these lexicostatistic results. Conservatively, we present Bantu in figure 2.15 as a unity, while accepting the results of the Branch Average method for the rest of South Bantoid. It should be noted that a consequence of accepting the basic split in Bantu between North-west and the rest is that the reconstructions of Bantu, such as Guthrie's (1967–71) Common Bantu or Meeussen's (1980) Proto-Bantu, will need to be revised to give more weight to North-west Bantu. Table 2.13 summarises the linguistic features of Bantoid.

Table 2.13. *Linguistic features of Bantoid*

Noun classes	Full (Bantu)/reduced (Vute)/remnant (Mambila)
Verbal extensions	Widely attested
Pronouns	3rd person concord with noun classes
Sentence order	SMVOA, SVMOA; Prepositions
Noun phrase	N + Gen; N + Poss; N + Adj; N + Num; N + Dem; N + Definite

2.5.8   *Unclassified languages*

In the Niger-Congo domain, there are some languages whose affiliation remains to be determined; some are apparently Niger-Congo but so far not assigned to a family, others are of uncertain classification.

Bɛrɛ = Pre. The Pre language, spoken in northern Côte d'Ivoire, was first reported by Creissels (n.d.) and although it has many Mande loans, it appears to be closer to West Volta-Congo.

Mpre. This language, once spoken in Ghana, is known only from an article by Cardinall (1931). Unrelated to Pre, its numerals resemble those of the Guang languages, but the other vocabulary is hard to recognise.

Laal. Spoken in south-central Chad, this language has been described by Boyeldieu (n.d.) and contains substantial Chadic and Adamawa elements as well as a core vocabulary of unknown provenance.

2.6   Typology and reconstructions

In this section, typical features will first be noted under each heading. Then proposed reconstructions, as distinct from typological resemblances, will be discussed.

2.6.1   *Phonological system*
2.6.1.1   *Vowels*

Niger-Congo languages often show vowel harmony based on the size of the pharynx, controlled by advancement or retraction of the root of the tongue and raising or lowering of the larynx (Ladefoged 1964; Stewart 1967; Lindau 1975). In a maximal system of this type, the expanded or [+ATR] vowels are /i e ɜ o u/ and the non-expanded or [−ATR] ones are /ɪ ɛ a ɔ ʊ/. It is also common to find systems which lack /ɜ/ and in which /a/ is opaque, combining with either set, and systems which lack /ɜ ɪ ʊ/ and in which /a i u/ are opaque. Some systems have only oral vowels, others both oral and nasalised. It is common for there to be fewer nasalised than oral vowels; there are never more.

Westermann (1927), followed by Mukarovsky (1976–7), reconstructed #a, #i, #u for Proto-West Sudanic (or Proto-West Nigritic), with mid vowels as later developments from coalescence or assimilation. In a careful reconstruction of the common ancestor of Proto-Potou-Tano (part of Kwa) and Proto-Bantu (equivalent to Proto-East Volta-Congo in the present classification), Stewart (1998) presents evidence for at least five oral vowels *i *ɪ *a *ʊ *u and five nasalised vowels *ĩ *ɪ̃ *ã *ʊ̃ *ũ. Outside Volta-Congo, Doneux (1975) has reconstructed a system of ten oral vowels with ATR harmony for Proto-Northern Atlantic; thus it is possible that Proto-Mande-Atlantic-Congo and even Proto-Niger-Congo had as many as ten oral vowels.

2.6.1.2   *Consonants*

Typical Niger-Congo consonant systems have five contrasting places of articulation: labial, dental/alveolar, palatal (including post-alveolar), velar, and labial-velar. Labial-velars are rare in Kordofanian and Bantu and absent in Atlantic and Dogon. Kordofanian has lamino-dental contrasting with apico-alveolar/retroflex. There are almost always voiceless and voiced plosives (and often affricates); usually voiced implosives, except in Kordofanian, Dogon, and parts of Benue-Congo, and occasionally unvoiced ones; frequently labialisation as a secondary articulation, less often palatalisation and very rarely velarisation; at least /m/, sometimes /n ɲ ŋ ŋm/; often prenasalised voiced stops, occasionally also voiceless ones; usually /f s/ and less often /v z/, sometimes /h/ or other fricatives; usually /l r y w/.

Westermann (1927) reconstructed a very small consonant inventory, Mukarovsky (1976–7: 37) a richer one including a series of consonants, represented as Ch, 'which might have been an aspirated plosive or an implosive, an affricate or a fricative'. Stewart (1973), reconstructing the consonants of Proto-Bantu-Potou-Tano from the sound correspondences, first proposed four series of stops; voiceless and voiced lenis plosives, voiceless and voiced non-lenis plosives. Later (1993) he proposed that the 'lenis' consonants were rather implosives, which is more promising given the wide distribution of voiced implosives in Niger-Congo. Neither of his two non-implosive/implosive contrasts has, however, been confirmed as going farther back than Proto-Potou-Tano, and it now seems possible that Proto-Bantu-Potou-Tano had voiced implosives to the exclusion of voiced plosives and that in general the voiced plosives found in the daughter languages go back to voiced implosives. Stewart has also proposed that Proto-Bantu-Potou-Tano had both simple nasals and voiced nasal continuants, and that these go back to double nasals and single nasals respectively in Pre-Bantu-Potou-Tano. Before the Pre-Bantu-Potou-Tano single nasals were reduced to nasalised voiced continuants, however, all vowels were already nasalised in the environment of nasal consonants, and the new nasalised voiced continuants thus became subphonemically nasalised variants of their oral counterparts. In daughter languages the nasalization may be completely lost, as in the eastern Bantu languages, or the nasalised voiced continuants may revert to simple nasals, frequently with the result that synchronically, as for instance in the Potou language Ebrié, simple nasals appear to be predictable variants of the implosives; a number of languages in various families of Niger-Congo have been synchronically analysed without phonemic nasals.

Stewart's work shows regular sound correspondences between Potou-Tano and Bantu and it is also possible to do this between Proto-Ịjọ and Bantu (table 2.14).

Table 2.14. *Regular sound correspondences in Proto-Ịjọ to Bantu voiceless plosives*

	'blow (with mouth)'	'sweep'	'hit'	'breathe, rest'
Common Bantu p-	*-púd-	*-píáŋg-	*-pám- 'strike'	*-púúm-
Proto-Ịjọ f-	*ófúró	*ófị́	*fámú 'beat'	*fúmú 'faint'
	'three'	'bedstead'	'pick up'	'tree'
Common Bantu t-	*-tátù	*-tándà	*-tóód-	*-tí
Proto-Ịjọ t-	*táárú	*tàndà' 'platform, bed'	*tɔ́lɔ́	*tẹ́ị́
	'five'	'choose'	'slice'	'wash'
Common Bantu c-	*-cáánò	*-cád-	*-cèŋg-	*-cùkud-
Proto-Ịjọ s-	*sɔ́ŋɔ́rɔ́	*-sèlě	*sẹ̀ŋgǐ	*sókɔ́rí
	'obstruct'	'become strong'	'wrap (up)'	'neck'
Common Bantu k-	*-kíík-	*-kód-	*-kút-	*-kiŋgɔ̀
Proto-Ịjọ k-	*kìkì'	*kòrɔ̌	*kútá⁺	*kɔ̀ŋgɔ̌

Sources: Guthrie (1967–71); Williamson (in prep.).
⁺ West Ịjọ only.

2.6.1.3   *Tone*

With few exceptions, Niger-Congo languages make use of register rather than contour tone systems, according to Pike's (1943) terminology. They often have complex morphophonemics and grammatical tone as a result of the survival of tones from deleted syllables. It is generally believed that Proto-Niger-Congo had at least two tones, but no serious reconstruction has yet been done.

2.6.2   *Noun-class prefixes*

Proto-Niger-Congo must have had a noun class system, already grammaticalised, because every family shows at least some traces of the system. Mande is often cited as an exception, but the initial consonant mutation in nouns, compared with that in other branches, suggests conditioning by earlier prefixes; even clearer evidence is the tonal alternation in Sembla:

	Mande	Sembla	*bī*	pl.	*bî*	'goat'	(Prost 1971: 72)
cf.	Bantoid	Esimbi	*i-bi*	pl.	*í-bí*	'goat'	(Stallcup 1980)

Comparative work in Southern Atlantic (Childs 1983) and Gur (Manessy 1965–6) shows that prefixing languages can change to suffixing ones by concord elements attaching themselves to a final demonstrative or article. This is part of the process of 'renewal' of demonstrative or definite markers which have weakened (Greenberg 1977; (ed.) 1978; 1978: cf. Williamson 1989b). The same affixes can be traced from family to family; see table 2.15, where the classes are numbered according to Bantuist conventions.

Systems with such a degree of similarity betray their common origin.

2.6.3   *Verbal extensions*

Surprisingly, Voeltz's pioneering unpublished study (1977) remains the only serious comparative work on verbal extensions in Niger-Congo. He shows that a number of extensions have reflexes in almost all families, including Kordofanian, and should therefore be reconstructed to Proto-Niger-Congo; these include #ed 'applied (directive, benefactive, applicative, relative, prepositional, etc.)', #ci and #ti 'causative' and #na 'reciprocal'. Suffixes with such specific forms and meanings are unlikely to occur accidentally, nor is borrowing likely when the verbal systems are otherwise so varied.

2.6.4   *Syntax*

Kordofanian, Atlantic, Kwa and Benue-Congo languages are SVOA languages while Mande is SMOVA. Ịjọ, Dogon, and Senufo are SOV; at least Ịjọ is SAOVM. North Volta-Congo is SVO, SMOV. Most scholars consider that these variations reflect developments from an original SMVO order, with the V of SOV languages having developed from a nominalisation (e.g. Claudi 1993). A minority view is that the original order was SOV, with independent developments into SVO. The position of nominal modifiers varies considerably, with a demonstrative element at the end of an NP in many groups, perhaps providing an original base to which other modifiers could attach themselves (cf. section 2.6.2).

2.6.5   *Basic vocabulary*

Westermann's 'West Sudanic' reconstructions essentially correspond to proto-Mande-Congo in modern terminology. Although his data sources excluded Kordofanian, Ịjọ, Dogon and Adamawa-Ubangi it is possible to find cognates in these groups for many of his reconstructed items. In terms of

Table 2.15. *Noun class affixes compared in five families of Niger-Congo*

Class pairs	1sg	2pl	3sg	4pl	5sg	6pl	6A	9sg	10pl
Typical items	human beings		trees, rope, tail, road, fire		egg, head, name, eye, tooth, breast		single liquids, mass	animals	
Kordofanian Heiban	gu-		gu-	j-	li-	ŋu-	ŋ-		
Atlantic *Northern		a-ba-		i-Ci-	e-de-	a-ga-	a-ma-	i̩-i̩/n-	a-na-
Gur *Oti-Volta	ʊ -a	ba	-u, ŋu	i-, ɲi	di	a, ŋa	mu		
Kwa *TR	o-	ba-	o-	i-	i̩-		N-		
Benue-Congo *Bantu	mù-	bà-	mù-	mì-	ɪ̩-	mà-	mà-	ʼn-	ʼn-

Sources: Proto-Heiban: Schadeberg (1981a); Proto-Northern Atlantic: Doneux (1975); Proto-Oti-Volta: Manessy (1975); Proto-Togo Remnant: Heine (1968a); Proto-Bantu: Meeussen (1967).

reconstruction, Kordofanian cognates represent evidence that a specific lexical item can be taken back as far as the Niger-Congo proto-language. Table 2.16 illustrates the likely Kordofanian cognates of some PWS items with initial n-.

Table 2.16. *Items proposed by Westermann (1927) with likely Kordofanian cognates: #n-*

	'come'	'elephant'	'tooth'	'hear'	'mouth'
West Sudanic	#na	#-ni-	#-ni, -nin	#nu-	#-nu, -nua
Kordofanian	nda	yu:ɲi	t-inyèn	-eenu 'ear'	*-uuɲu
	Rashad (RCS)	Lafofa (S2)	Orig (SE)	*Talodi (S2)	*Heiban (S1)

Sources: RCS: R. C. Stevenson (n.d.); SE: Schadeberg and Elias (1979); S1: Schadeberg (1981a); S2: Schadeberg (1981b).

2.7 Conclusion

Given the size and importance of the Niger-Congo language phylum, the many uncertainties and lacunae in basic data constitute an unfortunate limitation on any full-scale reconstruction. Nonetheless, the fragments of morphological and lexical evidence presented should clarify the genetic unity of Niger-Congo and indicate the next steps in a passage towards a full-scale reconstruction.

Notes

1 The following abbreviations have been used throughout this chapter:

A	Adverbial/Adjunct
Adj	Adjective
ATR	Advanced tongue root
CAR	Central African Republic
Dem	Demonstrative
DRC	Democratic Republic of the Congo
Gen	Genitive
M	Modality (tense/aspect/mood)
N	Noun
NP	Noun phrase
Num	Numeral
O	Object
Poss	Possessive
PWS	Proto-West Sudanic
S	Subject
TR	Togorestsprachen
V	Verb
V	Vowel

The convention for reconstructions used in Bendor-Samuel (1989) distinguishes those established by regular sound correspondences (*) from quasi-reconstructions derived by quick inspection of cognates (#). A double line in a genetic tree, thus:

indicates an ancient dialect continuum (Ross 1988). A dotted line in a genetic tree, thus:

indicates a tentative placement.

2 The authors would like to thank Bruce Connell, Bernd Heine, Derek Nurse, John Stewart and Erhard Voeltz for useful comments and corrections on an earlier draft.

3 Other publications by Mukarovsky show that he considered Mande and Fulfulde not to be Niger-Congo.

3

Nilo-Saharan

M. LIONEL BENDER

3.1   The Nilo-Saharan languages: phylum or collection of unrelated groups?[1]

Much scepticism has been expressed about the genetic classification of African languages into four phyla, that is maximal stocks which in our present state of knowledge cannot be brought into genetic relationship to each other by acceptable methodology. Of the four 'Greenbergian phyla' (Greenberg (1963a)), Nilo-Saharan is probably the least widely accepted. Let us first survey the proposed phylum from several points of view and in later sections consider some of the evidence for the existence and subgrouping of the putative phylum. Controversial languages such as †Meroitic and Shabo, which might be Nilo-Saharan, are not listed below (see section 3.2.2).

3.1.1   *Brief gazetteer of Nilo-Saharan languages*

Following is a revision of the listing of Nilo-Saharan languages in Bender (1996–7: 20–37). The reader is urged to consult the original for details and sources and refer to the family tree in section 3.2.2. The use of letters A–L for highest-level families is a modification of Greenberg's original west-to-east listing. Sudan herein refers to Republic of Sudan. Approximate geographical locations are given; see also map 3.3. Abbreviations NE, NC, etc., will be used where convenient (C for 'Central').

Population estimates are also given herein (mostly from Grimes (1996)). For totals by groups and discussion, see section 3.1.4. For large populations, M is used for millions so that, for example, 1.113M means 1,113,000; otherwise numbers of thousands is given, so that, for example, 880 means 880,000, 43 means 43,000, 1.5 means 1,500. 1 is used for 1,000 or less down to 500 and 'few' is used

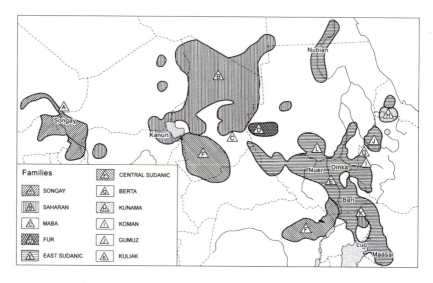

Map 3.3. Nilo-Saharan.

for vanishing languages with less than 500 speakers. The dagger symbol † means extinct or believed so.

Three independent families: A, B, K

A. *Songay*. A dialect cluster in central West Africa with six Western varieties along Niger River and four Northern varieties, the latter interspersed among Twareg (Berber) peoples of the desert north of the Niger. Songay 1.113M, Zerma 2M, Dendi 72, Tadaksahak 42.

B. *Saharan*. A language cluster extending east of Lake Chad to NW Sudan. Kanuri-Kanembu 4.128M, Daza 300, Teda-Tubu 73, Zagawa-Bideyat-†Berti 182.

K. *Kuliak*. Three languages of the NE corner of Uganda: Ik (Teuso) 6, Soo (Tepes) few, and †Nyangi.

A fourth large family with six branches: C, D, F, G, H, Core

C. *Maban*. Five languages along the middle Chad–Sudan border: Bora-Mabang 300, Masalit 250, Aiki (Runga and Kibet) 43, Kendeje 1.5, Surbakhal 6, 'Mimi' 5.

D. *Fur (or For)*. Neighbours of Maba in Dar Fur, Sudan: Fur 502 and Amdang 15.

F. *Central Sudanic*. A very large and complex language and dialect cluster found from Cameroon to southern Sudan, northern Uganda, and NE Zaire. Language names and classification are not entirely clear in many cases. Some names cover disparate languages, for example Sara, Kaba, Kara. The main groups are:

F1. Sara-Bagirmi. The first major group is in SE Chad along Chari River. Without going into details of subclassification, there are Sar 200, Mbai 100, Bedjond 36, Barma or Bagirmi 67, Bilala 137, Jaya 20, Gula 15, Gulay 163, Kuka 77, Kenga 30; Laka 57, Ngam 60, Ngambai 600, Dagba 40, Sara-Kaba 14, Kaba of Gozé 158; Doba 250; Kaba-Dunjo 4; Lutos (Ruté) 19, Medogo 19, Valé 5.5. The remainder are in Chad or Sudan or Central African Republic near where their borders come together. Yulu/Binga 7; Fongoro 1; Shemya (Sinyar) 7.5; Fer (Kara) 5, Furu 16.

F2. Bongo 7.5, Kara 15. In northern Central African Republic and SW Sudan.

F3. Modo-Baka: B'eli 8, Baka 26, Moda 1, Jur Modo 15.5, Morokodo 3.5. In southern Sudan, north of Zaire.

F4. Moru-Madi, in extreme southern Sudan and northern Uganda. Moru 70, Avokaya 40, Logo 210, Kaliko 15, 'High' Lugbara 488, 'Low' Lugbara 589, Luluba 15, Nyamusa 1, Okollo 48, Madi 150.

F5. Mangbutu-Efe, in NE corner of Zaire. Mangbutu 15, Efe 20, Ndo 300, Mamvu (Tengo) 60, Balese 50.

F6. Mangbetu-Asua, in NC and NE Zaire. Mangbetu 650, Lombi 12, Asua few.

F7. Kresh-Aja, in SW Sudan. Kresh 16, Aja few.

F8. 'Lendu' (Bantu name for people), in NE Zaire, near Lake Albert. Ba(le)dha 760, Bendi 32, Ngiti 100.

G. Berta. A dialect cluster in the middle Sudan–Ethiopia border area: 100.

H. Kunama. A dialect cluster in south-west Eritrea: 140.

The Core is the sixth branch of the fourth large family of Nilo-Saharan. It in turn has four branches.

E. East Sudanic. Here the numbering is my own, following on Greenberg's original. This large and complex family can be divided into two parts:

Ek (1 sg. pronoun with k):

E1. Nubian in S Egypt, N, SC and SW Sudan. Nobiin 545, Midob 30, †Birgid, Kenzi-Dongola 280, Hill Nubian (a dialect cluster): Dair 1, Dillinj 5, Gulfan 16, Karko 13, Wali 1.

E3. Nera ('Barya' or 'Barea') in southern Eritrea (63).

E5. Nyima, in Nuba Hills of SC Sudan. Ama (Nyimang) 74.5 and Dinik (Afitti) 4.5.

E7. Tama, in SC and W Sudan. Tama 63, Erenga-Sungor 38.5, Merarit 42.5.

En (1sg. pronoun with n):

E2. Surmic in SW Ethiopia and neighbouring Sudan: Majang (Mesengo) 50, Didinga-Murlé-Tennet 136, Suri (Mursi, Tirma, etc.) 36, Me'en or Mekan (Tishena, Bodi) 50, Balé (Zilmamu) 7.5, Kwegu-Muguji perhaps .5.

E4. Jebel or East Jebel, E Sudan. Gaam (Ingessana, Tabi) 100, Aka (Sillok) 1, Kelo (Tornasi and Beni Sheko) 1, Molo (Malkan) 1.

E6. Temein of Nuba Hills. Rongé or Temein 10, Doni (Jirru, Tesé) 1.5.

E8. Daju, W Sudan and E Chad. Daju 23,000, Shatt 15, Liguri 2.5, Nyala-Lagowa 80, Nyolgé (Nyalgulgulé) 1, Mongo 31, Sila 38, †Beygo.

Nilotic: E9 family of En

E9 Nilotic is part of En but is so vast that it deserves separate listing. There are three subgroups, usually referred to as West, East and South, for which I prefer the neutral (a), (b), (c), since the geographical locations are overlapping. In general, Nilotic (a) is found from S Sudan to NW Kenya, Nilotic (b) from S Sudan and Uganda to N Tanzania, Nilotic (c) in W Kenya and NW Tanzania.

(E9a) 1. Northern: Burun 18, Mebaan 37.5, Jumjum 37.5; 2. Luo: Northern: Colo (Shilluk) 175, Anywa (Anuak) 78, Jur 54, T(h)uri 7, Bor 8; Southern Luo: Acoli 774, Alur 920, Lango 978, Kumam 113, Adola 250, Kenya Luo 3.408M; 3. Dinka-Nuer: Jieng (Dinka) 1.35M, Naadh (Nuer) 840, Atuot 25.

(E9b) 1. Bari 286, Kakwa 147, Mandari 36; 2a. Lotuko-Maa: Lotuko 135, Lopit 50, Lokoya 13, Lango (not Lango of E9a) 20, Maa (Maasai), 883, Samburu 147, Ongamo few; 2b. Teso-Turkana: Toposa 100, Turkana-Nyangatom 345, Karimojong (incl. Jie, Dodoth) 370, Teso 1.217M.

(E9c) 1. †Omotik (not to be confused with the Omotic family of Afroasiatic languages in Ethiopia) and Datooga 175; 2. Kalenjin dialect clusters: Nandi 262, Keiyo 111, Kipsigis 472, Tugen 144, Endo-Marakwet 47.5, Okiek-Sogoo few, Sapiny-Sebei 120, Päkot 264.

Three small families

I. Koman. Two languages of E Sudan: T'wampa (Uduk) 20, now re-settled because of Sudanese repression into extreme W Ethiopia and †Gulé; three languages of middle Sudan–Ethiopian border area: Komo 11.5, Kwama 15, Opo (Shita) 3.5.

J. Gumuz. Dialect cluster of W Ethiopia on Sudan border north of Berta (90).

L. Kadu or Kadugli-Krongo in Nuba Mountains of SC Sudan. Kanga 8, Kadugli-Katcha-Miri 75, Keiga 6, Krongo 22, Mudo (Tulishi, etc.) 5.5, Tumma 6.5.

3.1.2   **Notes on nomenclature**

Problems in naming languages are created by historical confusions, for example a locality for a people inhabiting it or the use of pejorative names by outsiders such as 'stranger, non-believer, slave'. Another kind of difficulty is that some peoples call their languages by such non-ethnic names as 'talk-of-hill' (*kor-e-gaam*, E4 Gaam) or 'language of home' (*t'wa-m-pa*, I T'wampa or Uduk) or have no overall name recognised by all but go by clan or local names (e.g. J Gumuz, some of whom accept 'Gumuz', but many of whom do not).

No comment is necessary for groupings which take their names from prominent languages, for example Songay, Maba, obvious geographical features, for example Saharan, Nilotic, or well-established historical usage, for example Nubian. The name 'Songay' is often seen as 'Songhai', using French spelling. It is actually *soŋay*, with the velar nasal for which neither French nor English has a single letter, and one should be wary of confusing it with Somrai, a small Chadic language of Chad. Saharan has also been called 'East' or 'Central Saharan', but these distinctions are not needed. Maban (the group including Maba) should not be confused with Mebaan, a Nilotic language of E9a. 'Fur' is also seen as 'For'; in fact, interchange of *o* and *u* is common in Nilo-Saharan languages and is seen also in such names as Kado vs. Kadu. There is no 'West Sudanic' family corresponding to 'East' and 'Central'. There is no satisfactory name for the three small languages of family K of NE Uganda. Kadu (or Kado) is a name Roland Stevenson suggested for the family usually known as 'Kadugli-Krongo' and formerly assigned to Niger-Congo (when it was referred to as 'Niger-Kordofanian'; see chapter 2 above). *kadu* or a variant of it is the common word for 'person' in these languages.

Several 'Mimi' languages are reported in Chad near the middle Sudan border. One of these is a C Maban language, another is Amdang of the Biltiné area, related to D Fur, and it is possible that there is still another as yet unclassified 'Mimi'. Note has already been made of the confusion of names in the Central Sudanic family: various languages are known as 'Sara, Kaba, Sara-Kaba, Kaba-Dunjo, Kara', etc. A definitive survey is needed. Baledha is usually called 'Lendu', a name given by nearby Bantu-speakers, reinterpreting *ɓalɛndru*, name of the people, as having a Bantu prefix *ba-*. Berta has been called 'Gamila', based on Berta *ga mili*, 'people black', supposed to have been the reply to the question 'Who lives over there?' Another name applied to G Berta was 'Wetawit', supposedly (but dubiously) meaning 'bats' because the people were seen as nomadic and flitting from place to place.

Within East Sudanic and even crossing over into Central Sudanic, there is also repetition of names, for example Jur Luo of E9a, Jur Modo and Jur Beli of F3 (listed above as simply Modo and Beli), and several other 'Jur' languages (based on use of a Jieng word for 'strangers'). There is a large Lango language under E9a and a much smaller one under E9b, in addition to which Surmic Didinga has been called 'Lango' and Opo of Koman 'Langa'. The name 'Luo' ~ 'Lwo(o)' is widespread in Nilotic.

The E3 language *nəra bana* ('Nera talk', where Nera is 'sky, heaven') was formerly referred to as Barea, a variant of Barya, the Amharic word for 'slave'. E5 Ama gets the name Nyimang from a prominent *jebel* (from an Arabic term for 'hill') in the area. Dinik has been referred to by the clan name Afitti. For E2, once referred to by individual languages 'Didinga-Murle', Muldrow suggested 'Surma', a name used for SW Ethiopians speaking the languages in question; later Unseth suggested changing this to 'Surmic' because some specific groups use 'Surma' for themselves exclusively. In fact, 'Surma, Suri, Shuro', etc. are variants of a name for black people of the area. E4, the Jebel family, is my invention, based on examining the lexica and grammars of Gaam and several smaller local languages, formerly considered to be part of Berta, spoken around several prominant jebels ('hills') in eastern Sudan. I renamed Evans-Pritchard's languages of Jebels Sillok, Malkan and Tornasi as Aka, Molo and Kelo according to the self-names of the peoples. The big E4 language, Gaam (see first paragraph in this section), was known as Tabi (a locality) or Ingessana (said to be Arabic for 'the thankless ones' for people who did not accept Islam). In Nilotic, we have the curious coincidence of the extinct E9c language †Omotik (self-name *laamot*), once spoken in SW Kenya, with the name of the Afroasiatic Omotic family, located along the Omo River of southern Ethiopia. In Koman, T'wampa has already been mentioned: their usual name 'Uduk' is an outsiders' name with no known meaning. The extinct †Gulé (a few older speakers still alive in 1979) is named after a huge jebel: the self-name seems to have been 'Anej', a variant of 'Hamej', a name applied to supposed survivors of the former East Sudanese political state of Funj. Opo settlements exist on both sides of the Sudan–Ethiopia border under various names such as Ciita, Ansita, or Shita, Langa and others. J Gumuz and L Kadu have already been mentioned above, but note here that Gumuz (and many other groups of W Ethiopia) were also called 'Shank'illa' from a pejorative for black people in Amharic (and the languages 'Shank'illinya' in the Amharic formation).

3.1.3 *Cultural survey*

I condense here the data of appendix A2 and its discussion in Bender (1996–7: 54–6), which deals with subsistence, political organisation and ideological systems, as well as population estimates, for which see sections 3.1.1 and 3.1.4. These are all 'opportunistic' dimensions in the sense that they are the result of environmental adaptation and historical accident. Other important sources are Murdock (1959) for a continent-wide synthesis of subsistence bases and political organisation, Schneider (1981) for an economic approach to traditional African societies, and Bender (1975a) for detailed Ethiopian examples.

Pre-urbanised Nilo-Saharan people can be divided into three main groups: hunter/gatherers; hoe agriculturalists; and primary pastoralists. The former are rare today, found among Nilo-Saharan peoples only in a few forest-dwelling Central Sudanics, although many peoples supplement their diets by hunting/gathering. Primary pasturalists are also rare, found among Saharans (e.g. Zagawa), Surmics and Nilotics.

There are several agricultural complexes, based on origins of plant and animal resources, which prevail among Nilo-Saharans as well as other African peoples. These vary according to environment and routes of diffusion. Nilo-Saharan peoples generally depend on hoe agriculture with the Sudanic and Prenilote complexes predominant. In the desert areas and the upper Nile valley, conditions have necessitated an emphasis on herding and different agricultural strategies, those of Saharan oases and Nilotic grain-raising. A few areas, notably the Nuba Hills of central Sudan, require terracing and irrigation. Other economic activities such as trade, fishing, hunting, gathering, also follow environmental lines, both ecological and social.

Political organisation was generally of the egalitarian band-level type, with charismatic hunters or shamans with little real power, or of the village headman or chiefdom type. Because of the herding, raiding and semi-nomadism of the herding adaptation, herding peoples such as the Nilotes and Surmics have developed kin-based characteristics: clans, lineages, age-grading, shamans-cum-mediators, occasionally charismatic prophets. The development of state-level societies apparently was inspired by the Egyptian and West Africa models based on grain surpluses and later by contact with Islam. Their distribution on the western and northern periphery of Nilo-Saharan territory follows from this. Subsidiary petty kingdoms began to arise in the more interior areas, for example among the Colo (Shilluk) and Mangbetu.

The distribution of ideological systems has three major components. All of these can be called 'religious', because no predominantly secular societies have yet arisen in Nilo-Saharan Africa. Islam was spread by Arab imperialism from the north and the East African coast. Christianity in its Orthodox version survived in the Coptic Church of Egypt and the related, but not identical, Monophysite variety in Ethiopia, but was displaced along the upper Nile by Islamic invasions. Later, Christian missionisation occurred along the southern frontier with Islam and in such areas as Eritrea and southern Sudan. Elsewhere, traditional belief systems survive and even in nominally Christian and Islamic areas, they are very much alive in various degrees of syncretisation. Judaism had little impact in Nilo-Saharan areas.

Another dimension of variation is that of physical type, the so-called 'race' of older literature. The modern view is to look at *populations*, defined by frequencies of large numbers of different genes, not by external appearance, though the latter imperfectly reflects the former. In physical terms, there are two distinctive minority populations among Nilo-Saharan speakers: a few 'Pygmies' or people of very small stature (and other characteristics), found among some forest-dwelling Central Sudanics (and other non-Nilo-Saharan peoples), and 'elongated Africans', unusually tall people found among E2 Surmic and E9 Nilotes, as well as among some other East Africans speaking Afroasiatic or Bantu languages. In fact, the world's tallest people on average are the Naadh or Nuer (Nilotic-speakers). The remainder and the great majority of Nilo-Saharan speakers are generalised Sudanic peoples, whose genetic make-up in detail remains to be worked out.

3.1.4   *Demographic estimates*

It is difficult to arrive at accurate estimates of populations of Nilo-Saharan-speaking peoples for the usual reasons: lack of census data, a high degree of multilingualism, insufficient knowledge of dialect boundaries, displacements by migrations and raiding, etc. Without trying to do a detailed update, I base the estimates of section 3.1.1 on Grimes (1996) and my appendix (A1 of Bender (1996–7)). All figures cited should be taken as approximations. Note that the intention is to list *first-language speakers*, though this is another hard-to-control variable in the sources. Some languages may serve as local or regional linguae francae and thus have much larger numbers of speakers, as is often noted by Grimes (1996). For totals by groupings and a list of leading languages (with 500,000 speakers or more), see table 3.17.

Populations and positions in genetic classifications do not necessarily show much correlation. It can easily be seen that there are great disparities in Nilo-Saharan-speaking populations and little homogeneity across major genetic groupings. There are significant changes in the table from Bender (1996–7), including an overall increase of about 5,000,000.

A listing of individual leaders depends on how one treats dialect clusters. Lumping dialects which might be considered separate languages for political or ethnic reasons, the leaders with half a million or more speakers are listed in table 3.18.

The top three are from three of the major families: Saharan, Satellite-Core and Songay. The fourth major family, Kuliak, is not represented, since it is tiny. Below the top three, the dominance of Nilotic languages is easily seen, though four Central Sudanics, and one each from Nubian and Fur have their places also.

Table 3.17. *Total Nilo-Saharan speakers by major families*

A Songay	3,227,000	F C Sudanic	5,851,500
B Saharan	4,683,000	F1 Sara	2,108,000
C Maban	605,500	F2 Bongo	22,500
D Fur	517,000	F3 Modo	54,000
E E Sudanic	16,166,500	F4 Moru	1,652,000
Ek	1,177,000	F5 Mangbutu	445,000
E1 Nubian	891,000	F6 Mangbetu	662,000
E3 Nera	63,000	F7 Kresh	16,000
E5 Nyima	79,000	F8 'Lendu'	892,000
E7 Tama	144,000	G Berta	100,000
En	14,989,500	H Kunama	140,000
E2 Surmic	280,000	I Koman	50,000
E4 Jebel	103,000	J Gumuz	90,000
E6 Temein	11,500	K Ik	6000
E8 Daju	190,500	L Kadu	123,000
E9 Nilotic	14,404,500		
E9a Nil. (a)	9,073,000	Core:	16,435,000
E9b Nil. (b)	3,736,000	Satellite-Core:	23,649,000
E9c Nil. (c)	1,595,500	Nilo-Saharan:	31,565,000

Table 3.18. *Demographically leading Nilo-Saharan languages*

1.	Kanuri-Kanembu	4,128,000	9.	Maa	883,000
2.	Kenya Luo	3,408,000	10.	Naadh	840,000
3.	Songay	3,227,000	11.	Baledha	760,000
4.	Acoli, etc.[2]	3,035,000	12.	Mangbetu	650,000
5.	Jieng	1,350,000	13.	Ngambai	600,000
6.	Teso	1,217,000	14.	Nobiin	545,000
7.	Lugbara	1,077,000	15.	Fur	517,000
8.	Kalenjin[3]	989,000			

Nilo-Saharan languages are spoken in significant numbers in fifteen African countries: Eritrea, Ethiopia, Kenya, Tanzania, Zaire, Uganda, Sudan, Egypt, Chad, Central Africa Republic, Nigeria, Niger, Benin, Burkina Faso, Mali, plus 'spill-overs' in Algeria, Libya and Cameroon. The greatest variety in terms of genetic goupings are found in Chad, Sudan and Ethiopia. I will not attempt a country-by-country population count here: for any one country, Grimes (1996) can be consulted. One might ask how many Nilo-Saharan languages there are. Obviously this depends on the delicate question of how to separate language from dialect (see above, chapter 1). In my 1996–7 listing, in which I freely lumped dialects, I arrived at 108, and in the genetic family listing of Grimes (1996), which is much more a splitter's approach, there are 195.

3.2   **History of Nilo-Saharan studies and recent classifications**
3.2.1   *Older studies and classifications*

The story of Nilo-Saharan classification has two phases: prior to and after Greenberg's continent-wide genetic classification, which developed in the 1950s and was summed up in his 1963a book. After Greenberg (1963a), there is general (though not universal!) agreement that the languages of Africa today fall into four maximal units, known as *phyla* (plural of *phylum*, a term taken from biology).

In what follows I draw especially on Bender (1996–7) and Ruhlen (1987). The earlier period of Nilo-Saharan classification meshes with the general history of African classification and is covered in the Afroasiatic (Afrasian), Niger-Congo and Khoisan (Click) chapters in this book. As starting point, consider Westermann's revised classification of 1940:

1.   Khoisan: (a) Nama, (b) Bushman
2.   Hamito-Semitic: (a) Hamitic, (b) Semitic
3.   Negro: (a) Nilotic, (b) Bantu, (c) Sudanic: (i.) Nigritic (ii.) Mande (iii.) Semi-Bantu
4.   Inner Sudan

This classification continues some of the misconceptions of the past century, including special high-level places for Nilotic and Bantu and a 'Hamitic–Semitic' phylum having a split into co-ordinate 'Hamitic' and 'Semitic' halves, based on ancient near-eastern mythology. Most of what Greenberg called 'Eastern Sudanic' (except Nilotic) is found in 4: Inner Sudan.

In his 1955a collection of articles, Greenberg presented a continent-wide classification with sixteen units as follows:

1. Niger-Congo	5. Eastern	9. Mimi[4]	13. Koman
2. Songhai	Sudanic	10. Fur	14. Berta
3. Central	6. Afroasiatic	11. Temainian	15. Kunama
Sudanic	7. Click	12. Kordofanian	16. Nyangiyan
4. Central	8. Maban		
Saharan			

No less than twelve of these groups (excluding 1, 6, 7 and 12) are now considered to be Nilo-Saharan; all of them (except Nilotic) were in Westermann's Nigritic and Inner Sudan group. Although Greenberg may have been unhappy about having such vast families as Niger-Congo and Afroasiatic alongside single languages such as Fur and Kunama in the scheme, he took a conservative view about combining the latter (1995a: 100). But combine he did: nos. 8 and 9 were combined and five other smaller groups were put together into a 'Macro-Sudanic' unit with three branches: Berta, Central Sudanic and Kunama plus East Sudanic.

In the 1963a book, Kordofanian was co-ordinated with Niger-Congo and a slightly altered 'Macro-Sudanic' was renamed 'Chari-Nile' following a suggestion of Welmers. This created a Nilo-Saharan phylum as follows:

A. Songhai	E. Chari-Nile
B. Saharan	1. Eastern Sudanic
C. Maban	2. Central Sudanic
D. Fur	3. Berta
F. Koman	4. Kunama

One may wonder why Nilo-Saharan lagged behind the other three phyla in classification work. Ruhlen (1987: 107–9) suggests several reasons: relatively late European contact, little descriptive literature, relatively fewer languages than Afroasiatic or Niger-Congo, great internal heterogeneity, small and isolated groups.

As with Bantu within Niger-Congo, Nilotic has been at the centre of Nilo-Saharan studies. First recognised by Lepsius, Nilotic was divided by Johnston into two groups (presumably 'West' vs. 'East' and 'South'). Meinhof took a big step backwards and declared against common sense that 'West' was not co-ordinated to the others, which he considered to be 'mixed languages', namely 'Nilo-Hamitic'. Greenberg restored all of Nilotic as a family and Köhler reaffirmed the 'West' vs. 'East' and 'South' division. The 'Nilo-Hamitic' aberration was based on outmoded concepts of using racist and other extraneous criteria in language classification and casually accepting 'mixed' languages.

Several extensions of Nilotic to include obviously related languages were suggested: Nubian, Kunama, and perhaps Berta by Westermann, Nubian, Nera, Gaam, and Kunama by Murray, several East Sudanic languages by Conti Rossini and Murlé by Westermann. As seen above, all these were included in Greenberg's 'Chari-Nile'. Tucker and Bryan's (1956; 1966) survey and analysis volumes are a great landmark in Nilo-Saharan studies in terms of presenting a still useful gazetteer and a very valuable collection of descriptions. The volumes include a number of non-Nilo-Saharan languages of the area and even an excursion in the 1956 volume to South Africa. But the classification scheme and methodology are another step backwards: extreme conservatism in uniting groups (e.g. the old 'Nilo-Hamitic' is preserved as 'Paranilotic') and mixing of typological and genetic traits (see sections 3.2.3 and 3.3).

Something must be said of Greenberg's methodology also. Greenberg eschewed reconstructions and 'starred forms' and relied on 'mass comparison', looking for similarities across large databases of lexicon and grammatical morphemes. Unfortunately his databases are sometimes inadequate or biased, for example overuse of Nilotic and Nubian in his Nilo-Saharan comparisons, although this is at least partly because of lack of data in many areas, a situation which has been much improved in recent decades. There are also more errors in data-entering than one expects in such work. Nevertheless, he got it right for the most part and his African classification culminating in the 1963a book is a tremendous advance in African classification.

3.2.2   *Recent developments in genetic classification*

Since 1963, there have been many suggested refinements in the details of the Greenberg classification, two serious overall genetic classifications, and several radical proposals involving the relationships among Nilo-Saharan, Niger-Congo and Afroasiatic, less so as regards Khoisan. I take most of these matters up here in the framework of my own proposed genetic classification and then refer briefly to the other proposal by Ehret and to several radical suggestions (see also chapter 11 below).

My classification (Bender 1989c, 1991, 1996–7) is based on surveys of lexicon, segmental phonology and grammatical morphemes in all well-documented Nilo-Saharan languages accessible to me. I must emphasise the preliminary nature of this work, but I do think it is a start in the right direction. I followed the principle of historical-comparative linguistic methodology that the best evidence for grouping languages is their sharing of *innovations*, that is items which they innovated in a common period of development, not items *retained* from a more distant ancestor. In figure 3.16 I present my result in the form of a family tree for the proposed Nilo-Saharan phylum.

To summarise the structure shown in figure 3.16, A, B, and K (Songay, Saharan and Kuliak respectively) are independent branches of Nilo-Saharan, with S-C (Satellite-Core) being a fourth branch. Within S-C, there are six independent branches, C, D, F, G, H, Core (Maban, Fur, Central Sudanic, Berta, Kunama and Core). Core consists of four families E, I, J, L (East Sudanic, Koman, Gumuz and Kadu). The justification for this proposed structure is summarised in section 3.3.

Perhaps the most controversial unit in this classification is A Songay. The problems here are the geographical separation from other Nilo-Saharan and the strong influences of Mande languages of Niger-Congo and Berber languages of Afroasiatic. Various attempts have been made to sort out these influences, of which the most interesting is the thesis of Robert Nicolaï: see especially his 1990 book in which he argues that Songay is a post-Creole with a Berber base. Other scholars,

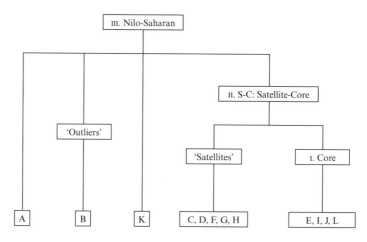

Fig. 3.16. Genetic classification of the Nilo-Saharan phylum.

notably Creissels and Mukarovsky, revived the old Delafosse arguments for classing Songay with Mande.

B Saharan has usually been seen as a divergent member of Nilo-Saharan, but some (notably Mukarovsky and Petracek) have suggested Afroasiatic affinity. K Kuliak still poses a problem. It was one of Greenberg's ten East Sudanic members (known also as 'Nyangiya'). I found Kuliak to be quite distinctive, though perhaps having a special relationship with Saharan and Fur. A problem is created by the fact that Kuliak is surrounded by Nilotic languages which have had strong influences and in fact are replacing the Kuliak languages.

C Maban and D Fur have not been very problematical. Both are entangled with the various 'Mimi' languages of the Chad–Sudan border. Greenberg showed that one 'Mimi', namely Amdang (or Biltiné), is a separate language of D Fur. Paul Doornbos provided data which shows that Kibet, formerly grouped with Tama of East Sudanic, is part of Maban.

Although still found as an accepted unit in many reference works, 'Chari-Nile' was criticised by several investigators and now seems to be an invalid grouping (see especially Goodman 1970). F Central Sudanic and E East Sudanic do not seem to be particularly close despite their similar names and H Kunama is rather distinctive on many counts. Of Greenberg's 'Chari-Nile' members, G Berta and East Sudanic seem to be closest, but in my classification I take a conservative view and have all four as distinct, with East Sudanic joining three others (I, J, L) to form a new family, for lack of a better name, the 'Core Family'. It might seem strange to unite East Sudanic to Koman, Gumuz and Kadu, the first two of which were formerly considered as isolates and the last of which was not even in Greenberg's 1963a Nilo-Saharan. The evidence for the grouping is from grammatical innovations. Incidentally, I now see I Koman and J Gumuz as being quite distinct, not showing a special relationship in a 'Komuz' family as I once suggested. Here, as in the case of Kuliak and Nilotic, geographical contact poses a problem.

As for Kadu, Greenberg had noted (1963a: 149) that the Tumtum group (= Kadu) diverged widely from other Kordofanian languages. Schadeberg and I were the first to suggest that Kadu is not part of Niger-Congo.

There are several still not satisfactorily classified languages which some see as being potential Nilo-Saharan members. The most notorious example is †Meroitic, the extinct language of the ancient Meroé Empire of the Khartoum area in Sudan, which is preserved in sparse formulaic written records. Greenberg and others have suggested East Sudanic affinity, others have made less plausible suggestions of Saharan, Tokharian (extinct languages of Indo-European), etc., but the evidence is too slight to arrive at a definitive answer. My studies suggest that Meroitic, as the language of a state-level civilisation, influenced languages of the Sudan–Ethiopia border area, but cannot as yet be linked genetically to any of them. Two recently documented languages of SW Ethiopia, Shabo (formerly known as 'Mikeyir') and Ongota (formerly known as 'Biralé'), both have very hybrid appearences and cannot satisfactorily be classified, though the former seems to be a potential Nilo-Saharan member, while the latter is linked to Cushitic of Afroasiatic.

Central and East Sudanic are the largest families in Nilo-Saharan. The former has been most extensively studied by Francophone scholars, who have produced much excellent recent work, including tonal analyses and some full-length descriptions. There is a large subfamily, called 'Bongo-Bagirmi' by Tucker and Bryan, which I refer to as Fc for 'Core Central Sudanic' for lack of a better term. The remainder are dealt with by Tucker and Bryan (1966) as 'Moru-Mangbetu' and 'Moru-Madi' plus 'Lendu' in detail in Tucker (1940) (under the name 'Eastern Sudanic'!). I call the entire group Fp for 'Peripheral Central Sudanic' to emphasise that they might not be a genetic group. Some changes in details of membership, etc. have taken place since 1966. East Sudanic has a similar split between a genetic family which can be easily characterised by an innovated 1sg. independent pronoun of general form *ani* (family En comprising Surmic, Jebel, Temein, Daju and Nilotic) and the rest, which have 1sg. pronoun of general form *aka* (Ek consisting of Nubian, Nera, Nyimang and Tama). Since the *aka* pronoun is a retention from Nilo-Saharan, one cannot be sure that Ek is a single genetic family on this basis.

Ehret's alternative genetic classification (see chapter 11 below) follows the methodology of his previous classifications of Afroasiatic, Cushitic, etc., building up phonological isoglosses from comparison of an extensive lexical database. In the resulting scheme, the family tree of Nilo-Saharan is strongly bilaterally branching, with small families being set off at each level vs. 'everything else' (see chapter 11 below, also Bender 1996b and 1996–7 for a critique).

One last topic which should be addressed here is that of whether Nilo-Saharan might be part of a still larger phylum. Resemblances to Niger-Congo have often been noticed and pointed out in passing. The first systematic suggestion along these lines is that of Gregersen 1972. More recently, Roger Blench (1995) has suggested that Niger-Congo may be a branch of Nilo-Saharan, co-ordinate with Central Sudanic. This is based on his observations concerning vowel-harmony systems, labio-velars, some lexical isoglosses and remnants of Niger-Congo noun-class systems in Nilo-Saharan. However, although I think that Niger-Congo and Nilo-Saharan are part of a single larger phylum, I am not convinced that Blench's structure with all of Niger-Congo co-ordinate to Central Sudanic is correct: once again there is a very large problem of extensive geographical contact, in this case of Central Sudanic and the Adamawa-Ubangi languages of Niger-Congo.

3.2.3   *Typological and areal survey*

Languages can be classified very usefully according to external criteria, for example geographical locations, political boundaries, numbers of speakers (as in section 3.1.4), degree of literacy and many others. For example, a classification according to writing systems in use is very important to literacy workers. External classifications may be misleading and even harmful if assumed to be based on language-intrinsic properties. A notorious example is the 'Hamitic' classification of Meinhof, in which he classified languages according to a mixture of such external properties as cattle possession by their speakers and internal typological features (see below, paragraph after next) such as marking for sex gender. This resulted in a 'Hamitic' family which contained, among others, Fula, 'Hottentot', Maasai, and Somali, that is representatives of all four genetic phyla!

Internal criteria are usually of more interest to linguists (scientific scholars of language). Genetic classification of languages is non-arbitrary in that it reflects history (descent through common ancestors), and thus it is the favourite classification system of linguists. But two other language-internal kinds of classification are also of great interest and are favoured in turn for particular functions. These are typological and areal. The first is based on properties of language which may not reflect historical connection or contacts, for example kinds of tonal systems, presence of particular morphological features, word-order phenomena, and the second is based on diffusion of linguistic features, allowing one to establish the existence of linguistic areas, for example the Balkans, South India or Afroasiatic-speaking Ethiopia.

Meinhof used such typological features as sex gender and presence of noun prefixes as basis of his classifications (see Greenberg 1963a *passim* for devastating criticism of Meinhof's methodology). There are few serious studies of typological classification in Nilo-Saharan, but two British practitioners stand out in this area: Tucker and Bryan. Working independently and together, they produced some work which is more useful than one might expect because their use of typology sometimes involves a mixture of typological and genetic criteria. For example, Bryan compared Surmic and Tama languages (thus, two East Sudanic groups from En and Ek respectively) on the basis of the way they form agglutinated verb complexes. This work would be purely typological and of no use for showing genetic relationship, except that she did consider some specific morphemes and so achieved some sound-meaning correspondences.

Tucker used morphological traits in his 'East Sudanic' book, for example 'defining' Sudanic languages by such traits as having monosyllabic roots and being tonal. This is typological: what actually establishes genetic groups is the occurrence of a stock of morphemes relateable through reconstruction to common ancestors. Similarly, Tucker and Bryan give detailed treatment of word shape in terms of consonant and vowel skeletons, for example CV, CVC or VC, in their 1966 book. In this book, they also discuss various pronoun patterns, for example 'block pattern' in which plurals are formed from singulars (found in Nilo-Saharan, but also all over the world) and 'interlocking patterns' in which, for example, 3f.sg. is like 2sg. (an Afroasiatic trait). The interlocking pattern is seen to be genetic when phonological substance is connected to it, namely 2sg. and 3f.sg. *t*, 3m.sg. *y* (the same pattern also applies in some cases in plurals).

Bryan also discovered the existence of singular/plural *n/k* and singular/plural *t/k* patterns in various morphological categories, which she considered substrata (thus areal) underlying many languages. *t/k* is found in most of En plus Tama of E7, Kadu, Fur, Soo (Tepeth) of Kuliak and Iraqw (Tucker and Bryan 1966: 22). *n/k* is found in most of En and Ek plus Kadu, Central Sudanic, Maba, Fur and several Kordofanian groups (24). Actually, singular *n* is mostly found in En plus Nubian, Central Sudanic and Fur, so that plural *k* alone accounts for most of the distribution, especially outside of Nilo-Saharan. I offer an alternative analysis in section 3.3.1.

Perhaps the most useful basis of typology has been ordering phenomena, and here again Greenberg has been one of the outstanding pioneers. Starting with Greenberg's basis, Heine (1976a) arrived at a continent-wide word-order typology of African languages, using a sample of 432 languages. I summarised these results for Nilo-Saharan and checked the representation in my 1996–7 book. Heine refined Greenberg's types, which are based on the dominant sentence order of S(ubject), O(bject), and V(erb), as follows: Type A: SVO; Type B: partly SVO, partly SOV; Type C: VSO; Type D: SOV. Dominant order means that a preponderance of simple sentences in a language follows the order in question. The typology may be refined, since any order may be statistically more-or-less dominant. The remaining possible orders (VOS, OSV, OVS) are rare as primary orders; they appear in Nilo-Saharan only as non-dominant orders in some constructions. It can be seen that both SVO and SOV languages are included in Heine's Type B, which is defined by dominant orders GenNom (i.e. possessor precedes possessed noun) and Postpositions (further details may be found in Heine (1976a) or briefly in Bender (1996–7)). Note, however, that Type D has SOV order with all the other correlated word-order phenomena pointed out by Greenberg; for this reason, it may be called 'rigid' D.

To summarise, in Nilo-Saharan, Type A is found in families EnFGIJL (i.e. all of Core except Ek and also in F, G), while Type D is found in ABCDEkH. This distribution fits well with my genetic classification in that all of Core except Ek is Type A and all the Satellites and Outliers except Kuliak are D. This leaves Ek as Type D, while Kuliak and parts of E2 and E9b,c are Type C (VSO). The exceptions are Bari of E9b and Datooga of E9c, both Type A. The logical interpretation is that Nilo-Saharan was Type D and that an innovation to Type A spread through most of Satellite-Core (as will be seen, this agrees well with the spread of morphological innovations). Type C is also an innovation, found among neighbouring parts of Surmic, Nilotic and also in Kuliak, which, as already noted, is surrounded today mostly by E9b languages. Finally, Songay must be singled out because it has dialects of Type B(A) and also B(D), recessive orders in parentheses. These may perhaps be explained by contact with Berber (SVO or VSO) in the north and Niger-Congo languages (Mande and others) in the south.

Genetic, typological and areal classifications are not always independent 'on the ground'. For example, it happens that Ethiopia is overwhelmingly Afroasiatic-speaking, having three subfamilies: Ethio-Semitic, Cushitic and Omotic. All these languages are rigid Type D. Here genetics and typology coincide. Because word order is relatively subject to diffusion, language areas may share a common word order even if there are several genetic families or even phyla present.

Lexicon presents a major problem in sorting out the genetic from the areal. There seem to be three puzzling situations: (1) neighbouring languages or families with lexical items which may have been borrowed but the direction is unclear; (2) '*Wanderwörter*' or words which seem to be found in many languages in a phylum or in several phyla; (3) 'pan-Africanisms' which seem to be found in most or all phyla and which may be symbolic in origin. For examples, see section 3.3.3.

There is not a wealth of typological or areal studies in the Nilo-Saharan realm. Greenberg dealt with Africa as a language area in another pioneering work (1959), drawing on phonology, grammar and semantics. French scholars, notably Boyeldieu, are studying Central Sudanic tonal systems and applying their evolution and relationships to classification. Insofar as segmental phonology as well is included and 'sound-meaning' complexes are compared, this work can be used for genetic classification. A synthesising study of typological/areal classification in Nilo-Saharan is badly needed.

3.3	**Some reconstructed morphology and lexicon**
3.3.1	*Nilo-Saharan as a phylum; archaising languages and grammatical retentions*

We now come to the question posed at the very beginning of this chapter: is Nilo-Saharan really a phylum or just a collection of unrelated groups? It has been emphasised in the text to this point that what characterises Nilo-Saharan as a phylum is not a collection of typological attributes such as monosyllabism or tonality, but rather a collection of lexical and grammatical morphemes reconstructable to a common ancestor by the comparative method. Actually, there is another step which is sometimes overlooked: showing that it is separate from what is reconstructed for the other established phyla – Niger-Congo, Afroasiatic and Khoisan. Only in the case of Afroasiatic is there a comparable body of work which allows this separation to be made. Niger-Congo and Nilo-Saharan are probably part of a super-phylum, so that the task for these two is ultimately to show the innovations separating them. Because of its relative geographical remoteness and lack of comparable studies, I shall ignore Khoisan in this discussion.

In my 1989c and 1991 articles, I established seven major retentions and thirty-nine other retentions which serve to define Nilo-Saharan. Incidentally, many of these were discovered by Greenberg and presented in his 1963a book. Forty-six retentions are too many to be taken up here, so I limit the exemplification to a sampling of the more striking ones. Examples are sometimes given without diacritics which are unnecessary to the exemplification and without details of variants. In some cases more recent analysis here supersedes the listings in the articles.

(1) Pronoun pattern Pi: 1/2/3 independent subject pronouns (especially in the singular) having vowels *a/i/e*, respectively. The third person *e* is often lacking. Found in families ADEkEnFcFpHIK, traces in B and C. Thus the pattern is lacking in G Berta, J Gumuz, L Kadu, which use the Po pattern instead or have innovated

away from both patterns. Examples are singular independents unless otherwise indicated.

A	Songay	*ay/ni*	En	Acoli	*aan/iin/ɛɛn*	
B	Zagawa	1sg.: *ai*	Fc	Bagirmi	*mal(y)i/ne*	
	Kanuri	2sg.: *ɲi*	Fp	Mangbetu	*ima/imi/inɛ*	
C	Maba	*am/mi/te*	H	Ilit	*aba/ena ~ ina*	
D	Fur	*ka/ji/ie*	I	Kwama	*ga/ɪk*	
Ek	Nyimang	*a/i/ɛn*	K	Ik	*ŋka/bi*, Nyangi	
					3sg.: *ikiet*	

(2) Pronoun pattern Po: 1/2/3 *a/o ~ u/e*, especially in singular, but more often in plural than Pi. Assuming that Pi is primary, the Po pattern may have been generalised to independents in some families. Found in CFcFpGL, traces in ABEkEnHIJ.

A	Dendi	*a/u*	Fp	Kresh	*ama/umu/ɛtɛ*	
B	Kanuri	2pl. poss.: *-ndo*	G	Berta	pl.: *haθaŋ/haθu/mɔre* (?)	
		2pl. vb. af.: *-w-*	H	Kunama	vb. sufs.: *-na/-nu*	
C	Masalit	*am(a)/muuŋ*	I	T'wampa	pl. 1 excl.: *am/um*	
Ek	Dongola	pl.: *ar/ur/ter*	J	Sai	poss.: *-(a)m/-u*	
En	Gaam	*aan/oon/een*	L	Miri	*aʔa/ɔʔɔ*, 3pl.: *ɛgɛ*	
Fc	Mangbetu	poss.: *-andr-a/-u-/ɛ*				

(3) First person singular pronoun **akwai*. This could also be treated as *aka ~ (w)ai*, since it is quite possible, even likely, that there were alternative pronouns in *Nilo-Saharan. Sometimes the plural pronoun is based on this also (Tucker and Bryan's 'block pattern'). Found in ADEkIKL, traces in BEn. Proto-Afroasiatic has prefix **ank~ink*, suffix *ku~ni*.

A	Songay	*ay*, emph.: *agay*	En	Nyala	*aaga*
B	Kanuri	*wu*, vb. af. *-k-*	I	Komo	*aka*
D	Fur	*ka*, Amdang *kai*	K	Ik	*ŋka*
Ek	Dongola	*ay*	L	Miri	*aʔa* (?)
	Nera	*ag*			
	Tama	*wa*			

(4) Second person singular **ini*. Found in ABEkEnFcHI, trace in Fp. It is possible that *m* forms in BDK belong with this also, but for the present I treat these as innovations (they were the basis for a postulated family BDK I once set up). The *n* sometimes disappears, for example in Nyimang and Tama, retaining only the *i*, which is part of Pi. *Afroasiatic **nt-*, *-kV*.

A	Zerma	*ni*	Fc	Modo	*ni*
B	Kanuri	*ɲi*	Fp	Mangbutu	*ini*
Ek	Midob	*iin*	H	Kunama	*e'na*
En	Majang	*in*	I	Komo	poss.: *-ini*

Despite this prevalance of *n*, Ehret (forthcoming a) sets up *Nilo-Saharan as *bi*, which is found only in Fur (plural) and Kuliak, trace in Saharan.

(5) Deictic pattern near/far or to/away *a/u ~ u/a*, where *a* and *u* stand for a reasonable range of phonemes which are phonetically close to the ones given. Here and in no. 6, 'polarity' of representation seems common, something which I do not accept in the pronouns of nos. 1 and 2 above. Found in ABEkEnFpGIK, trace in Fc. Afroasiatic has demonstratives in *n, t, d* but no vowel-patterned demonstratives.

A	Songay	to/away: *a/ɔ*	Fp	Miza	to/away: *a-/ɔ-*
B	Kanuri	*a-/tu-*	G	Berta	to/away: *-o/-a*
Ek	Ama	to/away: *kwu/kwa*	I	Opo	loc.: *-o/-a*
En	Luo	here/there: *ka/ku*	K	Nyangi	to/away: *-ac/-u*
Fc	Bagirmi	*ɛnna/nuu*			

(6) Singular/plural *a/i~i/a*, found in all grammatical categories. Examples are given from occurrences with nouns, unless otherwise indicated. Found in ABH, traces in CDEnFcFpIK. *Afroasiatic has a sing. *-aan, aam*, one type of plural *-aa(n)*.

A	Songay	*-a/-ey*, prn. 3sg./pl.: *a/i*
B	Teda	*-i/-a*
C	Maba	demon.: *-i/-a*
D	Fur	prn. 1sg./pl.: *ka/ki*
I	T'wampa	animate: *i-/a-*
En	Maa	*-a/-i*
Fc	Yulu	pl. demon.: *i-*
Fp	Mangbetu	1/2 prns. sg./pl.: *i-/a-*
H	Kunama	*-a/-e*
K	Kuliak	demon.: *na/ni*

(7) Copula *y(E)*[5]. Found in all families except GHJ. Copula *k* is even more widespread (in all families except L Kadu) and *T* and *n* are nearly as widespread, but show more variation in forms.

A	Zerma	'become': *tyi* (?)	Fc	Yulu	*ya(da)*
B	Kanuri	'and': *ye . . . ye* (?)	Fp	Miza	*ya*

C	Masalit	*yɛ*	I	T'wampa	*(ʔ)e*
D	Fur	*ii*	K	Ik	*iy*
Ek	Nera	*ya*	L	Kaca	*a*
En	Acoli	*ayɛ*			

(8) Verbal negation *mV*, found in AEkEnHJK. Afroasiatic has **m, n, b(aa), la(a)*.

A	Songay	*mana*	H	Kunama	*mme*
Ek	Nera	*ma*	J	Sai	*mɪ . . . je*
En	Murlé	*maa*	K	Ik	*maa*

(9) Verbal transitive/causative or factitive ('cause someone to do') *t*, found in ABCEkEnFcGʔK. In Afroasiatic, on the other hand, *t* is the usual marker of intransitive/passive and *s* of transitive/active.

A	Songay	factitive: *-andi*	En	Gaam	*-d ~ -t*
B	Kanuri	*tu*	Fc	Yulu	*t-*
C	Maba	*nd- ~ nj-*	G	Berta	factitive: *-(θ)iŋ* (?)
Ek	Dongola	*-(i)d(d)i*	K	Ik	*-it*

With the continuing output of thorough grammars of Nilo-Saharan languages in recent years and similar work going ahead in the other phyla, the task of firmly establishing Nilo-Saharan is proceeding. The disadvantage of grammatical morphology is that grammatical morphemes tend to be small so that similar forms recur even in unrelated phyla; for example see the Afroasiatic first person singular pronoun and the verbal negative *m* above. But with more sophisticated work, highly idiosyncratic patterns which are not subject to borrowing may be discovered to help make the case. Lexicon has the advantage of longer forms but is more subject to borrowing (see section 3.3.3).

3.3.2 *Innovating languages*

In this section I present some evidence of the kind needed to justify the subgrouping found in figure 3.16. Obviously one has to look at the whole picture in order to decide what is retained and what is innovated. I must stress how preliminary this work is and how much work lies ahead.

In Bender (1991), I identified seven major innovations and forty-five other innovations setting off the Satellite-Core group (S-C). Of these fifty-two, only eighteen are strictly limited to S-C. There are another thirty-five applying to few groups and even single languages (in the article there are thirty-six, but nos. 26 and 27 are the same). A selection of the best from the fifty-two S-C innovations is presented below (with some modifications from more recent analysis). The first three are chosen from major innovations.

(1) Singular/plural *n/g* (Bryan's 'substratal' *n/k*; see section 3.2.3) in many grammatical categories, often only in plural. The full pattern *n/g* is especially strong in En, finding its apex in Surmic, where in some cases possessive pronouns are even separately marked for number of possessor and possessed. The occurrences in Maba and Fur are weak and one cannot be sure that plural *-k* is the same plural as that of the *n/g* pattern. Unspecified forms below are pronouns. Not found in ABHK.

C	Maba	prn. pl.: *-ŋ* (?)	Fp	Kresh	*-m-/-g-*
D	Fur	demon. pl.: *k-*	G	Berta	demon. pl.: *-gu*
Ek	Nubian, Nera	demon. pl.: *-gu*	I	T'wampa	demon. pl.: *gw-, kw-*
En	Murlé	*-n-/-g-*	J	Kokit	'this' pl.: *-ŋe* (?)
Fc	Bagirmi	prn. pl.: *-ge*	L	Kaca	vb. af.: *n-/k-*

(2) Gender markers, usually in third person singular pronouns: masculine/feminine/neuter *r/b/n*. Found in EnIL, traces in EkFc, making this a Core innovation except for the occurrences in Bongo and Modo of Fc. J Gumuz has other gender markers. As seen in the examples, the masculine marker is fairly strong (assuming that *r ~ l* and *r – > y* in Kaca), neuter is uncommon but consistent, and feminine is inconsistent. (Perhaps Bongo masc. *ba* is polarised from fem.?). In a forthcoming article, Unseth makes a case for Majang (Surmic) plural *-ir* being originally a masculine marker; perhaps the masculine marker has its origin in plural. Greenberg (1963a: 114) exemplifies Nubian and Nilotic animate plural *-r*. Proto-Afroasiatic has the very different masculine *k^w-, (k)u*, feminine *t-*.

Ek	Birgid	*tar/idi* (?)	I	Komo	*har/hap/hen*
En	Bari	*lɔ-/na-*		Kwama	*hal/hap*
	Maa	articles: *ol/en*	L	Kaca	concord markers: *y-/m-/n-*
Fc	Bongo	*ba/ho/ne*			

(3) Demonstrative pattern near/far *i/e*, polarised to *e/i* in Berta.

D	Biltiné	*idi ?/dɛnne*	G	Berta	*'(e)lel-(e)θi*
Ek	Nera	*-yil-te*	I	Komo	masc.: *ne/di*
	Ama	*nil̪de*			

(4) Demonstrative formative *l*, especially 'far'. Proto-Afroasiatic is based on *d, n*.

C	Maba	*wa-k/illɛ-k*	G	Berta	*'(e)lel-(e)θi*
D	Fur	*in/illa*	J	Kokit	*-la/lɛt*

(5) Interrogative formative *ŋ*. Proto-Afroasiatic has 'who?' *mi-*, 'what?' *ma-*, 'where?' *na*.

C	almost all Maban interrogatives have *ɲ* or *ŋ(g)*-	
Ek	Nubian, Nera, Nyimang, Tama all have plentiful interrogatives with *n(d)* or *ŋ*	
En	Plentiful; typical is Nilotic (a) with 'what?' *(a)ŋo*, 'who?' *(a)ŋa*	
Fc	Bagirmi	'who?' *naŋa*, 'how many?' *ndo*
Fp	Lugbara	general interrogative marker *ŋgo*
G	Undu dialect	'what?' *naano*, 'who?' *ndolo*

(6) Negative *kV*. Proto-Afroasiatic is **m, n, la, b(aa)*.

Ek	Nera	pres., cont., fut.: *ka*
En	Majang	*ko-, ku-*
Fc	Kara	*-ku*
Fp	Miza, Madi, etc.	*ku*
I	Komo	*ɛk-, yak'-*

(7) Passive-intransitive *n*. Proto-Afroasiatic is **t*.

D	Fur	*iŋ, uŋ*	Fc	Yulu-Binga	*n-*
Ek	Nera	some verbs: *-nu*	Fp	Kresh	*-ine*
En	Rongé	*an*	L	Krongo	*-An-*

There is little resemblance to Afroasiatic, except for the unremarkable fact that both Nilo-Saharan and Afroasiatic have interrogatives with *n*. Of course the above examples are only a start on the massive task of reconstructing Nilo-Saharan morphology.

3.3.3 *Some remarks on lexicon and phonology*

3.3.3.1 *Lexicon*

As noted in section 3.2.2, the major problem of lexicon is not in separating typological from genetic but in separating areal from genetic. In Bender (1996–7), I used a lexical base of over 600 items divided into fifty semantic sets, explicitly excluding grammatical formatives, for example quantity, size, distance; earthlike and locus; bark and skin. The resulting reconstructions are divided into five classes: (A) isoglosses of three qualities – excellent, good and fair – and on three levels – Nilo-Saharan, Satellite-Core and Core; (B) symbolic forms, that is forms for which the arbitrary relationship between sound and meaning breaks down; (C) areal or 'Pan-African' forms found in three phyla (I did not investigate Khoisan); (D) items linking Nilo-Saharan and Niger-Congo; (E) items linking

Nilo-Saharan and Afroasiatic. The numbers of each are: 258, 21, 25, 30 and 26 respectively. Given space limitations, I exemplify these groupings by a few examples as follows. For the large families Ek, En, Fc, Fp, individual languages are not always identified. In the examples, the first gloss applies unless otherwise specified.

(1) *ar- 'rain', unless otherwise specified. An excellent Nilo-Saharan isogloss, found in all outliers, all satellites (Fc, but not Fp), and in two of the four Core families. Not found in my inspection of Niger-Congo and Afroasiatic.

A	Gao, Zerma	'water': har-i	Fc		'rainy season': ar(-a) (?)
B	Zagawa	'river': ɔr-ʊ-i	G	Berta	(r)rɔ
K	*Kuliak	*(w)ar-	H	Kunama, Ilit	(ŋ)oo'r-a
C	Aiki	'lake': ar-ɛ	E		ar
D	Fur	'river': roo	I	T'wampa	'river': wɔrr

(2) *kOr- 'rib, side', unless otherwise specified. An isogloss for Satellite-Core.

C	Maba, Aiki	kol-on, kol(l)-ɔŋ	I	T'wampa	gwar
Fp		-gar-a	J	Sesé	'horn': k'al-a
G	Berta	'bone': k'aar-a			

(3) *go 'frog, turtle'. A Core isogloss, but the semantics is a bit worrisome.

Ek	g(w)o-	I	Gulé	gɔ
En	gɔ-gi	L	Kaca, Krongo	-gɔ

(4) *tuf- 'spit'. A sound-symbolic item, also found widely in Niger-Congo (Mande, Ijoid, Atlantic-Congo) and Afroasiatic (Semitic, Chadic, Cushitic, Omotic). Note the metathesised variants in Kwama, Krongo.

A	all	tuf-a	H	Kunama	tif-o-, tof-o-
B	Kanuri, Tubu	təf-a-, tefa	Ek		tuf
C	Masalit	tuf	En		tuf ~ tuw, tuy
Fc		tiɓ-i	I	Kwama	tu-, pʊt
Fp		tu	L	Krongo	pʈu

(5) *kulol- (?) 'round or ring'. A much-discussed 'pan-African' item (e.g. Mande kulu, koori, Afroasiatic three families, including Cushitic kʷal). If this root is symbolic, it is in a non-obvious sense. Otherwise it is hard to explain its wide spread. The root is even more widespread if one accepts the extensions (which I reject for now) to meanings such as 'left-hand, (curved) stick, tree'.

A	Songay	gur-, kɔr-	H	Kunama	-gul-
B	Teda, Tubu	-kuli-, -kuri-	Ek		kɔr
	Zagawa	kuru-	En		kUr

K	*Kuliak	*mu-kuɬ*	I	T'wampa	*k'ol-*
D	Fur	'curved': *kɔrr-*	J	Sai	*-k'ul-*
	Komo	'curved': *-k'ɔul*	L	Tulishi, Kaca	*gull-, gu(u)l-u*
G	Berta	*-gol-, -gor-*			

(6) *TVR-* 'moon'. An areal form, also found in Chadic (all three branches), Cushitic and forms such as *tela* 'bright, day', etc., widespread in Niger-Congo (cf. example 2 in section 3.3.3.2).

A	Gao	*-dar-*	F	all	'moon, time': *TVr*
	Kaado, Zerma	*-diri,* 'star': *-daria*	H	Kunama, Ilit	*teel-, teer-*
K	Ik	'star': *ðòle-*	I	Kwama	*a-dwəi, a-dwoi*
D	Fur, Amdang	*duwʌl,* 'sun': *dul-*	L	all	*ṭar-, ṭɛr-*

(7) *tom-* 'ten, one'. Areal form also found in Niger-Congo: Mande and Volta-Congo, Afroasiatic: Cushitic and Omotic. Connection between 'ten' and 'one' is 'unit in counting'.

B	Zagawa	*tim(m)-i*	Ek		*tUm-un*
K	Nyangi, Ik	*tɔm-in, tom-in*	En		*tOm-On*
C	Maba, Mas.	'one': *too(m)*	J	all	'one': *me-ta(m)*

(8) **kon-* (?) 'elbow'. The semantic spread below is a bit wide. This item links Nilo-Saharan and Niger-Congo, compare the word for 'knee' (*kʰon*) in Niger-Congo languages, Mande 'head' (knee as head of leg?) *kon*, Volta-Congo *kona, ekun*, in Bantu as 'arm, hand' *kono*.

A	Gao	*kɔŋ-kor, hon-koro* (?)
C	Masalit	*-koŋ*
F		*kon, (k)ɔɲ*
	Fc	'knee': *gomo*
	Fp	*kum-*
G	Berta	*k'on-, kwɔn-*
H	Kunama	*ukun-*
	Kun., Ilit	'hand': *kona*
Ek		*kum*
En		*kɔm-,* 'elbow, knee': *kuun*
I	Kwama	'claw': *-kump'*
J	Sai	'knee': *kumb-*

(9) **bUr-* 'earth or country or land'. This item links Nilo-Saharan and Afroasiatic. The wide semantics seems justified by parallel items with the same

ranges. Found in four Afroasiatic families as *br ~ mr*; there is also Niger-Congo Mande 'mud' *bɔrɔgɔ* (cf. Fc below).

A	Gao, Kaado	*bor-, bur-*
B	†Berti	*bur* (also 'charcoal')
C	Masalit	'sand': *bor-*
D	Fur	*bar-u, bor-u*
Fc		*buruku* (also 'mud')
Fp		*vuru*
G	Berta	*-bor-*, 'down': *bul-*
H	Kunama	'down': *'buur-*
Ek		*buur*
En		'ashes': *puL*
I	T'wampa	*-bura*, 'dust': *-pura*
	Opo, Kwama	'dust': *burr, bul-*

3.3.3.2   *Phonology*

As touched on in section 3.2.2, there are two interrelated processes involved in the setting up of proposed cognate sets: (1) finding comparable items in sound and meaning, (2) checking to see if there is regularity in phonological correspondences. The latter means that segments in comparable items correspond in the same ways according to environments. This can be extended to non-segmental features such as tone and stress. At this early stage in proto-Nilo-Saharan reconstructions, I arrived (in Bender 1996–7: 66–71; see also Bender 1996c) at a set of proposed proto-phonemes and correspondences mostly of the equality type (e.g., *k* to *k*). The proposed Nilo-Saharan proto-phonemes are as follows, where the convention X/Y means 'occurs in outliers/Satellite-Core':

Labials	*b, f, m, w*	Also, in Satellite-Core only: *d/d, ɲ*
Alveolar/dentals	*d, t, s, n, l, r*	
Palatals	*j-, y*	
Velars	*g, k, kʰ, ŋ*	In Core only: *p, b, d, ʃ*
Vowels	*i, e/i, e, a, au, o, u*	

Not reconstructable: *z ~ s, sʼ, c, kʼ, h, ʔ, a ~ i, a ~ u, o/a, ai, ei, ie, oi, -ui*
Best interpreted as sequences: *mb, nt, nd, ŋg*, etc.
s ~ ʃ often; *j* is rare and initial only; *g, k, kʰ* mostly initial; *n, r* very rare initially, *-R* non-initial; initial vowels other than *a-* are rare

The correspondences across languages are of the equality type *except* for

> *D*   *d* in ABK, occasionally K has *t*; *d* ~ *t* in Satellites, *t* in Core
>
> *T*   *t* in ABK, *t* ~ *d* in Satellites, but *d* in G, *d* in EIJ, *d* ~ *t* in L
>
> *R*   *r* in ABK, *r* ~ *l* in Satellites, *r* in D, *l* in H, *l* in Core
>
> *k^h*   *k* ~ *h* in AB, *k* in K, *k* in Satellites, *k* ~ *h* in IJ, *k* in EL

A few examples will have to suffice to illustrate the correspondences. Others can be seen in the examples of section 3.3.3.1. Consonants are exemplified in initial positions where possible, since this is the position of greatest contrast. Other segments are also illustrated, for example *l* in the first example.

(1) *d*: Nilo-Saharan **dOl(m)* 'tree, branch, club, throwing stick, boomerang'

B	Kanuri	'branch': *dalam*	D	Fur	*dolm-a*, 'club': *dorm-a*
	Berti	'club': *dolm-ai*	H	Kunama	var. of tree: *daar-a*
C	Maba	'club': *dol-o*	I	Opo	*dor-oʔ*
	Masalit	'club': *dall-ɨɲi*			

(2) *t*: Nilo-Saharan **tAr-* 'sky, up, god, lightning, outside' (cf. example 6 in section 3.3.3.1)

A	Gao, Kaado	'outside': *tar-Ey*	Fc		*tor-o* ~ *dar-o*
B	Kanuri	*tol-ila*	Ek		*tell-i*; *dOr*
	Zagawa	*tao*, 'outside': *terr-i*	En		*tɛl*; *der*
C	Maba, Mimi	*ta(a)l*	I	Komo	'outside': *-til-a*
	Masalit	*dol-e*	L	Krongo	'lightning': *tal-*
D	Fur	'lightning': *taur-a*			'outside': *-taar-a*
	Amdang	*tɛrr-e*			

(3) *D* and *o*: Nilo-Saharan **Dog* 'mud, earth, field, mountain'

B	Teda, Tubu	'field': *doog-e*	Ek		*tOg*
K	Soo	*dɔg*	En		'earth': *tɔk* ~ *dɔk*
G	Berta	*atok'-oŋ, adok'-oŋ*	J	Sesé	*tok'-wa, ko-togw-a*

For an example of *r*, see example 1 of section 3.3.3.1, **ar* 'rain, etc.'.

(4) *l*: Nilo-Saharan **lUl-* ~ *lum-* 'cold'

B	Kanuri	*lol-onim*	Ek		*ɔr* (?)
D	Fur	*lull-a*	I	Gulé	*a-lum-di*
H	Ilit	*sul-lum-a*	L	Tulishi, Krongo	*-lim-*
				Kaca	*leʔmɛ*

(5) *R*: Nilo-Saharan **koR-* 'elbow, claw, foot, hand or arm, finger'

A	Gao	-kor(-o)	G	Berta	'foot': kol-ɔ
B	Tubu	kur-u	H	Kunama	-kul-a
	Kanuri, Tubu	'foot': -kol-	E		
K	Ik	'finger': kɔr-ɔk			'claw': -kol-
C	Maba, Mimi	'finger': kar-		Ek	-kol-
	Masalit	'hand': koro		En	kɔl-
	Aiki	kɔrɔ-	I	Komo	'hand': kol-o
D	Fur	'claw': ka(a)r-u	L	Kaca	-gɔɔr-ɔ
				Krongo	-koor-o

(6) *kʰ*: Nilo-Saharan **kʰay* 'big, all, full, very'

A	Zagawa	hai	En		kəi; 'full': gaay-
C	Masalit	'all': kwoy-	I	Kwama	'very': kyaa
	Aiki	kwɔy-e, kway-ɛ	J	Sai	'very': haai
Ek		kay			

(7) *u*: Nilo-Saharan **Tul-* 'smoke, hearth, hot'

A	Gao, Zerma	dull(-u)	H	Kunama	vb.: dullu
B	Kanuri	təl-in	Ek		tuL
C	Aiki	dur-i, 'hearth': -tur	En		toor
D	Amdang	'hot': tul	I	Gulé	dur-ɛd, jur-ɛd

The above examples are chosen for their representativeness and clarity, but most correspondence sets are not perfect. There are many reasons for this: for example, doubtful elicitations, questionable semantics, undiscovered phonological conditioning factors. No verbs (except adjectival verbs 'big', 'cold') are included among the examples. There are plenty of verbs in the data set, but in general verbs tend to be more complicated and problematical semantically.

The only comparable work in this area is that of Ehret (forthcoming a; see also chapter 11 below). In fact, Ehret's work is based much more on setting up a proto-phonology and establishing phonological correspondences than mine is (see section 3.2.2).

Notes

1 The following abbreviations are used in this chapter:

A	Songay	F4	Moru-Madi
af.	affix	F5	Mangbetu-Efe

B	Saharan	F6	Mangbetu-Asua
C	Maban	F7	Kresh-Aja
C	Consonant		
cont.	continuous	F8	'Lendu'
CS	Central Sudanic	G	Berta
D	Fur	H	Kunama
demon.	demonstrative	I	Koman
E	East Sudanic	incl.	inclusive
Ek	1sg. pronoun *k* subfamily of E	interr.	interrogative
emph.	emphatic	J	Gumuz
En	1sg. pronoun *n* subfamily of E	K	Kuliak
ES	East Sudanic		
excl.	exclusive	L	Kadu
E1	Nubian	loc.	locative
E2	Surmic	M	million
E3	Nera	masc.	masculine
E4	Jebel	neut.	neuter
E5	Nyimang	N-S	Nilo-Saharan
E6	Temein	Pi	pronoun pattern sg. 1/2 *ali*
E7	Tama	pl.	plural
E8	Daju	Po	pronoun pattern sg. 1/2 *alo*
E9	Nilotic	poss.	possessive
E9a	North or West Nilotic	prn.	pronoun
E9b	Central or East Nilotic	pres.	present
E9c	South Nilotic	S-C	Satellite-Core
F	Central Sudanic	sg.	singular
Fc	Core Central Sudanic	SOV	Subject–Object–Verb
fem.	feminine	suf.	suffix
Fp	Peripheral Central Sudanic	SVO	Subject–Verb–Object
fut.	future	vb.	verb
F1	Sara-Bagirmi	V	Vowel
F2	Bongo	VSO	Verb–Subject–Object
F3	Modo-Baka	†	extinct

2 Acoli-Alur-Lango-Kumam-Adola.
3 Nandi-Keiyo-Kipsigis-Tugen, according to Grimes (1996); if one included Endo-Marakwet, Sapiny-Sebei, and Päkot, the total would be 1,420,500; fifth place in the list.
4 The Mimi described by Nachtigal, now classed with Maban.
5 Capital letters are 'archiphonemes'; they are to be understood as 'something close to . . .', e.g. T is something close to t, it could be d or t (dental or alveolar), maybe a fricative. E is a vowel in the range of e or a.

Further reading

The references above cover the main sources for current Nilo-Saharan studies, but completeness or even thorough coverage would require many pages. The following reading guide for students supplements the above.

Nilo-Saharan languages in general

Tucker and Bryan (1956, 1966); Greenberg (1963a); Ruhlen (1987); Bender (1996–7); Grimes (1996).

Culture, history, etc.

Murdock (1959); Martin and O'Meara (1986) and chapters therein for references to specific areas such as prehistory, history, belief systems; Schneider (1981).

History of Nilo-Saharan studies, classifications, methodology

Anttila (1989) (methodology); Greenberg (1957) (methodology), (1959) (areal), (1963a) (history and method); Heine (1976a) (typological); Ruhlen (1987); Bender (1996–7).

Songay

Nicolai (1981, 1990).

Saharan

Cyffer (1996).

Maba

Edgar (1991).

Fur

Jakobi (1993).

Berta

Bender (1989a); Andersen (1992, 1993).

Kunama

Bender (1996a).

Koman

Bender (1984, 1994).

Gumuz

Bender (1979); Unseth (1985).

Kuliak

Heine (1976b, 1999).

Kadu

Reh (1985); Schadeberg (1994).

East Sudanic

Dimmendaal and Last (eds.) (1998); Bender and Ayre (1980); Bender (1997); Rottland (1982); Vossen (1982).

Central Sudanic

Tucker (1940); Bender (1989b).

Bibliography

Unseth (1990); Jakobi and Kümmerle (1993).

4

Afroasiatic

RICHARD J. HAYWARD

4.1 Introduction

Afroasiatic (AA) is probably the least controversial of the four phyla of languages proposed by Greenberg for the African continent. Long prior to Greenberg (1950a) a core of what we now call AA had been recognised, and subsequent to that publication there has been no serious suggestion that the AA concept should be called into question. There has not been universal agreement about the internal structure of the phylum nor complete unanimity about the membership of every language group proposed, but regarding the overall AA hypothesis there has been wide satisfaction.

In some ways AA presents rather special features. For a start it is the only phylum that includes some languages spoken exclusively outside of Africa. This is, of course, the rationale for calling it 'Afroasiatic' – or as some prefer 'Afro-asiatic', or yet others 'Afrasian' or 'Afrasan'.

Then in terms of the history of mankind it is incontrovertible that some of the earliest and greatest human achievements have been accomplished in civilisations founded and headed by AA peoples.[1] The Egyptians, Assyrians, Phoenicians, Hebrews and Arabs, to mention only some peoples whose architecture, mathematics and astronomy, religions and philosophies have contributed so vastly to human progress, have been speakers of AA languages.

Yet another special feature of AA is its great time-depth. In the case of Semitic, we have written specimens of language going back 4,000 years; nevertheless, the differences between these and any twentieth-century Semitic language are considerably less than that between either of them and, say, any modern Chadic or Omotic language. There are of course cognate forms and structures – without them there would be no substance to the AA Hypothesis – but the purpose in making these comparisons is to point up the extreme antiquity of AA. It has been proposed by Diakonoff (1988: 25) that the AA proto-language has to be assigned to a period prior to 8,000 BC; compare also Hodge (1976: 61f). Such a time-depth must be borne in mind when we consider linguistic reconstruction in section 4.3.

4.1.1   *A survey of AA languages*
          Currently the most neutral reckoning divides the AA phylum into six major branches, usually called 'families': Chadic, Berber, Egyptian, Semitic, Cushitic and Omotic. There are those who argue for one less branch, as well as those who argue for one, two, or even five more. Regarding Chadic, Berber, Egyptian and Semitic there has been general agreement that they are clear-cut entities. The disagreements concerning Cushitic will receive more attention in section 4.2, but for the present purpose we shall adopt the conventional position with its six independent families.

Map 4.4 directs attention to the fact that the spread of AA languages within Africa is largely to the north of the continent; only in Tanzania are AA languages spoken south of the Equator. The map also shows up the geographical continuity into Asia of these languages. Nevertheless, the map could be misleading in two respects. It includes no indication of Arabic. This omission is the result of an artifice facilitating demonstration of the relatively discrete locations of the six families within

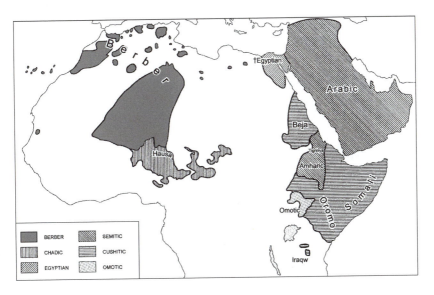

Map 4.4. Afroasiatic.

Africa. If we restored the reality by putting Arabic back onto the map, it would be immediately obvious how vast an area makes use of varieties of this single Semitic language, either as a first language or as a lingua franca (cf. the map in Heine 1970). Also the map is asynchronous: it shows the present-day distribution of five of the families, but the area designated for Egyptian represents a situation which would probably have obtained about 5,000 years ago. It would of course be very exciting to be able to define the territorial extents of all the other AA families contemporaneous with that stage of Egyptian – and there may well have been some we do not know of, but it is most improbable that we shall ever be able to do so.

To avoid the well-known difficulty in distinguishing 'language' and 'dialect', in what follows I shall often use the term 'variety'. According to Grimes (1996) AA comprises 371 extant linguistic varieties – and we also need to include those extinct ones we do know of. In this overview it would be tedious to list them exhaustively. Within each lower-end taxonomic group only those varieties with the highest numbers of speakers will normally be listed.[2] From a comparative point of view, mere numbers of speakers will naturally be of less importance than the actual properties or other special status factors of a variety, and for this reason any varieties of special interest will also be mentioned.

4.1.1.1   *Berber (or Libyco-Berber)*

Compared with other AA families Berber is peculiar in exhibiting no deep linguistic differences such as to require subfamilies. Indeed, the overall similarities of extant Berber varieties even led earlier investigators to speak of 'the Berber language' (Basset 1929), though this was certainly going too far. Specialists generally distinguish four main groups of languages and dialect clusters as spoken today, though the division probably represents more of a present-day geographical distributional than one based on strictly linguistic criteria. It is generally true of Berber speech communities that they tend to be widely dispersed and isolated from each other – though this is unlikely always to have been the case. The four groups are as follows.

1. Varieties spoken from north-western Morocco, through northern Algeria and Tunisia into Libya. They include: Tashelhit (3,000); Tamazight (3,000); Tarifit (2,000); and Kabyle (3,074).

2. Isolated varieties spoken in eastern Libya and in the Siwa Oasis in Egypt; they include: Awjilah (2,000); and Siwa (5).[3]

3. Sahara-Sahelian varieties spoken by communities scattered across a largely desert territory taking in parts of southern Algeria, Niger, Mali and Burkina Faso. The languages of the celebrated Tuareg, known

as Tamahaq to the north of the range and Tamajeq further south
(25–76) belong here.

4.   A quite distinct variety spoken by the Zenaga (25) living to the
south-west of the Berber range in parts of Mauritania.

To these living languages is usually added an extinct branch in the shape of
Old Libyan, a language (or languages) attested in inscriptions dating from the sec-
ond century BC found in Algeria, Tunisia and Morocco. What is fairly clearly another
AA language, Guanche, was once spoken by the indigenes of the Canary Islands.
It is believed by some linguists (Diakonoff 1988: 19) to have constituted a third
major subdivision of Libyco-Berber. Guanche lost out in the competition with
Spanish three or four centuries ago.

4.1.1.2   *Chadic*

According to Newman (1992: 253) there are approximately 140
Chadic languages.[4] As the map shows, they spread out in three directions from
Lake Chad – whence the family name originates – and are spoken in parts of Nigeria,
Chad, Cameroon, Central African Republic and Niger. The best known and most
widely spoken Chadic language is Hausa, which, if we include the millions of
second-language speakers, probably ranks as the largest African language, if we
exclude Arabic. For most other Chadic languages, speakers are numbered only
in thousands, and some are extremely small. Newman's (1977) classification of
Chadic into four branches has not been disputed; the necessarily abbreviated
gazetteer presented here follows the slightly revised version of Newman 1992.

1.   West Chadic languages, all spoken in Nigeria, fall into two subbranches.
One contains the four groups to which Hausa (22,000), Bole (100),
Angas (100) and Ron (115) respectively belong; the other contains
three groups, represented by Bade (250) and Ngizim (80), by Warji
(70) and by Boghom (50).

2.   Biu-Mandara languages are spoken in an area overlapping northern
Cameroon, north-eastern Nigeria and Chad. There are three sub-
branches. One of these comprises eight groups, represented by Tera
(50), Bura (250), Kamwe (300), Lamang (40), Mafa (138), Sukur (15),
Daba (36) and Bachama-Bata (300) respectively. The two groups of
the second subbranch may be represented by Buduma (59) and by
Musgu (75). The third subbranch consists of a single language,
Gidar (66).

3.   East Chadic languages are spoken in southern Chad and neighbouring
parts of Cameroon and Central African Republic. It has two subbranches,

each comprising three groups. The three groups of subbranch A are represented by a cluster of varieties called Tumak (25), by Nancere (72), and by Kera (51). Those of subbranch B may be represented by Dangaleat (27), by Mokulu (12), and by Sokoro (5).

4. Masa is an independent branch consisting of nine varieties spoken in south-western Chad and northern Cameroon. It includes Masana (212) Musey (120), and the nearly extinct Zumaya.

4.1.1.3 *Egyptian*

Egyptian presents an unprecedented situation; namely four and a half millennia of written records enabling us to trace the course of a 'single' language up to its demise in the fourteenth century. It is only the sense of this continuity over time that licenses our speaking of a 'single' language, for Egyptian, like every other language, underwent diachronic changes, and it needs to be appreciated that in distinguishing 'varieties' we are thinking about variation over time. More-over, terms encountered in the literature, such as Old Egyptian (3,100–2,000 BC), Middle Egyptian (2,000–1,300 BC), Late Egyptian, Hieratic, Demotic, Coptic, etc. are often associated with literary and graphic matters rather than with linguistic features *per se*, though of course these are there as well.

4.1.1.4 *Semitic*

Semitic is the most studied and consequently best understood branch of AA, though even here some languages remain very poorly known. Adding together both extant and (known) extinct ones, Semitic exhibits some fifty distinct varieties. On account of their origin, more than a dozen of these might be subsumed under the umbrella of 'Arabic', though general lack of mutual intelligibility suggests it would be unrealistic to do so.

Most authorities agree in recognising a threefold partitioning of Semitic, namely into North-east, North-west and South subfamilies. There is however a pervasive division of opinion over whether Arabic belongs with the North-west or with the South subfamily. In the ensuing outline I follow Hetzron (1972: 15–16),[5] who argues for the former position.

1. A North-east subfamily is required by Akkadian, the extinct language of the ancient civilisations of the Assyrians and Babylonians. Akkadian was in continuous use for some two and a half millennia up to the time of Christ.

2. Hetzron divides North-west Semitic into Central and South Central branches. The former represents Aramaic in its ancient and modern forms. Varieties of Aramaic have been spoken since the tenth

century BC, and during the first six centuries of the Christian Era Aramaic was the dominant language of the Near East. In modern times descendants of earlier Aramaic varieties still persist, though some of their speech communities are quite scattered globally. Western Neo-Aramaic/Ma'lula (15), Turoyo (70) and a language called by its speakers 'Assyrian' (200) represent just three such descendants. The South Central branch has a Canaanite division representing important extinct Near Eastern languages such as Phoenician and (Biblical) Hebrew. Phoenician, originally spoken in the area of Lebanon, was later spread by its colonising speakers so as to become the language of Carthage, where it was known as Punic. Also here of course is Israel's revived and thoroughly renovated Modern Hebrew (4,510). The intriguing language of Ras Shamra, Ugaritic, known from texts of the fourteenth and thirteenth centuries BC, probably belongs here.

The other branch of South Central Semitic is Arabic. The Classical language of the Qur'an, is attested from the fourth century AD, though its roots go back into the fifth century BC; it is no longer spoken. Today however there are many regional varieties of Arabic spoken throughout the Middle East and North Africa. Within Africa at least the following have to be clearly distinguished: Egyptian (42,500); Hassaniya (2,230), spoken in Mauritania and parts of Mali, Senegal and Niger; Moroccan (19,542); Shua (1,031), spoken in parts of Chad, Cameroon, Nigeria and Niger; Sudanese (16,000–19,000), spoken mainly in northern Sudan but with speakers in Egypt and Eritrea; Algerian Colloquial (22,400), spoken also in Tunisia; and Sulaimitian (4,500) spoken in parts of Libya and Egypt. Distinct from all these regional forms is Modern Standard/Literary Arabic, which is based on Classical Arabic and is the language of education, administration and wider communication; it is learned as a second language by many whose first language is one of the regional Arabics. This special form of bilingualism inspired the first description of diglossia (Ferguson 1959). Maltese (330), spoken on the island of Malta and elsewhere, is basically a form of North African Arabic that has been heavily influenced by Italian.

3. South Semitic comprises South Arabian and Ethio-Semitic. The former consists of dead varieties such as Ḥaḍrami, Minaean, Qatabanian and Sabaean, known only from south-west Arabian inscriptions dating from the eighth century BC, together with Modern South

Arabian Soqotri (70), Mehri (77), Jibbali (25) and Harsusi (700) –
though not all scholars accept this unified grouping.

Ethio-Semitic consists of a North Ethiopic branch comprising the
purely literary and liturgical Gi'iz, Tigre (683) and Tigrinya (6,060)
and a South Ethiopic branch with Transversal and Outer divisions.
Amharic (20,000), the national language of Ethiopia, belongs in the
former, as does Harari (26), a fascinating tongue indigenous to the
city of Harar. The Outer group consists of the extinct Gafat together
with northern 'Gurage' varieties such as Soddo (104) and a Central
Western group with Chaha, Mäsqan, etc. speakers (1,856). Another
'Gurage' variety, which includes Silt'i (493), is properly classified in
the Transversal group. It is important to appreciate this point as
'Gurage' has often been presented as a single language.

4.1.1.5   *Cushitic*

To see Cushitic as a single family involves putting together six
groups of languages, some of which are very distinct from each other and one of
which exhibits a number of substantially different internal subgroups. It also includes
the nearly extinct Yaaku language, spoken by a few elderly members of a hunter-
gatherer group in Kenya. The six groups commonly have the geographically based
labels given below, though Highland East Cushitic, Lowland East Cushitic,
Dullay and Yaaku have sometimes been subsumed under an 'East Cushitic' node.

1.   Northern Cushitic contains a single language, Bedawi/Beja (1,148),
     which is spoken in an area overlapping portions of Sudan, Egypt and
     Eritrea.

2.   Central Cushitic refers to the Agaw languages, a well-defined group
     of varieties spoken in north-western Ethiopia and in Eritrea. It com-
     prises the living varieties Bilin (70), Kemant and Kwara (jointly
     1,000), Xamtanga (80), Awngi (490), and some extinct varieties.

3.   With the possible exception of Burji, Highland East Cushitic consti-
     tutes another quite close-knit cluster. Its speakers generally live in the
     fertile mountainous areas of central southern Ethiopia, though there
     are speakers of Burji in northern Kenya. The group includes: Burji
     (87), Sidamo (1,500), and Kambata and Hadiyya with a million or
     so speakers each.

4.   Lowland East Cushitic comprehends three distinct subgroups:
     (i)   a northern subgroup consisting of closely related Saho (144)
           and Afar (1,200)

(ii) the Oromoid subgroup comprises all the varieties of Oromo proper (13,960) as spoken from the Tana River in Kenya to the Sudan borders and Tigrai zone of Ethiopia, and Konsoid, a dialect chain west of the southern Rift Valley of Ethiopia; its main variety is Konso (200)

(iii) Omo-Tana comprises eastern and western divisions. The former consists of northern Kenyan Rendille (32) and Boni (5), together with the numerous varieties of Somali (8,335) spoken in Somalia, Djibouti, eastern Ethiopia, and north-eastern Kenya. The western division consists of Daasenech (30), Arbore (1,000–5,000) and the probably now extinct Elmolo language. There is also the geographically isolated Bayso (500) spoken on and around Lake Abaya in the Ethiopian Rift Valley, which shares features with both eastern and western divisions.

5. Dullay represents a linguistic chain in the vicinity of the Wäyt'o valley to the west of Konsoid (cf. 4(ii) above). There is a distinct southern variety, Tsamay (7), and a more close-knit group lumped together in *Ethnologue* as 'Gawwada' (65–76).

6. Southern Cushitic languages are mostly spoken in Tanzania, where they are represented by the Iraqw cluster, for example Iraqw (365), Gorowa (30) and Burunge (31), by Mbugu/Ma'a (32) – often cited as a genuine example of a 'mixed language',[6] and the extinct Asax and probably extinct Kw'adza. The non-Tanzanian member is Dahalo (3,000), spoken by a community near the mouth of the Tana River in Kenya.

4.1.1.6 *Omotic*

All scholars concerned recognise the existence of two major groups of languages here. Those holding the Omotic Hypothesis see these as North and South Omotic subfamilies.

South Omotic comprises Aari (109), Hamer-Banna (25) and the less numerous varieties Karo (600) and Dime (2,128).

North Omotic falls into at least two main divisions: Dizoid and Gonga-Gimojan.

1. Dizoid consists of a cluster whose principal varieties, Dizi (18), Nayi (12) and Sheko (23), are spoken in south-west Ethiopia in the Kafa region.

2. The Gonga-Gimojan division includes Gonga proper, the most prominent varieties of which are Kaficho (500), Shakacho (70), Boro

(7) and the now almost certainly extinct Anfillo. The Gimojan division comprises Yemsa (500) and Gimira-Ometo. Gimira varieties share typological features in phonology with the geographically close Dizoid languages, though their genetic affinities are with Ometo. The main variety is Bench (80). Ometo is an extensive and long recognised cluster comprising a score of varieties; some of the better known are Wolaytta (2,000), Gamo (464), Gofa (154), Basketto (82), Male (20) and Chara (13). Ometo also includes some quite vulnerable minor varieties spoken on the southern Rift Valley lakes.

This account leaves a residue in the shape of the Mao varieties of the extreme west of Ethiopia and the Sudan borderland. The under-investigated state of the grammar of these languages makes it impossible to say where they fit within North Omotic (Bender 1990: 589). Mao divides into eastern (Bambassi (5)) and western (Hozo (3,000), Seze (3,000)) groups.

4.1.2   *A cultural survey*

It is next to impossible either on the one hand to offer any overall characterisation of the AA peoples in terms of culture or on the other hand to do any justice in this short section to the cultural achievements of certain of them. Nevertheless, a brief survey is in order.

Throughout pre-industrial times, and always subject to the general ecological constraints of the regions occupied,[7] it is clear that AA peoples learned to exploit every habitable niche and to adopt every possible way of life. It is likely that for most of their history the majority have been pastoralists and agriculturalists, as indeed – though as an ever-diminishing minority – some are today. But others moved far away from this life, engaging in trade and, in the case of the Phoenicians and later the Arabs, developing a highly successful maritime trade economy complete with colonial trading posts.

Where conditions were especially favourable, as in the Nile Valley, Mesopotamia and the Fertile Crescent, AA peoples early evolved what figure among the greatest and most enduring urban civilisations the world has seen. Their achievements are still visible in the architectural monuments that continue to amaze today's tourists, but at the less superficial level available to researchers they emerge in a rich complexity of detail that surrounds every aspect of government, civic infrastructure and religion.

Linguists will be peculiarly aware of the enormous breakthrough attained in the expression of language in written form and should be able to appreciate more than most the intellectual debt owed by the western world to those AA speakers whose varied efforts preceded and made possible alphabetic writing. Daniels' (1996:

21–30) objective evaluation of the relationships between and the relative merits of the writing systems of the ancient Near East emphasises the importance of the Semitic 'abjad' or 'consonantory' as a conceptual prerequisite for the independence of consonant and vowel as seen in alphabets.

All three major monotheistic world religions originated with Semitic peoples. But the roots of monotheism in the shape of belief in a supreme (male) Sky-God pervades the AA peoples, though it is not unique to them. The same rather weak conclusions would have to be drawn with regard to the practice of circumcision, to rituals directed towards spiritual entities associated with trees, wells and mountains, and with regard to belief in the 'evil eye'. There is also a widespread absence of rituals connected with ancestors, and a lack of totemism. But such matters are all subject to areal factors and widely open to substratal influences.

4.2 **A history of the concept of Afroasiatic**

Any claim that a given set of languages has genetic affinity is a hypothesis. Linguists who subscribe to the *AA Hypothesis* do so because they believe that it offers the best explanation for the linguistic facts as we know them. The evolution of the hypothesis (under a variety of names) has had a relatively long history. It began with the quite early recognition of the relatedness of the Semitic languages. It then developed over more than a century by an intermittant series of moves that admitted various individual African languages, or groups of them, to the status of 'poor relations' of Semitic. Since the criteria for admission were generally determined by reference to features common to Semitic, clear thinking about the nature of the original linguistic ancestor was inevitably skewed. Furthermore, for much of the time the process was bedevilled by racial (even racist) prejudices, as well as by certain linguistic misconceptions characteristic of the period. The following very brief synopsis attempts to identify some of the main events and shifts in thinking that have shaped the AA Hypothesis.

'Semitic', derived from the name of Noah's eldest son, Shem (Genesis 7:10), was first coined as a generic term for languages such as Aramaic, Hebrew and Arabic by von Schlözer in 1781. But a realisation of this affinity on the part of Jewish scholars went back for best part of a millennium. European scholars too had recognised the relatedness considerably earlier than 1781 (e.g., Postel 1538) and had even extended it to include Ethiopian languages such as Amharic and Gi'iz (Ludolph 1702). The present-day canon of Semitic languages includes many others not known at the time the name was introduced. Among these are languages of the South Arabian, Gurage and Neo-Aramaic groups, though pride of place here belongs to Akkadian, which was rediscovered and linguistically identified only in the 1850s.

Champollion's decipherment of hieroglyphic Egyptian in the 1820s revealed many similarities between that language and the old Semitic ones. Some later scholars even claimed it as Semitic (Erman 1892, Sethe 1899–1902, Albright 1923). Earlier opinions however had emphasised the differences and saw African traits in Egyptian. Among the earliest here were Renan (1855) and Lottner (1860/1). The former is sometimes said to have been the first to use the term 'Hamitic' (derived from the name of Noah's second son, Ham[8]). Renan considered Cushitic languages such as Galla (= Oromo) and Saho-Afar as 'sub-Semitic'.

By 1877 Müller's dichotomous 'Hamito-Semitic' had added Berber and the then-known Cushitic languages. Although acknowledging the similarities of Hausa to Hamitic, Müller did not include it. Lepsius (1880), however, was convinced of a special affiliation of Hausa to Berber and incorporated a Berber-Hausa group into his Hamitic family. But he blurred the picture by lodging Hottentot (Nama) and Oigob (= Maasai) here as well, adducing some disarmingly convincing – albeit incorrect – comparisons in the case of the former for close grammatical ties with Egyptian and Beja (1880: lxv).

In addition to proper comparisons involving language forms, all these earlier taxonomists employed physical anthropological and linguistic typological features in reaching their judgements, and this methodological flaw was to persist. Cust (1883) added a geographical criterion, so that for him Hamitic membership required: (a) being not Semitic; (b) having grammatical gender; (c) a location in north/north-east Africa (p. 94). While this enabled him to exclude any Khoisan languages – he did not know of Sandawe! – the criteria permitted the inclusion of some Nilo-Saharan ones.

Things got worse before they got better. In 1912 Meinhof wrote *Die Sprachen der Hamiten*. It employed a classification that relied on a mixture of genetic, typo-logical and anthropological criteria. The latter project the Hamites as a master race in Africa (though originally of Caucasian stock) who from a linguistic point of view both influence and are influenced by black Africans. The typological criteria include gender, the employment of ablaut, and the exhibition of a certain type of phonetic inventory and word structure. But where these were absent, the racially based criteria won out. The resulting Hamitic ended up embracing representatives from every linguistic phylum of Africa.

Throughout this protracted debate there was an implicit assumption that the binary branching Hamito-Semitic represents two comparable entities. That this is not the case should have been obvious to any Semiticist looking at Hamitic – and many of those who did so were Semiticists. Compared with the demonstrable unity of Semitic, any survey across the various groups under the Hamitic node reveals such colossal disparities that one must conclude it had only the status of a rag-bag. Any attempt to see a special unity in a lot of languages that do not quite qualify as Semitic is misguided. Once the Semitic yardstick was removed and the assumption of a binary branching was dropped, the true nature of the problem emerges as one of accounting for the fact that several distinct families – of which Semitic is just one – share some discernible linguistic forms. Delafosse (1914) did just this in presenting the internal classification of his 'afro-asiatique' in terms of several co-ordinate descent lines. Chadic was not yet included by Delafosse however, nor by Cohen (1924), who was otherwise so effective in securing wide acceptance of the restructuring. Unfortunately Cohen's 'chamito-sémitique', along with similar nomenclatural conservatism on the part of many subsequent writers, did much to enshrine a potentially misleading name.

In 1950 Greenberg carried appraisal of the problem one stage further by the introduction of a five-branched Afroasiatic phylum. *Inter alia* his uniform application of lexical mass comparison revealed the true affiliations of languages such as Maasai and Fulfulde and nicely underscored most of the family divisions within the phylum. Very importantly, it claimed unambiguous AA membership for Chadic (Greenberg 1950a).

Further refinement took place in 1969 when Fleming argued for a reassessment of West Cushitic. His arguments, together with Bender's (1971) conclusions, showed the need to excise this group entirely from Cushitic and to accord it the status of an independent family, Omotic; see also Fleming 1974, Bender 1975b.

Subsequent efforts have taken a number of directions. One of these has been to focus on the reconstruction of the linguistic features of various of the African families and their constituent groups. Within this category Newman and Ma 1966, Newman 1977, Hetzron 1972, Black 1973, Dolgopolsky 1973, Heine 1978, Sasse 1979, Jungraithmayr and Ibriszimow 1994, Ehret 1980, Ehret 1987 and Arvanites 1990 are of special note. Others have been attempting to reconstruct features of two or more families (e.g. Hodge 1966; Bynon 1984; Dolgopolsky 1983, 1987). In 1995 two full-scale dictionaries of AA reconstructions appeared quite independently of each other (Ehret, and Orel and Stolbova). Bold in conception and full of interest as to content as these are, both will at this stage have to be regarded as 'working documents', as indeed their authors are at pains to note.

Such work has clearly relied upon descriptive grammars and lexical materials. New research publications adding to this database have continued steadily to appear, though the details are too numerous to list here. Yet it nevertheless remains a fact that far too many languages remain undescribed; and there is urgent need for more basic lexicography.

Nor has the classification story come to an end. A phylum with five or six co-ordinate branches presents an irresistible temptation for subgrouping. The status of Omotic figures large here, and debate has waxed fierce. While some still wish to keep this group within a larger Cushitic (Lamberti 1991; Zaborski 1986a, 1997: 49), others argue from the paucity of AA features in Omotic grammar that Proto-Omotic must have arisen as the very earliest split in the phylum (Fleming 1983, Ehret 1995: 489).

Beja – orthodoxly regarded as a subfamily of Cushitic – has also been a bone of contention, being excluded from Cushitic by some (Hetzron 1980: 101), but vigorously retained by others (Zaborski 1984, 1997).

The reader should have noted that the controversies all seem to centre on Cushitic. Hetzron 1980 is valuable in highlighting what exactly the linguistic phenomena are that underlie the disagreements, though not all will accept his conclusions. Orel and Stolbova (1995: x–xiii) go considerably further than anyone else in deciding – pending better evidence[9] – to abandon 'Cushitic' altogether and to treat it, together with Omotic, as a *Sprachbund* of seven independent AA families. Bender (1997) proposes a 'Macro-Cushitic' comprising Berber, Semitic and 'Cushitic proper' and even speculates on the possibility of accommodating Indo-European under this new umbrella.

Quite clearly, much still remains to be done!

4.3   Evidence for the Afroasiatic Hypothesis

Up to this point in our discussion a common ancestry for the six linguistic families considered in section 4.1.1 has simply been assumed; it is now necessary to set out the key evidence for this assumption.

As we have seen in section 4.2, many scholars had a 'gut feeling' that these languages had a similar design plan, some common genius that implied an ultimate relatedness. But, as is well understood, whenever similarities are observed between languages they have to be evaluated in ways that will disentangle signals of genuine shared linguistic parentage from those that are merely typological or are simply traits resulting from a shared geography. The only admissible evidence is where similarities of meaning or function are accompanied by regular patterns of similarity in form, that is, cross-linguistic sound-meaning correspondences which are repeated to the point where it is possible to predict further instances. This principle, the so-called 'comparative method' (see chapter 10 below), has to be held to whether we consider lexicon or morphology.

Now it was on the basis of 'mass comparison', rather than the comparative method, that the canon of AA languages was established by Greenberg, and although this methodology avoids reliance on typological features, and has, in the present writer's view, come up with the right conclusions, a methodology that does not invoke the rigour of the principle stated in the last paragraph cannot make predictions, and so falls short of true theoretical status. Pragmatically, too, it is quite crude for it incorporates no filter for rejecting unrelated 'look-alikes' nor any means of recognising highly dissimilar, albeit cognate, items. Nevertheless, even allowing for loanwords, a high proportion of the look-alikes registered in mass comparison will in fact be the result of regular sound correspondences, so the method works as a heuristic device. But then it becomes the task of the comparative and historical linguist to uncover the detail, and in the case of AA this has been going on steadily for three decades.

It is generally agreed that shared morphology is the surest proof of genetic relatedness. Phonemes have no meaning in themselves and their organisation into systems and their phonetic realisations are all too prone to areal influences. Lexicon moreover is always open to infiltration by borrowing. Such problems are far less common with morphology, and this is why it will be our chief concern here.

Of the many aspects of comparative morphology that might be considered, space limitations will permit the presentation of only a few in any detail. Certain other cases will also receive a rather more cursory mention.

4.3.1   *The personal pronouns*

As in the case of other proto-languages, the personal pronouns provide some of the strongest support for the hypothesis. Comparative accounts and reconstructions that have appeared show some differences of detail and emphasis but there is substantial agreement on the main points. As in most other matters, Omotic languages show less agreement in pronominal forms, though even here some AA forms have been clearly retained.

Leaving aside for the moment prefixal verb agreement markers (cf. section 4.3.3) identification of the oldest pronominal elements across the entire phylum requires looking for them in forms with possessive determiner and object complement functions,[10] rather than in forms with subject function. Diakonoff refers to this set as 'dependent' (1988: 70–8), Newman as 'non-subject' (1980: 15), Hetzron as 'oblique' (1990: 586); but since precisely similar forms in some languages function also as independent subjects, such syntactically based labels may be inappropriate, and I shall simply refer to them as 'primary'. With the exception of Chadic and Omotic, there is evidence for another 'independent' set of pronouns, which had a topic-like role and so came to act as subjects complete with nominative marking. Since however, the independent series is not attested in all six families, it is not included here. The reconstructions cited finally in each case are taken from Ehret (1995).

The primary series:[11]

> 1sg 'me, my': E: *-ay*; P-S: *-ii*, *-ya'*, *-n(i)* (as object complement);
> B: *-i, -i-n*; P-C: **yi ~ *yu ~ *ya*; Ch: *wa, ni*;[12] O: *yi-n*;[13] P-AA: **i ~ *yi*.
> 2sg 'you, your': P-E: m. ***-ku*, f. ***-ki*; P-S: m. **-ka*, f. **-ki*; B: m.
> *-k*, f. *(k)m*; P-C: m. **ku*, f. **ki*; Ch: m. *ka*, f. *kim*; O: no obvious cog-
> nates; P-AA: m. **ku, *ka*, f. **ki*.[14]
> 3sg 'him, his, her': P-E: m. ***-su*, ***-si*; P-S: m. **-šu*, f. **-ši*; B: m. &
> f. *-s*; P-C: m. **ʔi-su(u) ~ *ʔi-sa(a)*, f. **ʔi-sii*; Ch: m. *ši*, f. *ta*; O: m.
> *iz-n*, f. *iž-n*; P-AA: m. & f. **si, *isi*.[15]
> 1pl 'us, our': P-E: ***-ina*; P-S: **-na ~ *-nu ~ *-ni*; B: *-nɣ*, P-C: **na ~
> *nu ~ *ni, *ʔina ~* etc.; Ch: *na*;[16] O: *in*.
> 2pl 'you': P-E: ***-kina*; P-S: m. **-kumu*, f. **-kina*; B: m. *-un*, f. *-unt*;[17]
> P-C: **kun(V) ~ *kin(V)*; Ch: *kun*; O: no obvious cognates; P-AA:
> **kuuna*.
> 3pl 'them': P-E: ***-sina*; P-S: m. **-šumu*, f. **-šina*; B: m. *-sn*, f. *-snt*;
> P-C: **ʔisunV ~ *ʔi-sinV*; Ch: **sun*; O: íš-n; P-AA: **su ~ *usu*.[18]

4.3.2   *Case markers*

In concluding an analysis of the Cushitic case system, Sasse (1984) goes on to argue that essentially the same system could be postulated for Semitic and Berber. He was not moreover, simply talking about typological similarities, for clear formal identity in the actual case markers is involved. Subsequent work has also made it possible to recognise an identical set of markers in Egyptian.

Within the hypothesised P-AA system, the 'basic' nominal form is termed the 'absolutive', and it is most generally characterised by final **-a*. Cross-linguistically, the core role of the absolutive is to mark the head of a NP functioning as the direct object of a verb. In Cushitic however and, as Sasse demonstrates, in Semitic and Berber too, the distribution of the absolutive is considerably more extensive, which justifies treating it as the least-marked, or basic, term.

Opposed to the absolutive is a nominative in **-u*, found in subject NPs that are unfocused.[19] This statement requires refinement in two respects. Firstly, a distinct nominative often occurs only in the masculine declension.[20] Secondly, within Cushitic a nominative in *-i* is far more widespread than one in *-u*. Indeed, Hetzron (1980: 16–17) suggests that the **-i* nominative is a Cushitic innovation. This seems to be extremely likely, and may result from an identification with the Cushitic masculine genitive reconstructed by Appleyard (1986b: 372) as **-i (~ *-ii)*. Support for absolutive **-a*: nominative **-u* (and P-C **-i*) is seen in the following:

S – Akkadian: nom.sg *šarr-u-m*, acc.sg *šarr-a-m* 'king', – Classical Arabic: nom.sg *malik-u*, acc.sg *malik-a* 'king'; B – Shilha: nom *u-šlḥi*, abs *a-šlḥi* 'a Berber man', C – Afar: m.nom *awk-i*, m.abs *áwk-a* 'boy' (cf. f.nom & abs *sagá* 'cow'); – Kemant: m.nom *gərw-i*, abs *gərw-a* 'man' (cf. f.nom & abs *gän-a* 'mother').

The Egyptian evidence for the nominative consists mainly of non-functional relic labial-velar glide formatives on vowel-final nominal stems, for example **ḥaf3aw* (< **ḥaf3a+u*) 'snake', **ḥaaruw* 'Horus', **masdiw* 'enemy'; but it survives for phonological reasons as a vowel in certain monosyllables, for example P-E: ***nib-u* 'lord'. The absolutive in *-a* is best preserved in certain syntactic constructions based on deverbal nominalisations (Callender 1975; see also Satzinger 1997: 35ff).

There are now no obvious traces of this system in Chadic. If it is the case that Chadic generalised the primary pronouns to subject function, one may speculate that prior to this it would have done the same thing with nouns.

What about Omotic? The Ometo cluster and Gimira certainly do have a case system of the type described, and masculine nouns do mark the nominative with an *-i* suffix; feminines however indicate nominative case with *-a*, though this is not identical to the absolutive. But this system is better seen as a secondary development, for earlier Omotic has almost certainly to be reconstructed with an accusative-marking case system (Hayward and Tsuge 1998: 26).[21] There may however be some traces of the **-u* nominative. In section 4.3.1 the Dizi first person singular pronoun was adduced as a reflex of the P-AA form. If that identification is correct, it might be speculated that the nominative form of this pronoun *yinu* carries a relic of AA case.[22] Furthermore, throughout the Gonga group, we find masculine nouns marking subject case with *-o* and *-u* (Lamberti 1993a: 65).

The case form referred to above as the genitive may more appropriately be called the 'oblique', for in addition to indicating possessive relationships it often also serves to mark a noun as an adpositional complement. The evidence for a P-AA oblique **-i* begins with Semitic forms such as Akkadian: gen.sg *šarr-i-m* 'king', Classical Arabic: gen.sg *malik-i* 'king'. Appleyard's reconstruction of Proto-Cushitic masculine genitive forms as **-i ~ *-ii* has been noted earlier. Egyptian reflexes have been reconstructed before pronominal possessive suffixes, for example ***ḥar-i-f* 'his face' and in a formation deriving adjectives from nominal genitives by suffixation of *-y*, for example ***ḥar-i-y* 'related to the face' (Loprieno 1995: 56).

Possessives are now expressed in other ways in Chadic and Berber languages and there is no good evidence for P-AA **-i*. In the case of Omotic, some items occur that may just possibly reflect this case formative. Genitives in *-i* (and *-e*) have been recorded for some Gonga varieties (Zaborski 1990: 619, Lamberti

1993a: 65) and an *-i* termination can be extracted from the wide functioning oblique *-nì* in Yemsa (Lamberti 1993b: 73). An oblique case in *-i* is found in Ometo; thus some *e*-final nouns in Koorite mark possessive with *-i* (Hayward 1987: 220), and feminine nouns in Gamo employ an *-i* oblique both as genitive and as a base for postpositions, for example *aayi* 'mother's', *aayi-ppe* 'from mother'; compare *aayo* 'mother (abs)'.

4.3.3   *Conjugational features of the verb*

One striking feature that emerges in considering the verb, especially for those trained as Semiticists, is the so-called *Prefix-Conjugation* (P-Cj). This is familiar from the imperfect of most modern Semitic languages, and is characterised by a prefixal pattern of subject agreements whose forms are not obviously relatable to either of the pronoun series discussed in section 4.3.1. The type is exemplified by an (abbreviated) imperfect paradigm of Arabic 'write', viz.: 1sg *ʔ-aktub-u*, 2m.sg *t-aktub-u*, 3m.sg *y-aktub-u*, 3f.sg *t-aktub-u*, 1pl *n-aktub-u*, etc. The perfect paradigm in modern Semitic does not have these prefixes, though at an earlier stage of Semitic, attested in Akkadian, both perfect and imperfect conjugated prefixally. Just such a conjugation pattern appears in Berber and also in certain verbs in some Cushitic languages, where it is clearly an archaism, and when found, occurs for both the perfect and imperfect – as in Akkadian; thus, Arbore 'come', perfect: 1sg *ʔ-eečč-e*, 2sg *t-eečč-e*, 3m.sg *y-eečč-e*, 3f.sg *t-eečč-e*, 1pl *n-eečč-e* etc.; imperfect: 1sg *ʔ-aačč-a*, 2sg *t-aačč-a*, 3m.sg *y-aačč-a*, 3f.sg *t-aačč-a*, *n-aačč-a*, etc.

The P-Cj is not attested in Egyptian, and whether or not this is interpreted as a loss (Klingenheben 1956, Rössler 1950) or the failure to share in an innovation (Diakonoff 1988: 22, Bender 1997: 22) has clear implications for how we view phylum-internal relationships.[23] Although Chadic has preverbal pronominal elements, formally these seem to relate to the primary pronouns (cf. section 4.3.1.), rather than to the pattern under discussion (Newman and Schuh 1974: 5ff; Schuh 1976: 2ff). The Omotic evidence is slight, being confined to Yemsa, where a partial resemblance to the P-C pattern shows up in suffixes which may once have been prefixal person markers on a (now eroded) postposed auxiliary verb,[24] for example Yemsa 'do', preterit: 1sg *zag-i-n*, 2sg *zag-i-t*, 3m.sg *zag-i*, 3f.sg *zag-ì*, 1pl *zag-i-ni*.

Egyptian does have, however, another archaic verb pattern known as the *Stative Conjugation*. Its reflexes are seen in the Akkadian 'stative': 1sg *-aa-ku*, 2m.sg *-aa-ta*, 2f.sg *-aa-ti*, 3m.sg *-ø*, 3f.sg *-at*, 1pl *-aa-nu*, etc.;[25] the Egyptian 'pseudoparticiple': 1sg *-kw*, *-ky*, 2sg *-ty*, 3m.sg *-y*, *-w*, 3f.sg *-ty*, 1pl *-wyn*, etc.; the Kabyle (Berber) 'qualitative perfect' 1sg *-əɣ*, 2sg *-əḍ*, 3m.sg *ø*, 3f.sg *-at*. The attempt to link the neatly reconstructed Cushitic 'stative' to these forms (Banti 1987) has proved questionable to some (Hetzron 1990: 584); and the putative cognates from East Chadic Mubi adduced by Diakonoff (1988: 93) seem, once again, just reminiscent of the primary pronoun series.

It was Greenberg (1952) who first drew attention to two features of what he termed the 'present stem' so widespread as to suggest their assignment to P-AA. The features concerned are: (i) internal ablaut to -*a*-; and (ii) medial consonant gemination.[26] In languages having the P-Cj, one or both features show up clearly, for example (3m.sg forms are shown throughout):

> S – Akkadian imperfect *ikabbit*, cf. preterit *ikbit* 'become heavy'; – Tigrinya: imperfect *y-əsäbbər*, cf. perfect *säbärä* 'break'; B – Tuareg: habitual *iffəy*, cf. past *ifəy* 'go out'; C – Beja: 'old' present *ʔis-dabil*, cf. 'old' past *ʔii-dbil* 'collect';[27] – Afar: imperfect *y-ard-e*, cf. perfect *y-erd-e* 'run'; see also the earlier Arbore forms.

In languages without the P-Cj, the gemination feature may nevertheless be present. The Egyptian 'imperfect participle', with its connotations of plurality of action (Loprieno 1995: 87) is such a case, for example *mrr* 'he who loves', compare perfective *mr*. In Chadic, however, both gemination and ablaut occur in Migama, though in other 'Ancient Stage' languages only ablaut is attested (Jungraithmayr 1978), for example (1sg forms are shown throughout):

> East Chadic – Migama: imperfect ná *ʔàpàllá*, cf. perfect ná *ʔápìlé* 'wash'; – Mubi: imperfect ní *ʔūwát*, cf. perfect ní *ʔēwít* 'bite'; West Chadic – Ron-Daffo: 'habitative' *ʔí mwáat*, cf. 'Grundaspekt' *ʔí mot* 'die'.

Schuh (1976) carries the argument further in identifying fossils of the ablaut in one set of verbal nominalisations found in both West and East Chadic branches. Wolff (1977), however, shifts the emphasis away from considering these forms as primarily concerned with tense/aspect and relates them at a wider level to plural categories of events and actions marked in the verb – which could, of course, actually be closer to their original AA role.

The Omotic data can neither be included nor excluded as evidence. The imperfect is certainly marked by stem reduplication in S. Omotic Aari, and an -*a(a)* stem termination appears in the imperfect in Yemsa, Shinasha (Gonga) and in Zayse and other Ometo varieties, but the subject awaits a proper analysis.

4.3.4   *Plural formatives*

It is a characteristic of many AA languages to display multiple plural formatives. Nevertheless it is possible to recognise certain formations as so widespread as to belong to P-AA.

Once again it was Greenberg (1955a) who demonstrated a likely AA pattern of plural formation involving ablaut to *a*, usually in the last stem syllable of a noun. The process is sometimes accompanied by reduplication, and sometimes triggers dissimilation or assimilation of other stem vowels of the plural. Greenberg noted substantial traces of this *a* in four of the then recognised branches of AA.[28] In the following examples internal *a* is underscored.

> S – Proto-Hebrew: **malk* : **malak* 'king/s'; – Gi'iz *bərk* : *bərak* 'knee/s'; – Akkadian *šam-u* : *šamam-u* 'heaven/s'; B – Kabyle: *a-mqərqur* : *i-mqərqar* 'frog/s'; *a-γanim* : *i-γunam* 'reed/s'; C – Beja: *book* : *bak* 'goat/s'; – Rendille: *ur* : *urar* 'stomach/s'; *gob* : *gobab* 'clan/s'; Ch – Ngizim: *gimsik* : *gimsak* 'man/men'; – Logone: *gənəm* : *gənam* 'woman/women'; – Musgu: *gumur-i* : *gumar-ai* 'shield/s'.

In several cases there are good traces of what must be regarded as P-AA plural suffixes. In each case reflexes of the suffixes concerned occur across a majority of the six AA families. Zaborski (1976) argues convincingly for an AA plural suffix containing a labial-velar glide, *w*. For example:

> S – Akkadian: *šarruu* (= *šarru-w*); E: *ʕnḥ* (< ***ʕanaḥ-u*) : *ʕnḥ.w* (< ***ʕanaḥu-u*) 'oath/oaths'; *t3šj* (< ***taʒašij-u*) : *t3šj.w* (< ***taʒašiju-aw*) 'neighbour/neighbours'; B: *im-i* : *im-au̯-ʔ n* 'mouth/s'; *mess-i* : *mess-au̯* 'master/s'; C – Hadiyya: *kin-a* : *kin-uwwa* 'stone/s'; *min-e* : *minne-wa* 'house/s'; – Afar: *alil* : *alil-wa* 'chest/s'; *lubak* : *lubak-wa* 'lion/s'; Ch – Hausa: *itààc-èè* : *itaat-uuwà* 'tree/s'; *kunn-ee* : *kunn-uuwà* 'ear/s'.

That such occurrences of a -*w* are really cognate is supported by the fact that in several cases this particular formation also appears in certain derived abstract nominals and/or collectives. This would be a very peculiar coincidence unless common inheritance were concerned.

There was almost certainly another plural formation involving a -*t* suffix, but it is not always easy to disentangle this from the -*t* of feminine gender (cf. section 4.3.5.3), so that careful analysis will be required to reconstruct the linguistic history involved. The formative here is of particular interest however, for it appears to have attestations in Omotic, where reflexes of none of the other formatives discussed are apparent.

4.3.5   *Other morphological evidence*

In this section certain selected features shared widely across AA will simply be presented with a minimum of comment. It must be emphasised that the features cited are far from exhaustive. Moreover, the fact that more commentary and exemplification accompanied the cases selected for review in sections 4.3.1–4 does not imply that less credibility attaches to the cases considered here; indeed, the forms considered first, in section 4.3.5.1, should be recognized as especially significant on account of the attestations of them in Omotic, which, as we have seen, has often had less solid support than the other families.

4.3.5.1 *Verb derivation*

AA languages all exhibit word-formation processes for creating new verbs from existing ones by means of affixes, often in combination. Verbs so derived differ from their bases in terms of syntactic argument structure, voice and the like. There are some recurrent affixal elements involved in this that are certainly of P-AA provenance. A transitivising/causative *s-* ~ *-s* is found in all six families,[29] for example E: **si-min-* 'establish', compare **man-* 'to be stable'; S – Amharic: *as-wässädä* 'he caused to take', compare *wässädä* 'he took'; B: *ss-xdm* 'cause to work', compare *xdm* 'work', *ss-isin* 'inform', compare *isin* 'know'; C – Sidamo: *raʔ-is-* 'boil (tr)', compare *raʔ-* 'boil (intr)'; Ch – Ngizim: *dəɓs-* 'hide (tr)', *dàas-* 'pour (tr) through a narrow opening'; O – Aari: *lanq-s-* 'tire (tr)', compare *lanq-* 'feel tired', Gamo: *gup-iss-* 'cause to jump', compare *gupp-* 'jump'.

Other widespread derivational affixes are: *m-* ~ *-m*, *n-* and *t-* ~ *-t*, associated variously with notions of reflexivity, reciprocity, and/or intransitivising/passivising formations – the last formative listed also often appears as a middle voice in Cushitic.

A long-standing issue concerns whether the P-AA verb root was originally tri-consonantal, as in Semitic generally, or biconsonantal, as it most frequently appears in Chadic, Cushitic and Omotic (cf. Hodge 1969: 244). One way of re-conciling the difference has been to propose that the third consonant is actually a derivational suffix. The fruitfulness of this proposal was demonstrated for Hausa by Jungraithmayr (1970, 1971). Ehret (1989) represents a *tour de force* in applying the idea to Semitic. Whether or not most of the derivational formatives Ehret reconstructs will gain acceptance within the field, his proposals have certainly facilitated a great many of the otherwise problematic reconstructions in his recent (1995) opus.

4.3.5.2 *Further case markers*

Diakonoff (1988: 61) lists a number of more peripheral case elements. Among these what he calls a locative-terminative, dative in *-Vš*, *-šV*,[30] a direct-ive in *-l* and an ablative/comparative in *-kV* are all attested in at least three AA families.

4.3.5.3   Gender and gender markers

Much has been written on this subject (Klingenheben 1951, Green-berg 1960a, Castellino 1975). Newman (1980: 17ff) goes well beyond previous work in demonstrating a remarkable constancy across five of the AA families with regard to nominal gender, even when the nouns concerned are not cognate (see chapter 10 below).[31]

A feminine gender marking element, -(a)t, is commonly noted in the literature for Semitic, Egyptian, Berber, Cushitic and Chadic; but it has also been noted in S. Omotic Aari (Hayward 1990: 445) and argued for in N. Omotic (Hayward 1989).

4.3.6   **Lexicon and phonology**

Among the hundreds of lexical items reconstructed for P-AA, the fol-lowing short selection seem unlikely to be disputed.[32]

> *ba 'not be there, negative' (Eh.2); *bak- 'strike, squeeze' (O&S.194 + O – Gamo bak- 'strike'); *pir- 'fly (v.)' (Eh.51); *-fir- 'flower, bear fruit' (Eh.85); *dim-/*dam- 'blood' (Eh.140, O&S.639 + S.O – Aari: zomʔi 'id.'); *-dar- 'enlarge, increase' (Eh.150); *-tuf- 'to spit' (Eh.162, O&S.2413); *-zaaʃ- 'rend, tear' (Eh.208 + O – Gamo zaʔ- 'split'); *sum-/*sim- 'name' (Eh.220, O&S.2304); *sin-/*san- 'nose' (Eh.222, O&S.2194); *gad-/*gud- 'be big' (Eh.265, O&S.867); *-geh- 'speak' (Eh.274, O&S.911 *gay-); *kop- 'sole' (Eh.327, O&S.1406 *kab- 'shoe, sandal'); *kamaʔ-/*kamay- 'food' (O&S.1424 + E.C – Afar: -okm- 'eat'); *k'ar- 'tip, point' (Eh.424, O&S.1549 *k'ar- 'horn'); *s'am- 'to sour' (Eh.535); *man-/*min- 'house' (O&S.1723); *nam-/*nim- 'man' (Eh.621, O&S.1841).

Regarding consonants, the preceding reconstructions involve quite straightfor-ward sound correspondences. P-AA *b in the first example above is reconstructed on the basis of E: b : C: *b : Ch: *b : N.O: *b.[33] But P-AA seems to have had a rich consonant inventory, just as many of its descendants do today.[34] There is general agreement that obstruents must have been organised in triads contrast-ing glottalised with plain voiced and voiceless series, not only for most places of articulation but also for certain other articulatory parameters, for example, among lateral obstruents, sibilants and labialised velars. A guttural series com-prising pharyngeals and laryngeals is also always postulated for the proto-language. During the various family evolutions, and at every lower level, the hypothesised inventories have been whittled down as a result of numerous mergers. The details of these events have not as yet been agreed upon however. Thus both Ehret and Orel and Stolbova attribute a glottalised coronal stop, *t'/*ṭ, to P-AA. But according to the one, the Egyptian reflex of this was *s*, which requires mergers of the original sound with six other phonemes (**s, *š, *c, *ts, *s'* and sometimes **tl'*); but according to the others, the Egyptian reflexes were *d* and *t*, with four and six etyma apiece. Again, all these authors reconstruct an ancestor language with a glottalised lateral affricate, **tl'/*ĉ*; but while Orel and Stolbova adduce for this Arabic forms having an emphatic *ḍ*, Ehret adduces Arabic forms having emphatic *ṣ*. Such examples could be multiplied. Large-scale, phylum-wide comparison stimulates the imagination and serves to inject a sense of purpose into the AA enterprise, but the most pressing need continues to be that of detailed and extensive lexical reconstruction within the constituent families.

4.4   The *Urheimat*

Apart from Semitic incursions into Africa, the present distribution of the six AA families has not changed significantly over the period known to history, and any discussion of the AA homeland involves speculation about prehistorical events. Clearly the two candidates are Africa and south-west Asia, and both have their advocates.

Given that five language families, now very distinct from each other, are exclusive to Africa, it is easier to envisage a scenario having an original epicentre in Africa. In his earlier work, Diakonoff (1988: 21ff) located the P-AA homeland in what is now the south-east Sahara. The north-eastwards migration of the ancestral Semitic speakers into Asia was then seen as an event that took place some 9,000 years ago. Recently however he has revised this somewhat by placing the proto-Semites from an early age between Palestine and the Nile Delta, where they would remain in contact with the African-based Berbero-Libyans and Proto-Bedauye/Beja speakers (Diakonoff 1998: 216f).

Those who argue for an Asian *Urheimat* (Militariev and Shnirelman 1984) do so largely to explain the existence of lexis shared by AA languages of Africa, Sumerian, and languages of the Caucasus. Assuming these to be loans, one has then to ask where the contact for this occurred; and clearly a non-African locale would be favoured.

Much has been written on the subject, and the interested reader will find guidance in an overview by Isserlin (1975).

Notes

1 The term 'AA peoples' will often be used as a shorthand for the more accurate, though cumbersome, phrase 'communities of speakers of AA languages'; the abbreviation is always, however, to be understood in this fuller sense.

2 Numbers of speakers are based on the 13th edition of *Ethnologue* (Grimes 1996). Grimes advances a number of reasons as to why estimates for numbers of speakers of a language may not be accurate (pp. viii–x) and the entries for many of the countries where AA languages are spoken are assigned an accuracy grading of 'B', which Grimes glosses as 'Based on good published sources but with need for further investigation by linguists on the field', or even 'C', which means 'Needs extensive checking by linguists on the field and more research in published sources'; this point must be constantly borne in mind by the reader. In presenting *Ethnologue* figures, the following abbreviatory convention will be observed. Except in the case of languages with 3,000 or less speakers (where the *Ethnologue* figure will be cited as given, and underlined) the figures will be presented in multiples of a thousand; thus, 3,050,000 would appear as 3,050. Intermediate figures will be rounded upwards. Names of varieties also normally follow *Ethnologue* spelling; alternative names and spellings can then readily be accessed in that work.

3 Naima Louali has drawn my attention to a publication (Miller (1996)) claiming that the Siwa number is twice this figure.

4 *Ethnologue* lists 192 Chadic languages. In some cases, too, the numbers of speakers given in Newman (1992) and *Ethnologue* show wide discrepancies. For consistency in this survey of AA languages, I have adhered to the *Ethnologue* figures.

5 Faber (1997) presents a clear explanation of the linguistic reasons underlying this classification, and also incorporates certain modifications based on more recent work.

6 See, however, Mous (1994).

7 The constraints have not remained constant; we know for example that earlier conditions in and around the Sahara were much more favourable than they are today.

8 The biblical account of Ham (Genesis 10) has often been misconstrued in representing him as the ancestor of the African races.

9 Judging by their remarks about the need for 'Proto-Cushitic' reconstruction, Orel and Stolbova (1995: x) must have been unaware of the enterprise of Ehret (1987).

10 Other functions are found on a more language-specific basis.

11 The following abbreviations have been adopted in the presentation of data:

(1) for the names of languages and language groups

B	Berber	P-AA	Proto-Afroasiatic
C	Cushitic	P-C	Proto-Cushitic
Ch	Chadic	P-E	Proto-Egyptian
E	Egyptian	P-S	Proto-Semitic
O	Omotic		

(2) for grammatical categories

abs	absolutive	3sg	3rd person singular
acc	accusative	1pl	1st person plural
gen	genitive	2pl	2nd person plural
nom	nominative	3pl	3rd person plural
NP	noun phrase	m.	masculine
1sg	1st person singular	f.	feminine
2sg	2nd person singular		

Except in a few cases – which are indicated – the sources of the forms presented here are as follows. Proto-Egyptian, marked with double asterisks, and vocalised Egyptian, marked with a single asterisk: Loprieno (1995: 63–7); Proto-Semitic: Diakonoff (1988: 70–8); Berber: Applegate (1971: 112). (Applegate does not actually specify the variety from which his forms are taken so that it is assumed they are intended to represent some sort of Common Berber); Proto-Cushitic: Appleyard (1986a); the Chadic forms, which are designated 'Old Hausa': Newman (1980: 15); the Omotic forms are from Dizi: Allan (1976: 383).

12 Chadic *ni* here in 1sg is cognate with the Semitic object pronoun form *-ni*. This element may also perhaps be preserved in Omotic Yemsa as the verb agreement for 1sg subjects (Lamberti 1993b: 185); cf. examples in section 4.3.3. Diakonoff adduces the E. Chadic Mubi possessive suffixes as putative reflexes of P-AA *$*i$ (1988: 77). The consonantal bases of the pronoun series appear also in subject function in Chadic: thus, 1sg Hausa *ni*, Mubi *ni*. Interestingly Ron-Daffo (W. Chadic) has 1sg subject *yi* (Schuh 1976: 6) or *ʔi* (Jungraithmayr 1978: 388).

13 Proto-Omotic *$*i$, seen here in Dizi *yi-n* (the *-n* is a fossil case marker) has reflexes also in S. Omotic Aari *ʔi*. The rest of N. Omotic has a new 1sg pronoun *ta*; though earlier *$*i$ still persists as a pronominal agreement marker in the verb in part of Ometo.

14 Newman (1980: 15) reconstructs the P-AA 2f.sg as *$*kim$ arguing that the *-m* element attested in Chadic, Berber and Egyptian is an AA retention. This seems convincing, for any suggestion that *-m* represents a shared innovation would suggest a subgrouping, which is not supported on other grounds.

15 Ehret (1995: 487) maintains that P-AA did not differentiate gender, but that this appeared later as an innovation in his 'Erythraean Branch', a branch consisting of all of AA minus Omotic. Ehret's position on gender in Omotic has also been my own (Hayward 1987: 227); see however my remarks in note 31 below.

16 As Newman points out (1980: 17), Chadic has an innovative (non-cognate) form *$*mu(n)$ for 1pl, and this has resulted in *$*na$ now having a restricted distribution.

17 The Berber forms are included here for inspection only, as the absence of any velar element should argue for their omission.

18 See note 15 above.

19 Focused NPs are generally nominal predicates in cleft constructions, which appear in the absolutive.

20 For those groups where the nominative came to be the citation form, for example Semitic and Egyptian, the occurrence of this *-u* is often spoken of as a marker of masculine gender. Furthermore, as the citation form is the nominative, it explains why it has been usual to see the absolutive as an accusative.

21 Furthermore, the actual nominative case markers of Gimira-Ometo have an altogether different etymology.

22 This would be analysed as *yi-n-u* where *yi* reflects P-AA *$*i$, *$*yi$ and *-n* represents the fossilised general N. Omotic accusative marker to which a relic of the still surviving P-AA nominative *$*-u$ is attached. 2sg pronoun *yetu* also shares this termination. A structural parallel occurs in many of the Ometo languages where the new nominative case in *-i* attaches to a relic of the old accusative marker in *-n*; e.g. *ta-n-i* 'I', cf. *ta-n-a* 'me'.

23 If the P-Cj is not original, it is difficult to see where the prefixes (presumably pronominal in origin) could have come from. This question seems not to be addressed by those who view this conjugation as an innovation.

24 This scenario mirrors that proposed by Praetorius (1894) for the development of the Cushitic Suffix Conjugation, which has had a universal acceptance. The differences between Yemsa and the general Cushitic pattern suggest parallel rather than shared evolution.

25 This paradigm replaced the earlier prefix-conjugated perfect in the rest of Semitic.

26 There seems to be variation here; in Berber biconsonantal verbs it is the first consonant, and in Chadic Migama it is the final consonant. The associations of geminated/reduplicated forms and the semantic categories of habitual, frequent and on-going (i.e., present) activities – which is easily extended to notions of plurality – have often been noted.

27 Ablaut to -*a*- is seen well in derived stems in Beja; the habitual of the causative stem is shown here. Greenberg's attempt to demonstrate the gemination feature in Beja is invalidated by failure to appreciate that original present-tense forms have to be sought in today's past-tense – hence his bewilderment about the derived stems (1952: 7); cf. the discussion by Zaborski (1975: 13ff).

28 Greenberg does cite a few instances from Coptic, but they seem less than satisfying.

29 It is also to be noted however that a causative in -*s* is found in Bantu (Niger-Congo) and is reconstructed for Proto-Central Khoisan.

30 Given that the forms found in most of the languages concerned have -*s*, rather than -*š*, the non-palatal sibilant might be closer to the original.

31 At the time Newman did not accept Omotic as Afroasiatic and did not include it in the survey. Had he done so it would have confirmed his disbelief, for Omotic languages seem largely to have abandoned grammatical gender. Nevertheless the distinction is always present in third-person pronouns, even though the actual morphology has undergone several group-specific replacements. More significantly, gender – albeit natural gender – is generally expressed in verb agreement.

32 The sources for reconstructed forms given here are indicated as: Eh (= Ehret 1995), O&S (= Orel and Stolbova 1995); the accompanying numbers refer to the numbering of the reconstructions in those works. When an attestation in a particular AA family has been weak or missing, and I happen to be aware of a likely cognate form, I have added it.

33 If the item had been attested in Semitic, the correspondence would have also been *b*.

34 Ehret posits forty-two P-AA consonants (1995: 72); Orel and Stolbova have ten less (1995: xvi).

5

Khoisan

TOM GÜLDEMANN AND RAINER VOSSEN

5.1   **Introductory remarks**[1]

For a long time the Khoisan languages were labelled and commonly known as 'Bushman' and 'Hottentot' languages. According to a widely accepted albeit controversial hypothesis, they represent the smallest of the four language phyla in Africa (Greenberg 1963a). In the past the number of languages and dialects may well have exceeded 100, but today only 30 or so still exist. That is, most Khoisan languages were already extinct or in process of extinction before sound scholarly interest in them could develop.

Geographically, the majority of modern Khoisan languages are distributed over much of Botswana and Namibia. There are also pockets of speakers in adjacent regions: in southern Angola and Zambia, western Zimbabwe as well as in northern South Africa. In former times probably the larger part of present-day South Africa was Khoisan-speaking territory (see map 5.5). Two isolated languages also considered to be of Khoisan stock are located in distant Tanzania.

5.2   **Research history and internal classification**

Despite the considerable number of adherents to the so-called macro-Khoisan hypothesis, which was set up first under the name of 'Click languages' by Greenberg (1950b), none of the several attempts at proving the genetic relatedness of all putative Khoisan languages has been convincing, as the evidence appears to be extremely meagre. Thus, the large proportion of missing links caused by the fact that too many of the extinct languages forever escaped our notice and that still too many of those which are alive have not been studied in detail, may pose an insoluble problem for the small number of Khoisanist linguists in the world.

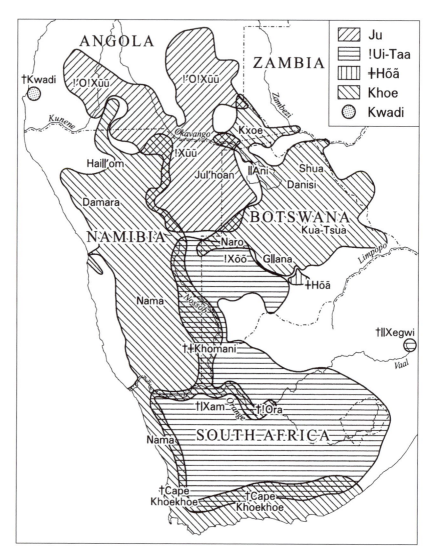

Map 5.5. South African Khoisan (pre-colonial situation). (Note: "†" = language now extinct.)

Greenberg's macro-Khoisan hypothesis, which is largely a result of lexical comparisons based on the criterion of resemblance in shape and meaning, implies the following internal classification: first, a dividing line is drawn between South African Khoisan (SAK) and the two East African isolates, Hadza and Sandawe. Within SAK three major branches are distinguished, that is Northern, Central and

Southern. Northern Khoisan presents itself as a dialect cluster consisting of three or four major units, with a considerable degree of mutual intelligibility. The Central branch comprises around twenty different languages and dialects, whereas Southern Khoisan today has virtually only one member (!Xõõ dialect cluster). It would seem, however, that most of the extinct languages of South Africa belonged to that latter branch. Furthermore, there is one language (ǂHõã) whose position within SAK is still unclear.

While members of each of Greenberg's three SAK branches can more or less be shown to share genetic relationship, such affiliations between the branches are highly questionable. When one moves beyond lexical comparison, similarities appear to be mainly phonological: complex inventories with clicks, a word structure of predominantly CVCV, CVV and CVN sequences and a distinctive distribution of consonants in which obstruents are restricted to C_1 position (cf. section 5.5). However, at the grammatical level there are major differences. For example, Northern Khoisan has little morphology compared to Central Khoisan in particular, but it has a fairly elaborated syntactic structure. The Central languages have a unique nominal and pronominal person-gender-number (PGN) system (cf. section 5.6.2) as compared to Northern and Southern (cf. section 5.6.1), and a large variety of verbal extensions unattested elsewhere in Khoisan (cf. section 5.6.2). In the Southern branch and in ǂHõã the bilabial click influx (cf. section 5.5) is unique.

However controversial Greenberg's hypothesis and classification of macro-Khoisan may be, they surely mark a turning point in the roughly 200-year-old history of Khoisan linguistics insofar as they were established on purely linguistic grounds. For previous comparative attempts tended to rely to some extent on extralinguistic, mostly physical and other anthropological criteria (e.g. Müller 1877; for more detailed accounts, see Köhler 1975 and Winter 1981). Partially for the same reason, the close genetic relationship between 'Hottentot' and the central group of 'Bushman' languages (i.e. Greenberg's Central Khoisan) remained for a long time undiscovered. As it were, the fundamental difference in subsistence economies – cattle-keeping on the one side ('Hottentots') and hunting and gathering on the other ('Bushmen') – combined with the typological observation of a nominal and pronominal PGN system in the 'Hottentot' languages which the then known 'Bushman' languages were lacking, was widely regarded as sufficient justification to keep the two entirely apart and even to relate 'Hottentot' to other gender languages in Africa and beyond (e.g. Bleek 1851 and Lepsius 1880).

Curiously, it was a physical anthropologist – Leonhardt Schulze – who, in 1928, coined the term 'Khoisan' (composed of 'Hottentot' *khoi* 'person' and *san* 'foragers') to point to a somatic-racial commonality between the 'Hottentot' and the

'Bushmen' people. Shortly thereafter, the cultural anthropologist Schapera further elaborated on the concept of 'Khoisan' and extended its meaning towards a
holistic view of 'Hottentot' and 'Bushman' as a racial, cultural *and* linguistic unit
(Schapera 1930). Truly Greenberg popularised the label which, however, was not
exclusively looked on benevolently by Africanist linguists, chiefly for one essential reason: it lacked concrete linguistic substantiation.

This situation has not changed a lot in the post-Greenbergian era. In principle,
two positions can be identified: roughly 'lumpers' versus 'splitters'. Whereas the
'lumpers' (e.g. Argyle 1994; Ehret 1986; Honken 1977, 1988; Ruhlen 1994) believe in deep relationships in a Khoisan phylum (and even beyond), the 'splitters'
(especially Westphal 1962, 1971) take more conservative views. Yet a third group
of scholars (e.g. Köhler 1975, 1981; Sands 1998; Traill 1980, 1986) decided to use
the term 'Khoisan' as a cover for all non-Bantu as well as non-Cushitic click
languages of eastern and southern Africa, but without explicitly adhering to the
genealogical implications. This latter opinion is shared by the present writers who,
in this chapter, start out from the following (pragmatically oriented) Khoisan
groupings:

(1)	Non-Khoe		
	(1.1)	Ju (*Northern*)	(!'O)!Xũũ, ‖X'au‖'e, Ju‖'hoan (DC)
	(1.2)	!Ui-Taa (*Southern*)	
		(1.2.1) !Ui	†|Xam, †|'Auni, †‡Khomani, †‖Xegwi, etc.
		(1.2.2) Taa	!Xõõ (DC); †Kakia
	(1.3)	‡Hõã	‡Hõã (isolate)
(2)	Khoe (*Central*)		
	(2.1)	Khoekhoe	
		(2.1.1) North	Nama/Damara, Hai‖'om, ‡Aakhoe (DC)
		(2.1.2) South	†!Ora; †Cape Khoekhoe varieties (DC)
	(2.2)	Kalahari Khoe	
		(2.2.1) West	Kxoe, Buga, ‖Ani (DC); Naro (DC); G‖ana, G|ui, ‡Haba (DC)
		(2.2.2) East	Shua, Ts'ixa, Danisi, |Xaise, †Deti; Kua-Tsua (DC)
(3)	*Sandawe*		Sandawe (isolate)
(4)	Kwadi		†Kwadi (undetermined)
(5)	*Hadza*		Hadza (isolate)

Note: DC = dialect cluster; [†] = (presumably) extinct; *italics* = Greenberg's major branches.

The term 'Non-Khoe' subsumes three SAK language groups which to this day cannot be shown to be genetically related but, nevertheless, share a considerable number of linguistic features, some of which are fairly rare from a cross-linguistic point of view. These are the !Ui-Taa language group, the Ju dialect cluster, and the genetically as yet unassigned ǂHõã language.

5.3 State of documentation

Although several groups commonly subsumed under the cover term 'Khoisan' have anthropologically been studied most intensively, their languages are in general still very poorly documented. Table 5.19 gives a brief overview of the state of documentation for those languages which are fairly well known from the literature. It does not include a number of languages which are so little known that they can hardly contribute to an overall assessment of Khoisan. Excluded are, for example, Kwadi and most !Ui varieties which are, or must be, believed to be extinct, and Kalahari East Khoe and northern Ju varieties that are spoken languages to this day.

Table 5.19. *State of documentation for the better-known Khoisan languages*

Language	Phonetics/ phonology	Lexicon	Grammar	Raw texts	Glossed texts
Hadza	T S	(S)	(S)	(S)	
Sandawe	T T S	M U (S)	S (S)	(S)	U
!Ora	M	(S)	(M S)	(M S)	
Nama/Damara	M S	U (M S)	M T (M)	U (M)	
Haiǁ'om-ǂAakhoe		U	U	U	(S)
Hiecho		(S)	(S)	(S)	
Kxoe		S U	M	M	M
Buga, ǁAni	S	S U	S	U	U
Gǀui, Gǁana	S	S			
Naro	S	M M	S		
!Xũũ	S	S	M	(S U)	S U
Juǀ'hoan	M S	M M	M M M	S U	
ǂHõã		S	S		
!Xõõ	M S	M	S (U)		U
ǀXam		(M U)	(S)	(M S U)	
ǁXegwi	(S)		(S)		

Note: M = monograph; S = short treatment; T = thesis; U = unpublished manuscript; ( ) = outdated.

This presentation aims to differentiate between more extensive works such as monographs or unpublished manuscripts and shorter treatments such as word lists, grammatical sketches, articles on specialised topics, or information within studies with a scope wider than one language only. On the one hand, there is a strong bias towards up-to-date phonetic-phonological analyses. On the other hand, there are immense gaps in the grammatical and discourse-oriented documentation. Here, even longer treatments are often far from being sufficient. Also remarkable is the large amount of data that are known to exist but still remain unpublished. Although some works may have been overlooked, this does not affect the general picture showing that the large majority of languages are essentially inaccessible to the wider linguistic public. In fact, only three languages are described in readily available sources to such an extent that linguists unfamiliar with these languages can gain a fairly good understanding after a reasonable amount of work. The languages are Standard Khoekhoe (alias Nama/Damara), Kxoe and Juǀ'hoan. This situation is all the more regrettable as Khoisan languages have been shown to add new fascinating facets to our general knowledge of human languages.

5.4 Sociolinguistic situation

Determining the number of Khoisan speakers is a difficult task, both for the past and present. While nothing is known for the pre-colonial and colonial periods, the present-day situation can only be described vaguely. On the one hand, most of the figures contained in the literature are outdated, on the other hand recent population census tend not to single out ethnic groups or languages. As a consequence, hardly more than a rough estimate – 200,000 – can here be given. This figure includes, however, the over 100,000 Khoekhoe speakers (available figures vary between 120,000 and 200,000), who represent by far the largest and only officially recognised Khoisan speech community. As second largest group, the Sandawe of Tanzania (several 10,000 speakers) may be mentioned. For other speech communities figures range from a few hundred (e.g. ǂHõã, Ts'ixa, Hadza) to several thousand (Juǀ'hoan, !Xõõ, Naro, Kxoe).

Whereas many Khoisan languages are known or assumed to have died out in earlier centuries, today some of the smaller groups of Khoisan speakers seem to be seriously threatened by extinction. Nevertheless, degrees of threat cannot be concluded immediately from the size of the speech community, as in some areas the overall conditions for a survival of small languages are more favourable than in others. Generally speaking, chances of survival are not good because of the rapid and on-going social, economic and political changes which accompany the process of nation-building (cf. Barnard 1992, Batibo 1998).

From a historical point of view, today's sociolinguistic situation may be said to have come into existence gradually over a period of roughly 2,000 years or more, the beginning of which was marked by first waves of Bantu immigrants from the north. In southern Africa, these intrusions initiated an enormous expansion of Bantu speakers which, as a consequence, triggered – and decisively contributed to – the partial destruction, displacement or absorption of the formerly autochthonous Khoisan-speaking population. From the mid-seventeenth century onwards the arrival of European settlers and traders further complicated these unfortunate developments. In modern times, social marginalisation and stigmatisation largely characterise the life of the Khoisan-speaking minorities. In Botswana, for instance, low social prestige and political insignificance find a formal expression in the contemptuous label 'Basarwa', which in a wider sense denotes people at the lowest level of the social ladder, but in a narrower sense refers to Khoisan speakers in particular. Very recently, however, in both Namibia and Botswana a change in thinking has begun to show, and an increase in political awareness also within the Khoisan-speaking population is slowly assuming tangible form (cf. Vossen 1997b).

5.5 Phonetics and phonology

5.5.1 *Types of sounds, phonological systems and typology*

It is safe to say that Khoisan sound systems are not only unique in Africa but figure among the most complex in the world. Although clicks are the most prominent token of this complexity, these languages possess many other features which are rare cross-linguistically and add to their great variety of phonological distinctions.

The mechanism underlying the articulation of clicks is well understood since Beach (1938) and many more details about the large variety of different click types have been added subsequently (see, e.g., Traill 1985, 1993, 1997). For a proper understanding of variation among these ingressive consonants it is important to clarify the distinction between click 'influx' and 'efflux'. In the production of the so-called suction mechanism, the tongue is moved against the roof of the mouth creating a closure in the oral cavity. The central tongue body is then lowered while blade and back of the tongue maintain the closure. Thus, the pressure of the air trapped in the cavity decreases. Then the front closure is released, the air rushing in being responsible for the loud noise typical of clicks. The way the anterior tongue body is manipulated determines the type of the click influx. There are five such influxes, commonly symbolised and labelled as follows: ☉ = bilabial, | = dental, ! = alveolar, ǂ = palatal, and ‖ = lateral. However, the terms are inadequate for an exhaustive description and explanation of the internal relations between the different types (cf. Traill 1993, 1995). The click efflux or accompaniment is shaped by the manner of release of the posterior closure. Here, the diversity of types is even greater (cf. Ladefoged and Traill 1994) and Khoisanists still diverge in their description and representation (cf. Köhler *et al.* 1988). The combinations of various influx and efflux types sometimes lead to excessively large click inventories.

The places of articulation of egressive sounds are *labial*, *alveolar*, palatal, lateral, *velar*, uvular and *glottal* (common ones in italics). While approximants, fricatives and nasals play a minor role, stops (plosives and affricates) are the backbone of any system. Consonants are regularly voiced, glottalised or aspirated. Posterior co-articulations like velar fricative or ejective are also frequent in SAK languages.

The characteristics of vowels also confront the researcher with an unexpected variety of types. The normal case is a system of five vowel qualities. These vowels can have a wide range of distinctive colourings: nasalisation is found in almost every language; glottalised, breathy and pharyngealised vowels are also fairly common. Again different combinations of these features can make up for a large inventory of distinctive vowel segments. Last but not least, tone is also a very important distinctive feature.

The above sound types combine in various ways to build up very complex phoneme systems. Some basic structural principles can be found all over Khoisan. Yet, Traill (1980) has shown that differences between languages can be dramatic; compare, for example, the inventory size of Standard Namibian (North) Khoekhoe with the one of eastern !Xõõ: 20 vs. 83 clicks, 12 vs. 43 nonclicks, and 10 vs. 44 vocalic monophthongs, respectively.

However, the extraordinarily high number of phonemes in !Xõõ and other languages results from the assumption that all complex segments are to be analysed as units. Traill (1985, 1993) challenges this view systematically and brings forward strong arguments in favour of a cluster analysis for many complex consonants. This reduces the number of primary segments considerably. Güldemann (2000) elaborates on this approach and adds another hypothesis, viz. that clicks and nonclicks can be analysed phonologically in one integrated system of consonants. Future research must show whether this holds against an increasing amount of data from other languages. The advantage is that these analyses can do away with two unprecedented typological anomalies of Khoisan associated with the traditional approach: the consonant inventory no longer comprises two disjunct systems and has a size much closer to cross-linguistically normal figures.

A final remark should be made about the way this multiplicity of sounds is distributed in lexical morphemes. With the exception of Hadza, the phonotactic constraints in a canonical stem are as follows:

C(C)$_1$	–V$_1$	–C$_2$	–V$_2$
strong stop	short/oral/back	sonorant or anterior voiced stop	short/oral

However marked this pattern appears, Traill (1985: 164ff) has shown that in conforming to cross-linguistic principles it is rather 'a variation on a universal theme'. Significant is yet another fact: given the very large number of strong consonants which are restricted to C$_1$ (a cluster is indicated by the bracketted C) and the small number of segments in all other slots, it is the phonological variation in the first consonantal stem position in particular that is crucial for the distinction of lexical meaning in Khoisan languages.

5.5.2	***Sound correspondences and changes***

In view of the immense irregularity of change and the distance in sound shape between allegedly related lexical items in their cross-Khoisan comparisons, some scholars without first-hand experience of these languages seem to imply that it is in the nature of the complex sounds that correspondences in Khoisan are not as tight and predictable as one would wish them to be. Undoubtedly, there are problems with both the empirical data and the analytical tools applied to them. However, Khoisanists founding their comparative work on their own material have shown that (a) the enormous sound complexity is not intrinsically unstable (Traill 1974b: 39–40), (b) correspondences and changes conforming to predictable patterns are discernible (Köhler 1973/4: 185ff; Snyman 1974: 40ff; Traill 1975, 1986; Traill and Vossen 1997; Honken 1998), and (c) working in a straightforwardly genetic group of languages permits the application of the methodology of historical/comparative reconstruction (Vossen 1997a). In presenting the most important findings on sound change in Khoisan, it is useful to make reference to the above phonotactic slots in stems. In the first consonant position, one is confronted with different types of what is called here 'strength oscillation' of the consonant. This neutral term is intended to include both lenition and strengthening. Clicks, the strongest and most frequent initial segments, replace each other according to the acoustic cross-classification of influxes (natural pairs are ǂ ~ |, ! ~ ‖, | ~ ‖, ǂ ~ !) or are replaced by cognate egressives (attested changes are | > ts, ǂ > c, ! > k/kL). They also lose or weaken co-articulation gestures or get lost completely, leaving behind their former accompaniment only. The latter two phenomena are also relevant to egressive stops. Interactions between the C$_1$ slot and the following vowel(s) are observed in Traill (1975) and can be described as an absorption of a feature of one slot by the other. This led Traill to the important assumption that at least some vowel colourings may not have been features of earlier language states, but originated in a process of feature displacement from the C_1 slot. It is significant in this respect that vowel colourings and consonant features can be related to each other. We find nasality, aspiration and glottalisation with both types of segment and, according to Traill (1980: 185–6) and Vossen (1992: 368), even a correlation between uvular consonants and vowel pharyngealisation dimly emerges. Another process in the V_1 position is its assimilation to a particular C_1–V_2 sequence (Traill 1985: 90–1). In the C_2 position, one can frequently observe an alternation between a nasal and a non-nasal sonorant (*n ~ r/l*) or the complete loss of the consonant. The latter process gives rise to long oral or nasal vowels. Nasals and nasality are also involved in changes taking place in the stem-final V_2 position. Traill (1975: 79–80) describes a possible absorption of a final vowel by a preceding nasal consonant and the consonantalisation of suprasegmental vowel nasalisation. The result of both phenomena is a final and often syllabic nasal.

Obviously, this cannot be an exhaustive treatment of sound change in Khoisan. However, it may suffice to demonstrate that, as in any other language group, there exist changes which are regular and frequent, and changes which must be viewed as less likely or even unnatural. The accumulating knowledge on this complex topic will form the future basis for more reliable historical work on Khoisan as a whole.

5.6   Grammatical characteristics

5.6.1   *Non-Khoe*

As mentioned before, the term 'Non-Khoe' denotes, parallel to the discussion in Güldemann (1998), a set of languages of a particular 'structural type' that is not necessarily tied to a common genetic origin. This can be outlined with reference to just a few basic structural properties.

One feature distinguishing Non-Khoe languages from all other Khoisan is that they have a SVO clause order and a nominal head–modifier structure with the important exception of associative constructions where the reverse order modifier–head is found. Thus, they are quite prototypical type B languages in Heine's (1976a) terms.

Non-Khoe languages possess little inflectional morphology; a phonological word is most often a bare lexical stem. Only in !Xõõ do we find frequent morphological alternations triggered by noun-class agreement. Most grammemes are particles which often do not conform to the phonotactic pattern of lexemes. Due to the sparseness of bound grammatical morphemes, many syntactic relations are expressed by analytic structures the order of which is closely tied to the above word-order configurations.

A salient characteristic in Non-Khoe is the syntactic behaviour of the verbal word(s) serving the expression of the state of affairs in a clause. There can be a fairly long chain of such stems after the subject which is not interrupted by any grammatical material. On the other hand, these verbal stems have a very restricted valency for all following nominal constituents. This feature, which is typical for so-called verb-serialising languages, helps to explain some peculiarities of the basic clause structure.

Thus most grammatical particles which express functions such as tense, aspect, modality, focus, negation and other notions modifying the state of affairs or the predication, are placed between the subject and the verb (chain). This consistent syntactic position can be explained if one assumes that such function words emerged via grammaticalisation of earlier verbal lexemes used as auxiliaries. This can be observed in modern Non-Khoe languages like, for example, Juǀ'hoan (cf. Dickens n.d.: 5–6, 59ff).

As mentioned above, the verbal predicate establishes a very special relation to all following constituents that refer to a nominal entity. Almost all verbs can be followed by only one noun phrase unless additional linguistic material is introduced. If a verb does not inherently entail a complement, certain grammatical devices must be used. This is not simply a question of verb transitivity, as these formal changes are not only triggered by objects but by any kind of nominal, including adverbial phrases of place, instrument or time. Time adverbs do not trigger such a marking when appearing at a place before the verb (chain). Juǀ'hoan, for instance, has *inter alia* recourse to a verb suffix *-a* to index the presence of a valency-external noun phrase – here a time adjunct:

ha	*kú*	*ú*	vs.	*ha*	*kú*	*ú -á*	*ǀám-à*	*hè*
CLI.PRO	IPFV	go		CLI.PRO	IPFV	go-VE	day-R	(be) this

'He was going.' 'He will be going today [day which is this].'

(Dickens n.d.: 19–20)

Another possible means by which to introduce an additional noun phrase in a clause is a serial verb construction whereby the respective noun phrase is subcategorised by verbs like 'have', 'take', 'give' or 'make'. If these precede the noun phrase directly, they may potentially develop into grammaticalised prepositions with a specialised meaning. In !Xõõ, they often look like inflected adpositions since they incorporate a marker agreeing in class with the nominal referent. Moreover, a considerable number of verbs in this language have come to prescribe the use of a particular element and occasionally this also leads to a special meaning of the whole phrase. In the following example the bare verb 'speak' is followed by the comitative marker and, then, means 'scold'. The element ‡'V itself presumably originated from the verb ‡'á(-u) 'have/take possession of'.

> ń   bà àhn   tâna   ‡'é'è
> 1SG.PRO FUT   speak   COM:CL3.AGR
> 'I will scold him.'   (Traill 1994: 19)

Less common from a cross-linguistic perspective is the existence of a type of preposed relational grammeme devoid of semantic specificity as regards the function of the noun phrase it serves to introduce. Such a versatile element marks by default all kinds of valency-external noun phrases and is, therefore, called here multipurpose oblique (MPO) marker. It can be identified in Ju|'hoan (*kò*), !Xũũ (*kè*), ‡Hõã (*kì*), !Xõõ (*kV* or *tV*) and possibly also |Xam (*au*). The following example from Ju|'hoan shows that the order of two post-verbal noun phrases can even be reversed without any effect neither on the occurrence and order of the grammatical elements signalling their presence (i.e., VE and MPO marker) nor on the assignment of their semantic roles (possible changes in the information structure have not yet been subject to investigation):

> ha   kú ||ohm-a   !aìhn   kò   g|úí
> CLI.PRO IPFV   chop-VE   tree   MPO   forest

or

> ha   kú ||ohm-a   g|úí   kò   !aìhn
> 'He was chopping the tree in the forest.'   (Dickens n.d.: 22)

The unusual result is that the direct object *!aìhn* 'tree' – the nominal participant which is semantically tied to the verb more closely – ends up detached from the latter and introduced by the MPO marker (cf. also Heikkinen 1987: 29 for !Xũũ).

As mentioned earlier, associative constructions which *inter alia* serve to express possessive relations are head-final. The majority of Non-Khoe languages have two types of structure: one characterised by the mere juxtaposition of the two nominal constituents and the other showing a medial attributor. Such a structural difference is sometimes, but not always, tied to a distinction 'alienable' vs. 'inalienable' possession.

Common to all Non-Khoe languages is the use of the associative type that lacks a segmental marker for a number of other linguistic functions. Thus, specific locative relations are commonly expressed with the help of relational nouns as heads of such constructions. Sometimes these postpositional elements are no longer transparent lexically. If, and only if, such a complex construction is integrated into a syntactically satiated clause may it be preceded by the above MPO marker, whereby a kind of circumpositional structure emerges. This can be seen in an example from ǂHõã:

ìa	ky"ào-áá	kì	ǀ'óõ̃-qà	!qhà'ne
3SG.PRO	go	-TA	MPO	tree-PL	beside

'He has gone beside the (group of) trees.'   (Gruber 1975: 38)

Another important application of this associative structure lies in the derivation of nominals expressing meanings like diminutive, natural sex, human agent, etc. from bare lexical stems. Again, the lexical stems serving as the structural head like, for example, 'child', 'man', 'woman', may later grammaticalise into lexically opaque noun suffixes.

A domain where Non-Khoe is less homogeneous concerns noun categorisation. Two groups, that is Taa (cf. Traill 1974a) and Ju (cf. Köhler 1971, Snyman 1970), are found to possess a noun-class system; for !Ui and ǂHõã this has not been reported. It should be borne in mind though, that in principle all research carried out before the 1970s failed to discover the existence of noun classes even in Taa and Ju. Therefore, it cannot be concluded that the extinct !Ui languages, none of which has been described sufficiently, did not have this feature. The reader is referred to the relevant sources for a more extensive discussion of the functional and formal properties of the systems in Taa and Ju. Here only the basic shared features are given. This helps to relate them to other types of noun categorisation found in Khoisan and to the typological discussion of this topic in general.

A first shared feature of the systems is that they are formally and semantically largely opaque in the sense that the class assignment of a considerable number of lexical items cannot be predicted from their meaning or phonetic shape. However, those semantic clues which are discernible clearly distinguish the Non-Khoe systems from those found elsewhere in Khoisan insofar as natural sex does not play any role. Features which can be shown in Non-Khoe to establish a kind of semantic core for a given class are animacy and, in Ju, also shape, food characteristics, or body parts. The grammatical category of number – and this marks yet another dividing line between Non-Khoe and other Khoisan languages – is only poorly integrated in these systems for most inanimate entities. This insensitivity towards number has been discussed by Traill (1994: 22f) for !Xóõ and by Köhler (1971: 517ff) for Juǀ'hoan. It is unfortunate that all other treatments of Juǀ'hoan (Snyman 1970, Dickens n.d.) – apparently inspired by the well-known type of noun categorisation found in neighbouring Bantu languages – have described the system exclusively in terms of singular–plural class pairs (*alias* genders). Yet a more basic form-oriented analysis considering the elements index-ing class membership, that is distinctive pronouns, leads to four agreement classes where number is only partly relevant. If described in these terms, the sys-tem turns out to be structurally very similar to the one found in Taa. Table 5.20 gives such a restatement for Juǀ'hoan as described by Dickens (n.d.: 12ff).

Table 5.20. *The noun class system of Juǀ'hoan*

Noun class	Free pronoun	Pronoun as possessum	Relatively stable core meaning	
			For inanimate nouns	For animate nouns
1	*ha*	*mà*	plant and plant food	singular
2	*sì*	*hì*	—	plural/own social group
3	*ká*	*gá*	body parts, deverbal nouns	
4	*hì*	*hì*	long objects	plural/all other animates

That number plays only a minor role in noun class systems does not mean that it is an unimportant category in Non-Khoe languages. On the contrary, it not only pervades nominal categories but even verbal expressions referring to states of affairs (see section 5.7.1). For nominal plurals it can be generalised that they are formally fairly diverse and often unpredictable (cf., e.g., Dickens n.d.: 8f for Juǀ'hoan and Traill 1994: 22f for ǃXõõ). Formal devices repeatedly found to be used are suffixation, segmental or suprasegmental stem changes, stem suppletion and reduplication.

The complicated treatment of number in Non-Khoe is also observable in unusual morphological effects when associative structures lacking a segmental marker (and expressions derived thereof) are pluralised. The particularly complex and still poorly understood case of ǂHõã was made the exclusive topic of discussion in two of only three existing papers on the grammar of this language (Gruber 1975, Collins 1998). The examples show that plurality of the head noun is also indexed by an element detached from the former and that this marker can even be the only sig-nal of this feature.

ǂ'amkoe	ǃkoa	ǂ'amkoe	kí	ǃkoa -qa
person	house	person	PL.POSSM	house-PL
'the person's house'		'the person's houses'		

tcon-ǃka'e	kí	ǃkoa (-qa)	
people	PL.POSSM	house(-PL)	
'the people's houses'			(Collins 1998: 10f)

As an adpositional phrase is syntactically identical with this associative structure, the above phenomenon has also repercussions here: the postposition is
marked for plurality!

> kyeama-qa 'a kì koloi na . . . kì koloi-qa kí   na
> dog -PL be MPO truck INE   MPO truck-PL PL.LOC INE
> 'The dogs are in the truck.'   '. . . in the trucks.'

> (Collins 1998: 24)

Unexpected complexity in plurals of nominal compounds – again structurally
related to associative phrases – can also be identified in |Xam. Bleek and Lloyd
(1911: 151ff) give several cases where derivational compounds for natural sex and
lexicalised compounds denoting body parts in the plural have a structure different
from their singular counterparts. The example, although lexically opaque, also shows
that, similarly to ‡Hõã, plurality may be expressed detached from the head of the
complex structure.

> !kāu-ttú 'belly' vs. !kau!kaú-těn-ttu 'bellies'
> ? -hole   ?:PL -? -hole

> (Bleek and Lloyd 1911: 153)

5.6.2   **Khoe**

Khoe languages have a rich morphology. Both particles and bound
morphemes exist. Derivation and inflection govern the word-formational processes;
suffixation is the major tool (cf. Vossen 1997a).

A word is identified unambiguously as a noun when it is marked by a person-
gender-number (PGN) suffix, which indicates a third (in Khoekhoe even first and
second) person in the combination of gender and number. There are three such
genders – masculine, feminine, common (i.e., both masculine and feminine) – and
three number categories: singular, dual and plural. The following example from
Naro illustrates the facts:

Table 5.21. *The noun class suffixes of Naro*

	M	F	C
SG	ba	sa	—
DU	tsara	sara	khoara
PL	‖ua	dzi	na

Under certain conditions the SG and 3C/PL suffixes can be shortened to the mere consonant. East Khoe languages of the Kalahari branch tend to make little use of the noun class system. Some of them (e.g. Deti, |Xaise, Kua) have even lost certain formatives.

In principle, the Khoe noun class system is sex-oriented; yet a number of other semantic connotations such as size, shape, collectivity or metonymic association are possible. One may term the former usage 'marked–specific', the latter 'unmarked–generic' (Vossen 1986). Compare the following examples from Naro: *yìi-bá* (M/SG) 'wood' – *yìi-sá* (F/SG) 'tree'; *dìní-sá* (F/SG) 'bee swarm'.

Adjectives, numerals, demonstratives, possessives and interrogatives are in grammatical agreement with the governing noun. In addition, a few languages (‖Ani, Buga, Deti) have object concord markers encoded in the finite verb (cf. Vossen 1985). Agreement markers are mostly identical in shape with the PGN suffixes. In some languages PGN marking and grammatical agreement are obligatory (e.g. Nama) or nearly obligatory (e.g. Naro), in others they appear to be obligatory under certain circumstances only (e.g. ‖Ani) or even optional. On the majority of Kalahari Khoe languages more research is needed to clarify this point.

Nominal case marking does not exist in Khoe but a morpheme *'a* (~ *a*) can be used noun-finally to indicate an object role. Nominal possession is expressed by an associative particle *di* (Nama *tì*, Buga *da*). If the order is possessor–possessed, it is placed between the two and may be marked for gender and number in agreement with the governing noun, for example

!Ora	*xoasao-b*	*di*	*kx'oo-b*	'leopard meat'
	leopard-M/SG	POSS	meat-M/SG	
Kxoe	*Gòàbá-m*	*dì*	*ŋgúú*	'house of Mbukushu man'
	Mbukushu-M/SG	POSS	house	
‖Ani	*|õãn*	*dì-m*	*|xéé-mà*	'child's body'
	child	POSS-M/SG	body-M/SG	
Naro	*hàúgù-m*	*dì(-s)*	*|'óán-sà*	'dog's bone'
	dog-M/SG	POSS(-F/SG)	bone-F/SG	

In a possessed–possessor word order the associative particle is placed after the possessor and, as a rule, marked for gender and number:

Naro   *|'óán-sà   hàúgù-m   dì-sà* 'dog's bone'

The two Naro examples describe the case in which the bone is considered a 'toy' of the dog (alienable possession). If inalienable possession (i.e., the bone as body-part of the dog) is aimed at, either juxtaposition or *status constructus* apply:

Naro   *hàúgù-m |'óán*   or   *hàúgù=|'óán*

Personal pronouns in Khoe are self-standing. They occur in preverbal position. Khoekhoe and Naro, alternatively, make use of short forms which are placed after the verb. Person, gender and number (PGN) are contained in each pronominal form. Third person pronouns are basically the nominal PGN suffixes. In Kalahari Khoe, these are immediately preceded by a demonstrative formative. Inclusive and exclusive forms are distinguished for the first person plural in Naro, and dual as well as plural in Khoekhoe.

Object pronouns are largely identical in shape with the subject pronouns. In Kxoe, ‖Ani, Buga and Naro they are mostly followed by the object marker *'a* (see above) or one of its allomorphs (in Naro only). In some languages (e.g. ‖Ani, Naro, ǂHaba) object forms are tonally distinct from the subject ones. They are independent forms in Kalahari Khoe and !Ora, whereas in Nama they appear as verbal suffixes. For a full range of pronominal paradigms in Khoe, see Vossen (1997a: 232–51).

As for demonstratives, the deictic features [near] and [far] are attested throughout the Khoe family. More detailed studies on Nama (cf., e.g., Hagman 1977) and Kxoe (Köhler 1981) especially have shown though, that the system of deictic functions of demonstrative formatives is probably more complex than this in all of Khoe. In Nama, for instance, the use of demonstratives is primarily dependent on discourse, the deictic function being of secondary importance. The term 'discourse' is to be understood here in a wider sense insofar as it implies both the immediate speech situation and the text (e.g., a narrative). In the former case a distinction is made between presence and absence of referent; moreover, the relative degree of distance plays an important role. In Kxoe, the differentiation of speaker and addressee partially determines the deictic properties.

Possessive pronouns do not exist in Khoe. In order to express pronominal possession two constructions are generally possible: (1) juxtaposition of a personal pronoun and a referential noun (e.g. Nama *tí ǀʼápé-s* 'my decision'), and (2) use of the associative particle *di* (Nama *tì*, Buga *da*) or yet another morpheme of the same function (*'ã, 'a, ka*) which always follows the personal pronoun. Together they can be placed either before or after the referential noun. Grammatical agreement is possible though apparently not obligatory between the associative particle and the referential noun, e.g. G‖ana *kí dì(-m) ɲúú-mà* vs. *ɲúú-mà kí dì(-m)* vs. *kí kà ɲúú(-mà)* 'my house'.

In its non-finite form, the verb in Khoe is identical with the verbal base (infinitive/imperative). In its finite form, it is marked minimally for tense (Kalahari Khoe) or aspect (Khoekhoe), but derivative suffixes, a 'non-passive' or passive juncture (Kalahari Khoe only), object suffixes (Nama) or concord markers (‖Ani, Buga, Deti) as well as a negative formative may be added.

All languages (except ǂHaba) distinguish morphologically the primary tenses past, present and future. Secondary tenses are characteristic, above all, of the past tense where different degrees of remoteness are formally differentiated. A clear-cut dividing line between perfect and imperfect can be drawn at least in Deti. The negative present tense is a specific feature of Kalahari East Khoe. Possibly more frequent than hitherto attested are gerunds. The richest paradigm of tense markers presents itself in Kxoe. This situation, however, may be the result of the as yet relatively poor state of documentation of Kalahari Khoe languages in general.

Tenses are formally expressed by particles in Khoekhoe and by suffixes in Kxoe, Buga and ‖Ani. In Kalahari East Khoe, suffixes mark the past tenses, the negative present and gerunds, whereas present and future are represented by particles. The latter also applies to Naro, G‖ana, G|ui and ǂHaba, which in the past, however, show mixed formations.

Aspect as a morphological category in its own right exists only in Nama, where perfective and imperfective are distinguished.

Derivative verbal extensions as semantic and/or syntactic modifiers of basic verbs are very typical of all Khoe languages. Throughout attested are causative (1 = *ka*), reflexive, reciprocal, and probably dative/benefactive and repetitive, too. Kalahari Khoe languages make use of a terminative-itive suffix; also widely found are the functions of causative (3 = reduplication) and directional-locative. Restrictively distributed are the functions of diminutive (Nama), instrumentative (!Ora, Kxoe, ‖Ani, Buga), permansive-intensive (Kxoe), negative (= stem negation; Kxoe, ‖Ani), alternative (Kxoe, ‖Ani), frequentative-iterative (Kxoe, Danisi), passive (Khoekhoe) and causative (2 = *si*) (Khoekhoe, ‖Ani).

Passive in Khoekhoe occurs as a verbal extension, whereas in Kalahari Khoe it takes the place of the juncture (see below). At the present stage of investigation it is hard to determine the semantic differences between the three types of causative on the one hand, and between repetitive and frequentative-iterative on the other. Both causative (3) and repetitive are formed by reduplication. Non-conjugable are verbs extended by the intentional suffix. The most productive derivative functions are causative (1/3), repetitive, dative/benefactive, reflexive, reciprocal, terminative-itive and passive (Khoekhoe only). Combinations of derivative extensions are common throughout the family.

The juncture morpheme denotes 'non-passive' action. It exists in Kalahari Khoe only where it is suffixed to the (basic or extended) verbal stem followed by the tense marker. In a passive construction the passive marker takes its place. In general, -*a*- is the formal basis of juncture. It can be replaced by a variety of allomorphs whose number varies from language to language. Formally, these allomorphs are partially the result of progressive vowel assimilation and partially historically motivated. The broadest spectrum of such allomorphs appears to occur in Kxoe, ‖Ani and Kua.

Negation is formally expressed by particles (e.g. Khoekhoe *tama*; G‖ana, G|ui and ǂHaba *tàmà* ~ *tema*) or affixes (Kxoe, ‖Ani, Buga *-bé*), sometimes by a combination of both. In Kalahari East Khoe, a negative present tense has been noted.

The following examples illustrate the formation of finite verb forms in some selected languages:

!Ora	(SUBJ)	*ko*	*‖xa*	*=‖xa*	*-sen*	'. . . learned'
		PAST	be capable=CAUS(1)-REFL			

‖Ani	(*tsá*	*tí*	*di*	*ŋúú* *-mà*	*'à*)	*múùn-m* *-tè*	(*rè*)?
	PRO	PRO	POSS	house-M/SG	OBJ	see -OBJ/-PRES	INT
	2M/SG	1SG				M/SG	

'Do you (M/SG) see my house?'

Ts'ixa	(*tí*	*khoe*	*|xòà*)	*‖'áé-* *ku* *-na* *-tà* *-íté*.	'I've met nobody.'
	PRO	person	with	meet-REC-JUNC-PAST/-NEG	
	1SG			[near]	

In Khoe syntactical structure, co-ordination prevails over subordination. An example may be seen in the formation of 'relative constructions' as in, for example, ‖Ani:

n|né -m	*khoe -mà*	*‖ùrú-biye*
DEM/-M/SG	person-M/SG	bush-horse
[near]		
this	man	zebra
|x'ùún-a *-‖'òm -mà*	*kx'áò=khòè*	*tóòta**
kill-JUNC-PAST/-M/SG	male=person	real
[near]		
the having killed one	man	real

'This man who (recently) killed a zebra (is) a real man.'

* (< Setswana)

In this phrase the 'relative clause' is placed between the subject ('this man') and the complement ('real man') of the non-verbal predicate ('is'), which itself is not formally expressed. The 'relative clause' consists of an unmarked nominal object ('zebra') that is followed by the verb which it relates to. This verb in its finite form is nominalised by means of a PGN marker that is in grammatical agreement (M/SG) with the subject of the phrase.

The dominant order of chief constituents is SOV but for reason of emphasis, for instance, the object may likewise precede the subject; compare ‖Ani

tsá	di	‖xáó -má	tí	séè -m	-tà	kx'ò=xúú	ǀx'ùún-kà.
PRO	POSS	spear-M/SG	PRO	take-OBJ/	-PAST	eat=thing	kill-INSTR
2M/SG			1SG		M/SG [rec]		
your		spear	I	have taken it today		meat	kill with

'I have taken your (M/SG) spear (this morning) to kill game with it.'

Nominal qualifiers such as adjectives, numerals and demonstratives precede the noun; postpositions, rather than prepositions, are used as adpositions. Adverbial phrases are mostly placed at the beginning of a sentence, though sentence-final occurrence is also not uncommon.

5.6.3   *Sandawe*

Sandawe has an elaborated suffixing morphology which interacts closely with the similarly complex clause syntax. The latter is determined by segmental (PGN markers) as well as suprasegmental elements. According to Elderkin (1989: 25ff), two major classes of clause are to be distinguished – the basic clause and the nominal clause – the difference being described as follows:

> Within the *basic clause*, the favoured sequence of constituents is Temporal, Subject, Object, Verb, (TSOV). One of these constituents is marked in the sense that it has a morpheme suffixed to it; the marked constituent has some sort of semantic prominence as a point of information. If the subject is marked, the suffixed morpheme is the nominative morpheme -*á:*. If any other constituent is marked, the morpheme which is suffixed is of the suffixed subject pgn series and it agrees with the subject . . . The *nominal clause* consists of two NPs in juxtaposition and has a copular function. As there is no verb, there is no subject; the NPs are labeled NP₁ and NP₂. Typically, when possible, the NP₂ carries a pgn morpheme from the nominal series. [Italics are ours; T. G. and R. V.]

Compare the following examples from Elderkin (1989: 27f):

basic clause

marked subject				marked object			
'útè	sándá -á	sómbá	thíímé.	'útè	sándá	sómbá-sà	thíímé.
yesterday	Sanda-NOM	fish	catch	y.	Sanda	fish-3F/SG	catch

'Yesterday Sanda caught the fish.'

nominal clause

tsí	ɬáá-sì.
1SG	good-1SG

'I am well.'

As can be seen from table 5.22, only two genders (masculine and feminine) and numbers (singular and plural) are distinguished in Sandawe; moreover, gender distinction is confined to the third-person singular. The PGN-inflected sequential marker occurs in so-called narrative conjunctions in which the 'suffixed subject PGN (is) combined with the conjunction *pu*' [italics are ours; T. G. and R. V.].

Table 5.22. *PGN markers in Sandawe (after Elderkin 1989)*

Person	Free pronoun	Nominal PGN suffix		Subject PGN suffix	PGN-inflected sequential marker
		High	Low		
1SG	*tsí*	*sé*	*sì*	*sì*	*síí*
2SG	*hàpú*	*pó*	*pò*	*ì*	*pí*
3M/SG	hèwé	*éé*	*è / w / m / Ø à*	*à*	*páá / kwáá*
3F/SG	*hèsú*	*(éé)sú*	*sù*	*sà*	*sáá / swáá*
1PL	*súún*	*súún*	*sùùn*	*ò*	*póó*
2PL	*síín*	*síín*	*sìin*	*è*	*péé*
3PL	*hèsó*	*só*	*sò*	*'à*	*'áá*

The dominant word order SOV contained in the above quotation from Elderkin allows for certain, mostly pragmatically motivated, permutations. Like in Khoe, nominal qualifiers precede the governing noun; but unlike Khoe, Sandawe has suppletive verb forms for plurals, for example: *hik'(i)* / PL *ni'* 'go'; *ie* / *ne* 'stay'; *ǁume* / *hlee* 'stand'; *siee* / *tlaa* 'carry' (Kagaya 1993: ix).

5.6.4 *Kwadi*

Kwadi is almost unknown to linguists. The only published information on grammar can be found in Westphal (1971). All other material known to exist consists of largely unanalysed unpublished field notes.

What can be extracted from the scanty information available is that Kwadi appears to be a SOV language with a head-final noun phrase. Compare the following examples:

> *ta*   *mɛsa*   *ɬálaɬála*   'I raise the table.' (Westphal 1971: 396)
> 1SG.PRO   table   raise

> *ʧì*   *nyunga*   *ŋǀwiʃi*   *ya*   *-dɛ*   *phela*   *tçéá'ɛ*
> my   brother   small:?   thing-M.SG   house   inside
> 'my brother'   'small thing'   'in the house'   (Westphal n.d.)

In this respect it can be aligned typologically with Sandawe and the Khoe family. The similarity is further strengthened by the fact that Kwadi has sex-based gender suffixes.

A phenomenon not at all understood are complex predicate patterns with frequent stem reduplication which is discernible in the first example.

5.6.5   *Hadza*

Athough Hadza is also very insufficiently described in available sources, it can be said with some certainty that it stands out against all other Khoisan languages in some basic typological features. It is the only language where a basic clause order VSO is attested. As SVO sentences are also found it is possible that we are confronted in fact with a borderline case extensively discussed *inter alia* in Dik (1980: 152ff), where for pragmatic reasons certain constituents tend to be placed at a position before the verb:

unu	boha:taya	mana:-ko	or	boho:taya	unu	mana:-ko
man	hide:3M.SG	meat -F.SG		hide:3M.SG	man	meat -F.SG

'The man hides meat.'   (de Voogt 1992: 14)

Associative constructions are head-initial and can be rendered either by juxtaposition or a medial attributor. The functional difference between the two structures is not clear.

ǀ'ets'a-ko	sa:'akuti-ko	vs.	ǀ'ets'a-ko	ma	unu
house -F.SG	woman -F.SG		house -F.SG	ASS	man
'the house of the woman'			'the house of the man'		

(de Voogt 1992: 12f)

Function words and affixes mostly follow their grammatical host, although preposed elements also exist. Morphology in general seems to be rather complex both on verbs and nouns. A similarity to Kwadi, Sandawe, and the Khoe family is that Hadza distinguishes two sex-based genders. However, this would seem to be achieved through nominal suffixes which do not have a syntactic significance comparable to PGN markers in Khoe and Sandawe.

5.7   Lexical characteristics

5.7.1   *Non-Khoe*

Lexical stems can usually be distinguished from grammatical morphemes by their sound shape. While lexemes largely conform to the phonotactic pattern outlined in section 5.5.1, grammemes often have a CV form in which the consonant is very rarely a click or a complex consonant.

Regarding the classification of lexical items, it must be stressed that traditional concepts of word categories typical for European languages turn out to be problematic in Non-Khoe languages. In principle, one can draw a basic distinction between stems that denote a referential entity and stems that express a state of affairs, which corresponds to a canonical noun–verb distinction. However, even this distinction is occasionally blurred when the specific meaning of a stem is determined only by its syntactic context in an utterance. Even in a language like !Xõõ with a considerable amount of morphology, stems can express a verbal or a nominal notion; for example, *ǂ'án* means 'to think/guess' or 'thought'.

Another interesting fact is that the class of verbal stems comprises a fairly wide range of conceptual notions. Non-Khoe languages lack, for instance, a large class of proper adjectives and use stative verbs as sentential modifiers instead. Stems with a syntactic behaviour of predicates even serve to express what in other languages is usually rendered by question words and demonstratives (see the first example in section 5.6.1 for a verbal demonstrative in Juǀ'hoan). The following example from !Xõõ is an instance of an interrogative verb:

ta	*te*	*'ããh'ã*	*ke*	'Which person?'
person:CLI	R:CLI.AGR	(be) which	R:CLI.AGR	

(Dickens 1997: 111)

Finally, another widespread characteristic of Non-Khoe is the phenomenon of number-sensitive suppletion of lexical stems. The following examples for a transitive verb, an intransitive verb and a noun are taken from ǂHõã: 'take/get/receive' SG *!kù*, PL *ǂq'áí*; 'fall' SG *!q'áo*, PL *ǀqhéé*; 'person' SG *ǂ'àm-kõè*, PL *čòõ-!ka'e* (Gruber 1975: 6f, 31).

5.7.2   **Khoe**

Very generally speaking, Khoe languages have simple and complex words. Simple words are as a rule identical with lexical roots. Complex words are either extended (by affixation or reduplication) or compounded, or both.

Many lexical roots can serve as a base for creating both nouns and verbs. Nouns are created by extending the root by means of PGN suffixes. Verbs are formed by extending the root through derivative suffixes, which modify or alter the meaning and/or syntactic role of the verbal, or by bringing them into a finite form (cf., e.g., Naro *kx'ùí* 'speak(ing)': *kx'ùí-kù* [V/REC] 'to quarrel', *kx'ùí-sà* [F/SG] 'language/law').

Reduplication of nominal stems is relatively rare and leads to semantic change within the same semantic field, for example ǁAni: *ǀxám-dzì* [F/PL] 'urine' vs. *ǀxám=ǀxàm-hè* [F/SG] 'bladder of the urine'. With verbal stems, reduplication conveys iterative or causative meaning: *kóm-kù* [REC] 'to hear one another' vs. *kóm=kòm-kù* 'to inform one another'. Nominal compounds usually derive from N + N sequences (cf. ‖Ani *g‖ùú* 'chest' vs. *g‖ùú-ǀʼóán* 'breast-bone'), whereas the structure N + V in most cases points to verbal quality (e.g., *nǂnôm* 'to form/ mould' vs. *ǀʼúù-nǂnôm* 'to comb' [lit.: to form hair]).

Khoe does not have many proper adjectives. The few that exist can be used both attributively and predicatively. When qualifying a noun they are placed before it (e.g. ‖Ani *ǀáu ǀʼóán* 'big bone'); in non-verbal predications, however, they follow the noun without the copula itself showing up on the surface (e.g., *ǀʼóán ǀáú* 'the bone is big').

Note

1   The following abbreviations have been used throughout this chapter:

AGR	agreement	NEG	negative marker
ASS	associative	NOM	nominative
C	common (gender); consonant	NP	noun phrase
CAUS	causative	O(BJ)	object
CL	agreement class	PAST	past tense
COM	comitative	PGN	person-gender-number
DC	dialect cluster	PL	plural
DEM	demonstrative	POSS	possessive
DU	dual	POSSM	possessum
F	feminine	PRES	present tense
FUT	future	PRO	pronoun
INE	inessive	R	relative
INSTR	instrumentative	REC	reciprocal
INT	interrogative	REFL	reflexive
IPFV	imperfective	SAK	South African Khoisan
JUNC	juncture morpheme	SG	singular
L	liquid	S(UBJ)	subject
LOC	locative	T	temporal
M	masculine	TA	tense/aspect
MPO	multipurpose oblique	V	verb; vowel
N	nasal; noun	VE	valency-external NP

6

Phonology

G. N. CLEMENTS

6.1   **Introduction**

The African continent offers a generous sample of the great variety
of phonological systems to be found in the world's languages, as well as some
original features of its own. African phonological systems range from the relatively simple to the staggeringly complex. Those on the more complex end of the
spectrum contain phonemic contrasts little known elsewhere in the world, rich patterns of morphophonemic alternation, and intricate tonal and accentual systems,
all offering stimulating grounds for phonetic and phonological study. This chapter offers a synthesis of recent work on African language phonology, focusing especially on their phoneme inventories, feature contrasts, syllable structure and tone.
A brief overview of this sort cannot hope to be complete, and many important
topics receive little attention (see further reading list at the end of this chapter).

The linguistic study of vernacular African languages dates back to Fr Giacinto
Brusciotto's grammar of the Bantu language Kongo (or Kikongo),[1] published in
Rome in 1659. However, the study of African languages began in earnest only in
the nineteenth century under the impulse of a few pioneering linguists. These early
studies had two chief goals: to provide practical descriptions and to lay a basis
for comparative-historical studies. Some of this work was of excellent quality
and is still useful today. (For historical overviews, see Greenberg 1965 and Cole
1971.)

The scientific study of African languages received a major impetus in the first
part of the twentieth century from the enormous amount of descriptive work
carried out by linguists based in Africa, Europe and (since about mid-century)
North America. In all this work, the study of phonology – the necessary preliminary to any complete grammatical description – was pre-eminent. More recently,

the study of African languages has interacted fruitfully with advances in linguistic theory. A new emphasis, inspired by the research perspective of generative grammar (Chomsky and Halle 1968) and its various offshoots, has been placed on examining African languages in order to obtain a better understanding of universal properties of the human language faculty itself. New data from Africa has provided a corrective to the often Eurocentric bias of earlier linguistic theories, and has stimulated many recent developments in linguistic theory (see Clements 1989).

Largely in response to challenges raised by African language data, phonological theory over the last two or three decades has attempted to develop more adequate models in areas such as feature theory, syllabification, vowel harmony, and tonal phonology, to name just a few (see Goldsmith 1990 and Kenstowicz 1994 for overviews). It is a striking fact that many of the contributors to the new phonology have themselves been Africanists, or linguists who have immersed themselves deeply in the study of African language data. A result is that the interaction between theory and description has been especially close in the Africanist domain.

African languages continue to present many puzzles, challenges and surprises to the phonologist. With the large majority of African languages still poorly (if at all) described and many smaller languages menaced by extinction, the importance of continuing research for descriptive, comparative and theoretical purposes cannot be overemphasised.

6.2   Structure of phoneme inventories

Phoneme systems in Africa, as elsewhere, are structured by the principle of *economy* – the use of a few features to create a large number of phonemic contrasts.

Let us consider a simple illustration. If we were to build a 'prototypical' African language by selecting phoneme types occurring commonly[2] across African languages, we would obtain the inventory shown in table 6.23. This table lists phonemes in a conventional format, with places of articulation listed from left to right, and degrees of stricture and other 'manners' of articulation from top to bottom. Here and below we will generally adopt the phonetic symbols suggested by the International Phonetic Association except, in deference to widespread Africanist usage, for the use of *y* for the palatal glide (semivowel). Where relevant to the discussion, phonemes will be enclosed in slants / . . . / and their phonetic realisations in brackets [. . .].

Symbols in this table represent phoneme *types* rather than particular phonetic segments. For example, *c* represents any voiceless postalveolar stop (including sounds

Table 6.23. *A 'prototypical' African phoneme system*

p	t	c	k		i		u
b	d	ɟ	g		e		o
m	n	ɲ	ŋ		ɛ		ɔ
f	s	ʃ	h			a	
	z						
	l						
w	r	y					

such as [ʧ tɕ č]), ʃ represents any postalveolar fricative, and *r* represents any rhotic ('r-sound').

The principle of economy is well illustrated here. In consonants, we find oral and nasal stops at four places of articulation: labial, dental/alveolar, post-alveolar and velar. Voiceless fricatives and voiced approximants (liquids and glides) occur at the first three of these, and the voiced fricatives /v/ and /ʒ/, though absent in the table, are also not uncommon. In the commonest vowel system, shown at the right, three front vowels are paralleled by three back vowels, while the low vowel /a/ is unpaired. This table contains no 'exotic' segments; all its sounds occur widely in the languages of the world. Some of these, however, are better represented in Africa than elsewhere. For example, /ɟ f z ɲ ŋ/ would not be included in a similar table constructed for non-African languages, while the glottal stop /ʔ/ would.

The phoneme system in table 6.23, while indicating commonly encountered phonemes, is not very typical of actually existing phoneme systems. Most familiar African languages lack some of its phonemes, and most add further phonemes of other types. Thus, for example, Diola lacks /ʃ z/ while having the lower high vowels /ɪ ʊ/ and the mid central vowel /ə/, and Birom lacks /ʃ ɲ/ but has the labial-velars /k͡p g͡b/ as well as /v/. Indeed, many African languages have rather large numbers of less common phoneme types. Some of the commoner of these minority types are listed below, with some relatively under-represented types included for comparison:

Phoneme types commoner in Africa than elsewhere

- implosives
- labial-velar stops
- initial nasal clusters (NC)
- clicks
- lower high vowels /ɪ ʊ/

Phoneme types rarer in Africa than elsewhere

- uvular consonants
- retroflex stops and fricatives
- diphthongs
- front rounded vowels
- the high central vowel /ɨ/

Of the sounds in the first column, implosives are very well represented in African languages, while the clicks are, as far as we know, found *only* in African languages; these less usual sounds will be described in more detail below. These sounds, too, tend to conform to the principle of economy: if one such sound occurs in a language, others of the same type are likely to occur as well, especially if they fill in what would otherwise be 'gaps' in a regular pattern. To take a particularly famous example, languages that have one click tend to have large numbers of them, characterised by the same manners of articulation found in non-click consonants.

Competing with the principle of economy is that of *markedness*: some types of sounds are more complex than others, and tend to be less well represented in phoneme systems than their less marked counterparts. Thus, for example, voiced fricatives are more marked than voiceless fricatives and, as table 6.23 shows, are commonly missing even when their voiceless counterparts are present. Failures of the principle of economy can often be explained in terms of the relative markedness of the missing sounds.

These generalisations about phoneme frequency, based on data pooled across all African languages, do not reflect important genetic and areal preferences, and we will comment on some of these in the more detailed discussion of consonant and vowel features which follows.

6.3   Features of consonants

Phoneme systems can be defined in terms of a small number of *distinctive features*. A distinctive feature is a sound property, such as [+nasal], that serves to distinguish one phoneme (or phoneme series) from another. Besides accounting for phonemic contrasts, features define *natural classes* of sounds that commonly function together in phonological patterns; in many African languages, for example, all consonant clusters are of the form NC, where N is a [+nasal] sound and C a consonant. The choice of features needed to define phoneme contrasts and phonological classes typically differs only little from one language to another.

Distinctive feature theory originated in the work of Trubetzkoy in the 1930s and Jakobson and his colleagues in the 1940s and 1950s, and has continued to evolve as new information has become available. Below, we will generally use the features described in Halle and Clements (1983), as revised to include the articulator features of Sagey (1990). In general, these features provide a good account of African phonological systems. However, we will call attention to several cases where these features may have to be revised or extended to handle African data.[3]

6.3.1   ***Place of articulation features***

The major places of articulation in consonants are characterised by the features [labial], [coronal] and [dorsal], defined in terms of the articulators that execute them:

- *labial* sounds involve the lips as active articulator
- *coronal* sounds involve the tongue tip, blade or front (that is, the 'crown' of the tongue) as active articulator
- *dorsal* sounds involve the body or back ('dorsum') of the tongue as active articulator

Within each of these general categories, further distinctions are created by articulator-dependent features, specifying the precise positioning of the articulator in question.

Labial consonants. This category includes bilabial and labiodental sounds, as well as labial-velar sounds, treated separately below. Most African languages have no minimal contrasts between bilabial and labiodental sounds, since plosives and nasals are usually bilabial, while affricates and fricatives are generally labiodental. However, these two places of articulation do contrast in a few languages. For example, Tsonga and Ewe have contrasts between bilabial and labio-velar fricatives /ɸ β/ and /f v/, and Teke (Kukuya) contrasts bilabial and labiodental nasals /m/ and /ɱ/, the latter produced with strong lip protrusion. Furthermore, while in most languages the labial glide is the labial-velar /w/, several languages (including Kresh, Gbeya and Mbum) have a contrasting labiodental flap, sometimes symbolised ⱱ̆, which appears to be unknown outside Africa. The feature [±strident] is sometimes used to distinguish the relatively noisy labiodental fricatives from the less noisy bilabials, although this feature cannot distinguish the contrasting types of nasals and glides just cited, all of which are non-strident.

Evidence for features can often be drawn from systems of consonant and vowel harmony in which all (or a subset of) the consonants or vowels in a given domain agree in a given feature. In Classical Arabic, for example, no native lexical root contains two different labial consonants /b f m/. This pattern, which treats the bilabials /b m/ and the labiodental /f/ as a single class, confirms the functional reality of the feature [labial].

Coronal consonants. The commonest distinction among coronal sounds is one between *anterior* sounds (dental, alveolar and denti-alveolar) and *posterior* sounds (palato-alveolar, alveolo-palatal, retroflex and palatal). These two large classes are distinguished by the coronal-dependent feature [±anterior]. A further common contrast among coronal sounds is one between sibilants such as [s] or [ts] and non-sibilants such as [t] or [θ] (the initial sound in *thin*), for which the feature [±strident] is commonly used. In some languages, the features [±anterior] and [±strident] combine to create three- or even four-way contrasts. Zayse, for instance, has a three-way contrast between anterior non-sibilants /t d ḍ/, anterior ('hissing') sibilants /ts dz s z/ and posterior ('hushing') sibilants /tʃ dʒ ʃ ʒ/. According to a rule of consonant harmony in Zayse, all [+strident] consonants in a root must agree in their value for [±anterior]. Thus we find roots like *zatsts* 'lead' containing only anterior sibilants and roots like *ʔiʃiʃ* 'five' containing only posterior sibilants, but none mixing anterior and posterior sibilants.

A less common contrast among anterior coronal sounds is that between apical (tongue-tip) and laminal (tongue-blade) sounds, distinguished by the coronal-dependent feature [±apical].[4] When contrasting in a single language, apical sounds tend to be alveolar and laminal sounds dental or interdental, though this pattern is reversed in a few languages (for example, Temne and Shilluk). Posterior cor-onals are usually non-apical, but some languages, such as Maba and Beja, have an apical or retroflex series, sometimes transcribed [ṭ ḍ]. Like the other features described above, the feature [±apical] is sometimes involved in systems of conson-ant harmony. In Shilluk, for example, all anterior stops in the root must be either apical (dental) or non-apical (alveolar). Thus we find apical-stop roots like *ṭiṇ* 'small' and non-apical stop roots like *tin* 'today', but no roots mixing these two categories. The Bench (or Benchnon) variety of Gimira has an unusual four-way contrast among two anterior series of consonants, plain /t d t'/ and sibilant /ts ts' s z/, and two posterior series of sibilants, apical (retroflex) /tʂ tʂ' ʂ z̨/ and laminal (palato-alveolar) /tʃ tʃ' ʃ ʒ/. According to its system of harmony, all pos-terior sibilants in a root must agree in the feature [±apical]; we thus find apical consonant roots such as *tʂ'utʂ'* 'louse' and non-apical roots like *ʃaʃ* 'stretcher', but none containing both.

Dorsal, laryngeal and pharyngeal consonants.   All African languages have one or more series of dorsal sounds, commonly including velars such as /k g x/ and more rarely uvulars such as /q ɢ χ/. Most African languages also have laryngeal sounds such as the glottal stop /ʔ/, the voiceless aspirate /h/, or the voiced aspir-ate /ɦ/, though the latter two rarely contrast.

The pharyngeal consonants /ħ ʕ/, in contrast, are mostly restricted to the Afroasiatic languages of N and NE Africa. Here they often pattern with uvular fricatives and laryngeals as a natural class of so-called 'guttural' sounds; in Tigrinya, for example, the mid-central vowel /ä/ is lowered to [a] in any syllable containing a 'guttural' consonant. The feature defining the full class of guttural sounds has been a matter of some controversy, due to the fact that no single articu-lator, such as the tongue root or glottis, is activated in the production of all its members. In response to this problem, Hayward and Hayward (1989) and

McCarthy (1994) have proposed a 'zone of constriction' feature (named [guttural] by the Haywards and [pharyngeal] by McCarthy) to characterise articulations produced anywhere in the pharynx from the uvula down to the larynx, inclusively. Further features distinguish the various types of guttural sounds: thus, the pharyngeals [ħ], [ʕ] are characterised as [guttural] and [constricted pharynx], the uvulars [χ], [ʁ] as [guttural] and [dorsal], and the laryngeals [h], [ʔ] as [guttural] as well as [spread glottis] vs. [constricted glottis], respectively.

Labial-velar stops are made with overlapping, near-simultaneous closures at the lips and velum (Connell 1994a). These sounds occur in many sub-Saharan languages across a broad belt extending from the Atlantic coast in the west as far as the Upper White Nile in the east, crossing major genetic lines. The oral stops [k͡p ɡ͡b] are the commonest representatives of this class, but a labial-velar nasal [ŋ͡m] occurs phonemically in several languages such as Isoko, Idoma and Gwari. Labial-velar stops usually contrast with simple labial and dorsal stops. As shown in table 6.24, Kalaḅarị I;ọ has surface contrasts among labial, dorsal and labial-velar stops as well as implosives and labialised velars (though the latter can be analysed as stop + /u/ sequences underlyingly):

Table 6.24. *Surface contrasts among Kalaḅarị Iọ stops*

Voiceless explosive stops	p	t		k	k͡p	kw
Voiced explosive stops	b	d	dʒ	ɡ	ɡ͡b	ɡw
Voiced implosive stops	ɓ	ɗ				

Labial-velar sounds can be characterised by the features [labial] and [dorsal]. Both of these features play a role in defining natural classes of sounds. In Kalaḅarị Iọ, for example, nasals assimilate to the place of articulation of a following stop, being realised as labials before labials (e.g. [mb]), coronals before coronals (e.g. [nd]), and so forth. Before labial-velars, nasals are realised as labial-velars [ŋ͡m]; thus we find the doubly-articulated nasal + stop clusters [ŋ͡mk͡p] and [ŋ͡mɡ͡b]. As a further example, the Ngbaka language has the labial, velar and labial-velar stop phonemes /p b k ɡ k͡p ɡ͡b/ and the corresponding nasal clusters /mb ŋɡ ŋ͡mɡ͡b/. In this language, a rule of consonant harmony requires any two [labial] consonants in a simple word to have the same characterisation for [dorsal]. Thus while words like *k͡pàk͡pō* 'hook' with two labial-dorsal sounds are well formed, hypothetical words such as *pVk͡pV* combining labial-dorsals with simple labials are strictly excluded, outside compounds and loanwords.

The major places of articulation reviewed above are often supplemented by concomitant *minor* (or *secondary*) articulations such as labialisation Cʷ, palatalisation

Cʸ, velarisation Cˠ, or (as in Berber and Arabic) uvularisation, usually termed 'emphasis'. Labialisation often arises historically in the context of [u] or [w], and palatalisation in the context of [i] or [y]. It is often hard, in synchronic analysis, to determine whether a phonetic sequence such as [kw] should be analysed phonemically as /ku/, /kw/ or even as the single segment /kʷ/. Sometimes, however, one or more of these alternatives can be eliminated by paying close attention to phonological patterning. In Ikwere, for example, the non-finite verbal prefix is realised as a non-high copy of the first root vowel, as in *à-yá* 'to come in', *è-bé* 'to find', *è-sí* 'to cook', *ò-dú* 'to arrive'. The choice of *a-* as prefix in verbs such as *à-byá* 'to come' or *à-gwá* 'to refuse' shows that *y* and *w* function as part of the syllable onset, and not as underlying vowels /i/ and /u/.

6.3.2   *Laryngeal features*

The commonest stop system across Africa has a contrast between [−voice] and [+voice] sounds such as /t/ vs. /d/, as we saw in table 6.23. Close behind in frequency are systems which add a further series, most often implosive (e.g. /ɗ/) but sometimes laryngealised (/ɗ̰/), preglottalised (/ˀd/), or voiceless ejective (/tʼ/). The first three of these sounds, all voiced, are not known to contrast with each other in any language, and should probably be considered alternative phonetic realisations of a single phonological category.

The feature [±constricted glottis] commonly distinguishes implosives and ejectives from other types of stops. *Implosives* are produced by enlarging the oropharyngeal cavity during the stop closure so as to reduce intraoral air pressure, offsetting any increase due to airflow through the glottis during voicing; a common way of achieving this effect is to lower the larynx. The result is a sound that is often noticeably imploded (producing a 'popping' sound) at its release. Implosives are found widely across West, Central and East Africa, with a special concentration, crossing genetic boundaries, in Nigeria, Chad and Cameroon.

Implosives, like other sounds, are structured by the principle of economy: if a language has one implosive, there is a good chance that it will have another.[5] But here too, economy is constrained by markedness. As observed by Greenberg (1970), implosives are increasingly marked as we proceed from the front to the back of the mouth, in the order 'ɓ (labial) – ɗ (apical) – ʄ (palatal) – ɠ (velar)'. As a result, the implosive series in any given language is usually incomplete, with one or more implosives at the right end of the scale normally missing.

While implosive sounds are usually voiced, voiceless glottalised implosives such as bilabial /ɓ̥/ contrast with corresponding voiced implosives in such widely separated languages as Owere Igbo, Lendu and Seereer-Siin. Though implosive sounds are generally stops, some Central Sudanic languages (including Mangbetu) have a very unusual contrast between plain and implosive labiodental fricatives, the latter of which, according to Demolin (1988: 68), are 'strongly imploded, the lower lip briefly pulled back in the mouth'. Implosive stops are said to pattern as a natural class opposed to explosive stops in Kalaḅarị Ịjọ (table 6.24), where voiced implosives and explosives exclude each other within the morpheme. Thus we find *ɓaɓa* 'calabash', *bábā* 'cut', *dụɓárị* 'stone', *badara* 'be very wide', but no 'mixed' forms such as **badʼara*.

Ejective stops are found commonly in Chadic languages and, as an areal feature crossing genetic boundaries, in the north-east (especially Ethiopia). Ejective stops are produced by forming an oral closure with the lips or tongue, raising the larynx while keeping the glottis tightly closed (compressing the air between the glottal and oral closures), and then releasing the oral closure, causing the air to explode rapidly outward. Ejectives contrast with implosives in several languages, such as Koma, Dahalo, Ik, Uduk, Kullo and Goemai. While ejectives are normally voiceless, voiced ejectives have been reported in some Khoisan languages.[6]

Relatively uncommon in Africa are minimal contrasts involving the feature [±spread glottis], typically realised as aspiration or, in the case of voiced stops, breathy voice. An unusual system involving this feature is that of Owere Igbo, shown in table 6.25. Here, the features [±spread] and [±constricted] cross-classify the binary voicing distinction to produce a six-term contrast among labial stops. This is a striking example of economy: all possible combinations of the three laryngeal features are employed, except for the combination [+spread, +constricted], which is excluded on grounds of physical incompatibility. We have no information on whether the implosive /ɓ/ is normally produced with laryngealisation, hence our question mark in the table. Ladefoged *et al.* (1976: 154) observe that this sound is not necessarily produced with implosion at release, or even with negative oral air pressure during the stop phase; rather, 'it seems that [ɓ] contrasts with [b] simply by having no increase (rather than by having an actual decrease) in oral pressure during the closure'. It is further distinguished from /b/ by the fact that it is auditorily velarised.

Table 6.25. *Labial stop contrasts in Owere Igbo (after Ladefoged et al. 1976)*

	p	pʰ	β	b	bɦ	ɓ
Voice	−	−	−	+	+	+
Spread	−	+	−	−	+	−
Constricted	−	−	+	−	−	?

6.3.3   *Languages without nasal consonants*

An unusual feature of a number of West African languages is the absence of [+nasal] consonants at the phonemic level. In such languages, though consonants such as [m n] exist phonetically, they can always be derived from non-nasal consonants in the context of nasalised vowels. For example, Ebrié, a Kwa language described by Bole-Richard (1983), has the nasalised vowel phonemes /ɛ̃ ã ɔ̃/ as shown by minimal contrasts like [pʰá] 'climb' vs. [pʰã́] 'give off'. The nasal consonants [m n ɲ ŋ] are in complementary distribution with their oral counterparts [ɓ l y w], the nasals occurring only before or after nasalised vowels as in [á-nɛ̃̀] 'hoe' and [ɛ̃́-ná] 'sleep' while the oral sounds occur only in other contexts. This pattern gives rise to many regular alternations, as in [á-ɓɛ́] 'cord' vs. [ɛ̃́-mɛ́] 'cords' (underlyingly /ɛ̃́ 'plural' + ɓɛ́ 'cord'/). Given these facts, we can derive the surface nasal consonants from underlying /ɓ l w/ by a rule nasalising implosives, liquids and glides in the context of nasalised sounds.

6.3.4   *What kind of speech sounds are implosives?*

The phonological behaviour of implosives raises a special challenge for feature analysis. As just noted, these sounds behave like liquids and glides in Ebrié in undergoing the regular rule of nasalisation. Why should this be so?

Further study shows that implosives in African languages pattern with sonorant consonants (nasals, liquids and glides) in many respects:

- implosives, like sonorants, are often fully nasalised in the context of nasalised vowels (as in Ebrié)
- implosives, like sonorants, are often excluded in nasal clusters (NC, CN)
- implosives, like sonorants, are often excluded from the class of 'depressor consonants' which in many languages cause the lowering of tones of adjacent vowels
- implosives are often in complementary distribution with sonorants (thus /l/ is realised [ɗ] before high vowels and glides in Ebrié)
- the unmarked or usual value of voicing in implosives, as in sonorants, is [+voice]

These patterns strongly suggest that implosives are not obstruents after all, but sonorants. Indeed, implosives satisfy the definition of sonorants as stated by Halle (1992: 208): 'SONORANT sounds are produced without a pressure build-up inside the vocal tract; non-sonorant sounds are produced with pressure in the vocal tract that exceeds the ambient atmospheric pressure.' This definition holds whether the implosive is actually imploded, or simply not exploded, as in the case of Owere Igbo /ɓ/ described above.

Table 6.26. *A proposed feature classification of oral stops*

	Exploded				Non-exploded			
	p	p'	b	b'	ɓ	ɓ'	ɓ	ɓ'
Sonorant	−	−	−	−	+	+	+	+
Voice	−	−	+	+	−	−	+	+
Constricted	−	+	−	+	−	+	−	+

Consequently, following earlier suggestions by Stewart (1989) and Creissels (1994), we propose to treat implosives as sonorants.[7] Generalising this approach to related sounds, we arrive at the feature classification of various oral stops shown in table 6.26, in which exploded stops ('explosives') are classified as [−sonorant] and non-exploded stops, including implosives, as [+sonorant]. (In this table, traditional symbols for implosives are extended to all non-exploded stops.) The first three exploded stops in this table are the familiar voiceless, ejective and voiced stops, and require no special comment. The fourth [b'] is the voiced ejective found in some Khoisan languages (see note 6). The non-exploded stop [ɓ] is the apparently non-glottalised 'soft' or lenis voiceless stop described by Bole-Richard (1983) for Ebrié.[8] The sound represented [ɓ'] is the voiceless implosive stop, produced with tight glottal constriction during closure and implosion at release; this class of sounds may also include the partly voiceless glottalised stops of several Atlantic languages including Fula, and perhaps the partly voiceless, non-exploded laryngealised stops described for several Chadic languages, including Hausa (Ladefoged and Maddieson 1996: 85). [ɓ] is the fully voiced, non-laryngealised implosive found widely in West African languages (e.g. Degema, Kalaḅarị Ịọ), which appears to involve no more glottal constriction than is involved in normal voicing (Lindau 1984). The last category [ɓ'] represents the rarer fully voiced, laryngealised implosive, recorded for one speaker of Owere Igbo by Ladefoged (1968: 16). It seems that no language distinguishes more than two types of non-exploded stops, one from the first pair /ɓ ɓ'/and one from the second /ɓ ɓ'/.

This analysis directly accounts for the close relationship between implosives and sonorants. The implosive [ɗ] differs from [l] only in being non-lateral, and from [n] only in being non-nasal, explaining the frequent allophonic relationship among these sounds.

6.3.5   ***Do we need the feature fortis/lenis?***

The preceding discussion has shown that the distinction between non-ploded stops and exploded stops can be subsumed under the feature [sonorant], and does not require further features such as [imploded], [suction] or [fortis]/

[lenis]. We consider here two other types of contrast sometimes described in terms of fortisness or lenisness.

First, some Edoid languages have an unusual contrast between normal-length and extra-short (tapped) sounds. Yẹkhee (Etsakọ), for example, has minimal contrasts between normal-length /k g k͡p g͡b m/ and extra-short /kh gh k͡ph g͡bh mh/, and Ghotuọ contrasts normal-length /m n l y/ with extra-short /mh nh lh yh/ (*h* is here used to transcribe shortness, not aspiration). According to Elugbe (1989) and other writers, the extra-short sounds involve a shorter, laxer articulation. Such contrasts may require a new feature, for which Elugbe (1989) suggests [±lenis] and Stewart (1989) [±short].

Second, in many languages long or geminate consonants (see section 6.5) are realised with redundant tenseness or fortition, often accompanied by a particularly strong release burst. This type of articulation can sometimes be directly observed in bilabial sounds, in which the lips are visibly more tightly pressed together in geminates than in their singleton counterparts. Many linguists have preferred to take the length distinction as underlying and the tenseness distinction as a derived, secondary cue in such cases (see Dell and Elmedlaoui 1997 for discussion of Berber). However, in fast speech and in diachronic change, articulatory tension may entirely replace duration as the primary phonetic cue to an original length distinction (see Gilley 1992: 37–9 for discussion of Shilluk and other Nilotic languages). In such cases, some linguists have favoured a feature such as [±fortis]. In some languages, however, the fortis sounds continue to pattern as geminates, in which case gemination, rather than fortition, can be retained as the underlying feature; in many other languages, the fortis–lenis distinction reinforces other features such as aspiration or voicing, which can be taken as the basis of the underlying contrasts. The phonetic correlates of a feature [±fortis] are still poorly understood, and its status as a genuine phonological feature remains highly controversial.

6.4   Vowel features and vowel harmony

The following vowel systems, and variants thereof, are widely found in Africa:

(1)   5 vowels   7 vowels   9 vowels

5 vowels		7 vowels		9 vowels	
i	u	i	u	i	u
				ɪ	ʊ
e	o	e	o	e	o
		ɛ	ɔ	ɛ	ɔ
a		a		a	

All these systems have a symmetrical set of front and back vowels and a low central vowel /a/. Variants of these systems with an additional non-low central vowel, commonly transcribed /ə/, are also not uncommon. Several languages have systems like the 7- and 9-vowel systems above but without /ɛ/, in which case /a/ tends to take its place as the front counterpart of /ɔ/.

In general, the 5-vowel system shown in (1) and variants thereof is well represented in Afroasiatic, Bantu and Khoisan languages, as is the 7-vowel system in Nilo-Saharan and Niger-Congo languages, including Bantu. The 9-vowel system, sometimes expanded with /ə/, is also widely found in Nilo-Saharan and Niger-Congo, though rare in Bantu. Besides these systems, the 3-vowel system /i u a/ is also found in some Afroasiatic languages. These generalisations represent trends, and many other, often less balanced systems are found as well, though no other types seem as widely favoured as these.

In many African languages, there are good grounds for viewing the five vowel qualities [i u e o a] as a basic 'unmarked' set and defining fuller sets of vowels with additional features. The feature [ATR] provides a good illustration of this principle. We shall introduce this feature through a discussion of a characteristic system of vowel harmony, widespread among Nilo-Saharan and non-Bantu Niger-Congo languages.

6.4.1 *ATR (advanced tongue root)*

In vowel harmony systems, all (or a subset of) vowels in the word tend to agree in a given distinctive feature [±F]. One value of this feature is said to be 'dominant' if it always spreads to all other vowels in the word, never yielding to the opposite value. In *dominant harmony* systems, dominant vowels occur in both roots and suffixes (but rarely in prefixes, at least in Africa). In these systems, roots harmonise with any suffixes bearing the dominant value of [±F] and vice versa. In *root-controlled systems*, dominant vowels are restricted to roots, and consequently roots never harmonise with suffixes.

A typically African pattern of dominant harmony can be illustrated by Diola (Sapir 1965), whose ten vowel phonemes, assigned to two harmonic sets A and B, are shown below:

(2)   set A   set B
    i   u   ɪ   ʊ
    e   o   ɛ   ɔ
      ə   a

In Diola, set A vowels (whose harmonic feature [±F] remains to be determined) are dominant. Examples of alternations are given in (3), illustrating the effect of two dominant-vowel morphemes, the root ɟitum (column 1) and the suffix -ul 'toward the speaker' (rows d, e).

(3)   set A root /ɟitum/   set B root /baɟ/
    (a)   ɟitum   'lead away!'   baɟ   'have!'
    (b)   ɟitum-en   'cause to lead away'   baɟ-ɛn   'cause to have'
    (c)   ni-ɟitum-en-u   'I caused you   nɪ-baɟ-ɛn-ʊ   'I caused you
                             to be led away'   to have'
    (d)   ɟitum-ul   'bring!'   bəɟ-ul   'have from'
    (e)   ni-ɟitum-ul-u   'I brought you'   ni-bəɟ-ul-u   'I have for you'

As these examples show, both of these morphemes require set A vowels to the exclusion of set B vowels throughout the word, causing alternations not only in prefixes and suffixes but also in the root baɟ, realised as [bəɟ] (column 2, rows d, e).

A characteristic *root-controlled* vowel harmony system, in which dominant vowels are restricted to roots, can be illustrated by Akan. Akan has four dominant set A vowel phonemes /i u e o/, underlyingly restricted to roots, and five set B phonemes /ɪ ʊ ɛ ɔ a/, found in roots and suffixes (Stewart 1967, Clements 1985). As shown by the examples in (4), if the root contains only set A vowels, affix vowels are realised with their set A alternants (column 1), while if the root contains only set B vowels, affix vowels take their set B alternants (column 2). (Roots are underlined, tones are omitted.)

(4)   set A roots   set B roots
    e-<u>bu</u>-o   'nest'   ɛ-<u>bu</u>-ɔ   'stone'
    o-<u>kusi</u>-e   'rat'   ɔ-<u>kɔdɪ</u>-ɛ   'eagle'
    o-<u>fiti</u>-i   's/he pierced'   ɔ-<u>cɪrɛ</u>-ɪ   's/he showed'
    o-be-<u>tu</u>-i   's/he came and dug'   ɔ-bɛ-<u>tʊ</u>-ɪ   's/he came and threw'

The harmonic feature [±F] underlying vowel harmony systems such as those of Diola and Akan long eluded linguists, who tended to resort to vague or inaccurate terms such as 'relative tongue height' or 'tension' to describe it. In the case of so-called *cross-height* vowel harmony systems – those in which both high and mid vowels alternate, as in Diola and Akan – the feature clearly cannot be one of tongue height in any obvious sense, since in such an analysis the raising of /ɪ ʊ/ to /i u/ would be triggered not only by the higher set A vowels /i u/ but also by the lower set A vowels /e o/, a curious type of assimilation. Nor are the set A vowels in such systems characterised by features such as tenseness, length or diphthongisation, which distinguish English vowels like [i:] vs. [ɪ] (e.g. *bead, bid*) or [ey] vs. [ɛ] (e.g. *raid, red*).

X-ray studies of Igbo, Akan and Ịọ vowels published by Ladefoged (1968), Painter (1973) and Lindau (1975) showed that the primary articulatory basis of vowel harmony in these languages is the volume of the pharyngeal cavity, which is considerably greater in set A vowels than in set B vowels. Since the volume of the pharyngeal cavity is mainly controlled by the advancement or retraction of the tongue root, the feature underlying vowel harmony is most often termed [advanced tongue root], or [±ATR] for short (Stewart 1967). Articulatorily, [+ATR] vowels are often somewhat fronted, due to the fact that root-advancing tends to push the tongue body forward; acoustically, they have a lower first formant frequency than their [−ATR] counterparts. In many languages, especially in the Nilotic group, this difference in timbre is reinforced by a further distinction in voice quality, which is variously described by such impressionistic terms as 'breathy/hollow/bright/ muffled' for the [+ATR] set as opposed to 'creaky/hard/dull/ brassy' for the [−ATR] set. In some languages (e.g. Agar Dinka), the breathy/creaky distinction seems to have completely replaced the original [+ATR]/[−ATR] contrast. The articulatory basis of these voice quality distinctions is still poorly understood.

While 10-vowel systems like that of Diola are not uncommon, most languages within the wide area characterised by ATR vowel harmony have 'reduced' vowel systems lacking /ə/ and often /ɪ ʊ/ as well, yielding 9- and 7-vowel systems as shown in (1) above. Such reduced systems often result from the historical merger of these relatively rare vowels with more widely occurring counterparts, for example /ə/ with /a/ or a mid vowel, /ɪ/ with /i/, /e/, or /ɛ/, and /ʊ/ with /u/, /o/ or /ɔ/. These mergers often create *opaque* vowels – vowels which can occur with vowels of either harmonic category in roots, but which govern the harmonic category of adjacent affixes.

It is useful to recognise two types of opaque vowels. In some languages, opaque vowels are *ambivalent*, functioning as [+ATR] vowels in some roots and as [−ATR] vowels in others. Thus in Okpẹ, with a 7-vowel system of the type shown in (1), the upper mid vowels /e o/ function as [+ATR] vowels in the roots *sé* 'fall' and *só* 'steal', as is shown by the [+ATR] prefixes in the infinitives *è-sé, è-só*. However, these same vowels function as [−ATR] vowels in the roots *ré* 'eat' and *só* 'sing', as is shown by the [−ATR] prefixes and suffixes in the infinitives *ɛ̀-ry-ɔ́, ɛ̀-sw-ɔ́* (in these forms, the root vowels undergo a later rule of glide formation). To explain these patterns, Hoffmann (1973) proposed to assign roots like 'eat' and 'sing' the abstract underlying vowels /ɪ ʊ/, accounting for their [−ATR] harmony and other properties, and to set up a late realisation rule, applying after vowel harmony, which lowers these vowels to their [+ATR] surface values [e o].

More commonly, opaque vowels are *monovalent*, always requiring the same value of [±ATR] in affix vowels, regardless of what root they occur in. In Akan, for example, the opaque [−ATR] low vowel /a/ occurs freely with [+ATR] vowels in roots, where it shifts to [ə] before a [+ATR] vowel in the following syllable (as in *kari* [kəri] 'weigh') and is otherwise realised as [a] (as in *bisa* [bisa] 'ask'). Whatever the root, however, this vowel always requires [−ATR] vowels in neighbouring affixes, as is illustrated by the prefix in [ɔ-kəri-i] 's/he weighed' and the suffix in [o-bisa-ı] 's/he asked'; thus it always functions as a [−ATR] vowel, in accordance with its basic phonetic value.

It is currently a controversial question whether all African vowel systems with four or five vowel heights should be described with the feature [±ATR]. At present, the best phonological and phonetic evidence for the feature [±ATR] comes from languages with cross-height vowel harmony, such as Igbo and Akan. In other languages, the evidence for the feature [±ATR] is much less secure. For example, X-ray tracings of vowels in Ngwe [ŋ̀wɛ́], a Bamileke language of Cameroon lacking cross-height harmony, show that the differences between the vowels /i e ɛ æ/ involve not only tongue root displacement but also equally important differences in degree of constriction between the front of the tongue and the anterior part of the palate, caused, at least in part, by the raising and lowering of the jaw (see Ladefoged 1968: 34). This way of implementing vowel height distinctions resembles that found in some non-African languages, such as French.

Furthermore, patterns of vowel alternation in languages outside the cross-height harmony zone offer little direct phonological support for the feature [±ATR]. For example, Southern Sotho (Sesotho), a southern Bantu language, has recently developed a 9-vowel system of the type shown in (1) above. (The upper mid series /e o/ was originally non-phonemic, but has come to acquire phonemic status through subsequent phonological change and borrowing.) This system superficially resembles that of Akan. However, instead of cross-height vowel harmony, Southern Sotho has a regular rule raising the lower mid vowels /ɛ ɔ/ to [e o] when followed in the next syllable by any of the vowels /e o ı ʊ i u/ (Clements 1991); compare, for example, [bɔn-a] 'see' and [sɛb-a] 'gossip', in which the root vowels have their basic value, with [bon-ı] 'to have seen' and [mʊ-seb-i] 'gossiper', in which these vowels have been raised (tones are omitted in these examples). The problem for an ATR-based analysis is to explain why both /ı/ and /i/, which have different values for this feature, induce raising. It seems much more straightforward to treat vowel height as a scalar or hierarchical feature in Southern Sotho; we can then state that lower mid vowels rise one degree in height when followed by any *higher* vowel.

6.4.2   *Other vowel features*

We review other vowel features more briefly. Another feature that can multiply a set of vowels by a factor of two is [+nasal]. Phonemic nasality is widely found in non-Bantu Niger-Congo languages, as well as Khoisan. A few languages, such as Lelemi and Likpe, have a full complement of nasalised vowels. More often, however, some oral vowels have no nasalised counterpart. Commonly missing are the upper or [+ATR] mid vowels [ẽ õ], while the peripheral vowels [ĩ ũ ã] are usually, though not always, present (Williamson 1973). Nasality has a strong propensity to spread to neighbouring sounds; a fully fledged system of nasal harmony, requiring all vowels in multisyllabic roots to be either nasal or oral, has been reported in the Maxi variety of Gbe.

Voice quality functions as a distinctive feature in many Nilotic languages such as Nuer and Agar Dinka, where seven basic vowel qualities /i u e o ɛ ɔ a/ occur in both breathy and non-breathy varieties. Bor Dinka has developed two phonemically distinctive voice qualities described as 'breathy vs. normal' and 'hollow vs. harsh', whose articulatory bases (and feature characterisation) are still uncertain. 'Whispered' or voiceless vowels are reported in a number of languages including Ik (Teuso), Teso and Turkana, though in some cases they can apparently be derived from underlying voiced vowels. Perhaps the most remarkable development of voice quality contrasts occurs in some of the Khoisan languages, however. Thus in one of the richest systems of vowel contrasts known among the world's languages, !Xóõ multiplies its five basic vowels /i u e o a/ by features of nasalisation, breathiness, glottalisation, and pharyngealisation to achieve a total of forty-four contrastive vowel qualities, not counting phonemic length (Traill 1985).[9]

Phonetically fricative vowels – high vowels realised with frication noise – have been reported in several languages, notably the Central Sudanic languages Ngiti and Lendu, several languages in the Grassfields Bantu area of Cameroon, and at least two NW Bantu languages, Fang and Ewondo. In Mambila, a North Bantoid language, a high unrounded fricative vowel /i/ is reported to contrast minimally with the (non-fricative) high vowels /i ɯ/. Such vowels have occasionally fed speculation that the Proto-Bantu high vowels /i u/ might have been accompanied by frication.

6.5   Syllables and phonological quantity

We next turn to the question of how speech sounds are organised into larger structures. Recent advances in phonological theory (recovering insights of earlier traditions) have shown that consonants and vowels are organised into syllables (see e.g. Goldsmith 1990, Blevins 1995), and syllables into a hierarchy of larger prosodic categories such as the phonological word, the phonological phrase, the intonational phrase and the utterance (e.g. Selkirk 1986). This higher-level organisation helps to determine the overall shape of each utterance, including the manner in which prosodic information, such as tones and accents, aligns with segmental material.

This section takes up two fundamental aspects of prosodic organisation, syllable structure and phonological quantity.

6.5.1   *Syllable structure*

In most African languages, words can be exhaustively divided into a sequence of syllables. That is, each word can be analysed into a succession of units of the same general form, typically containing a peak of prominence *V* (representing a vowel, diphthong or 'syllabic' consonant), usually preceded and sometimes followed by a less prominent margin *C* (representing a consonant or consonant cluster). An initial margin is termed an *onset* and a final margin, a *coda.*

The preferred syllable type in most languages is CV. Languages can be further typologised according to whether they allow syllables without onsets (V), syllables with codas (CVC), or both (V, CVC and VC). Onsetless syllables, when allowed, are often restricted to word- or phrase-initial position. Coda consonants often result from the loss of a following vowel, and may retain some of the characteristics of the missing vowel, as in Engenni (E̱ge̱ne̱) where [èsánì] 'pepper' varies freely with [èsáɲ̀], whose final consonant bears the syllabicity and tone of the elided vowel. A further syllable type found in many African languages is the syllabic nasal N̩. This sound usually agrees in place of articulation with a following consonant; it can sometimes be derived from an underlying nasalised vowel, and sometimes from a full underlying NV syllable.

What constitutes a well-formed syllable varies from language to language, and within a language it may also vary according to grammatical status and position. The stem-initial syllable typically hosts the largest number of phonemic contrasts. Khoisan languages, for example, normally restrict their clicks to this position, and many Bantu languages deploy their full set of vowel contrasts only in the stem-initial syllable; indeed, Hyman (1998) identifies stem-internal syllables in Bantu as a 'prosodic trough' subject to constraints that hold nowhere else.

Constraints on morpheme structure can often be directly explained in terms of constraints on syllable structure. In many Bantu languages, for instance, prefixes typically have the form (C)V-, roots CV(N)C-, derivational elements (extensions, suffixes) -VC-, and the obligatory final vowel suffix -V. These apparently idiosyncratic constraints make sense once we recognise that the core syllable in most Bantu languages is open (that is, vowel-final), and that the only permissable cluster is NC, syllabified as a syllable onset when occurring between vowels. The constraints on morpheme structure thus 'conspire' to allow any Bantu word to be fully parsed as a sequence of open syllables (for example, a word made up of the formatives

CV+CVNC+VC+V can be exhaustively syllabified as a sequence of four syllables CV.CV.NCV.CV). If Bantu prefixes could have the shape VC, or suffixes CV, many words could not be fully parsed into open syllables unless their form were radically adjusted by processes of epenthesis or deletion.

Many African languages give striking evidence for the psychological reality of the syllable in patterns of loanword adaptation, or in word games involving syllable permutation. An interesting example of the latter has been developed by speakers of Ganda (Luganda), a Bantu language which has the syllable structures described just above. In the children's play language known as Ludikya, Ganda words are transformed by a rule requiring syllables to be produced in reverse order. Some examples are given below:

(5) Ganda   Ludikya
     mukóno   *nokómu*   'arm'
     muvúbúká   *kabúvúmú*   'young man'
     mubínikilo   *lokínibimu* 'funnel'
     bágeenda   *ndágeeba*   'they are going'

Notably, NC clusters are transposed together with the following vowel, as is shown by the last example whose input form must therefore be syllabified as *bá.gee.nda*; this behaviour confirms their status as syllable onset.

6.5.2   ***Quantity and mora structure***

In studying phonological systems, we commonly find that one long segment patterns like two short segments with regard to phonological rules sensitive to segment count (hence the formula '1 long = 2 short'). Phonological theory has captured this generalisation by representing segmental quantity on an independent *quantity tier* (also known as the *timing tier* or *skeleton*), where short segments are linked to one unit and long segments to two.

In Hausa, for example, where length is distinctive in both vowels and consonants, the word *tállée* 'soup-pot' can be represented as follows (tones omitted):

(6)   Syllable tier

       Quantity tier

       Segmental tier

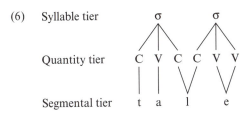

In such representations, quantity units are often represented as 'V' or 'C' depending on their function in the syllable, V functioning as peak and C as margin. The

V unit and any following V or C in the same syllable are sometimes further grouped into a 'rhyme' (or 'rime') constituent. This approach allows us to define the notion of *syllable weight* (to a first approximation) in terms of quantity units: light syllables typically contain a single quantity unit in their rhyme, and heavy syllables two.[10] By this definition, for example, *tállée* in (6) consists of two heavy syllables.

The 'bipositional' representation of long segments illustrated in (6) allows a considerable simplification of Hausa syllabification rules. Hausa has only three syllable types: CV, CVV (where VV is a long vowel or a diphthong) and CVC (where the final C can be the first member of a cluster or the first part of a long (or *geminate*) consonant, which we write as C=). These three types can be described by the syllable template CV(X) shown in (7), where the optional term X represents either C or V.

(7)

C	*V*	*(X)*	Example	
d	*a*		*dámóo*	'monitor'
r	*a*	*a*	*ràagóo*	'ram'
t	*a*	*u*	*tàusái*	'pity'
j	*i*	*r*	*jírgíi*	'train, plane'
t	*a*	*C=*	*tállée*	'soup-pot'

All Hausa words are exhaustively parsable by the template (7).

Given this template and representations such as (6), we can directly explain the fact that neither long vowels nor diphthongs can be followed by a consonant in the same syllable; this follows from the fact that template (7) does not provide for 'extra-heavy' syllables, that is, syllables whose rhymes contain three quantity units (or *moras*). Similarly, the fact that consonant sequences and geminates occur only between vowels follows from the fact that in any other position they cannot be fully syllabified by the template in (7). (See Newman 1972 and Leben 1977 for further discussion of syllable representations in Hausa and other Chadic languages.)

Syllable constraints often trigger regular phonological *alternations*, that is, variations in the phonological shape of morphemes. In Hausa, for example, extra-heavy syllables created by the morphology are usually brought into conformity with the template in (7) by shortening or deleting a vowel, as in *bàutáa* 'slavery', deriving from the underlying form /baaw+taa/ (compare *báawàa* 'slave', which preserves the long initial vowel). Shilluk, which also has contrastive length in vowels and consonants (in consonants it is realised with redundant 'fortis' articulation, as discussed above), has an interesting variant on this approach. In this Nilotic language, vowel sequences are disallowed. If such sequences are created by the morphology, the first vowel is deleted and the preceding consonant is lengthened in compensation, as is shown by the bracketed phonetic form in (8a). Since Shilluk also disallows extra-heavy syllables, a preceding long vowel, if present, must shorten to make room for the lengthened consonant, as shown in (8b). However, there is a (superficially) unpredictable subclass of 'stable' long vowels that never shorten. Since their length is always preserved, the following consonant cannot acquire derived length, and is realised short as shown in (8c). (Underlined vowels have distinctively breathy voice; tones are omitted.)

(8) (a) *ḍɔŋɔ*   'basket'   *ḍɔŋɔ-e*   'his basket'   [ḍɔŋŋe]
     (b) *ciino̱*   'intestine' *ciino̱-e* 'his intestine' [ci̱nne]
     (c) *gɔɔlɔ*   'hook'   *gɔɔlɔ-e* 'his hook'   [gɔɔle]

These various constraints 'conspire' to preserve the preferred CV(X) syllable type in surface forms. (See Gilley 1992 for a fuller analysis.)

In summary, the bipositional representation of phonological quantity correctly predicts for Hausa, Shilluk and many other languages that long vowels and consonants typically pattern as bisegmental sequences in respect to rules and principles sensitive to the segment count. The independence of the quantity tier can be quite strikingly confirmed by the study of language games, as further examples from Ganda will demonstrate. Like Hausa and Shilluk, Ganda has long vowels and consonants, and its full syllable template is (C)V(X), where C can be a cluster NC, and X is either V or C=. When syllables containing long segments are transposed in Ludikya, only the segments switch position, and length is left in place. This behaviour is illustrated by examples such as the following:

(9) Ganda   Ludikya
     báana   *náaba*   'children'
     kiwúúgúlû   *lugúúwúkî*   'owl'
     jjúba   *bbáju*   'dove'
     muyízzi   *ziyímmu*   'hunter'

In some cases, consonant and vowel length are exchanged: *muggá* → *gaamú* 'river'. In terms of the bipositional analysis of quantity, then, we may say that Ludikya involves a permutation of the segmental content of syllables alone, leaving the units of the quantity tier intact. Such examples offer striking support for the psychological validity of quantity units, as distinct from segments *per se*.[11]

Most languages distinguish no more than two degrees of vowel length within the syllable, and some linguists have assumed that this is a universal upper limit.

Agar Dinka, however, has three degrees of distinctive vowel length, as shown by the following minimal set (Andersen 1987; the subscript tilde indicates creaky voice):

(10) *ạ-tɔ̰ŋ*   'you are lighting it'
      ạ-tɔ̰ɔŋ   'he is lighting it'
      ạ-tɔ̰ɔɔŋ   'he is knocking at it'

That such sequences are indeed monosyllabic is confirmed by the fact that short, long and extra-long vowels all bear the same three distinctive tone melodies (H, L, HL):

(11)		Short		Long		Extra-long	
	L	*mòc*	'man'	*tìik*	'woman'	*raạan*	'person'
	H	*kɔ́c*	'people'	*cíin*	'hand'	*liɛ́ɛt*	'sand'
	HL	*tɔ̂ŋ*	'eggs'	*nɔ̂ok*	'feather'	*tìịim*	'trees'

In contrast, bisyllabic sequences bear sequences of these basic tone melodies, for example *àrɔ̂w* 'tortoise' (L+HL), *àboɔ́or* 'flood' (L+H). In Dinka, then, quite exceptionally, vowels may contrast in terms of linkage to one, two or three quantity units, and the preferred syllable type in this language can be represented CV_i^3C.

The analysis of syllables and phonological quantity has generated a large theoretical literature, and there are many competing theories of syllable organisation to which we cannot do justice in this brief introduction. The approach presented above is developed more fully in this writer's analysis of quantity and mora structure in Ganda (Clements 1986), as well as in Clements and Keyser (1983). One of the better-known alternatives is an approach which suppresses the distinction between C and V units in favour of uniform X units, as in Gilley's (1992) analysis of quantity in Shilluk; see further Blevins (1995). A further alternative is a mora-based approach which suppresses the onset and rhyme constituents, and treats quantity in terms of uniform weight units (x) or moras (μ); see for example Hyman's (1985) weight-unit analysis of Gokana, or Odden's (1996) mora-based treatment of Matuumbi (Kimatuumbi).

6.6   **Clusters**

        It is often believed that African languages disfavour consonant clusters. While this statement is not entirely incorrect, it is an oversimplification. Many African languages have consonant clusters, and many others are in the process of acquiring them. Clusters raise difficult problems of analysis. In some cases, they can be shown to behave as single, phonetically complex consonants (a 'monosegmental analysis'), while in others they pattern as phoneme sequences (a 'bisegmental analysis'). We shall see here that a satisfactory analysis may depend on how a given cluster is syllabified.

Consonant clusters – by which we mean any phonetic sequence of consonants, without prejudice as to their eventual analysis as one or two phonemes – generally lend themselves to one of the four analyses shown in (12), illustrating a hypothetical cluster *nd*. In (12a) the cluster is analysed as a sequence of two onsets separated by a phonologically 'empty' syllable peak (V_e), in (12b) as a coda + onset sequence, in (12c) as a complex onset consisting of two phonemes, and in (12d) as a simple onset consisting of one phoneme, whose features are sequenced only at the phonetic level.

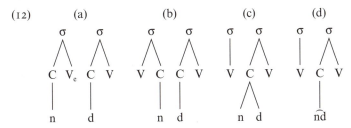

Analysis (12a) is often appropriate when either member of the cluster bears features of a missing vowel, such as tone or syllabicity. The choice between (12b) and (12c) can frequently be determined by the rules of syllabification. (12b) can be justified, for example, if the cluster creates a heavy syllable on its left, as it does in Hausa, while (12c) or (12d) is motivated if the cluster can be shown to form a single syllable onset, as in Ganda.

It is often more difficult to decide between the bisegmental analysis (12c) and the monosegmental analysis (12d). The bisegmental analysis may be acceptable if the language tolerates other onset clusters as well, and it is clearly preferred if:

- the two members of the cluster can be separated by processes of epenthesis or reduplication (satisfying the test of *separability*)
- each member occurs on its own as an independent onset consonant (satisfying the test of *compositionality*)

or

- each member forms part of a substitution class which combines with the other member (satisfying the test of *commutation*)

The monosegmental analysis (12d) is usually preferred if none of these conditions is satisfied.

A further property of the bisegmental analyses (12a–c) is that they predict that a cluster will pattern differently on its left and right edge. For example, under these analyses we expect that a cluster *nd* will pattern as a nasal segment only with regard to material on its left and as an oral segment only with regard to material on its right; that is, it will display so-called 'edge effects'. Under the monosegmental analysis (12d), in contrast, *nd* can also pattern as a nasal segment on its right and as an oral segment on its left (creating so-called 'anti-edge effects').[12] Examples of these effects will be given below.

6.6.1 *Liquid clusters*

Many West African languages have liquid clusters CL, where L is realised as *l* or *r*. Often, these arise historically from the loss of a vowel: CVLV > CLV. However, the liquid shows varying degrees of affiliation to the preceding consonant in different languages. In the Fante variety of Akan, for example, vowel deletion is a synchronic process, and a brief transitional vowel can still be heard at the intersection between the consonant and the liquid. In many words, such as *ɔ-práà* 's/he swept', the liquid bears the tone (and sometimes other features) of the deleted vowel. As a consequence, the CLV sequence continues to pattern tonally like a bisyllabic CVLV sequence. In such cases, as suggested by Welmers (1973), it is plausible to analyse the root as an underlying CV_eLV sequence as in (12a), with the liquid reassociating to the V_e position in the surface realisation.

Not all CL clusters lend themselves to this analysis, however. In most Gbe languages, which have a single liquid phoneme /l/, vowel deletion has progressed further, and the postconsonantal liquid bears no vowel features or tones. CLV roots still bear some traces of their earlier CVLV status, however. For example, the liquid combines freely with the glides *w*, *y* in roots like *wlu* 'dig', *yrá* 'bless', in gross violation of normal sonority constraints on complex onsets; and falling (HL) tones are largely restricted to CLV syllables in the native lexicon (*èklâ* 'soul'), betraying their origin as H + L tones on separate syllables. Furthermore, there are few if any CVLV roots in which $V_1 = V_2$, from which CLV roots are thought to derive. However, further observations show that CLV sequences pattern differently from CVLV sequences in the modern phonological system. First, /l/ is realised as [r] if the immediately preceding consonant is coronal, as in [dzrá] 'buy', but as [l] in all other contexts, even following a coronal onset across a vowel: [àdzàlɛ̀] 'soap'. Further, in several varieties of Gbe, while nearly all bisyllables show full reduplication (e.g. *sùbɔ́-súbɔ́* 'worship'), CLV roots consistently reduplicate only the CV sequence, just as do monosyllables:

(13)	(a)	CV roots			(b)	CLV roots		
		ɖu	*ɖu-ɖu*	'eat'		*tró*	*to-tró*	'turn down'
		ko	*ko-ko*	'laugh at'		*klɔ́*	*kɔ-klɔ́*	'wash'

These facts suggest that the historical bisyllabic sequences CVLV have become synchronically reanalysed as a single CLV syllable with a complex onset as shown in (12c). These onsets have not become further reduced to single segments as in (12d), however, since as shown in (13b), the clusters are separable under reduplication (recall the separability test). See Capo (1991) for further discussion of these and related facts.

In other languages, liquids are much more restricted in their distribution than in Akan or Gbe. In Madi, for example, the only clusters are /ʈr ɖr ts dz/ and NC clusters. Here, /ʈr ɖr/ are realised phonetically as retroflex stops with a trilled or fricative release. Given the absence of any other retroflex sounds in Madi, these sounds can be considered as single segments – retroflex affricates – as in (12d), paralleling the strident affricates /ts dz/ (Andersen 1986).

6.6.2   ***Nasal clusters***

Nasal clusters of the form NC (more rarely, CN) in which N and C share the same place of articulation are widely distributed across sub-Saharan Africa, crossing genetic boundaries. In many languages, such as Ganda, NC clusters are the only occurring clusters. (For overviews see Welmers 1973, Herbert 1986, and Creissels 1994.)

In some languages, NC clusters have a synchronic source in underlying NVC sequences from which the vowel has been deleted (12a), in which case the nasal is usually realised with the syllabicity and perhaps other characteristics (tone, stress) of the absent vowel.[13] In Swahili, for example, the noun prefix /mu-/ is regularly realised as syllabic [m̩] before a consonant, and bears stress if the following stem is monosyllabic, as in [m̩-ke] 'wife'. We may compare this form with [mw-ána] 'child', in which the underlying /u/ is glided to [w] before the stem-initial vowel *a*.

In other languages, however, NC clusters are underlying. In some cases, they can be analysed as coda + onset sequences as shown in (12b). An example can be cited from the Chadic language Bole (also known as Bolanci; see Newman 1972). In this language, NC clusters occur both word-initially and word-internally. Word-initially, they function as onsets. Intervocalically, however, they pattern like all other CC sequences in making the preceding syllable heavy. This is shown by verbs ending in -*u*, which have the tone pattern LH if the first syllable is heavy (*mòyyú* 'wait for') and HH if the first syllable is light (*móyú* 'see'). Intervocalic NC clusters always make the preceding syllable heavy (*wùndú* 'call'), and so must be analysed as a coda + onset sequence.

In the closely related Kanakuru language, however, NC clusters behave consistently as onsets, since they never add to the weight of the preceding syllable. This is shown by tone patterns of verbal nouns formed with the productive suffix

-ǝk. These nouns have the tone pattern HH if the first syllable of the root is light (*mónǝk* 'forget'), but HL if it is heavy (*yáhjǝk* 'sift'). Verbal nouns with inter-vocalic NC clusters always have HH tone (e.g. *ɓíndǝk* 'squeeze'), showing that the first syllable is light. Further facts in this language show that the single-segment analysis (12d) may be preferable to the sequence analysis (12c). First, Kanakuru never allows a sequence of more than two consonants within the word; exceptions created by the morphology are broken up by epenthesis. However, NC clusters occur freely after consonants, as in *kúrnjé* 'baobab', *gúlŋgì* 'intestines'; under the single-segment analysis (12d), they are not exceptions to this generalisation. Second, while ordinary nasals trigger the nasalisation of certain consonants to their left (thus /ar-ni/ 'his hand' is realised *an-ni*), NC clusters fail to do so – an 'anti-edge effect'. This behaviour would be quite unexpected under the sequence analysis in (12c), in which NC clusters are formally indistinguishable from simple nasals N on their left edge. To explain such facts, Newman (1974) proposes that NC clusters are underlying nasal obstruents in Kanakuru, constituting unit phonemes with no internal sequencing. Nasal obstruents can be excluded from the nasalisation rule by restricting it to nasal sonorants (*m*, *n*, etc.). The fact that obstruent nasals are realised as NC sequences at the phonetic level can be accounted for by phonetic realisation rules.

6.6.3   *Obstruent clusters*

From a typological point of view, one of the most unusual phonetic cluster types found in African languages involves sequences of obstruents (stops, fricatives). Such clusters are commoner than is often suspected. Thus, Meinhof (1932) lists a variety of obstruent clusters such as *px, ps, pʃ, fx, fs, ff* and their voiced counterparts as among the 'commonest Bantu sounds', and similar sounds are found quite widely in other parts of Africa as well. While sounds such as *pʃ* are sometimes labelled 'heterorganic affricates', suggesting an analysis as unit segments, this treatment does not readily generalise to comparable fricative clusters like Sotho *fs ff vʒ* or Kutep *fx, sf*, nor to stop clusters such as !Xóõ *tkx', dzkx'*, Zezuru Shona *pk, ʧk*, Margi *pt, bdz*, Eggon *kb, bg*, and so forth. It seems, rather, that we are dealing with genuine phoneme sequences.

One common source of obstruent clusters is vowel loss, by which CVC > CC. In some cases, the elided vowel is still present underlyingly, or in a variant realisation. For example, some clusters in Margi arise synchronically through an optional process eliding high vowels between coronal and velar consonants, giving rise to free variants such as *sùkùdɔ̀* ~ *skùdɔ̀* 'push'. Here the underlying representation clearly involves successive onsets as shown in (12a). In other cases, obstruent clusters form coda + onset sequences, as in Bole where, as we saw above, all clusters (including obstruent clusters) render the preceding syllable heavy. For these cases the coda + onset representation in (12b) is appropriate.

'Tighter' onset clusters of types (12c) and (12d) are also not uncommon. In some cases, fricatives arise to reinforce aspiration, as in Nama *kh*, realised [kxʰ]. In many other languages, as Meinhof (1932) points out, stop + fricative clusters can be traced to earlier C + high vowel + V sequences via a series of historical changes in which the high vowel becomes a glide (perhaps fusing with the consonant as a secondary articulation) and eventually conditions the appearance of a fricative. (14) is a possible representation of some of the stages in such a chain of events, where (a) and (b) represent possible beginning points and (d) and (e) possible end points.

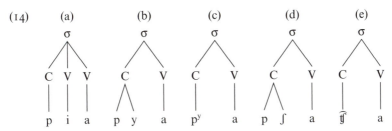

A variant scenario produces fricatives from 'intrusive' glides inserted into simple consonant + high vowel sequences, for example *ku > kwu > kfu*. Obstruent clusters such as *pʃ* (14d) are unstable and tend to be replaced by unit sounds such as *pf* or *ʧ* (14e).

Obstruent clusters such as those in (14d, e) have triggered off a lively debate regarding their representation. Let us start with the most familiar case: affricates such as *ts* or *ʧ*. These sounds are (by definition) stop + fricative sequences that pattern as unit phonemes, and have the single-segment representation shown in (14e). Some linguists have attempted to represent their phonetically complex nature directly in the phonology by treating these sounds as single segments with internally sequenced features [−continuant], [+continuant], while others have treated them as [+strident] stops at the phonological level, whose fricative release is introduced only in the phonetics.

Consider next the labial-velar sounds *k͡p*, *g͡b*. There are several good reasons for considering these sounds as single segments with the structure shown in (14e). One comes from the fact that labial-velars are inseparable under reduplication. Thus in some varieties of Gbe, as shown in (13), monosyllabic verb stems are reduplicated by copying the first C and V, while the second member of a CC cluster is dropped, as in words like *kɔ-klɔ́* 'wash'. In contrast, the labial-velar /k͡p/ is always reduplicated as a whole, as shown by forms like *k͡pɛ-k͡pɛ́* 'meet', consistently with a single-segment analysis.

Another argument comes from the absence of expected 'edge effects'. In many languages, nasal consonants assimilate to the place of articulation of an immediately following consonant, but in none, as far as we know, do they assimilate to a non-adjacent consonant. Now in some languages, nasals assimilate to *both* the labial and velar articulations of a following labial-velar (an 'anti-edge effect'), yielding the phonetic sequence [ŋm͡kp]. If we analysed /k͡p/ as two successive units /k + p/ as in (14d), we would expect the nasal to assimilate to the *k*, but not to the *p*, which is not adjacent to it.

Thirdly, in at least one language, Eggon, labial-velar stops *k͡p*, *g͡b* contrast with the otherwise similar bisegmental sequences *kp*, *gb*: compare *k͡pu* 'die' vs. *kpu* 'kneel', or *g͡bu* 'arrive' vs. *gba* 'divide'. Here, bisegmental sequences such as *kp* are phonetically distinguished from their labial-velar counterparts *k͡p* by their longer duration and the fact that their first consonant is audibly released.

While affricates and labial-velar stops can therefore be treated as single segments, most other obstruent clusters appear to behave as bisegmental sequences wherever good evidence is available. This is obviously true of the bisegmental clusters *kp*, *gb* of Eggon; but such an analysis is equally motivated in other languages as well. The members of other obstruent clusters are usually clearly phonetically sequenced one after the other, and the first member of a sequence of stops is often audibly released, as in Eggon. Furthermore, obstruent clusters generally show the 'edge effects' expected of true bisegmental sequences. Thus, in clusters composed of nasals followed by obstruent clusters (NCC), the nasal assimilates to the place of articulation of the first obstruent, never the second, as in Venda *mmbwa* 'dog', realised [m̩bɣwa] and not [m̩ŋbɣwa]. (See Maddieson 1987, 1990 for further discussion of problems in cluster analysis.)

6.6.4   *Clicks and their accompaniments*

A click is a multiply articulated sound produced by forming one closure in the front of the mouth with the lips or tongue front and another in the back of the mouth with the tongue dorsum. The air pocket trapped between the two closures is expanded by drawing the tongue body downward and backward while maintaining both closures, and the front closure is then released to produce the characteristic click burst as air rushes into the mouth (the 'influx'). Outside Khoisan, clicks are known to occur only in south African Bantu languages such as Zulu, Xhosa, Southern Sotho and Yeyi, and in the Cushitic language Dahalo (Sanye). Clicks are often treated as single, complex segments, but as we shall see below, at least some of them can be analysed as clusters.

Table 6.27 illustrates the five basic click sounds of !Xóõ, a Southern Khoisan language, following the description of Traill (1985). (The click symbols, which

Table 6.27. *Click places of articulation in !Xóõ (after Traill 1985)*

Symbol	Conventional label	Front closure	Release
ʘ	labial	bilabial	affricated labiodental
ǀ	dental	laminal dental-alveolar	affricated
ǃ	alveolar	apical post-dental	abrupt
ǁ	lateral	apical post-dental	affricated lateral
ǂ	palatal	laminal dental-to-palatal	abrupt

designate the nature of the front closure only, are those of the International Phonetic Association.)

Most click languages lack the labial click, and often one or more of the others. Bantu languages usually have at most three clicks, represented in their orthographies by the letters *c* (dental), *q* (alveolar), and *x* (lateral), though Yeyi has the palatal click as well.

Clicks are produced together with a variety of back-of-the-mouth articulations, collectively termed the accompaniment (or efflux). The simplest accompaniment is a voiceless velar closure. More complex accompaniments involve voicing, aspiration, glottalisation, nasalisation, uvularisation, affrication and various combinations of these. Accompaniments are often symbolised by the sound(s) that would be heard if the front closure of the click were removed, for example *k*, *g*, k^h, *k'*, *ŋ*, *q*, *kx*, *qx*, etc., though for simplicity the symbol *k* is generally omitted. In !Xóõ, the five clicks of table 6.27 combine freely with sixteen accompaniments to create at least eighty contrastive click complexes.[14]

From a phonological point of view, most clicks and their accompaniments can be analysed as multiply articulated sounds consisting of a simultaneous back [dorsal] component and a front [coronal] or [labial] component, satisfying the unit analysis shown in (14e). However, Traill (1985) points out that at least some click + accompaniment complexes can be analysed as phoneme sequences. A telling argument for this view is that most Khoisan languages admit many rather complex obstruent clusters outside the click system; for example, few linguists would maintain that a cluster such as !Xóõ *dt'kx'* constitutes a single phoneme. If this cluster is a phoneme sequence, it is reasonable to suppose that an ejected affricated uvularised click such as *!kx'*, which ends in the same cluster as *dt'kx'*, can also be analysed as a phoneme sequence.

It seems unlikely, however, that all click + accompaniment clusters can be decomposed in this manner. Certain accompaniments, as Traill notes, have no parallels in the non-click system; in !Xóõ, for example, there is no independent phoneme /ŋ̊/ corresponding to the voiceless nasalised accompaniment transcribed *ŋ̊*. Even more problematically, a thoroughgoing sequence analysis 'peeling off' all accompaniments as separate phonemes would leave the front closures as residue, with no obvious counterparts in the non-click system. Though we might, for example, treat the anterior closures of ǂ and | as positional variants of /t/ and /ts/, there would still be no obvious non-click sources for the anterior closures of ‖ and !. In several important respects, then, a thoroughgoing sequence analysis of click complexes would fail the test of compositionality. However these problems are to be solved, the parallels between click accompaniments and independent non-click consonants are too striking and thoroughgoing to be a matter of pure coincidence, and future work will no doubt throw more light on how they are best expressed.[15]

The last two sections have shown how a variety of complex facts can be explained in terms of a model of syllable organisation in which the quantity units C, V function as onsets, peaks and codas, and in which the onset, and perhaps other syllable constituents, can contain phoneme sequences. This model is highly constrained and strongly predictive. In such a model, there appears to be little need to assume 'compound' onsets or codas containing two or more C units, nor to recognise internally sequenced segments (so-called 'contour segments'), as has been commonly done in the past (e.g. Sagey 1990). Further research will show whether a constrained approach of this type, perhaps allowing a restricted use of extra-syllabicity (i.e., segments that remain unsyllabified at the edges of the syllabification domain), can be maintained generally for languages in Africa and elsewhere.

6.7   **Prosodic systems and tone**
        The majority of African languages are tone or tonal-accent languages, in which differences in relative pitch are used to convey lexical and grammatical distinctions. The commonest type of system, widely found in Niger-Congo and Nilo-Saharan languages, opposes two distinctive tone levels, high (H) and low (L), and often allows two or more of these tones in succession on single syllables, creating what are known as contour tones. In Mende, for example, we find five contrastive tone patterns on monosyllabic nouns alone, as illustrated by kɔ́ 'war' (H), kpà 'debt' (L), mbû 'owl' (HL), mbǎ 'rice' (LH), and mbǎ 'companion' (LHL). Most often, as in these Mende examples, H tones are transcribed with the acute accent (´), L tones with the grave accent (`), and contour tones with appropriate sequences of these (for example, a HL falling tone is transcribed with the circumflex accent (ˆ), consisting of the acute and grave accents joined together).

Perhaps the most outstanding characteristic of tones in African languages is their independence with respect to their segmental support. Tones behave very much as though they exist in a separate 'dimension' from consonant and vowel segments, as is shown by typical characteristics such as those listed in (15).

(15) Some typical properties of African tone systems
  - *Tone melodies* Significant generalisations can often be stated over tone sequences ('melodies') in abstraction from the segments that bear them
  - *Contour tones* Rising and falling tones can usually be analysed as combinations of two or more level tones (H, L, etc.)
  - *Spreading tones* Single level tones may spread over several syllables at once
  - *Floating tones* Some tones 'float' between other tones, often causing raising of the preceding tone, or lowering ('downstep') of following tones
  - *Tone shift* Tones characterising one morpheme can be realised on other morphemes, sometimes at a considerable distance away

One of the most influential recent developments in phonology is the theory known as *Autosegmental Phonology*, an approach initially motivated by the desire to explain properties of tone such as those listed in (15) (see Goldsmith 1990 and references therein). The basic premise of autosegmental tonology is that tones are represented on a line (or 'tier') parallel to that of consonants and vowels, and are synchronised with the units that bear them (such as syllables or moras) by means of association lines.

All the properties listed in (15) are well exemplified in the tonal system of Bambara, which also illustrates the distinction between lexical tones and grammatical tones. We shall examine tone in one variety of Bambara below, following the autosegmental analysis of Rialland and Badjimé (1989). We will restrict our attention to nouns of one and two syllables, but the analysis given below is compatible with the fuller analysis required for the complete system.

The forms in (16) illustrate the tonal patterns of Bambara nouns in citation form, and when forming complete utterances with the particles *don* 'it's' and *tɛ* 'it's not'. Notice that the tones of nouns in citation form are different from their tones in context.

(16)

Citation form	__*dòn* ('it's X')	__*tɛ́* ('it's not X')
bâ 'the river'	*bá dôn* 'it's a river'	*bá tɛ́* 'it's not a river'
	bá dòn 'it's the river'	*bá ꞌtɛ́* 'it's not the river'
bǎ 'the goat'	*bà dôn* 'it's a goat'	*bà tɛ́* 'it's not a goat'
	bǎ dòn 'it's the goat'	*bǎ ꞌtɛ́* 'it's not the goat'

bálâ 'the balaphone'	*bálá dôn* 'it's a balaphone'	*bálá té* 'it's not a balaphone'
	bálá dòn 'it's the balaphone'	*bálá ˈté* 'it's not the balaphone'
bàlâ 'the porcupine'	*bàlà dôn* 'it's a porcupine'	*bàlà té* 'it's not a porcupine'
	bàlá dòn 'it's the porcupine'	*bàlá ˈté* it's not the porcupine'

It will be observed that the definite article in Bambara has no segmental realisation. In the second and third columns of (16), the definite form of each noun is distinguished from the indefinite form shown just above it by tonal alternations in the noun (in the case of 'goat' and 'porcupine'), tonal alternations in the particle (column 2), and downstep preceding the particle (indicated by the raised exclamation point in column 3).

As the examples in (16) show, one-syllable nouns fall into one of two tone classes, illustrated by the nouns 'river' and 'goat'. Two-syllable nouns also fall into two tone classes, illustrated by 'balaphone' and 'porcupine'. These examples are representative of the vast majority of one- and two-syllable nouns. We will now show that the various surface realisations in (16) can all be derived from underlying tone melodies in which tones are not yet associated with syllables.

Consider first the indefinite forms of columns 2 and 3. Observing that the nouns 'river' and 'balaphone' bear only H tones in the indefinite while 'goat' and 'porcupine' bear only L tones, we may assign these nouns a 'floating' H tone and a L tone, respectively, in their lexical representations, as shown in (17a). These floating tones associate to the single syllable of monosyllabic nouns and to both syllables of bisyllabic nouns, giving the surface forms shown in (17b).

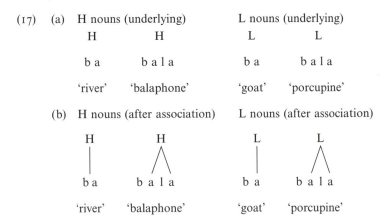

(17) (a) H nouns (underlying)   L nouns (underlying)

      (b) H nouns (after association)   L nouns (after association)

In these autosegmental representations, tones are represented on separate lines, or tiers, from the segments that bear them. Tones are linked to vowels by association lines; tones that are not so linked are floating tones. (In a fuller syllable-based representation, tones would be linked to syllables instead of to vowels.)

Given the analysis in (17), the four 'tone classes' of (16) can be derived from a basic two-way distinction between H-tone nouns and L-tone nouns in underlying representation. This type of analysis can be extended to the great majority of non-derived one- and two-syllable lexemes – nouns, verbs, particles such as *don* and *tɛ*, etc. – in Bambara.

But how then can we explain the falling tone of *dôn* in the indefinite forms of column 2 of (16)? The L-tone realisation of *dòn* in the definite forms suggests that this particle may belong to the L tone class underlyingly. If this is true, the falling tone would be a composite H + L tone. But where does the H come from? A clue comes from the fact that a similarly mysterious H appears at the end of nouns of the L tone class in the definite form in columns 2 and 3, where it forms the second component of a rising (L + H) tone in the monosyllabic noun 'goat', and a simple H tone on the final syllable of the bisyllabic noun 'porcupine'. Further study of Bambara shows that a H tone occurs at the end of the underlying tone melody of all lexemes. This tone is realised phonetically on an immediately following L-tone item such as *dòn* in the indefinite forms in (16), or on a preceding L-tone item such as the nouns 'goat' and 'porcupine' in the definite forms. To explain these facts, Rialland and Badjimé postulate a morphological 'H-tone affix' whose function is to mark the right edge of lexical categories.

It remains, then, to explain the tonal modifications introduced by the category 'definite'. For this purpose Rialland and Badjimé posit a grammatical L tone marking definiteness, which follows all tones of definite nouns (including the H tonal affix just discussed). This tone is a tonal suffix, not associated with any vowel. However, it makes its presence felt through two effects: (1) it prevents the H-tone affix from associating to a following L-tone particle such as *dòn*, as shown in the definite forms of the second column, and (2) it induces downstep between two successive H tones, as shown in the definite forms of the third column. Though a 'phantom' tone in the sense that it is not actually pronounced, the presence of the floating L tone is sufficient, through these indirect effects, to distinguish definite nouns from indefinite nouns in *all* cases.

Example (18) represents the analysis of the indefinite forms of column 2 in (16), after tone association.

(18)

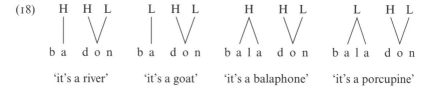

ba don	ba don	bala don	bala don
'it's a river'	'it's a goat'	'it's a balaphone'	'it's a porcupine'

In these examples, the first tone is the lexical tone of the noun, the second tone is the H tone affix, and the third tone is the lexical L tone of *dòn*. Notice that apart from the choice of H vs. L for the noun, the tone melodies are identical in all cases.

Consider next the forms with *té* 'it's not'. The only crucial difference between these forms and those with *dòn* 'it's' is that the lexical tone of *té* is H. The representation of these forms, after tone association, is shown in (19).

(19)

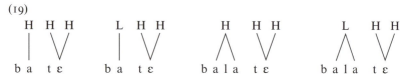

'it's not a river'   'it's not a goat'   'it's not a balaphone'   'it's not a porcupine'

Here it seems reasonable to assume that two H tones linked to a single vowel are phonetically indistinguishable from a single H tone linked to the vowel (or we might alternatively suppose that they are automatically collapsed into one by a general convention).

The only novelty introduced by the definite article is its floating L tone, inserted just after the H-tone affix. The representations after tone association are shown in (20) and (21). (The L tone of the article is underlined for clarity.)

(20)

'it's the river'   'it's the goat'   'it's the balaphone'   'it's the porcupine'

(21)

'it's not the river' 'it's not the goat' 'it's not the balaphone' 'it's not the porcupine'

Here we see in graphic terms the important effects of the floating L tone. In (20), its presence is sufficient to cause the H-tone affix to associate leftward (note that if it associated rightward, it would 'trap' the floating L tone between the H and L components of a falling tone, creating a highly awkward configuration). In (21), it falls between two H tones, inducing downstep on the second.

We may finally consider the citation forms in (16). The reader can now easily appreciate that these forms bear three tones in succession: the lexical H or L tone of the noun, the H-tone affix, and the L article tone. Surface representations are shown in (22).

(22)

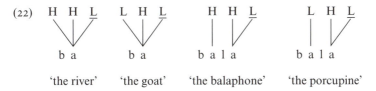

'the river' 'the goat' 'the balaphone' 'the porcupine'

These forms provide striking evidence of the reality of the floating L tone, which has up to now led a chimerical existence. As we now see (and as further forms confirm), it associates to a word-final vowel in just one context: when it is utterance-final.

In sum, Bambara illustrates many aspects of the characteristic independence of tones from segments in African languages, such as tone melodies, contour tones, spreading tones, floating tones and downstep. The independence of tone is further illustrated, in many languages, in word games in which segments or syllables are permuted, while tones stay in place; see the Ludikya forms in (5) and (9) for examples. Bambara is by no means, however, representative of all African tone systems; African tone languages tend to reshuffle the properties we have observed in Bambara in many different combinations and with infinite variations.

Thus, while Bambara tone can best be described by assuming that tones are initially unlinked to vowels, associating by principles depending on the tonal composition of the melody and the number of syllables, other tone languages are better described by assuming that tones are already linked to syllables at the outset. Further, while Bambara has just two lexical tone levels, many other African tone languages have three, four or even five distinctive tone levels. Again, while Bambara is a true tone language in the sense that it has an underlying opposition between two distinct tone levels, H and L, in *tonal accent languages*, characteristic of NE Africa as well as many Bantu languages, we find a lexical opposition between the presence and absence of a tone (usually, but not always H); in such systems there is no reason to posit a second tone at all. And finally, while contour tones in Bambara and most other West African languages lend themselves readily to decomposition into sequences of H and L tones, this type of analysis seems less appropriate for Khoisan languages, whose contours tend to behave as units.

We conclude this discussion with a brief (and very incomplete) typology of African prosodic systems in (23), specifying a number of basic parameters underlying their diverse surface realisations.

(23) Some parameters of African prosodic systems
    (a) Number of lexically contrastive tone levels
        0 = predictable stress or accent (e.g. Arabic, Wolof, Swahili)
        1 = tonal accent (e.g. Somali, Tonga, (Ki)Matuumbi)
        2 = H vs. L (e.g. Hausa, Luo, Temne, Bambara, Gbe, Kikuyu)
        3 = H vs. M vs. L (e.g. Tera, Moru-Madi, Bedik, Bobo, Yoruba, Zande)
        4 = e.g. Lendu, Moba, Grebo, Igede, Fe'fe'-Bamileke
        5 = e.g. Gimira (Benchnon variety), Wobe, Dan (Santa variety), Ashuku
    (b) Tone-bearing unit: syllable or mora
    (c) Types of contour tones: HL, LH, LHL, MH, etc.
    (d) Function of floating tones (lexical, phonological, grammatical, syntactic)
    (e) Tone association: lexical or derived
        if derived: domain of tone association (root, stem, word, phrase, etc.); manner of association (left-to-right, right-to-left, edge-in)
    (f) Downstep: present or absent
        if present: source (lexical, grammatical, phonological, syntactic)
    (g) Intonational characteristics:
        downdrift, suspension of downdrift, final lowering, boundary tones, etc.

All these topics, and many more, provide a fascinating ground for investigation and deserve fuller discussion than we can give them here. For an excellent recent overview of African tonal systems, see Odden (1995).

Notes

I would like to express special thanks to the following friends, colleagues and scholars who have helped by returning useful comments, corrections, and suggestions on an earlier draft of this chapter, often at very short notice: Chet Creider, Gerrit Dimmendaal, Bernd Heine,

Larry Hyman, Paul Newman, Derek Nurse, Annie Rialland, Thilo Schadeberg, John Stewart, Tony Traill, Rainer Vossen and Kay Williamson. I hope they will find their efforts repaid. Any remaining errors are of course my own.

1 In this chapter, alternative language names will be cited in parentheses.

2 All statements of phoneme frequency in this chapter have been cross-checked with the African data in UPSID (Maddieson 1992), a database consisting of 451 phoneme systems drawn from a genetically balanced sample of the world's languages. UPSID contains 106 phoneme systems from Africa alone, including 55 Niger-Congo languages, 24 Afroasiatic languages, 23 Nilo-Saharan languages, and 4 Khoisan languages. The phonemes listed in table 1 occur in at least half these languages.

3 For expository purposes, we adopt two-valued features throughout, except in the case of the (one-valued) place of articulation features. Many phonologists believe that other features should be treated as one-valued as well. The descriptions that follow can generally be recast in alternative feature frameworks with little difficulty.

4 This feature is also known, with values reversed, as [±distributed].

5 Thus, of the 106 African languages listed in the UPSID sample (see note 2), 37, or 35 per cent, have the labial /ɓ/, while only 17, or 16 per cent, have the apical /ɗ/. If these two sounds were distributed across languages purely on the basis of their individual frequencies – that is, if the principle of economy did not apply to them – we would expect only 16 per cent of the 37 languages with /ɓ/ to also have /ɗ/, predicting a total of 6. In fact, 17 of the languages that have /ɓ/ also have /ɗ/.

6 !Xũ and !Xóõ are described as having minimal contrasts between voiced and voiceless ejectives such as /dz'/ vs. /ts'/. The voiced ejectives are produced by first voicing and then glottalising the stop, and can be represented [dts'], etc., in a narrower transcription. Snyman (1970) and Traill (1985) treat these sounds as unit phonemes, rather than clusters. In !Xũ, at least, /dz'/ cannot be analysed as a cluster /dz+ʔ/ since /ʔ/ does not occur as an independent phoneme.

7 See also Kaye (1981) for a related proposal.

8 Bole-Richard describes this type of sound as follows (p. 330): 'articulation faible, pas d'élévation de la pression de l'air qui semble retenu au moment de la post-occlusion, donc pas d'aspiration ni d'affriction [*sic*]' (weak articulation, no increase in air pressure which seems held back at the moment of release, thus no aspiration or affrication).

9 Pharyngealisation, however, combines only with back vowels. Ladefoged and Maddieson (1996) view the combination 'breathy + pharyngealisation' as an independent articulatory type, which they term 'stridency'.

10 See, however, Hyman (1985, chapter 1) for a critical discussion of rhyme-based accounts of syllable weight.

11 The importance of quantity units in Ganda is further confirmed by a principle of drum accompaniment to songs and poems which counts moras (quantity units in the rhyme). According to this principle, each drum beat has the value of one mora, and a long syllable is given two drum beats; thus *kimuli* and *baana* have three beats, *bageenda* and *muyizzi* four.

12 This prediction does not hold, however, if *n̄d* is analysed as a 'contour segment' with internally sequenced features, a currently controversial issue. The terms 'edge effect' and 'anti-edge effect' are taken from Sagey (1990).

13 Similarly, the relatively rare CN clusters found in languages like Gwari and Ikwere often have a source in CVN sequences, at least historically.

14 In more recent work on !Xóõ, Traill has reported three further complexes.

15 This writer favours an intermediate view in which the uvular fricative component *x* of the accompaniments written *(k)x*, *kx'*, *gx*, and *gkx'*, and perhaps the laryngeal

components written *h*, ', are identified with the phonemes /χ/, /h/, /ʔ/, all of which occur independently in !Xóõ, while the other accompaniments are treated as phonologically simultaneous features of the click (see also Traill 1993). Once these components are segmented out, all remaining clicks except those with voiceless nasal accompaniments fall into the same manner of articulation series as non-click consonants.

Further reading

Fuller surveys of African language phonology can be found in Westermann and Ward (1933), Welmers (1973) and Creissels (1994). Bendor-Samuel (1989) includes surveys of Niger-Congo phonology. At a more advanced level, the collection edited by Goldsmith (1995) contains chapters on African tone systems (Odden, Newman), Ethiopian language phonology (Hudson), and Semitic phonology (Hoberman), as well as many other topics illustrated with African data. More specialised treatments of tone include Clements and Goldsmith (1984) and Hyman and Kisseberth (1998), both focusing on Bantu; Pulleyblank (1986), emphasising Nigerian languages; and Clark (1990), presenting a detailed study of Igbo. Hyman (1994) discusses morphological conditioning in the phonology of Bemba (Cibemba). Two classic studies of the syntactic conditioning of phonological rules are Selkirk (1986), discussing examples from Mwiini (Chi Mwiini) and Ewe, and Odden (1987), with examples from Matuumbi (Kimatuumbi).

General works on phonology and phonetics often contain substantial discussion of African languages. For introductions to contemporary phonological theory from the perspective of Africanists, see Pulleyblank (1989), Katamba (1989), and Paradis (1993). Hyman's classic textbook of phonology (1975b) introduces basic concepts from an early generative perspective. Halle and Clements (1983) contains an introductory essay and many data-based exercises. More advanced readings include Sagey (1990), Goldsmith (1990, 1995), and Kenstowicz (1994). Archangeli and Pulleyblank (1994) present an extended study of the feature [ATR], with many detailed phonological analyses. Ladefoged and Maddieson's comprehensive *Sounds of the World's Languages* (1996) presents a wealth of data on phonetic description with much attention to African languages.

7

Morphology

GERRIT J. DIMMENDAAL

7.1 **Basic concepts**

7.1.1 *Language types*

Amongst the commonly taught African languages at universities across the world is Swahili, a major language in terms of number of speakers. After some practice, a novice to the language may claim the following with some justification:[1]

(1) Swahili, Bantu, Niger-Congo[2]
     ni-me-ji-funza   *Ki-swahili*
     1SG-ANT-REFL-learn   CL7-Swahili
     'I have learned/taught myself Swahili.'

By then the apprentice will have learned that Swahili words can be decomposed into smaller meaningful elements. Such minimal signs composed of the unity of a constituent of form with a constituent of meaning are called morphemes. The interlinear glossing in the example above shows that there are different position classes or slots in Swahili, for example for a morpheme marking person (1SG), or completion of an action (the anterior marker -*me*-). Also, nouns in Swahili usually take a noun class marker. Nouns referring to language names take a marker *ki*- (compare also *Ki-ingereza* 'English'). This contrasts with 'Swahili person', *M-swahili* (singular), *Wa-swahili* (plural).

The sequential (or horizontal) domain of the utterance is generally referred to as the syntagmatic dimension. It contrasts with a paradigmatic (or vertical) axis, involving so-called relations *in absentia*. Instead of a first person singular, the speaker could have made reference to another person. By considering the entire paradigm (from the Greek term for 'pattern', *paradeigma*), that is the set of all the related forms, we get a clearer picture of position classes.[3]

(2)   Swahili, Bantu, Niger-Congo
       1SG   *ni-me-ji-funza*   'I have learned/taught myself' etc.
       2SG   *u-me-ji-funza*
       3SG   *a-me-ji-funza*
       1PL   *tu-me-ji-funza*
       2PL   *m-me-ji-funza*
       3PL   *wa-me-ji-funza*

It turns out that in Swahili the person marker always precedes the marker expressing information about the time at which the verbal action or process takes place. Further comparison with paradigms expressing a different 'tense', as it is commonly referred to in the study of Swahili and other Bantu languages, makes this clear. Compare the general present (or indefinite) forms:

(3)   1SG   *n-a-ji-funza*   'I learn/teach myself' etc.
       2SG   *w-a-ji-funza*
       3SG   *a-ji-funza*
       1PL   *tw-a-ji-funza*
       2PL   *mw-a-ji-funza*
       3PL   *w-a-ji-funza*

The first person singular marker in the general present is *n-*, rather than *ni-*. Since *ni-* and *n-* have identical meanings, we could try and account for their variant forms by looking at the environment in which they occur. Amongst the set of alternants with identical meaning, the form which cannot be predicted from the environment is to be taken as the more basic ('underlying') form. As it turns out, the person-marking form lacks a vowel whenever the following morpheme itself starts with a vowel, and so structurally it is in complementary distribution with *ni-*. Since the vowel quality in the latter element is unpredictable (compare, for example, the high back vowel in the case of the first person plural), we take *ni-* to be the basic form, and *n-* to be an allomorph of the first person singular marker. These examples also show that morphological analyses of languages usually involve a phonological (or more properly, morphophonological) component as well.

But things are not always that easy. If the novices had started out in another major language south of the Sahara, Hausa, their perspective on morphology as the study of word formation might have developed in a different direction. Compare the following paradigm from this Chadic language. (In these and other examples below, the following tone-marking convention is used: ′ for high tone, ` for low tone, and ⁻ for mid tone.)

(4) Hausa, Chadic, Afroasiatic

1SG	*náá kòòyí Háúsá*	'I (have) learned Hausa.'
2SG:M	*káá kòòyí Háúsá*	'You (have) learned Hausa.'
2SG:F	*kín kòòyí Háúsá*	'You (have) learned Hausa.'
3SG:M	*yáá kòòyí Háúsá*	'He (has) learned Hausa.'
3SG:F	*táá kòòyí Háúsá*	'She (has) learned Hausa.'
1PL	*mún kòòyí Háúsá*	'We (have) learned Hausa.'
2PL	*kún kòòyí Háúsá*	'You (pl) (have) learned Hausa.'
3PL	*sún kòòyí Háúsá*	'They (have) learned Hausa.'
4PL	*án kòòyí Háúsá*	'One (has) learned Hausa.'

Apparently, Hausa belongs to a different language type, where words cannot always be cut up into separate morphemes as easily as in Swahili. When providing utterances with an 'interlinear glossing' by separating morphemes with hyphens, this works quite well for a language like Swahili. But for a language like Hausa we see that single morphemes do not necessarily form the most useful basis for morphological analysis. First, it is not always easy to determine where the boundary or juncture between two morphemes lies. Second, whereas in the case of Swahili we could easily detect an anterior marker -*me*-, it is not immediately obvious from the Hausa paradigm above what the shape of the perfective marker is; is it -*aa*, -*in*, or -*n* maybe? Third, a particular morpheme may be an exponent of more than one meaning; by exponent we mean a marking expressing a property in a word. Since the segmentation into discrete morphemes is rendered difficult in Hausa, we have to find an alternative way of describing the various meanings, or sememes, involved. The element *taa* in the paradigm above is an exponent of gender (being a feminine, rather than a masculine form), number (singular, rather than plural), person (third, rather than first or second person), and aspect (perfective, i.e. a process that has been completed, contrasting with an imperfective and future-marking form). Since these meanings overlap in one unit, a so-called portmanteau morpheme, we are dealing with cumulative exponence. It is important, from a descriptive point of view, to represent such information in our interlinear glossing; the common way of doing this is by way of a colon.

(5) Hausa, Chadic, Afroasiatic

táá	*kòòyí*	*Háúsá*	'She has learned Hausa.'[4]
3SG:F:PERF	learn	Hausa	
tá-nàà	*kòòyó-n*	*Háúsá*	'She is learning Hausa.'
3SG:F:IMPF	learning-M:GEN	Hausa	

Fused exponence applies when a marker can be shown to result from the fusion
or (partly) phonological merger of two adjacent morphemes. This is commonly
represented by way of a dot between the interlinear glossings. This we find in the
Nilotic language Turkana, where the third person marker for past tenses *a-* fuses
with the high front vowel of one class of verbs.

(6)   Turkana, Nilotic, Nilo-Saharan (Dimmendaal 1983c: 120)
        à-ɲám   '(s)he has eaten (solid things)' (verb root *-ɲám*)
        3:PAST-eat
        èmúj   '(s)he has eaten (fluid things)' (verb root *-ìmúj*)
        3:PAST.eat

It is not always easy to distinguish cumulative from fused exponence synchronically; diachronically, such morphologically complex markers, for example
the commonly observed portmanteau markers combining gender, case, definiteness and number in Afroasiatic languages, may be interpreted as a way of
economising on morphological distinctions.

Another deviation from the one meaning-one form pattern or simple exponence
is that of extended exponence. As the following examples from Rundi show, this
Bantu language uses alternative forms to express one and the same tense (zero
marking, Ø) when the verb has a conjunctive meaning, versus *-r(a)-*, or *-da* (after
a nasal consonant), when the verb expresses a disjunctive meaning. The conjunctive helps to put 'en évidence le mot suivant' (Meeussen 1959: 109), whereas the
disjunctive expresses a 'forme sans rapport spécial avec un mot suivant éventuel'
(p. 109). The conjunctive marker itself involves a so-called 'suprasegmental' morpheme, namely a low tone on the verb root (as a result of which the root *-ààmùr-*
becomes *-ààmùr-*), whereas the disjunctive verb form involves either a high tone
on the verb root or its lexical tone.

(7)   Rundi, Bantu, Niger-Congo (Meeussen 1959: 119)
        n-ø-ààmùùrà   *ìntòrè*   'I am picking the prune.'
        1SG-IMPF:CONJ-pick:CONJ   prune

(8)   *n-d-áàmùùrà*   *ìntòrè*   'I am picking prunes.'
        1SG-IMPF:DISJ-pick:DISJ   prune

This distinction is well-attested in Bantu languages, but it may be much more
widespread in Niger-Congo, as pointed out by Creissels (see chapter 9 below). The
main exponent of disjunctive versus conjunctive meaning is to be found in the
tonal structure of the verb root, but it extends into and overlaps with tense marking in Rundi and other Bantu languages. Thus, even in languages which at first

sight appear to represent classic instances of a one-to-one exponence, as is true for Bantu in general, a closer investigation reveals that the relationship between form and meaning, that is between signans and signatum, can be many-to-many.

7.1.2   *Units of morph analysis*

The markers expressing a combination of person, number, aspect and mood, and preceding the verb 'learn' in the Hausa examples above, belong to a closed or finite set of functional morphemes. Content (or lexical) morphemes (for example, nominal or verbal roots) belong to open sets, that is they can be extended with ever more entries, for example through borrowing. In the case of Swahili, the functional morphemes are attached to the verbal root, that is they are bound morphemes. Since they precede the (verb) root, they are referred to as prefixes. Alternatively, languages may use suffixes or circumfixes, the latter involving a discontinuous grammatical construction consisting of a prefix and a suffix. This variation occurs in Atlantic languages to noun class affixation (data on Diola-Fogny from Sapir 1965; data on Fulfulde and Serer from Mukarovsky 1983).

(9)	Diola:	*a-jɔla*	'a Diola person'
	Fulfulde:	*gor-ko*	'person'
	Serer:	*o-kor-oxa*	'person'

As we saw above, languages may also use suprafixes (i.e., tonal or other suprasegmental markers). Alternatively, infixes may be used:

(10)	Hausa, Chadic, Afroasiatic (Newman 1990)
	gúlbíí / *gúl-àà-béé* 'stream (SG/PL)'
	wúríí / *wúr-àà-réé* 'place (SG/PL)'

According to Newman (1990: 38), 'internal *a*' in Hausa is derived historically from external suffixes.

In the case of the anterior in the Swahili examples above we saw that markers, for example subject-marking prefixes, with identical meanings, may be realised through slightly different forms, so-called allomorphs. Morphological analyses of undescribed languages usually start with an attempt to identify morphs, in the same way that a first analysis of their sound structures involves identification of phones (sounds). Both ultimately should lead to a structural analysis whereby systematic oppositions are investigated, including the question whether morphs are representations of one and the same morpheme, that is its allomorphs, parallel to phonemes and their allophones. But what if two (or more) functional morphemes are identical in form, and vary in meaning? How do we decide whether we are dealing with one form covering an array of related meanings, that is with poly-semy, or distinct meanings which happened to be expressed by way of the same form, that is with homonymy (or homophony)? This problem frequently occurs in Omotic and Cushitic languages where some plural nouns take the same inflectional suffix as singular feminine nouns, while other plural nouns take the same suffix as singular masculine nouns, a feature that has come to be known as gender syncretism or polarity. As rules of thumb, two general principles may be invoked for such analytical problems: relatedness of meaning; and relatedness of morphosyntactic function. Where two formally identical markers are diametrically opposed in meaning, for example one expressing a definite singular form, and the other an indefinite plural, they should be treated as separate morphemes.

When speaking of allomorphs, authors usually mean phonologically conditioned alternants of a particular morpheme, that is a unit with one and the same mean-ing. Allomorphs of one and the same morpheme may differ in their vowel qual-ity, consonant shape, tone, or a combination of these. Vowel harmony, for example commonly conditions the morphological variants of one and the same morpheme, as Clements shows in chapter 6 of this volume. Alternatively, languages may have morphological or lexically determined allomorphs. For example, abstract nouns in the Nilotic language Turkana are formed by way of a set of formally unrelated suffixal forms whose distribution depends on the canonical shape of the stative verb or adjectival root from which they are derived. (Vowels between parentheses are devoiced before pause.)

(11)   Turkana, Nilotic, Nilo-Saharan (Dimmendaal 1983c: 270–4)
       á-réŋ-ìs(í)   'redness'   (*-réŋ* 'be red')
       á-jɔ́k-ìs(í)   'kindness'   (*-jɔ́k* 'be kind, good')

       á-gógóŋ-(ù)   'strength'   (*-gógóŋ* 'be strong')
       á-bábár-(ù)   'saltiness'   (*-bábár* 'be salty')

       á-cúkúl-úl   'depth'   (*-cúkúl* 'be deep')
       á-ŋáráb-áb   'roughness'   (*-ŋáráb* 'be rough')

The distribution of such contrasting suffixes is predictable from the shape of the root to which they are added, even though their actual shapes cannot be pre-dicted from their phonological environment. The suffix *-ìs(ì)* is used after CVC roots, whereas $C_1V_1C_1V_1C$ roots take a suffix *-(ù)*. (The prefix *a-* is a feminine nominal gender marker; the vowels between parentheses are devoiced before pause.) The Turkana nouns for 'depth' and 'roughness' are formed through a repetition of part of the segments of the base form, in this case a root vowel and consonant, rather than through affixation of a morpheme. This process is known as (partial) reduplication. Reduplication is quite common cross-linguistically. Although its function or meaning may vary, there is also a widespread tendency to use reduplicative patterns 'for the expression of meanings that have something to do with the quantity of referents' (Moravcsik 1978: 330). The formal expression accordingly may be argued to be non-arbitrary or iconic.

Other languages use complete reduplication. Ewe is a language with a rich array of reduplicative processes.

(12) Ewe, Kwa, Niger-Congo (Ameka, 1999)
      sí   'to escape'   *sì-sí*   'escaping, escape'
      súbɔ́   'to worship' *sùbɔ́-súbɔ́*   'worshipping'

Ewe also has triplication; compare: *gbǎ* 'first'; *gbǎgbàágbǎ* 'the very first'. Reduplication in this Kwa language may even involve words operating as independent syntactic units otherwise, such as *ŋútsù*.

(13) *ŋútsù   gbɔ́   ŋútsǔ*   'emasculated man'
      man   vicinity man

The form *ŋútsǔ* involves a high tone suffix which combines with the low tone on the last syllable of the noun, yielding a rising tone (Ameka, 1999: 96). As further pointed out by Ameka (1999: 88), 'The vacillation in the mode of writing [as separate words or as one word; GJD] reflects the problem of the status of these forms.' This relates to a more common analytical problem. It is useful for Ewe and other languages to draw a distinction between phonological words and grammatical words in such cases. Whereas phonologically *ŋútsǔ* is still an independent unit, it has ceased to be an independent referent grammatically in that it can no longer be modified separately or referred to independently; instead, the newly formed (grammatical) word 'emasculated man' has acquired these properties.[5]

7.1.3 *Compounding*

Compounds, that is grammatical units involving two or more lexical roots, also tend to function as single words grammatically, even though they may contain forms otherwise functioning as independent words, as the word for 'tear-gas' in Hausa.

(14) Hausa, Chadic, Afroasiatic (Newman, in press)
      bàřkòònó-n   *tsóóhúwáá*   'tear-gas [lit. pepper of the old woman]'
      pepper-M:GEN   old woman

In compounds, the constituent members cannot be split up, and components such as 'pepper' cease to be referents to which one can refer independently (e.g.

by way of a demonstrative). But there is an additional, interesting semantic dimension to such morphologically complex forms. Whereas a literal reading ('(the) pepper of an old woman') is possible, this Hausa example also has a non-literal reading. The meaning of an expression is a function of the meaning of its parts and the way they are combined. It is the semantic unpredictability (specialisation) in this Hausa compound which needs to be learned or stored separately in the Hausa lexicon.

In a classic in linguistics, Bloomfield (1933) distinguished between endocentric and exocentric compounds. In the former type, it is the head of the compound which determines the categorial status (and other features like declension class or gender, if these occur). Thus, in the example from Banda-Linda below, the construction 'hair on head (head-hair)' refers to a kind of 'hair', which accordingly is the head of the construction passing on its category features to the entire word. Endocentric compounds usually are systematically head-final or head-initial in languages. Exocentric compounds on the other hand generally lack this formal property as well as semantic compositionality, because their meaning usually cannot be inferred from the meaning of their parts, and must be learned separately instead. As is common cross-linguistically, many names for plants and trees in Banda-Linda are exocentric.

(15)   Banda-Linda, Adamawa-Ubangian (Cloarec-Heiss 1986: 132–53)
        sù-kūmù   'hair on head'   *tū-mbʌ̀là*   'Culcasia n. gen. (botanical
        hair-head   ear-elephant   species)'

Apart from compounds with a lexical head and a modifier, there are co-ordinate (serial, appositional) compounds. This we find, for example, in Turkana adjectives such as *-ɲáɲá-rèŋan(ì)* 'orange (lit. yellow-red)'. Languages like Turkana are not particularly rich in compounding if one considers performance in face-to-face interactions. But in narrative discourse, for example in trickster tales, speakers make creative use of circumscriptions in order to refer to animal characters; for example, instead of *ékósòwán(ì)* 'buffalo' the following compound may be used in Turkana:

(16)   Turkana, Nilotic, Nilo-Saharan
        ló-dyó-ŋàráb   *à*   *èkúmè*   *ló*
        REL-bit-rough   of   nose:GEN   this
        'the somewhat rough-nosed one'

In (16) we have a so-called synthetic compound, containing a derived but not necessarily independently occurring member; compare also English 'left-hand-ed', an adjective whereby 'hand-ed' does not exist. In Turkana, the sequence 'rough of nose' only occurs in this kind of construction. This type of speaker's creativity is a poorly understood aspect of African languages. Also, unearthing word games and special purpose languages no doubt will further our understanding of the morphological structure of these languages.

Compounds may straddle the border between morphology and syntax, compare the following examples from Hausa and Chewa:

(17) Hausa, Chadic, Afroasiatic (Newman, in press)
háálí-n   *k̀ààk̀àà-ní-kàà-yí*
condition-M:GEN   how-1SG-RHET do
'dilemma, hard times [lit. a condition of how shall I act]'

(18) Chewa, Bantu, Niger-Congo (Bresnan and Mchombo 1995: 222)
à-mw-à-ndí-ón-èr-á   *pà-tì*
CL2-you-PERF-me-see-APPL-FI   CL16-where
'San people [lit. the where-did-you-see-me-from people]'

A common feature in particular of Cushitic languages is a construction involving a verbal base with some nominal complement (usually a bare root). This complex predicate construction, which is much more widespread cross-linguistically (see Mithun 1986; Aikhenvald, in press) has come to be known as noun incorporation. An example:

(19) Dullay, Cushitic, Afroasiatic (Sasse 1994)
an-wošo   *tayad'a*   'I am a field-guard, engaged in
VF:1SG-field   guard:IMPF:1SG   field-guarding.'

(20) *wošo*   *an-tayad'a*   'I guard a (particular) field.'
field   VF:1SG-guard:IMPF:1SG

Whether noun incorporation needs to be distinguished from compounding or not in a particular language depends on whether there are separate phonological or morphological rules involved.

When a linguistic phenomenon is extremely regular and productive, the most efficient way for the mind to deal with it is to store it as a rule of the grammar that can be implemented on-line in a rapid way. On the other hand, it appears that when the linguistic phenomenon contains a number of differing, non-productive patterns, the most efficient way for the mind to deal with it is to simply store the various forms and index their relationships to each other as part of the lexicon. Constructions may be 'lexicalised' because of their non-literal semantics. Avoidance of semantic computation is the main advantage of storage in the lexicon (as against parsing). Alternatively, retrieval from a memory system, the lexicon, is advantageous, because formally irregular alternations are involved. Formal rules governing genitive or nominal associative constructions may be complex but nevertheless regular, as they in fact are in many Niger-Congo languages. Compare, for example, the construction of compound nouns described by Bearth and Link (1980) for the Kru (Niger-Congo) language Wobe, which involves a series of complex tonal changes on the head noun. (Integers represent tone levels; note that the authors do not use interlinear glossing.)

(21)   Wobe, Kru, Niger-Congo (Bearth and Link 1980)
   kwlɔ⁴⁵   *gbe⁴⁵*   'village dog' (*gbe⁴³* 'dog')
   village   dog:GEN
   kwlɔ⁴⁵   *dei⁴⁻¹*   'village friend' (*dei²⁻¹* 'friend')
   village   friend:GEN

The establishment of a small set of formal rules in Wobe allows for the generation of an infinite set of new noun plus noun combinations. Accordingly, these associative constructions are regular, that is they can be produced 'on-line', and so there is no need to list all of these separately in the lexicon.

Associative (possessive, genitive) constructions of this type usually involve semantic subdivisions such as part-whole relations, kinship terminology, or body part nomenclature. Whether these need to be listed in the lexicon depends on their semantic and/or formal transparency. For an interesting account of this in 'Donko-ko, an Ubangian (Niger-Congo) language, see Pasch (1985).

Many African languages have a special construction expressing 'owner of' consisting of a possessor showing connections with a wide array of forms, for example 'chief', 'self', 'father', 'mother' plus the possessed item (in either order); thus, Eastern Luba *mfùmwá bàànà* 'one who has children' (*mfùmù* 'chief') (Meeussen 1975: 2).

7.1.4   *Inflection and derivation*

   In morphology, a distinction is usually drawn between compounding, inflection and derivation. Inflectional and derivational markers involve bound, functional morphemes with a partly different grammatical status. There are a number of tendencies – none of which are necessarily universally valid – that help us in determining whether a particular morpheme in a language is part of the derivational or inflectional system.

A major motivation of derivation consists in the adaptation of units to new syntactic functions. Accordingly, morphological operations involving a change in word class (category shift) typically are derivational in nature. Examples from Hausa:

(22) Hausa, Chadic, Afroasiatic
    Verb   Derived noun
    hàìfáá 'give birth'   *má-háif-áá* 'place of birth'
    búúɗèè 'open'   *má-búúɗ-íí* 'key'
    nóómàà 'farm'   *má-nòòm-íí* 'farmer'

Inflectional processes usually do not change word class. They also tend to be more regular and productive than derivation. In inflection, difference in meaning between basic and the morphologically complex forms is usually predictable, in derivation only partially so. One of the rare instances of inflection involving transposition, that is category change without a functional change, is found with so-called primary verbal nouns in Hausa, which are used to express imperfective aspect with one class of (transitive) verbs.

(23) Hausa, Chadic, Afroasiatic
    yáá   *hàřbí*   *bàrééwáá*   'He shot a gazelle.'
    3SG:M-PERF   shoot   gazelle
    yá-nàà   *hàřbá-ř*   *bàrééwáá*
    3SG:M-IMPF   shooting:PVN-GEN   gazelle
    'He is shooting a gazelle.'

Derivational markers frequently form the inner layer of word formation, and inflectional markers tend to appear on the outside of derivational markers. (See also Aikhenvald, in press, for further examples.) This we see in Swahili, where derivational suffixes precede the so-called inflectional 'final' vowel of verbs:

(24) Swahili, Bantu, Niger-Congo
    -som-a   'read, study'
    read-FI
    -som-ek-a   'be decipherable'
    teach-NE-FI
    -som-esh-a   'teach, send to school'
    teach-CAUS-FI

Prototypical inflectional properties of nouns are the marking of case, definiteness, gender or number. For Indo-European languages, the expression of degree in adjectives (e.g. *thick*, *thick-er*, *thick-est*) tends to be part of their inflectional morphology. Unlike these Indo-European languages, many African languages have only few adjectives, that is a syntactic category formally distinct from nouns or verbs, and expressing property concepts ('bald', 'old', 'beautiful'). In most African languages, such concepts tend to take the shape of nouns or verbs. Compare Hausa:

(25)   Hausa, Chadic, Afroasiatic

　　　tá-nàà　　　*dà*　　*k̃ář̃fíí*　　'She is strong.'

　　　3SG:F-IMPF　with　strength

　　　táá　　　*fí*　　　*Múúsá*　*k̃ář̃fíí*

　　　3SG:PERF　surpass　Musa　strength

　　　'She is stronger than Musa.'

Possibly as a corollary of the fact that they have few adjectives as a separate syntactic category, many African languages tend to express comparatives by way of a verb 'surpass' rather than by way of a separate inflectional category (parallel to 'she eats more than I do' = 'she eats surpasses me').

Inflectional properties of verbs include the marking of tense, aspect, mood or modality, voice (diathesis), polarity (negation marking), person and number. They are typically syntactically driven word formations. Person and number marking in the verb paradigms shown above, for example, are obligatory, otherwise ungrammatical constructions would occur. Such cross-reference marking or co-indexing on verbs for pronominal subject (and object) including accumulation of the person-number categories ('we inclusive/exclusive', 'dual' and 'trial') is common in African languages (see the studies in Wiesemann 1986). In the Khoisan language Nama, for example, a series of pronominal markers occurs whose form depends on person (first, second, third), number (singular, dual, plural), gender (masculine, feminine, common), as well as on the various syntactic contexts in which these forms occur (Haacke 1977). Across Nilo-Saharan one finds languages marking pronominal subject as well as object on the verb, often in a fused form. Occasionally, this type of cross-reference marking on verbs results in the non-distinctness of forms as a result of phonological processes, as in Maasai. By adding independent (subject and/or) object pronouns, the degree of ambiguity can be reduced.

(26)   Maasai, Nilo-Saharan (Tucker and Mpaayei 1955: 201)

　　　kí-dɔ́l　　　　*'nánʊ́*　　　'you see *me*'

　　　2SG>1SG-see　me:ABS

　　　kí-dɔ́l　　　　*nínyè*　　　'*(s)he* sees you'

　　　3SG>2SG-see　(s)he:NOM

This type of (formal) neutralisation is to be distinguished from syncretism (or inflectional homonymy), which involves neutralisation of one or more inflectional features, simply because they are not expressed. In Swahili, there is a distinction for example between an anterior verb form (marked with -*me*-) and a past tense (marked with -*li*-) in the affirmative. When one negates these verb forms, the two types merge for many speakers, that is there is inflectional homonymy (although an alternative form *sijajifunza Kiswahili*, 'I have not learned Swahili yet' is used in many contexts).

(27)   Swahili, Bantu, Niger-Congo
       nimejifunza Kiswahili   'I have learned swahili.'
       nilijifunza Kiswahili   'I learned Swahili.'
       sikujifunza Kiwahili   'I haven't learned/didn't learn Swahili.'

Finding the productive rules of inflectional and derivational word formation in a language is not always an easy descriptive task, particularly in languages with opulent morphologies. Sometimes the investigator has to go through hundreds of forms to find out about regular versus irregular alternations. Moreover, it may not always be possible to identify basic versus non-basic forms. Two or more forms may be equally complex, requiring replacement of morphemes. This is common with descriptive kinship terminology, as in Turkana (Nilo-Saharan) *lò-káàtó* 'brother', *nà-káàtó* 'sister'. The direction of the derivational change may not be immediately obvious, because languages sometimes employ zero derivation (conversion), that is change in syntactic class or category without any formal modification. This phenomenon is common in English, where numerous nouns may also be used as verbs, for example '(to) cow', '(to) cream'.

Generally speaking, it is useful to distinguish between derivation and inflection as morphological processes, in spite of occasional difficulties in determining whether a particular morphological property is part of the derivational or inflectional system of a language.[6] Some linguists have gone as far as to argue that inflection and derivation constitute separate subcomponents of grammar with minimal interaction (cf. Booij 1996 for a discussion). Unless we get to know more about the storage of inflectional and derivational features in the brain of speakers, however, this quest for compartmentalisation of these morphological components remains little more than a metaphor. At the same time, historical-comparative research has revealed that a derivational marker in one language may have a status as an inflectional marker in a related language and vice versa. In other words, whatever their psycholinguistic status is, it is obvious that the two components interact, and that morphological properties may be reallocated or reinterpreted. For example, Eastern Nilotic languages distinguish between masculine and feminine gender (as well as neuter gender in the Teso-Turkana group within this branch of Nilotic) as an obligatory inflectional category of the noun. Southern and Western Nilotic languages on the other hand, have gender marking as a derivational category for certain nouns (in particular those referring to names of animals) as well as for personal names. Compare the Lango names *ò-cén* (masculine) / *à-cén* (feminine) 'second of twins' (from *cén* 'behind, back') (Noonan 1992: 77). This pattern for naming also exists in Eastern Nilotic languages such as Maasai, but here the masculine–feminine distinction is an obligatory inflectional property of virtually all nouns (see also Payne 1996). Accordingly, there must be historical processes leading to the reinterpretation of their respective morphological status. These phenomena do not invalidate the distinction, but rather force us to look for mechanisms that can help explain reinterpretation of the grammatical status. How and why such reinterpretations of derivation as inflection or vice versa take place is not known.

A related question is that of inflectional or derivational obsolescence. Although the historical 'dynamics' behind this is little understood, there appear to be at least two factors involved. When morphemes enter into a collocation, they may influence each other not only formally, but also semantically. This semantic specialisation potentially increases with the frequency of usage or productivity of a morpheme; the result may be loss of semantic transparency. Compare causative marking by way of tonal modification in Ngiti:

(28)   Ngiti, Central Sudanic, Nilo-Saharan (Kutsch Lojenga 1994: 298)
        īmɔ̀tā 'to be soaked in water (of cassava)'
        īmɔ̀tá 'to soak (something) in water'

Another cause of loss of productivity and, eventually, obsolescence, may be formal neutralisation of basic and derived forms. In the following example, the derived causative in Ngiti (involving tonal modification) is not or no longer formally distinct from the root form from which it is derived:

(29)   *īkɔ̀tá* 'to be pierced'   *īkɔ̀tá* 'to pierce'

Complex alternations in verb morphology are common in many Nilo-Saharan languages (compare, for example, Novelli 1985 on the Nilotic language Karimojong). The presence of such complex systems with (potentially) thousands of verb forms, raises the question to what extent acquiring such a language involves memorisation versus on-line production by applying a rule-based approach.

Suppletion – the use of two or more quite different shapes within the same paradigm – constitutes an extreme case of lexical irregularity; it is often found with high frequency words, as in Hausa *àkwíyàà* (SG)/*áwáákíí* (PL) 'goat'. There may be a number of reasons for this: high frequency words may be subject to sporadic sound changes; in addition, when they constitute basic vocabulary, the alternation may be acquired at an early age through memorisation, rather than being rule-based. An exhaustive listing of exceptions and irregularities next to productive systems is crucial for historical/comparative purposes, since the former commonly represent the more archaic features. Also, in the case of verb paradigms, negative and verb forms in dependent clauses tend to conserve a more archaic structure, which is less rule-bound than those in main clauses as a consequence of communicative dynamism. Usually, however, the regular verb paradigms can be grouped together in a macroparadigm, with a set of rules and hierarchical relations between the various paradigms. Many African languages also have a separate set of verb forms used in consecutive constructions (see chapter 8 below). Ordering of paradigms is similar to ordering of sound systems. For example, when the segments *s* and *m* occur in a language, they usually constitute different structural units (*sic*). But it is at least as interesting to know with which segments they form a pattern, that is whether either *s* or *m* share features, or are in systematic opposition with other structural units in the language. Verb paradigms deserve a similar approach in grammatical descriptions. (See Dimmendaal 1991 for some suggestions.)

Frequently, one member in a morphological paradigm is not marked, or, phrased differently, marked by way of a 'zero' morph, for example the third person, as against first and second person, in a verbal paradigm. Also, cross-linguistically imperative (as against indicative mood) verb forms tend to be stripped of inflectional properties such as tense or person marking, at least in the singular. As in phonological systems, certain oppositions may be privative, that is there is an unmarked member and a marked (morphologically more complex) form. For a survey of principled exceptions to general markedness conventions in languages, see Koch (1995).

7.1.5   ***Morphological typology***

As we saw above, languages may employ different strategies to express conceptual relations; they may use separate words, affixation, internal modification (e.g. through tone), reduplication or compounding. Occasionally, metathesis comes in as part of an inflectional or derivational process. This can be observed sometimes with imperfective versus perfective verb forms in Nilo-Saharan languages; compare imperfective *eŋet*, perfective *teŋ* 'ask' in Me'en, a Surmic language spoken in Ethiopia (Will 1998).

Whereas languages like Swahili make extensive use of deriving one verb from another and less extensive use of compounding, a language such as Ewe lacks verbal derivation, and fully exploits compounding. Students of language have been aware of such typological differences between languages at least since the beginning of the nineteenth century. 'Language type' in those days of necessity referred to 'morphological type', since neither syntax nor phonology in the modern sense had come to be established in the nineteenth century. Languages were assumed to be isolating (e.g. Chinese), agglutinating (e.g. Turkish), or inflectional (e.g. Latin or Greek).

Edward Sapir, a leading linguist of the twentieth century and eminent specialist of American Indian languages, tried to rid these concepts of their valuative and evolutionary connotations. His view, still adhered to today, is that language change is a cyclic process; languages may develop bound morphemes, which in due course become eroded, after which independent morphemes may develop again; alternatively, reinterpretation of existing systems may take place within relatively short time spans (Heath 1997).

Sapir (1921) proposed to replace the older morphological concepts with a number of logically independent classificatory parameters: (1) the number of morphemes per word, and (2) the degree of phonological alteration of morphemes in combination. As stated by Sapir, languages may be characterised as belonging to the analytic, synthetic or polysynthetic type, in an ascending order of complexity based on the number of morphemes per word. By investigating the degree of alteration of morphemes, languages may be called isolating, agglutinative, fusional or symbolic. Agglutinative languages such as Swahili have a high degree of synthesis, that is ratio of number of morphemes per word. The degree of synthesis is highest for so-called polysynthetic languages. Compare the following example from Siberian Yupik with the corresponding English translation:

> (30)   Siberian Yupik (Comrie 1981: 42)
> *angya-ghlla-ng-yug-tuq*
> boat-AUGM-acquire-DES-3SG
> 'He wants to acquire a big boat.'

In polysynthetic structures, several roots and affixes are combined into a single (phonological) word, sometimes corresponding to a whole sentence in English, although major syntactic boundaries such as that between the nominal agent of a transitive verb tend to be expressed in a separate word from the verb and its complements. Polysynthetic structures appear to be common in American Indian languages, as well as Australian, Paleo-Siberian and Papuan languages, but not in African languages.

Because many African languages use internal morphology (especially tone) as the sole marker of grammatical relations, they are easily mistaken for isolating languages. An elegant illustration of this pitfall is given by Andersen (1992–4), who shows how the Nilotic language Dinka, traditionally assumed to be an isolating language, actually has a rather elaborate system of 'vertical' morphology, expressed by (combinations of) tonal, vocalic and consonantal modifications. This only becomes obvious from a comparison of paradigms. Compare:

(31) Dinka, Nilotic, Nilo-Saharan (Andersen 1992–4)
      à̠-wɛ̠́ɛ̠́c   'you are kicking it hither'
      D-kick:CP:2SG

      à̠-wɛ̠̀ɛ̠̀-c   '(s)he is kicking it hither'
      D-kick:CP:3SG

      à̠-wɛ̠́ɛ̠́c   '(s)he is kicking'
      D-kick:AP

Greenberg, also renowned for his important contribution to African linguistics, elaborated upon Sapir's typology. Greenberg's (1954) quantitative index allows languages to be ranked on some parameter (relative to other languages) rather than being classified into discrete types. By comparing features on a quantitative scale instead of the whole language (as Sapir did), one can measure the degree of development of each feature by a numerial index. For example, the degree of synthesis or gross complexity of the word (based on the ratio morpheme/word) is 2.55 for Swahili, 1.68 for English, and 3.72 for Inuit (Eskimo), according to Greenberg (1954: 193). The ratio of agglutinative constructions to morph juncture (morpheme boundaries) is the index of agglutination; a language with a high value for this index will be agglutinational, a language with a low value, fusional. Similarly, the number of root morphemes per word (compounding), or the proportion of derivational or inflectional morphemes to a word could be calculated. Also, the ratio of prefixes and suffixes can be established, alternative strategies being rare in Greenberg's sample languages.[7] Languages employ different techniques for relating words to each other, for example inflectional morphemes without concord ('pure inflection'), concord (agreement), or a combination of these, and constituent order. All languages presumably have ways of indicating grammatical relations, for example by using juxtaposition of elements. Alternatively, or in addition to that, languages such as Swahili use relational (agreement or concord) markers (see chapter 8 below). Accordingly, Swahili would be referred to as an agglutinative, concordial language in Greenberg's terms.

Languages as wholes tend to involve greater or lesser mixtures of different sorts of strategies. Hausa morphology is characterised by affixation with and without fusion, as well as suprasegmental processes, for example tonal inflection, as we saw earlier. Accordingly, Sapir might have characterised this Chadic language as fusional-agglutinative, with a symbolic tinge.

A technique, which has come to be known as non-concatenative morphology (also referred to as non-agglutinative morphology), is commonly found in Semitic and other Afroasiatic languages. A student of Classical Arabic may be brave and claim: *darastu alʕarabiyya(tu)* 'I have learned/studied Arabic.' When changing these into imperfective forms, one notices that a portion of the morphological material precedes the root and another portion is incorporated or contained in the root (with the three 'radicals' *drs*): *adrusu al ʕarabiyya(tu)*, 'I am studying Arabic'. This is different from English alternations such as *take/took*, since the latter are non-recurrent; it therefore is not useful to speak of infixes in English.

There is a problem in visualising the processes or alternations involving partly discontinuous morphemes in languages like Arabic. Following an influential study by McCarthy (1981) on Classical Arabic verb morphology, it has become fashionable to represent such non-affixal morphemes on separate tiers. In this approach towards morphology, morphemic units (e.g. vocalic and consonantal 'melodies') are segregated on separate, autosegmental tiers (or planes); these are mapped onto so-called prosodic templates or CV skeletons; these templates carry the grammatical meaning, for example of roots (CVCVC) or causative stems (CVCCVC).

This model has been extended towards other prosodic phenomena such as reduplication by McCarthy (1981: 407ff). Historically, this approach to problems of root and pattern morphology grew out of autosegmental approaches to tone and other prosodic features (see chapter 6 above).

Whereas there is tremendous variation morphologically between African languages, areal types usually cutting across genetic boundaries, tonal changes as exponents of some inflectional or derivational process are widespread; compare Wolff (1983) on the Chadic (Afroasiatic) language Lamang, Haacke (1998) on the Khoisan language Khoekhoe, Hutchison (1981) on the Nilo-Saharan language Kanuri, or Ikoro (1996) on the Niger-Congo language Kana.

Linguists, like other human beings, like to think in metaphors as we saw above in the discussion of non-concatenative morphology, because 'they are good to think with'. Let us look upon morphology, then, as a theory of house-building. When travelling across Africa, one may observe different architectural traditions. In some areas, one first sets up the skeletal frame (including the overarching roof construction), and then starts to fill up the intermediate space. Whereas with some homes, the building blocks (bricks, stones or other construction materials) may still be visible after completion (e.g. the agglutinative type), others (e.g. the fusional type) have plastered walls. And, to extend our metaphor of the housing to the notion of compounds (as units with more than one major building), some languages have them and treasure them, others do quite well without.

The housing, whatever shape or structure it takes, contains a storage area, a lexicon consisting of a list of lexemes, as Matthews (1974) has called them, and a set of rules expressing systematic relations between them. The concept of 'lexeme' refers to abstract 'vocabulary words'. They are the fundamental elements in the lexicon of a language (sometimes written in capitals). For Swahili verbs this would coincide with the basic root plus final marker *-a*, as in -SOMA, 'read, study'. For Arabic, it is common to use the third person masculine singular past (perfective) verb form (e.g. KATABA 'read, study').

A lexeme may also need to be represented with two entries, as with perfective versus imperfective verb roots in the Nilo-Saharan language Me'en: *am* (perfective), *us* (imperfective) 'eat', or *mat* (perfective), *ir* (imperfective) 'drink' (data from Will 1998: 457); suppletive or partly irregular perfective/imperfective alternations are common in Nilo-Saharan languages. A lexeme may also consist of syntactically discontinuous elements. Alternatively, a complex lexeme may consist of a sequence of two verbs (not necessarily contiguous to each other), reflecting an idiomatic collocation, as with certain serial verb constructions in West African Niger-Congo languages.

7.1.6 *Phonological and grammatical words*

The concept of 'word' is needed regardless of the morphological type to which a particular language belongs, and so from a cross-linguistical perspective the most fruitful way of studying morphology is by taking the word as a key notion or sign. The psycholinguistic reality of the notion of the word becomes evident, for example, when looking at the orthography used for different languages. How and why did those developing orthographies for Swahili and Hausa decide to write a four-word utterance in English such as 'I have learned Swahili', with two words in Swahili, and with three in Hausa (both in the Arabic and the Roman orthographic tradition)? In other words, how did those developing these orthographies decide whether one is dealing with one or two words? Obviously, this would not have been possible without a concept of what constitutes a word psychologically. Traditionally, a number of formal and semantic criteria are invoked in establishing the bound or free status of morphemes. For example: can a particular element occur on its own, or does it always require the presence of another marker? Can it be followed by pause? Does the element have a fixed position with respect to other clausal elements? Can it be separated from those elements? Is permutation possible? Can other elements intervene (and does the whole then operate as a new word)? Does the constituent operate as a unit of reference, that is is there cohesiveness? Does it constitute a prosodic unit (in terms of intonation or tone)?

Whereas phonological and grammatical words tend to coincide, this is not always the case. As we saw above, potential mismatches between these notions may apply with reduplication and compounding, since these potentially involve elements which also can occur as independent words. Alternatively, conundrums concerning the definition of wordhood frequently centre around clitics, as data from Swahili help to illustrate. In Swahili, words usually receive stress or prominence on the penultimate vowel, as in *ku-íta* 'to call'. When deriving a verb stem from a basic root in Swahili, for example by adding an Applicative suffix *-i-*, one observes how stress automatically shifts: *ku-it-í-a* 'to call for'. Now compare the following examples (data from the author):

(32) *wa-li-ni-it-i-a*   'They called me.'
3PL:SU-PA-1SG:OB-call-APPL-FI

(33) *wa-li-ni-it-i-á-ni*
3PL:SU-PA-1SG:OB-call-APPL-FI-what
'What were they calling me for?'

The morpheme *-ni* also occurs as a longer form with its own penultimate stress, that is as a phonologically and grammatically independent word *níni* 'what'. Because the element *ni* is prosodically deficient in the clause above, we may refer to this phonologically bound element as a 'simple clitic', which becomes anchored to a host (usually a major lexical category). Clitics are (typically, though not uniquely, functional) elements requiring a host or anchor for prosodic reasons. Their bound status becomes clear from their phonological interaction with an adjacent word. When attached to a preceding (grammatical) word, they are called 'enclitics'; when anchored onto a following word, they are 'proclitics'. Another example is the use of the short form of the third-person plural pronoun in Hausa in combination with a proper name, as in *su-Audu* 'Audu cum suis, Audu and his companions'; this phenomenon, sometimes called 'totalisation', is common across Africa (see also Meeussen 1975: 4).

'Simple clitics' are sometimes contrasted with 'special clitics' or 'phrasal affixes', elements which are always attached to a host. Postpositions, conjunctions or negation markers frequently belong in this category as prosodically deficient markers which become syntactically attached to a major category such as a noun phrase or verb phrase. (See also Anderson 1992: *passim*.) Alternatively, both morphemes may belong to a closed set, that is both may be function morphemes, together forming a phonological word or clitic group. This is common, for example, in languages where subject pronouns and markers for tense, aspect, and mood tend to cluster in prosodic units, as in the Hausa examples above.

As argued by Creissels (see chapter 9 below), pronominal subject markers in various West African languages are probably bound, rather than free, morphemes. Their status either as affixes or clitics thus needs further investigation. This obviously has consequences for the morphological typology of these languages.

7.1.7 **The lexicon**

A central task in the description of morphological systems is the identification of productive, as against semi-productive and unproductive, alternations. Productive word formation processes are regular in terms of form. What is more important, since unproductive alternations may also be regular, is the readiness with which an element enters into new combinations. A productive marker often applies to larger sets of words, and is available for the creation of new forms. One test case for productivity would be, for example, whether a particular inflectional or derivational marker can be applied to recent borrowings in a language. The formation of new words is constrained by existing words in the lexicon. Usually, one has to be specific about the environment, subject to semantic restrictions, and so productivity comes in degrees. A related aspect is that of creativity. Obviously, one has to respect what is in store, that is in the lexicon, when coining new words, otherwise such innovations will be pre-empted by the conventional terms in the language.

Applying productive rules of word formation is but one of several methods of vocabulary extension. The Hausa word for 'reactionary person/ideology', *kòòmàà bááyá* (lit. 'return back') is an exocentric compound, consisting of a verb plus (adverbial) complement, which was created by analogy with an existing and highly common pattern of exocentric compound formation in the language.

(34) Hausa, Chadic, Afroasiatic (McIntyre 1995)
      bùgà zààbíí   'short-toed eagle'
      beat guineafowl
      gààgàrà báámíí 'tongue twister'
      defy novice

Borrowing, including the formation of calques (loan translations), is another technique. Heavy borrowing may affect the existing inflectional and derivational system of a language, as is true for many Germanic languages which borrowed extensively from Latin and Greek. Such external influence on the morphological structure is not uncommon in Africa, where multilingualism constitutes the norm rather than the exception. Elwana, a Kenyan Bantu language closely related to Swahili, has borrowed heavily from a neighbouring Cushitic language, Orma (Nurse 1999); apart from the more common Bantu noun-class prefixes, there are numerous suffixal pairings for plural in this language, as in Orma and other Cushitic languages.

New words may also be coined through processes such as clipping ('lab' from 'laboratory'), the formation of acronyms (PET study, instead of Positron Emission Tomographic study), folk etymology ('sparrow grass' instead of 'asparagus'), back formation (by deleting material from existing words, 'sulk' from 'sulky', by analogy with 'bulk' and 'bulky') and blending ('stash' from 'stop' plus 'dash'). To what extent these word-formation processes play a role in African languages is not known.

The lexicon is sometimes contrasted with grammar (or syntax). There is, however, no principled reason why phrases or sentences could not be stored in a lexicon; on the contrary, they probably are. The lexicon may also involve potentially complex structures and relations, not only because of the type of derivational, inflectional and compounding rules discussed above (involving phrasal elements), but also because of idiomatic expressions one has to learn in primary as well as in secondary language acquisition. When studying Ewe, Hausa or Swahili, one also learns about utterances that are grammatically correct but not idiomatic. 'This is not the way to say such-and-such in this language', is a frequently heard comment, as second-language learners will confirm.

Knowledge of a body of institutionalised or 'lexicalised' utterances, including syntactic idioms, is part of the competence of native speakers. This implies that the distinction between the lexicon and grammar of a language is scalar, rather than binary. Memorised sequences, characterised by formal or semantic irregularity, thus may include complete clauses and sentences.

7.1.8   ***Beyond the morpheme***

Any language is the result of an historical development, consequently it may contain the remains of an earlier productive system of alternations. Across Niger-Congo, for example, there are languages that have abandoned the productive system of singular/plural alternations of nominal class affixes. Petrified noun-class affixes no longer provide a detectable independent contribution to meaning in these languages, except maybe in nouns derived from verbs or some other major category. Alternatively, one may find meaningless morphs in verbal systems. For example, Bynon-Polak (1975: 150–151) has shown that in the Bantu language Shi there are roots plus meaningless, formal extensions; these need to be distinguished on a purely formal basis into a root and a formal suffix or expansion, since they deviate from the common -CV(V)C root pattern in the language, Some of these expansions (e.g., *-ik-, -id-, -uk-*) are morphologically identical to actual suffixes, others (e.g., *-um-, -in-, -ut-*) have no parallel among the recurrent derivational suffixes of Shi.

(35)   Shi, Bantu, Niger-Congo (Bynon-Polak 1975: 150f)
         -súnìk-   'push' (* *-sun-* not attested)
         -pásh-ìk-   'be possible' (*-pash-* 'be able'; *-ik-* neutro-passive)

Apart from such 'empty morphs', there are other lexical quirks which play a role in morphology, but which cannot be identified with morphemes *per se*. These sound-symbolic elements, sometimes called 'phonaesthemes', occupy a position intermediate between the morpheme and the phoneme. The sound symbolism is usually discovered, not by paradigmatic contrast, but rather by recurrent association of meaning for example with particular consonants, clusters or vowel type. In the Nilotic language Alur, the voiced velar implosive gɓ is relatively rare, except in ideophonic words.

(36)   Alur, Nilotic, Nilo-Saharan (Ukoko *et al.* 1964)
        ɓlέ   'deeply'   ɓlɔ́ɓlɔ̀   'stealthily, negligently'

(37)   gɓě   'imitates the thud of a heavy body falling over backwards'
        gɓàk   'till, at the terminus'
        gɓiá   'imitates the gliding of feet on the slippery roads after rain'

The basic linguistic assumption that the relationship between sound and meaning in languages is arbitrary does not apply to such words; their aberrant phonotactics are motivated instead. The restricted distribution (markedness) of these segments is exploited in the language in order to mark a particular class of words expressing sensorial experiences. Variation in tone as well as pharynx size (ATR harmony) is also used sometimes for sound symbolic reasons (see also Hinton, Nichols, and Ohala 1994).

Compare also examples from Nembe, where the underscoring in the second example expresses [-ATR] vowels.

(38)   Nembe, Ijoid, Niger-Congo (Madugu 1988)
        kágùlúù   'twisted, rugged'
        kágu̱lu̱ù   'twisted, rugged (but of smaller object)'

If we continue to assume that word structure is essentially agglutinative with a disposition towards the morpheme as the core notion, and if we were to apply such an analysis to Hausa, for example, we would need rather abstract underlying forms and processes or rules. Such an approach towards morphological structure has come to be known as the Item and Process approach (Hockett 1958), whereby 'item' refers to 'morpheme'. This tradition contrasts with a morpheme-based concept of morphology in which statements about morphophonemic processes are avoided, an approach referred to by Hockett as the Item and Arrangement theory. When considering the various complicating factors discussed above, all of which appear to be part and parcel of human language, a word-based model of morphology indeed appears to be an attractive alternative.

As we saw earlier, many-to-one and one-to-many links between form and function or meaning seriously complicate strategies for decomposing words into their component morphemes. Accordingly, one may assume that useful statements can be made only at the word level, an approach that has come to be known as the Word and Paradigm model (Hockett 1958, Robins 1959).

7.2   Some issues in the descriptive and theoretical study of African languages

7.2.1   *Syntactic typology and morphological type*

Modern technology allows us to do advanced psycholinguistic research by using PET scans in order to investigate the storing and computation as well as parsing of morphological structures. No doubt these techniques will be applied in the near future in the investigation of African languages whose morphological structures are already reasonably well understood. But there still remains a wide variety of more basic analytical problems facing the Africanist with an interest in morphology. First and above all, there is a considerable amount of elementary descriptive work still to be done, in particular on Khoisan languages, but also for various languages in other families; this empirical issue should therefore receive highest priority. It requires the serendipity of the analyst and a (not necessarily electronic) notebook.

Such widening of our understanding should build on the conventional wisdom emerging from previous scholarship on these African languages and families, with an open mind for phenomena hitherto unaccounted for, and without trying to force newly discovered structures into existing models or conceptualisations. Also, the parameters of typology help us to identify groups of correlated properties that co-vary with one another, as shown by Creissels elsewhere in this volume (chapter 9). The present section elaborates upon the morphological dimension of this inductive method.

Languages may differ considerably, also in their morphological typology. These differences may result from distinct genetic ancestries, from areal contact with different languages, or from independent historical changes. On the other hand, languages may be typologically similar due to chance or areal contact resulting in the borrowing of structures. But we now know that these factors are not quite enough to explain typological differences or similarities between languages. Let us survey a number of such non-accidental clusterings of features.

As observed by Masica (1976) in his typological survey of South Asia, languages in this area share amongst others a verb-final syntax, but also the use of converbs and so-called verbal root compounding. The same clustering of properties is found in East African and Central African Nilo-Saharan languages, in Afroasiatic as well as Central Khoisan, all with a verb-final syntax. Compare the Omotic (Afroasiatic) language Maale, where converbs in adjoined (dependent) clauses share the agent role with the agent of the main clause, but lack inflection of tense, person or number, unlike the main verb ('load' in the example below).

(39) Maale, Omotic, Afroasiatic (Azeb Amha, in press)
ʔízí   mís-'ó   tík '-í   màkìin-àà   c 'ààn-é-nè
3SG:M:NOMtree-ACC cut-CV car-LOC   load-PERF-DECL
'He cut the tree and loaded it on a car.'

Root compounding is also common in Omotic languages such as Maale:

(40) èkk-í mùkk-   'bring' (èkk- 'take'; mùkk- 'come')
take-CV come

Alternatively, root compounding appears to be a natural outcome in languages employing verb serialisation. (See also Durie 1997 for a cross-linguistic survey.) The latter type of complex predicate formation is common in West African languages mainly belonging to Kwa, western Benue-Congo and Ijoid (Lord 1993).

(41) Igbo, Benue-Congo, Niger-Congo (Lord 1975)
tí-wá   'shatter (tr)'   tí   'hit, beat'   wá   'split open (intr)'
fù-nyú 'blow out'   fù   'blow'   nyú 'be off'

Since one of the two juxtaposed verb roots is selected from a small set, usually expressing an aspectual (resultative) or directional meaning, one could argue that there is a head-modifier relation involved in these examples.

7.2.2 *Iconicity and its limits*

Cross-linguistically, there is constructional or diagrammatic iconicity in that elements that function together tend to occur together, also at the morphological level. This observation has been formulated into a general principle of relevance by Bybee (1985). Lexical or grammatical independence of a marker often reflects the conceptual independence of that entity. The relevance order tends to be mirrored in the position of function morphemes relative to lexical roots cross-linguistically. For example, because the temporal or aspectual categories are highly relevant to verbal acts or processes, these inflectional categories are often expressed as bound morphemes on the verb. The diminution of their conceptual distance usually correlates with their closeness. It in turn may be reflected in morphophonemic alternation, even in languages that are otherwise agglutinating. This can be seen in the fusional process between verbal roots and perfective markers, known as 'imbrication' in Bantu studies (cf. Bastin 1983).

Other principles occasionally override the iconicity principle. This may be illustrated with examples from the Bantu language Rundi, which has an extremely rich morphological system, for example an extensive system of verbal derivation by way of suffixation. The reciprocal formation (*-an-*) requires a verb to be transitive; this function is performed, if the basis is not transitive already, by a causative suffix *-ị-* ('get wet (intransitive)' ->'cause to get wet/wet (transitive)'). This derivational order, however, is not reflected in the sequential order. Verbal suffixes consisting of a single vowel in Rundi tend to appear after other types of derivational suffixes (e.g. -VC- types).

(43)   Rundi, Bantu, Niger-Congo (Meeussen 1959: 57–60)
    -tsàp-   'get wet'
    -tsàp-ị-   'wet something'
    -tsàp-àn-ị- 'wet each other'

Such exceptions to the general principle of constructional (diagrammatic) iconicity appear to be relatively rare.

The notion of relevance has been developed into a more general system of dependency by Aikhenvald and Dixon (1998). Grammatical systems may operate independently of each other. Alternatively, the choice of one category depends on another, for example there is a dependency relation. Aikhenvald and Dixon have carried out an extensive cross-linguistic survey, thereby concentrating on eight types of grammatical systems. On the basis of their study, they arrive at the following dependency hierarchy between these systems:

    1. Polarity (i.e. negation marking) (I)
    2. Tense; Aspect: Evidentiality (II)
    3. Person; Reference classification (gender, etc.) (III)
    4. Number (III)
    5. Case (IV)

According to this hierarchy, the formal expression of case may depend on the presence of tense and/or negation marking, but not the other way round. This may be illustrated by way of the Nilotic (Nilo-Saharan) language Turkana, where the noun (phrase) expressing the goal or patient in a transitive clause would occur in the absolutive case, except when the verb occurs in the negative present perfective, in which case the same noun (phrase) requires nominative case. This suggests that case marking depends on tense/aspect and negation in this language.

(44)   Turkana, Nilotic, Nilo-Saharan (Dimmendaal 1983c: 444)
    ɲ-ɛ̀-ɲám-à   ákìríŋ   'the meat has not been eaten (by somebody)'
    NEG-3-eat-MImeat:NOM

Of course, the validity of such cross-linguistic generalisations needs to be checked for individual languages. As it turns out, Turkana also presents some counter-evidence to the presumed universality of the dependency relations formulated by Aikhenvald and Dixon. In this Nilotic language, there are two negation markers, *pɛ-* and *ɲi-*, which have different syntactic scope. In certain tense-aspect forms, there is a choice between the two negation markers, corresponding to a difference in meaning. But the present perfective (which requires a middle voice marker, as shown in (44) above) is only compatible with the negation marker *ɲi-*; in other words, negation marking here depends on, or at least is in interaction with, tense/aspect. This would seem to contradict the proposed unilateral dependency relation. Since the generalisations arrived at by Aikhenvald and Dixon (1998) are based on a large sample of languages across the world, the somewhat exceptional situation for Turkana requires a separate explanation.[8]

7.2.3   *Head-marking and dependent-marking languages*

A further example showing how syntax and morphology may interact, sometimes giving rise to similar results in genetically unrelated languages, comes from the following. As pointed out by Nichols (1986: 56), morphological marking of grammatical relations may appear on either the head of a syntactic phrase (e.g. the verb in a verb phrase, rather than complements such as objects), or the dependent member of the constituent (or on both, or on neither). Head-marking languages favour verb-initial constituent order, that is the initial constituent of an utterance, the verb or predicate, tends to express information on argument structure and semantic roles. This is exactly what one observes in Nilo-Saharan groups with a verb-initial syntax, for example Nilotic and Surmic, where cross-reference markers for pronominal subject and object, voice, valency-changing devices (dative, instrumental, comitative and other operations) tend to be expressed on the verb, as in Maasai.

(45)   Maasai, Nilotic, Nilo-Saharan (Tucker and Mpaayei 1955: 155)
        áà-ìpʊ̀t-àkìn-yé-kì   *ènkúkúrí*   *ɛ̀nkɔ̀tí*
        3>1SG-fill-DAT-INST-PASS   small calabash   big calabash
        'A small calabash is used to fill the big calabash for me.'

Verb-final Nilo-Saharan languages have a strong propensity for dependent-marking strategies, that is they use case on syntactic arguments and adjuncts in order to express semantic roles such as dative or instrumental; a similar strategy is found in Cushitic and Omotic languages.

Head-marking structures of course are not restricted to verb-initial languages. Various Niger-Congo languages typically are head-marking languages, that is they lack case, and instead mark syntactic relations by using verbal valency markers. These languages have SVO or S-AUX-OV as their basic order.

The case of Maasai above and other languages allowing for sequences of bound morphemes in, what appear to be fixed, slots or position classes for various semantic roles expressed on the verb, raises the question of whether morphological layers or strata are added at different levels in the lexicon, that is whether there is hierarchical ordering. As we saw above, iconicity has its limits, so we cannot go entirely by the position relative to the root. Nevertheless, the more relevant the meaning of a morpheme to some other morpheme, the closer its expression unit will occur to that morpheme cross-linguistically. If affinity tends to be reflected in the position relative to the root, this raises other questions, for example how many strata are there, can morphemes belong to just one stratum or not? For reasons of space, this issue cannot be further discussed here; the interested reader is referred to Katamba (1993, part II) for a lucid discussion.

7.2.5   ***Morphology or phonology?***

Beside the morphology–syntax 'interface', there is an obvious link between morphology and phonology. It is not always clear on a priori grounds whether particular alternations between related forms are to be treated as lexical or as phonological phenomena. Such a classic analytical problem occurs in languages that have undergone a reduction from nine (or ten) vowels to seven *υ > o, *$\imath$ > e), without losing all the alternations that go along with the former system. Consider how to predict the form of 3SG in the Benue-Congo language Okpe (data from Hoffmann 1973):

(46)	Imperative		3SG:PAST
	se	'fill'	*o seri*
	so	'steal'	*o sori*
	re	'eat'	*ɔ rere*
	so	'sing'	*ɔ soro*

One could set up an abstract underlying form (thereby recreating the historical process of vowel merger) for 'eat' and 'sing', *rɪ* and *sʋ*. This would make the phonological alternations regular in that classic ATR harmony rules are obeyed (see Clements, chapter 6 above). The presumed phonological elegance of this solution still requires a lexical–phonological rule changing *ɪ* into *e*, and *ʋ* into *o*; see also Archangeli and Pulleyblank (1994: 250ff) for an assessment of phonological objections to an abstract approach for languages that have lost vowel harmony as a productive system of alternations between morphemes. Rather than relegating the dregs to morphology, one might start out from the assumption that certain verbs with *e* and *o* are irregular (analogous to saying that verbs such as 'hang' in English have an irregular past-tense form).

What this discussion should make clear is that any description involves choices in how and where to allocate such alternations. Languages can only be properly understood by treating them as wholes, consisting of partly independent but interacting subsystems.

7.2.6 *Noun classification*

There is a long tradition in the study of Niger-Congo languages of looking for semantic principles underlying the at times rich system of noun classification. That there is a certain semantic basis can hardly be denied, for example when looking at nouns derived from verbs (which require the use of noun classes), or when investigating reduced systems such as pidginised varieties of Bantu languages. Here, there is a tendency for nouns to become invariable, except for classes 1/2, the gender containing human beings as its prototypical referents (Heine 1973). A similar pattern is common elsewhere in Niger-Congo groups (e.g. Kru) where reduced noun class systems have come about probably as a natural historical process of morphological simplification. (See also Demuth *et al.* 1986 for an interesting survey also in relation to language acquisition.)

When investigating borrowings in languages with noun classes, there is also some evidence for semantics as a factor in the allocation of words. At the same time, it is clear from such borrowings that other, formal, principles may play an important role as well; new or borrowed terms are often assigned to classes on phonological grounds (compare the Swahili word for 'book' *ki-tabu* from Arabic *kitaab*), or put into a default class. (See Nurse and Hinnebusch 1993: 351–5.) If children were using semantic criteria as a means for learning Bantu noun class and agreement systems, for example, we would anticipate cases of overgeneralisation. However, language acquisition by children does provide no evidence for overgeneralisation of (presumed) semantic criteria (Demuth 1988).

In a number of more recent approaches towards the potential semantic basis of such systems, alternatives have been proposed to the somewhat simplistic human/non-human, animate/inanimate type of analysis. On the basis of a study of noun classification in Moore (Gur, Niger-Congo), Delplanque (1995) has argued for more abstract common denominators than binary distinctions such as concrete/abstract, human/non-human, countable/non-countable by invoking notions underlying notions such as 'compact', 'discret', 'dense'. Along a different line of research, Breedveld (1995) has argued for prototypical meanings in Fulfulde, an Atlantic language with more than twenty noun class markers and an intricate system of morphophonological alternations or consonant gradation in word-initial position, accompanying noun class suffixation. On first encounter, the *-ki* class (realised through a number of allomorphs, all ending in a high front vowel), for example, contains semantically rather diffuse items such as names for trees, body part terms such as 'armpit' and words such as 'goodness'.

(47)   Fulfulde, Atlantic, Niger-Congo (Breedveld 1995: 400)
     lekki   'tree, medicine'   *keeci*   'lower back'
     ʔoroowi 'baobab'   *moɉɉuki* 'goodness'

As argued by Breedveld (1995: 400–1), these and other terms belonging to this class, share a domain of experience, which can be expressed by way of associative connections, for example body parts on which a child is carried (like a fruit on a tree) and qualities such as 'goodness' (achievable with medicine derived from trees). Additional evidence in favour of such a semantic network is derived by the author from the allocation of loan words and dialect variation within Fulfulde.

Number marking in Nilo-Saharan languages probably involves a semantic dimension of a partly different nature. With the exception of Central Sudanic languages, Saharan and Songhai, singular versus plural distinctions in this language family tend to be rich. What is more, nouns whose referents naturally congregate in large numbers or collectives (e.g. 'bees'), or pairs (e.g. 'breasts') tend to be locally unmarked in the plural, the singular being expressed by way of a suffix.[9]

(48)   Turkana, Nilotic, Nilo-Saharan (Dimmendaal 1983c: 223–58)
     singular   plural
     é-síkín-á   *ŋí-síkín*   'breast'
     á-ŋásép   *ŋá-ŋàsèp-á* 'placenta'
     (The prefixes in these examples are gender markers.)

Occasionally, there is a three-way alternation between singular, plural and collective, as in Turkana *í-twáán(ì)* 'person', *ŋí-tóŋá* 'persons', *ŋ(ì)-tóŋà-sínéí* 'mankind'. Similar three-way distinctions also occur in Niger-Congo languages with noun classes, as in the Atlantic language Limba: *hú-bíní* '(one) breast'; *má-bíní* '(a pair of) breasts'; *má-bíníìnì* 'breasts (in general)' (data by the author). It is also important, from a typological point of view, to keep in mind that the distinction between countable and non-countable nouns in Niger-Congo and other language families does not necessarily correspond to what is common for example in Indo-European languages. Compare Moore (Gur, Niger-Congo) *koo-m* 'water', *koom-de* 'a drip of water', *koom-a* 'several places containing water' (Delplanque 1995). Such a contrast between countable and mass nouns is absent in languages with numeral classifiers, as shown by Ikoro (1996: 85–102) for Kana

(Cross-River, Niger-Congo); this type of classificatory system was long thought to be absent in Africa.

7.2.4   ***Lexicalisation patterns***

In a brilliant study on (Agar) Dinka, Andersen (1992–4) has shown that stratum ordering can be necessary even in an essentially monosyllabic language. As argued by the author, the root in Dinka is the deepest layer, followed by a derivational layer, which in turn is followed by an inflectional layer. Whereas derivation (for example, the expression of movement towards or away from the deictic centre, or the Benefactive) in Dinka is expressed by non-concatenative morphology, inflection involves affixation, non-concatenative morphology, or a combination of these.

(49)   Dinka, Nilotic, Nilo-Saharan (Andersen 1992–4)

à-mïït	'(s)he is pulling (transitive)'
D-pull	
à-mḯïìt	'(s)he is pulling (transitive) thither'
D-pull:CF	
à-m i̯ i̯ ït	'(s)he is pulling (transitive) hither'
D-pull:CP	
à-m i̯ ït	'(s)he is pulling (transitive) for'
D-pull:BEN	
à-m i̯ i̯ ì-t	'(s)he is pulling (intransitive) for'
D-pull:BEN:AP	
à-m i̯ ì-t	'(s)he is pulling (intransitive)'
D-pull:AP	

Whereas semantic roles may be conflated in one structural unit by way of a verb root plus some morphological element, as in Dinka, other languages, for example English, may require separate words. Compare the inverse situation in the following example from Ewe (Westermann 1930: 107–8) and its translation in English: *zɔ dabodabo* 'waggle, walk shakily (like a duck)'. All this suggests that languages may use widely different techniques of mapping units of meaning (sememes) onto morphology and syntax. In order to get to grips with such different lexicalisation patterns, in particular with respect to the conceptualisation of spatial expressions in languages, Talmy (1985) has developed a set of concepts such as Figure, Ground, Motion, Manner, Path. It would be interesting, both from a genetic and an areal point of view, to know how African languages conceptualise spatial expressions as well as other universal linguistic notions. This comparative research programme has been initiated for African languages by Schaefer and Gaines (1997).

Acquiring a language implies learning the fixed formulas for reporting events. Routine culture-specific patterns of usage can harden into language-specific morphosyntactic constructions, 'tailor made' to meet the communicative needs of the speech community. That culture-related semantics can be built into a morphological or morphosyntactic construction is clear from location-marking systems; languages spoken in mountainous regions, for example, tend to have extensive ways of referring to location. The extent to which culture is linked more generally with morphosyntactic organisation again is a perspective barely investigated for African languages.

Given the considerable typological diversity between African languages in the way they actually build words, it would seem that these languages could play and should play a major role in our conceptualisation of morphological systems.

Notes

This chapter was written when the author was a visiting scholar at the Research Centre for Linguistic Typology, Australian National University (Canberra). I am deeply indebted to the directors of the centre, Sasha Aikhenvald and Bob Dixon, for their invitation, as well as for their inspiration and encouragement. Their comments on this chapter, as well as comments and suggestions by Nick Clements, Bernd Heine, Maggy Konter-Katani, Paul Newman and Derek Nurse, are gratefully acknowledged here.
1 Any unmarked data are from the author's own notes.
2 The following abbreviations have been used in this chapter:

ACC	Accusative	INST	Instrumental
ANT	Anterior	INTR	Intransitive
AP	Antipassive	LOC	Locative
APPL	Applicative	M	Masculine
AUGM	Augmentative	MI	Middle voice
BEN	Benefactive	MU	Multiplicative
C	Consonant	NE	Neuter(-passive)
CF	Centrifugal	NEG	Negative
CL	Class marker	NOM	Nominative
CONJ	Conjunctive/conjoint	PAS	Passive
CP	Centripedal	PA	Past
CV	Converb	PERF	Perfective
D	Dependent	PL	Plural
DAT	Dative	PVN	Primary verbal noun
DECL	Declarative	REFL	Reflexive
DES	Desiderative	REL	Relative
DETR	detransitive	RHET	Rhetorical
DISJ	Disjunctive disjoint	SG	Singular

F	Feminine	SVN	Secondary verbal noun
FI	Final vowel	V	Vowel
GEN	Genitive	VEN	Ventive
IMPF	Imperfective	VF	Verb focus

3 The important linguistic concept of paradigm apparently was known already by the ancient Sumerians 3,500 years ago.

4 The Hausa verb form 'learn' also provides information on its morphosyntactic function through its vowel-final ending, a fact which needs to be represented in interlinear glossing in a descriptive grammar of the language.

5 For an interesting account of phonological consequences of reduplication, and the role played by the morpheme and prosodic structure, see Mutaka and Hyman 1990 on the Bantu language Kinande.

6 It is to be kept in mind that what is inflectional in one language, may be derivational in another. As argued by Sapir (1921: 103), number marking in the American Indian language Nootka involves concept formation more similar to derivation than to inflection, since it is not required by the syntactic context, although it may have syntactic relevance.

7 For a critical assessment of this quantificatory method, see Comrie (1981: 39–49).

8 This typologically odd feature may be due to the fact that negation marking in Turkana is syntactically fixed (immediately preceding the verb), that is scope variation (and, corresponding to this, focus marking) cannot be rendered by varying the position of the negation marker relative to the verb, and so negation marking has to interact with typical verbal parameters such as tense/aspect and (middle) voice.

9 An analysis whereby the singular form is assumed to be basic, and the plural 'derived' by way of subtraction or deletion of phonological material, can only be defended if one assumes a Standard Average European perspective on language structure (Dimmendaal, to appear). Subtraction as such appears to exist in certain languages (see, for example, Dressler 1987 for a description of Icelandic nouns formed by a rule of final vowel truncation from the base infinitive: *hamr* 'hammering', < *hamra* 'to hammer' < *hamar* '(a) hammer').

Further reading

Apart from classic introductions in morphology such as Nida (1946; or later reprints), there are various modern handbooks: Anderson (1992), Aronoff (1994), Bauer (1988), Carstairs-McCarthy (1992), Dressler *et al.* (1997), Katamba (1993), Matthews (1974), Mel'čuk (1996), Spencer and Zwicky (1998). For typological approaches to morphology, the reader is referred to Greenberg (1978), as well as various contributions in Shopen (the 1985 edition, or the revised version, in press). A modern scientific journal devoted to the synchronic and diachronic study of morphology is the *Yearbook of Morphology*.

8

Syntax

JOHN R. WATTERS

8.1 Introduction

In the study of syntax we are concerned with how words and morphemes combine to form grammatical sentences. We study how they are placed in a linear order, how they group into larger, patterned units to form phrases and clauses, and how those units relate to one another to form a hierarchy of structures within structures. We seek to understand how similar structures might derive from a more basic, shared structure. We also note that such structures do not exist in a vacuum or in isolation, but are used in social contexts to convey meanings and communicate messages.

With regard to linear order, all languages have more than one way to order words. When we study a language we want to compare how and why word order varies within that language. Languages have a basic word order that serves as the most common way to form a sentence and express or assert the idea (technically the 'proposition') associated with it. In Africa, nearly all languages have a basic word order that is fixed and not free – the subject and object occur in fixed positions in relation to the verb in the basic word order. This is not the case in all languages around the world.

Besides the basic word order, other, less common word orders will also be found in every language. The basic word order is used to form affirmative sentences, among other things. The less common orders, however, are often used for more specialised functions. These include functions such as to form negative sentences, ask questions, indicate what the sentence is about (i.e. change the 'topic'), place the emphasis on a particular part of the sentence (i.e. indicate the 'focus'), and so on. The specific word order used in a given sentence depends on how the speaker packages the idea (i.e. the 'semantic information') associated with the sentence. How the sentence is packaged will be sensitive to its place in the context of the current dialogue or monologue and the content it brings to that context. The relationship between the different word orders and the reasons for the variations serve as important input for developing syntactic theories.

In presenting a brief overview such as this one, we have to be selective, so we will concentrate primarily on sentences with active verbs. They are the prototypical sentences and provide the larger context in which noun phrases, verb phrases and other syntactic constructions operate. For word order in non-verbal sentences and noun phrases, see chapter 9 below. In presenting verbal clauses, we will first consider simple sentences in section 8.2. These consist of a single clause. Then we will consider compound and complex sentences in section 8.3. These consist of multiple clauses.

8.2 Simple sentences (sentences with single clauses)

8.2.1 *The primary units: word categories*

The words we use to form grammatical sentences in languages around the world belong to various classes of words. These include nouns, verbs, adjectives, adpositions and adverbs. Adpositions further subdivide into prepositions and postpositions. Prepositions precede the noun they associate with, and postpositions follow the noun. Other classes include pronouns, determiners, conjunctions, intensifiers and interjections. The specific ways in which these word classes are used need to be defined for each language rather than assumed from their use in English or other European languages.

Words can modify other words and in the process serve as 'specifiers', 'complements' and 'modifiers' to form a string of words[1] called 'a phrase'. The main word of the string serves as the 'head' of the phrase. If the main word is a verb, then the verb and the words that modify it form a 'verb phrase', if it is a noun, then they form a 'noun phrase', and so on.

In African languages, nouns and verbs are the important lexical word classes. African languages tend to use verbs frequently, more often than English and other European languages do. Many descriptive adjectives in European languages are expressed by verbs in African languages. Sentences like 'he is big' and 'she is beautiful' are often expressed by a single verbal word rather than the verb 'to be' plus an adjective, as in 'is + big'. Consider the following where 'red' in (1) and 'ill' in (2) are treated as verbs:

(1) Aghem, Grassfields Bantu, Benue-Congo, Niger-Congo (Hyman 1979: 32)[2]

nwín　 'fí-**báŋà**　　 nò　 'The bird is red.'
bird　 C I I-**red**:PRS:IC　 FOC

(2)   Ngiti, Lendu, Central Sudanic, Nilo-Saharan (Kutsch Lojenga 1994: 228)

    mǎ   *m-àndɪ*   'We are ill.'

    1PL:EXC   SC-**ill**:PFV:PRS

Verbs may also be used where English speakers might use adverbs (e.g. 'frequently', 'not yet', 'still', 'again') and conjunctions (e.g. 'and then'). Consider (3) and (4) below. The verb 'repeat' in (3) carries the sense of 'again', while the verb 'continue' in (4) carries the sense of 'still' in (4a) and 'not yet' in the negative form of the sentence in (4b).

(3)   Yoruba, Defoid, Benue-Congo, Niger-Congo (Welmers 1973: 377)

    ó   **tún**   *ń*   *lọ*   'He is going again.'

    3SG   **repeat**   is going

(4)   Ejagham, Ekoid Bantu, Benue-Congo, Niger-Congo

    (a)   *à-**nyɔ́nè***   *à-chòr-á*   'She is still talking.'

          3SG:PFV-**continue**   3SG:HAB-speak-IMPFV

    (b)   *à-**nyɔ́nè***   *á-kà-chŏt*   'She has not yet talked.'

          3SG:PFV-**continue**   3SG-NEG-talk

African languages tend to have fewer prepositions/postpositions than European languages. Finally, African languages are known for a class of words known as 'ideophones'. They are usually phonologically distinct from most other words in the language, many being onomatopoeic in form. Ideophones commonly contain reduplicated syllables, or one of the vowels or consonants is extra long. See Welmers (1973: chapter 15) for further discussion. Consider these examples of ideophones where *bɔ̀ɔ* in (5a) intensifies the redness, and *tɔ́ tɔ́ tɔ́* in (5b) describes how the running was done:

(5)   Babungo, Grassfields Bantu, Benue-Congo, Niger-Congo (Schaub 1985: 385)

    (a)   *ŋwɔ́*   *báy*   *lāa*   *bɔ̀ɔ*   'He was very, very red.'

          3SG   red:IMPFV   that   IDEO

    (b)   *ŋwɔ́*   *nyíŋ*   *máa*   *tɔ́ tɔ́ tɔ́*   'He ran quickly and continuously.'

          3SG   run:IMPFV   at   IDEO

8.2.2   *Basic word order: simple sentences*

To describe the basic word order we commonly use the terms 'Subject' (S), 'Verb' (V) and 'Object' (O). We usually find the basic word order of any language by studying sentences with all the following characteristics: they are main, declarative, affirmative, active sentences containing a transitive verb. Such sentences also have nouns (or noun phrases) serving in the S and O positions, rather than pronouns. Sentences with the basic word order do not have any words or phrases marked for emphasis or for any other special role. The basic word order is the most common word order found in sentences of the given language, often those used to express the main sequence of events in a story or narrative (Longacre 1990: 1). However, caution is needed in determining the basic word order of a language since the above criteria may lead in more than one direction as in some Central Sudanic languages (see Andersen 1984 and Watson 1997). For more details concerning basic word order, see chapter 9 below.

One study of basic word order in African languages (Heine 1976a) found that of the 300 languages included in the study, 71 per cent were SVO, 24 per cent SOV, and 5 per cent VSO. So the variations on the theme of basic word order may include:

> SVO
> SOV (some languages display a SVOV or S AUX OV order)
> VSO

The SVO order is common in Afroasiatic language subgroups such as the Chadic languages (see Hausa below), in nearly all Niger-Congo subgroups (as in Swahili below) except Mande, Senufo and Ijo, in a number of Nilo-Saharan languages (such as Bari below), and in many Khoisan languages except the Khoe group.

(6) Hausa, Chadic, Afroasiatic (Caron 1991: 15)

```
---S---    ---------V---------    ----O----
àbduu      yaa          ci        naamàa
Abdou      3SGM:COMP    eat       meat        'Abdou ate meat.'
```

(7) Swahili, Bantu, Benue-Congo, Niger-Congo (Vitale 1981: 32)

```
----S----   -----V-----   --O--
Halima      a-na-pika     ugali
Halima      3SG-PRS-cook  porridge    'Halima is cooking porridge.'
```

(8) Bari, Eastern Nilotic, Eastern Sudanic, Nilo-Saharan (Nyombe 1993: 78)

```
---S---   ------V------   --O--   --ADV--
teleme    a      kop      kene    'de'de
monkey    TNS    catch    branch  quickly
```
'The monkey caught the branch quickly.'

The second most common basic word order in Africa is SOV. It is found in the Ethio-Semitic, Cushitic and Omotic languages within Afroasiatic; in the Senufo,

Mande and Ijo languages of Niger-Congo; in numerous Nilo-Saharan languages; and all the Khoe subgroup within Khoisan (Tom Güldemann, p.c.). Consider the following:

(9) Silt'e (Silti), Ethio-Semitic, Afroasiatic (Gutt and Mussa 1997: 900)

---s---   -------o-------   ---v---
išaam   ziiṭṭañe gilgil čeeñeet
she:and   nine   kids   she:gave:birth
'And she gave birth to nine kids.'

(10) Supyire, Senufo, Gur, Niger-Congo (Carlson 1994: 370)

--s--   --o--   --v--
kile   ù   kùni   pwɔ̀
God   3SG   path:DEF   SBJ:sweep
'May God sweep the path (=blessing).'

(11) Aiki, Maban, Nilo-Saharan (Nougayrol 1989: 34)

--s--   -----o-----   ---v---
gɔ̀ŋ   yàŋ   sám   tɔ̀rmè
farmer   place   good   3SG-occupy:IC:ASRTV
'The farmer occupies a fertile plot.'

The third basic word order, VSO, is uncommon. It is found primarily among the Berber and Chadic languages of Afroasiatic; the Nilotic, Surmic and Kuliak languages of Eastern Sudanic, as well as languages of Southern Sudanic, all of Nilo-Saharan; but also in Hadza, a purported Khoisan language. Consider (12):

(12) Maasai, Eastern Nilotic, Eastern Sudanic, Nilo-Saharan (Tucker and Bryan 1966: 468)

-v-   ----s----   ----o----
ɛ́dɔ́l   ɔltúŋání   eŋkolii
see   person:NOM   gazelle:ACC   'The person sees a gazelle.'

Some linguists argue that these VSO languages are actually SVO in their initial or underlying form, but that the V(erb) is eventually moved to the front of the sentence to produce the VSO order on the surface (Creider 1989 and Nyombe 1993).

A common issue concerning basic word orders concerns the presence of auxiliary (AUX) verb forms. Auxiliary verbs relate to the primary verb in a sentence usually by indicating a tense or aspect or mood, but sometimes they have an adverbial function. Depending on how the given auxiliary verb behaves in the language, it may either serve as a 'specifier' in the verb phrase, as in [AUX O V], or it might be the head of a larger 'auxiliary phrase' with the verb phrase as its complement, as in [AUX [O V]]. Whatever the structural details may be for a specific auxiliary verb, various languages with SVO as the basic order use the order S-AUX-OV when an auxiliary is present. These languages have the equivalent of two verbal positions in the sentence: the first position lies immediately after the S(ubject) and the second after the O(bject). For the first position, preference is given to the auxiliary, giving the S-AUX-OV order. However, if no auxiliary is present, then the main verb occurs in the first position, giving the basic SVO word order. Such variations in word order are found in some subgroups of Nilo-Saharan languages such as in Central and Eastern Sudanic languages, subgroups of Niger-Congo such as Kru (see Marchese 1986 and Koopman 1984) and the Wider Bantu of Cameroon, and in !Xun, a North Khoisan language.

SOV languages also tend to place the AUX immediately after the S(ubject), as we see in Supyire (13), also producing an S-AUX-OV order.

(13)   Supyire, Senufo, Gur, Niger-Congo (Carlson 1994: 239)

     -S-   -AUX-   -O-   ----V----

     u   màha   suro   shwɔhɔ

     she   HAB   mush cook   'She cooks mush.'

However, in Ethio-Semitic languages of Afroasiatic, the AUX is suffixed to the verb so comes in the final sentence position: SOV-AUX.

Sometimes the variation in word order depends on the aspect[3] of the verb. So in a Central Sudanic language like Ma'di (Tucker and Bryan 1966: 47), the perfective requires SVO and the imperfective SOV. Word order in subordinate clauses may also differ from the basic word order in main clauses. In Western Nilotic, the basic word orders are SVO and S-AUX-OV, but in relative and interrogative clauses they are VSO and AUX-SVO (Nyombe 1989: 76).

Besides auxiliaries, word order involves the linear placement of additional objects (such as benefactives and locations) and adjuncts (such as adpositions, which we refer to often as 'prepositional' or 'postpositional' phrases). In the case of languages that can have two or more objects, languages with the more common SVO pattern usually place the additional object following the verb. This gives a SVOO word order. Most often the first object has a benefactive semantic role (i.e. the one who benefits from the action) and is often referred to as the 'indirect object'.

In a VSO language such as Turkana, the second object follows the first object and so follows the verb also, giving a VSOO order, as we see in (14):

(14)   Turkana, Eastern Nilotic, Eastern Sudanic, Nilo-Saharan (Dimmen-
       daal 1983a: 252)

       ------V------   --S--   --O--   ---O---
       à-ɪn-a-kɪn-ì   *ayɔ̀ŋ*   *ŋɪdè*   *akìmuj*
       1SG-give-to-DAT-ASP   1SG   children   food
       'I will give the children food.'

As for locational and temporal phrases, sometimes they serve as the complement of a verb. An example would be 'in the box' in the sentence 'She put the
money in the box', where the verb 'put' requires a locational phrase. Many times,
however, locational and temporal phrases are not complements but adjuncts of
the sentence. They provide optional clarification as to the place or time of the
action. Adjuncts of sentences in SVO languages generally follow the O(bject), giving a SVOX word order, where 'X' represents one or more adjuncts. In some SOV
languages, on the other hand, the adjuncts precede the verb, giving an SXOV or
SOXV order, as shown below in Aiki, where the adjunct is a LOC(ative) postpositional phrase *tàk gɔ́n* 'at the pond' (literally 'water at').

(15)   Aiki, Maban, Nilo-Saharan (Nougayrol 1989: 34)
       ------S------   ---------O---------   -------LOC-------   -----V-----
       kàikài   *tí*   *tíɲíŋ*   *gá*   **tàk**   **gɔ́n**   *tàndàrkè*
       child   ANA   3SG:mother   ACC   **water:SG** **LOC**   3SG:join:C:ASRTV
       'The child joined its mother at the pond.'

Otherwise an SOV language may use the SOVX order for adjuncts, as seen in
Mende with the instrumental prepositional phrase *à bóa* 'with a knife'.

(16)   Mende, Western, Mande, Niger-Congo (Givón 1984: 214)
       -S-   --O--   -V-   ---INST---
       è   *wúru*   *tèe*   *à*   *bóa*
       he   stick   cut   **with** **knife**   'He cut the stick with a knife.'

8.2.3   *Basic word order: noun phrases and adpositional phrases*
8.2.3.1   *Order within noun phrases and adpositional phrases*
       Like simple sentences (or clauses), noun phrases and adpositional
phrases (i.e. prepositional and postpositional phrases) also have basic word
orders. Some languages display a tendency of being either head-initial or head-
final languages. However, in other languages these head-initial and head-final correlations do not hold so neatly. Significant exceptions include the Gur languages

of West Africa (Bendor-Samuel 1971: 157, 171), and the Kru, Kwa and Mande languages (see chapter 9 below for more discussion).

8.2.3.2   *Cross-referencing noun phrases in verb phrases*
Within the sentence, noun phrases may be cross-referenced in the verb phrase. Most commonly these would be the subject and object noun phrases. For example, in the Benue-Congo languages, particularly the Bantu languages, and among the Ethio-Semitic languages, a verb usually contains an affix that cross-references it to the subject noun phrase. This kind of obligatory cross-referencing is often referred to as 'agreement'. It is exemplified in (17a), where the *à-* prefix in the verb agrees in number and gender with the subject noun phrase. In such languages, the subject noun phrase may also be absent, but the verbal affix must still be present, as in (17b). In such cases, the verbal affix serves as an affixed or dependent subject pronoun. When an independent subject pronoun is used such as with *yê* in (17c), it generally serves to place emphasis (the 'focus') on the subject or to clarify what the discourse is about (the 'topic').

(17)   Ejagham, Ekoid Bantu, Benue-Congo, Niger-Congo
    (a)   *ǹ-tèm   òmé   à-kpâŋ   è-bhĭn   èj-ê*
          C1-friend C1:my C1:PFV-hoe C5-farm C5-POSS:3SG
          é-nyàné
          C5-yesterday
          'My friend hoed her farm yesterday.'
    (b)   *à-kpâŋ   è-bhĭn   èj-ê   é-nyàné*
          C1:PFV-hoe C5-farm C5-POSS:3SG C5-yesterday
          'She hoed her farm yesterday.'
    (c)   *yê   à-kpâŋ   è-bhĭn   èj-ê   é-nyàné*
          C1:3SG C1:PFV-hoe C5-farm C5-POSS:3SG C5-yesterday
          '**She** hoed her farm yesterday.'

In other languages throughout Africa, however, agreement between the subject noun phrase and the verb phrase is not present. These include Niger-Congo languages in subgroups such as Mande, Adamawa-Ubangi, Kru, Kwa, Gur and some Benue-Congo subgroups like Mambiloid languages, as well as many Chadic languages and various Nilo-Saharan languages. These languages generally require an independent pronoun as the explicit subject when a subject noun is not present. For example, in (18a) a subject noun is present, but in (18b) an independent subject pronoun is used.

(18)   Linda, Banda, Adamawa-Ubangi, Niger-Congo (Cloarec-Heiss 1986: 44)

(a)   *kōʃē   ɔ́   kpè*
       person   IC   flee   'The person flees.'

(b)   *mɔ́   kpè*
       1SG:IC   flee   'I flee.'

Various languages go beyond agreement between the subject noun phrase and the verb phrase. They include the optional cross-referencing of the object noun phrase in the verb phrase, as well as optional cross-referencing of noun phrases used for other roles such as benefactive and instrumental. In these latter cases, the noun phrase has typically moved from an adjunct noun phrase function to an object function. The use of such agreement is common in Bantu and West Atlantic languages, as well as Kru, Ethio-Semitic and Nilo-Saharan languages. It appears that no African language has obligatory agreement between the object noun phrase and the verb phrase.

8.2.3.3   *Noun phrases and noun class concord systems*

Besides cross-referencing between noun phrases and verb phrases, the most pervasive cross-referencing or agreement systems are found in the Niger-Congo languages, particularly the Benue-Congo languages. These languages have what are referred to as 'noun-class systems'. In these systems, the subject noun not only determines what affix is used for agreement on the verb, but the noun also determines the agreement affixes on modifiers within the noun phrase as well as on pronouns that refer back to an earlier noun reference (i.e. 'anaphoric' pronouns) within the larger discourse. Consider the two sentences below.

(19)   Ejagham,[4] Ekoid Bantu, Benue-Congo, Niger-Congo (Watters 1981)

(a)   *è-yù   èj-â   j-ɔ́t   n̂j-í   n̂j-ì*
       c5-yam   c5-your   c5-one   c5-this   c5-which
       n̄nàmé″,   n̂j-ɔ̀nè   é-bhìp
       I:bought, c5-it   c5:PFV-bad
       'This one yam of yours that I bought, it is spoiled.'

(b)   *bì-yù   ìbh-â   ì-bhá'é   m̀b-í   m̀b-ì   n̄nàmé″,*
       c8-yam   c8-your   c8-two   c8-this   c8-which   I:bought,
       m̀b-ɔ̀nè   ì-bhìp
       c8-they   c8:PFV-bad
       'These two yams of yours which I bought, they are spoiled.'

As can be seen with the presence of all the 'C5s' (class 5) in (19a) and 'C8s' (class 8) in (19b), agreement with the noun in such languages is pervasive. Modifiers in the noun phrase must agree with the head noun, as well as the subject ('anaphoric') pronoun of the second clause. (Please see chapter 7 above for details of noun-class systems.)

8.2.4   *Commands and questions*

The basic word order of simple sentences such as those presented above refers only to declarative sentences – sentences in the indicative mood. Sentences in the indicative mood involve situations that are presented as fact through the use of statements or assertions. But what happens when those sentences become commands or questions? Commands represent the imperative mood in which the speaker wants the given situation to be different and so commands someone to change it. Questions represent the interrogative mood in which the speaker is not sure if a given situation is a fact, or what the details of the situation are, and so asks someone to clarify.

As for commands (or 'imperatives'), the relevant points for syntax are that the subject noun phrase is usually absent even though the subject number (singular or plural) is often marked in the verb.

In the case of questions, three types should be considered. There are the 'yes/ no' questions, information word questions, and indirect questions. In African languages yes/no questions most commonly involve only a question marker or morpheme at the end or the beginning of the sentence.

Linda (20) is typical of many Niger-Congo and other languages that use a question marker at the edge of the sentence. The question marker is simply added.

(20)   Linda, Banda, Adamawa-Ubangi, Niger-Congo (Cloarec-Heiss 1986: 464f)

(a)   *cè*   *gú*
      he/she   arrived   'She arrived.'

(b)   *cè*   *gú*   *à*
      he/she   arrived   QM   'Did she arrive?'

In a language such as Silt'e (Silti) in (21), a rise in intonation at the end of the sentence or the interrogative particle *way* also at the end of the sentence may be used to mark a yes/no question.

(21)   Silt'e (Silti), Ethio-Semitic, Afroasiatic (Gutt and Mussa 1997: 955)
        akkum   *tisiikbiňaaš*   ***way***
        now:and   you:F:laugh:at:me   QM
        'And are you now laughing at me?'

In Hausa, the same two ways of asking a yes/no question exist as in Silt'e (Silti). However, in Hausa, use of the sentence-final question marker requires question intonation (Caron 1991: 34).

In many languages in West Africa from the Mande, Gur and Kwa groups, however, the intonation used is not rising but falling. In Konni, a Gur language of Ghana, the initial pitch of the question sentence is higher than with an assertion, and the last segment of the question sentence, whether vowel or nasal, is lengthened and has a slow fall in pitch. Consider the example in (22) where the pitch on the final vowel is falling:

(22)   Konni, Gur, Niger-Congo (Mike Cahill, p.c.)
    nì   díè sààbú-ò   'Are you (pl.) eating porridge?'
    you eat porridge-?

As with each of the examples above, most African languages use their basic word order to form yes/no questions.

Yes/no questions may also be formed with a negative as in 'Didn't he go to Accra?' In English, if we answered 'yes', we would be answering that he did indeed go to Accra. If we answered 'no', we would mean that he did not go. The opposite is true in African languages. Consider the following example.

(23)   Ejagham, Ekoid Bantu, Benue-Congo, Niger-Congo
    (a) *ó-kà-jĭ*   *ògə̀m*   *à*   'Didn't you go to the market?'
        2SG-NEG-go market QM
    (b) *ǹǹ̀ǹ, (ń-kà-jĭ)*   'Yes, (I didn't go).'
        yes, (1SG-NEG-go)
    (c) *éè, (ǹ-jǎk)*   'No, (I went).'
        no, (1SG-go)

When we look at information word questions (also known as 'WH-questions', 'content questions', and 'constituent questions') the situation is similar to that of yes/no questions: the basic word order is often maintained. In English we place the interrogative word 'who', 'what', 'where', 'how', and so on, at the beginning of the sentence. African languages also typically have these interrogative words. However, they most commonly remain in their subject or object position (or other position) in the basic word order rather than being placed at the beginning of the sentence.

In some languages the interrogative word question is doubly marked: the interrogative word is accompanied by a sentence-final question word, such as the yes/no question word, as in Supyire (Carlson 1994: 533), a Gur language, and Ngie, a Grassfields Bantu language.

Some languages, on the other hand, do use alternative word orders. In Vata (Koopman 1984: 35), an SVO (or SOV) Kru language, the interrogative word occurs at the beginning of the sentence. In other SVO languages the sentence-final position, or a position immediately following the verb, is used for interrogative words. The Niger-Congo languages Aghem, Noon and Mambila are examples. Of interest is how each of these languages treats the subject-interrogative noun phrase. In Aghem, a Grassfields Bantu language (Watters 1979: 144ff), and in Noon, a West Atlantic language (Maria Soukka, p.c.), the subject-interrogative takes the same sentence-final position as other interrogative words. In both cases, however, an indefinite pronoun occurs in the normal subject position and serves as a cross-reference to the subject-interrogative word. In Mambila, a Benue-Congo language (Perrin 1994: 237f), the subject-interrogative also acts differently from other interrogatives. It occurs in the normal sentence-initial subject position rather than in the expected sentence-final position. However, in this case, a marker of emphasis that cross-references with the subject-interrogative word is placed in the sentence-final position.

Besides the normal interrogative word questions, indirect interrogative word questions are also used. In English we can take the question 'What did she buy?' and ask it indirectly as in 'Please tell me what she bought.' In both sentences the interrogative word 'what' is used, and it occurs at the beginning of the clause. In African languages, however, the indirect question would often not use the interrogative word. Instead, a relative clause would be used with a generic head noun like 'thing' in 'Please tell me the thing that she bought', contrasting with 'She bought what?' However, in East Africa, a Bantu language like Swahili, an Ethio-Semitic language like Amharic, and various Eastern Sudanic languages such as Turkana use interrogative words in indirect questions.

8.2.5   *Negation*

The basic word order of simple sentences presented above referred to affirmative sentences. But what happens when those sentences become negative ones?

Two different kinds of negation should be distinguished. First, the sentence as a whole may be negated ('predicate negation'). Secondly, a particular constituent of the sentence may be negated, such as a noun phrase ('constituent negation'). For constituent negation, many African languages use a cleft-like construction of the shape 'It is not X who/which did it' as in 'It is not **Ina** who became chief.' What we discuss below will concern sentence negation.

General sentence negation is marked either internally to the verbal word or externally to it. In the first case, a verbal affix is included in the verbal word.

In the latter case, a negative particle is placed adjacent to or in place of the auxiliary, or the particle occurs at the end of the verb phrase, or both occur simultaneously.

8.2.5.1   *Negation internal to the verbal word: verbal affixes*
    One common way to negate a sentence is to modify the verbal word. This modification uses an affix in the formation of the verb, changing it from a positive to a negative verb. This type of negation is found throughout the Benue-Congo languages, for example. Consider the following example from Aghem:

(24) Aghem, Grassfields Bantu, Benue-Congo, Niger-Congo (Anderson 1979: 86, 118)
    (a) *ò bò   fí-ghâm*   'He has hit the mat.'
         3SG hit   C7-mat
    (b) *ò kà bó   ghâm-fɔ*   'He has not hit the mat.'
         3SG NEG hit mat-C7   (demphasised noun form required with negatives)

In Lobala, the verbal word is doubly marked in the negative, with negative particles preceding and following the subject affix as seen in (25).

(25) Lobala, Bantu C, Benue-Congo, Niger-Congo (David Morgan, p.c.)
    (a) *ba-tub-aka*   'They sang.'
         3PL-sing-PST
    (b) *te- ba- ik-   aka   tuba*   'They did not sing.'
         NEG-3PL-NEG:AUX-PST   sing

A rare pattern among the world's languages is found among the Omotic languages. Various ones have three distinct conjugations of a given verb: positive, interrogative and negative (Lionel Bender, p.c.). Instead of attaching a negative affix to a single base form of the verb, these Omotic languages have a specifically negative form of the verb that parallels a positive and an interrogative form.

8.2.5.2   *Negation external to the verbal word: auxiliary and*
            verb phrase particles
    Another modification of the verb can involve changes to the verbal auxiliary. For example, in Igbo (Welmers and Welmers 1968: 107) as shown in (26) below, the negative suffix *ghí* is attached to the incompletive particle *nà*.

(26)   Igbo, Igboid, Benue-Congo, Niger-Congo (Welmers 1973: 405)

    (a) ọ̀   nà   èri ń'ri   'She is eating.'

        he/she IC   eat food

    (b) ọ̀   ná-'ghí èri ń'ri   'She is not eating.'

        he/she IC-NEG   eat food

Negative particles outside the verbal word and auxiliary provide another common way to negate a sentence in African languages. These particles occur at the verb phrase level. For example, in the SVO language Fer, a Central Sudanic, Nilo-Saharan language of the Central African Republic and Sudan, the negative particle occurs at the end of the verb phrase (and sentence), forming the pattern S V (O) NEG.

(27)   Fer, Central Sudanic, Nilo-Saharan (Boyeldieu 1987: 90)

    jùwà   *līf*   *ɔ̃ʔ*   'We do not see the moon.'

    we:see   moon   NEG

Various Chadic languages in Nigeria and Cameroon also use the pattern S V O NEG. In such languages, when the negative particle comes at the end of a complex sentence which consists of a main clause followed by a final subordinate clause, the interpretation of the negation is ambiguous. The negative particle could be negating either the main clause or the subordinate clause. Consider the Tera example in which the negative particle *ɓa* can negate either the main clause with the verb 'insult' or the subordinate clause with the verb 'belong'.

(28)   Tera, Chadic, Afroasiatic (Newman 1970: 102)

    nduk   *kə*   *pəz*   *ndib* *nə*   *kə*   *hlugdə* *a xa*   *nda* *ɓa*

    person   SUB   insult   man   REL   SUB   knife   belong   him   NEG

    'A person should not insult a man who has a knife.' OR

    'A person should insult a man who does not have a knife.'

Another Chadic language, Hausa, uses a double negative, but not in the imperfective or 'present tense'. Where it does use the double negative, the first negative particle is adjacent to the auxiliary and the second is verb-phrase (and sentence-) final. They form the pattern S NEG V O NEG, as follows:

(29)   Hausa, Chadic, Afroasiatic (Kraft and Kraft 1973: 310)

    yaarinyàa **bà**   *tà*   *tàfi*   *goonaa*   **ba**

    girl   NEG   3fs:C   go   farm   NEG

    'The girl did not go to the farm.'

Double negatives also occur in Gur languages.

At times negative particles that occur at the level of the verb phrase may also involve changes in the word order. For example, in Logbara the SOV word order in positive sentences changes to an S-V-O-NEG word order in negative ones.

(30)   Logbara, Central Sudanic, Nilo-Saharan (Crazzolara 1960: 92, in Payne 1985: 230)

    (a) *drùsĭ*   *mâ* *zâ* *ɲaa* *rá*   'Tomorrow I shall eat meat.'
       tomorrow I   meat eat ASRTV

    (b) *drùsĭ*   *á* *ɲaa* *zá*   **kö**   'Tomorrow I shall not eat meat.'
       tomorrow I eat meat NEG

In Kru, the strategy is the reverse. The basic SVO word order used in positive sentences is changed to S-NEG-O-V. The negative (NEG) particle behaves like an auxiliary.

(31)   Kru, Kru, Niger-Congo (Hyman 1975a: 125, also in Payne 1985: 229)

    (a) *ɔ́*   *tɛ̀* *kɔ́*   'He bought rice.'
       he:C buy rice

    (b) *ɔ́*   *sé* *kɔ́* *tè*   'He did not buy rice.'
       he:C NEG rice buy

A more radical and unusual negative formation occurs in Linda. In this case, the negative particle occurs sentence-final, outside the verbal word (32b, c, d). However, the verb is also modified by the reduplication of the first syllable (32b, c). In addition, in transitive sentences, the verb may either be reduplicated or it may be repeated just before the negative particle (32c, d).

(32)   Linda, Banda, Adamawa-Ubangi, Niger-Congo (Cloarec-Heiss 1986: 356f)

    (a) *àndà*   *ʒú*   'A house burned.'
       house C:burn

    (b) *àndà*   *ʒúʒú*   *nē*   'A house did not burn.'
       house C:NEG:burn NEG

    (c) *mɔ̄* *mámâ*   *kòsárà* *nē*   'I did not work.'
       I   C:NEG:do work   NEG

    (d) *mɔ̄* *má*   *kòsárà* *mâ*   *nē*   'I did not work.' (preferred)
       I   C:do work NEG:do NEG

8.2.6   *Topics, passives and voice*

        The basic word order of simple sentences presented in section 8.2.2 referred to active sentences. But what happens when those sentences become passive ones? And how do passive sentences relate to 'topics' of sentences and to other changes in the number of participants present in the situation expressed in the sentence?

Syntactically, passive sentences are those in which the object of an active sentence becomes the subject. In the process, the subject of the active sentence is relegated to a secondary position, such as an adpositional phrase, or may be deleted altogether. Passive sentences thus bear a syntactic relationship to their active counterparts. In fact, passive sentences relate to two larger systems: topic and voice.

8.2.6.1   *Passives and topics*

In the case of topics, when the object noun phrase of an active sentence becomes the subject noun phrase of a passive sentence, it thereby becomes more topical in the sentence, that is 'what is under discussion'. In a language like English we can take a simple, active sentence like (33a) and change it in the various ways demonstrated in (33b) through (33f).

(33)	(a)	My neighbour grated cassava yesterday.	NEUTRAL
	(b)	Cassava my neighbour grated yesterday.	TOPICALISATION
	(c)	As for cassava, my neighbour grated some yesterday.	LEFT-DISLOCATION
	(d)	Cassava was grated yesterday.	AGENTLESS PASSIVE
	(e)	Cassava was grated by my neighbour yesterday.	AGENT PASSIVE
	(f)	Someone/they grated cassava yesterday.	INDEFINITE PERSONAL

Though each of the sentences may refer to the same event, the way the situation is presented by the speaker in (33) varies from sentence to sentence. The first noun phrase in each sentence could be treated as 'what is under discussion' or 'the topic', while the remainder of the sentence could be considered the relevant information or 'comment' the speaker wants to make concerning the topic. So the variation is sensitive to how the speaker wants to package the information – the pragmatic or discourse dimension. All the sentences from (33b) through (33f) serve to make the original object 'cassava', which is semantically the patient of the event of grating, more topical than it is in (33a), where it serves as part of the comment on the topic of 'my neighbour'.

In African languages we find all of these variations on the simple active sentence in order to make those noun phrases which are not subjects (and not agents) more topical. We can summarise as follows:

(1)   some languages have no passive and use only indefinite constructions like (33f)

(2)   some languages have only agentless passives as in (33d)

(3)   some languages use passives of the type (33d) and (33e), and some
       may also use indefinite constructions like (33f)

(4)   most languages have some form of (33b) or (33c), or both

Those languages which have no passive sentences like (33d) and (33e), but only
an indefinite form like that in (33f), are exemplified by Babungo:

(34)   Babungo, Grassfields Bantu, Benue-Congo, Niger-Congo (Schaub 1985:
        209)

        ví   jìa   ŋwɔ́
        3PL:INDF hold:PFV   3PS
        'They/someone caught him.' = 'He was caught.'

As we see from the English examples in (33d–f), indefinite constructions can
occur in languages with passive constructions. However, many African languages
do not have a passive but only use the indefinite construction. These languages
are found largely in the following groups: Benue-Congo (but not Bantu), Kwa,
Gur, Mande, as well as Chadic.

For another set of languages, only the agentless passive, like (33d), is possible.
Such languages include Sonrai/Songhai in West Africa, Tamazight (Berber),
Nandi (Nilo-Saharan) (see Keenan 1985a: 249), as well as many Kru languages
(Marchese 1989: 134). West Atlantic languages such as Fulfulde, in which pass-
ives are commonly used, also behave this way. Consider example (35) from the
Fulfulde of western Niger:

(35)   Fulfulde, West Atlantic, Niger-Congo (Steve White, p.c.)

        (a)   *debboo*   *wadani*   *jama'aare*   *neema*
               woman:the   bring:BEN:PFV   group   food
               'The woman brought food for the group.'

        (b)   *so   nii   neema   waddaama   nder   jama'aare*
               if   thus   food   bring:PASS:PFV   to/in   group
               'If food is brought to the group.'

The first sentence (35a) includes the subject (and agent) 'woman' and two objects:
the indirect object (and benefactive) 'group', and the direct object (and patient)
'food'. In sentence (35b) the agent is absent, the patient 'food' serves as the subject, and the benefactive 'group' is expressed by a prepositional phrase, so the benefactive affix (BEN) is lost on the verb. Some languages, particularly in West Africa,
take this process the next step. Not only is the sentence agentless, but also the
verb has no passive morphology (PASS), that is it remains unchanged. Nawdm
in (36) provides an example.

(36) Nawdm, Gur, Niger-Congo (Jacques Nicole, p.c.)

    (a)   *nídbá*   **nyìrá**   *dáám*   *wèém*

         people:PL **drink:PFV** corn.beer   quickly

         'The people drank the beer quickly.'

    (b)   *dáám*   **nyìrá**   *wèém*

         corn.beer **drink:PFV** quickly

         'The beer was drunk quickly.'

Other languages have a full passive system represented by (33d) and (33e). These include the majority of Bantu languages as well as Afroasiatic languages such as various Ethio-Semitic and Berber languages. Consider the passive in Chewa in (37), where the verbal suffix *–idw* indicates the passive.

(37) Chewa, Bantu, Benue-Congo, Niger-Congo (Mchombo 1993: 17)

    (a)   *alenje*   *a-na-gúl-ír-á*   *mbidzi*   *mikéka*

         C2:hunters C2:SM-PST-buy-APPL-FV C10:zebras C4:mats

         'The hunters bought the zebras some mats.'

    (b)   *mbidzi*   *zi-na-gúl-í-idw-á*   *mikêka*   *ndí alenje*

         C10:zebras C10:sm-PST-buy-APPL-PASS-FV C4:mats   by C2:hunters

         'The zebras were bought mats by the hunters.'

In Silt'e (Silti), an Ethio-Semitic language, passive forms equivalent to (33d) and (33e) exist, but the indefinite form like (33f) is more commonly used in texts and speech (Gutt and Mussa 1997: 918). In Tamajaq (Tamazight), full passives like (33e) also exist, though they are most often agentless, as in (33d). In the Tamajaq example in (38), basic verb roots and affixes consist only of one or more consonants, with *TW* serving as the passive (PASS) affix.

    (38)   Tamajaq (Tamazight), Berber, Afroasiatic (Christian Grandouiller, p.c.)

        (a)   *TW* + *NN* → *itawannu*

            PASS + say → 'He/it is said.'

        (b)   *N* + *TW* + *SNFRN* → *nətiwasanafran*

            1PL + PASS + choose → 'We have been chosen.'

        (c)   *obaran*   *nana* *shənnanan*

            they:scratched   us,   thorns   'Thorns scratched us.'

        (d)   *nətiwabar*   *əs*   *shənnanan*

            we:were:scratched by:means:of thorns

            'We were scratched by thorns.'

A more common counterpart to the active sentence in Tamajaq is that in (39b). It involves shifting the noun phrase *talamt* in the object role to the subject role, and simultaneously replacing the original object with an independent object pronoun *tat*. The object (or patient) in this way becomes the sentence topic, perhaps functioning more like the topic construction in (33b) above.

> (39)   Tamajaq (see preceding example)
>   (a)   *amadan   izzag   talamt*
>   herder   he:has:milked   camel-F
>   'The herder milked the camel.'
>   (b)   *talamt   izzag   tat   amadan*
>   camel-F   he:has:milked   3SGF:OBJ   herder
>   'The camel the herder milked.'

Sentences such as (33b) and (33c), in which an object noun phrase is fronted and so marked as the topic of the sentence, are found in most African languages. They generally occur in sentence-initial position. They may be marked by a topic word, such as the 'As for' in (33c), or be marked simply by virtue of their position in the sentence, as in (33b). Topic words may be extended as in Zulgo (Chadic, Afroasiatic) to mark not only noun phrases but also subordinate clauses with a variety of relations to the main clause (Haller and Watters 1984). Some Bantu languages such as Chewa, however, may place a topic noun phrase that is cross-referenced with the object-pronoun prefix in every possible noun phrase position in the sentence. It may occur in sentence-initial, -medial or -final positions (see Bresnan and Mchombo 1987: 745).

8.2.6.2   *Passives and voice*

Besides marking topic, passives also participate in a second system having to do with 'valence'. This system involves the rearranging of grammatical relations in a given sentence. The rearranging may involve addition, deletion or modification. As we have seen above in section 8.2.6.1, the passive may involve a modification in which the agent changes from its subject role to a secondary role in an adpositional phrase. At other times, the passive involves the deletion of the agent altogether. These are two forms of the passive voice.

Another way of rearranging the grammatical relations is to use reflexive and reciprocal sentences. In reflexive sentences, the agent and patient refer to the same participant rather than to two different ones. In reciprocal sentences, the agent and patient refer to a set of participants that mutually affect one another in the same way. Many African languages mark the reflexive in the verb, as in Swahili *Ahmed a-na-ji-penda* 'Ahmed loves himself' (Vitale 1981: 137) where *–ji-* is the object prefix that refers to the same participant as the subject noun phrase *Ahmed*. Other languages indicate it by means of a pronoun or noun that has been assigned a reflexive meaning, as in Supyire *u a ù-yé bání* 'he has wounded himself', where *ù-yé* is the third person singular reflexive; or as in Ejagham *agbo a-kôt biji ibhê* 'Agbo loves himself', where the noun phrase *biji ibhê* 'his body' is reflexive. In fact, 'body' is used in many languages across Africa as the reflexive, as well as 'head', 'heart', and 'soul'. Similarly for the reciprocal: some languages use verbal affixes while others use nouns such as 'friends' or 'fellows' or pronouns in special ways to indicate the reciprocal. Consider the reduplication of the third person plural pronoun in Babungo along with 'bodies' in (40).

(40) Babungo, Grassfields Bantu, Benue-Congo, Niger-Congo (Schaub 1985: 199)

vɔ̌ŋ   gàŋtɔ̀   yìŋwáa   vɔ̌ŋ,   vɔ̌ŋ   vɔ̌ŋ
3PL   help:PFV   bodies   3PL,   3PL   3PL   'They helped each other.'

Another important change in grammatical relations involves causatives. With causatives, an additional participant is specified in the sentence, specifically the participant who is responsible for causing the given situation. Causatives are marked either by verbal affixes or through the use of two clauses, as in 'he made her sing', where 'made' serves as the causative. Bantu, West Atlantic, Gur, Ethio-Semitic and Nilo-Saharan languages often use verbal affixes. Some languages use a combination of these strategies. Consider the following examples of causatives. Oromo uses a verbal affix, as in (41b), while Ejagham has a subclass of verbs that use an affix, as in (42), but most verbs require a two-clause construction, as in (43).

(41) Oromo, Cushitic, Afroasiatic (Dubinsky, Lloret, and Newman 1988)
(a) *aannan-ni   daanf-e*
milk-NOM   boil-AGR
'The milk boiled.'
(b) *terfaa-n   aannan   daanf-is-a*
Terfa-NOM   milk   boil-CAUS-AGR
'Terfa made the milk boil/boiled the milk.'

(42) Ejagham, Ekoid Bantu, Benue-Congo, Niger-Congo (also true for (43))
(a) *èbhĭn   ábhǒ   é-rík*
C5:farm   3PL:POSS   C5:PFV-burn
'Their farm burned.'
(b) *yê   à-ríg-ì   èbhĭn   ábhǒ*
C1:3SG   3SG:PFV-burn-CAUS   C5:farm   3PL:POSS
'He burned their farm.'

(43)   Ejagham (see (42) above)
   (a)   *ǹtèm*   *òmé*   *à-sôn*
       CI:friend   CI:my   3SG:PFV-become.well
       'My friend is well.'
   (b)   *à-yîm*   *ǹtèm*   *òmé*   *à-sôn*
       3SG:PFV-**make**   CI:friend   CI:my   3SG:PFV-become.well
       'She made my friend well.'

On another point: some languages have verbal affix systems that allow them to mark additional participants such as instrumentals and locatives as objects of the verb. Instrumentals and locatives are normally marked by adpositional phrases and function as simple additions ('adjuncts') to the core of the sentence comprised of the verb, the subject and the objects. However, many Bantu, West Atlantic, Ethio-Semitic and Nilo-Saharan languages have verbal affixes that mark instrumentals, locatives and other relations. When these affixes are used, the instrumental or locative may change from an adpositional phrase to become an object noun phrase. Potentially it may become a subject noun phrase if the language allows full passives.

Finally, a number of Nilo-Saharan languages do not use verbal affixes to indicate the grammatical relations of the noun phrases. Instead, the verb is unmarked for any grammatical relations and each noun phrase is instead marked. We refer to these noun phrase affixes as marking 'case'. They are prominent in verb-final, SOV, Nilo-Saharan languages (Gerrit Dimmendaal, p.c.).

8.2.7   *Emphasis or 'focus'*

The basic word order of simple sentences presented in section 8.2.2 referred to sentences without any special emphasis ('focus'). But what happens when a particular constituent in a sentence is the focus of that sentence? 'Focus', like 'topic', is a discourse or pragmatic function. 'Focus' refers to the most important or salient information in the sentence, and usually is the information that the speaker assumes the hearer does not share with him or her.

The basic word order and intonation of a language may be altered to emphasise a part of the sentence. In English we primarily use intonation, specifically higher pitch, to emphasise one word or phrase over the others in a sentence. We may also use cleft-type constructions such as 'It was the lion that killed our goat' to indicate the focus, which in this case would be the noun phrase 'the lion'. Some African languages sometimes use intonation, but more commonly focus involves one of the following alterations: (1) changes in the form of the main verb or use of auxiliary verb forms; (2) use of special words ('particles'); (3) use of cleft-type constructions; and (4) actual change in the basic word order in which case specific positions within the sentence serve as marking emphasis or focus. It is common for a language to use more than one of these means to mark the emphasis or 'focus' of a sentence. Some languages have complex systems to indicate various types of focus.

Ejagham below exemplifies the use of changes in the verb form. The first sentence uses the common word order and verb form, while the second (a question) and the third (an answer) use the form that indicates a marked focus is present. Bolding shows the focus of the given sentence.

(44)　Ejagham, Ekoid Bantu, Benue-Congo, Niger-Congo (Watters 1981)

    (a)　*à-nâm*　　　*bì-yù*
        3SG:PFV-buy　c8-yam
        'She bought yams.'

    (b)　*à-nàm-é"*　　　**jěn**
        3SG:PFV-buy-Focus　**what**
        '**What** did she buy?'

    (c)　*à-nàm-é"*　　　**bì-yù**
        3SG:PFV-buy-Focus　**c8-yam**
        'She bought **yams**.'

An important point highlighted by the examples in (44) is that question words such as 'who', 'what', and 'where' are always the focused constituent in questions of this type. The constituent that answers the question word then serves as the focus of the response.

Aghem has a complex focus system. In some cases it uses a focus particle *nô* 'focus (FOC)' that places emphasis on the phrase just preceding it.

(45)　Aghem (Grassfields Bantu, Benue-Congo, Niger-Congo) (Watters 1979: 167)

    (a)　*fú*　*kí*　*mɔ̂*　*nyìŋ*　*á*　*kí'-bé*
        rat　it　PST　run　in　c7-compound
        'The rat ran in the compound.'

    (b)　*fú*　*kí*　*mɔ̂*　**nyìŋ**　*nô*　*á*　*kí'-bé*
        rat　it　PST　run　FOC　in　c7-compound
        'The rat **ran** (did not walk) in the compound.'

    (c)　*fú*　*kí*　*mɔ̂*　*nyìŋ*　**á**　**kí'-bé**　　*nô*
        rat　it　PST　run　in　c7-compound　FOC
        'The rat ran **inside the compound** (not inside the house).'

Sentence (45a) uses the basic word order with no particles. The second and third sentences, (45b) and (45c), have emphasis or focus placed on the verb and the location, respectively, by placing the particle *nô* immediately after the constituent in focus.

Languages may use combinations of verb changes and particles, as in Vute.

(46)   Vute, Benue-Congo, Niger-Congo (Thwing and Watters 1987: 103)

    (a)   *mvèìn*   *yi*   *ɓwáb-na*   *tí*   *ŋgé*   *cene*

          chief   PST   buy-IO   PFV   3SG   chicken

          'The chief bought him a chicken.'

    (b)   *mvèìn*   *yi*   *ɓwáb-na-**á***   *ŋgé*   ***cene***   *ʔá*

          chief   PST   buy-IO-FOC   3SG   **chicken**   FOC

          'The chief bought him a **chicken**.'

In Vute, the focus marker on the verb indicates only that the noun phrase marked with the other focus marker *ʔá* is in focus. Other languages that use particles in their focus systems include the Eastern Cushitic languages Somali and Oromo.

Probably all languages in Africa have a form similar to the cleft-type construction in English. For information questions and focus, a language such as Ngie (Grassfields Bantu) appears to use only cleft-type constructions. Busa, an Eastern Mande language, uses cleft-type constructions for subject and object focus, but for verb and adjunct focus the focus marker immediately follows the focused item (Wedekind 1972: 34).

Many languages in Africa use changes in the basic word order to mark focus. In Turkana, a VSO language, if the subject or object noun phrase is emphasised, it occurs before the V(erb), potentially giving SVO or OVS word order (see Dimmendaal 1983a: 256). In contrast, in a group of languages with the basic word order SVOX along the Cameroonian and Nigerian border (e.g. Aghem and Noni), the syntactic position immediately following the verb serves as the focus position. In Mambila, another SVO language from the same area (see 47a), it is the sentence-final position that serves as the focus position. If a noun phrase is in focus, then any other post-verbal noun phrases will be moved to a pre-verbal position, as seen in (47b, c). If the verb itself is focused, as in (47d), it occurs sentence-final like the noun phrases.

(47)   Mambila, Mambiloid, Benue-Congo, Niger-Congo (Perrin 1994)

    (a)   *mè*   *ŋgeé*   *naâ*   *cɔ̀gɔ̀*   *léilé*

          1SG   buy   PST   cloth   yesterday

          'I bought cloth yesterday.'

(b) *mè   léilé   ŋgeé   naâ   cɔ̀gɔ̀*
ISG yesterday   buy   PST   **cloth**
'I bought **cloth** yesterday.'

(c) *mè   cɔ̀gɔ̀   ŋgeé   naâ   léilé*
ISG cloth   buy   PST   **yesterday**
'I bought cloth **yesterday**.'

(d) *mè   naâ   cɔ̀gɔ̀   ŋge*
ISG PST   cloth   **buy**
'I **bought** cloth.'

8.3   Compound and complex sentences (sentences with multiple clauses)

So far we have looked at simple sentences, that is sentences with only a single clause. Sentences may, however, consist of more than one clause. Such sentences may be referred to as 'compound' and 'complex'. Compound sentences involve the linking of two or more clauses of equal rank. Complex sentences involve the linking of two or more clauses in which one clause is the 'main' or 'matrix' clause and the other is the secondary (i.e. 'subordinate', 'dependent', or 'embedded') clause. However, as we will see below, the classical dichotomy between compound and complex sentences really involves a gradation of multiple ways to link two or more clauses to one another, but the dichotomy will serve us for matters of presentation.

Some of the syntactic issues raised by sentences with multiple clauses concern: (1) the means used to connect the two (or more) clauses; (2) the relationship between the two clauses; (3) the tracing of participants or noun phrases from one clause to the next; (3) the semantic relationship of the verbs in each clause to one another; (4) the omission of words in one of the clauses that are implied by some in the other clause, and so on.

8.3.1   *Compound sentences: linking clauses of equal importance*

To form compound sentences, African languages use various strategies: co-ordination, juxtaposition, 'consecutive' constructions and 'serial verb' constructions. Some languages use more than one of these strategies.

8.3.1.1   *Co-ordination*

Languages that use co-ordination are those that formally indicate the linkage between the two clauses by using a co-ordinating word such as 'and' for conjunction, 'but' for contrast, and 'or' for disjunction. Some languages have a word meaning 'and' but nothing meaning 'but' or 'or'. Other languages have a word for contrast and disjunction, but nothing for conjunction. Take Nawdm, a Gur language, for example. It does not have a word for contrast but it does have three different words for conjunction. One conjunction *n* means the two clauses have the same subject, another *te* means the clauses have different subjects, and a third *ka* means the two clauses are part of single, global event.

(48)   Nawdm, Gur, Niger-Congo (Jacques Nicole, p.c.)

(a)   *bà   dìirá   díité   n̂   nȳim   dáám*
        they   ate   food   **and**   drank   beer
        (= two events in sequence, same subject)

(b)   *bà   dìirá   díité,   wíi   té   nȳim   dáám*
        they   ate   food,   he   **then** drank   beer
        (= two events in sequence, different subjects)

(c)   *bà   dìirá   díité   ká   nȳi   dáám*
        they   ate   food   **and**   drank   beer
        (= one single event; 2nd verb changed aspect)

In other Gur languages, the conjunctions may carry tense and aspect functions as well. A simpler system of co-ordinating conjunctions is found in Aiki, using *sà* 'then'.

(49)   Aiki, Maban, Nilo-Saharan (Nougayrol 1989: 36)

nár   kádè   gá   màndài   tí-sín   t-ík   sà
day   certain ACC   lion   3SG-find:C 3SG-go:C   **then**

t-òòs   sà   tì-ɲààn-è̀
3SG-kill:C **then**   3SG-eat:C-ASRTV

'A certain day, a lion went and found (it), then killed (it), and then ate (it).'

The co-ordination of clauses within a sentence in African languages is generally different from co-ordination within the noun phrase. Noun phrases often use a conjunction 'and' that may also serve as the adposition 'with'.

8.3.1.2   *Juxtaposition*

Many languages in Africa do not use co-ordinating words. Instead, the two (or more) clauses are simply strung together. Nawdm uses juxtaposition for contrast as in 'but'. The first clause has an affirmative adverb such as 'certainly, truly', with no other special indicators in the rest of the sentence. So one could say: 'He went to the market for certain, he did not buy yams' to mean 'He went to the market but did not buy yams.'

Juxtaposition is prominent in many languages in place of using the conjunction 'and'. Consider the examples below from Ejagham (50) and Silt'e (51).

(50) Ejagham, Ekoid Bantu, Benue-Congo, Niger-Congo
      à-tûp   *ǹnyàm,*   *à-kân*   *kǎ èték,*
      3SG:PFV-shot   C9:animal   3SG:PFV-carry   to C5:village
      à-bhâ   *à-yâm*   *á-dî*
      3SG:PFV-butcher   3SG:PFV-cook   3PL:PFV-eat
      'He shot the animal, carried it to the village, then he butchered it, cooked it, and they ate.'

(51) Silt'e (Silti), Ethio-Semitic, Afroasiatic (Gutt and Mussa 1997: 947)
      surreenee   *beetanaane*   *afeetata*
      trousers:ACC:my   he:took-apart:CONV   he:made-wider:CONV
      sofeňň
      he:sewed:for:me
      'He took my trousers apart and made them wider for me.'

Note the conspicuous absence of conjunctions in both (50) and (51). In Ejagham (50), an SVO language, each of the five verbs is fully inflected for aspect, mood and subject agreement, just like verbs in any main clause. In Silt'e (51), an SOV language, the use of converbs for a sequence of clauses is the most common way to co-ordinate clauses. The converbs are marked for person, number, gender and aspect, but not for tense. The main (and final) verb *sofeňň* 'he:sewed:for:me' is the only one marked for tense. The clauses with converbs derive their tense from the main clause, forming a type of clausal chain in which some clauses are marked as non-final and one clause as final (Thompson and Longacre 1985: 175). This type of clausal chaining is common among the Ethio-Semitic, Cushitic and Omotic languages (Bender *et al.* 1976: 75).

8.3.1.3   *Consecutive constructions*

Some languages use a 'consecutive clause' construction in which each clause shares the same subject noun phrase, but the sequencing of the events is overtly marked in the verb of the second clause. This structure is the mirror image of the Ethio-Semitic chaining in which 'non-final' verbs are followed by a final verb, as seen in (51). With consecutive constructions, an initial verb is followed by a marked 'non-initial' verb. The sequence of actions is overtly marked in the second clause. In the Fe'fe' example (52), the nasal on the verb 'come' marks this sequencing, while the high tone on the final verb of the Igbo example (53) does the same. The Nupe example (54) uses a separate morpheme 'and' to indicate the sequencing.

(52)   Fe'fe', Grassfields Bantu, Benue-Congo, Niger-Congo (Hyman 1971)

ā   kā   láh   cāk   **n**-sā
he   PST   take   pot   **and**-come
'He took the pot and came.'

(53)   Igbo, Igboid, Benue-Congo, Niger-Congo (Hyman 1971)
ó   wèrè   ìtè   byá
he   took   pot   come
'He took the pot and came.'

(54)   Nupe, Nupoid, Benue-Congo, Niger-Congo (Hyman 1971: 29)
u   lá   dùkũ   **ci**   bé
he   took   pot   **and**   came
'He took the pot and came.'

8.3.1.4   *Serial verb constructions: from co-ordinate clauses and verb phrases
to compound verbs*

Sometimes two linked clauses behave like a sequence of verb phrases rather than a sequence of clauses. In these cases we can talk of 'serial verb constructions' or 'serialisation'. (See chapters 5 and 9 in this volume for further discussion and examples. See also the past debate about identifying the source of serial verb constructions in Awobuluyi (1973), Bamgboṣe (1974, 1982), Schachter (1974), Stahlke (1970, 1974), George (1975), and van Leynseele (1975), among others.)

Consider this example from Igbo.

(55)   Igbo, Igboid, Benue-Congo, Niger-Congo (Manfredi 1989: 353)
àdá   gàra   áhya   zúọ   úwe
Ada   go   market   buy   dress
'Ada went to market and bought clothes.'

Serial verb constructions are commonly found in some of the Benue-Congo, Kwa and Gur languages of Niger-Congo, but they are not limited to Niger-Congo. These sequences of verbs share the same subject noun phrase and may have an intervening object between the verbs. Often one of the verbs serves more as an auxiliary verb with a meaning different from its core meaning. They differ from co-ordinated and juxtaposed clauses in that the verbs agree in tense and aspect, and they allow only one negative.

Using Bamgboṣe (1982) as a guide, serial verb constructions have the following variation. First, in some cases the two verbs are so semantically fused that they are best considered a single lexical item in the dictionary. So in the example below, the verbs 'receive' and 'hear' combine to form a new compound verb 'believe' (< 'receive' + 'hear').

(56) Yoruba, Defoid, Benue-Congo, Niger-Congo (Bamgboṣe 1982: 5)

olú	gba	ọmọ	náà	gbọ
Olu	received	child	the	hear

'Olu believed the child.'

In some other cases the two verbs maintain their primary meanings. For example, 'go' and 'buy' in (55) above, or 'buy' and 'eat' in (57).

(57) Yoruba, Defoid, Benue-Congo, Niger-Congo (Bamgboṣe 1982: 4)

-NP-	---------VP---------		-VP-
olú	ra	ẹ̀pà	jẹ
Olu	bought	groundnuts	eat

'Olu bought groundnuts and ate them.'

In other cases one of the verbs takes a secondary or auxiliary meaning. Thus, the verb *maa* in (58), whose primary meaning is 'give', is interpreted here as having a secondary 'benefactive' meaning: namely, 'do for the benefit of'. The other verb *yɛɛ* maintains its primary meaning 'do'.

(58) Akan, Kwa, Niger-Congo (Bamgboṣe 1982: 5)

kofi	yɛɛ	adwuma	maa	amma
Kofi	did	work	gave	Amma

'Kofi worked for Amma.'

In some languages, verbs with such an auxiliary meaning can also become tense and aspect markers, and not just be used to mark grammatical relations, as in (58). In still other cases the two verbs reflect the reduction of a clause and an embedded purpose clause. So, in (59), 'came in order to take' is simplified as 'came take'. Compare (59) with (54) to see how (59) differs from a consecutive construction.

(59) Nupe, Nupoid, Benue-Congo, Niger-Congo (Bamgboṣe 1982: 5)

tsoda	bé	lá	egbà
Tsoda	came	take	axe

'Tsoda came in order to take the axe.'

8.3.2   ***Complex sentences: linking clauses of greater and lesser importance***
Complex sentences involve the linking of two or more clauses in which one clause is the 'main' or 'matrix' clause and the other is the secondary

(i.e. 'subordinate', 'dependent', or 'embedded') clause. The secondary clause may clarify the time, place or manner of the main clause ('adverbial' clauses). It may specify the identity of one of the noun phrases in the main clause ('adjectival' or 'relative' clauses). It may also be embedded as one of the noun phrases in the main clause or the verbal complement ('nominal' or 'complement' clause).

8.3.2.1 *Adverbial clauses: clauses as modifiers of verb phrases or other clauses*

Adverbial clauses modify verb phrases or other clauses. They often link the main clause of a given sentence to the preceding discourse. They use special morphemes, special verb forms, word order, or a combination of these to indicate that a particular clause is subordinate and adverbial (see Thompson and Longacre 1985: 206–34 for most points made here). Consider this example from Babungo in which the adverbial clause (bolded) uses a subordinating conjunction *fáŋ* and links the previous sentence to its own main clause.

(60)   Babungo, Grassfields Bantu, Benue-Congo, Niger-Congo (Schaub 1985: 38)

làmbí   gə̀   táa   gáy.   **fáŋ**   **ŋwɔ́**   **tó'**   **fí**
Lambi   go:PFV   in/to   grass   **when**   **he**   **walk:IMPFV** **from**
táa   **gáy**,
in   **grass**,
'Lambi went to the bush. **When he was walking through the bush,**
yè   nyáa   túŋ.
see:PFV animal   shoot:IMPFV
he saw an animal and shot it.'

Sometimes languages use the simple juxtaposition of clauses or auxiliary verbs to express adverbial notions, while other languages use subordination. While it is common for adverbial clauses to follow the main clause, an important generalisation regarding S-AUX-OV languages is that these languages permit adverbial clauses to precede or follow the main clause. However, SOV languages with postpositions in eastern Africa only permit adverbial clauses to precede the main clause (Heine 1976a). Ethio-Semitic languages are such a case, with adverbial clauses generally preceding the main clause. In many African languages, relative clauses are often used instead of adverbial clauses to express temporal, locative and manner adverbials, often without the head NP present (see section 8.3.2.3 on relative clauses). Consider these Hausa and Swahili examples:

(61)   Hausa, Chadic, Afroasiatic (Thompson and Longacre 1985: 180)
       Yara-n   sun   ga sarki (lokaci-n) da   suka   shiga   birni
       kids-the   they   see king **(time-the)** REL **they   enter   city**
       'The kids saw the king **when they visited the city**.' (lit. 'The kids saw
       the king **the time that they visited the city**.')

(62)   Swahili,   Bantu,   Benue-Congo,   Niger-Congo   (Thompson   and
       Longacre 1985: 181)
       Baba   a-na-po-pika   *chakula,   kuna pilipili*
       father   CI:SM-PRS-REL-cook   food,   there is pepper plenty
       '**When father cooks**, there is plenty of pepper.'

To mark adverbial clauses as being simultaneous with the main clause, African
languages often use a non-perfective verb form (i.e. continuative, durative, imperfective, habitual) to signal that relationship. This is especially true of Benue-Congo
languages. In conditional clauses, conditional morphemes are commonly used, but
some languages use relative clauses (Efik, Benue-Congo) and nominalised clauses
(Ngizim, Chadic).

8.3.2.2   *Nominal clauses: clauses as arguments of predicates*

In languages of the world, nominal or 'complement' clauses function
as noun phrases and complements of the main clause. They may take the role of
a subject noun phrase, as in '**The drumming for the procession** was great' or '**To
drum for the procession** is an honour'; of an object noun phrase, as in 'He enjoyed
the drumming for the procession'; or serve as a complement to the main clause verb,
as in 'He told him **that he should drum in the procession**.'
Nominal types vary from language to language and each language usually has
more than one type. The types found depend on the absence or presence of words
that link the main clause to the complement clause ('complementisers'). The types
also depend on the form of the verb in the complement clause. The verb forms
are either infinitives, or are inflected in the subjunctive or indicative mood.
It is fairly common in Africa to find nominal clauses using complementisers as
well as being simply juxtaposed, that is clauses placed in sequence, with no conjunction joining them. Some languages have more than one complementiser, such
as Kabre (Gur), which uses both *né* and *zì* 'that', the first implying that the complement clause took place, the second carrying no such implication (Noonan 1985:
44–8). In Ejagham (Ekoid Bantu), the complementisers are marked for person and
number to agree with the subject of the main clause: *bɔ̀rɛ̀* 'that:first person singular', *sè* 'that:second and third person singular', and *sê* 'that:first, second, third

plural'. Complementisers in African languages are at times related to the verbs of 'saying', as in Silt'e where *baala* 'say' is used (Gutt and Mussa 1997: 954).

Verbs in complement clauses are in the indicative mood for situations taken to be fact, and in the subjunctive mood for situations that are not yet realised. If the subject of the complement clause has the same referent as the subject (or object for some languages) in the main clause, then the complement clause takes an infinitival form. For example, with purpose clauses, many languages use infinitival verbal forms in the second clause (i.e. purpose clause) when the subject of the complement clause has the same referent as the subject in the main clause, as in (63):

(63)   Kinyarwanda, Bantu, Niger-Congo (Thompson and Longacre 1985: 187)
        tuagiiya   muli   parika   kureeba   uiyamasure
        we:went   in/to   zoo   INF:see   animals
        'We went to the zoo to see the animals.'

Languages without infinitival verb forms often use subjunctive-type moods, for example Godie, a Kru (Niger-Congo) language, uses the 'volitive' mood in purpose clauses. Some languages, such as Ngizim, a Chadic (Afroasiatic) language, use the same verbal morphology for both purpose and reason clauses, while other languages, such as Kanuri, a Saharan (Nilo-Saharan) language, use different verb forms for purpose and reason clauses.

Nominal clauses in African languages most commonly occur as complement clauses. Nominal clauses in subject and object noun phrases are much less common, but when nominal clauses do occur in these roles they usually take the form of infinitival clauses. More commonly, however, relative clauses are used in the place of nominal clauses, as in '**The time when Musa caught the thief** brought joy to the village' or 'The village rejoiced **the time when Musa caught the thief**.' African languages generally do not use participial clauses or complement clauses as subject or object noun phrases. So the following types of nominal clauses (bolded) are not common in Africa: '**Musa's catching the thief** brought joy to the village' or '**That Musa caught the thief** brought joy to the village.' Probably as common as relative clauses is the use of parataxis or co-ordination as in '**Musa caught the thief**, (and) the village rejoiced.'

The noun phrases in the different types of complement clauses lead to different pronoun strategies. In the case of infinitives, the subject pronoun is absent in the complement clause because it refers to the same entity as the subject (or object) of the main clause. In juxtaposed or co-ordinated clauses, the pronoun references follow the normal rules of pronouns within a discourse. However, in the case of indicative and subjunctive clauses that follow a complementiser, some languages make use of what is referred to in the literature as 'logophoric' pronouns. Such pronouns are found in some of the Nilo-Saharan languages of north-east Africa, some Adamawa-Ubangi, Benue-Congo and Kwa languages of Niger-Congo, and some Chadic languages of Afroasiatic. Consider the following example:

(64)   Mupun, Western Chadic, Chadic, Afroasiatic (Frajzyngier 1989: 201)

    (a) *wu*   *sat*   *nɔ́*   ***dí***   *nas*   *an*
        3SGM   say   that   **3SGM:LOG**   beat   1SG
        'He(1) said that **he(1)** beat me.'

    (b) *wu*   *sat*   *nɔ́*   ***wu***   *nas*   *an*
        3SGM   say   that   **3SGM:ANA**   beat   1SG
        'He(1) said that **he(2)** beat me.'

The logophoric pronoun *dí* in (64a) signals that the subject of the complement clause 'he beat me' is identical to the third person singular of the main clause: the usual 'anaphoric' pronoun *wu* in (64b) signals a different subject between the two clauses. Logophoric pronouns may also involve object pronouns and possessive pronouns, as well as second person.

8.3.2.3 *Adjectival clauses: clauses embedded within noun phrases*

When we speak of adjectival, or 'relative', clauses, we refer to a type of structure in which a noun phrase includes a clause that modifies the head of the phrase, just as adjectives in a noun phrase modify the head of the phrase. (See Keenan 1985b: 141ff for discussion.) In fact, relative clauses in African languages are frequently used for adjectival functions where European languages would use adjectives: for example 'the tall man' as 'the man who is tall'.

Languages in Africa generally have some form of relative clause. Relative clauses may be divided into restrictive relatives, as in 'the woman that I married', and non-restrictive relatives, as in 'my mother, who gave me birth long ago'. Restrictive relatives reduce the set of items that the head noun refers to, so above, of 'all women' it is restricted to 'the one that I married'. Non-restrictives do not narrow the identity of the head noun. They simply provide additional information, as in 'the one who gave me birth'. This distinction between restrictive and non-restrictive relatives is generally not marked in African languages, and many only have restrictive relative clauses, with non-restrictive senses expressed through apposition, as in 'my mother, the woman who gave me birth'. Those that do not have relative clauses in the sense of a noun phrase with an embedded adjectival clause at least have some functional equivalent that can restrict the identity of the head noun. African languages display a range of ways to form relative clauses. Compare the following:

(65)   Swahili, Bantu, Benue-Congo, Niger-Congo (Vitale 1981: 92)
---s--v---PredNom-

      [--s--   ------v------   ---o---]

watu   *[amba-o   wa-li-m-piga   Ahmed]   ni   washenzi*

people [REL-C2   they-PST-him-hit Ahmed] are savages

'The people who hit Ahmed are savages.'

(66)   Afar, Cushitic, Afroasiatic (Bliese 1981: 21)
--s--   --o--- --v--

    [-s- --o-- ---v---   ]

'usuk [a'tu   bah-'t-e   ] **duy'ye** *'be-e*

he   you   bring-you-PFV **things** took-he:PFV

'He took the things which you brought.'

In the Swahili example (65), the structure of the noun plus a relative clause is similar to English. The head noun (bolded) comes first, followed by the relative clause, indicated by the square brackets [. . .]. The clause begins with a relative pronoun *ambao*. In languages with a basic SVO word order, the relative clause typically follows the head noun, as in Swahili.

In the Afar example (66), the order of the head noun and relative clause is reversed, with the clause preceding the head noun. This order is common in SOV languages. The head noun 'things' is the direct object of the main clause and also the direct object in the relative clause. In both (65) and (66), where the head noun is realised outside the relative clause, its matching noun phrase in the relative clause is absent, even in the form of a pronoun, whether the clause follows or precedes the head noun. This lack of a pronoun in the relative clause to cross-reference with the head noun of the relative clause is common when the head noun correlates with the subject or object of the relative clause.

The strategy of having the head noun external to the relative clause is not used in Bambara.

(67)   Bambara (SOV), Mande, Niger-Congo (Bird 1968: 47)
*[n   ye so   **mìn** ye] tyè   ` be ò   dyɔ*

[1SG C **house** REL see] man the IC that erect

'The house that I saw, the man is building it.'

In (67) the embedded clause retains the noun *so* 'house' while the main clause uses the pronoun *ò* 'that' as an anaphoric pronoun reference to 'house'. What would be the head noun in other languages is actually internal to the relative clause, as is the relative marker *mìn*. Further, the relative clause is not embedded in the main clause like the relative clauses in examples (65) and (66). Rather than serving a restrictive function, the relative clause in (67) appears to serve more like a topic construction. This form of relativisation is unusual in Africa, found among the northern Mande languages, and among the Gur languages (Anne Kompaore, p.c.).

Structures used for relativisation not only vary from language to language, but also within languages. So languages may have more than one form of relative clause. Consider the examples in (68) for Swahili.

(68)   Swahili, Bantu, Benue-Congo, Niger-Congo (Vitale 1981: 99, example (78))

    (a)   *mtoto*   *amba-ye*   *a-na-lala*
           child   REL-CI   s/he-PRS-sleep
           'the child who is sleeping'

    (b)   *mtoto*   *a-na-ye-lala*
           child   s/he-PRS-REL-sleep
           'the child who is sleeping'

    (c)   *mtoto*   *a-lala-ye*
           child   s/he-sleep-REL
           'the sleeping child'

(68a) has the same structure as the Swahili relative verb in (65), with the head noun preceding the embedded adjectival clause, and the two being linked by a relative pronoun, namely *ambaye*. In (68b), however, the relative pronoun no longer connects the head noun with the relative clause. Instead the relative marker *-ye-* appears as an affix on the verb and marks the clause as a relative clause. In (68c) the verb is tenseless, with the relative marker *-ye* attached as a suffix to the verb. Example (68a) serves as a full relative clause while (68c) parallels a 'noun + adjective' construction. Yet all three use the *ye* relative (REL) marker. Variation of this type found in Swahili is not common in the Bantu languages. Yet there is considerable variation across Bantu as to how relatives are formed (Nsuka Nkutsi 1982). Most Bantu languages use a clause-initial relative marker.

As has been noted in earlier sections of this chapter, relative clauses or similar constructions, such as cleft-type sentences, are often used in focus constructions. Information questions may use the cleft sentence involving a relative clause. In addition, many languages have specific verb forms that are used both in relative clauses and in information questions and answers to those questions. In this way, relative clauses and information questions are formally linked. This is particularly true of Niger-Congo and Chadic languages (see Hyman and Watters 1984).

Finally, relative clauses may also be used in indirect questions, and to function in place of nominal clauses, as well as locative, temporal or manner adverbial clauses.

8.4   Conclusion

In a chapter concerning the syntax of hundreds of languages spread throughout at least four major language families across a vast continent, the coverage has to be spotty and selective. The four families included in this book do not form a natural group of languages except for the fact that they share one continent and have been in contact with one another along their borders for thousands of years.

Yet we have seen some relevant syntactic features of African languages. We noted the centrality of verbs and nouns in African languages, particularly by comparison to European languages, and the presence of ideophones. We observed the basic word order of simple sentences, including SVO, SOV and VSO languages. We noted the process of cross-referencing noun phrases in verbs, using agreement and other systems such as the concord systems found in many of the Niger-Congo languages.

We then observed how the basic word order may be altered when assertions are changed into commands or questions, or negation is used. We also discussed the presence of passive-like constructions, from true passives to constructions using indefinite pronouns, and their relation to topics and voice. We saw the variety of ways to focus on particular constituents within a sentence.

In the final section we moved from simple to compound and complex sentences. We noted that two or more clauses of equal rank may be linked through coordination or juxtaposition. Related constructions included consecutive and serial verb constructions. Two or more clauses of different rank may be linked, most commonly through particles, verb forms or juxtaposition to form adverbial, nominal and adjectival ('relative') clauses. Throughout we noted the significant use of relative clauses in place of adverbial and nominal clauses.

In the end, we must say that many African languages still remain poorly studied or have not been studied at all. We know little of their syntax. If we are to make further progress in our understanding of the syntax of African languages, studies of individual languages and overviews of language subgroups are needed. The next generation will be a critical time for progress to be made if we are to preserve for humanity the richness and diversity of the languages of Africa.

Notes

I want to thank the following people for their very helpful comments and suggestions on an earlier version of this chapter, or for other information provided in its writing: Thomas

Bearth, Lionel Bender, Mike Cahill, Rod Casali, Bernard Comrie, Gerrit Dimmendaal, Inge Egner, Derek Fivaz, Leoma Gilley, Tom Güldemann, Eeva Gutt, Ernst-August Gutt, Robert Hedinger, Bernd Heine, George Huttar, Anne Kompaore, Ruth Mason, David Morgan, Paul Newman, Jacques Nicole, Derek Nurse, Okoth Okombo, Ken Olson, Ronnie Sim, Maria Soukka, Pete Unseth, Rene Vallette, Dick Watson and Klaus Wedekind. Their comments and suggestions have made the chapter more accurate and informative. I regret that space did not permit me to indicate which person contributed to a particular sentence, paragraph or item of information. I usually indicated 'personal communication (p.c.)' when language data I used was provided by an individual. To the extent that this chapter proves helpful and informative, it is in very good measure due to the contributions of the above individuals. In some cases I did not follow the advice of the reviewers, in some cases their advice suggested competing directions, in other cases time or space did not permit incorporating their comments. In the end, I had to make the choices of the final form of the chapter. I accept full responsibility for its shortcomings.

1 To get an idea of what it means to talk about 'strings of words' composed of items such as a 'specifier', 'complement' and 'modifier', consider the following exemplary phrases from English:

(i)	is rapidly **hoeing** the field	(= VERB PHRASE)
(ii)	two professional **drummers** of the band	(= NOUN PHRASE)
(iii)	very considerately **gentle** with the child	(= ADJECTIVE PHRASE)

In phrase (i) the head of the phrase is the verb 'hoeing', so it forms a verb phrase. In (ii) it is the noun 'drummers', so it forms a noun phrase. In (iii) it is the adjective 'gentle', so forms an adjective phrase. In the verb phrase (i), the verb 'is' would be the specifier, 'the field' the complement, and 'rapidly' the modifier. In the noun phrase (ii), the numeral 'two' would be the specifier, 'of the band' would be the complement, and 'professional' would be the modifier. In the adjective phrase (iii), 'very' is the specifier, 'with the child' is the complement, and 'considerately' is the modifier.

2 The following abbreviations have been used in this chapter:

*	ungrammatical	HAB	habitual
1PL	first person plural	IC	incompletive
1SG	first singular	IDEO	ideophone
2SG	second singular		
3SGF	third singular female	INF	infinitive
3SGM	third person masculine singular	LOC	locative
3SG	third person singular	LOG	logophoric
ACC	accusative	NEG	negative
AGR	agreement marker	NOM	nominative
ANA	anaphoric	O	object
APPL	applicative	OBJ	object
ASP	aspect		
ASRTV	assertive	PART	verbal particle
AUX	auxiliary	PASS	passive
BEN	benefactive	PFV	perfective
C	completive	POSS	possession
C2	noun class 2 concord	PRS	present
C4	noun class 4 concord	PROG	progressive
C7	noun class 7 concord	PST	past
C10	noun class 10 concord	QM	question marker
C11	noun class 11 concord	REL	relative marker

CAUS	causative	S	subject
COMP	complemetiser	SBJ	subjunctive
DAT	dative	SC	subject concord
DEF	definite	SG	singular
DET	determiner	SM	subject marker
EXC	exclusive	STAT	stative
F	female	SUB	subordinate marker
FOC	focus	TNS	tense
FUT	future	V	verb
FV	final vowel	X	adjuncts

3 'Aspect' differs from 'tense'. Tense refers to the point in time identified with the situation referred to by the clause, such as past, present or future. Time is seen as a sequence of points along a time line. Aspect refers to how the situation is viewed in itself: as a complete, bounded situation in itself (i.e. 'perfective') or a situation with an internal temporal structure, with a beginning, middle and end (i.e. 'imperfective'). (See Comrie 1976 and Givón 1984: 272.)

4 Ejagham has the following tones: low, high, down-stepped high, rising, falling-to-low, and falling-to-mid. The falling-to-mid is marked as '''.

Further reading

General books to read that touch on issues discussed in this chapter include Welmers (1973), Greenberg (1963a), Gregersen (1977) and Heine (1976a). Studies of specific languages or language groups are worth looking at for more details on syntactic constructions. Among those works might be more general works like Bender (1976), Creider (1989), and Bendor-Samuel (1989), which includes notes on syntax at the end of various chapters covering the different subgroups of Niger-Congo. If you read French, another excellent overview would be Creissels (1991).

9

Typology

DENIS CREISSELS

9.1 Introduction

When linguistic typology started developing in the nineteenth century, its aim was to account for the structural diversity of languages by classifying them into a small number of types. In such classifications, each language taken as a whole was considered as belonging to a particular language type. However, modern research has made it clear that typology must begin with establishing types of structures in the individual subsystems that constitute a language, and not types of languages, since two languages may have the same type of structure in certain domains but different types of structure in other domains. One may subsequently observe that certain logically possible types of structure are rare, or even not attested at all. Correlations between a priori independent structural types may also be investigated: certain combinations of logically independent features turn out to be rare, or even not attested at all. But these correlations are not restrictive enough to make possible a reduction of the structural diversity of languages to a small number of language types not limited to some particular aspects of language structure.

The structural diversity of African languages is not as great as that of the languages of the world, but it is nevertheless sufficient to exclude the possibility of classifying them into a small number of language types without arbitrarily selecting a few typological features and excluding others the consideration of which could lead to a different classification. Consequently, the possibility of classifying African languages into a small number of language types will not be considered here.

Another preliminary question that deserves some discussion is the possibility of correlations between phonological and morphosyntactic features. Such a correlation was proposed by Houis (1970) for the languages of Africa, but consideration of a wider sample of African languages does not corroborate it. More generally, phonology turns out to be an autonomous component of language structure in the sense that correlations between phonological and morphosyntactic features seem to exist only within very limited groups of languages and therefore have no general significance. Since phonological typology deserves a separate account, in this chapter, I shall limit myself to a discussion of a set of morphosyntactic features the importance of which for a typological characterisation of languages is agreed on by most authors.

This typological sketch of African languages will thus mainly consist of a review of the form taken in African languages by the notions generally viewed as essential in the syntactic organisation of languages, in order both to give an overview of the structural diversity of African languages and to compare the structural diversity of African languages with that observed elsewhere in the languages of the world. This implies taking a position on the possibility of defining a set of syntactic notions both universal (i.e. which play a role in the organisation of every language) and fundamental (i.e. which constitute, in the descriptions of individual languages and from a logical point of view, the primitive notions on the basis of which the other notions relevant to the description are built). The following hypotheses, which are more or less explicitly accepted in most current work on language typology, are adopted here:

- The most general characteristic of natural language syntax is the existence of two major types of phrases: noun phrases and clauses.
- Noun phrases typically consist of a noun, which relates the referent of the noun phrase to a notion available in the lexicon, and of a variable number of modifiers.
- With the possible exception of particular types of clauses typically specialised in the expression of identification, existence, location or attribution of qualities (see section 9.6), clauses result from the combination of a variable number of noun phrases with a verb, and this construction can be at least partially analysed in terms of predicate–argument structure: the verb (the predicate) assigns semantic roles to some of the noun phrases with which it combines (the arguments).
- The syntactic relations between the verb and the nominal terms of a clause are universally organised according to a contrast 'subject (S) / (direct) object (O) / obliques (X)'. The notion of subject relies on various syntactic mechanisms (relativisation, reflexive pronoun control, etc.) that imply a hierarchy of the nominal terms of a clause: the subject in a particular language can be defined as the formal type

of relation with the verb characteristic of nominal terms that, in the language in question, occupy the highest rank in this hierarchy. There are also syntactic mechanisms that reveal a variable degree of solidarity between the verb and the nominal terms of the clause other than the subject (indexation, passivisation, etc.), and the (direct) object in a particular language can be defined as the type of formal relation with the verb characteristic of nominal terms other than subjects that, in the language in question, show the highest degree of solidarity with the verb in such mechanisms. With verbs representing actions involving an agent and a patient, the subject typically represents the agent, and the object typically represents the patient.

- The genitive can be universally characterised as a noun phrase with the function of noun modifier in a construction that minimally specifies the semantic nature of the relation between the referent of the head noun and the referent of the noun phrase in modifier function.

Note that the dative (or 'indirect object') is not viewed here as a universal notion on the same level as subject and (direct) object: some languages have a particular type of syntactic relation distinct both from the (direct) object and from the obliques, typically associated with the semantic role of goal, but in many languages, the nominal term commonly called 'indirect object' is not clearly distinct from the obliques, and in some other languages (in particular in languages with double object constructions, which are very common in Africa) it may have the syntactic behaviour characteristic of (direct) objects.

9.2   Subject/object

In addition to clause constituent order (see section 9.5), the distinction between subject and object may involve case marking and indexation, and voice morphemes included in verb forms may modify the valence of the verb (intransitive/transitive/ditransitive) and the semantic roles it assigns to its subject and/or object(s).

9.2.1   *Subject/object case marking typology*

In the majority of African languages, both subjects and objects are unmarked for case, that is they do not exhibit any marking (affix, adposition or prosodic contour) distinguishing noun phrases in subject or object function from noun phrases quoted in isolation. This is in particular true of the overwhelming majority of Niger-Congo languages. However, in a number of Central Chadic languages, nouns in object function are introduced by prepositions, and case-marked subjects or objects are common in north-east Africa, in the Cushitic and Semitic branches of Afroasiatic and in certain branches of Nilo-Saharan.

Among the languages that have case marking systems distinguishing the subject from the object, the most common type, both worldwide and at the level of the African continent, is that in which the subject is unmarked for case (i.e. coincides with the quotation form of nouns), whereas the object takes a particular case form, called accusative.

Another fairly common type at world level is the ergative type of case marking, in which the object of transitive clauses and the subject of intransitive clauses are unmarked for case, whereas the subject of transitive clauses takes a particular case form, generally called ergative. A few African languages have been claimed to have some ergative properties, but no clear case of ergative type of case marking has been reported to my knowledge. This is consistent with the strong predominance of the clause constituent order SVO in the languages of Africa (see section 9.4), since it has been observed that the ergative type of case marking occurs only in languages that have either SOV or VSO as their basic clause constituent order.

By contrast, the type of case marking in which the object is unmarked for case and the subject takes a particular case form (irrespective of the transitive vs. intransitive distinction), which is very rare at world level, is not uncommon among the African languages that have distinct case forms for subjects and objects. It occurs for example in Somali, Oromo, Maasai.

Kanuri illustrates another rare type of case marking, in which both the subject and the object may be case-marked, irrespective of the transitive vs. intransitive distinction.

In the African languages that have case marking systems distinguishing the subject from the object, cases are often marked by tonal differences only. For example, the citation form of the Somali noun meaning 'knife', which is used also when the noun is in object function, is *mindí*, and its form in subject function is *mindi*.

'Tone cases' have been reported for some Western Bantu languages too, and it is interesting to notice that they result from an evolution in the course of which a distinction between a definite and an indefinite form of nouns lost its original function, each form becoming attached to certain syntactic contexts – see Blanchon (1998). More generally, the languages of Africa confirm the existence of a relation between definiteness and case marking: languages in which the use of an accusative marker correlates with the definiteness distinction include Amharic, Tigre and some Cushitic languages.

9.22   ***Subject/object indexation typology***

Most African languagues have subject markers attached to verb forms, and a number of them have also object markers. Note that many descriptions of West African languages do not mention the existence of subject markers attached to verbs, but in most cases the morphemes termed 'subject pronouns' in descriptions of West African languages are not really separate words and should be reanalysed as prefixed to the verb.

Subject markers and object markers may be obligatory; in such cases, they are usually termed agreement morphemes. But their presence may also depend on the discourse structure of the clause. Among African languages, one encounters both languages with obligatory subject markers and languages with discourse-dependent subject markers. By contrast, object markers functioning as pure agreement morphemes are rare in Africa. Tswana, example (1), illustrates a situation in which the object markers included in the verb forms always represent topics and are therefore in complementary distribution with noun phrases in object function, the choice between an object marker and a free pronoun in object function being pragmatically significant.

(1)   Tswana (Bantu, Niger-Congo)[1]
  (a)   *kì-χὼ-bíd-ìtsè*   'I *called* you.'
        SM.1S-OM.2S-call-ANT   (how is it possible that you didn't hear me?)
  (b)   *kì-bíd-itsé*   *wèná*   'I called *you*.' (and nobody else!)
        SM.1S-call-ANT   YOU

Swahili illustrates an intermediate situation, in which definite objects (including pronouns and proper nouns) trigger the presence of an object marker irrespective of their discourse function, whereas no object marker accompanies indefinite noun phrases in object function (example (2)). Note that in Swahili, definiteness is not overtly marked at noun phrase level, and consequently the presence of an object marker constitutes the only clue to the definiteness of common nouns in object function.

(2)   Swahili (Bantu, Niger-Congo)
  (a)   *ni-me- ku-ona*   'I have seen you.'
        SM.1S-ANT-OM2S-see
  (b)   **ni-me-ona*   *wewe*
        SM.1S-ANT-see   you
  (c)   *u-me-leta*   *chakula?*   'Have you brought (some) food?'
        SM.2S-ANT-bring   CL7.food
  (d)   *u-me-ki-leta*   *chakula?*   'Have you brought the food?'
        SM.2S-ANT-OM.CL7-bring   CL7.food   (which I told you to bring)

Duranti (1979), Kidima (1987) and Morolong and Hyman (1977) show that the use of object markers in languages with double object constructions supports the hypothesis of a 'topicality hierarchy' conflating distinctions in person, semantic role and animacy, which more generally accounts for various aspects of the behaviour of noun phrases in object function.

In a number of African languages, even among those that have no case distinction between subjects and objects, subject markers differ from the corresponding object markers, at least in some persons. But I am aware of no African language with intransitive subject markers identical to the object markers and different from the transitive subject markers, that is with a system of subject and object markers following an ergative pattern (see above).

The distinctions expressed by subject and object markers almost always parallel those expressed by free pronouns. They always include distinctions in person and number. In the first person plural, a distinction between 'we including you' and 'we excluding you' occurs sporadically in several groups of African languages. As a rule, additional distinctions in the third person (sometimes in the second person) are encountered in languages in which identical distinctions are involved in the agreement between nouns and modifiers, as illustrated here by Swati, example (3).

(3)   Swati (Bantu, Niger-Congo)

    (a)   *in-dvodza   len-dze   i-yabaleka*   'The tall man is running away.'
          CL9-man   CL9-tall   SM.CL9-run

    (b)   *um-fana   lomu-dze   u-yabaleka*   'The tall boy is running away.'
          CL1-boy   CL1-tall   SM.CL1-run

There are however exceptions to this rule. For example, Wolof has 'noun class' distinctions at the noun phrase level, but these distinctions do not manifest themselves in the variations of personal pronouns or of subject and object markers. Conversely, Zande is devoid of any gender distinction at the noun phrase level, but in the third person, the personal pronouns and the subject markers of Zande have different forms for masculine human, feminine human, non-human animate and inanimate.

9.2.3   *Voice*
    Descriptions of African languages often mention passive, reciprocal, causative and applicative verb forms. In particular, most West Atlantic and Bantu languages make very wide use of the applicative voice. In these languages, several semantic types of complements that cross-linguistically tend to be treated as obliques can occur only as (direct) objects of applicative verb forms, and

consequently adpositions or case affixes encoding the meanings in question are rarely used or even totally absent, as illustrated here by Tswana, example (4).

(4) Tswana

    (a) *kì-bíd-ítsé*   *bàná*
          SM.1S-call-ANT   CL2.children
          'I have called the children.'

    (b) *kì-bíl-éd-ítsé*   *bàná*   *dìjɔ́*
          SM.1S-call-APPL-ANT   CL2.children   CL8.meal
          'I have called the children for meal.'

    (c) *kì-bíl-éd-ítsé*   *bàná*   *ŋàkà*
          SM.1S-call-APPL-ANT   CL2-children   CL9-doctor
          'I have called the doctor for the children.'

As regards voice, it is worth also mentioning the following two points:

(a) African languages often have verb forms that assign a 'passive' role to their subject, but, in contrast with true passive forms, do not imply the existence of an agent triggering and/or controlling the process (see chapter 8 above). From a general linguistics point of view, this is a particular variety of middle voice, but in most descriptions of African languages where such a voice occurs, it is either not clearly distinguished from a true passive voice, or it is referred to by terms (such as 'neuter') that do not identify it as a voice at all. Tswana – example (5) – illustrates here this distinction between (true) passive and mediopassive.

(5) Tswana

    (a) *màí*   *á-thùb-íl-w-è*   *[kíŋwàná]*
          CL6.egg   SM.CL6-break-ANT-PAS-ANT by   CL1.child
          'The eggs were broken (by the child).'

    (b) *màí*   *á-thúb-èχ-ìlè*   'The eggs broke.'
          CL6.eggs   SM.CL6-break-MEDPAS-ANT

(b) The distinction between reflexive morphemes and middle voice markers is not always clear-cut, due to the well-known fact that reflexives tend to rapidly acquire middle voice uses, and verb forms referred to as 'reflexive' should often be identified rather as 'middle', since they have a variety of uses that cannot be reduced to the notion of reflexive proper.

9.3 The verb

9.3.1 *Presence vs. absence of verbal inflection*

In most languages, the verb has an inflection considerably more complex than that of any other category. The verb may have a rich inflection system even in languages in which nominal inflection proper does not exist (which means that all of the grammatical morphemes operating at noun phrase level have the status of phrasal affixes (see section 9.4) rather than that of affixes of the head noun). This situation is for example common among Kwa languages.

Languages really devoid of verbal inflection are very rare. Note that on this matter, the available documentation on African languages may be misleading, since in many descriptions of West African languages, as already mentioned in connection with subject markers, verb prefixes are wrongly identified as free morphemes, with the result that languages with an entirely prefixal verb inflection (which is a fairly common situation among West African languages) are wrongly presented as languages devoid of verbal inflection.

There are however a few African languages that are really devoid of verbal inflection, for example Zarma, a language that has no subject or object indexation in verb forms, and in which tense, aspect, modality and negation markers cannot be analysed as verb affixes, since they may be separated from the verb by a noun phrase in object function – example (6).

> (6)   Zarma (Songay, Nilo-Saharan)
> *fà:tí   sí   fòjŏ: hìnà* 'Faati won't cook the soup.'
> Faati   IMPERF.NEG   soup-DEF   cook

9.3.2   *Types of verbal inflection*

The proportion of languages with a predominently or even exclusively prefixal verbal inflection is higher in Africa than in most other parts of the world. Another striking characteristic of African languages is the high proportion of languages with a verbal inflection involving not only segmental morphemes but also tonal alternations. In Kposo, the perfective vs. imperfective and positive vs. negative distinctions may rely exclusively on tonal variations of the subject marker prefixed to the verb – example (7).

> (7)   Kposo (Kwa, Niger-Congo)
> *ū-dzí* 'we are eating'   *úū-dzí* 'we are not eating'
> *ù-dzí* 'we have eaten'   *ūù-dzí* 'we have not eaten'

As regards the nature of the distinctions expressed through verbal inflection, three types of verbal inflection can be distinguished:

> (a)   in a vast majority of African languages, verbal inflection involves both subject or object markers and other types of morphemes
> (b)   as already mentioned in section 9.2.2, languages with a verbal inflection involving no subject or object marker are not very common in

Africa, but a number of Mande languages (Mende, Soso, Soninke, etc.) illustrate this situation

(c) systems of verbal inflection consisting exclusively of subject and object markers are extremely rare at world level, and among African languages, the only case I am aware of is that of the Sara languages

TAM (tense, aspect, modality) distinctions are certainly the type of semantic distinctions most commonly expressed through verbal inflection, but systems of verbal inflection involving additional types of semantic distinctions are not rare in Africa. Systems of verbal inflection expressing negation are common, but systems of verbal inflection expressing distinctions relating to various types of focus phenomena are particularly interesting, since such systems are found in a number of languages belonging to various branches of the Niger-Congo phylum but seem to be very rare outside Africa. For further details on the relation between verbal inflection and focus in African languages, see Creissels (1996), Creissels and Robert (1998), Faraclas (1984), Givón (1975a), Hyman and Watters (1984).

9.3.3 *Auxiliaries*

Complex verb forms of the type commonly encountered in European languages (i.e. complex verb forms consisting of an auxiliary verb and a dependent or nominalised form of another verb, traditionally called main verb) are quite common in African languages too, and comparative data very often suggest that TAM markers that have synchronically the status of inflectional morphemes originate in ancient auxiliary verbs (future markers originating in an auxiliarised form of a verb 'come' or 'go' are particularly common in African languages).

A very general characteristic of African languages is that they tend to have auxiliary verbs expressing meanings commonly taken up by adverbial expressions in European languages, that is auxiliary verbs with meanings such as 'to do first', 'to do again', 'to do often', 'to have previously done', 'to have done the day before', 'not to have done yet', etc. – see Creissels (1998a) and (1998b).

Note that there may be some variation in the use of the notion of 'auxiliary' in descriptions of individual languages: this term may apply to auxiliary verbs only (i.e. to items exhibiting at least certain morphological characteristics of verbs), or to any TAM marker that is not strictly speaking affixed to the verb. For example, constructions of the type illustrated by (6) above, in which TAM markers are separated from the verb by a noun phrase in object function, are common in Mande languages too; in the Mandeist tradition, such TAM markers are called 'predicative markers', but in other traditions, similar morphemes would be called 'auxiliaries' – and in fact, historically, at least some of these 'predicative markers' are decategorialised auxiliary verbs.

9.3.4   ***Serial verbs***

The type of complex predicate known in the literature as 'serial verb' is a sequence of two or more verbs with the three following properties (see also chapter 8):

- there is a single subject for the whole sequence
- each verb may have its own complement
- the sequence as a whole has the behaviour of a single predicate, and not that of a construction involving distinct predicates in some dependency relation

It is difficult to say exactly which languages really have serial verbs. The point is that manipulations are necessary in order to establish the precise nature of verb sequences, since at first sight, there is most of the time no obvious distinction between serial verbs and verb sequences in which each verb constitutes a distinct predicate, in particular consecutive constructions (i.e. constructions in which two or more successive clauses represent successive events – see section 9.7). Unfortunately, in many descriptions of African languages, any more or less 'exotic' verb sequence (i.e. any sequence of verbs that does not exhibit every characteristic of the sequences of verbs found in European languages) is loosely termed 'serial verb'.

Baule – example (8) – illustrates a particularly clear case of serial verb: in this construction, both *fa* 'take' and *kle* 'show' combine with verbal affixes, which in particular excludes the analysis of *fa* as a preposition in a monoverbal sentence with the SOV constituent order, but this verb sequence cannot be viewed as reflecting the decomposition of a complex event into elementary ones (one does not 'take' a house before showing it to somebody else), and it is obvious that the complement of the verb 'take' does not receive its semantic role from it, but from the other component of the serial verb.

(8)   Baule (Kwa, Niger-Congo)
       ɔ-à-fà   í   swǎ   n   à-klè   mí̋
       he-ANT-take his   house DEF   ANT-show me
       'He has shown me his house.'

One may argue that the only true serialising languages are those that have constructions similar to that illustrated by (8), and that even in typical serialising languages, many constructions commonly viewed as particular types of serial verbs are not serial verbs at all.

In Africa, uncontroversial cases of serial verbs are found mainly in Kwa languages (e.g. Ewe) and in Benue-Congo languages previously classified as Eastern Kwa (e.g. Yoruba).

9.3.5 *Complex verb form reanalysis and syntactic change*

Reanalysis of constructions involving auxiliarisation or serialisation is often put forward as an explanation of changes in clause constituent order and/or case marking. In particular:

(a) In languages having SVOX as their basic clause constituent order, if at the noun-phrase level the genitival modifier precedes the noun, noun phrases corresponding to the object of finite verb forms precede nominalised verb forms, since they are treated as their genitival modifier; consequently, with complex verb forms consisting of an auxiliary verb and a nominalised form of the main verb, the noun phrase corresponding to the object of a finite verb form precedes the nominalised form of the main verb. Subsequently, the decategorialisation of the auxiliary verb may lead to the reanalysis of such constructions as involving a finite verb form preceded by a noun phrase in object function. The presence of TAM markers between the subject and the object in clauses with the constituent order SOVX can be viewed as a strong hint that such a process of reanalysis took place in the history of the language in question.

(b) In serialising languages having SVOX as their basic clause constituent order, one often finds combinations of the verb 'take' with another verb in which the second verb is devoid of object but assigns to the object of 'take' the semantic role it could assign to its own object, as in (8) above; here again, the generalisation of the serial construction and the decategorialisation of 'take' may lead to reanalysing 'take' as an accusative marker in a construction with the constituent order SOV.

There is some evidence that such processes played and continue to play a role in the evolution of African languages. For further details and/or competing views on this much debated issue, see Claudi (1988, 1993, 1994), Gensler (1997), Givón (1975b, 1976, 1979), Heine (1980), Heine and Reh (1984), Hyman (1975b), Jarvis (1981), Longacre (1990), Lord (1977, 1993) and Tosco (1993).

9.4 The structure of noun phrases

9.4.1 *Nominal classification*

Classifier systems of the type encountered in languages of East Asia or of the Pacific are extremely rare in Africa. Pasch (1985) describes a system of genitival classifiers in the Ubangian language Dongo-ko, and Ikoro (1994) describes a system of numeral classifiers in the Cross-River languague Kana, but these are quite exceptional cases. By contrast, one commonly finds in Africa noun classification systems in which nouns are divided into several subsets on the basis of the fact that several types of noun modifiers have alternate forms to indicate agreement with the noun they modify.

As discussed in Corbett (1991), there is no essential distinction between 'gender' systems and 'noun class' systems, and 'gender' could conveniently include types of nominal classification traditionally referred to as 'noun class systems'. However, in African linguistics, the term 'gender' tends to be used only when sex figures among the bases of classification.

As already mentioned in section 9.2.2, gender systems manifested within the limits of noun phrases through agreement between the head noun and its modifiers usually go with similar agreement phenomena involving morphemes or words external to the noun phrase but anaphorically linked to it (pronouns, subject markers, object markers), but these two phenomena should be distinguished, since they do not necessarily co-occur: languages may have gender distinctions manifested only at the level of the relation between the noun and its modifiers, or only at the level of the relation between the noun phrase and morphemes or words anaphorically linked to it.

Two types of gender systems are common among African languages:

(a) Systems with two genders mainly based on the sex distinction (masculine vs. feminine) are common in all branches of Afroasiatic and in some branches of Nilo-Saharan; in Khoisan, such systems are found in Khoe languages and in the isolated languages Sandawe, Kwadi and Hadza. A third gender similar to the Indo-European neuter has been reported to exist in Eastern Nilotic languages and in Khoe languages. A few Niger-Congo languages (Ijo, Zande) are reported to have a masculine vs. feminine distinction, but it concerns only 'pronominal' gender and does not manifest itself at the level of the relation between the noun and its modifiers. These languages do not correspond to any grouping definable in genetic or geographic terms: they are sporadically found in several branches of Niger-Congo, in areas very distant from one another.

(b) Different types of gender systems, in which the sex distinction plays no role, are encountered in all major branches of the Niger-Congo phylum, with the only exception of Mande, and in Northern Khoisan.

In addition to the irrelevance of the masculine vs. feminine distinction, Niger-Congo gender systems, usually referred to as 'noun class systems', share the following characteristics:

- the number of genders is relatively high; gender systems with something like twenty genders are not exceptional among Bantu or Atlantic languages
- the semantic distinction most transparently taken into account in the allocation of nouns to genders is always the human vs. non-human distinction
- gender and number interfere in a particularly intricate way: it is impossible to isolate plural markers as distinct from gender markers; nouns that belong to the same gender in the singular often belong to different genders in the plural, and conversely; alternate plural forms (with sometimes more or less subtle shades of meaning) corresponding to the same singular form are not uncommon
- in Niger-Congo gender systems, the distinction between inflection and derivation tends to blur, since on the one hand gender cannot be dissociated from number, which is a typically inflectional notion, but on the other hand allocation of nouns to genders largely relies on typically derivational notions or distinctions, such as augmentative, diminutive, concrete vs. abstract, tree vs fruit, etc., and in deverbative nouns, gender markers straightforwardly express distinctions usually conveyed by distinct derivational morphemes (deverbative nouns in the 'human' gender denote agents, etc.)

The complexity of the interaction between gender and number in Niger-Congo gender systems explains why most descriptions do not focus on the possibility of classifying lexemes into genders, but rather on the inventory of possible agreement patterns; they consequently group nominal forms into 'noun classes' on the basis of their agreement properties, which leads one to consider the singular and the plural of the same noun as two distinct units belonging to distinct 'noun classes', since they enter into different agreement patterns. For example, the singular form *mò-thò* of the Tswana noun meaning 'human being' is said to belong to class 1, whereas its plural form *bà-thò* is said to belong to class 2. Genders in the usual sense of this term may subsequently be defined as pairs of 'noun classes', the alternation of which may express the singular vs. plural distinction.

9.4.2   *Definiteness and referentiality*

Definite articles are quite common in African languages. African languages provide considerable comparative evidence that in the overwhelming majority of cases, definite articles originate in demonstratives. However, some language groups confirm also the possibility of articles originating in third-person possessives. Indefinite articles originating in the numeral 'one' are also attested, but they are far less common than definite articles.

Languages with and without definite articles are encountered virtually in all language families and in all parts of the African continent. This distribution shows that the grammaticalisation process 'demonstrative > definite article' is very frequent in the evolution of languages, but also that definite articles are relatively unstable: processes leading to their loss or to a change in their status are also frequent. There is a very general tendency of definite articles proper towards expanding their use to include both definite determination and non-definite referential uses, giving rise to what Greenberg (1978) calls 'stage II of the definite article'. Articles at this stage of their evolution are particularly common in Africa. Subsequently, since the proportion of referential noun phrases in discourse greatly exceeds that of non-referential ones, in languages with 'stage II definite articles', the definite form of nouns tends to become obligatory in most contexts, the indefinite form occurring only in contexts favouring a non-referential interpretation, for example in negative context, as illustrated here by Mandinka – example (9).

(9)   Mandinka (Mande, Niger-Congo)
      (a)   i   yè   kúlúŋ-ò   jè   'They saw a/the boat.'
            they PERF boat-DEF   see
      (b)   *i ye kuluŋ je
      (c)   i   máŋ   'kúlúŋ-ò   jè   'They did not see the boat.'
            they PERF.NEG boat-DEF   see
      (d)   i   máŋ   kùlùŋ jè   'They did not see any boat.'
            they PERF.NEG boat   see

A possible evolution at this stage is that the definite form of nouns generalises in syntactically defined contexts but becomes impossible in syntactic contexts in which the indefinite form is relatively frequent, giving rise to a case distinction (see section 9.2.1). But another possibility is a general increase of the tendency to reduce the number of contexts in which the indefinite form of nouns is possible; as the final outcome of such an evolution, what is historically the definite form of nouns becomes their only possible form, the former article no longer having any connection with definiteness or referentiality. Three possibilities must then be distinguished:

      (a)   In cases where there was no gender-like distinction in the demonstrative in which the former article originated, the article at the last stage of its cycle becomes a marker of nominality as such, giving rise to situations in which, for example, every common noun in the language exhibits the same ending.

(b)   In the case of languages devoid of gender proper but with some gender-like distinction in the demonstrative in which the former article originated, the result of the generalisation of the former article is that nouns acquire classifying markers, which may subsequently favour the development of a gender system. However, there is no evidence that such processes took place in the history of African languages: if they ever did, it must have occurred in a very remote past, and is no more accessible to reconstruction.

(c)   In languages with a gender system, if the former article expressed the gender distinction, the evolution described above results in the reinforcement or renewal of gender morphology, and may in particular compensate for the phonological erosion of older gender markers. Niger-Congo languages provide considerable evidence of such evolutions. In particular, there is a tendency towards replacing older class suffixes by newer class prefixes in many subgroups of the Gur branch of Niger-Congo, and a tendency towards replacing older class prefixes by newer class suffixes in many subgroups of the Atlantic family, and in both cases there is comparative evidence that the newer class affixes originate in definite articles.

An interesting observation concerning definite articles is the relatively high proportion of African languages with drastically eroded 'stage II articles'. In a number of African languages, 'stage II articles' manifest themselves only through a change in tone at the beginning or at the end of the word they are attached to, which results from the erosion of former prefixes or suffixes, as shown by comparison with closely related languages in which a segmental form of the article is maintained. For example, Swati *sitiɓa* (indef.) / *sítiɓa* (def.) 'well' may be compared with Zulu *siziɓa* / *i-síziɓa* (< *í-siziɓa*), and Kita Maninka *básá* (indef.) / *básà* (def.) 'lizard' may be compared with Gambian Mandinka *básá* / *básò:* (< *básá-ò*).

In the available descriptions of African languages, definite articles are analysed either as free morphemes or as affixes, but in most cases, this decision turns out to rely exclusively on the absence vs. presence of a specific phonological interaction with the neighbouring words, and closer examination of the distribution of definite articles shows that they are in fact neither really free morphemes nor true affixes, but rather 'phrasal affixes', that is bound morphemes differing from prototypical affixes in that they are not attached to a particular type of stem but rather to the first or to the last word of the noun phrase, irrespective of the precise nature of this word. For example, in Mandinka, the definite form of 'woman' is *mùsô:* (< *mùsú-ò*), but 'the/a one-eyed woman' is *mùsù nyá:-kílíŋ-ò*, literally 'woman eye-one-the'.

Arabic illustrates the somewhat exceptional case of a language with a definite article really affixed to nouns and with agreement in definiteness between the noun and the adjectival modifiers, as in *al-baytu l-kabiːru* 'the big house', literally 'the-house the-big'.

9.4.3   *Number*

Virtually all African languages have bound morphemes encoding plurality without particular restrictions on the semantic nature of nouns, that is plural markers the use of which takes into account the count vs. mass noun distinction without however being restricted to noun phrases that occupy a relatively high position in the animacy hierarchy.

However, the total lack of plural markers is illustrated by Igbo. Apart from the personal pronouns, two non-derived Igbo nouns only have suppletive plural forms: *ŋ̀ŋwá* pl. *ớmɔ̀* 'child' and *ónyé* pl. *ńdí* 'person', and in the case of nouns that are not compounds with 'person' or 'child' as their first formant (such as *ŋ̀ŋwá ớnɔ̀ ákwɔ́kɔ́* 'schoolchild', lit. 'book house child' or *ónyé á·ˈfíá* 'trader', lit. 'market person'), plurality can be expressed only by adding numerals or quantifiers with meanings such as 'several', 'a few', 'many', etc. Such a situation is found also in some languages of the Chadic family (Gwandara, Pero), but on the whole, it is rather exceptional in Africa. The same can be said of systems of plural markers restricted to a narrow range of nouns (mainly humans and animates), but here again, such a situation is found in some languages of the Chadic family, for example in Masa – see Frajzyngier (1977).

As regards the use of plural markers, two opposite tendencies emerge among African languages, which largely correlate both with the morphological nature of plural markers and with the presence vs. absence of a gender system:

(a)   languages devoid of a gender system generally have a single plural marker with the morphological status of a phrasal affix (see section 9.5.2), and such plural markers tend to be used on a 'pragmatic' basis, that is to be employed only when plurality is both communicatively relevant and not implied by the context, at least in the case of nouns that do not refer to persons

(b)   languages that have gender generally have a morphologically complex form of plural marking, characterised by a fusion of gender markers and number markers, and variations in gender and number manifest themselves through morphemes affixed to the head noun and to (some of) its modifiers, in an agreement relationship. In these languages, plural marking tends to function on a 'semantic' basis, which means that plural markers tend to be present in every noun phrase referring to a plurality of individuals, irrespective of their communicative relevance.

Extreme cases of morphologically complex plural marking are encountered in the Eastern Sudanic branch of Nilo-Saharan and in all branches of the Afroasiatic phylum. For example, Hausa plurals divide into six basic types or so, most of them with two or more subtypes, and there are a few entirely irregular plurals; plural formation in Hausa involves not only various suffixes, but also vowel insertion (e.g. *gàrma:* pl. *garè:mani:* 'large hoe'), consonant reduplication (e.g. *ko:fà:* pl. *ko:fo:fi:* 'doorway'), and changes in tone.

In Africa, a three-way number set-up (singular/dual/plural) for both nouns and pronouns exists only in the central and northern branches of the Khoisan phylum. In the other language families of Africa, dual is extremely rare, and always restricted to pronouns. Several languages of the Sara-Bongo-Bagirmi subgroup of Central Sudanic and some Chadic languages have a distinct dual form in the first person only.

In many African languages, number does not manifest itself in nominal morphology only, but also in the existence of plural (or 'pluractional') verbs expressing frequentative or iterative action – see in particular Newman (1990).

9.4.4   *Case affixes and adpositions*

Morphologically, variations affecting the function of a noun phrase in larger constructions in which they are included may bring into play three types of morphemes:

(a)   adpositions, that is free morphemes that precede (prepositions) or follow (postpositions) the noun phrase with which they combine

(b)   phrasal affixes, that is bound morphemes attached to the first or to the last word of the noun phrase irrespective of the precise nature of this word

(c)   bound morphemes affixed to the head noun and to (some of) its modifiers, in an agreement relationship

Case systems of type (c) (i.e. systems in which nouns are inflected for case, and where modifiers agree in case with the noun they modify) have not been reported for any African language to my knowledge. Morphemes analysed as case affixes in descriptions of African languages are mostly phrasal affixes, and in current practice, they are not consistently distinguished from adpositions. What has been said above about the identification of definite articles as free or bound morphemes can be repeated here for the distinction between adpositions and case affixes: in

African languages, case morphemes often have the status of phrasal affixes, which is not a traditional notion in descriptive linguistics, and the decision to label them 'case affixes' or 'adpositions' in descriptive grammars seems to rely mainly on the degree of their phonological interaction with neighbouring words – and even from this point of view, the decisions taken in descriptions of individual languages are not very consistent. For example, Bambara 'postpositions' and Kanuri 'case suffixes' exhibit no significant difference in their morphological properties: both are bound morphemes with the distribution characteristic of phrasal affixes, and both exhibit a moderate degree of phonological interaction with the last word of the noun phrase with which they combine.

African languages provide a considerable amount of comparative evidence that reanalysis of genitival constructions involving body part nouns is a major source of adpositions – see Heine (1989), but they provide also evidence for other possible origins, in particular the reanalysis of serial verb constructions – see in particular Lord (1993). In this connection, it is interesting to observe that a comitative preposition or prefix occurs in many West African languages in which all the other case markers are postpositions or suffixes. Since this occurs in languages in which the verb precedes its complements and the noun follows its genitival modifier, a possible explanation is that these comitative prepositions or prefixes do not result from the reanalysis of a genitival construction, but rather from the reanalysis of a serial verb construction involving a verb meaning 'be with', 'accompany', etc.

The question of 'tone cases', found exclusively in languages that have an overt case distinction between subjects and objects, has already been dealt with in section 9.2.1.

A feature common to serialising languages and to languages that have an applicative voice is that, in comparison with other languages, they make only a limited use of adpositions and case affixes, since both serialisation and applicative voice result in giving the status of direct objects to various semantic types of complements that tend to be treated as obliques in languages devoid of these mechanisms.

9.4.5   *The genitival modifier*

The genitival construction may involve a genitive marker attached to the genitival modifier and/or so-called 'possessive affixes'. Case-marked genitives are common even in languages devoid of case contrast between subject and object.

Possessive affixes in complementary distribution with noun phrases in genitive function may be analysed as cliticised personal pronouns in genitive function.

But in some cases, the presence of a genitival modifier implies the presence of a possessive affix, which therefore may be viewed as an agreement morpheme. Cliticisation of personal pronouns in genitive function and agreement of the noun with its genitival modifier are much less common in African languages than cliticisation of personal pronouns in subject function and agreement of the verb with its subject. Note however that the available documentation is not always reliable regarding the distinction between 'possessive adjectives (or pronouns)' and 'possessive affixes'; once again, the reason is the lack of consistency in the way phrasal affixes are accounted for in descriptive grammars: so-called 'possessive adjectives' often turn out to be phrasal affixes that do not really differ in their behaviour from morphemes identified as 'possessive affixes' in other traditions.

A number of African languages have more than one possible way of combining a noun with a genitival modifier, most commonly with a distinction in meaning so that the variant with more morphological material (genitive markers or possessive affixes) is used with 'non-intimate' (or 'alienable') types of relations, and that with less morphological material with 'intimate' (or 'inalienable') types of relations. As a rule, the inalienable form involves mere juxtaposition. Prototypically inalienable relations are those between a person and the parts of his/her body or between a person and his/her relatives, whereas the relation between a person and the objects he/she disposes of (without necessarily owning them) is a prototypically alienable relation.

9.4.6 *The adjectival modifier*

As regards adjective as a category, a striking particularity of a number of African languages (particularly in the Niger-Congo phylum) is that they have a very small number of non-derived adjectives (sometimes less than ten), and no possibility of deriving adjectives from other categories at all. For example, Igbo has eight adjectives, semantically four pairs of antonyms: *úkwú* 'large' / *ńtà* 'small', *ɔ́hɔ́'rɔ́* 'new' / *ócyê* 'old', *ɔ́má* 'good' / *ɔ́jɔ́'ɔ́* 'bad' and *ɔ́cá* 'light-coloured' / *ójí·'í* 'dark-coloured'.

A situation in which adjectives are morphologically very similar (or even identical) to nouns is not uncommon in Africa. For example, in most Bantu languages, the gender-number prefixes attached to adjectives are identical to those attached to nouns; by contrast, the other types of modifiers have distinct gender-number prefixes at least in some classes.

Another particularity found in many African languages, which is consistent with their tendency towards having very limited inventories of adjectival lexemes, is that many notions typically encoded through adjectives in the languages of the world tend to be encoded through verbs. Wolof illustrates the borderline case of a language that properly speaking does not have a category 'adjective', and in which even the notions most typically encoded through adjectival lexemes are encoded through lexemes that fulfil the predicate function exactly in the same way as typically verbal lexemes.

9.5   Word order typology

Among the logically possible clause constituent orders, only those in which the subject (S) precedes the object (O) commonly have the status of basic constituent order. Malagasy (a Malayo-Polynesian language) clearly has a basic VOS order, and the Western Nilotic language Pari has been claimed to have a basic OVS order, but no other case of exceptional constituent order pattern has been reported to my knowledge among African languages. In this respect, African languages do not differ from languages in other parts of the world. But in many other respects, clause constituent order is typically a domain in which the diversity observed at the level of the African continent differs from that observed at world level. (See map 9.6.)

First of all, the proportion of African languages with a particularly rigid clause constituent order is relatively high. Sandawe, a poorly documented language spoken in Tanzania, has been reported to have a relatively flexible clause constituent order – see Dalgish (1979), but such cases are exceptional in Africa, and none of the relatively well-documented African languages exhibits a 'free' clause constituent order (i.e. a constituent order pragmatically rather than syntactically determined) of the type encountered in Russian, in Hungarian or in some Australian languages. Second, the proportion of African languages with a basic VSO order is roughly comparable to that observed at world level, but the proportion of languages with a basic SVO order is considerably higher (and the proportion of those with a basic SOV order considerably lower) among the languages of Africa than at world level, at least from a strictly numerical point of view (note however that genetically balanced samples show a higher proportion of verb-final languages). Even more importantly, Heine (1976a) has shown that a strict dichotomy between an SVO and an SOV type cannot be held in African linguistics, and that a satisfying account of the patterns of word-order variation observed in African languages requires recognising four main types, in the definition of which the position occupied by the genitive modifier and by noun phrases in oblique function is more important than that of the object.

Type A corresponds to what is often considered as the 'consistent' SVO type. Languages of this type have a basic SVOX clause constituent order, prepositions, and, within the noun phrase, all of the modifiers (including the genitival modifier) follow the head noun. This type is particularly predominant in Niger-Congo (in

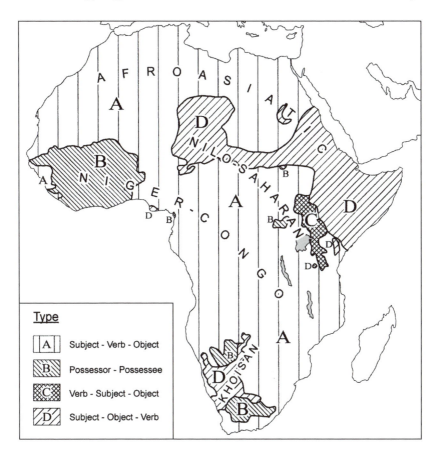

Map 9.6. Basic word order types (according to Heine 1976).

particular, virtually all Atlantic and Benue-Congo languages belong to it), but it is found also in Nilo-Saharan, Afroasiatic and Khoisan.

A minor type, viewed as a subtype of type A, differs from type A proper in the position of the adjectival modifier: in this subtype, the adjectival modifier precedes the head noun (but all other kinds of modifiers follow it, as in type A proper). This subtype is found in a geographically definable area including mostly Adamawa-Ubangian languages, but also some Benue-Congo and Chadic languages (in particular Hausa).

Type B is defined by the following characteristics: languages of this type have postpositions; within the noun phrase, the genitival modifier precedes the head noun, but all other kinds of modifiers follow it; at clause level, type B languages may have an SVOX order, or an SOVX order, or both. In other words, this type groups together SVO languages that differ from the 'consistent' SVO type in putting the genitival modifier before the noun it modifies, and SOV languages that differ from the 'consistent' SOV type by putting the obliques after the verb. The reason for grouping together these two sets of languages and for considering as irrelevant the position of the object is that there is considerable evidence that:

(a)   clause constituent order SVOX is unstable in languages that put the genitival modifier before the noun it modifies, since the reanalysis of constructions involving auxiliaries automatically leads to the emergence of an alternative SOVX order (see section 9.2.5)

(b)   languages with SOVX as the only possible clause constituent order share more properties with SVO languages than with 'true' SOV languages (i.e. SOXV languages); for example, they have the order 'auxiliary – main verb', whereas 'true' SOV languages have the order 'main verb – auxiliary'; moreover, in languages with SOVX as the only possible clause constituent order, one often finds evidence supporting the reconstruction of an ancient SVOX order subsequently modified by evolutions of the type just mentioned

Type B is widespread in Africa, but relatively uncommon outside Africa. It is mainly located in West Africa, in a geographically compact area including the languages of the Kru, Kwa, Gur and Mande branches of Niger-Congo and Songhay, but it occurs also sporadically in others parts of the African continent. Mande languages, with their rigid SOVX clause constituent order, can be viewed as its most typical representatives.

Type C corresponds to the type known in the literature as VSO. It differs from type A in the position of the subject only. It shares with it the use of prepositions and the position of the noun modifiers (including the genitival modifier) after the noun they modify. Apart from Ancient Egyptian and a few Chadic languages, uncontroversial examples of this type are largely confined to the Eastern Sudanic group of Nilo-Saharan. It has been reported to exist also in the Berber and Semitic branches of Afroasiatic, but this question is somewhat controversial. The point is that there may often be hesitations in identifying the basic constituent order of individual languages as SVO or VSO, due to the fact that languages that have a basic VSO constituent order always have at least SVO as a possible alternative. Dimmendaal (1983b) provides interesting insights into the properties of verb-initial languages; Reh (1983) describes an exceptional case of a verb-initial language with postpositions.

Type D is subdivided into two subtypes. Type D1 corresponds to what is generally considered as the 'consistent' SOV type. In this type, not only the object, but also the obliques precede the verb. Postpositions are used, and at the noun phrase level all kinds of modifiers (including the genitival modifier) precede the head noun. This type is relatively widespread in other parts of the world, but in its most extreme form, it concerns only a few African languages: Ijo, Central Khoisan and Sandawe. Type D2 shares with D1 the position of obliques before the verb and the use of postpositions, but it differs from it in that, at the noun-phrase level, all kinds of noun modifiers follow the noun they modify. In Africa, type D2 is found in the Nilo-Saharan phylum (e.g. Kanuri) and in the Cushitic branch of Afroasiatic (e.g. Somali, Oromo). Most Ethiopian Semitic languages occupy an intermediate position between type D1 and type D2.

Taking noun modifiers as a whole, it is possible to say that, in the languages of the world, word order within the noun phrase tends to be harmonic with clause-constituent order: in languages in which the verb precedes its complements (objects and obliques), the noun tends to precede its modifiers, and in languages in which the verb follows its complements, the noun tends to follow its modifiers. But in languages with an SOXV clause constituent order, this tendency may be offset by a strong tendency of certain types of modifiers to follow the noun they modify rather than preceding it. This is particularly striking for relative clauses, but also, although to a lesser degree, for adjectival modifiers. In this respect, the patterns of word order variation presented above call for the following remarks.

(a) In a number of African languages with an SVOX or SOVX clause constituent order, the genitival modifier is the only type of modifier that precedes the noun, whereas at world level, the tendency of the genitival modifier towards preceding the noun is not particularly strong in comparison with other types of modifiers, such as numerals or demonstratives.

(b) In some other languages with an SVOX or SOVX clause constituent order, the adjectival modifier is the only type of modifier that precedes the noun, which contradicts the fact that in the languages of the world, the adjectival modifier is among the types of modifiers that exhibit a marked tendency towards following the noun they modify.

(c) In African languages with an SOXV clause constituent order, the tendency towards a harmonic order at the noun phrase level (i.e. an order in which the noun occupies within the noun phrase the same place as the verb within the clause) is very weak: in Africa, SOXV languages in which all types of modifiers follow the noun they modify are even more numerous than those in which all types of modifiers precede the noun.

As regards adpositions, African data confirms that, with very few exceptions, languages in which the genitival modifier precedes the noun generally have case morphemes at the right edge of the noun phrase (postpositions or bound morphemes suffixed to the last word of the noun phrase), whereas those in which the genitival modifier follows the noun generally have case morphemes at the left edge of the noun phrase (prepositions or bound morphemes prefixed to the first word of the noun phrase). The obvious explanation for this correlation is that, historically, the reanalysis of 'genitive + noun' constructions is the main source of 'noun phrase + adposition' constructions.

9.6   **Non-verbal predications**

Non-verbal predications do not necessarily occur in individual languages, but they are commonly encountered in clauses expressing identification, existence, location or attribution of qualities, with a TAM value identical to that expressed in verbal predication by the verb tenses commonly labelled 'indicative present'.

Uncontroversial examples of non-verbal predications are those (not particularly frequent in Africa) involving mere juxtaposition of noun phrases or adposition phrases, as illustrated here by Kanuri – example (10).

(10)   Kanuri (Saharan, Nilo-Saharan)

    (a)   *bíntu   féro*   'Bintu is a girl.'
           Bintu   girl

    (b)   *músa   káno-lan*   'Musa is in Kano.'
           Musa   Kano-LOC

    (c)   *nyí   kúra*   'You are big.'
           you   big

There is a problem of interpretation with constructions involving predicative words devoid of morphological properties that would identify them as verb forms: certain traditions tend to analyse such predicative words as irregular verbs, but labels such as 'non-verbal predicative' or 'non-verbal copula' are also current in descriptions of African languages. For example, *bé* 'be located at' is analysed as a non-verbal predicative in most recent descriptions of Bambara, but this analysis accounts only for its limited combinability with TAM morphemes; its syntactic distribution is clearly that of a verb, and it combines at least with the TAM marker *tùŋ* 'past'; consequently, one may prefer to view it as an irregular verb. Such predicatives are particularly common in West African languages. Historically, there is in many cases comparative evidence that they originate in decategorialised verbs, but this is not their only possible source (they may in particular originate also in demonstratives).

Tswana – example (11) – illustrates a construction involving a predicative element attached to nouns. This predicative element is identical to the verbal prefix expressing agreement with the subject in positive tenses of the indicative. It may be analysed as a cliticised form of the verb 'to be', since Tswana has a verb 'to be' devoid of indicative present, and this construction occurs only in the indicative present.

(11)   Tswana
　　　　(a)   *ŋw-àná*　　*ó-fà*　　　　　'The child is here.'
　　　　　　　CL1-child　SM.CL1-here
　　　　(b)   *b-ánà*　　　*bá-fà*　　　　'The children are here.'
　　　　　　　CL2-child　SM.CL2-here

Such a construction is fairly common in Bantu languages, but the variations of the predicative element affixed to nouns are always limited to person-number(-gender), and possibly negation. Other cases of cliticised copulas have been reported outside the Bantu family (for example in the Cross-River language Kana), but to the best of my knowledge, in African languages, the use of predicative elements affixed to nouns is always restricted to a limited range of TAM values.

9.7　　　　**Complex constructions**
　　　　　As regards the combination of clauses into complex structures, I shall limit myself here to a brief summary of what seem to be the most salient features of African languages.

Bambara illustrates a type of relativisation strategy in which the relative clause is not embedded in the main clause, which constitutes the only available relativisation strategy in most Northern Mande languages; it occurs only sporadically in other groups of African languages (some authors exclude this type from relative clauses proper). Example (12) shows that in Bambara, relativisation entirely relies on the presence of the relative marker *mìŋ* within the relative clause, the location of *mìŋ* signalling the relativised position. When the relative clause precedes the main clause (which is the most common construction), the main clause includes a demonstrative (*ò*) representing the term the referent of which is determined by the relative clause. There is an alternative construction in which the relative clause follows the main clause (see also chapter 8 above).

(12)　 Bambara (Mande, Niger-Congo)
　　　　(a)   *wùlú*　*yé*　　*démìsɛ́ŋ*　　*'kíŋ*
　　　　　　　dog　PERF　child　　　bite
　　　　　　　'The dog bit the child.' (independent clause)

(b) *n   y'   ó   bòlìtɔ   'yé*
  I   PERF   this.one   running   see
  'I saw this one running away.' (independent clause)

(c) *wùlú   'mìŋ   yé   démìsɛ́ŋ   'kíŋ,   n   y'   ó   bòlìtɔ   'yé*
  dog   REL   PERF   child   bite   I   PERF   this.one   running   see
  'I saw the dog that bit the child running away.'

(d) *wùlú   yé   démìsɛ́ŋ   'mìŋ   kíŋ,   n   y'   ó   bòlìtɔ   'yé*
  dog   PERF   child   REL   bite   I   PERF   this.one   running   see
  'I saw the child that the dog bit running away.'

Among African languages, I know of no sure attestation of the relativisation strategy in which a relative clause embedded in the main clause includes the noun the referent of which is determined by the property expressed by the relative clause. In an article published thirty years ago, an example of this type was reported for Bambara, and since that time this example has been reproduced in every typological account of relativisation, making Bambara famous among typologists for its alleged head-internal relatives embedded in the main clause. Unfortunately, this paper was based on wrong data: no first-hand study of Bambara or of any other variety of Manding has confirmed the existence of this construction, and every informant I asked categorically rejected it. Note that the absence of embedded head-internal relatives in African languages is consistent with their relation with word order typology: a well-known generalisation is that embedded head-internal relatives are encountered in 'consistent' SOV languages (i.e. in languages in which the verb always occurs at the end of the clause and the head noun at the end of the noun phrase), and, as already mentioned, languages of this type are rare in Africa.

Embedded relatives treated as noun modifiers that precede the noun they modify are found for example in Amharic, but this is a very exceptional case among African languages. This is not surprising given the general tendency of African languages towards postposing the modifiers to the noun and the well-known fact that, in comparison with other types of modifiers, relative clauses are particularly prone to follow the noun they modify.

Consequently, the predominance of the relativisation strategy in which embedded relatives are treated as noun modifiers that follow the noun they modify, already noted at world level, is particularly strong among African languages.

As regards the issue of accessibility to relativisation, an interesting observation is that cases of languages in which only subjects and direct objects can be relativised are relatively frequent in Africa, which certainly correlates with the possibility of treating virtually every semantic type of complement as the direct object of an applicative verb form.

Many groups of African languages exhibit a marked tendency towards encoding dependency relations between clauses through the use of verb forms distinct from those fulfilling the predicate function in independent assertive clauses, rather than through conjunctions. In particular, many African languages use special verb forms (often termed 'consecutive' or 'sequential') in sequences of clauses reflecting a chronological presentation of events, as illustrated here by Tswana – example (13).

(13)   Tswana

    (a) *kì-ìlé*   *tòrópó-ŋ,*   *kì-rék-ílé*   *dítɬhàkó*
          SM.1S-go.ANT town-LOC SM.1S-buy-ANT CL8.shoes
          'I went to town, I bought shoes.' (independent clauses)

    (b) *kì-ìlé*   *tòrópó-ŋ,*   *k-à-réká*   *dítɬhàkó*
          SM.1S-go.ANT town-LOC SM.1S-CONS-buy CL8-shoes
          'I went to town and I bought shoes.' (consecutive construction)

Note also in this connection that, in contrast with European languages, many African languages make a strict distinction between noun phrase co-ordination and clause co-ordination: the equivalent of 'and' between noun phrases (which is generally the same morpheme as the comitative adposition) cannot link clauses in a way similar to English 'and'.

As regards complementation, one notes first the relatively high proportion of African languages in which the clausal complement of verbs of saying, perceiving, thinking and of verbs expressing desire, intention, command, etc., is introduced by a complementiser that is quite transparently a grammaticalised form of a verb 'to say' (or of a non-verbal predicative used in quotative constructions). Second, complementation confirms the extreme rarity of strict SOV languages in Africa. In typical strict SOV languages, such as Turkish or Japanese, the verb is systematically preceded not only by its nominal complements, but also by its clausal complements, whereas in African languages, clausal complements follow the verb even in languages that have a strict SOXV clause constituent order and a strong tendency towards harmonic order at noun phrase level, as illustrated here by Ijo – example (14).

(14)   Ijo (Ijoid, Niger-Congo)

    (a) *erí* *kɛnɪ* *dóω*   *gbaamɪ*   'He told a tale.'
          he   one   tale   told

    (b) *erǐ* *gba* *ámɛɛ* *erǐ* *boŋgimi*   'He said that he would come.'
          he   said that   he will come

9.8   **Conclusion**

The main concern of linguistics, which distinguishes it from every other approach to language, is to characterise as narrowly as possible what is (and what is not) a possible human language. Language typology aims at a comprehensive account of the structural diversity observed in attested human languages, and therefore provides linguistics with indispensable empirical evidence. In this typological sketch of African languages, I have tried to make apparent the contribution of African language data to language typology, and consequently to general linguistics. This contribution is particularly crucial on issues such as applicative voice, serialisation, nominal classification, word order typology, focalisation. By way of a conclusion, I would like to emphasise that the contribution of African language typology to general linguistics could certainly be even greater if the documentation on African languages were more abundant and of better quality. In particular, many grammatical mechanisms found in the languages of Africa, for example the encoding of focus phenomena through verbal morphology, crucially often bring into play tonal variations of verb forms – see Creissels (1996) – but, unfortunately, the proportion of African languages for which a comprehensive and reliable description of the tonal morphology of the verb is available is, to put it mildly, not very high. Therefore, improvement in the description of individual African languages is a necessary condition for any further improvement of our understanding of African language structure, and consequently for a better contribution of African language typology to general linguistics.

Notes

I gratefully acknowledge the helpful comments and suggestions provided by Thomas Bearth, Ulrike Claudi, Bernard Comrie, Gerrit Dimmendaal, Zygmunt Frajzyngier, Colette Grinevald, Tom Güldemann, Bernd Heine, Paul Newman and Derek Nurse.

1 The following abbreviations have been used throughout this chapter:

1S	1st person singular	MEDPAS	mediopassive
2S	2nd person singular	NEG	negative
ANT	anterior	OM	object marker
APPL	applicative	PAS	passive
CL	class	PERF	perfective
CONS	consecutive	REL	relative
DEF	definite	SM	subject marker
IMPERF	imperfective	TAM	tense-aspect-modality
LOC	locative		

10

Comparative linguistics

PAUL NEWMAN

10.1 **Introduction**

The aim of historical/comparative linguistics is to provide information about the past history of languages and groups of languages. In Africa, where, with few exceptions such as Ancient Egyptian, languages were not written until historically recent times, determination of facts about the past requires reconstruction and interpretation based on a careful analysis of languages as spoken at the present time. Most often the reconstruction of language history depends on the comparison of different languages; but it is sometimes possible to deduce aspects of the past from looking at a single language.

The aim of this chapter is to describe types of problems that historical/comparative linguists deal with and to give a general idea of the methodologies employed. The substantive results of these endeavours throughout Africa are described elsewhere in this book (see chapters 2 through 5). The focus here is on linguistic techniques *per se*, regardless of the language area or language groups under investigation. To avoid detracting the reader from the principles being elucidated by an over-abundance of scattered data, the examples in this chapter will be relatively few in number, and will be limited to Hausa and other languages in the Chadic family.

The four major areas of historical/comparative work to be treated here are: (1) classification and subclassification; (2) reconstruction; (3) establishment of sound laws; and (4) treatment of loan words.

10.2 **Classification**

Language classification, sometimes referred to as genetic or phylogenetic classification, involves putting together related languages into families or language groups that can be presumed to have been derived historically from a common ancestor. For example, Spanish, Portuguese and Italian are closely related languages that have been grouped into the Romance family while Hebrew, Arabic and Aramaic have been classified as members of the family known as Semitic. Whereas the method of classification involves the comparison of occurring languages, the result is a claim about their historical origins, thus the commonly used term 'historical/comparative' linguistics.

In describing linguistic relationships, the long-established practice has been to use kinship terminology. Hebrew, for example, is described as a 'daughter' language of Proto-Semitic, the source language of the family, with Arabic and Aramaic as 'sister' languages. Proto-Semitic, however, is not described as the 'mother' language, as one might expect, but rather as the ancestor language, or proto-language, or 'Ursprache'.

The relationship between languages is sometimes close and evident, as with Spanish and Portuguese or Dutch and German or Yoruba and Igala, and sometimes more distant, as with English and Hindi or Shona and Fulani. The terminology for describing degrees of relationship is not fixed, but one tends to find labels such as the following, going from the most inclusive, highest level groups to the most narrow: super-phylum (or stock), phylum, family, subfamily, group, subgroup, dialect cluster. The relationship between languages is typically represented by means of family tree diagrams built on the model of family genealogical trees and biological cladograms (see, for example, chapters 2 and 11).

The methodology of classification as exemplified in the treatment of African languages is best described with reference to the work of Joseph H. Greenberg, whose classification (Greenberg 1963a) has served as the point of reference for Africanists for a generation. Greenberg's approach implicitly or explicitly makes use of the following principles and guidelines:

(a) Language classification must be based on linguistic evidence alone and not on racial or cultural criteria. This seemingly obvious principle was in fact ignored by many linguists in the late nineteenth and early twentieth century, who allowed themselves to classify languages on the basis of the speakers' skin colour and factors such as whether they were pastoralists or members of a ruling class or simple sedentary agriculturalists. A particularly egregious case of this mixing of linguistic and non-linguistic factors was Meinhof's supposed 'Hamitic' family (Meinhof 1912; with discussion by Sanders 1969).

(b) Language classification must be based on *specific* points of resemblance and not on the presence or absence of general features of a typological nature. Thus whether two or more languages are tonal or not or whether they have an odd number vs. an even number of vowels might be interesting from a typological or areal point of view, but in and of itself is irrelevant in determining relatedness. The classification of Westermann and Bryan (1952) in which Chadic languages were divided into two separate families because one group had grammatical gender while the other did not is an example of the misuse of typology in classification.

(c) Relatedness adheres to the rule of transitivity. That is, if a language A can be shown to be related to a language B, and B can be shown to be related to C, then A is necessarily related to C. A consequence of this principle is that one may be able to ascertain a relationship between two languages A and C even when they appear very different on the surface and it is difficult to see points of resemblance between them.

(d) Classifications based on vocabulary and those based on morphology and grammar will normally lead to the same results. (This principle holds for establishing relatedness as such; it is less reliable in determining subgroup relationships.) Early scholars used to argue vehemently about whether one should use lexical or grammatical evidence in arriving at a classification, the assumption being that one approach might show that a language A belonged to a family with language B where the other approach might indicate that A belonged to a different family with language Z. According to this principle, the results of both approaches can be expected to coincide. Classifiers may choose to look first at lexical evidence or at morphological evidence because something significant catches their eye; but if they are on the right track, the evidence from the other area can be expected to support and reinforce the proposed classification. The reason for this is the observation noted long ago by Weinreich (1958: 377): 'In the well-known comparative fields, basic vocabulary and basic grammar have always been found to develop together.'

(e) The job of the comparative linguist is to provide the best explanation possible consistent with the facts. In proposing a classification, it is *not* necessary that the linguist 'prove' that the classification is absolutely certain by the presentation of conclusive evidence. In response to widely speculative classifications that had been offered at various times by irresponsible scholars, many careful, empirically based linguists jumped to the opposite extreme and took the position that all languages should be treated as unrelated unless and until proved otherwise. This was thought to be a prudent scientific requirement. However, on closer inspection, this requirement turns out to be untenable and not in keeping with standard scientific procedures. All that the comparative linguist can be expected to do is look at a pair or group of languages. If resemblances show up that appear to be greater than could be expected by chance, the linguist has to ask why. Could the resemblances be accounted for by universal sound symbolism, could they reflect areal characteristics, could they perhaps be due to borrowing from one language into another, or are the resemblances of the kind that are indicative of common origin? If the latter is the case, the linguist is justified in postulating a genetic relationship even if the evidence is still somewhat on the weak side. For example, in the opinion of some scholars, the evidence supporting the relationship between the Chadic language family and other language groups in the Afroasiatic phylum, such as Semitic and Berber, is not compelling. Nevertheless, some points of resemblance in morphology and lexicon are so striking that if one did not assume relationship, they would be impossible to explain away. The classification of Chadic within Afroasiatic is thus fully justified, not because it has been 'proved' as in a court of law, but because it is the explanation most consistent with the facts as a whole (Newman 1980, see also chapter 4 above).

Up to now we have been considering general principles of classification rather than linguistic techniques *per se*, to which we now turn. Here I will limit myself to two methods: (a) mass comparison of vocabulary, and (b) comparison of grammatical morphemes.

10.2.1   *Mass comparison*

Mass comparison (now sometimes termed 'multilateral comparison') is an approach expounded by Greenberg (1955b) nearly a half century ago in his original work on African language classification. In essence, the method determines relatedness, that is classifies languages into families, by the comparison of similar looking vocabulary items. In this method, there is no requirement that regular sound correspondences have been established by the Comparative Method (see below), only that words look alike. Previous scholars had reservations about classifying languages on the basis of lexical comparisons for two main reasons. First, in depending on vocabulary, as opposed to morphology or grammar, one runs the risk of assuming cognacy between similar words when the real explanation is borrowing. Second, since one is dealing with look-alikes rather than words that one has determined to be cognates on the basis of regular phonological correspondences, there is no guarantee that the resemblances are of real significance and not just due to accident. Three aspects of mass comparison are designed to meet these problems. To begin with, vocabulary is limited to fundamental, basic vocabulary, such as body parts, core colour terms such as 'white', 'red' and 'black', essential verbs such as 'die' or 'drink', and lower numerals, where experience has shown that borrowing is relatively uncommon. Second, one takes into account a considerable number of words at the same time rather than trying to make decisions about cognacy with individual word pairs. Thus, if two languages have very similar words indicating 'mouth', for example, one cannot immediately conclude that the words are cognate and that they qualify as evidence of relatedness. However, if one finds a good number of pairs of phonologically similar items, this justifies classifying them together. Finally, one looks at a number of languages at the same time in order to better spot patterns and to identify cognates whose similarity is far from evident. For example, if one compares words in the Chadic languages Tera and Margi [T] *wuzən* and [M] *psar* 'grass', one might not recognise that they are related. However, if one looks at these languages plus a dozen other Chadic languages such as Bole, Gude, Kotoko and Ngizim, and, for contrast, words from a few non-Chadic languages such as Kanuri and Fulani, intersecting patterns of lexical similarity emerge such that the relationship between Tera and Margi becomes evident. Moreover, by treating a number of languages at the same time, one can take advantage of the principle of transitivity in a way that is more effective than trying to work out all relationships in a pairwise fashion.

10.2.2   ***Comparison of grammatical morphemes***

Because grammatical morphemes and such paradigmatic classes as pronouns are much less prone to borrowing than vocabulary, similarities between them can be strong evidence of relatedness. There are two drawbacks, however. First, since grammatical morphemes in the languages of the world tend to be short, compare English 'to', 'me', 'un-' (as in 'untrained'), '-s' (as in 'cats'), etc., there is always the possibility that similarities between languages could be due to chance. On the other hand, the likelihood of multiconsonantal words such as English *brother* and German *Bruder* being accidentally similar is infinitesimally small. Second, grammatical morphemes tend to employ universally 'unmarked' sounds (such as /t/, /k/, /s/, /n/) rather than the full set of phonemes found in individual languages, again increasing the possibility of accidental resemblance. The solution is to focus on *detailed* resemblances in morphology, where possible looking at patterns and paradigms rather than at individual items. Especially important in establishing relationship is the identification of shared asymmetries and irregularities. For example, as evidence in support of the Afroasiatic phylum, one can cite the fact that the Chadic second person feminine pronoun **kim* not only looks like the corresponding pronoun in Berber and Egyptian, but shares with these other languages the curious feature of being the only singular pronoun with the shape CVC, a shape that is typical of the plural pronouns in these languages. In the case of the Bantu family, which was already well recognised in the nineteenth century, the pattern of corresponding singular/plural noun class markers served as the key to their classification (see chapter 2 above). Particularly decisive when it can be found, which is not all that frequent, is 'suppletion', that is the use of distinct stems in morphosyntactically related constructions. Comparing English *good/better* with

German *gut/besser* and Dutch *goed/beter*, or English *I/me* with German *ich/mich* and Dutch *ik/mij* would permit one to postulate relatedness between these languages even in the absence of other evidence.

10.2.3   *Subclassification (linguistic subgrouping)*

Once various languages have been determined to be related and have been classified as members of the same family or phylum, the next task is to figure out the precise nature of the relationships, that is, to work out the relative closeness of the relationships such as could be reflected on a family tree diagram. This job of subclassification turns out to be both very easy and very hard. In some cases, closely related languages can naturally be assigned to different subgroups by simple inspection. For example, if you take a quick look at Russian, Polish, Spanish and Italian, four Indo-European languages, it is immediately obvious that the first two constitute a group as opposed to the latter two. Similarly, the Bantu languages Zulu and Xhosa can be put together as opposed to Tiv or Efik, more distantly related languages, and the Kru languages Grebo and Bete easily fall together as opposed to Yoruba or Igbo. In other cases, however, the evidence is ambiguous and subclassification is difficult. Languages may look alike to a greater or lesser extent because of their ultimate membership in the same family, but it is not clear who goes with whom.

The best, most reliable indicator of subgrouping relationship is 'shared innovation'. If some languages have undergone a distinctive change not found in other members of the family, this suggests strongly that the languages in question shared a common ancestor and thus constitute a subgroup. This innovation could involve phonology, morphology, syntax, lexicon or even semantics. As an example in the lexical domain, one finds that in Hausa and Bole the widespread Proto-Chadic words for 'fire' *aku (or *akwa) and 'two' *sər- have been replaced by the stems *wuti and *bulu, respectively, thereby justifying their subclassification into a common group ('West-Chadic-A') as opposed to other Chadic languages such as Ngizim and Ga'anda, which have retained reflexes of the original words. In practice, the reliance on shared innovation in determining subclassification can be problematic since one cannot always tell which features found in two languages are innovations as opposed to retentions and which innovations are due to a shared historical event as opposed to being the result of drift or parallel independent change. Moreover, different innovations do not always coincide, that is, there are cases where a shared phonological innovation points to one subgrouping relationship whereas a shared lexical replacement points to another. Nevertheless, the shared innovation principle is sound and when used with care provides the most reliable means of determining subclassification.

Because of the difficulties in applying the principle of shared innovation, some scholars have tried to determine subgroups by means of lexicostatistics, namely the calculation of the percentage of shared cognates in a basic word list. This approach, however, is so fraught with weaknesses of a conceptual, analytical and practical nature that it cannot be counted on to provide results that are any better than one would get by simple impressionistic comparisons.

10.3   **Reconstruction**

By comparing evidence from related current-day languages, it is possible to reconstruct what the ancestor language looked like to a greater or lesser extent. This reconstructed ancestor language is referred to as a 'proto-language'. Given data from Zulu, Kongo and Bemba, for example, one can reconstruct aspects of the vocabulary, phonology and grammar of Proto-Bantu. Similarly, given good descriptions of Turkana, Luo and Maasai one can piece together a picture of Proto-Nilotic.

10.3.1   *The Comparative Method*

The main technique for doing reconstruction, especially of phonology and vocabulary, is called the Comparative Method. The Comparative Method is typically carried out on languages already presumed or demonstrated to be related; it is not an essential classificatory tool in establishing relationships as such. This method involves comparing similar words in related languages in order to establish regular sound correspondences, by which one means that some sound X in one language regularly matches some sound Y in a sister language. Sometimes the X and the Y are identical or nearly so, but this is not required. What is essential is that the sounds systematically correspond. For example, in the Chadic family, if one compares Karekare, Bura and Hausa, one finds that non-initial /r/ in the first language is regularly matched by /l/ in the second and by /y/ or /i/ in the third, for example [K] *carafu*, [B] *kilfa*, [H] *kiifi* (< *kiyfi*) 'fish'; non-initial /ɗ/ in Karekare is matched by final /r/ in Bura, but by /ɗ/ in Hausa, for example [K] *poɗu*, [B] *nfwar*, [H] *fudu* 'four'; whereas initial /m/ appears as such throughout, for example [K] *mar*, [B] *mal*, [H] *mai* (< *may*) 'oil'. When additional examples are taken into consideration, one is able to reconstruct the Proto-Chadic form for these words, namely, **kirfi* (or **kirif*) **fadu* and **mar*, respectively. Once one has reconstructed enough words, one can then take stock of the phonological elements found in the proto-lexicon and thereby reconstruct the original phonological inventory, which in principle could have been richer or skimpier than that of the various daughter languages. Modern Hausa, for example, has /ʔ/ and /h/ in its phonological inventory, but these two gutturals cannot be reconstructed for Proto-Chadic. Conversely, Hausa does not have the affricates /ts/ and /dz/, nor does it have the velar fricative /x/, all of which were likely present in Proto-Chadic.

The Comparative Method can be extended from content words such as nouns and verbs to grammatical morphemes, thereby allowing the reconstruction of aspects of the morphology and grammar of a proto-language. Thus in Chadic, one has been able to establish /n/ and /t/ as gender markers (masculine and feminine respectively) and *mV-* as a prefix forming agentive/locative/instrumental nouns. Similarly, in Bantu one has been able to establish a full set of corresponding singular/plural noun class markers (see chapter 2 above).

It should be pointed out that it is sometimes possible to reconstruct things about grammatical morphemes and patterns in a proto-language even though one cannot reconstruct the exact forms *per se* using the Comparative Method. For example, one can assert with confidence that plurals of nouns in Proto-Chadic were formed with suffixes, rather than prefixes or infixes, and that verbal extensions were also formed with suffixes, even though one still lacks precise information about the form of the morphemes in question. Perhaps even more striking is the fact that it is possible to reconstruct the gender of many words in Proto-Chadic without necessarily being able to reconstruct the words themselves. Thus we know that 'fire' and 'scorpion', for example, were feminine, 'crocodile' and 'nose' were masculine, whereas 'water' was plural.

The Comparative Method in the strict sense of the term is not applied in the case of syntactic reconstruction. Rather, one compares a number of current languages from a broader perspective, taking general knowledge of linguistic typology and normal directions of change into account. One then postulates grammatical structures for the proto-language that allow the easiest and most natural pathways to arrive at the occurring language forms. For example, current Chadic languages exhibit a variety of word orders for the placement of direct and indirect objects. However, the diversity lends itself to a simple explanation if one assumes that Proto-Chadic had two different structures depending on whether the indirect object was a personal pronoun or not. If the indirect object was pronominal, the order was Verb + immediately following pronoun + direct object (comparable to English *He told me the news*). If the indirect object was not a personal pronoun, the order was Verb + direct object + a preposition-like marker + the object (comparable to English *He told the news to John*). Unlike English, where *me* and *John* can be used in sentences of either type, in Proto-Chadic, the choice of structures was rigidly tied to the word class of the indirect object.

A major problem in syntactic reconstruction relates to the paucity of choices – the word order for adjectival modifiers, for example, is basically restricted to

Adjective-Noun or Noun-Adjective – and the difficulty in reconciling observed facts about specific languages with established findings about typological consistencies and correlations. Thus scholars continue to debate whether the basic sentence order of Proto-Niger-Congo was S-O-V (subject-object-verb) (Givón 1979) or S-V-O (subject-verb-object) (Heine 1980; see also Claudi 1993). Similarly, it is still an open question whether Proto-Chadic was V-S-O, as proposed by Frajzyngier (1983), or S-V-O, which is my own opinion.

In comparing similar morphological or grammatical items in related languages, one has to be aware that they may not reflect a shared retention from the common ancestor, but rather may be due to parallel independent development or drift. Thus two languages which look to have the same item for the preposition 'on' or the future marker may have undergone independent processes of grammaticalisation, internally developing the former from the noun 'head' and the latter from the verb 'go' (Heine and Reh 1984). Similarly, two related languages that have double negatives (like French *ne . . . pas*) may not reflect the original archaic state of affairs, but rather may have independently added a second reinforcing negative morpheme.

10.3.2   ***Internal Reconstruction***

Another method often used as an alternative to or in conjunction with the Comparative Method is Internal Reconstruction. The basic notion here is that morphemes or words in a language ideally should have a unique shape. When one finds the same item with different shapes in different phonological or grammatical environments, it suggests that something historical has happened and thus it is often possible to postulate an historical scenario even in the absence of comparative evidence. For example, in Kanakuru, where a number of verbs have corresponding forms for singular and 'pluractional', that is, indicating the plurality of the action, the word 'die' has the paired forms *muri/mute*; 'take out' has *pori/pode*; and 'tie' has *dowi/dope*. When one takes other examples of Kanakuru consonant change into account, one can reconstruct the original forms of these verbs as **muti, podi* and **dopi*, where the pluractionals were formed by geminating the second consonant (the change in the final vowel not being completely understood), for example *mutte, podde* and *doppe*. What then happened is that intervocalic consonants in the language weakened: single consonants underwent lenition to corresponding 'soft' consonants, for example /t/ and /d/ > /r/, /p/ > /w/, etc. and geminate/double consonants altered into single consonants, resulting in the strange alternations found in the current-day language (Frajzyngier 1976).

Internal reconstruction can also be used when faced with other unexplainable irregularities and asymmetries in a system. For example, in Hausa, the demonstratives meaning 'some', namely *wani* (masc. sg.), *wata* (fem. sg.) and *wasu* (pl.), all contain a formative *wa-*. The *ta* can be equated with the identical third person feminine pronoun, and *su* can be equated with the identical third person plural pronoun. Curiously, the form *ni* is identical to the first-person singular (gender unmarked) pronoun. Why should this be? One could look for some strange psycholinguistic explanation, but viewing things historically, a reasonable hypothesis would be that Hausa originally had a third person masculine pronoun **ni* which has subsequently been lost in the language. In fact comparative evidence shows conclusively that this internally deduced hypothesis is true: Hausa used to have a bound third person masculine pronoun *ni*, which differed from the first person only in tone, but this was eventually replaced by expansion in the use of the coexisting pronominal forms *sa* and *shi*.

10.4   **Sound laws**

Implicit in the operation of the Comparative Method, discussed above in section 10.3.1, is the regularity of sound change. When one reconstructs a Proto-Chadic word such as **mar* 'oil' and says that Hausa */may/* (= [*mai*]) is a current-day reflex of that original form, one assumes that there has been a general change of **r* to *y* and that this is not just an isolated, idiosyncratic phenomenon. The development of historical/comparative linguistics in the nineteenth century was marked by the discovery of regular changes, that is 'sound laws', affecting European languages. Among the better-known changes are Grimm's Law, which describes changes in the consonantal system of Germanic languages from their Indo-European origins, and the Great English Vowel Shift, which accounts for the change in English vowels from their pronunciation in Old English, as reflected to a great extent in current English spelling, to the pronunciation found today. Scholars working on African languages have also discovered regular sound laws affecting different languages or groups of languages. Two of the best known are Dahl's Law (Meinhof 1903) and Klingenheben's Law (Klingenheben 1927/8).

Dahl's Law refers to a change affecting a number of East African Bantu languages whereby the first of two voiceless obstruents dissimilates and becomes voiced. In Kikuyu, for example, where the change is restricted to the consonant /k/, the name of the language is pronounced *gikuyu*. Other examples include *githaka* 'bush' (< **kithaka*), *gukua* 'die' < **kukua*, and *kugwata* 'catch' < **kukwata*. Note in this last example that /kw/ changes to /gw/ before it has a chance to affect the initial /k/.

Klingenheben's Law refers to the systematic weakening of syllable-final obstruents into sonorants or glides that took place in the historical development of Hausa. According to the law, velars such as /k/ and labials such as /p/ changed to /w/ (and later to /u/), whereas coronals such as /t/ changed to /ʀ/ (a rolled sound that was distinct from the original flap /ɾ/ in the language), for example *ɓakna > ɓauna 'buffalo', *sapka > sauka 'get down'; *fatkee > faɾkee 'trader'. Interestingly, whereas it is the convention to speak of Klingenheben's Law in the singular, as if there were a complex but single change, the reality is that there were three different changes that happened at historically different times, the last change, namely labials to /w/, affecting only a few dialects in the language. What this illustrates is that sound laws often begin in one part of the phonological system and then generalise to other areas rather than necessarily taking place in a sudden and inclusive manner.

10.5   **Analysis of loan words**

It is well known that languages in contact influence one another. Sometimes the impact of one language on another is minimal, as with Japanese influence on English, which is limited to a few words such as *tempura* and *sushi*; in other cases it can be massive, as with Arabic influence on Berber. In addition to studying the 'vertical' development of languages over time, comparative/historical linguists are also concerned with changes that reflect processes of 'horizontal' linguistic transfer. In principle, the transfer can extend to morphology, syntax and semantics, but most commonly the influence manifests itself in the area of loan words. The analysis of loan words involves a number of interrelated questions such as who borrowed from whom? what adjustments took place in accepting the loan words? and what impact did the loan words have on the recipient language?

If two languages A and B share a word that appears to be a loan word, one has to ask whether A borrowed the word from B or vice versa. I am assuming for the sake of the discussion that the two languages are unrelated. If they are related, albeit distantly, as with Arabic and Hausa, there is the added problem of determining whether the similar looking words are loan words or retentions from a common ancestor. There are a number of good indicators that help determine the direction of the borrowing. (a) To begin with, if the term is widely found in languages related to A but not in languages related to B, then one can assume that language B was the borrower. (b) If the loan word is morphologically or lexically analysable in language A but not in language B, then again B must be the borrower. On this basis, one could determine, what we already know to be the case, that Hausa borrowed its word *cingam* from English *chewing gum* and not vice versa. (c) Phonological mismatches between two languages can also serve to indicate the direction of borrowing. Arabic has a contrast between /h/ and /χ/, a voiceless uvular fricative, whereas Hausa only has /h/. The word for 'pretext, excuse' in these two languages is *χujja* and *hujja*, respectively. If Arabic were the borrower, there is no reason why it wouldn't have adopted the word as *hujja* with the regular /h/. Since Hausa was the borrower, it is only natural that it would replace /χ/ by the closest sound it had available in its phonological inventory, namely

/h/. Note, moreover, that geminate/doubled obstruents were essentially non-existent in the indigenous Hausa vocabulary, again marking this item as a recently introduced loan word in the language.

A difficult matter that is often neglected in the study of loan words is determining the true avenue of borrowing. For example, many Arabic loan words found in English were not borrowed directly, but rather came into English via Medieval Latin or French. Similarly, many Arabic loan words in Hausa, such as *kasuwa* 'market', from Arabic *suq*, had Kanuri as an intermediate source. We also find that many English loan words in Hausa, such as *tasha* 'station', were borrowed via some southern Nigerian language. The conclusive evidence here is provided by the treatment of the /st/ cluster, which is simplified to /t/ in indirectly borrowed words as compared with directly borrowed words where it is retained but broken up by an epenthetic vowel; compare *suto* 'store(room)'.

Finally, in analysing loan words in two languages, there is always the possibility that neither language borrowed from the other, but rather that they both adopted the words from some third language. For example, Hausa (Chadic) and Swahili (Bantu) have a large number of words in common. The explanation in this case is not that one of the languages was influenced by the other, but rather that they both independently borrowed heavily from Arabic (Baldi 1988).

One interesting phenomenon that has affected African languages because of the colonial experience has been the borrowing of different words in the same language from different European sources. For example, Hausa as spoken in Niger has taken many of its recent loan words from French whereas comparable loan words in the Hausa of Nigeria have come from English, for example 'driver's licence': *parmi* vs. *lasin*; '(flashlight) battery': *pil* vs. *batuʀ*; 'lawyer': *aboka* vs. *lauya*; and 'cake': *gato* vs. *kyat*.

When languages adopt loan words, they typically modify the new items in keeping with the pre-existing structure of the language. External influence, especially when heavy, may also bring about significant changes in the phonology and grammar of the borrowing language. Before the influx of Arabic loan words, Hausa did not have /h/ as a separate phoneme. The sound [h] existed, but only as an allophone of /f/ before back-rounded vowels, for example *dafu* = [*dahu*] 'be cooked'. As a result of the wide-reaching Arabic influence, subsequently reinforced by loan words from English, /h/ emerged as a fully functional consonant in the language. In the area of grammar, Hausa at one time had an almost exceptionless system whereby all words with feminine gender ended in the vowel /a/. However, since the gender of loan words has been assigned on semantic or analogical criteria regardless of the form of the words (cf. Heine 1968b for the assignment of loan words in languages with noun classes), the original fit between phonology and gender has started to break down. Thus one now finds numerous non /a/-final feminine words such as *goggo* 'aunt' from Fulani and *gwamnati* 'government' from English (feminine by analogy with the earlier Arabic loan word *hukuma* 'governing authority').

10.6   Conclusion

Historical/comparative linguistics is concerned with languages as they have developed over time. It treats their evolutionary creation and development as reflected in current-day phylogenetic relationships, the nature of their internal linguistic changes, and the way in which they have been influenced by other languages. By extrapolating back from the present, linguists comparing present-day language in detail have been able to reconstruct a picture of what various proto-languages looked like hundreds and thousands of years ago.

In the African area, the techniques of historical/comparative linguistics have led to the postulation of four major phyla with complex internal subgroupings. The techniques have also allowed linguists to do significant reconstruction of lexicon and phonology, most notably in the Bantu family (Guthrie 1967–71). Further methodological refinements and additional work can be expected to answer questions such as: (a) are there any linguistic isolates in Africa apart from the four major phyla? (b) does Mande really belong in Niger-Kordofanian, and if so, why does it look so different from other languages in the phylum? (c) what was the original noun class pattern for basic proto-Niger-Congo? (d) what was the basic word order for Proto-Afroasiatic and for its constituent branches such as Chadic and Cushitic? (e) in the past, were there language families in Africa other than Khoisan that had click consonants as part of their phonological inventories? (f) what kind of time depth would be required to account for the considerable diversity in the Nilo-Saharan family, assuming that it is indeed a valid phylum?

Greenberg's monumental contribution to African historical linguistics is now fifty years old: the field is clearly ready for a new leap forward. This challenge awaits a new, younger generation of African linguists.

Further reading

Most discussions of historical linguistic methodology are concerned with languages outside of Africa. These general sources, which commonly focus on Indo-European languages, are nevertheless important for anyone who intends to go deeper into the question of African language history and classification. Here is a brief selected list of essential works. (a) On classification and subclassification: Greenberg 1957, 1963a; Hetzron 1976; Hoijer 1962; Lackner and Rowe 1955; Newman 1995b; Nurse 1997. (b) On reconstruction and sound change: Bloomfield 1965; Hoenigswald 1963, 1990; Kuryłowicz 1964. (c) On contact phenomena: Greenberg 1960b; Sapir 1963; Thomason and Kaufman 1988.

11

Language and history

CHRISTOPHER EHRET

11.1   Language history and human history

From the history of any language can be read the history of the people who have spoken that language in past eras. Why is that so? And just how do we read this kind of historical document? To answer these questions, we will draw on examples from the continent of Africa, not only because African languages and linguistics are our themes in this book, but because scholars of Africa, much more than those of other parts of the world, have made effective use of linguistic documentation in reconstructing the past. In our presentation we will deal with all four of the major African families of languages, Nilo-Saharan, Afroasiatic, Khoisan and Niger-Congo.

Language evidence is a very democratic historical resource. It does not normally allow one to identify individual characters in history, but it provides a powerful set of tools for probing the widest range of past developments within communities and societies as a whole, and it lends itself well to studies of history over the long term. For while linguistically based history does not allow precise dating, its data relate directly to the whole array of cultural elements that comprise the longer-term trends and the sustained courses of human development.

What are these data? Every language contains an extensive archive of many thousands of individual artifacts of the past. These artifacts are the words of the language; they are hard evidence, able to be rigorously situated in a linguistic stratigraphy. Each language contains the full range of vocabulary necessary to express the whole gamut of knowledge, experience and cultural practice pursued by the various members of the society that speaks the language. As ideas, behaviours and practices changed in the earlier history of that society, the vocabulary that described these elements of life necessarily underwent changes – in the meanings applied to existing words, in the adoption or deriving of new words, and in the loss or obsolescence of older words. The history of past change and development across that gamut of culture and economy is thus mirrored in the histories of the thousands of individual words with which the members of the society express all the various elements of their lives.

11.1.1   *Establishing a linguistic stratigraphy*

How does one uncover individual word histories in a language or in a group of languages? The essential first step is to establish what is often called a linguistic stratigraphy.

The most basic form of such a stratigraphy can be represented by a family tree of the relationships among the languages being studied. The technical linguistic aspects of establishing a family tree, and the complications that often arise in carrying out the task, are not something we have time or space to deal with here. But the historical meaning of such 'genetic' relationships among languages is something that does need explaining here if we are to understand how human history can be recovered from linguistic documentation.

At its most fundamental level, the genetic metaphor implies a linguistic relationship not unlike that found in many single-cell organisms. Two or more languages are related because they descend from a common mother language, called a 'proto-language'. This proto-language evolved at an earlier time in history into two or more daughter languages – it diverged into its daughters, much as the mother cell divides into daughter cells. The daughter languages each can subsequently become proto-languages themselves, diverging at later periods into daughter languages of their own; and this process can of course repeat again and again over the long-run of language history.

If we apply this schema to the early branchings of the important Nilo-Saharan family of African languages, we come up with the tree diagram that is figure 11.17.[1] With this diagram we identify a series of historical periods. First, the original 'mother' language, which we call proto-Nilo-Saharan, diverged into two daughter languages, proto-Koman and proto-Sudanic. Subsequently, Proto-Koman evolved into Gumuz and proto-Western Koman. Proto-Sudanic, the other original daughter language of proto-Nilo-Saharan, evolved into two daughters of its own, proto-Central Sudanic and proto-Northern Sudanic. Proto-Northern Sudanic then gave rise to Kunama and proto-Saharo-Sahelian, while still later proto-Saharo-Sahelian diverged into proto-Saharan and proto-Sahelian. A complex and varied array of later divergences took place in the history of this family of languages, but for the sake of clarity only the earliest developments are presented here.

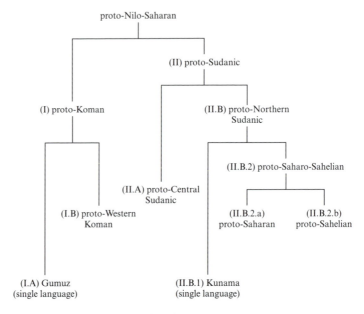

Fig. 11.17. Classification of Nilo-Saharan

This sequence of periods constitutes the basic linguistic stratigraphy of the early ages of Nilo-Saharan history. The first stratum, affecting all of the family, is the period of history represented by proto-Nilo-Saharan. Thereafter each branching line of descent forms its own separate stratigraphic sequence. For the Koman language group, the second stratum is the period of evolution of proto-Koman out of proto-Nilo-Saharan, and the third stratum covers the era during which Gumuz and proto-Western Koman became distinct. But if, in contrast, we follow the chain of eras that leads down to the Saharan subgroup, the second stratum is formed by the period in which proto-Sudanic came to be spoken; the third covers the evolution of the separate languages, proto-Central and proto-Northern Sudanic, out of proto-Sudanic; and the fourth is marked by proto-Northern Sudanic's divergence into its proto-Saharo-Sahelian and Kunama branches. The fifth stratum in this historical sequence comprises the period of the emergence of proto-Saharan, as well as proto-Sahelian, out of proto-Saharo-Sahelian.

It is very important when describing language history to use terms like 'diverged' and 'evolved', which imply extended processes of development. The straight lines of a family tree diagram sometimes mislead people into thinking that sharp language splits are involved. But in fact the break-up of a mother language into daughters is always gradual. Language change is an on-going process in any living, spoken language. It consists of the slow, progressive accumulation of many small changes – in vocabulary, in grammatical usages and in pronunciation – as time goes on. In the special case of linguistic divergence, a language begins initially to undergo different changes in different parts of its speech territory. These diverging courses of change lead at first to the emergence of different dialects of the language in the different areas, and then, over a period of centuries, to the evolving of these dialects into distinct languages, no longer intelligible to each other's speakers.

The mitotic metaphor of linguistic relationship and divergence is an apt one in most respects. The most important insight we discover is that the mother language diverges into its daughters, just as the microscopic mother single cell in biology splits into its own daughters. The proto-language does not 'give birth' to its daughters and remain distinct from them; it evolves directly into each of its daughters as part of a continuing historical process – it becomes its daughters. One significant difference between the metaphor and its concrete biological referent is that the mother language can sometimes give rise to several daughters during the same period of time, whereas mitotic division produces normally just two cells out of one mother cell.

11.1.2   ***Languages and societies***

There is one more step we must take before we can begin to situate our linguistic historical evidence in our linguistic stratigraphy: we must comprehend the social historical dimensions of language relationship. To do this we must first understand how language and society connect to each other. Through most of human history, a language could exist only because there was a society to which that language belonged and whose members used it as their vehicle of social and cultural communication. When, for whatever historical reason, people lose the sense that they belong to a commonality distinct from those of other peoples, the language they speak soon ceases to be passed down to younger generations and so begins to die out. Conversely, the continuing existence of a language over a long span of time reveals a corresponding long-term societal continuity of one kind or another among the speakers of the language, extending right across the different periods of its history.

The longer the period of time since the divergence of a daughter language out of the proto-language, the more varied and diverse the ways in which the accompanying history of social continuities is likely to be played out. Most often a language is transmitted through direct historical lines of societal descent, even though as the centuries pass the society itself may change out of all recognition, and even though at times the disruptions of war or internal societal strife, or the challenges of nature, may greatly attenuate the connection.

Much less commonly, a lateral transmission of a language can take place. Dahalo, a language of the Southern Cushitic subgroup of the Afroasiatic language family spoken in Kenya, provides a good example. Originally, sometime before 2,000 years ago, the Dahalo people were gatherer-hunters who spoke a language belonging to the Khoisan family. After a probably long period of close relations with a neighbouring, dominant Southern Cushitic-speaking farming society, the Dahalo gave up using their original Khoisan language. They began instead to speak the Southern Cushitic language of their neighbours, although they continued to follow their older food-collecting ways of life. They also took many words from their old language into their new one, and this is how we know today that they used to speak a Khoisan tongue. Then during the first millennium AD, the Southern Cushitic farmers were all assimilated into another Cushitic farming society, the Garree. Only the Dahalo continued to speak the Southern Cushitic language. Because they still maintained their economically distinct way of life, they were able to retain the adopted language, despite having a new society move in all around them (Ehret 1974).

So the history of related languages is at one and the same time a history of societies. When we reconstruct the relationships among a group of languages, we simultaneously establish the historical existence of the societies that spoke the languages. We also establish that some sort of societal continuity connects the histories of the speakers of each language right back in time to the people who spoke the ancestral language, the 'proto-language' of the family as a whole. Our tree of relationships among the Nilo-Saharan daughter languages is a history of a succession of Nilo-Saharan-speaking societies. It forms a social-historical as well as linguistic stratigraphy.

11.1.3   *Words as historical artifacts*

Once we have used the evidence of language relationship to lay out the historical links among the related societies and to formulate the linguistic stratigraphy of this history, we are ready to tackle the most challenging and most rewarding part of the enterprise of recovering history from language evidence. We are ready to position the individual artifacts of history, the words that make up the vocabularies of the languages of our topic of study, in our stratigraphy. Two criteria guide our placement of the artifacts.

11.1.3.1   *Locating words in a linguistic stratigraphy*

One criterion is the actual distribution of the words in particular modern-day languages. To derive an extant word from a root word used in an earlier proto-language, the modern-day forms of the root (its *reflexes*) must appear in at least one language in each of two primary branches of the family. To be considered a proto-Nilo-Saharan item, a root word must have reflexes in at least one language of each of the two primary branches of Nilo-Saharan, Koman and Sudanic.

The process of determining whether a modern-day word can be traced back to an intermediate daughter language, such as proto-Northern Sudanic, has an additional wrinkle. The most obvious basis for reconstruction would be for the root word, as before, to have reflexes in at least one language in each of the two primary divisions of Northern Sudanic, namely, in Kunama and Saharo-Sahelian. But the criterion could be satisfied just as well in another fashion. If the same root word occurred in a language of the Central Sudanic group, it would need only to be found either in Kunama or in any one of the Saharo-Sahelian tongues to be considered a proto-Northern Sudanic item. The reason is obvious if we refer back to the tree diagram of the Nilo-Saharan family. To trace a modern-day word back to an earlier proto-language is to say that the word was transmitted from that proto-language via the direct line of social and linguistic descent of the language in which it is found in later times. If we follow the outlines of the Nilo-Saharan family tree, we see that the lines of descent that link Kunama and proto-Saharo-Sahelian to Central Sudanic connect back through two successive intermediate daughter languages, proto-Northern Sudanic and proto-Sudanic. The only way a word could be part of the common inheritance of both a Central Sudanic language and Kunama, or of both a Central Sudanic language and a Saharo-Sahelian one, would be if it also was in use in the proto-Northern Sudanic language.

11.1.3.2   *Regular sound change in language history*

A second criterion must be met, however, if we are to consider such root forms to be fully valid reconstructions, and this is the criterion of regular sound correspondence. Regular sound correspondence allows us to determine whether two closely similar words are cognates or borrowings (or just chance resemblances).

What do we mean by regular sound correspondence? As part of the normal course of history in any language, there arise from time to time changes in how particular sounds are pronounced. When such a 'sound shift', as it is called, takes hold, it tends to effect all cases of the sound in question. For instance, if a *b* becomes a *p* at the end of one word in a language, it normally does so because of the operation of a sound shift rule that changes all cases of former word-final *b* into *p*. In other words, sound change in any language proceeds on the whole according to regularly formulatable rules (see chapter 10).

Because of this characteristic, history always creates a regular correspondence of sounds between related languages. To choose an example from the Bantu branch of the Niger-Congo language family, a proto-Bantu sound represented by linguists as *b regularly became a *w* in the daughter language Swahili and dropped out of pronunciation entirely in another daughter language, Gikuyu of Kenya. By other sound shifts, the proto-Bantu consonant sequence *nt changed into simple *t* in Swahili, while becoming *nd* in Gikuyu. And by two further sound-change histories, original Bantu *a remained *a* in both languages, and original *u stayed *u* in Swahili while producing a sound spelled *ũ* (but pronounced like *o*) in Gikuyu. Thus we say that Swahili *w* regularly corresponds to Gikuyu Ø (zero); that the instances of Swahili *t* that derive from proto-Bantu *nt correspond regularly to Gikuyu *nd*; and that Swahili *a* and Gikuyu *a* and also Swahili *u* and Gikuyu *ũ* show regular sound correspondences. Reflecting these regularities, the proto-Bantu root word *bantu 'persons, people' became modern-day *watu* in Swahili and *andũ* in Gikuyu.

Regular sound change allows us to identify the words in the related languages that have been preserved in a direct line of descent from the vocabulary of the common mother, or proto-language. It enables us, consequently, to distinguish from such inherited items the words that a particular language has adopted or, as linguists say, 'borrowed', from other languages over the course of its history. If the sound correspondences are regular *throughout* in the words being compared – as they are in the instance of Swahili *watu* and Gikuyu *andũ* just cited – then the probabilities are usually exceedingly high that the words are cognates, directly inherited in each language from their distant, ancestral proto-language – that each word is, in linguistic terminology, a regular reflex of the same root word. If sound correspondences fail even in any one of the sounds in the two items being compared, then some other kind of history, usually involving the borrowing of the word into one or both languages, may have to be invoked instead.

11.1.3.3   *Varieties of word histories*

Each kind of word history in some manner reveals a portion of the human history of the speakers of the language. Some words occurring today in the daughter languages will prove to have been in use, with the same meanings, ever since the time the mother language was spoken. They will thus attest to long-term cultural continuities – to areas and elements of conservatism and retention in culture and life. The widespread use in Bantu languages of the Niger-Congo family, for instance, of an old, inherited word for 'goat', *-búlì, reconstructed back to the proto-Bantu period and in fact even earlier in Niger-Congo history, shows that the proto-Bantu people without a doubt knew of goats and that the knowledge was maintained from that period down to the present among each of the peoples who use the word today.

In contrast, the semantic derivations of words often reveal older, now lost, ways of thinking or former ways of doing things. For example, in the proto-Mashariki language, a daughter language of proto-Bantu spoken near the great Western Rift valleys of Africa at around 1000 BC, a new word for 'to plant (crops)' came into use. Because this verb previously in Bantu history meant 'to split', its new meaning tells us that the proto-Mashariki people continued to emphasise an earlier rainforest-based agricultural technique, protective of fragile soils, of cutting a narrow slit in the ground and planting a new cutting from a yam or other similar food plant in the slit. In the next several centuries after 1000 BC, the settlement of Mashariki people in lands with richer soils, along with changes in their crops led to the complete loss of this practice among their descendants. Without this piece of linguistic testimony, an insight about earlier agricultural technology might have been lost.

Other words of ancient use in a language family will have undergone meaning shifts in one or another daughter tongue. In the Horn of Africa, for instance, several words in the proto-Soomaali language of the Afroasiatic family originally referred to the different life-stages of cattle. In the daughter language, Maxay ('Northern Soomaali'), they came instead to refer to the equivalent life-stages of camels (Ali 1985). These meaning shifts reveal the replacement of cattle by camels among the early Maxay, who about 1,200 years ago spread their settlement into very dry parts of the Horn, where camels but not cattle could thrive.

In still other cases derivational affixes may be added to an old root word to create a new term. For example, among the early Mashariki Bantu of about 3,000–2,500 years ago in the African Great Lakes region, a new word for salt (*-*inò*) came into use. Its derivation from an older verb meaning 'to dip' (*-*in-*) indicates that the people of that region had begun by then to extract salt from certain briny lake deposits, somewhat earlier than the archaeology can yet confirm (Ehret 1998).

Other kinds of meaning change can reveal the appearance of new ideas or the development of new economic practices, as we will learn later in this chapter from several examples drawn from Nilo-Saharan history. Among these are an ancient Nilo-Saharan verb *k^hày* 'to break off, tear off', which, after the inception of cultivation, took on a more specific application to the clearing off of vegetation, and another early Nilo-Saharan verb *$n\d{d}$ɔ*, which shifted its application after the adoption of cattle-raising from 'to squeeze, press out' in general to the technical meaning 'to milk'.

Still other words will turn out to have been 'borrowed', that is adopted, into a particular language from another language, rather than inherited from the proto-language. Borrowed words, or loan words as they are also called, reveal cross-cultural influences. Many different kinds of word-borrowing have taken place in history. There is space here to mention just a few.

The borrowing of a single word often indicates the adoption of the item named by the word. For instance, the generic term *ŋikaal* for camel in Turkana of northern Kenya is a loan word from Soomaali or Rendille *gaal*, showing that the Turkana first learned of these animals from speakers of one of those two languages.

At the other extreme, a very large number of words may have been borrowed, all in a relatively short period of time, from one language into another. Very often this kind of word borrowing tells us that large numbers of the people who formerly spoke the donor language of the loan words were assimilated into the society of the people who adopted the words. Between these extremes lies a variety of other patterns of word-borrowing among languages, all of which require a delicate interpretive hand. The differing kinds, quantity and rapidity of borrowing in such instances can reflect a great variety of different kinds and intensities of intersocietal contact, and it is in fact essential to an adequate historical interpretation of word-borrowing that such wider historically linked sets of loan words in a language be identified (for a preliminary categorisation of the types of borrowing that occur in language history, see Ehret 1981).

A very different, but equally productive approach to grouping word histories takes account of the findings of ethnoscience. Scholars of this branch of anthropology have shown that societies, each in their own various culture-specific ways, systematise their knowledge and understanding of the cultural and natural worlds in which they operate. These folk understandings are expressed in the semantic patternings of the words that deal with the different subsets of folk knowledge. Because of that fact, it becomes possible to elicit the modern folk systems of peoples speaking related languages and then to seek to reconstruct from these data the earlier systems of their common ancestors. From the individual word histories within a semantic subset, further inferences may then be drawn about the course of change in ideas and beliefs between earlier and more recent periods. Both inherited and borrowed vocabulary may figure in this type of investigation, with borrowed words in particular revealing whether the cultural shift owes wholly or in part to influences from neighbouring societies. (The techniques and potentials of this approach are discussed at some length in Ehret 1978; some applications in reconstructing religious history appear in Ehret 1972.)

11.2 Building a stratigraphy: the Nilo-Saharan example

It is now time to see in a more practical manner how these principles have been used in African historical studies. Our examples will deal primarily with very early history. Beginnings have been made towards uncovering the early historical developments among the speakers of each of the major language families of the continent – Nilo-Saharan (especially Ehret 1993); Niger-Congo (e.g., Blench 1993, Ehret 1982, Klieman 1997, Vansina 1990, Williamson 1989a, 1993, among others); Afroasiatic (Ehret 1976, 1979, 1995); and Khoisan.

We will begin our survey with the Nilo-Saharan languages. Nilo-Saharan societies took on key roles in the earliest creation and spread of agricultural ways of life in the African continent, and the evidence for that history provides striking illustrations of the power of linguistic evidence in unveiling the ancient past.

11.2.1 *The Nilo-Saharan family in historical perspective*

This family has undergone a complex history of repeated divergence into subgroupings and languages, a history that took at least the past 12,000 years to unfold. Over those thousands of years, great shifts in human economies and in customary life and political and social institutions have taken place in Africa as well as all across the world, and Nilo-Saharan-speaking peoples have been at the centre of many of the most important reshapings of life and livelihood in the African continent. Their languages, as would be expected, have time and again mirrored those changes. A particularly striking and telling range of examples of how linguistic historical methods and techniques work out in practice can be adduced if we restrict ourselves to the period 11,000–7,500 years ago, when most Nilo-Saharan peoples shifted from gatherer-hunter to herding and cultivating economies.

The actual evidence and arguments for Nilo-Saharan history are quite complex, and the history itself is long and immensely varied, and so only a simplified sampling of the relevant data can be presented. In the word evidence cited here, the regularity of sound correspondences can be assumed to have been established (in Ehret forthcoming), unless irregularities are specifically noted, as is done for word borrowings from one Nilo-Saharan language to another. The reader should refer to the Nilo-Saharan family tree (section 11.1.1) for the linguistic stratigraphy with which to trace the lines of descent of the particular reflexes of each root word. To assist the reader in identifying the descent lines, each citation of a reflex and its language has its branch of Nilo-Saharan also listed. The examples that illustrate this story are drawn from the history of the Sudanic branch of the family.

In the first two stages of this history, represented by the proto-Nilo-Saharan and proto-Sudanic strata, the societies that spoke the Nilo-Saharan languages were still all probably gatherer-hunters in economy. No vocabulary diagnostic of any type of food production can be traced to those two eras. To the proto-Northern Sudanic period can be traced the first words that may indicate the deliberate raising of domestic animals, while the earliest stratum in which words indicative of cultivation can be identified is the subsequent proto-Saharo-Sahelian era (Ehret 1993). Finally, at the proto-Saharan and proto-Sahelian eras, sheep and goats were added to this economy.

11.2.2   *A stratigraphy of Nilo-Saharan word evidence*

The histories of the individual root words that make up this body of evidence are of several types. Sometimes we simply cannot as yet track the words back before the beginnings of food production; the earliest term for a cultivated field, traceable to the proto-Saharo-Sahelian language, is such a case:

*ɔɗomp 'cultivated field'
II.B.2.a. Saharan: KANURI *də́mbà* 'bed for sweet potatoes, small irri-
gation dike'
II.B.2.b. Sahelian: TEMEIN *ɔjɔm*, PL. *kɔjɔm* '(cultivated) field'
Nilotic: JYANG *dom*, PL. *dum* '(cultivated) field'

In many other instances, however, the words turn out to be older roots shifted in meaning to express activities or things connected to livestock raising or to the cultivation of crops. An example of this kind of history is a proto-Nilo-Saharan (PNS) root word that originally referred in a general way to breaking or tearing off, but at the Saharan-Sahelian stage took on the technical meaning of cutting and clearing away plant material, particularly in relation to cultivation:

*kʰày 'to break off, tear off (tr.)'
I. Koman: OPO *kai* 'to break'
II.A. Central Sudanic: proto-Central Sudanic **kɛ* OR **k'ɛ* 'to tear off'
II.B.2.a. Saharan: KANURI *cè, kè* 'to plow, remove earth'
II.B.2.b. Sahelian: FOR *kauy-* 'to weed; to skin'
SONGAY *kèyè* 'to weed field a second time'
NYIMANG *kai* 'to chop (with axe)'
Nilotic: proto-Western Nilotic **kay* 'to harvest'
Rub[2]: IK *kaw-* 'to cut (e.g., with axe), to clear land'

These two examples, as well as the many other Nilo-Saharan word histories related to agricultural activities but not cited here, are consistent with the conclusion that cultivation of crops began as a set of independent inventions among the proto-Saharo-Sahelians.

If we turn our attention to word histories relating to livestock raising, a more varied picture emerges. Again some root words cannot yet be traced back to earlier pre-food-producing periods, as, for example, a verb for 'to drive herd' used as early as the Saharo-Sahelian period:

> ****yókw* 'to drive herd'**
> II.B.2.a. Saharan: KANURI *yók* 'to drive, herd'
> II.B.2.b. Sahelian: SONGAY *yógó* 'to bustle, stir, move about to gather the herd and send it to pasture'
> Nilotic: proto-Eastern Nilotic **-yok* 'to herd'
> proto-Southern Nilotic *yakw 'to herd'
> proto-Rub [*yakw, *eakw 'to herd': probable loan from Southern Nilotic (expected **yokw-?*)]

But again also, other old root words specifically do reveal in their histories the transition to animal domestication. For instance, the earliest verb indicative of driving livestock to pasture, which can be tracked back to proto-Northern Sudanic in our linguistic stratigraphy, was formed by attaching the Nilo-Saharan causative suffix *k to the older proto-Nilo-Saharan (PNS) verb *ṣu 'to lead off, to start off':

> ****ṣʻúːk* 'to drive (animals)'** [PNS *ṣu 'to lead off, start off' plus old *k causative]
> II.B.1. KUNAMA *sugune-* 'to cultivate, to raise animals' [back-formation from noun, consisting of stem plus *n noun suffix]
> II.B.2.a. Saharan: KANURI *sùk* 'to drive (many things), to speed horse'
> II.B.2.b. Sahelian: Nubian: DONGOLAWI *šuːg* 'to drive along, off'

The particular animals driven by the people of the proto-Northern Sudanic stage appear to have been cattle, as the following old cognate indicates:

> ****yáːyr* 'cow, head of cattle'** [PNS *yaːy 'meat' plus **-(V)r* noun suffix]
> II.B.1. KUNAMA *aira, aila* 'cow'
> [*ara* 'wild cow, antelope, small buffalo': loan apparently from early form of the Nera (Nara) language]
> II.B.2.a. Saharan: BERTI *eir* 'cow'
> II.B.2.b. Sahelian: SONGAY *yàarù* 'bull; brave; to be brave'
> NARA *ar*, PL. *are* 'cow'
> Nilotic: proto-Southern Nilotic **(y)eːʀ* 'male cattle'

Most interestingly, this root word can be derived, by addition of a Nilo-Saharan noun suffix *-(V)r*, from a still earlier, proto-Nilo-Saharan term **ya:y* for 'meat'. This history suggests that cattle may well have been domesticated by Northern Sudanic people themselves, rather than having been introduced from elsewhere, and that the Northern Sudanic people used cattle as their main source of meat.

Still other root words dealing with livestock raising have histories that include their having been borrowed from one language to another. Histories of this kind, of course, indicate the diffusion of the things or ideas from one early society or group of societies to another. A most instructive instance is provided by the earliest verb for 'to milk', because its history involves both its semantic derivation from an earlier Nilo-Saharan pre-food-production root word and its later spread by borrowing from one Nilo-Saharan branch to another. Originally meaning 'to squeeze', the root added a verb suffix at the Northern Sudanic stage in our linguistic stratigraphy and, along with that suffixation, a further meaning 'to milk'.

> ***nd͡ʒ 'to squeeze'**
>
> II.A. Central Sudanic: proto-Central Sudanic **nʐɔ* 'to squeeze out, press out'
>
> proto-Central Sudanic [**jo* 'to milk': loan from Sahelian language]
>
> II.B.1. KUNAMA *šu-* 'to milk' [stem plus **w* focused-action extension]
>
> II.B.2.b. Sahelian: TAMA *juw-* 'to milk' [stem plus **w* focused-action extension]
>
> GAAM *ɖən-* 'to milk' [stem plus **w* focused-action extension plus **n* durative extension]
>
> Rub: proto-Rub **'jut* 'to milk' [stem plus **w* focused-action extension plus **t^h* continuative extension]

In the Central Sudanic branch, this verb appears in two forms – with regular sound correspondence and the meaning 'to press out', and in a borrowed form with the meaning 'to milk'. Its history is one of a number of similar word histories in Central Sudanic languages indicating that the early Central Sudanic people, who diverged along a separate line of historical development before the Northern Sudanic period, did not participate in the original establishment of livestock raising among Nilo-Saharan peoples and that those ideas and practices diffused to them from other Nilo-Saharan societies only much later in time.

Even more arresting is the evidence dealing with the raising of sheep and goats. Here the histories of a number of key early root words show that the raising of these two animals did not originate among the Nilo-Saharans at all, but spread to them after the proto-Saharo-Sahelian period in our stratigraphy. The sources in each case were languages of the Afroasiatic family. For instance, the generic term *tam for 'sheep' in the proto-Saharan language was an ancient loan word from the Chadic branch of the Afroasiatic language family. Similarly, the proto-Sahelian root word for 'goat', *ay, came originally from the northern, Beja branch of the Cushitic branch of the Afroasiatic family (Ehret, 1993; 1999):

> *áy 'goat'
> II.B.2.b. Sahelian: FOR *déi*, PL. *keita* 'he-goat'
> > TEMEIN *kai* 'goats (suppletive plural)' [*k^h plural affix plus stem]
> > Daju: proto-Daju *aiše 'goat' [stem plus *s noun suffix]
> > Surmic: Didinga-Murle *ɛ:θ 'goat' [stem plus *s noun suffix]

This conclusion fits the zoological and archaeological evidence, which shows that goats and sheep did indeed spread into Nilo-Saharan-speaking areas from the Afroasiatic-speaking societies to the north, and that they spread after cattle raising had already developed among peoples of the Northern Sudanic branch of the family (Ehret 1993; Ehret forthcoming a; Wendorf and Schild 1998).

To recapitulate, these sets of evidence are part of a much larger body of data demonstrating that, in the earliest periods of the linguistically recoverable history of Nilo-Saharan peoples, their societies were gatherer-hunters in economy. Food production took hold in a three-stage process. First, a tending in some fashion of cattle began among the proto-Northern Sudanic communities. Next the cultivation of crops was taken up by the proto-Saharo-Sahelians, and finally goats and sheep were added to the economy at the proto-Sahelian and proto-Saharan stages.

11.3 Locating past societies: examples from Nilo-Saharan history

To turn the linguistic findings into satisfactory history we must correlate them with other datable evidence of the past, such as archaeology or written documents. To accomplish this correlation, two other lines of linguistic historical argumentation must be applied. One is to use the more recent locations of the languages of a family to argue for the most probable areas in which their earlier proto-languages would have been found. The other is to apply a tool called 'glottochronology' to estimate the broad timeframe within which particular proto-languages would have been spoken.

11.3.1   ***Locating societies in place***

In arguing for earlier language locations, the most probable historical scheme is the one that requires the least population displacement and fewest
population movements to account for the modern locations of the languages of
the family. The sequence of argumentation begins with the most recent branchings among the languages and moves backwards in time.

What does this method tell us about the geographical history of the Nilo-Saharan
development of food production? The latest of the three stages we have identified
for this history took place among the proto-Sahelians (see the Nilo-Saharan family tree above). With the exception of a single subgroup, Eastern Sahelian – the
languages of which extend from the Nubian tongues spoken along the Nile in the
northern Sudan to the Maasai of north-central Tanzania – all the Sahelian
groups today are located in the sahel geographical belt, along the southern edges
of the Sahara Desert, extending from Songay spoken in Mali in the interior delta
of the Niger River to the For language of the Marra Mountains in Sudan. The
simplest history of population movements is therefore one that places the lands
of proto-Sahelian broadly somewhere along the southern edge of the Sahara region.

At the next previous stage in this history, proto-Sahelian diverged as a sister
language of proto-Saharan out of their common ancestor, proto-Saharo-
Sahelian. The modern-day distribution of the daughter languages of proto-
Saharan reaches from the Sahara Desert fringes north of the Marra Mountains,
where Zaghawa and Berti are spoken, to the Tibesti region of the east-central Sahara
Desert, occupied by the Tibu people, to the Lake Chad Basin at the south edge
of the central Sahara, in which the Kanuri language is spoken. The proto-
Saharan speech territory therefore most probably lay in the southern or south-
eastern parts of what is today the central Sahara Desert. If we combine the arguments
for locating the proto-Saharan and proto-Sahelian territories, the simplest history
we can construct would attribute the wide spread of the Sahelian languages to
a single early east–west expansion, with that expansion beginning from a region
adjacent to the proposed proto-Saharan lands in the east-central or south-east-
central Sahara.

Finally, we consider the first of the three stages. In that period the proto-Northern
Sudanic language diverged into two branchings – proto-Saharo-Sahelian, whose
lands on our reckoning would best be placed in the east-central or south-east-
central Sahara, and Kunama, today a single language spoken just beyond the far
south-east edge of the Sahara Desert, in the far north-western part of the Ethiopian Highlands. The simplest account of this historical stage would involve a single
expansion, either (1) of the speakers of the proto-Saharo-Sahelian daughter language of proto-Northern Sudanic westward from the south-eastern Sahara, or

(2) of the speakers of the earliest form of the Kunama language eastward from the south-east-central Sahara, or (3) of both groups outwards from a common centre somewhere in the eastern half of the southern Sahara regions.

11.3.2   *Locating societies in time*

One way to give a dating framework to this history is to apply a technique known by the unprepossessing name, 'glottochronology'. The approach is based on empirical observations, taken in a variety of language families from different parts of the world, which reveal a recurrent patterning of lexical change in what has been called 'basic' or 'core' vocabulary. Using a standard list of 100 or 200 meanings, sometimes called the 'Swadesh' list, that are basic and nearly universal in the world's languages, scholars have found that the percentages of words replaced by new words for the same meanings tend towards similar outcomes over similar periods of time in each language.

The method has been widely criticised, but the criticisms only too commonly have been expressed as a kind of disbelief, a very unscholarly substitute for argumentation from evidence (Embleton 1986: 61 makes a similar point). A possible reason behind this 'unbelief' is that both the detractors of glottochronology and many of its early supporters misunderstood it as a phenomenon involving *regular and predictable* change. But in fact what is involved here is the accumulation of many changes that are individually *random and unpredictable*. This sort of accumulated change in the different languages then becomes describable by statistics and bell curves. It is a phenomenon that is of course quite familiar to sociologists studying human behaviour, but perhaps a bit exotic to linguists of recent decades, who seem, at least in many cases, to have thought a mystical regularity was being attributed to language change.[3]

Glottochronology has been shown to fit well with known language histories in the Americas, Europe, Asia and Africa. It works well for languages of the very distantly related Semitic and Cushitic branches of the Afroasiatic family, for the Turkic language group, for Carib, and for Japanese, among others, as well as for a variety of Indo-European cases (see Ehret 1988a: 569 for some of the relevant sources). Nor does the size or social complexity of the speech community appear to modify the long-term outcome of this kind of vocabulary change. The applicability of glottochronological estimation to societies of widely varying demography and culture is amply evident in the variety of solidly based correlations of archaeology with language that have been developed in the past three decades for eastern Africa (Ambrose 1982; Ehret 1998; Ahmed 1995, among others).

Roughly speaking, in the 100-meaning list the proportion of words that a language will retain with the same meaning over a 500-year period will tend to range around a median of 86 per cent. Two related languages that have been diverging from their common mother language for 1,000 years can therefore be expected to have both kept the same words in around 74 per cent of the cases, give or take several percentage points. After 2,000 years of divergence, the range of percentages will distribute around a median of 53 per cent; after 3,000 years, around 39 per cent; and so on down the scale:[4] see table 11.28.

Table 11.28. *Median dating and retention rates*

Rough median dating [BP]	Median common retention rate between related languages [in percentages]
1000	74
2000	55
3000	40
4000	30
5000	22
6000	16
7000	12
8000	9
9000	7
10000	5

In the case of the Northern Sudanic branch of Nilo-Saharan, the languages of its Kunama and Saharo-Sahelian subbranches are separated by cognation figures centring around 3–6 per cent, indicative of a time period for the divergence of proto-Northern Sudanic of more than 9,000 years ago – in other words, somewhere very, very roughly in the range of about 8000 or 9000 BC.

For just that period in the history of the Sahara, which was then a land mostly of steppe, grassland and dry savanna environments, a strikingly close set of parallels can be identified between the archaeology and the linguistic history of early Nilo-Saharan food production. In areas that included far south-western Egypt, a three-stage development of food production took place between about 9000 and 5000 BC (Wendorf *et al.* 1984; Wendorf and Schild 1998 brings this work up to date). It began with the tending of cattle before 8000, followed by the appearance of *prima facie* evidence for a second development, of cultivation, by the second half of the eighth millennium, and at a still later point in time, possibly about 6000 BC, by the first evidence of sheep and/or goats. The archaeological dates of the three stages fit within the general range of time proposed for the proto-Northern Sudanic society and its next two strata of descendant societies, the proto-Saharo-Sahelians and the proto-Saharans and proto-Sahelians. Moreover, the locations of the finds lie in a part of the same overall region, the southern half of the eastern

Sahara, in which the linguistic arguments would place these peoples (Ehret 1993). The same succession of economic changes appear, from the beginnings of cattle tending among the proto-Northern Sudanians, to the adding of crop cultivation by their proto-Saharo-Sahelian descendants, to the adoption of sheep and goats by the still later proto-Sahelian and proto-Saharan daughter societies of the proto-Saharo-Sahelian people.

11.4 **Early history among the Khoisan, Afroasiatic and Niger-Congo peoples**

The early history of the Khoisan language family is only sketchily understood so far. But fairly extensive study of the Afroasiatic family has been undertaken, and a variety of proposals on the courses of early Niger-Congo history have been mapped out by several scholars.

11.4.1 *The Khoisan family*

Proto-Khoisan was a very anciently spoken language, dating possibly as long ago as 20000 BP. The Khoisan peoples of recent centuries were heirs to a cultural tradition that once occupied much of the eastern side of the continent, from northern East Africa to the Cape of Good Hope.

Scholars who accept the membership of the Hadza language in this family usually favour a Khoisan family tree in which Hadza by itself forms one of two primary branches. The second primary branch comprising the rest of the family then split, in this view, into one branch consisting again of a single remaining language, Sandawe, and a second branch comprised of the rest of the Khoisan languages.

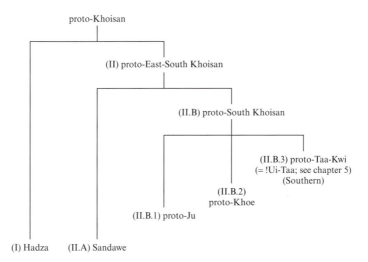

Fig.11.18. Classification of Khoisan

Hadza and Sandawe, which derive from the first two divergences in the family, are both spoken today in Tanzania in East Africa; the South Khoisan tongues, in contrast, all are or were spoken in southern Africa. The principles for inferring the locations of past societies (section 11.3.1) thus dictate that the earliest periods of Khoisan history must have been played out in eastern Africa and that the spread of Khoisan languages into southern Africa took place at a later time.

This linguistic historical inference supports the conclusion that the early Khoisan were makers of the Eastern African Microlithic tradition (Munson 1986). Tool assemblages belonging to this cultural complex date back to at least 17000 BP in the archaeology of East Africa. But not until the sixth millennium BC did the Wilton culture, an offshoot of the Eastern African Microlithic, spread south across southern Africa. This archaeological history thus matches well with the linguistic implication that Khoisan languages spread into southern Africa only after having been long established farther north.

11.4.2   *The Afroasiatic (Afrasan) family*

Afroasiatic, also known as Afrasan (and formerly known as Hamito-Semitic), is the family of African languages best known to non-specialists.[5] Along with the more than 250 languages of its Cushitic, Omotic and Chadic branches, it includes ancient Egyptian, the Berber languages of northern and Saharan Africa, and a single outlying subgroup of south-west Asian languages, Semitic (see Ehret 1995 for this subclassification).

Because of the association of the Semitic languages with several world religions, the Afroasiatic family has long been uncritically presumed by non-Africanist scholars to be of south-west Asian origin. But recent studies have put it beyond doubt that the ancestral language, proto-Afroasiatic, was spoken in Africa. The linguistic geography of early Afroasiatic language history, as depicted in the family tree (figure 11.19), confirms that conclusion. It shows us that the first divergence in the family gave rise to a narrowly spread branch, Omotic, consisting of languages spoken in later times entirely in the Ethiopian Highlands, and to the more widely spread Erythraic branch. The second period of this history, in which proto-Erythraic diverged into two groups, similarly produced one branch, Cushitic, with a more restricted spread – centring on the Horn of Africa and extending no farther north than the central Red Sea hills – and a geographically extended branch, North Erythraic. Only from the proto-North Erythraic stage onwards did the more northerly subgroups of the Afroasiatic family come into being, as the family tree shows us.

A linguistic stratigraphy of Afroasiatic word histories corroborates this locating of the early stages of Afroasiatic history. The proto-Afroasiatic vocabulary included terms for flour (*dzayj-*), for edible food taken from grasses (*ʕeyl-* and

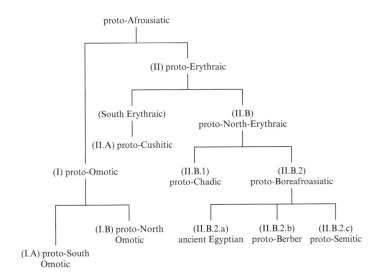

Fig. 11.19. Classification of Afroasiatic

zar-), for grindstone (*bayn*-), and also for donkey (*k*ʷ*er*-), but no words at all implying the herding of animals or the cultivating of crops. At the proto-Erythraic stage, a root word for cow (*ɬoʔ*-) was added, but still lacking in the proto-Erythraic language were any words specifically indicative of cultivation or herding (Ehret 1995; 1999). The presence of these root words shows us that the proto-Afroasiatics made use of wild grass bulbs or seeds for food and lived within the natural range of wild donkeys. Their proto-Erythraic descendants continued this way of life and – to judge from their having a word for cow – either moved to areas where wild cattle could be found or experienced an environmental shift that allowed the cow to spread into their lands.

This linguistically proposed history correlates remarkably well with developments in the archaeology of north-eastern Africa. Wild donkeys ranged the Red Sea hills and the far northern fringe of the Ethiopian Highlands, in just the regions where the arguments from linguistic geography would place the early Afroasiatic populations. In parts of the same broad region, the collection of wild grasses by people with grindstones took hold before 13000 BC, and remained a basic subsistence practice for several thousand years longer. As for wild cattle, these moved south from the Mediterranean as far as the north edge of the Ethiopian region after about 11500 BC, when wetter climates spread across the eastern Sahara. It seems therefore highly probable that the proto-Afroasiatics and their descendants, the proto-Erythraic people, are to be identified with the early wild-grass-collecting cultures of north-eastern Africa.

The first incontrovertible evidence found in the word histories for the appearance of livestock raising and cultivation appears only at the proto-Cushitic, proto-Chadic, proto-Berber and proto-Semitic periods. The proto-Cushitic language contained, for example, nouns for cultivated field (*paʔr-*) and cattle pen (*mawr-*) and the verbs for 'to milk' (*ʔilm-*) and 'to cultivate' (*ʔabr-*). Old Cushitic terms for finger millet (*dangawc-*) and t'ef (*tl'eff-*) identify two of the crops they cultivated. Similarly, the proto-Chadic people had words for cultivated field (*mar*) and sorghum (*dəwr*) and numerous domestic animal terms, such as for sheep (*tam-k-*), ram (*nzəl*) and goat (*bəkr*). In the archaeology, the first moves of the North Erythraic groups, such as the proto-Chadic people, towards food production may possibly coincide with the spread of livestock to the Capsian cultures of the northern Sahara, by 6000 BC. The roughly contemporaneous spread of proto-Cushitic communities into northern parts of the Ethiopian Highlands, required by the linguistic evidence (Ehret 1976), is as yet archaeologically unexplored.

The history of the Omotic languages has been little studied as yet. Still, certain broad elements of their history are clear enough. The earliest Omotic speakers were an offshoot of the proto-Afroasiatic grain collectors, because they maintained some of the wild-grass-collecting words used by their proto-Afroasiatic forebears. The early sites of grain collectors found in the archaeology of north-eastern Ethiopia may well have been theirs. But their descendants of the last several millennia have been pre-eminently cultivators, with their staple crop being the enset plant. The wide occurrence of Omotic loan words in modern-day Cushitic languages of Ethiopia reveals that Omotic agricultural societies formerly occupied most of the Ethiopian Highlands.

Other expansions of Afroasiatic languages took place in western parts of Africa. Proto-Chadic, a member of the North Erythraic branch, was taken by its speakers south from the central Sahara into the eastern Lake Chad Basin in about the sixth millennium. During the fifth to third millennia BC, descendant languages of proto-Chadic spread over a great part of today's northern Nigeria and central Chad. Well over 100 Chadic languages are currently spoken, the best known of which is Hausa.

The Berber languages, another subgroup of the North Erythraic branch, expanded at three different periods. First, in the third millennium BC, the speakers of proto-Berber spread across areas extending from the central Maghreb to the borders of Middle Kingdom Egypt. A second Berber expansion covered large parts of North Africa in the last millennium BC and gave rise to many of the Berber peoples known in the Roman records. A final Berber spread took place in the first millennium AD, when the Tuareg, by then possessors of camels, occupied the central Sahara (Ehret 1999).

The Semitic languages spread to far south-west Asia at an uncertain date, but surely well before 5000 BC. Two movements of Semitic languages from Asia back into Africa require mention also. The Ethiopic group, numbering today about fifteen languages, the most well known of which is Amharic, all derive from a dialect of Epigraphic South Arabian carried to Eritrea in about the sixth century BC by settlers from Yemen. Because of their central role in commerce and in the rise of early states in the Horn, these immigrants spread their language to many of the indigenous Cushites (Ehret 1988b). The older idea that South Arabian pre-eminence resulted from their bringing iron technology or plow agriculture into the region is simply not supported by the evidence. Plow cultivation, in fact, can be shown from Cushitic word histories to antedate the South Arabian arrival by as many as 3,000 years (Ehret 1979).

Dialects of another Semitic language, Arabic, are now spoken widely in North Africa, Sudan and the western Sahara. They spread to those regions through both conquest and population movement in the centuries since the rise of Islam in the seventh century AD.

11.4.3   *The Niger-Congo family*

Niger-Congo is another family with a very long history. The proto-language of the family may have been spoken as long as 15,000 or more years ago. The most widely followed subclassifications of the family divide it into a series of branches and subbranches (Bendor-Samuel 1989; see chapter 2 above[6]), a much simplified version of which is presented in figure 11.20.

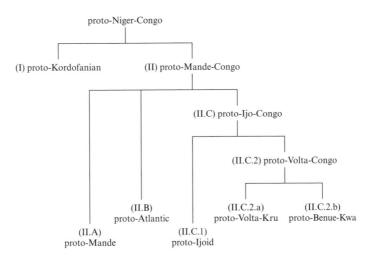

Fig. 11.20. Classification of Niger-Congo

The first expansion of Niger-Congo peoples appears to have stretched from as far east as the Nuba Mountains of Sudan, where proto-Kordofanian would have been spoken, to as far west as Mali, anciently the territory of the Mande and Atlantic-Congo branches. Just how long ago this period of expansion took place remains unknown.

A second, but still early and important stage in Niger-Congo history was the proto-Mande-Congo era. At this period, or so it appears from the evidence of word histories, the cultivation of the Guinea yam and possibly other crops, such as the oil palm, began among at least the peoples of the Atlantic and Ijo-Congo branches of the family (Williamson 1993 proposes the early words for these crops; Greenberg 1964 identifies an Atlantic and Ijo-Congo verb for cultivation, *-lim-*). Between possibly about 8000 and 6000 BC, these peoples spread across the woodland savannas of West Africa, the natural environment of Guinea yams. At that time, woodland savanna environments extended several hundred kilometres farther north into the Sudan belt than they do today.

Then at around 5000–4000 BC, at a period of shift to somewhat drier climate, the proto-Benue-Kwa descendants of the proto-Volta-Congo people expanded south into the rainforest belt of West Africa. The glottochronological dating of this spread of languages places it in about the sixth millennium (Armstrong 1964), and that dating correlates exceedingly well with an expansion into the rainforest, known from the archaeological record, of peoples who made polished stone axes (Shaw 1978/9). Yams and oil palms require sunlight to grow, and stone axes would have been the essential tools of the incoming Benue-Kwa cultivators for converting forest into clearings.

One offshoot of the Benue-Kwa peoples, the speakers of the Bantu languages, then expanded as early as 3000 BC from Cameroon into the equatorial rainforest of the Congo. Over the course of the next 3,000 years, various Bantu societies spread successively through many parts of the forest and into the edges of the southern woodland savanna to the south of the rainforest (Vansina 1990; Klieman 1997), bringing West African yam agriculture into those regions.

Over roughly the same time period, another grouping of Niger-Congo peoples, the Adamawa-Ubangians, carried the same agricultural way of life eastwards through the woodland savanna zone just north of the equatorial forest, across what is today the Central African Republic (Saxon 1982). The original proto-Adamawa-Ubangian language was a daughter of the proto-Volta-Kru language (see figure 11.20).

Then, during the early first millennium BC, one particular descendant people of the proto-Bantu, the Mashariki (or Eastern) Bantu, moved farther east, into the Great Lakes region of Africa. Around the last three centuries BC, the Mashariki communities began a relatively rapid expansion that scattered their descendants across eastern Africa, from Uganda and Kenya in the north to Natal in the south. Other Bantu peoples spread at about the same time more directly south from the equatorial rainforest into the savannas of what is today Angola and Zambia. In all of southern and in many eastern parts of Africa, Bantu expansion proceeded at the expense of Khoisan languages. In Uganda, Kenya and Tanzania, Southern Cushitic and Eastern Sahelian languages also were sometimes replaced by Bantu. The overall history of these developments is exceedingly complex. But the outcome is simply stated: because of these population movements, Bantu languages are today spoken across a third of the continent.

11.5   **Writing history for historians from language evidence**
        These examples from early African history are useful in illustrating the basic techniques of historical reconstruction of history from linguistics, and for showing how archaeology and linguistic findings can be combined. The cases cited from Nilo-Saharan history, in particular, familiarise us with some of the long-established methods and formats to follow in this kind of historical study. They give us a first awareness of just how far-reaching and valuable this work can be.

But the really important advances and the most sophisticated and original applications of linguistic methods in Africa have dealt with the history of the past 3 to 4,000 years. The most wide-ranging of these works are Vansina's *Paths in the Rainforests* (1990) and Ehret's *An African Classical Age* (1998). Each intertwines the evidence of many hundreds and, in the case of the Ehret's book, many thousands of word histories. Each marshals a great body of comparative ethnographic evidence to evoke and articulate the social and cultural changes those word histories encompass. Each engages the long-term social and political developments as well as the multiple trajectories of agricultural and technological history and the consequences of trade and the diffusion of things and ideas over longer and shorter distances.

The importance of these books reaches far beyond just the uncovering of the African past. Both are models for the writing of full and satisfying social and economic histories of large regions, applicable to any part of the world where written documentation is lacking and to many parts of the world where written documentation exists but is sparse and uneven. Both of them demonstrate the great power of language evidence in displaying the history of the inner as well as the outer lives of those societies. Vansina's work constructs the history of the Bantu peoples of the equatorial rainforest regions of Africa, a story of ancient genesis and great complexity and longevity. Ehret's book depicts the complex unfolding of cross-cultural interactions in eastern Africa in the last millennium BC, which involved peoples of all four of the major African language families, and the emergence out of those interactions of a new cultural world and its spread in the early first millennium AD all across the eastern and southern sides of the continent. It sets that history, as well, within the wider African and world historical contexts of its times.

Other, younger scholars are now pursuing the same kinds of directions in their work, and we can confidantly expect further exciting advances in the coming years. What has been discussed here only scratches the surface of what linguistic techniques can bring to the study of history in Africa and to the building of rich and deep understandings of all the neglected histories of preliterate or otherwise underdocumented societies around the world.

Notes

1 An alternative Nilo-Saharan subclassification different in several key aspects is followed by Bender ed. 1997 and in chapter 3 in this volume and elsewhere. The differences derive primarily from the fact that his works use a less wide range of classificatory evidence and a more incomplete phonological reconstruction of proto-Nilo-Saharan than is found in Ehret forthcoming a.

2 'Rub' corresponds to what other authors call 'Kuliak'.

3 Very few studies have sought to apply actual evidence to disprove glottochronology. One kind of substantive work dealt with languages in which the apparent rate of change in basic vocabulary was significantly less than expected by the method (in particular, Bergslund and Vogt 1962). But these languages each had a long history of being associated with the special social preservation and recital of the older literary forms, a situation that provided a strong and recurrent potential for feedback from those ancient literary sources to the spoken language, thus reinforcing the use of older vocabulary and slowing the replacement of old words by new. The results of these studies in fact fit in with the expectations of the method and do nothing that brings into question the utility of glottochronology in the study of unwritten languages.

Other scholars have been bothered by the fact that lesser apparent rates of change apply to neighbouring languages in a chain of contiguous, closely related dialects. But these instances derive from histories in which the society that spoke the mother language underwent an incomplete divergence into daughter communities and in which the intersocietal boundaries never became well defined. They regularly produce a recognisable patterning of percentages allowing them to be easily identified and understood. Normally the dialects located farthest apart, at opposite ends of the chain, have cognate percentages with each other that fit well with the glottochronological expectations. The dialects located in between then have percentages that are skewed higher in direct proportion to how close they are to each other, with adjacent dialects sharing the highest percentages of all.

4 It has been argued that, because the words for some meanings on the list tend to be retained longer than others, very ancient periods of language divergence will be reflected mainly by retentions of the words most resistant to replacement, with the consequence that over very long spans of time the rate of change in the 100-word list will seem to slow down (the literature on this point is reviewed by Embleton 1986). The point is a reasonable one,

but the experience of correlating linguistic findings and archaeology in eastern Africa suggests that this element may be a relatively minor distorting factor in interpreting what is, after all, a very, very rough measurement indeed. For that reason, the simple list of approximated datings is being relied upon here.

5 The name 'Afrasan' would be more appropiate here in part because it is shorter and easier to pronounce, but more importantly it is a name that gives proper emphasis to the African origins of the family.

6 In chapter 2, a geographically misleading and more complex name, 'West Volta-Congo', is used for the grouping Volta-Kru. The term is misleading because it includes languages spread far to the east of West Africa, in far southern Sudan, as well as languages in West Africa. Similarly the older name Benue-Kwa is to be preferred to the alternative name 'East Volta-Congo' of Williamson and Blench, because the Benue-Kwa group includes languages spoken almost as far west as the westernmost Volta-Kru ('West Volta-Congo') languages.

12

Language and society

H. EKKEHARD WOLFF

12.1 Introduction

African sociolinguistics is about the social and cultural dimensions of language in Africa. It studies the patterns of *language use* on the one hand, and the factors involved in *language variation* on the other. Being concerned with actual *speech acts*,[1] sociolinguistics seeks to answer several 'big *Whs*': *Who* speaks *What* to *Whom*, *When* and *Where*, and *Why* in *Which* particular language variety? The big Whs reflect some of the major social factors involved when two or more individuals are speaking to each other, that is engage in verbal as much as social interaction:

- *participants*: who speaks to whom?
- *topic*: what are they speaking about?
- *setting* and the *sociocultural context*: where and when (at any particular social occasion or cultural event?) do they speak?
- *pragmatic function*: why are they speaking, what is language used for?
- *variety*: which particular 'lect', 'code', or 'register' are they using?

Differences in language use and language variation are due to complex patterns of interlocking factors, mainly historical, geographic, ethnic, cultural and social (section 12.2). The study of language variation can only be conducted against the background of these variables. Since language changes over time and in space alongside cultural and social changes in society, African sociolinguistics, therefore, also deals with the social and cultural dimensions of *language change* (section 12.3; cf. also chapter 10 above) in Africa.

Since we find widespread multilingualism[2] in Africa (see section 12.4), that is individuals or groups of people who use two or more languages regularly and who often apply the languages they use for different purposes or switch between them in very systematic ways, the study of language use and language variation among multilinguals is also an integral part of African sociolinguistics. Multilingualism is linked to the rise, spread and decline of *linguae francae*[3] (12.4.3) and the emergence of *pidgins* and *creole* languages (12.4.3.1), various types of *code-mixing* (12.4.1.1), the extinction of languages (*language death*, 12.4.4.1) and the emergence of new languages in Africa (12.3.2.1).

In the course of becoming multilingual, individuals or groups of speakers will either maintain their original first language ('mother tongue') or eventually give it up in favour of exclusively using languages acquired simultaneously or learned at later stages in life, that is shift to their second or third language ('other tongue'). African sociolinguistics thus also deals with instances and strategies of *language maintenance* and *language shift* when languages come under 'stress' (section 12.4.4).

One of the major characteristics of the language situation in Africa is the functional rivalry between African languages and the imported languages which are usually those of the former colonial masters and which are still being used for official purposes of nationwide communication and in formal education. African sociolinguistics, therefore, studies the *status* and *functions* of each and every language in a given African society or state, and the *politics* and *implementation* strategies of maintaining or changing the status and functions of language. Since the status of a language within a society can be planned and implemented, APPLIED AFRICAN SOCIOLINGUISTICS deals with all aspects of *language planning* (section 12.5), *language standardisation* (12.5.1) as well as *language and politics* (12.5.2), in Africa.

12.2 Language variation

12.2.1 *Language vs. dialect*

No two speakers of the same language speak alike, nor does the same speaker use his/her language the same way all the time: variation is part of language and language behaviour.[4] Whereas two speakers are said to differ in terms of their particular *idiolectal* varieties, the same speaker is said to use different *codes* or *registers* on different occasions and for different communicative purposes. However, the most common way of identifying a speaker linguistically is by his or her *dialect*, since most speakers of a language are aware of regional varieties within their language. For an experienced speaker of Hausa in West Africa, for instance, it may not be difficult to identify another speaker of Hausa as coming from Tahoua in Niger (speaking a dialect of Hausa which the speakers in Tahoua call Aderanci) or from the Katsina or the Bauchi area in Nigeria (speaking dialects of Hausa which the speakers call Katsinanci and Guddiranci). Dialects of a language typically have names.

Ideally, the notion of 'dialect' should be clear, and one would assume that linguists know how to tell a dialect from a 'language' and identify any particular dialect as belonging to a particular language. However, this is a problematic theoretical issue in linguistics and leads to the unsatisfactory admission that nobody knows exactly how many 'languages' are spoken around the world in general, and in Africa in particular (see chapter 1 above).

Language and *dialect* are terms which may be clear in everyday conversation, but prove to be problematic and ambiguous when applied in a technical sense. We could say that the Hausa language has several dialects, among them Aderanci, Katsinanci and Guddiranci. In this sense, language is the sum total of all its varieties (dialects, sociolects, idiolects, including all possible codes and registers). However, when a person from Katsina is referred to as a 'dialect speaker', it is often implied that this person does not speak Hausa in some particular 'good' or accepted way, meaning that there is a 'better' and more acceptable way of speaking Hausa, and the frame of reference alluded to would be the so-called Standard Hausa. Compared to the Standard Hausa variety,[5] the Katsinanci variety is considered to represent non-standard or even substandard Hausa. This relates to a notion of dialect as something inferior to or even outside of, the language which itself becomes automatically identified with the 'standard'. In this sense, language versus dialect reflects degrees of social acceptance and prestige. Further, we still hear people say that compared to Europe with its sixty or so 'languages', Africa has about 2,000 or more 'dialects'.[6] This implies a linguistic as well as cultural superiority of Europe over Africa, and an (often subconscious) attempt to belittle African languages and cultures. The reasons given are often related to factors such as writing traditions and standardisation: a proper 'language' in this evaluative sense has a standard or high variety and a relatively long history of writing – a 'dialect' has neither of these.

Also, in particular with reference to Europe, 'languages' tend to be identified with national borders and sovereign states, and 'dialects' with regional varieties largely within national borders, consequently 'languages' are said to be 'dialects with a national anthem, a flag, and a navy'. A similar situation is found in southern Africa: the languages Sotho, Swazi and Tswana are more likely to be considered 'languages' because they can be associated with the politically independent states of Lesotho, Swaziland and Botswana. On purely linguistic grounds, they are more likely dialects of just two languages which have several mutually intelligible dialects: Nguni (with varieties like Ndebele, Swati, Xhosa, Zulu) and Sotho (Northern Sotho, Southern Sotho, Tswana). Even within South Africa, Zulu and

Xhosa, for instance, are considered to be different languages for several non-linguistic reasons:

(a) members of the respective speech communities consider themselves to be 'different' on ethnic, social and historical grounds

(b) each of them has large numbers of speakers

(c) they have been aggressively treated as 'different' because the *apartheid* system insisted on the differences rather than the commonness of features among the population groups, their cultures and languages

(d) they are listed as different 'official' languages in the South African constitution of 1996

Yoruba in West Africa is another language with mutually unintelligible dialects which, however, share a commonly recognised standard (Ayọ Bamgboṣe, p.c.). This situation is characteristic for any so-called *dialect chain* (or *dialect continuum*) when speakers do understand immediately neighbouring dialects but have severe problems communicating with speakers of far-away dialects of the same language.

12.2.2   *Social stratification, identity and language*

Language behaviour is social behaviour and reflects social stratification, which is part of every society. It is impossible to conceive of any more or less permanent system of cohabitation of human beings which would not be governed by social rules. Social stratification implies a hierarchical relationship of 'higher' and 'lower' in terms of prestige, power and privileges – in sociological terms: *status* and *roles*. Even within what seem to be rather 'homogeneous' societies, human social behaviour will reflect and thereby reinforce, differences of status and roles. Social, ethnic,[7] cultural and linguistic homogeneity, however, are the exception rather than the rule in most countries and societies. Yet, many ideas about a 'nation-state' which are shared by intellectuals and political and educational elites in Africa appear to imply homogeneity as a necessary prerequisite of successful nation-building.

Ethnic and linguistic differences often coincide, that is, people with different ethnic background often also speak different languages or different varieties of a language. Language can thus be used as a reliable criterion for *ethnic identity* in both directions – group-internal and group-external: by their language behaviour, speakers identify themselves as members of the same group as much as they are identified by others as belonging to a different group.[8] This makes language not only an ideal target for assimilation policies, as for example in the former French and Portuguese colonies in Africa, but also an effective instrument for apartheid as, until quite recently, in Namibia and South Africa. It is a widespread misconception among policy makers that linguistic homogeneity will imply or foster social homogeneity. This is simply not so. Ethnically different groups may share the same language and patterns of language behaviour, such as the Hutu and Tutsi in Ruanda and Burundi or the various Somali-speaking clans. Their recent history has shown, however, that a shared language does not prevent societies from suffering from severe internal conflicts, civil war and even genocide.

Social identity in its most general sense is reflected in linguistic behaviour. It relies on kind and degree of social stratification, that is on the existence and recognition of 'social groups' within society. Social identity is not necessarily the same as ethnic identity. In some cases, however, the two may coincide as, for instance, in the case of Ruanda and Burundi referred to above: based on racial and thereby racist considerations, German and later Belgian colonial politics elevated members of Tutsi groups to higher social status as functionaries of the colonial administration and thereby created a social class which ran along the lines of 'ethnic' = racial criteria. But even in societies which appear to be ethnically more or less homogeneous, linguistic differences exist which can be linked to cultural and social differences within that society such as, for instance, social class and caste. Social stratification may be based on some combination of the following criteria, which are often reflected in differences in language behaviour: age, sex, ethnic/clan/lineage/family background, kinship relations within clan/lineage/family, religion, occupation, economic status, migrant versus permanent resident status and 'race'. In Africa's multi-ethnic societies, social stratification is not necessarily related directly to ethnic composition, although there are always strong tendencies to create such relationship between power and ethnic origin – the strongest case is commonly referred to by the term 'apartheid'.

Language usage, as any other *symbolic* feature a given culture may recognise, creates and permits the identification of social stratification. Younger members of society address elder members in particular ways and vice versa, men speak differently from women, and both sexes tend to speak differently to members of the other sex. Certain traditional occupations such as blacksmiths, native doctors and priests, as well as people with a background in modern formal education, will signal their social identity (willingly or subconsciously) by their way of speaking. Even within the same family, among husband and wife, parents and children, grandparents and grandchildren, different patterns of language behaviour can be observed. *Social variation of speech* is observed, for instance, as in whether one should speak or rather be silent, who to speak to and who never to speak to directly, the choice and avoidance of certain terms of address, the choice and avoidance of certain vocabulary items, the choice and avoidance of certain formulaic expressions, social *accents* (i.e. particular pronunciation features), and patterns of *code-mixing* (12.4.1.1). Social change will also change language behaviour: children will change their speech habits when growing older to become adults and, later, 'elders'. Once following the father or being elected as a traditional ruler, a person's linguistic behaviour will change, too. In some West African societies, a ruler's voice must not be heard (nor his mouth be seen, which is therefore veiled) by the ordinary member of society, the ruler will only whisper into the ear of his 'spokesman' who will then announce publicly what the ruler has said. Even with regard to modern politics: when democratisation became a big issue in the early 1990s, politicians swiftly changed their language behaviour, for instance, in the Republic of Niger. Before, they would address any crowd of people in French, the only official language of the country; they could not be bothered by the fact that more than 90 per cent of the people they talked to were not able to understand French! Speaking French, the official language, in public was part and parcel of being a politician. Now, the same politicians make sure that they speak Hausa or Zarma to larger audiences because they want to be re-elected, and had better make themselves understood!

In addition to the ethnic and social identity of speakers as members of particular social groups, every speaking human being has his/her own individual habits and patterns of speech and of reacting to the usage of language by others. The linguistic system associated with a single speaker is referred to as *idiolect*. There are as many idiolects in any language as there are speakers of that language. The idiolect is an inseparable part of and key to, the personality and individual identity of a speaker. As one can tell the truth or a lie in the same language, language behaviour reveals much of a speaker's identity and personality, but it may also be used by the speaker to 'cheat' on the addressee by disguising the real or original personality and pretending a false or adopted identity.

12.2.3   *Sociophonetics and linguistic accommodation*

Probably the first differences a speaker notices in the linguistic behaviour of some other speaker(s) relate to pronunciation: we easily detect a foreign *accent* (section 12.3.1) and are sometimes able to locate a foreigner in terms of her/his mother tongue. The same is true for accents within the same language because the various *lects* (i.e. dialects, sociolects) are not homogeneous. They all come with their different accents which allow other speakers to locate a person more precisely even within one dialect (12.3.2) or sociolect (12.3.2.1), that is each idiolect is automatically characterised by a certain accent. There is no completely accent-free production of natural language utterances.

Speakers are aware of linguistic variation and how social hierarchies are reflected by different lects. They have strategies to accommodate to other lects if need arises (sometimes subconsciously). Such *linguistic accommodation* is observed in both directions along the social hierarchy scale: same speakers can adapt to 'higher' varieties (for instance, when working as sales assistants dealing with higher-class customers) or to 'lower' varieties (when, for instance, stressing solidarity and group cohesion speaking to people back home in the village without, however, being condescending or arrogant). In the attempt to accommodate to higher varieties, speakers at times exaggerate and create *hypercorrect*[9] forms which, however, may eventually enter the general repertoire of social groups of speakers and become a give-away for such groups.

12.2.4   *Language as a social bond*

Language acts as a social bond, and language behaviour reflects *social* and *communicative distance*. Willingly or subconsciously, people signal degrees of intimacy, solidarity, respect, taboo, exclusion, discrimination by choice of language and/or by choice of variables of linguistic forms such as intonation and pronunciation, vocabulary and formulaic expressions. In multilingual environments, patterns of code-mixing (cf. section 12.4.1.1) can be used for signalling social nearness among speakers who share the same languages. A foreign accent, for instance, can result in more or less subtle acts of exclusion by native speakers. Switching to another language (for instance, to a *language of wider communication*, 12.4.2) in a group of people may be a wilful or subconscious act to include someone who has been left out of the conversations and social interaction as long as it was conducted in the shared native language of only a few members of that group. In dialogue, language behaviour is used to either bridge social gaps by linguistic accommodation (cf. above), or to create social distance by shifting to a linguistically more divergent variant, if not by even shifting to another language altogether.

Accordingly, different scales can be set up for certain social dimensions which are helpful in the analysis of social interaction through language:

(1)   the social distance or solidarity scale on which to locate the relationship of the participants in terms of

      intimacy $\Longleftrightarrow$ distance

    high solidarity   low solidarity

(2)   the status scale on which to locate the participants in terms of

      superiority $\Longleftrightarrow$ inferiority

    high status   low status

(3) the formality scale on which to locate the socio-cultural setting

      formal   ⟵⟹   informal

      high formality   low formality

(4) the referential scale on which to locate the function in terms of referential content, that is conveying new or important information on things, events, other people, etc.

      high referential   ⟵⟹   low referential

      information content   information content

(5) the affective scale on which to locate the function in terms of affective content, that is conveying information about how the participants feel about the topic or their personal relationship

      high affective content   ⟵⟹   low affective content

12.2.5   ***Language use in African cultural contexts***

In Africa as much as elsewhere in the world, various cultures have developed specific patterns of language use. There is, therefore, a scale of socio-cultural acceptance at a given instance of speaking. The Itsekiri and Okpe in the Delta area of Nigeria, for instance, have different terms for such words as 'blood', 'fire', 'firewood' according to whether the word is used at night or during daytime (Ayọ Bamgboṣe, p.c.). Among the best-known instances of culturally determined language use in Africa are the terms of avoidance (taboo) and respect among, for instance, the Xhosa and Zulu in Southern Africa, referred to as *hlonipa* (Finlayson 1978).

The cultural habit in certain societies of having to choose between at least two forms of personal pronouns for direct address is an immediate linguistic reflex of communicative distance as related to relevant social variables. Often quoted examples are the 'high' and 'respectful' and 'polite' forms of *vous* in French and *Sie* in German, which signal greater social distance than the corresponding 'low' forms *tu* and *du*, which are much more 'intimate'. The intimate forms can also be used in a condescending and even discriminating manner, thereby almost paradoxically changing a signal of social nearness into one of utter social distance. Observations of this kind open to the wide field of *political correctness* in verbal behaviour and how to talk about social groups, often minorities. Among the factors and strategies which govern lexical choice guided by the wish to behave socio-culturally or politically 'correct' are language *taboos* (i.e. avoidance of proper names and certain words, for instance sex/gender-specific pronouns and compounds) and the creation of *euphemisms* and *neologisms* (often circumscriptions and/or highly 'technical' words of foreign etymological heritage) to replace words with negative or too specific (for instance religious or obscene) connotations.

Social distance and politeness, as reflected in the above mentioned French and German choice of pronouns of address, are not much reported from Africa. In several Bantu languages spoken widely across southern Tanzania and Mozambique, second person plural pronouns are used much as in French and German, that is, plural forms are used when addressing a single person in order to indicate respect. Yoruba differentiates between *o* and *e* which signal age and/or status difference rather than familiarity (Ayọ Bamgboṣe, p.c.). Another instance is reported from the Mossi culture of Burkina Faso (Froger 1910; quoted from Reh 1981: 516): the pronoun *nyamba* (2nd pers. pl.) is used when addressing people who are higher on the social scale and among members of the aristocracy and for addressing strangers; the pronoun *fo* is used to address people lower in the social hierarchy and among members of the lower layers of Mossi society.

The Shilluk people in southern Sudan recognise a language variant referred to as the king's language (Pumphrey 1937; quoted from Reh 1981: 516) in which certain words and expressions are substituted by others: 'pebble' replaces 'head', 'dog' replaces 'donkey', and instead of 'going' or 'rising' someone is said to 'be led' and 'lifted' (by God).

The language of the Janjero in Ethiopia is reported (Cerulli 1938; quoted from Reh 1981: 516) to reflect a traditional three-step structure of society: the 'king's language' will differ somewhat from the 'language of respect', and both display differences from the 'common language'. Failing to address the king in the linguistically appropriate manner is considered an insult to the king and may result in lethal punishment.

A particular case of sociophonetics is reported from the Akan society in Ghana, where the 'royal accent' is identified with wilful stuttering and nasal articulation (Nketia 1971; quoted from Reh 1981: 517).

We find in Africa examples of 'sacred' language for special religious activities and of 'secret' language not allowed and often incomprehensible to non-members of a particular group of people who adhere to special cults of worship or belong to secret societies, who all tend to insist on keeping out the non-initiated. Verbal taboos are quite common also, and various strategies are being applied to avoid using certain words, often words connected to body parts like the genitals, sexual activities and other body functions associated with these body parts. The Nupe society in West Africa (Nigeria) is often quoted as being particularly prudish, and conscientiously so, speakers preferring to use technical terms borrowed from Arabic or very involved euphemisms and choosing to 'manipulate words in order to eliminate tasteless connotations' (cf. Farb 1975: 87).

12.2.6   ***Domains of language use***

Sociolinguists speak of 'domains' when several of the social factors and cultural dimensions of language use typically coincide, that is when the same set of participants typically use the same linguistic variety when they speak in a particular setting or sociocultural context on a topic which is also typical for that occasion. Such domains may be expressed in terms of participants and settings:

Table 12.29. *Domains, participants and settings*

Domain	Participants	Setting
Family	parents, spouse, children	home
Friendship	peer group, friends	home, street, sports, leisure
Religion	priest, imam	church, mosque
Education	teachers, principal professors, fellow students	school university
Business	bank manager, clerk	bank
Authorities	police officer, lord mayor	police station, town hall
Employment	colleagues, employer	workplace

In monolingual speech communities, speakers tend to use different varieties (codes, registers) of their mother tongue for different domains. In multilingual speech communities, speakers may use different languages altogether. The choice of the actual variety is further determined by other social factors and dimensions like social distance, status, formality and function, even though the topic may be the same. For instance, when speaking about sitting down for dinner among family members at home, speakers will choose different codes or registers when addressing their father, their spouse or their own children. At university, the registers used for speaking about examination problems to fellow students, professors or the vice-chancellor may vary considerably.

12.2.7   ***Language attitudes***

Being aware of the existence of different languages and the varieties of their own language, speakers will inevitably develop attitudes towards languages and language varieties. One may like or dislike a language or a particular dialect of one's own language: linguistic prejudice, that is culturally inherited positive or negative prejudices about languages and language varieties, is probably a universal human characteristic. Being able to speak a language L_x at all or even speak it well may tend to enhance a speaker's prestige in society, while obviously being a speaker of language L_y may hamper one's social upward mobility and make one the target of ridicule and being associated with backwardness and lack of sophistication. This latter negative prejudice is often encountered, or is feared to be encountered by its speakers, in the case of African 'vernaculars' or 'ethnic/tribal' languages *vis-à-vis* the more prestigious 'national' languages or even the 'official', often imported, language of the country.

Any attempt by language planners to change the functions and use of languages in a society, for instance by establishing an endoglossic language policy (section 12.5.2.1) and introducing African languages into the system of formal education will, first of all, have to deal with changing language attitudes. Failing to do so will, as experience shows, jeopardise all measures by governments and literacy agencies concerning the implementation of a new language policy.

12.2.8   ***Language as barrier***

The existence of 'language barriers' is a common human experience. Because of one's ability or inability to speak a language or particular variety of a language, geographical and social mobility may be dramatically restricted or enhanced. All sectors of 'participation' of the individual with regard to matters beyond the horizon of the native village or quarter of town where one was brought up are affected: international or even national (in the case of multilingual countries) politics and economics, dissemination of information and knowledge, formal and informal education, oral and written (tele)communication, even travelling, depend on the appropriate linguistic skills. Language barriers are overcome by two basic strategies:

(a)   bi- and multilingualism – a strategy already and traditionally widespread in Africa, more so in urban agglomerations and traditional centres of economic exchange than in rural areas of which many are still largely monolingual

(b)   linguistic assimilation and language shift, usually to a more prestigious lingua franca or language of wider communication – also widely practised in African societies

Language barriers can be said to be either vertical or horizontal. As vertical barriers, they block or impede social mobility, as horizontal barriers they block or impede geographic mobility (which in turn may have a blocking effect on social mobility).

Heine (1977) has classified languages in Africa as vertical or horizontal media of communication. *Horizontal media* stress solidarity and social equality, characteristically the case of African mother tongues. *Vertical media*, on the other hand, stress divergence and inequality, separate the elite from the masses and thereby serve for upward social mobility – characteristically the case with imported ex-colonial languages of wider communication in Africa. Horizontal media are traditionally handed down without access to the formal educational system and are acquired as first language at home (mother tongue) or are learned as second or third language (other tongue) in the streets or while conducting one's occupation or business. Vertical media are characteristically taught at school. Also, vertical media tend to have a tradition of writing and standardisation, whereas horizontal media are often confined to oral communication with little or no standardisation force behind them. Different from vertical media, an 'everything goes' attitude is associated with horizontal media which leads to increased variation and accelerated language change; they can easily become the subject of pidginisation.[10] Shift of a language from horizontal to vertical function is, however, possible, for instance when an African language becomes a national or even official language, replacing, or acting beside a vertical medium of European provenance.

12.3   The social and cultural dimensions of language change
12.3.1   *Language change in time: the diachronic perspective*

All languages change over time and space. Members of the speech community tend to notice and react to this. Older people complain about the falling standards of the language competence of the younger generation and often blame this on changes in social institutions such as schools, broadcasting (radio and TV), public appearances of modern leaders or on cultural imperialism by other cultures and the languages associated with those – like that of former colonial masters (as in the case of many African countries), or there are more general complaints about 'Westernisation' or 'Americanisation' as a correlate of ubiquitous globalisation and modernisation.

Language changes because society changes! Social change is one of the factors contributing to the inevitability of linguistic change (cf. chapter 10 above). Language change and linguistic heterogeneity therefore reflect the complex relationship between speaking, social background, functional aspects of language use and linguistic norms. The major largely non-linguistic factors which contribute to language change are (a) *isolation, migration, and language contact*, at times combined with (b) *imperfect language acquisition and learning*, (c) *modernisation*, and (d) *social mobility and prestige*.

> (a)   When people move away from each other or become separated by, for instance, political or ecological barriers, lack of everyday

communication will enhance differences in the kind and speed of linguistic changes (sound production, vocabulary, grammar), and here we speak of *divergence* processes. On the other hand, migration may lead to new contact situations in which other languages are likely to exert some influence and foster certain changes in terms of *convergence* processes.

(b)   Language is transmitted from generation to generation and children acquire language from adult speech around them. However, imperfect imitation of adult speech by children, once accepted and in turn imitated by adults, may contribute to the generalisation of such change. More common, however, appears to be the impact of imperfectly learning of a second language by immigrant groups, which tend to impose their particular speech habits on the newly learned language in situations of bilingualism.[11]

(c)   Vocabulary is particularly susceptible to changes due to new ideas and objects being introduced to the everyday experience of the speakers. The 'Words and Things' hypothesis (from German *Wörter und Sachen*) claims that groups of speakers tend to take over not only a new cultural item but quite often also the original designation in the language of origin, that is introduce a new ('borrowed') word as a *loan word* to their language. The introduction of masses of new words may lead to drastic changes in, for instance, the sound inventory and system (phonology) of the language.[12]

(d)   Ways of speaking are usually associated with more or less positive or negative prestige, depending on the social hierarchies within society. 'Stiff upper lip' pronunciation may stimulate as much emotional and social reaction as certain 'substandard' or 'jargon' ('argot') varieties. People tend to like (and imitate) certain ways of speaking and dislike others. Such preferences and avoidances in pronunciation, vocabulary and grammar may be conscious in some and subconscious in other cases. Once certain patterns become generalised, we state that, once again, language has changed.

These non-linguistic factors conspire with language-internal (linguistic) factors which initiate and/or speed up language change. These are (a) *ease of pronunciation*, that is the tendency to assimilate sounds to each other, simplify complex units, reduce or drop parts of words or word groups; (b) *analogical realignment*, that is the strategies to make conform to the rules what appear to be 'exceptions' to these rules within the linguistic system (cf. also *hypercorrect forms* further above);

(c) *grammaticalisation*, that is the functional (and sometimes also phonological) change of words and morphemes to become *grammatical markers* for pre-existing or even newly appearing grammatical categories; (d) *universal (implicational) typology*, that is the tendency of certain changes, once they occur, to trigger certain other changes within the linguistic system, such tendencies (sometimes called *drift*) may be independently shared by unrelated languages all over the world.

12.3.2   ***Language change in space: the dialectological perspective***
The study of regional variation makes up the long-established field of *dialectology* (also called *linguistic geography* or *dialect geography*). In socially stable environments as often in rural and 'traditional' areas, it is usually quite easy for people who have not met before, to identify each other by their *dialect*. Dialects, therefore, are abstractions from several idiolects which reflect the same regional background. Regional background, however, is not the only source of differences in speech habits and patterns: sex, age, occupation or any other social factor may go along with noticeable differences in linguistic behaviour which sociolinguistics have come to refer to as *sociolects*. Together with dialects and idiolects, they constitute the set of varieties (or simply lects) which make up the reality of one language.

In the light of the ever-increasing geographical mobility of people in industrial societies, and the observation that ethnically or linguistically homogeneous quarters (*ghetto*) in urban agglomerations become less and less the normal pattern, the *geographic identity* of speakers becomes more and more difficult to ascertain because increasingly we observe mixing of dialect forms by which the inherited distinct regional speech habits and patterns become blurred and give way to some pandialectal *koine*[13] used by some speakers, and to more or less standard forms used by other speakers under the continuous impact of standard varieties in education, the mass media and official nationwide communication.

Linguists tend to draw a sharp distinction between *dialect* and *accent*: whereas accent is usually limited to differences in pronunciation only (hence there are several regional or social accents noticeable in the pronunciation of a standard language), differences in grammar and/or vocabulary are usually considered to constitute different dialects of a language. For instance, in the Hausa language as spoken on both sides of the Niger-Nigeria international border, speakers from Niger are easily recognised by pronouncing [h] and [m], where Nigerian Hausa speakers would pronounce [f] and [u], for example

Niger/Non-Standard	Nigeria/Standard[14]	
[*tàhí*]	[*tàfí*]	'go'
[*zámnà:*]	[*záunà:*]	'sit, dwell'

These differences in pronunciation would characterise different accents of Hausa. In order to prove the existence of different dialects, we would have to refer to, for instance, the way to form the 'future tense' of the verb 'go', in which several structural differences[15] show up between the dialects; compare

Niger/Non-Standard   Nigeria/Standard
[zâ: ní tàhíyà:]   [zân tàfî]   'I will go'

Not surprisingly, both dialectal areas also differ in vocabulary items such as the referent of some traditional designations of coins and notes of currency which were introduced in the colonial period. In Niger, a former French colony, the Hausa terms refer to the metrical colonial currency of francs (fr CFA), whereas in Nigeria reference is now to the metric Nigerian currency of Naira and Kobo but originally the terms referred to the non-metrical British currency in terms of pound sterling, shilling (s) and penny (d):

	Niger	Nigeria	Origin
sisi	–	5 Kobo	sixpence (6d coin)
sule	–	10 Kobo	shilling (1s = 12d coin)
dala	5 fr CFA (coin)	25 Kobo	half a crown (coin: 2s 6d)
jikaljaka	1000 fr CFA	200 Naira	100 pound sterling

These examples of lexical dialectal differences at the same time testify to differences in the particular contact situation of the dialect areas as the result of differences of their colonial history. Niger Hausa has been considerably influenced lexically by French (e.g. *kile* < Fr. *clef* pronounced [*kle*] 'key'), Standard Hausa likewise by English (e.g. *tebur* < E. *table*). Both dialect areas, however, share the tremendous impact of Arabic as the language of Islam which has been present in the area for almost 1,000 years. This process is referred to as *borrowing* from a donor language, resulting in *loan words* (or simply *loans*) in the borrowing or receiving language (cf. chapter 10 above).

Several more or less objective linguistic criteria are used to establish dialect and language boundaries. The most widely used criteria are *mutual intelligibility* (also referred to as *intercomprehension*) and the identification of *isoglosses*.

Mutual intelligibility: When speakers from different parts of a country or even from different countries manage to understand each other with more or less difficulty when each of them uses their particular idiolect and dialectal variant, we may say that for this reason they share the same language. On the other hand, dialects of what is claimed to be the same language may be so different that spontaneous oral communication is no longer possible. This is true for many 'languages' in

Europe. However, since in the case of most European languages the speakers have access to a common written variety which is usually also used in nationwide oral communication (radio and TV broadcasting, cinema, theatre, but usually also in formal education), and which they recognise as their common 'standard', we are justified to say that we are dealing with dialects of the same language despite absence of mutual intelligibility between many of its dialects. This scenario is characteristic for what is called a *dialect continuum* or a *dialect chain*. For Africa, it has been claimed that many of the hundreds of Bantu languages, in particular those stretching from Kenya southwards into South Africa, form such a kind of dialect continuum, where it is difficult to tell where one Bantu language ends and another begins.[16]

Isoglosses: The classic method of dialectology is the mapping of dialectal differences, that is the identification of isoglosses and their representation on dialect atlases. The researcher chooses *points of elicitation*, for instance, neighbouring villages ideally over the whole language area, and in each village several speakers (*informants*, usually selected along some established parameters like sex, age, occupation) are interrogated usually by means of a questionnaire and accompanying tape recordings. Their utterances are meticulously transferred to an exact *phonetic transcription*. Whatever the linguistic features which come up as being different at certain points of elicitation, they are put on a map (one map per feature) and lines are drawn around points of elicitation which share a feature or the same difference in feature: these lines are called *isoglosses*. Isoglosses can be identified on all levels of linguistic structure: *isophones* would relate to phonetic and phonological features, *isomorphs* to morphological features, *isosemes* to semantic features, *isolexes* to lexical items, that is vocabulary. Ideally, several isoglosses should run parallel every now and then and form bundles. Such *bundles of isoglosses* would constitute a dialect boundary (if not a 'language' boundary, when very many isoglosses run parallel!).

Although isogloss maps are a useful visual aid, their relevance for establishing dialect boundaries rests on the distinction between features that are considered to be more or less significant. Any classification of languages or dialects rests on the criteria (i.e. isoglosses) which are chosen: there are several instances where isoglosses of one kind (or bundles of them) conflict with bundles of isoglosses of another kind which would disallow any unambiguous classification! Dialectologists and comparative linguists have to live with this dilemma.

12.3.2.1   Urban dialectology

Traditional dialectology heavily relied on relatively homogeneous rural areas and elderly people who were often formally uneducated and largely untravelled and were therefore considered to speak 'purer' dialectal variants than younger speakers who had been to school and to the bigger cities. Modern dialectology expands the geographical preoccupation to include social dialects (i.e. *sociolects*) as are more met with in urban agglomerations where regional background becomes less and less important. The creolisation of pidgins (section 12.4.3.1) like the Petit-Nègre and West African Pidgin (Wes Cos) in the major cities along the West African coast and its hinterlands is a still under-researched field of urban dialectology in Africa.

Particularly exotic in the urban African context are the newly emerging sociolects of juvenile delinquents and street gangs of semi-educated and jobless youth which are often imitated by more educated schoolchildren and students: for example Sheng in Nairobi (cf. Abdulaziz and Osinde, forthcoming), Nouchi in Abidjan, and the 'Black Urban Vernaculars' in South Africa (known as Tsotsitaal, Iscamtho, Pretoria Sotho, Tembisa Mixed Language; cf. Schuring 1985, Slabbert 1994) which involve heavy code-switching and thereby tend to 'mix' various linguistic systems, among them various standardised languages of African and non-African provenance. Their systematic study has barely begun. It remains to be seen and studied whether and how, maybe alongside the better known and very different case of Fanagalo (Fanakalo) of the South African mines and railways, they will eventually creolise and pose the same problems for the educational systems as the West African instances quoted above.

12.4   **Multilingualism**

In Africa, multilingualism is the norm rather than the exception. The vast phenomena of language contact, of which multilingualism is but one facet, can be approached from at least three different perspectives, each implying a particular set of methods, axioms and theories: the psycholinguistic, the sociolinguistic, and the historical-linguistic perspective. For easy reference, a distinction may be drawn between

    (a)   multilingualism as a feature of sociolinguistic *nation-state profiles*

    (b)   instances and forms of *institutional* multilingualism within a given nation-state

    (c)   *individual* multilingualism

Consider the following summarising statements drawn from a UNESCO working document prepared for the Intergovernmental Conference on Language Policies in Africa, in Harare, 17–21 March 1997 (p. 3):

According to the definition of languages and dialects there are between 1,250 and 2,100 languages in Africa . . . It is a trivial statement to say that monolingual countries are more the exception than the rule if we are to adhere to strict criteria. Even in an apparently monolingual setting, the geographical distance (dialects), the social distance (sociolects), the historical distance and other codes and registers will make the situation more complex.

Homogeneity is a fiction in the linguistic field more than in any other. Taking an arbitrary threshold of 90 per cent as the defining landmark of a monolingual country, only a handful of countries meets this criterion in Africa. The ones generally cited are Botswana (language: Setswana), Burundi (Kirundi), Lesotho (Sotho), Madagascar (Malagasy), Mauritius (Creole), Rwanda (Kinyarwanda), Seychelles (Creole), Somalia (Somali), Swaziland (Seswati).

The degree of multilingualism varies greatly. About 105 million people speak around 410 languages in Nigeria, 30 million people in [former] Zaire use 206 languages and Ethiopia has 97 languages for a population of about 45 million. Diversity is not the characteristic of giants alone. In Cameroon 185 languages are used by 8 million people, giving an average of 50,000 persons per language, 3 million inhabitants of Benin are spread over 58 languages while 2 million Congolese [Congo Brazzaville] have at their disposal 31 languages. On the other hand, Mauritania has four languages, Niger ten.

. . . these figures need to be scrutinised further, and they yield interesting and useful information. With a population of about 28 million Tanzania has 120 languages, among them Kiswahili which as a lingua franca is used by the vast majority of the population. Mali has 12 languages and 90 per cent of the population use four of them and 60 to 65 per cent use only one language, Bamanan, as first (L1) or second (L2) language. Twenty years ago this percentage was around 40 per cent; the increase is due more to growing numbers of users of Bamanan as L2 rather than the demographic increase of the ethnic Bamanan. Burkina Faso has about 60 languages for a population of 9 million, half of which is morephone (speaker of More language).

The numbers also conceal facts which need to be brought to light for a better understanding of the context and the challenge of multilingualism as a problem. In Nigeria 397 languages out of 410 are 'minority' languages, but the total number of their speakers account for 60 per cent of the population. Among them are several languages with more than 1 million speakers, with a few of them having a number of speakers close to 10 million. Similar phenomena are observed elsewhere and compel a departure from 'numerical muscle' as a decisive criterion in language planning . . .

Even in world terms, a mother tongue of another language with some 200,000 or so speakers is by no means a small language, given the fact that the overall population of the country of its usage may be much greater. Where, as in much of Africa, speakers of a certain language are not dispersed but tend to be restricted to well-defined geographical areas, even languages of some 50,000 speakers become significant for the purposes of development and use in national life. By the time one gets down to this level of languages with 50,000 speakers, one has taken into account well over 90 per cent of the population of almost any African country . . .

12.4.1   *Individual multilingualism*
We continue with a quotation from the same document, p. 4:

In a survey related to the case of Nigeria, the number of languages spoken by each of the subjects of the speech communities studied ranged from two to five as follows: 60 per cent of the subjects spoke two languages; 30 per cent three; and 10 per cent over four languages. A similar observation could be made regarding many if not all the African countries, where there is a widespread tradition of handling multilingualism. Often there is a complementary distribution of this multilingualism across languages by sectors of activities. The multilingualism is not only functional or commercial, it cuts across the whole social fabric. It forms a socio-political and socio-linguistic characteristic of most speech communities . . .

Despite the fact that individual multilingualism is an almost everyday phenomenon in Africa among adults, and given the 2,000 or so (see chapter 1 above) indigenous languages in Africa which are all candidates for individual multilingualism, there is little in-depth published research on this subject available.[17]

One of the major problems in the study of multilingualism is related to ascertaining the level of *proficiency* which the multilingual speaker has in any of the languages concerned – perfectly balanced equal competence in two or more languages is the rare exception rather than the norm. One language can be the *preferred* or *dominant* one (and will serve habitually as matrix languages in *code-switching*, cf. below), while others are more or less *dormant* or *specialised* for certain topics of conversation or verbal interaction with certain other speakers. In the course of a lifetime, a speaker may change his/her dominant language depending on education and social and geographical mobility (section 12.4.4).

The degree of multilingual competence among speakers of African languages varies again in relation to interlocking social factors. Men tend to be more multilingual than women, and people living in urban agglomerations tend to use more languages than people in the rural areas where one still finds large areas of monolingualism. Formal education also tends to add competence in another language since in many if not most African schools the medium of instruction is not the children's mother tongue or preferred language. One could guess that at least 50 per cent of the people living in Africa are multilingual. The official language, however, when it coincides with the language of the former colonial master, is often only understood and actively used by less than 10 per cent of the national population as in most 'Francophone' states, and somewhat higher (maybe up to 25 per cent) in 'Anglophone' countries.

12.4.1.1   *Code-mixing*

A particular phenomenon which is intimately linked to individual multilingualism and has attracted much attention, is referred to by terms such as *code choice*, *code-changing*, *code-mixing* and *code-switching*. For the purpose of this introduction, the term *code-mixing* will refer to any instance of interchanging usage of two or more languages within the same conversation or discourse by the same bilingual speaker. Code-mixing may thus take the form of either borrowing[18] or code-switching proper. Borrowing in this sense is an ad hoc strategy to remedy temporary or permanent lack of vocabulary. Code-switching as such is a third code in its own right which is available for bilingual speakers, besides the two other codes represented by the two languages as used in monolingual discourse. It is a code which is often favoured among bilingual speakers and is either used, as Carol Myers-Scotton (1993) sees it, as the *unmarked* choice of possible codes; as a special code it signals absence or conscious overcoming of tradition-controlled social distance, and indicates mutual recognition of belonging to a not exclusively ethnically nor linguistically defined group: 'Code-switching is a conversational strategy used to establish, cross or destroy group boundaries; to create, evoke or change interpersonal relations with their rights and obligations' (Gal 1988: 247). In a given situation, various factors contribute to the actual choice of language or code, for example the multilingual repertoires of the speakers involved and their respective degree of competence in the languages they use, the social setting in which the communication takes place, number and identity of the speakers, the social role and status of the speakers, the social distance between the participants, the topic, the referential, and affective content of conversation.

The varieties of code-mixing range from simple *tag switching* (i.e. throwing in a few words or fixed expressions from another language in which the speaker is not necessarily fully competent) via *interlarded speech* (i.e. happily switching between two languages within the same sentence, even within the same word) to complete switches between monolingual utterances. When a new participant enters the verbal interaction, speakers will often switch code (i.e. the language) when they do not share the same mother tongue or when they differ in status and social distance from the new participants. One may welcome and overtly involve a new participant by switching to the language higher on his/her affection scale, or – on the contrary – by switching introduce more social distance and less intimacy, in the extreme case for insult and abuse. A topic related to a particular domain (such as formal education, modern technology and communication) may also result in switching to another language (often the high variety in a diglossia situation; see section 12.4.1.1). Sociolinguists speak of *metaphorical code-switching* when multilingual speakers change the language within the same discourse in order to draw on the different associations and social connotations of status and prestige linked to the different codes, thereby overtly signalling their complex social identity.

Code-switching quite often takes place at turn-taking points in dialogue, but also in a speaker's monologue either between sentences (inter-sentential), or within sentences (intra-sentential), occasionally even within words at the juncture of two morphemes which make up the word. Code-switching is also used for pragmatic reasons such as warnings and admonitions, to attract the attention of other participants or to highlight parts of discourse, to mark off quotations either to report what somebody had said, or quoting a proverb or idiomatic expression from another language. Multilingual competence and code-switching strategies are acquired already by small children (cf. Khamis 1994).

In the absence of a generally accepted theory of code-mixing, figure 12.21 may do for the sake of illustration,[19] to highlight the fundamental differences one might like to draw between '(nonce) borrowing' and 'switching'.

Educators and language purists tend to disapprove of code-switching and take this rather natural linguistic behaviour of multilingual individuals to be an indication of deficiencies in the competence of one or all languages involved in it. Rather than accepting code-switching as enriching the linguistic competence of multilingual speakers, the speakers are at times stigmatised as speaking 'none of the languages properly'.

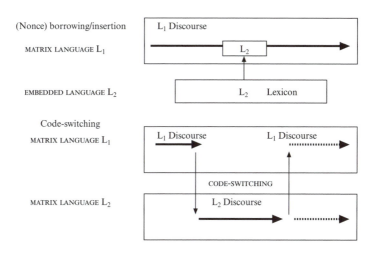

Fig. 12.2. (Nonce) borrowing and code-switching.

12.4.2   ***Language functions, institutional multilingualism and diglossia***

Language may serve different functions in society, and in multilingual societies several languages may be found to divide functions among them. Within multilingual societies,[20] different languages may have different legal status, and some of the society's institutions may require one or two particular language(s) to be used within its domain rather than any other language, hence we speak of institutional multilingualism. Institutional multilingualism may refer to

- societies or states which reserve certain functions to certain languages in their constitution or by decree, irrespective of the degree of implementation or actual usage by the people
- societies or states in which different institutions are identified with *de facto* different language uses; in Ethiopia, for instance, the Christian church is identified with the use of Geᶜez for liturgical and literary purposes, whereas Amharic and Oromo, for instance, are used both for fundamental education and for wider communication (also in the media), and English is a special purpose language for higher education and international communication
- institutions which demand the use of more than one language, for example educational systems which allow for mother tongues in the first years of primary education but require a national and/or foreign language for secondary and higher education

Table 12.30. *Function vs. legal status of languages*

Functional domains	Functional labels/ legal status	Functional description
Official communication	official language	nation-wide official communication for political, legal, administrative, educational, business, media purposes
Inter-group communication	vehicular language lingua franca	used for inter-ethnic communication whenever need arises, learned by large parts of populations with different mother tongues as second or third languages
	community language regional language	dominant language used in areas broader than their ethnic boundaries but not having a national scope
	national language	dominant language in multilingual environment used for regional or even nationwide communication (*de facto* national language); may be decreed to serve some of the official functions (*de jure* national language)
Intra-group communication	mother-tongue language vernacular language local language	learnt by African children through social interaction with members of communities to which they are linked by parentage
	ethnic language tribal language chtonolect	sometimes non-dominant or language of minority population in multilingual environment
International communication	language of wider communication	cf. Inter-African language, world language
	foreign language	imported languages with no or very few mother tongue speakers in the country
	cross-border language	language whose territory has been divided by an international border and is spoken on both sides of the border
	language of African intercommunication, Inter-African language	widely used across national borders for African intercommunication, e.g. Kiswahili, Pulaar/Fulfulde, Mandinka, Hausa
	world language	such as English, French, Portuguese, Arabic, which are used for communication among people of different countries and continents
Education	special-purpose language	(a) language as medium of instruction (b) language as subject of instruction
Literature		language used for literary production, print media
Religion		language used for religious purposes

Accordingly, societies or states can by classified according to the legal status of the languages spoken within its confines, and of how (many) languages are commonly used for which functions within its boundaries. Legal status is tied up with language functions. In most multilingual societies or states, however, legal status and language functions overlap: see table 12.30.

Apparently simple functional terms such as *mother tongue, national language* and *official language* are used with a confusing and conflicting range of interpretation, and quite often there is considerable functional overlap. Further, policy makers and language planners are tempted to combine mother tongue and community languages and to dilute dialects and minority ethno-linguistic groups into a homogeneous language and speech community for practical purposes. Other sociolinguistic typologies related to language functions distinguish between

(a) *first languages*, which are acquired in early years and normally become the speaker's natural instrument of thought and communication (often coinciding with mother-tongue languages above; in some multilingual societies there may be speakers who have acquired more than one language in this sense)

(b) *second languages*, which are acquired or learned at a later stage in life for commercial or other purposes, often through formal education

(c) *major or majority languages*, judged by number of speakers (usually reserved for languages which are not restricted to intra-group communication, but are also used for regional or wider communication and, therefore, as second languages)

(d) *minor or minority languages*, which are also judged by number of speakers (usually they are not used for inter-group communication and are, therefore, seldom learned by others as second language)

(e) *special-purpose languages*, which are usually second or foreign languages and largely restricted in use for religious and/or educational purposes like, for instance, Geᶜez in the Ethiopian Church, Classical Arabic for Qurᶜanic education, English and French for Western-type higher education; some special-purpose languages can rightfully also be referred to as *classical languages* (e.g. Geᶜez and Classical Arabic)

(f) *standard(ised) languages*, which have a relatively high degree of standardisation and normalisation; this is the case for only very few African languages but is true for the imported foreign languages which can or must, therefore, be used for official and educational purposes

(g) *non-standard(ised) languages*, which have as yet little or no standardisation and normalisation; this is the case for most African languages

(h) *pidgin languages*, which are a specific type of lingua franca resulting from a particular contact situation in a suddenly arising multilingual environment with no pre-existing shared language of wider communication, and which is nobody's mother tongue and has 'reduced' characteristics in vocabulary and grammar

(i) *creole languages*, which are usually, and often too narrowly, restricted to former pidgin languages which have expanded in lexicon and grammar and have become mother-tongue languages for at least some speakers.

12.4.2.1 **Diglossia**

Language behaviour in multilingual societies implies language choice for functional purposes: it may be more useful, profitable, comfortable, etc. to use different languages or varieties of the same language for different functions and develop corresponding patterns of language behaviour, often along a High–Low continuum related to social stratification and hierarchy. Following Ferguson (1959), such a situation is referred to as 'diglossia'. In many if not most African countries, the distinction between *official language*, possibly various *national languages* and a number of *local, ethnic, vernacular languages* (cf. section 12.4.2) tends to reflect a particular high–low continuum in which the 'high' variety is identified with the official language – this is quite often that of the former colonial master in Africa (English, French, Portuguese, Spanish).

In the case of Arabic,[21] the high variety is characteristically associated with the so-called *Classical Arabic*, that is the Qurᶜan, Islamic religious texts in general, and with WRITING, whereas the many mutually non-intelligible 'vernacular' or 'colloquial' or 'dialectal' Arabic varieties are characteristically associated with the low variety on the diglossia scale, and with SPEAKING. Some intermediate varieties have emerged largely through the media: film and TV productions largely of Egyptian provenance have dramatically contributed to the spread of the Egyptian, more specifically the Cairene dialect as a *koine*, whereas *Modern High Arabic* (based on Classical Arabic) is about to be accepted as a new standard for written communication and official rhetoric. In addition and particularly in the multilingual Maghreb countries (Morocco, Algeria, Tunisia), French enters at the high range both for speaking and writing and complicates the picture, involving also considerable Arabic-French code-mixing in the middle range. Even worse for the Berberophone populations, their languages, which are only spoken and practically never written,[22] enter at the lowest possible range and subject to social discrimination and ridicule. Table 12.31 represents a very schematic and as such a gross simplification.

Table 12.31. *Spoken vs. written varieties*

	Spoken varieties	Written varieties	Characteristic functional domain
High		Classical Arabic	Islamic religion
↑		FRENCH	school, official discourse, politics, French language media
		Modern High Arabic	cultural discourse, modern prose, Arabic language print media
↓	Cairo *koine*		modern popular culture
	Colloquial Arabic,		everyday life
Low	Arabic dialects		
	BERBER (Rif, Kabyle, Tashilhait, etc.)		family, intimate friends

In the whole African context – and not just in the Arabophone part of the continent – it is, therefore, useful to distinguish *multilingualism*, that is the general ability and habit of individual speakers or whole speech communities to use different languages, from *diglossia* (or even *triglossia*), that is the specific usage of either different varieties of the same language or different languages for different functional purposes as the accepted norm or habit of a speech community and usually related to a High–Low scale of social acceptance and prestige. Originally diglossia would exclude the use of the high variety in everyday conversation (such as Classical Arabic). Diglossia is nowadays also used to describe any situation where two different languages or varieties of the same language are used and spoken in everyday life for different, often complementary functions in a speech community,[23] one, however, being characteristically associated with sociolinguistically high, the other with low functions, that is one being considered more prestigious than the other.

In Africa, the High–Low distinction often refers to the official ex-colonial language *vis-à-vis* any vernacular language (cf. section 12.5). In this situation, several factors reinforce each other and almost allow for self-fulfilling prophecies: the high language is standardised and codified, that is, is a 'written language' with written literature, is used for prestigious official functions, and is employed on the upper levels of the educational system. It becomes associated with upward social mobility, money-getting and political power as is witnessed by the linguistic behaviour of the members of the political elite who use the high language on most occasions of public speech. The low language(s), often only deficiently standardised or not codified at all, with little or no written literature (other than possibly some translations of the Bible), find it difficult to compete in function and prestige, even though some of the African languages are being standardised and codified and increasingly develop written literature in addition to their rich oral literature. Even where they have been given official status in the constitution, as for instance, in South Africa with nine of the eleven official languages of the country being African languages, they are traditionally located towards the low end of the scale (cf. section 12.2.5 for language attitudes).

12.4.3   *Linguae francae*

Most of the 2,000 African languages are used as first languages (mother tongues, vernaculars) and, therefore, are being used largely or exclusively for intra-group communication. For inter-group communication, other languages need to be learned and used. Such languages which are habitually used by many non-native speakers for inter-group communication are referred to as *linguae francae* or 'vehicular' languages. Such vehicular languages, unless they are *pidgins* (cf. below), have also their own native speakers who may constitute a majority population or are 'rulers' in a given area or have otherwise higher socio-economic prestige, factors which may have contributed to the fact that their language was chosen by others to serve as a lingua franca. The coexistence of vernacular and vehicular varieties of African languages at a given time in history in terms of pidginisation and revernacularisation, creolisation and decreolisation, is a much neglected field of African sociolinguistics.[24]

Although African linguae francae were in existence long before the scramble for Africa by European colonial powers began and European languages came to be used in Africa, their precise earlier number is not known. Examples are, for instance, Amharic in Ethiopia, Hausa, Kanuri, Mandingo, More, Songay in large parts of West Africa, Sango in Central Africa, and Swahili in East Africa. A special role must be attributed to Arabic, which started to spread rapidly over large parts of northern Africa and beyond as early as the seventh century AD. It served not only the religious needs related to the dynamic spread of Islam, but also continuously threatened and in many instances finally replaced local African languages. Arabicisation, at times aggressive and as something entirely different from Islamisation, still creates considerable political problems in, for instance, the Sudan and much of Berberophone North Africa (Maghreb).

The spread of linguae francae in Africa can result in increasing instances of language shift, usually after periods of bilingualism involving the mother tongue language and the lingua franca. Large-scale language shift within a speech community may then result in language death of the mother tongue. Linguae francae are, therefore, at times accused of *glottophagia*. Likewise, language planners who propagate the further spread of a lingua franca through the educational system, for instance, may find themselves accused of assisting *linguicide* and thereby depriving a speech community of its primordial means of identification.

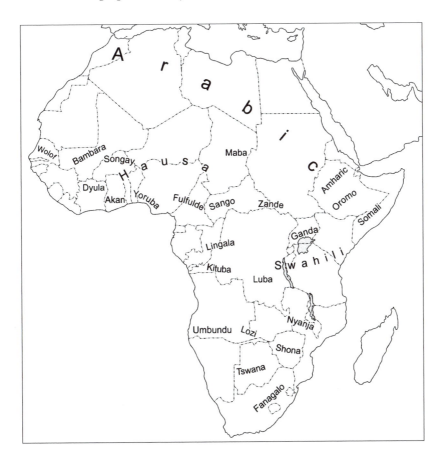

Map 12.7. The main African language-based linguae francae.

12.4.3.1   Pidgins and creoles

With the advent of European colonialism, new linguae francae emerged by *pidginisation* of local vernacular languages. Other linguae francae developed via pidginisation of European languages along the coast.

A *pidgin* emerges under certain socioeconomic conditions along trade routes and coastlines, particularly when several groups with different languages and no common lingua franca are forced to communicate in the presence of a newly arrived dominant language like that of seafaring traders and colonialists. A pidgin is characteristically only used as a second language for restricted communication. It is 'reduced' in vocabulary and is often said to 'lack' grammar, it is 'mixed' with words and structural elements from surrounding local languages and, most significantly, has no native speakers. Pidgins are restricted to a narrow range of functions and domains and only supplement the linguistic repertoire of its speakers by yet another variety. Speakers of pidgins tend to have one other fully fledged language at their disposal as mother tongue, that is they are, as a rule, bilingual. Pidgins tend to be stigmatised as 'marginal' languages or as 'corrupt', 'bad' or 'broken' variants of the standard language on which they appear to be based, that is they are often – but falsely – considered to be the result of imperfect language learning. They appear to have the majority of their vocabulary taken from the dominant, often European, standard language on which they are said to be 'based' (a misleading description) and to have taken the best part of what grammar there is from one or more of the local vernacular languages. However, there are elements in their structure which are not easily traceable to any of the languages immediately involved in their creation. Although geared towards restricted functions, pidgins are linguistic systems in their own right, but they cannot compete neither structurally nor functionally nor socially with fully fledged languages. Pidgins may be short-lived and cease to exist as soon as the particular socioeconomic situation changes which had originally brought them about, and they may persist or change when the situation changes. When one colonial power takes over the territory from another colonial power, this will be accompanied by a change of dominant language. Pidgins may accommodate to such changes by *relexification*, that is by replacing one source of their lexical 'base' by another, for example, French by English.

Some pidgins, however, eventually become mother tongues for sections of the population; when this happens we speak of *creolisation*. The most practical distinction, therefore, between a *pidgin* and a *creole* language is that of the existence of first language (mother tongue) speakers. Once a pidgin has become the first language of a generation of speakers and has become elaborated in terms of vocabulary and grammar, it is a fully fledged language and no longer restricted in function. This would be an instance of *language birth*, that is of a creole language.[25] Still, creoles are also often looked down upon, even by their own native speakers, as being inferior to the corresponding (European) standard language.

Crystal (1997: 340) lists the following pidgins and creoles for Africa, a list which needs careful checking but could probably still be expanded in particular with regard to yet undiscovered cases of pre-colonial African pidgins and creoles, that is such without interference from colonial languages.

Petit Mauresque	North African Pidgin French
Cape Verde Creole	Portuguese-based creole, Cape Verde Islands
Kryôl	Portuguese-based creole in Senegal
Gambian Krio (Aku)	English-based creole with only few first language speakers, gradually being ousted by English and pidginised Wolof

Crioulo	Portuguese-based creole in Guinea, widely used as lingua franca
Krio	English-based creole in Sierra Leone
(A)Merico (Settler English)	English-based creole along the Liberian coast
Liberian Pidgin English	English-based pidgin in Liberia, including Kru English used by Kru fishermen in Liberia and along the coast
Petit-Nègre	French-based pidgin in Ivory Coast and former French possessions along the West African coast
West African Pidgin English	chain of English-based pidgins along the West African coast
Gulf of Guinea Portuguese	group of creoles on the islands Annobon, Sao Tome, Principe
Cameroon Pidgin English	English-based pidgin, creolised in some urban centres
Ewondo Populaire	Ewondo-based pidgin used for trade in Cameroon
Barikanci	Hausa-based pidgin in northern Nigeria and along the pilgrims' route to Mecca (name derived from 'barracks')
Tekrur	Arabic-based pidgin in the area east of Lake Chad and in the Bodélé depression
Juba Arabic	Arabic-based creole in the southern Sudan
Galgaliya	Arabic-based pidgin in north-eastern Nigeria
Sango	Ngbandi-based creole in the Central African Republic
Congo Pidgins: Kituba (Munukutuba), Lingala,	Bantu language-based pidgins in Congo (former Zaire)
Asmara Pidgin Italian	Italian-based pidgin in Eritrea
Swahili Pidgins	pidginised and partly creolised varieties of Kiswahili in East Africa, among them *(Ki)Settla* in Kenya originally developed for communication between Africans and Europeans (Whiteley 1974: 55)
Afrikaans Pidgin	partly creolised Afrikaans-based pidgin in Namaland of Namibia
Cape Dutch (Taal Dutch)	Afrikaans-based varieties in the Cape Region of South Africa
Fanagalo (Fanakalo)	Xhosa-based English pidgin used in the South African mines; also known as Mine Kaffir and Kitchen Kaffir

Zambia Pidgins:	Bantu language-based pidgins in the Zambian
Town Bemba, Settla	copper belt
Réunionnais	French-based creole in the island of Réunion
Barracon	nineteenth-century pidgin spoken in the ports of
	Mozambique
Mauritian French Creole	French-based creole used in Mauritius, some also
	in Madagascar and the Comoro Islands
Morisyen	French-based creole also in Mauritius, with a dia-
	lect Rodrigues Creole in Rodrigues Island
Seychellois (Seselwa)	French-based creole used in the Seychelles

Pidgins and a creole language with the same language 'base' may coexist for quite some time, together with the language which is said to be their 'base'. Thus

Map 12.8. Pidgins and creoles (based on Crystal 1997).

Sierra Leone has Standard British English, Standard Sierra Leone English, Krio (as English-based creole), and West African Pidgin English. Creole studies use the term *post-creole continuum* to reflect this situation. Bickerton (1975) has suggested various terms to label ranges along the continuum, like *acrolects* for the highest varieties, *basilects* for the lowest, and *mesolects* for all the intermediate varieties.[26] The linguistic differences are considerable; compare the following three examples from the Jamaican creole continuum (Todd 1974; quoted from Wardhaugh 1992: 81):

acrolectal	*it's my book*	*where is it?*	*I didn't eat any*
mesolectal	*iz me buk*	*wier i de?*	*a in nyam non*
basilectal	*a fi mi buk dat*	*a we i de?*	*mi na bin nyam non*

Post-creole continua can be related to the process of *decreolisation*, which occurs when standard varieties maintain their influence on the creole and thus allow for a 'target' for moving sociolinguistically up the ladder. This results in diglossia, that is in recognising socially relevant 'higher' and 'lower' variants.

Pidgins and creoles are traditionally said to be based on a known local or international language. When we say that Krio is English-based and Sechellois is French-based, our judgement only reflects one source of the vocabulary of the language which we recognise easily in utterances such as (examples from Wardhaugh 1993: 66)

Krio	*i no tu had*	'it's not too hard'
Sechellois	*i pa tro difisil*	'it is not too difficult'

But beyond surface resemblance in vocabulary with their 'base', the languages share structural properties which cannot be explained with reference to English or French (cf. the negation and lack of a verb in the above examples). Since pidgins and creoles share overall structural resemblance, different theories concerning their origin have been proposed. Pidgins are definitely not the result of failing to learn some standard or other language (*imperfect learning theory*). Although pidgins and creoles share many structural properties with at least some African languages (*substratum theory*), the sad history of cross-Atlantic slave trade from Africa cannot explain the worldwide distribution of these features (for instance, in Hawaiian creole; cf. Bickerton 1977: 61f). This leaves us with two opposing hypotheses: *polygenesis* and *monogenesis*. Have all pidgins emerged from one single *proto-pidgin* and only subsequently become diversified depending on which other languages they were in contact with (monogenesis)? Or have they emerged independently from each other over and over again but always 'based' on some language of wider communication and commerce and spoken aboard ships which sailed the seven seas (polygenesis)? Support for the monogenesis hypothesis is sometimes sought from the observation of *relexification*, which has happened in some but not all cases of pidgins and creoles, and therefore cannot account for the far-reaching similarities of structure of all known pidgins and creoles. Relexification theory has become quite popular among sociolinguists and creolists but is challenged by Derek Bickerton (1981, 1983), who advances explanations based on his *bioprogram* and *universal language learning* theory: children have a bioprogram which enables them to learn language from the linguistic input provided by their immediate environment, that is, they match the input to some innate universal language acquisition apparatus which is part of their bioprogram. Bickerton claims that the shared grammatical structure of pidgins and creoles is similar to the innate universal language acquisition apparatus of the child. With the restricted input provided by a pidgin-speaking environment, children will develop their innate universal language acquisition apparatus to function as the full-fledged grammar of the language they are about to acquire, that is the creole. For Bickerton, therefore, pidginisation is second language learning with restricted input, and creolisation is first-language acquisition also with restricted input.

12.4.4   *Language under stress*
12.4.4.1   *Language shift and language death*

Multilingual settings differ considerably across the continents in terms of relative stability. Sociolinguists distinguish between 'stable' and 'unstable' diglossia. In such settings, languages seldom have equal status in terms of *dominance*, that is regarding frequency of use, degree of proficiency, prestige and array of functions (section 12.4.1). Dominant languages are therefore likely to threaten non-dominant languages to the verge of extinction.[27] We call such threatened languages 'endangered' when they lose communicative functions because, quite characteristically, the next generation no longer acquires the mother tongue language as first language. Languages die out for lack of active speakers – *language death*. In Africa, more than 100 languages are seriously endangered in this sense of approaching language death (Brenzinger 1992, 1998).

The major reason for language death besides genocide (which was largely responsible for the extinction of several Khoisan languages, together with their speakers, in southern Africa following European colonialisation after 1652) is *language shift*, which typically occurs in the case of migrant minorities who give up their language in favour of the language of their new environment. Individuals or whole groups of speakers shift to another language for everyday communication and make this their dominant language; their former first language becomes dormant and eventually forgotten. Language shift is the most drastic instance of *linguistic accommodation* (cf. above). In Africa, we may still find language 'rememberers', that is old people who remember having spoken a different language earlier in their lives but have since ceased to do so because of lack of other speakers.

Language shift may also be triggered by migration from rural to urban areas and upward social mobility, and it comes along with bilingualism and diglossia.[28] For large-scale language shift and eventually language death to occur, it is necessary that the speech community's *attitude* (section 12.2.7) towards their mother tongue (often a minority language) is predominantly negative, or that they are unaware of the threat imposed on their language by diglossia and large-scale bilingualism on the part of the next generation.

12.4.4.2 *Language maintenance*

The generally shared worry among the older generation that the children do no longer speak the mother tongue language at all or not well is hardly enough to prevent the language from extinction. Speakers develop strategies in order to avoid language shift and to support *language maintenance*. The prerequisite is a positive *attitude* (section 12.2.7) towards the mother tongue language as an important resource for pride and identity of the speech community. Bilingualism and diglossia (12.4.2.1) and concomitant code-mixing (12.4.1.1) must not be complained about but must be maintained and must become 'stable' in order to allow the minority language to fulfil at least complementary functions, that is in certain *domains* (12.2.6), in the life of the community. Language maintenance is supported, for instance, by discouraging inter-ethnic marriages and keeping the language alive at home as the first language for the next generation to acquire. Institutional support would involve active minority policies of regional or national governments by recognition as 'national language' in the constitution and by allowing for mother tongue instruction in local schools both as medium and subject of instruction.

In times of language stress involving heavy bilingualism and possibly diglossia, a minority language may extensively borrow from the lexicon and the grammar of a dominant majority language. Structural borrowing can be so extreme that the languages in contact, even if they are only distantly or not at all genealogically related to each other by common origin, become so similar in structure that linguists speak of a *Sprachbund*. In such cases, several adjacent languages develop and share a significant number of so-called *areal features*, which change or replace their original genealogical features, that is the languages are said to *converge* in terms of grammatical structure and vocabulary. Convergence may go as far as making one language an apparent dialect of the other, yet the speakers of that 'dialect' will insist on their ethnic and linguistic identity as being different.[29] Wolff (1979b) has suggested reserving the term *ethnolect* for cases of this kind, which he illustrates by the Cena and Gwara varieties of the Glavda and Margi languages in north-eastern Nigeria.

Language maintenance tends to result in cases of 'mixed' languages, that is languages with non-linear ancestry and broken transmission (Thomason and Kaufman 1988). One of the best known, but controversial, cases in Africa is that of Ma'a/Mbugu in Tanzania, where speakers 'maintain', for instance, parallel lexical repertoires which are related to different languages, one of Cushitic and the other of Bantu linguistic affiliation: according to M. Mous (p.c., see also Bakker and Mous 1994) this is a case of culturally established 'remembering' of a language even after a generalised language shift from a Cushitic ('Ma'a') to a Bantu ('Mbugu') language had occurred in the history of the speech community. Lesser known but no less intriguing are Tasawaq (Wolff and Alidou, in press) and its sisters of the so-called Northern Songay dialect group in the southern Sahara of Niger, Mali and Algeria. Nurse (1999) describes two particular contact situations in East Africa which have produced Ilwana and Daisu (Segeju).

12.5   Language planning

12.5.1   *Language standardisation*

African sociolinguistics has a wide range of practical applications, commonly referred to by the term *language planning*. This term, however, refers to at least two different sets of problems and activities:[30] *status planning* and *corpus planning* (cf. below). One of the major concerns of language planning in Africa, however, is *language standardisation*, that is turning linguistic varieties into *standard languages* in the sense of

(1)   an approved and accepted *norm* above all vernacular, colloquial and dialectal varieties for *generalised* and *normative* usage in certain domains such as literature, science, higher education, the media, the churches and all public sectors

(2)   a *regularised* and *codified* normative *system of reference* supported by a standard orthography, standard reference grammars and (preferably monolingual) standard dictionaries

A fully fledged standard language will, ideally, enjoy recognition as such by the whole speech community (for instance, as a prestigious high variety in a diglossia situation), reflect linguistic (and possibly national or even ethnic) identity, have or develop a rich writing tradition, and be potentially equipped to encode all necessary modernisation in its lexicon. It will be effectively used as high variety, predominantly for written communication in matters of official or semi-official concern on regional, national or international levels, besides and in addition to several low varieties, which will continue to be used orally and locally but are viewed as not up to the needs of modern communication, particularly not for writing and use throughout the formal education system.

In this sense, only a small number of the world's languages are standard languages (better: have a standardised norm), and the same is true for African languages. In Africa, the beginnings of language standardisation go back to pre-colonial and early colonial periods when missionaries began to have the Bible, or parts of it, translated into African languages and engaged in developing teaching materials for primary education in mission schools. The most illuminating and successful cases of language standardisation in Africa are, for various different reasons and possibly in that order, Afrikaans,[31] Swahili, Hausa, Somali and Shona.

Status planning is sometimes also referred to as 'social' or 'external' planning; it is geared at establishing and developing the functional usage of a particular language or languages within a state. It is part of national language politics which should ideally be based on the research of, and under consultation with, sociolinguists and educationists. In particular, status planning concerns the choice of languages to be used as official language(s) and/or of educational and other cultural purposes (media, religion). The status of these languages may be found codified in the constitution of the country.

For any language variety to be considered in language planning for the acquisition of particular functional roles or status in the society, it must fulfil certain requirements in terms of standardisation involving *modernisation* (section 12.5.1.3) and *cultivation* (12.5.1.5). There must be *codification* (12.5.1.2) in terms of a standard orthography, a reliable reference grammar, a comprehensive monolingual dictionary, sufficient and adequate reading materials, and teacher training manuals. In particular, its vocabulary should undergo continuous expansion in some controlled way with regard to new *terminology* for use of the language in education and regional or nationwide communication on all issues of the modern world. All these requirements of actual language material (i.e. the 'corpus' of the language) can be planned and implemented (12.5.1.4), so here we speak of *corpus planning*.

Corpus planning is sometimes also referred to as 'linguistic' or 'internal' planning; and is geared at establishing and developing spelling norms, setting norms of grammar and expanding the lexicon. Language standardisation involves several phases:

(1)   *determination* (12.5.1.1) of both language status and the norm within a chosen language, which is to serve as standard frame of reference

(2)   *codification* (12.5.1.2) of languages or language variants with no writing tradition at all, or choice among or unification of, competing writing systems already existing in the area[32]

(3)   *elaboration* (12.5.1.3) of vocabulary (*modernisation*) and grammar (*normalisation*) to serve as sources for reference and basic tools for the development of pedagogical materials for all levels of formal education

(4)   *implementation* (12.5.1.4) of both language status and the norms of standardisation, that is creating and enhancing acceptance in the speech communities

(5)   *cultivation* (12.5.1.5) of the so created standard languages by language authorities to ensure continued observance of the norms and control implementation. In Africa in particular, language cultivation would also be concerned with the creation and continuous production of post-literacy materials

(6)   special cases of language planning and standardisation involve language *harmonisation* (12.5.1.6), that is the unification of distinct and sometimes quite distant (i.e. mutually non-intelligible) dialects

12.5.1.1   *Determination*

In multilingual countries, 'determination' in terms of status planning refers to language policy (section 12.5.2) and involves, first of all, choice of which (one or several) of the country's languages should be selected to perform particular functions in regional, national and international communication (12.4.2). In terms of language standardisation, 'determination' refers to the norm which is chosen to serve as the standard frame of reference for any chosen language. This is usually a highly sensitive issue in most African societies. The determination of languages and norms becomes inevitably a question of power which will favour those who already use the chosen variety and disfavour those who do not. Selecting one existing language to acquire the status of 'official' or 'national' language, or selecting one particular lect to become the standard form of a given language, means that speakers of other varieties may feel that their speech forms are now being discriminated against as 'minority', 'ethnic', 'tribal', 'vernacular' languages or 'non-' or 'sub-standard' dialects. In some cases and in order to avoid social and political unrest based on determination of a 'standard', an *idealised norm* can be created, that is a pandialectal variant which is 'nobody's dialect' (e.g. Ewe, Igbo and Shona). In other cases, we are faced with a *de facto* norm when a language already possesses 'scripture' and a tradition of writing, often based on a Bible translation which may date from the nineteenth century. Some languages may even suffer from the coexistence of several standards in different traditions established by different missionary societies and for sociopolitical reasons (like apartheid) as, for instance, in the cases of Igbo (Nigeria) and the Nguni and Sotho languages in southern Africa.

When choosing a dialect or koine, various criteria could be used and must be weighed against each other because existing language variants will differ in the extent to which they conform to criteria such as the following:

- 'numerical muscle' in terms of number of mother tongue speakers, and the degree of *de facto* use in vehicular function by non mother tongue speakers
- degree of standardisation and quantity of post-literacy materials already available
- historical or cultural prestige among non-native speakers and/or linguistic 'purity' of the chosen variant in the eyes of mother tongue speakers
- historical, cultural or religious prestige of the mother tongue speakers themselves
- political and/or economic dominance of its mother tongue or non mother tongue speakers

Status planning in terms of norm determination can be a unifying factor in nation-building and can create a new feeling of identity and solidarity. It enhances the prestige of its users within society and tends to mark off members of a modern national elite. It is most often initiated from the top (governments) rather than from below (speech communities at the grass roots level) and can be a fairly rapid matter of just a few years or decades – the most cited African examples are Swahili in Tanzania, Hausa in northern Nigeria and Niger, and Somali. For Standard Swahili, for instance, the Unguja dialect of Zanzibar Town was chosen as a basis, and the explanation of the dynamic spread of Swahili in Tanzania and adjacent countries is often related to the observation that Swahili was not associated with a powerful speech community which would be feared to exert political, economic or cultural dominance. Accordingly, Swahili can be said to have become a symbol of national identity in Tanzania. Standard Hausa is based on the dialect of Kano (Nigeria), the major commercial centre in Hausaland. Unlike Swahili, however, Hausa is identified with a large economically and politically powerful population segment feared by non-Hausa linguistic and cultural entities in Nigeria and Niger as potentially dominating and threatening their identities. For Ewe, a language spoken in Togo and adjacent parts of Ghana and Benin, the standard created by missionaries was based on the coastal Aŋlo-Dialect but eventually became so different from spoken Aŋlo that it is only used for writing and on very formal occasions (Ansre 1971), that is it has become 'nobody's dialect' (except for non mother tongue missionaries!). Standard Shona in Zimbabwe rests on no less than six different dialects, and like Standard Ewe is mainly used for writing and is spoken by nobody (Ansre 1971). For Standard Shona orthography, however, the Zezuru dialect of the capital city unofficially serves as frame of reference after the 1967 Spelling Reform (Mkanganwi 1975).

12.5.1.2   *Codification*

The first step in codification is graphicisation, that is the creation or unification of a *standard orthography*. Hardly more than 10 per cent of the African languages can pride themselves on a writing tradition;[33] their beginnings usually coincided with the advent of missionaries and colonialists.[34] When linguists reduce spoken languages to writing for the first time, they use specially designed systems of *transcription* like the International Phonetic Alphabet (IPA) or modifications thereof like the 'Africa Alphabet' designed for the International Africa Institute (IAI) soon after its foundation in 1926. Such specialised alphabets adapt existing writing systems such as the Roman or Greek/Cyrillic or Arabic set of characters to the needs of any given language on the basis of some general principles and strategies such as:

(a)   use of diacritics, that is added marks above and below the ordinary graphic symbol for any kind of phonetic or phonological distinction, for example

   á   è   ŭ   î   ā   õ   ạ   ṣ   ä   ą

(b)   added index symbols for additional features like palatalisation, labialisation, aspiration etc., for example

   kʲ   kʷ   kʰ

(c)   graphic modifications ('tails', 'hooks', 'bars') added to basic letters of the alphabet for particular phonetic features, for example

   ŋ   ɲ   ɳ   ɓ   ɗ   ħ

(d)   upside-down or mirror-image modifications of basic letters, for example

   ɐ   ə   ɔ   Ч   ɯ   ʌ

(e)   ligatures, for example

   ʧ   æ   œ

(f)   difference in character type and capitalisation, for example

   ɑ, a   i, ɪ   z, ʒ   g, G

(g) addition of letters from different alphabets (Greek, Icelandic, Danish etc.)

β ɸ ɛ ɣ ð θ ø

(h) specially designed new symbols, for example

ʘ ʃ ɼ ɰ

(i) or any combination of the above strategies, for example

ɞ ʕ ʔ ʒ ɒ Œ ə

A further strategy is the use of *digraphs* and *trigraphs*, the use of combinations of two or three symbols to represent one sound, for example sh (instead of ʃ), ghw (instead of ɣʷ) or doubling a vowel symbol (or adding a ':') to indicate a 'long' vowel (e.g. aa = a: = ā), etc. For practical purposes of typing and printing, in particular in the pre-desktop publishing days of early orthography development for African languages, the 'dictatorship of the typewriter' ruled the choice of symbols and symbol combinations, and early corpus planners restricted the orthographic conventions to those symbols which were readily available on their typewriters.

12.5.1.3   *Elaboration*

African languages are often said not only to lack expressions to cope with the needs of modern technology and worldwide communication for commercial and other exchanges, but also for adequately teaching these languages in terms of normative grammar, stylistics and functional appropriateness (i.e. *normalisation*) throughout the formal education system.

There is, first of all and for all languages of the world, a constant need for elaboration of vocabulary by creating and expanding the appropriate terminology for commercial, professional and scientific domains as knowledge and technology progress. This is part of corpus planning and is usually the task of language academies (language boards or committees) and touches upon issues to be discussed under language cultivation. *Lexical innovation* is a constant and unplanned spontaneous and *ad hoc* process in any language, that is as communication needs change and expand, speakers develop strategies for creating or borrowing new terms which their language did not have until then. 'Modernisation', 'elaboration', 'language development', however, are terms used for planned lexical innovation which imply in a very pejorative sense that languages, particularly in Africa and which have not yet been submitted to language planning, are somewhat 'unmodern/traditional', 'primitive' or 'underdeveloped'.[35] Such discriminating statements must be rejected as obviously false. In the course of their long histories, African languages as well as all other languages have accommodated many instances of culture contact, and these have left lasting or only temporary traces in their vocabulary and other parts of linguistic structure. The following are some of the most commonly applied strategies of lexical innovation, illustrated with examples from Hausa:

    (a)   language-internal sources
          compounding

baƙin mai	'crude oil'		lit. 'black (of) oil'

expanding or narrowing down the meaning of an existing lexical item

cf.	*jirgi*	'canoe' → 'means of transport'	
jirgin ruwa		'boat, ship'	lit. '*jirgi* (of) water'
jirgin wuta		'steamship'	lit. '*jirgi* (of) fire'
jirgin iska		'sailing ship'	lit. '*jirgi* (of) wind'
jirgin ƙasa		'train'	lit. '*jirgi* (of) ground'
jirgin sama		'aircraft'	lit. '*jirgi* (of) sky'

          paraphrase

jirgin sama mai saukar ungulu	'helicopter'
	lit. 'aircraft landing (of) vulture'

    (b)   language-external sources
          borrowing

helikwapta	'helicopter'

          loan translation (calques)

bankin duniya	'World Bank'	lit. 'bank (of) world'

12.5.1.4   *Implementation*

Once the standard is established, usually by the co-operation of (socio)linguists, educators, poets and leaders of the speech community, it is for policy makers to provide for putting decisions into practice, and most effectively so through feeding the new standard norm into the educational system. A striking example of highly effective implementation was the masterplan for introducing Somali as official language and the new Standard Orthography in Somalia in 1972/3, after endless years of escaping decisions on which type of graphicisation to adopt. This rapid implementation scheme consisted of various simultaneous and follow-up activities. During the campaign, information pamphlets were dropped nationwide from army helicopters over practically all inhabited areas of the country at the moment the head of state announced the decision over the radio; schools and universities were closed down for considerable time and all students were trained and then engaged in large-scale literacy campaigns based on the new Standard Orthography; extensive nationwide radio programs propagated and supported the literacy campaigns; civil servants were compelled within three months to pass tests in writing the new orthography, failure resulted in loss of employment; Somali was instantly introduced as the medium of instruction in the first years of primary education and later was made compulsory also for secondary schools; the national newspaper changed to exclusive use of Somali within a few months.

12.5.1.5 *Cultivation*

After initial implementation, standardised languages need continuous support from language promotion agencies such as language committees, boards or academies. These advisory bodies are needed to

(a) create guidelines as to matters of style and acceptable variants mainly in literary production

(b) ensure that printed materials conform to the standard norms

(c) ensure that lexical innovation is continuously subjected to standardisation in order to avoid uncontrolled competition of terms with similar yet different meanings

Radio programmes, newspaper columns and award-winning competitions in oral as well as written skills in the standard variety will play an important role in creating positive attitudes (section 12.2.7) and boosting the literacy environment.

The most successful instance of language planning and standardisation in Africa particularly with regard to language cultivation is that of Afrikaans, which rose from an 'underdeveloped' and marginalised creole and mother-tongue language which had been heavily discriminated under colonial rule by members of the English-speaking colonial elite. Meanwhile and based on practically nothing but the will and activities of its speakers, it has risen to a fully fledged national language of South Africa spoken as mother tongue and lingua franca by people of very different ethnic backgrounds and is able to serve all the needs of modern technology and communication. It is an example well worth studying for any sociolinguist who is interested in questions of language planning, of both status and corpus.

12.5.1.6 *Harmonisation*

Harmonisation processes provide extreme challenges for applied sociolinguistics because they interfere with conflicting interests on the part of the populations involved who tend to be rather conservative and are normally not interested in changing the status quo.

National harmonisation of orthographies, for instance, aims at reducing and limiting the inventory of graphic symbols including use of diacritics used within one multilingual country for its various languages. The ultimate pedagogical aim of national harmonisation is to facilitate reading and writing in languages other than one's own spoken in the same country.

International harmonisation is concerned with the harmonisation of *cross-border languages*. In Africa, many territories inhabited by speakers of the same language are divided by national borders. National standardisation procedures often result in different standards being created on both sides of the border. In order to allow reading materials from one side of the border to be easily used on the other, international harmonisation aims at establishing a single unified orthography for each language across borders. Such international harmonisation of orthographies for the cross-border languages Fulfulde, Hausa, Kanuri, Manding, Songay-Zarma and Tamashek of the West African Sahel zone was intended at the 1966 UNESCO conference in Bamako, Mali. Of the languages considered at the conference, only Hausa, which is spoken on both sides of the border between Nigeria and Niger, has had a long and successful record of standardisation (beginning in 1911 in Nigeria). In a series of meetings across the Nigeria–Niger border, the competing orthographies which coexisted in Nigeria and in Niger were officially and finally harmonised at the 1980 Niamey meeting.

Language harmonisation is a special case of language standardisation. It involves the unification of distinct and sometimes quite distant, that is mutually non-intelligible, dialects which may have been considered different languages for historical, geographical or ethnic reasons, to converge on one standard which is at least written, if not spoken. It worked for Akan in Ghana by harmonising Akuapem Twi, Asante, Fanti and other linguistically closely related regional variants. However, in some instances it may be impossible to harmonise and bring about a new standard for language varieties which, for historical reasons, are considered to be separate 'languages' by its speakers, as is the case, for instance, with the linguistically viable Standard Nguni (harmonising the mutually intelligible varieties known as Ndebele, Swati/Swazi, Xhosa, Zulu) and Standard Sotho (harmonising Northern Sotho, Southern Sotho and Tswana) in southern Africa.

12.5.2   *Language and politics*

The politics of language are concerned with the status of languages within the state, language rights for minorities, and the implementation of status planning of languages: 'Language planning is a government's authorised, long-term, sustained, and conscious effort to alter a language's function in a society for the purpose of solving communication problems' (Weinstein 1980: 56). Language policies, therefore, can promote, prescribe, discourage or prevent the use of languages and thereby empower or disempower speakers of languages by giving higher or lower status to their languages. Language policies are guided by particular ideologies or ultimate goals, the following are listed by Cobarrubias (1983):

(a) *linguistic assimilation* is most clearly seen in Portuguese, Spanish and French colonial policies in Africa: every person was supposed to assimilate to the monolingual and monocultural behavioural patterns considered to be the norm in the colonial motherland[36]

(b) *linguistic pluralism* would accept non-monolingualism in its multifold manifestations as individual and/or institutional multilingualism, di- or triglossia, multi-monolingualism, etc.

(c) *vernacularisation* (cf. *endoglossic* language policy below)

(d) *internationalisation* (cf. *exoglossic* language policy below)

Language policies will establish a functional hierarchy of *official* language(s), *national* language(s), and other languages spoken within the state, and indicate their role and institutional support. However, the definitions for official language and national language can be quite different and can involve all or only some of the languages within the state.

The term *national language* may be used to refer to some or all languages of the state in order to stress their function for national unity and identity. In the current constitution of Niger, for instance, all indigenous African languages are listed as ('*de jure*') national languages. In South Africa under the apartheid regime, the nine major African languages which now rank among the country's eleven official languages could have been referred to as '*de facto*' national languages, that is as languages spoken by major populations within the country in its recognised national borders (i.e. disregarding the so-called homelands which were installed as artificial reservations for linguistically largely homogeneous populations). In the present constitution of the new South Africa, no 'national languages' are recognised besides the official languages. Both Niger's national languages and the new South Africa's official languages are utilised as symbols of national unity and reconciliation. But whereas the Niger constitution reflects and describes the functional difference between French as the country's only official language and the rest, the South African constitution is programmatic rather than descriptive: it idealises the situation by postulating equality in function and status for all official languages, while the sociolinguistic reality still mirrors inequality in status and functions with foremost English and then Afrikaans on the one hand, and the indigenous African languages on the other.

12.5.2.1   *Endoglossic vs. exoglossic language policies*

Choosing an African language as official language is referred to as an *endoglossic* language policy, opting for a foreign language is referred to as *exoglossic* language policy. Determination (section 12.5.1.1) of one or more official language(s) for the country is linked to considerations as to whether the choice enhances or endangers national unity by its consequences for the balance of power. Experience seems to show that endoglossic solutions will fail proportional to the extent in which the mother tongue speakers of the chosen language play a dominant political or economic role or can be associated with power in some other way. The subtleties of power balance between majorities and minorities will be dramatically effected by such a policy.

One of the major educational problems in post-colonial Africa concerns the double-faced character of the ex-colonial languages which are 'imported' as opposed to the indigenous African mother tongue languages. With a few exceptions of some former settler colonies like, for instance, Algeria, Namibia, South Africa and Zimbabwe, the languages of the former colonial masters have no significant populations of mother tongue speakers within modern nation-states of Africa – which makes them truly *foreign languages*. In most parts of Africa, however, these foreign languages have a peculiar status and must play different roles: despite the almost complete absence of native speakers, they are being used as official languages for nationwide communication and as medium of instruction on most if not all levels of the formal education system. In that sense, they are no longer treated as foreign languages since they are made to expand their original *special purpose function* (section 12.4.2), which was to enable international and worldwide communication for the commercial and political elites. Unlike in most countries outside Africa, the new African elites prefer to use the foreign language for many functions which are normally reserved for mother tongues or national languages. Upward social mobility is encouraged through use of the foreign language. This also allows the elite to control replenishment of their own ranks. On the other hand, these imported languages are associated with the former colonial masters and, therefore, are perceived by African intellectuals as instruments of dominance and cultural alienation which many of them would like to see replaced by one or more indigenous languages rather today than tomorrow. With a few exceptions, of which Ngugi wa Thiongo is the strongest voice, their complaints are launched paradoxically in exactly the languages they complain about! This dilemma situation makes language policy and planning in Africa a difficult matter and will not favour rapid changes from exoglossic to endoglossic policies for quite some time.

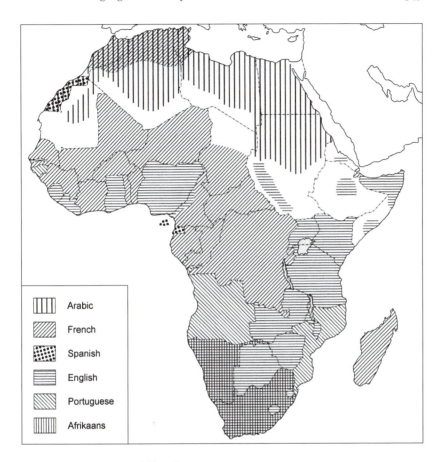

Map 12.9. Dominant non-African languages.

Notes

This chapter represents a drastically shortened version of a more general introductory text (Wolff 1999). I gratefully acknowledge valuable comments made by Ayọ Bamgboṣe, visiting professor at the Institut für Afrikanistik, University of Leipzig, in 1997–9, on an early version of the fuller text.

1 'Speech Act Theory' is connected with authors such as J. L. Austin and J. R. Searle.
2 The terms *bilingualism* and *multilingualism* are sometimes used interchangeably. Many authors, like the present one, apply the term *multilingualism* in a very general sense under which true *bilinguals*, speakers of just two languages, would be subsumed. Another common designation for multilingual individuals using more than two languages is *polyglot*, the fact of being polyglot is then referred to as *polyglossia*.

3 The term refers to any language which is used for inter-ethnic communication, that is among people who do not share the same mother tongue. Other terms used are *vehicular language, contact language, auxiliary language, trade language, international language, language of wider communication*. Also and characteristically, *pidgins* function as linguae francae.

4 *Variety, code, register* or *lect* are terms used to refer to variant manifestations of a speaker's linguistic competence and repertoire, be they variants of different languages or variants of a single language.

5 Standard Hausa is based on the dialect of Kano (Kananci) but is not identical with it; it is somewhat artificial and actually meant to be used for writing and printing. Accordingly, it is sometimes jokingly but correctly referred to as 'Gaskiyanci', that is the dialect of the *Gaskiya* newspaper and the products of a related publishing house which began its activities in the early colonial days.

6 This comment is made very much in the same sense that Europeans are said to have 'cultures' and Africans to have 'customs and rituals'.

7 The highly problematic term 'ethnic' is being used here in a non-technical sense and very much in order to avoid the even more problematic term 'tribal', which has acquired rather derogatory connotations. As used in this chapter, *ethnic* refers to social groups which draw their identity and feeling of solidarity from shared history, that is usually common descent relating to some (often mythological) ancestry and/or shared immigration traditions. Such ethnic identity is not necessarily paralleled by genetic, cultural or linguistic facts.

8 Ethnic or any other social parameter. Simultaneously they may be stigmatised or highly respected as the case may be, according to the motto 'Let me hear how you speak and I'll tell you who you are.'

9 Speakers who are not certain about the norms of pronunciation and grammar tend to overimitate other people's speech habits and thereby violate the norms.

10 The English-based pidgins along the West Coast of Africa and their Creole offsprings were built on oral varieties of the language to begin with – not on the standard of writing and Received Pronunciation.

11 It is claimed that the varieties of *Black English* in the USA reflect such substratum influences from West African languages due to several centuries of transatlantic slave trade. For a more detailed discussion of *substratum influence*, see Thomason and Kaufmann (1988: 37–48).

12 A spectacular case is the spread of the so-called click sounds from the Khoisan languages into neighbouring Bantu languages in southern Africa.

13 This Greek word originally referred to the 'Common Greek' spoken in much of the eastern Mediterranean region for 1,000 years from about the fourth century BC (and is also known as the language of the New Testament in Christian religious tradition).

14 Standard Hausa is based on but not identical with, varieties spoken in and around the important city of Kano in northern Nigeria.

15 These are

(a) the use of the verbal noun [tàhíyà:] in Niger as opposed to the verb stem [tàfí] in Standard Hausa (SH; the verbal noun in SH would have been [tàfíyà:])

(b) the non-contracted form [zâ: ní] 'I will' in Niger as opposed to the contracted form [zân] < *záa nì in SH

(c) the difference in tone melody (indicated by the diacritics: ´marking a High tone,` marking a Low tone) on the future marker + subject pronoun: [zâ: ní] = High-Low-High in Niger as opposed to [zân] < *záa nì = High-Low in SH

16 The uncertain status of the 500 or so Bantu languages in terms of 'languages' or 'dialects' accounts for much of the general uncertainty as to how many 'African languages' there are!

17 A maybe not fully exhaustive review of the literature conducted in 1993/4 revealed a rather poor picture. Practically all published work on Africa looks at the issue in terms of what I call 'colonial di- and triglossia', that is indigenous African languages in competition with the language of a former colonial master (for the full bibliographical references, the reader is referred to Khamis 1994):

Diglossia studies	Author(s)	Year of publication
Swahili-English	Scotton and Ury	1977
Kikuyu-English	Scotton	1979
Akan-English	Forson	1979
Adangme-English	Nartey	1982
Yoruba-English	Goke-Pariola	1983
Hausa-English	Madaki	1983
Lingala-French	Kamwangamalu	1984
Hausa-English	Bickmore	1985
Lingala-French, Swahili-English	Bokamba	1988
Swahili-English	Myers-Scotton	1990
Shona-English	Myers-Scotton	1991
Wolof-French	Deprez-de Heridia	in preparation
Senufo-French	Tabouret-Keller	in preparation
Shaba Swahili-French	De Rooij	in preparation
Swahili-English, Shona-English	Myers-Scotton	in preparation

Triglossia studies	Author(s)	Year of publication
Asu-Swahili-English	O'Barr	1971
Kipare/Kinyakusa-Swahili-English	Mkilifi	1972
Larteh-Twi-English	Johnson	1975
Luhya-Swahili-English	Scotton and Ury	1977
Luhya-Swahili-English	Myers-Scotton	1988
Lwidakho-Swahili-English	Myers-Scotton	1990
Lwidakho-Swahili-English	Myers-Scotton	in preparation

Only two projects were found not involving automatically one ex-colonial language:

Shaba Swahili-Swahili Bora	Myers-Scotton	in preparation
Lwidakho-Swahili	Myers-Scotton	in preparation

Given that millions of multilingual African adults and teenagers must have acquired their particular linguistic competence during childhood, it is hard to believe that we are also forced to note an almost complete absence of studies on early childhood language acquisition in general, and multilingualism in particular, in the African context. A notable exception is Khamis (1994).

18 This has been referred to more accurately as *nonce borrowing* (a term first used by Weinreich (1953) and later taken up by Sankoff, Poplack and Vanniarajan (1991)) or *ad hoc borrowing* or *insertion* – as opposed to ordinary lexical borrowing in the sense of using *loan words* which have become part of the language's lexicon through historical language contact.

19 L_1 and L_2 are used to refer to any number of languages available to any speaker/hearer. The symbols are not to be construed in terms of sequence of language acquisition or learning!

20 When describing the sociolinguistic situation of a given society or state, some authors find it useful to draw a distinction between multilingualism proper (with considerable individual multilingualism involved) and multi-monolingualism (with little or no individual multilingualism involved).

21 The Arabic-speaking world is a notorious and probably the best-described case of diglossia and even triglossia among varieties of the 'same language'. The Arabic dialect continuum prevents speakers from rather distant locations, for instance, Morocco and Egypt, from communicating easily in their everyday 'colloquial' varieties. They have to resort to the written form based on Classical Arabic or to some intermediate varieties.

22 With the exception of the old Berber alphabet *tifinagh*, which is sporadically used for informal messages and decoration purposes by some Tuareg in the southern Sahara, and more recent activities outside the Maghreb countries, particularly among exiled intellectuals and migrant workers, towards standardising Berber languages for use in formal education.

23 In analogy, *triglossia* will refer to a situation in which three languages are used in largely complementary functions; one of the earliest described cases of stable triglossia in Africa is that of Larteh in Ghana. Sometimes the term *polyglossia* is used to describe a society in which more than two or three languages are involved in the national communication landscape.

24 Notable exceptions are the sociolinguistic works of Robert Nicolaï on Songay.

25 The actual processes of pidginisation and creolisation, however, are much more complex than this rather simplistic scenario suggests. But basically pidginisation involves processes in the direction of *simplification*, whereas creolisation involves processes in the opposite direction, namely *elaboration* not only in terms of enriching the vocabulary, but also in terms of structural complexity and communicative functions. Note, however, at least one instance from the Nigerian Delta area where children grow up speaking Nigerian Pidgin as their mother tongue, even though this pidgin has apparently not become 'creolised' in the sense of linguistic elaboration (Ayọ Bamgboṣe, p.c.).

26 Cave (1973) has identified up to eighteen ways of rendering the same sentence in the Guyanese continuum.

27 This process is sometimes referred to as *glottophagia* (language swallowing) or *linguicide* (language murder) on the part of the *dominant* language in instances of *unstable multilingualism*. Such processes may be planned as part of a given language policy (for instance, in cases of assimilation policies like in former French and Portuguese colonies in Africa), or may just happen in arising situations of *language contact*.

28 Not all cases of diglossia involving bilingualism necessarily result in language shift.

29 Often in such cases, the investigating linguist will be told by speakers that 'we understand them, but they don't understand us'.

30 R. L. Cooper (1989) has added a third category, *acquisition planning*, which other authors would account for under the implementation stage of 'status planning'.

31 Afrikaans is considered here a language 'in Africa' but not an 'African language' in the narrow sense as used in this introduction. It is either a separate Germanic 'language' or a very distant overseas 'dialect' of Dutch, or it is considered a Dutch-'based' creole language.

32 These could be either pre-colonial adaptations of the Arabic script (like *ajami* for Hausa and many other languages under early Arabic influence such as Swahili, Fulfulde etc.) or Christian scripture using adaptations of the Roman alphabet created by missionary efforts in (pre-)colonial times.

33 Egyptian, with its long history and stages of writing traditions (known as Hieroglyphic, Demotic, and Coptic), Ethiopian Geᶜez, and the *tifinagh* script of the Tuareg (based on its Old Libyan precursor).

34 In rare cases, local writing systems have been created, for instance, along the West African coast and its hinterlands (e.g. the script of the Vai, Loma, Kpelle, Bamum etc.), which, however, are hardly ever considered for modern standardisation.

35 To avoid such negative connotations, Petr Zima (1974) has suggested using the term 'reorientation' instead, which would also signal the fact that it is not the process of lexical innovation and quantitative increase of vocabulary that is new, but the direction of the process.

36 This proves to be largely a myth. Thus, the case of purportedly monolingual and monocultural France with its Basque, Breton, Alsacian and Occitan linguistic minorities.

REFERENCES

Abdulaziz, Mohamed H. and K. Osinde forthcoming. Sheng and Engsh – development of youth mixed codes in Kenya. *International Journal of the Sociology of Language.*

Ahmed, Christine Choi 1995. Before Eve was Eve: 2200 years of gendered history in East Central Africa. Ph.D. thesis, University of California at Los Angeles.

Aikhenvald, Alexandra Y. in press. Typological distinctions in word formation. In: Shopen (ed.) in press.

Aikhenvald, Alexandra Y. and R. M. W. Dixon 1998. Dependencies between grammatical systems. *Language* 74: 56–80.

Alagoa, Ebiegberi J., Frederick H. Anozie and Nwanna Nzewunwa (eds.) 1989. *The Early History of the Niger Delta.* Hamburg: Buske.

Albright, William F. 1923. The principles of Egyptian phonological development. *Recueil de travaux relatifs à la philologie et à l'archéologie égyptiennes et assyriennes* 40: 64–70.

Alexandre, Pierre 1967. *Langues et langage en Afrique noire.* Paris: Payot.

Ali, Mohamed Nuuh 1985. History in the Horn of Africa. Ph.D. thesis, University of California at Los Angeles.

Allan, Edward J. 1976. Dizi. In: Bender (ed.) 1976. Pp. 377–92.

Alsina, Alex, Joan Bresnan and Peter Sells (eds.) 1997. *Complex Predicates.* Stanford: Center for the Study of Language and Information.

Ambrose, Stanley 1982. Archaeology and linguistic reconstruction of history in East Africa. In: Ehret and Posnansky (eds.) 1982. Pp. 104–57.

Ameka, Felix 1999. Reduplication in Ewe. *Anthropological Linguistics* 41.

Andersen, Torben 1984. Aspect and word order in Moru. *Journal of African Languages and Linguistics* 6: 19–34.

1986. The phonemic system of Madi. *Afrika und Übersee* 69: 193–207.

1987. The phonemic system of Agar Dinka. *Journal of African Languages and Linguistics* 9: 1–27.

1992. Aspects of Berta phonology. *Afrika und Übersee* 76.1: 421–80.

1992–4. Morphological stratification in Dinka: on the alternation of voice quality, vowel length, and tone in the morphology of transitive verbal roots in a monosyllabic language. *Studies in African Linguistics* 23.1: 1–63.

1993. Verbal roots and verbal inflection in Berta. In: Nicolaï and Rottland (eds.) 1995.

Anderson, Stephen C. 1979. Verb structure. In: Hyman (ed.) 1979. Pp. 1–72.

Anderson, Stephen R. 1992. *A-morphous Morphology*. Cambridge: Cambridge University Press.

Ansre, Gilbert 1971. Language standardisation in sub-Saharan Africa. In: Sebeok (ed.) 1971. Pp. 680–98.

Antilla, Raimo 1989. *Historical and Comparative Linguistics*. Second revised edition. Amsterdam, Philadelphia: Benjamins.

Applegate, Joseph R. 1971. The Berber languages. In: Hodge (ed.) 1971. Pp. 96–118.

Appleyard, David L. 1986a. Agaw, Cushitic and Afroasiatic: the personal pronoun revisited. *Journal of Semitic Studies* 31.2: 195–236.

    1986b. Gender in the inflexion of the noun in Agaw. In: Bechhaus-Gerst and Serzisko (eds.) 1986. Pp. 357–75.

Archangeli, Diana and Douglas Pulleyblank 1994. *Grounded Phonology*. Cambridge, Mass.: MIT Press.

Argyle, John W. 1994. Thinking the unthinkable: a possible genetic relationship between Khoisan and Niger-Congo. Paper read at the International Symposium on Khoisan Studies: Multidisciplinary Perspectives, Tutzing/Lake Starnberg, 11–14 July 1994.

Armstrong, Robert G. 1964. *The Study of West African Languages*. Ibadan: Institute of African Studies.

Aronoff, Mark 1994. *Morphology by Itself: Stems and Inflectional Classes*. Cambridge, Mass.: MIT Press.

Arvanites, Linda 1990. The glottalic phonemes of Proto-Eastern Cushitic. Ph.D. thesis, University of California at Los Angeles.

Awobuluyi, Oladele A. 1973. The modifying serial construction: a critique. *Studies in African Linguistics* 4: 87–111.

Azeb Amha in press. *The Maale Language*. Leiden: Centre for Non-Western Studies.

Baker, Mark 1988. *Incorporation: A Theory of Grammatical Function Changing*. Chicago: University of Chicago Press.

Bakker, Peter and Maarten Mous (eds.) 1994. *Mixed Languages: 15 Case Studies in Language Intertwining*. Studies in Language and Language Use, 13. Amsterdam: Institute for Functional Research into Language and Language Use.

Baldi, Phillip (ed.) 1990. *Linguistic Change and Reconstruction Methodology*. Berlin: Mouton de Gruyter.

Baldi, Sergio 1988. *A First Ethnolinguistic Comparison of Arabic Loanwords Common to Hausa and Swahili*. Supplement 57 to Annali dell'Istituto Orientale di Napoli 48/4. Naples: Istituto Universitario Orientale.

Bamgboṣe, Ayọ 1974. On serial verbs and verbal status. *Journal of West African Languages* 9: 17–48.

    1982. Issues in the analysis of serial verbal constructions. *Journal of West African Languages* 12: 3–21.

Banti, Giorgio 1987. Evidence for a second type of suffix conjugation in Cushitic. In: Jungraithmayr and Müller (eds.) 1987. Pp. 123–68.

Barlow, Michael and Charles A. Ferguson (eds.) 1988. *Agreement in Natural Language: Approaches, Theories, Descriptions*. Stanford: Center for the Study of Language and Information.

Barnard, Alan 1992. *Hunters and Herders of Southern Africa. A Comparative Ethnography of the Khoisan Peoples*. Cambridge Studies in Social and Cultural Anthropology, 85. Cambridge: Cambridge University Press.

Barreteau, Daniel (ed.) 1978. *Inventaire des études linguistiques sur les pays d'Afrique noire d'expression française et sur Madagascar*. Paris: Conseil International de la Langue Française.

Barreteau, Daniel and Yves Moñino 1978. Les langues oubangiennes. In: Barreteau (ed.) 1978. Pp. 195–208.

Basset, André 1929. *La langue berbère. Morphologie. Le verbe. Etude de thèmes.* Paris: Leroux.

Bassett, William and Melvin Herskovits (eds.) 1959. *Continuity and Change in African Cultures.* Chicago: Phoenix.

Bastin, Yvonne 1983. *La finale verbale -ide et l'imbrication en bantou.* Annales, 114. Tervuren: Musée Royal de l'Afrique Centrale.

Bastin, Yvonne, André Coupez and Michael Mann forthcoming. *Classification lexico-statistique des langues bantoues sur base de 542 relevés.* Tervuren: Musée Royal de l'Afrique Centrale, and London: School of Oriental and African Studies.

Batibo, Herman M. 1998. The fate of the Khoesan languages of Botswana. In: Brenzinger (ed.) 1998. Pp. 267–84.

Bauer, Laurie 1988. *Introducing Linguistic Morphology.* Edinburgh: Edinburgh University Press.

Baumann, Hermann (ed.) 1975. *Die Völker Afrikas und ihre traditionellen Kulturen.* Part 1, *Allgemeiner Teil und südliches Afrika.* Studien zur Kulturkunde, 34. Wiesbaden: Franz Steiner.

Bausi, Alessandro and Mauro Tosco (eds.) 1997. *Afroasiatica Neapolitana. Contributi presentati all'8° Incontro di Linguistica Afroasiatica (Camito-Semitica), Napoli, 25–26 Gennaio 1996.* Naples: Istituto Universitario Orientale.

Bayene, Taddese (ed.) 1988. *Proceedings of the Eighth International Conference of Ethiopian Studies.* Vol. 1. Addis Ababa: Institute of Ethiopian Studies.

Beach, Douglas M. 1938. *The Phonetics of the Hottentot Language.* Cambridge: W. Heiffer & Sons.

Bearth, Thomas and Christa Link 1980. The tone puzzle of Wobe. *Studies in African Linguistics* 11.2: 147–207.

Bearth, Thomas *et al.* (eds.) 1993. *Perspektiven afrikanistischer Forschung / Perspectives de recherches africanistes.* Cologne: Köppe.

Bechhaus-Gerst, Marianne and Fritz Serzisko (eds.) 1986. *Cushitic – Omotic. Papers from the International Symposium on Cushitic and Omotic Languages, Cologne, January 6–9, 1986.* Hamburg: Buske.

Bender, M. Lionel 1971. The languages of Ethiopia: a new lexicostatistic classification and some problems of diffusion. *Anthropological Linguistics* 13.5: 165–288.

1975a. *The Ethiopian Nilo-Saharans.* Addis Ababa: Artistic.

1975b. *Omotic: A New Afroasiatic Language Family.* University Museum Series, 3. Carbondale: Southern Illinois University Press.

Bender, M. Lionel (ed.) 1976. *The Non-Semitic Languages of Ethiopia.* Monograph no. 5, Occasional Papers Series, Committee on Ethiopian Studies. East Lansing: African Studies Center, Michigan State University.

1979. Gumuz: a sketch of grammar and lexicon. *Afrika und Übersee* 62.1: 38–69.

Bender, M. Lionel (ed.) 1983. *Nilo-Saharan Language Studies* (Monograph No. 13, Committee on Northeast African Studies). East Lansing: African Studies Center, Michigan State University.

1984. Proto-Koman phonology and lexicon. *Afrika und Übersee* 66.2: 259–97.

1989a. Berta lexicon. In: Bender (ed.) 1989. Pp. 271–304.

1989b. Central Sudanic lexical and phonological reconstructions. *Afrikanistische Arbeitspapiere* 29: 5–61.

1989c. Nilo-Saharan pronouns/demons. In: Bender (ed.) 1989. Pp. 1–34.

Bender, M. Lionel (ed.) 1989. *Topics in Nilo-Saharan Linguistics.* Nilo-Saharan Linguistic Analyses and Documentation, 3. Hamburg: Buske.

1990. The limits of Omotic. In: Hayward (ed.) 1990. Pp. 584–616.

1991. Sub-classification of Nilo-Saharan. In: Bender (ed.) 1991. Pp. 1–35.

Bender, M. Lionel (ed.) 1991. *Proceedings of the Fourth Nilo-Saharan Conference, Bayreuth, Aug. 30–Sept. 2, 1989.* Nilo-Saharan Linguistic Analyses and Documentation, 7. Hamburg: Buske.

1994. Comparative Komuz grammar. *Afrika und Übersee* 77.1: 31–54.

1996a. *Kunama.* (Languages of the World, Materials 59.) Munich: LINCOM Europa.

1996b. Nilo-Saharan 95. In: Bender and Hinnebusch (eds.) 1996. Pp. 1–25.

1996c. Nilo-Saharan phonology. In: Kaye (ed.) 1996. Pp. 815–38.

1996d. The sub-grouping of Eastern Sudanic. In: Bender and Hinnebusch (eds.) 1996. Pp. 139–50.

1996–7. *The Nilo-Saharan Languages: An Essay in Classification.* (LINCOM handbooks in Linguistics 06.) Munich: LINCOM Europa.

1997a. Upside-down Afrasian. *Afrikanistische Arbeitspapiere* 50: 19–34.

1997b. The Eastern Jebel languages of Sudan I: phonology. *Afrika und Übersee* 80: 189–215.

Bender, M. Lionel (ed.) 1997. *The Nilo-Saharan Languages: A Comparative Essay.* Munich: LINCOM Europa.

Bender, M. Lionel and Malik A. Ayre 1980. *Preliminary Gaam-English-Gaam Dictionary.* Carbondale: Southern Illinois University Printing Service.

Bender, M. Lionel and Thomas J. Hinnebusch (eds.) 1996. *Proceedings of the Sixth International Nilo-Saharan Linguistics Conference 1995.* Afrikanistische Arbeitspapiere, 45. Cologne: Institut für Afrikanistik, Universität zu Köln.

Bender, M. Lionel, J. Donald Bowen, Robert L. Cooper, Charles A. Ferguson 1976. *Language in Ethiopia.* London: Oxford University Press.

Bendor-Samuel, John 1971. Niger-Congo, Gur. In: Sebeok (ed.) 1971. Pp. 141–78.

Bendor-Samuel, John (ed.) 1989. *The Niger-Congo Languages: A Classification and Description of Africa's Largest Language Family.* Lanham, New York, London: University Press of America.

Bendor-Samuel, John, Elizabeth J. Olsen and Ann R. White 1989. Dogon. In: Bendor-Samuel (ed.) 1989. Pp. 169–77.

Bennett, Patrick R. 1983. Adamawa-Eastern: problems and prospects. In: Dihoff (ed.) 1983. Pp. 23–48.

Bennett, Patrick R. and Jan P. Sterk 1977. South Central Niger-Congo: a reclassification. *Studies in African Linguistics* 8: 241–73.

Bergslund, Knut and Hans Vogt 1962. On the validity of glottochronology. *Current Anthropology* 3: 115–53.

Bertho, Jacques 1953. La place des dialectes dogon de la falaise de Bandiagara parmi les autres groupes linguistiques de la zone soudanaise. *Bulletin de l'IFAN* 55: 405–41.

Bickerton, Derek 1975. *Dynamics of a Creole System.* Cambridge: Cambridge University Press.

1977. Pidginization and creolization: language acquisition and language universals. In: Valdman (ed.) 1977.

1981. *Roots of Language.* Ann Arbor: Karoma.

1983. Creole languages. *Scientific American* 249.1: 116–22.

Bird, Charles 1968. Relative clauses in Bambara. *Journal of West African Languages* 5: 35–47.

Black, Paul 1974. Lowland East Cushitic: subgrouping and reconstruction. Ph.D. thesis, Yale University.

Blanchon, Jean Alain 1998. Semantic/pragmatic conditions on the tonology of the Kongo noun-phrase: a diachronic hypothesis. In: Hyman and Kisseberth (eds.) 1998. Pp. 1–32.

Bleek, Wilhelm H. I. 1851. *De nominum generibus linguarum africae australis, copticae, semiticarum aliarumque sexualium.* Bonn: Adolph Marcus.

Bleek, Wilhelm H. I. and Lucy C. Lloyd 1911. *Specimens of Bushman Folklore*. London: George Allen.

Blench, Roger M. 1989. New Benue-Congo: a definition and proposed internal classification. *Afrikanistische Arbeitspapiere* 17: 115–47.

1993. Recent development in African language classification and their implications for prehistory. In: Shaw *et al.* (eds.) 1993. Pp. 126–38.

1995. Is Niger-Congo simply a branch of Nilo-Saharan? In: Nicolaï and Rottland (eds.) 1995. Pp. 83–130.

in press a. Further evidence for Niger-Saharan and the problem of pan-African roots. In: Cyffer (ed.) in press.

in press b. Revisiting Plateau. In: Cyffer (ed.) in press.

n.d. The North Bantoid hypothesis. Electronic ms.

Blench, Roger M. and Matthew Spriggs (eds.) 1999. *Language and Archaeology, IV*. London: Routledge.

Blench, Roger and Kay Williamson 1988. Bantoid revisited. Paper presented at the 18th Colloquium on African Languages, Leiden.

Blevins, Juliet 1995. The syllable in phonological theory. In: Goldsmith (ed.) 1995. Pp. 206–44.

Bliese, Loren F. 1981. *A Generative Grammar of Afar*. Dallas: Summer Institute of Linguistics and University of Texas at Arlington.

Bloomfield, Leonard 1933. *Language*. London: Allen & Unwin.

1965. *Language History*. Ed. by Harry Hoijer. New York: Holt.

Bole-Richard, Rémy 1983. Ebrié. In: Hérault (ed.) 1983a. Pp. 307–57.

Bole-Richard, Rémy and Philippe Lafage 1983. Etude lexicostatistique des langues kwa de Côte d'Ivoire. In: Hérault (ed.) 1983b. Pp. 201–4.

Booij, Geert 1996. Inherent versus contextual inflection and the Split Morphology hypothesis. In: Booij and van Marle (eds.) 1996. Pp. 1–16.

Booij, Geert and Jaap van Marle (eds.) 1995. *Yearbook of Morphology 1994*. Dordrecht: Kluwer.

1996. *Yearbook of Morphology 1995*. Dordrecht: Kluwer.

Boyd, Raymond 1989. Adamawa-Ubangi. In: Bendor-Samuel (ed.) 1989. Pp. 178–215.

1994. *Historical Perspectives on Chamba Daka*. Cologne: Köppe.

Boyeldieu, Pascal 1987. *Les Langues Fer ('Kara') et Yulu du Nord Centrafrican*. Paris: Laboratoire de Langues et Civilisations à Tradition Orale.

n.d. Présentation du láà: l ou 'Gori' (Moyen-Chari, Tchad). Unpublished ms. Paris: CNRS.

Breedveld, Anneke 1995. *Form and Meaning in Fulfulde: A Morphophonological Study of Maasinankoore*. Leiden: Centre for Non-Western Studies.

Brenzinger, Matthias (ed.) 1992. *Language Death: Factual and Theoretical Explorations with Special Reference to East Africa*. Contributions to the Sociology of Language, 64. Berlin, New York: Mouton de Gruyter.

1998. *Endangered Languages in Africa*. Cologne: Köppe.

Bresnan, Joan and Sam A. Mchombo 1987. Topic, pronoun and agreement in Chichewa. *Language* 63: 741–82.

1995. The lexical integrity principle: evidence from Bantu. *Natural Language and Linguistic Theory* 13: 181–254.

Bright, William (ed.) 1992a. *International Encyclopedia of Linguistics*. Vol. I. Oxford: Oxford University Press.

1992b. *International Encyclopedia of Linguistics*. Vol. III. Oxford: Oxford University Press.

Bybee, Joan 1985. *Morphology: A Study of the Relation Between Meaning and Form*. Amsterdam, Philadelphia: Benjamins.

Bynon, James 1984. Berber and Chadic: the lexical evidence. In: Bynon (ed.) 1984. Pp. 241–90.

Bynon, James (ed.) 1984. *Current Progress in Afro-Asiatic Linguistics. Papers of the Third International Hamito-Semitic Congress*. Amsterdam, Philadelphia: Benjamins.

Bynon, James and Theodora Bynon (eds.) 1975. *Hamito-Semitica. Proceedings of a Colloquium Held by the Historical Section of the Linguistics Association (Great Britain) at the School of Oriental and African Studies, University of London, on the 18th, 19th and 20th March 1970*. The Hague: Mouton.

Bynon-Polak, Louise 1975. *A Shi Grammar: Surface Structures and Generative Phonology of a Bantu Language*. Tervuren: Musée Royal de l'Afrique Centrale.

Calame-Griaule, Geneviève 1978. Le dogon. In: Barreteau (ed.) 1978. Pp. 63–9.

Callender, John 1975. Afroasiatic cases and the formation of Ancient Egyptian constructions with possessive suffixes. *Afroasiatic Linguistics* 2.6: 95–112.

Carlson, Robert 1994. A grammar of Supyire. Mouton Grammar Library, 14. Berlin, New York: Mouton de Gruyter.

Capo, Hounkpati B. C. 1991. *A Comparative Phonology of Gbe*. Berlin: Mouton de Gruyter.

Cardinall, A. W. 1931. A survival. *Gold Coast Review* 5.1: 193–7.

Caron, Bernard 1991. *Le haoussa de l'ader*. Berlin: Reimer.

Carstairs-McCarthy, Andrew 1992. *Current Morphology*. London and New York: Routledge.

Castellino, Giorgio R. 1975. Gender in Cushitic. In: Bynon and Bynon (eds.) 1975. Pp. 333–59.

Cave, G. N. 1973. Some communication problems of immigrant children in Britain. Unpublished paper (quoted from Wardhaugh 1992).

Černy, V. *et al.* (eds.) 1974. *Asian and African Languages in Social Context*. Diss. orientales, 34. Prague.

Cerulli, Enrico 1938. *Il linguaggio dei Giangerò ed alcune lingue Sidama dell'Omo (Basketo, Ciara, Zaissè)*. Studi Etiopici, 3. Rome: Istituto per l'Oriente. Colloque sur le multilinguisme. 1962. Brazzaville: CCTA.

Childs, G. Tucker 1983. Noun class affix renewal in Southern West Atlantic. In: Kaye *et al.* (eds.) 1983. Pp. 17–29.

Chomsky, Noam 1972. *Studies on Semantics in Generative Grammar*. The Hague: Mouton.

Chomsky, Noam and Morris Halle 1968. *The Sound Pattern of English*. New York: Harper & Row.

Clark, Mary M. 1990. *The Tonal System of Igbo*. Dordrecht: Foris.

Claudi, Ulrike 1988. The development of tense/aspect marking in Kru languages. *Journal of African Languages and Linguistics* 10.1: 53–77.

1993. *Die Stellung von Verb und Objekt in Niger-Kongo-Sprachen*. Afrikanistische Monographien, 1. Cologne: Institut für Afrikanistik, Universität zu Köln.

1994. Word order change as category change: the Mande case. In: Pagliuca (ed.) 1994. Pp. 201–41.

Clements, George N. 1985. Akan vowel harmony: a nonlinear analysis. In: Goyvaerts (ed.) 1985. Pp. 55–98.

1986. Compensatory lengthening and consonant gemination in Luganda. In: Wetzels and Sezer (eds.) 1986. Pp. 37–77.

1989. African linguistics and its contributions to linguistic theory. *Studies in the Linguistic Sciences* 19: 3–39.

1991. Vowel height assimilation in Bantu languages. *BLS 17*. Proceedings of the 17th Annual Meeting of the Berkeley Linguistics Society, special session on African language structures. Pp. 25–64.

Clements, George N. and S. K. Keyser 1983. *CV Phonology: A Generative Theory of the Syllable*. Cambridge, Mass.: MIT Press.

Clements, George N. and John A. Goldsmith (eds.) 1984. *Autosegmental Studies in Bantu Tone.* Dordrecht: Foris.

Cloarec-Heiss, France 1986. *Dynamique et équilibre d'une syntaxe: le banda-linda de Centrafrique.* Cambridge: Cambridge University Press and Paris: Editions de la Maison des Sciences de l'Homme for the Centre National de la Recherche Scientifique (SELAF).

Cobarrubias, J. 1983. Ethical issues in status planning. In: Cobarrubias and Fishman (eds.) 1983.

Cobarrubias, J. and J. A. Fishman (eds.) 1983. *Progress in Language Planning.* The Hague: Mouton.

Cohen, Marcel 1924. Langues chamito-sémitiques. In: Meillet and Cohen (eds.) 1924. Pp. 81–151.

Cole, Desmond T. 1971. The history of African linguistics to 1945. In: Sebeok (ed.) 1971. Pp. 1–29.

Cole, Jennifer and Charles Kisseberth (eds.) 1994. *Perspectives in Phonology.* Stanford: Center for the Study of Language and Information.

Collins, Chris 1998. Plurality in ǂHoan. *Khoisan Forum* 9. Cologne: Universität zu Köln.

Comrie, Bernard 1976. *Aspect.* Cambridge: Cambridge University Press.

   1981. *Language Universals and Linguistic Typology.* Oxford: Blackwell.

Comrie, Bernard (ed.) 1987. *The World's Major Languages.* London and Sydney: Croom Helm.

Connell, Bruce 1994a. The structure of labial-velar stops. *Journal of Phonetics* 22: 441–76.

   1994b. The lower cross languages: a prolegomena to the classification of the Cross River languages. *Journal of West African Languages* 24.1: 3–46.

   1998. Classifying Cross River. In: Maddieson and Hinnebusch (eds.) 1998. Pp. 17–25.

   in press. The integrity of Mambiloid. In: Wolff (ed.) in press.

Cooper, Robert L. 1989. *Language Planning and Social Change.* Cambridge: Cambridge University Press.

Corbett, Greville 1991. *Gender.* Cambridge: Cambridge University Press.

Crabb, David W. 1969. *Ekoid Bantu Languages of Ogoja.* Cambridge: Cambridge University Press.

Craig, Colette (ed.) 1986. *Noun Classes and Categorization.* Amsterdam, Philadelphia: Benjamins.

Crazzolara, J. P. 1960. *A Study of the Logbara (Ma'di) Language.* London: Dawson.

Creider, Chet A. 1989. *The Syntax of the Nilotic Languages: Themes and Variations.* Berlin: Reimer.

Creissels, Denis 1981. Songhay et Niger-Congo (mandé). In: Schadeberg and Bender (eds.) 1981. Pp. 307–27.

   1991. *Déscription des langues négro-africaines et théorie syntaxique.* Grenoble: ELLUG.

   1994. *Aperçu sur les structures phonologiques des langues négro-africaines.* 2nd edition. Grenoble: ELLUG, Université Stendhal.

   1996. Conjunctive and disjunctive verb forms in Setswana. *South African Journal of African Languages* 16.4: 109–15.

   1998a. Remarques sur l'auxiliarisation en tswana. *Le gré des langues* 13: 112–40.

   1998b. Auxiliaires et auxiliarisation: l'exemple du tswana. *Faits de langues* 11–12: 251–65.

   n.d. Liste de mots Pre. Unpublished ms.

Creissels, Denis and Stephanie Robert 1998. Morphologie verbale et organisation discursive de l'énoncé: l'exemple du tswana et du wolof. *Faits de langues* 11–12: 161–78.

Crozier, David H. and Roger M. Blench (eds.) 1992. *An Index of Nigerian Languages*. Abuja: Language Development Centre, Ilorin: University of Ilorin, and Dallas, Summer Institute of Linguistics and the University of Texas at Arlington.

Crystal, David 1997. *The Cambridge Encyclopaedia of Language*. Cambridge: Cambridge University Press.

Cust, Robert N. 1883. *A Sketch of the Modern Languages of Africa*. London: Trübner.

Cyffer, Norbert 1996: Who are the ancestors of the Saharan family? In: Bender and Hinnebusch (eds.) 1996. Pp. 53–63.

Cyffer, Norbert (ed.) in press. *Proceedings of the 7th Nilo-Saharan Conference in Vienna, 2–6th September, 1998*.

Dalgish, Gerard M. 1979. Subject identification strategies and free word order: the case of Sandawe. *Studies in African Linguistics* 10.3: 273–310.

Daniels, Peter T. 1996. The first civilisations. In: Daniels and Bright (eds.) 1996. Pp. 21–32.

Daniels, Peter T. and William Bright (eds.) 1996. *The World's Writing Systems*. New York and Oxford: Oxford Unversity Press.

Dell, François and Mohamed Elmedlaoui. 1997. Les géminées en berbère. *Linguistique africaine* 19: 5–56.

Delafosse, Maurice 1914. *Esquisse générale des langues de l'Afrique et plus particulièrement de l'Afrique française*. Paris: Masson.

1924. Langues du Soudan et de la Guinée. In: Meillet and Cohen (eds.) 1924. Pp. 737–845.

Delplanque, Alain 1995. Que signifient les classes nominales? L'exemple du mooré, langue Gur. *Linguistique africaine* 15: 5–54.

Demolin, Didier 1988. Some problems of phonological reconstruction in Central Sudanic. *Belgian Journal of Linguistics* 3: 53–95.

Demuth, Katherine 1988. Noun classes and agreement in Sesotho acquisition. In: Barlow and Ferguson (eds.) 1988. Pp. 305–21.

Demuth, Katherine, Nicholas Faraclas and Lynell Marchese 1986. Niger-Congo noun class and agreement systems in language acquisition and historical change. In: Craig (ed.) 1986. Pp. 453–71.

Diakonoff, Igor M. 1988. *Afrasian Languages*. Translated from Russian by A. A. Korolevana and V.Ya. Porkhomovsky. Moscow: Nauka.

1998. The earliest Semitic society. Linguistic data. *Journal of Semitic Studies* 4.3: 209–19.

Dickens, Patrick J. 1997. Relative clauses in Juǀ'hoan. In: Haacke and Elderkin (eds.) 1997. Pp. 107–16.

n.d. Juǀ'hoan grammar. Unpublished manuscript.

Dihoff, Ivan R. (ed.) 1983. *Current Approaches to African Linguistics*. Vol. 1. Dordrecht: Foris.

Dik, Simon C. 1980. *Studies in Functional Grammar*. London: Academic Press.

Dimmendaal, Gerrit J. 1983a. Topics in a grammar of Turkana. In: Bender (ed.) 1983. Pp. 239–71.

1983b. Turkana as a verb-initial language. *Journal of African Languages and Linguistics* 5.1: 17–44.

1983c. *The Turkana Language*. Dordrecht: Foris.

1991. The geometry of verb paradigms in Teso-Turkana. In: Plank (ed.) 1991. Pp. 275–306.

to appear. Noun classification in Nilo-Saharan languages. *Anthropological Linguistics*.

Dimmendaal, Gerrit J. and Marco Last (eds.) 1998. *Surmic Languages and Cultures*. Cologne: Köppe.

Dixon, R. M. W. 1997. *The Rise and Fall of Languages*. Cambridge: Cambridge University Press.

Dolgopolsky, Aharon B. 1973. *Sravnitelíno-istoricheskaya Fonetika Kushitskikh Yazykov.* Moscow: Nauka.

1983. Semitic and East Cushitic: sound correspondences and cognate sets. In: Segert and Bodrogligeti (eds.) 1983. Pp. 123–42.

1987. South Cushitic lateral consonants as compared to Semitic and East Cushitic. In: Jungraithmayr and Müller (eds.) 1987. Pp. 195–214.

Doneux, Jean L. 1975. Hypothèses pour la comparative des langues atlantiques. *Africana Linguistica* 6: 41–129.

Dressler, Wolfgang U. 1987. Subtraction in a polycentristic theory of natural morphology. In: Gussmann (ed.) 1987. Pp. 67–77.

Dressler, Wolfgang U., Martin Prinzhorn and John R. Rennison (eds.) 1997. *Advances in Morphology.* Berlin: Mouton de Gruyter.

Dubinsky, Stanley, Maria-Rosa Lloret and Paul Newman 1988. Lexical and syntactic causatives in Oromo. *Language* 64: 485–500.

Duranti, Alessandro 1979. Object clitics pronouns in Bantu and the topicality hierarchy. *Studies in African Linguistics* 10.1: 31–45.

Durie, Mark 1997. Grammatical structures in verb serialization. In: Alsina, Bresnan and Sells (eds.) 1997. Pp. 289–354.

Dwyer, David J. 1989. Mande. In: Bendor-Samuel (ed.) 1989. Pp. 47–65.

Edgar, John 1991: *A Maba Group Lexicon.* Berlin: Reimer.

Ehret, Christopher 1972. Language evidence and religious history. In: Ranger and Kimambo (eds.) 1972. Pp. 45–9.

1974. *Ethiopians and East Africans: The Problem of Contacts.* Nairobi: East African Publishing House.

1976. Cushitic prehistory. In: Bender (ed.) 1976. Pp. 85–96.

1978. Historical inference from transformations in cultural vocabularies. *Sprache und Geschichte in Afrika* 2: 189–218.

1979. On the antiquity of agriculture in Ethiopia. *Journal of African History* 20: 161–77.

1980. *The Historical Reconstruction of Southern Cushitic Phonology and Vocabulary.* Kölner Beiträge zur Afrikanistik, 5. Berlin: Reimer.

1981. The demographic implications of linguistic change and language shift. In: Fyfe and McMaster (eds.) 1981. Pp. 153–82.

1982. Linguistic inferences about Bantu history. In: Ehret and Posnansky (eds.) 1982. Pp. 57–65.

1986. Proposals on Khoisan reconstruction. *Sprache und Geschichte in Afrika* 7.2: 105–30.

1987. Proto-Cushitic reconstruction. *Sprache und Geschichte in Afrika* 8: 7–180.

1988a. Language change and the material correlates of language and ethnic shift. *Antiquity* 62: 564–74.

1988b. Social transformation in the early history of the Horn of Africa: linguistic clues to developments of the period 500 BC to AD 500. In: Bayene (ed.) 1988.

1989. The origin of third consonants in Semitic roots: an internal reconstruction (applied to Arabic). *Journal of Afroasiatic Languages* 2.2: 109–202.

1993. Nilo-Saharans and the Saharo-Sudanese Neolithic. In: Shaw *et al.* (eds.) 1993. Pp. 104–25.

1995. *Reconstructing Proto-Afroasiatic (Proto-Afrasian): Vowels, Tone, Consonants and Vocabulary.* University of California Publications in Linguistics, 126. Berkeley: University of California Press.

1997. Linguistics, historical. In: Middleton (ed.) 1997. Pp. 579–80.

1998. *An African Classical Age: Eastern and Southern Africa in World History, 1000 BC to AD 400.* Charlottesville: University Press of Virginia, and Oxford: James Currey.

forthcoming a. *A Historical-Comparative Reconstruction of Nilo-Saharan.* Cologne: Köppe.

forthcoming b. Who were the rock artists? Identifying the Holocene populations of the Sahara. In: Muzzolini (ed.) forthcoming.

Ehret, Christopher and Merrick Posnansky (eds.) 1982. *The Archaeological and Linguistic Reconstruction of African History.* Berkeley: University of California Press.

Elderkin, Edward D. 1989. The significance and origin of the use of pitch in Sandawe. Ph.D. thesis, University of York.

Elugbe, Ben O. 1989. *Comparative Edoid: Phonology and Lexicon.* Delta Series, 6. Port Harcourt: University of Port Harcourt Press.

Embleton, Sheila 1986. *Statistics in Historical Linguistics.* Quantitative Linguistics, 30. Bochum: Studienverlag Dr N. Brockmeyer.

Erman, Adolf 1892. Das Verhältniss des Ägyptischen zu den semitischen Sprachen. *Zeitschrift der Deutschen Morgenländischen Gesellschaft* 46: 93–129.

Faber, Alice 1997. Genetic subgrouping of the Semitic languages. In: Hetzron (ed.) 1997. Pp. 3–15.

Faraclas, Nicholas 1984. Tone, stress, and the Obolo verbal focus system. *Journal of African Languages and Linguistics* 6.2: 127–46.

1989. Cross River. In: Bendor-Samuel (ed.) 1989. Pp. 377–99.

Farb, Peter. 1975. *Word Play: What Happens When People Talk.* New York: A. A. Knopf.

Ferguson, Charles A. 1959. Diglossia. *Word* 15: 325–40.

Finlayson, Rosalie 1978. A preliminary survey of hlonipa among the Xhosa. *Taalfasette* 24.2: 48–63.

Fleming, Harold C. 1969. The classification of West Cushitic within Hamito-Semitic. In: McCall *et al.* (eds.) 1969. Pp. 3–27.

1974. Omotic as an Afroasiatic family. *Studies in African Linguistics,* supplement 5: 81–94.

1983. Chadic external relations. In: Wolff and Meyer-Bahlburg (eds.) 1983. Pp. 17–31.

Frajzyngier, Zygmunt 1976. Rule inversion in Chadic: an explanation. *Studies in African Linguistics* 7: 195–210.

1977. The plural in Chadic. In: Newman and Newman (eds.) 1977. Pp. 37–56.

1983. Marking syntactic relations in Proto-Chadic. In: Wolff and Meyer-Bahlburg (eds.) 1983. Pp. 115–38.

1989. Three kinds of anaphora. In: Haïk and Tuller (eds.) 1989. Pp. 194–216.

1997. Grammaticalization of number: from demonstratives to nominal and verbal plural. *Linguistic Typology* 1: 193–242.

Froger, F. 1910. *Etude sur la langue des Mossi, suivie d'un vocabulaire & de textes.* Paris: Leroux.

Fronzaroli, Pelio (ed.) 1978. *Atti del secondo Congresso Internazionale di Linguistica Camito-Semitica, Firenze, 16–19 aprile 1974.* Firenze: Istituto di Linguistica e di Lingue orientali, Università di Firenze.

Fyfe, Christopher and David McMaster (eds.) 1981. *African Historical Demography.* Vol. II.

Gal, Susan 1988. The political economy of code choice. In: Heller (ed.) 1988. Pp. 245–64.

Gensler, Orin 1997. Grammaticalization, typology, and Niger-Congo word order: progress on a still-unsolved problem. *Journal of African Languages and Linguistics* 18.1: 57–93.

George, Isaac (Madugu) 1975. A typology of verb serialization. *Journal of West African Languages* 10: 78–97.

Gerhardt, Ludwig 1989. Kainji and Platoid. In: Bendor-Samuel (ed.) 1989. Pp. 359–76.

Gilley, Leoma G. 1992. *An Autosegmental Approach to Shilluk Phonology.* Dallas: Summer Institute of Linguistics and the University of Texas at Arlington.

Givón, Talmy 1975a. Focus and the scope of assertion, some Bantu evidence. *Studies in African Linguistics* 6.2: 185–205.

1975b. Serial verbs and syntactic change: Niger-Congo. In: Li (ed.) 1975. Pp. 47–112.

1976. On the SOV reconstruction of Southern Nilotic: internal evidence from Toposa. *Studies in African Linguistics*, supplement 6: 73–93.

1979. Language typology in Africa: a critical review. *Journal of African Languages and Linguistics* 1.2: 199–224.

1984. *Syntax: A Functional-Typological Introduction.* Vol. 1. Amsterdam, Philadelphia: Benjamins.

Goldenberg, Gideon (ed.) 1986. *Proceedings of the 6th International Conference of Ethiopian Studies, Tel-Aviv, 14th–17th April, 1980.* Rotterdam: Balkema.

Goldsmith, John A. 1990. *Autosegmental and Metrical Phonology.* Oxford: Blackwell.

Goldsmith, John A. (ed.) 1995. *Handbook of Phonological Theory.* Oxford: Blackwell.

Goodman, Morris 1970. Some Questions in the Classification of African Languages. *International Journal of American Linguistics* 36.7: 117–22.

Gowlett, Derek F. (ed.) 1992. *African Linguistic Contributions.* Presented in honour of Ernst Westphal. Pretoria: Via Afrika.

Goyvaerts, Didier (ed.) 1985. *African Linguistics.* Amsterdam, Philadelphia: Benjamins.

Greenberg, Joseph H. 1950a. Studies in African linguistic classification: IV Hamito-Semitic. *Southwestern Journal of Anthropology* 6.3: 47–63.

1950b. Studies in African linguistic classification: VI The click languages. *Southwestern Journal of Anthropology* 6.3: 223–37.

1952. The Afro-asiatic (Hamito-Semitic) present. *Journal of the American Oriental Society* 72: 1–9.

1954. A quantitative approach to the morphological typology of language. In: Spencer (ed.) 1954. Pp. 192–220.

1955a. Internal a-plurals in Afroasiatic (Hamito-Semitic). In: Lukas (ed.) 1955. Pp. 198–204.

1955b. *Studies in African Linguistic Classification.* New Haven: Compass Publishing Company.

1957. *Essays in Linguistics.* Chicago: University of Chicago Press, and London: Phoenix.

1959. Africa as a linguistic area. In: Basset and Herskovits (eds.) 1959. Pp. 15–27.

1960a. An Afro-asiatic pattern of gender and number agreement. *Journal of the American Oriental Society* 80: 317–21.

1960b. Linguistic evidence for the influence of the Kanuri on the Hausa. *Journal of African History* 1: 205–12.

1963a. *The Languages of Africa.* Bloomington: Indiana University Center in Anthropology, Folklore, and Linguistics, and The Hague: Mouton.

1963b. Some universals of grammar with particular reference to the order of meaningful elements. In: Greenberg (ed.) 1963. Pp. 58–90.

Historical inferences from linguistic research in sub-Saharan Africa. In: J. Butler (ed.) *Boston University Papers from African History* 1: 1–15. New York: Praeger.

Greenberg, Joseph H. (ed.) 1963. *Universals of Language.* Cambridge, Mass.: MIT Press.

1965. Linguistics. In: Lystad (ed.) 1965. Pp. 416–41.

1970. Some generalizations concerning glottalic consonants, especially implosives. *International Journal of American Linguistics* 36: 123–45.

1977. Niger-Congo noun class markers: prefixes, suffixes, both or neither. *Studies in African Linguistics*, supplement 7: 97–104.

1978a. How does a language acquire gender markers? In: Greenberg (ed.) 1978. Pp. 47–82.

1978b. *Universals of Human Language*. Vol. III, *Word Structure*. Stanford, Calif.: Stanford University Press.

1983. Some areal characteristics of African languages. In: Dihoff (ed.) 1983. Pp. 3–21.

Gregersen, Edgar A. 1972. Kongo-Saharan. *Journal of African Languages* 11.1: 69–89.

1977. *Language in Africa: An Introductory Survey*. New York, Paris and London: Gordon & Breach.

Grimes, Barbara F. (ed.) 1996. *Ethnologue: Languages of the World*. 13th edition. Dallas: Summer Institute of Linguistics and the University of Texas at Arlington.

Grimes, Joseph E. and Barbara F. Grimes 1996. *Ethnologue Language Family Index*. 13th edition. Dallas: Summer Institute of Linguistics and the University of Texas at Arlington.

Gruber, Jeffrey S. 1975. Plural predicates in ‡Hõã. In: Traill (ed.) 1975. Pp. 1–50.

Güldemann, Tom 1998. The Kalahari basin as an object of areal typology – a first approach. In: Schladt (ed.) 1998. Pp. 137–69.

1999. Phonological regularities of consonant systems in genetic lineages of Khoisan. In: Keuthmann, Sommer and Vossen (eds.) 1999.

Gussmann, Edmund (ed.) 1987. *Rules and the Lexicon: Studies in Word-Formation*. Lublin: Redakcja Wydawnictw, Katolickiego Uniwersytetu Lubelskiego.

Guthrie, Malcolm 1948. *The Classification of the Bantu Languages*. Oxford: Oxford University Press.

1967–71. *Comparative Bantu*. 4 vols. Farnborough: Gregg.

Gutt, Eeva H. M. and Hussein Mohammed Mussa 1997. *Silt'e-Amharic-English Dictionary*. Addis Ababa: Addis Ababa University Press.

Haacke, Wilfrid H. G. 1977. The so-called 'personal pronoun' in Nama. In: Traill (ed.) 1977. Pp. 43–62.

1998. *The Tonology of Khoekhoe (Nama/Damara)*. Quellen zur Khoisan-Forschung, 17. Cologne: Köppe.

Haacke, Wilfrid H. G. and Edward D. Elderkin (eds.) 1997. *Namibian Languages: Reports and Papers*. Namibia African Studies, 4. Cologne: Köppe.

Hagman, Roy S. 1977. *Nama Hottentot Grammar*. Indiana University Publications, Language Science Monographs, 15. Bloomington: Indiana University Press.

Haïk, Isabelle and Laurice Tuller (eds.) 1989. *Current Approaches to African Languages*. Vol. VI. Dordrecht: Kluwer.

Halle, Morris 1992. Features. In: Bright (ed.) 1992b. Pp. 207–12.

Halle, Morris and George N. Clements 1983. *Problem Book in Phonology*. Cambridge, Mass.: MIT Press and Bradford Books.

Haller, Beat and John R. Watters 1984. Topic in Zulgo. *Studies in African Linguistics* 15: 27–46.

Hayward, K. M. and Richard J. Hayward 1989. 'Guttural': arguments for a new distinctive feature. *Transactions of the Philological Society* 87: 179–93.

Hayward, Richard J. 1987. Terminal vowels in Ometo nominals. In: Jungraithmayr and Müller (eds.) 1987. Pp. 215–31.

1989. The notion of 'default gender': a key to interpreting the evolution of certain verb paradigms in East Ometo, and its implications for Omotic. *Afrika und Übersee* 72: 17–32.

1998. The origins of the North Ometo verb agreement systems. *Journal of African Languages and Linguistics* 19: 93–111.

Hayward, Richard J. (ed.) 1990. *Omotic Language Studies*. London: School of Oriental and African Studies.

Hayward, Richard J. and Yoichi Tsuge 1998. Concerning case in Omotic. *Afrika und Übersee* 81: 21–38.

Heath, Jeffrey 1997. Lost wax: Abrupt replacement of key morphemes in Australian agreement complexes. *Diachronica* 14: 197–232.

Heikkinen, Terttu 1987. *An Outline Grammar of the !Xũ Language* (spoken in Ovamboland and West Kavango). South African Journal of African Languages 7, supplement 1. Pretoria: Via Afrika.

Heine, Bernd 1968a. *Die Verbreitung und Gliederung der Togorestsprachen.* Berlin: Reimer.

1968b. The allocation of loan-words within the nominal class systems of some Togo remnant languages. *Journal of African Languages* 7: 130–9.

1970. *Status and Use of African Lingua Francas.* Munich: Weltforum.

1973. *Pidgin-Sprachen im Bantu-Bereich.* Berlin: Reimer.

1976a. *A Typology of African Languages Based on the Order of Meaningful Elements.* Kölner Beiträge zur Afrikanistik, 4. Berlin: Reimer.

1976b. *The Kuliak Languages of Eastern Uganda.* Nairobi: East African Publishing House.

1977. Vertical and horizontal communication in Africa. *Afrika Spektrum* 77: 231–8.

1978. The Sam languages: a history of Rendille, Boni and Somali. *Afroasiatic Linguistics* 6.2: 1–93.

1980. Language typology and linguistic reconstruction: the Niger-Congo case. *Journal of African Languages and Linguistics* 2.2: 95–112.

1989. Adpositions in African languages. *Linguistique africaine* 2: 77–127.

1999. *Ik dictionary.* Nilo-Saharan, 15. Cologne: Köppe.

Heine, Bernd, Ulrike Claudi and Friederike Hünnemeyer 1991. *Grammaticalization: A Conceptual Framework.* Hamburg: Buske.

Heine, Bernd and Mechthild Reh 1984. *Grammaticalization and Reanalysis in African Languages.* Hamburg: Buske.

Heine, Bernd, Thilo C. Schadeberg and Ekkehard Wolff (eds.) 1981. *Die Sprachen Afrikas.* Hamburg: Buske.

Heller, Monica (ed.) 1988. *Codeswitching: Anthropological and Sociolinguistic Perspectives.* Contributions to the Sociology of Language, 48. Berlin, New York and Amsterdam: Mouton de Gruyter.

Hérault, Georges (ed.) 1983a. *Atlas des langues kwa de Côte d'Ivoire.* Vol. I, *Monographies.* Abidjan: Agence de Coopération Culturelle et Technique and Institut de Linguistique Appliquée, Université d'Abidjan.

(ed.) 1983b. *Atlas des Langues Kwa de Côte d'Ivoire.* Vol. II. Abidjan: Agence de Coopération Culturelle et Technique and Institut de Linguistique Appliquée, Université d'Abidjan.

Herbert, Robert K. 1986. *Language Universals, Markedness Theory, and Natural Phonetic Processes.* Berlin: Mouton de Gruyter.

1997. *African Linguistics at the Crossroads.* Papers from Kwaluseni (1st World Congress of African Linguistics, Swaziland, 18–22 July 1997). Cologne: Köppe.

Herbert, Robert K. (ed.) 1992. *Language and Society in Africa: The Theory and Practice of Sociolinguistics.* Johannesburg: Witwatersrand University Press.

Hetzron, Robert 1972. *Ethiopian Semitic: Studies in Classification.* Journal of Semitic Studies, monograph 2. Manchester: Manchester University Press.

1976. Two principles of genetic reconstruction. *Lingua* 38: 89–108.

1980. The limits of Cushitic. *Sprache und Geschichte in Afrika* 2: 7–126.

1990. Dialectal variation in Proto-Afroasiatic. In: Baldi (ed.) 1990. Pp. 577–97.

Hetzron, Robert (ed.) 1997. *The Semitic Languages.* London: Routledge.

Hinton, Leanne, Johanna Nichols and John J. Ohala (eds.) 1994. *Sound Symbolism.* Cambridge: Cambridge University Press.

Hoberman, Robert D. 1995. Current issues in Semitic phonology. In: Goldsmith (ed.) 1995. Pp. 839–47.

Hockett, Charles F. 1958. Two models of grammatical description. *Word* 10: 210–34.

Hodge, Carlton T. 1966. Hausa – Egyptian establishment. *Anthropological Linguistics* 8.1: 40–57.

1969. *Egyptian Amid Afroasiatic Languages*. American Oriental Society, Middle West Brands, Semicentennial volume. Bloomington: Indiana University Press.

1971. Afroasiatic: an overview. In: Hodge (ed.) 1971. Pp. 9–26.

1976. Lisramic (Afroasiatic): an overview. In: Bender (ed.) 1976. Pp. 43–65.

Hodge, Carlton T. (ed.) 1971. *Afroasiatic: An Overview*. The Hague: Mouton.

Hoenigswald, Henry M. 1963. On the history of the comparative method. *Anthropological Linguistics* 5.1: 1–11.

1990. Language families and subgroupings, tree model and wave theory, and reconstruction of protolanguages. In: Polomé (ed.) 1990. Pp. 441–54.

Hoffmann, Carl 1973. The vowel harmony system of the Okpe monosyllabic verb, or Okpe – A nine vowel language with only seven vowels. *Research Notes* (Ibadan, Nigeria) 6: 79–111.

Hoijer, Harry 1962. Linguistic sub-groupings by glottochronology [lexicostatistics] and by the comparative method: the Athapascan languages. *Lingua* 11: 192–8.

Honken, Henry 1977. Submerged features and Proto-Khoisan. In: Traill (ed.) 1977. Pp. 145–69.

1988. Phonetic correspondences among Khoisan affricates. In: Vossen (ed.) 1988. Pp. 47–65.

1998. Sound correspondence patterns in Khoisan languages. In: Schladt (ed.) 1998. Pp. 171–91.

Houis, Maurice 1970. Réflexion sur une double corrélation typologique. *Journal of West African Languages* 7.2: 59–68.

Hudson, Grover 1995. Phonology of Ethiopian languages. In: Goldsmith (ed.) 1995. Pp. 782–97.

Hutchison, John P. 1981. *The Kanuri Language: A Reference Grammar*. Madison: African Studies Program, University of Wisconsin.

Hyman, Larry M. 1971. Consecutivization in Fe'fe'. *Journal of African Languages* 10: 29–43.

1975a. On the change from SOV to SVO: evidence from Niger-Congo. In: Li (ed.) 1975. Pp. 113–47.

1975b. *Phonology: Theory and Analysis*. New York: Holt, Rinehart & Winston.

1979. Phonology and noun structure. In: Hyman (ed.) 1979. Pp. 1–72.

1985. *A Theory of Phonological Weight*. Dordrecht: Foris.

1994. Cyclic phonology and morphology in Cibemba. In: Cole and Kisseberth (eds.) 1994. Pp. 81–112.

1998. Positional prominence and the 'prosodic trough' in Yaka. *Phonology* 15: 41–75.

Hyman, Larry M. (ed.) 1979. *Aghem Grammatical Structure*. Southern California Occasional Papers in Linguistics, 7. Los Angeles: University of Southern California Press.

(ed.) 1980. *Noun Classes in the Grassfields Bantu Borderland*. Los Angeles: University of Southern California Press.

Hyman, Larry M. and Charles Kisseberth (eds.) 1998. *Theoretical Aspects of Bantu Tone*. Stanford: Center for the Study of Language and Information.

Hyman, Larry M. and John R. Watters 1984. Auxiliary focus. *Studies in African Linguistics* 15.3: 233–73.

Ikoro, Suanu M. 1994. Numeral classifiers in Kana. *Journal of African Languages and Linguistics* 15.1: 7–28.

1996. *The Kana Language*. Leiden: Centre for Non-Western Studies.

Isserlin, Benedikt S. J. 1975. Some aspects of the present state of Hamito-Semitic studies. In: Bynon and Bynon (eds.) 1975. Pp. 479–86.

Jakobi, Angelika 1993. *A Fur Grammar*. Hamburg: Buske.

Jakobi, Angelika and Tanja Kümmerle 1993. *The Nubian Languages: An Annotated Bibliography.* Cologne: Köppe.

Jarvis, Elisabeth 1981. Some considerations in establishing the basic word order of Podoko. *Studies in African Linguistics* 12.2: 155–67.

Jenewari, Charles E. W. 1989. Ijoid. In: Bendor-Samuel (ed.) 1989. Pp. 105–18.

Johnston, Sir Harry 1902. *The Uganda Protectorate.* London: Hutchinson.

Jungraithmayr, Herrmann 1970. On root augmentation in Hausa. *Journal of African Languages* 9: 83–8.

   1971. Reflections on the root structure in Chadohamitic (Chadic). *Actes du 8e Congrès de la Société Linguistique de l'Afrique Occidentales. Annales de l'Université d'Abijan.* Série H: Linguistique, Hors-Série, vol. 1: 285–92.

   1978. A tentative four stage model for the development of the Chadic languages. In: Fronzaroli (ed.) 1978. Pp. 381–8.

Jungraithmayr, Herrmann and Dymitr Ibriszimow 1994. *Chadic Lexical Roots.* Berlin: Reimer.

Jungraithmayr, Herrmann and Walter W. Müller (eds.) 1987. *Proceedings of the 4th International Hamito-Semitic Congress.* Current Issues in Linguistic Theory, 44. Amsterdam, Philadelphia: Benjamins.

Kagaya, Ryohei 1993. *A Classified Vocabulary of the Sandawe Language.* Asian and African Lexicon, 26. Tokyo: Institute for the Study of Languages and Cultures of Asia and Africa.

Kastenholz, Raimund 1991/2. Comparative Mande studies: state of the art. *Sprache und Geschichte in Afrika* 12/13: 107–58.

   1996. *Sprachgeschichte im West-Mande.* Cologne: Köppe.

Katamba, Francis 1989. *An Introduction to Phonology.* London and New York: Longman.

   1993. *Morphology.* London: Macmillan.

Kaye, Alan S. (ed.) 1996. *Phonologies of Asia and Africa.* Winona Lake: Eisenbrauns.

Kaye, Jonathan 1981. Implosives as liquids. *Studies in African Linguistics,* supplement 8: 78–81.

Kaye, Jonathan, Hilda Koopman, Dominique Sportiche and André Dugas (eds.) 1983. *Current Approaches to African Linguistics.* Vol. II. Dordrecht: Foris.

Keating, Patricia (ed.) 1994. *Papers in Laboratory Phonology 3.* Cambridge: Cambridge University Press.

Keenan, Edward L. 1985a. Passive in the world's languages. In: Shopen (ed.) 1985a. Pp. 243–79.

   1985b. Relative clauses. In: Shopen (ed.) 1985b. Pp. 141–70.

Kenstowicz, Michael 1994. *Phonology in Generative Grammar.* Oxford: Blackwell.

Keuthmann, Klaus, Gabriele Sommer and Rainer Vossen (eds.) 1999. *Essays in Honour of Anthony Traill.* Quellen zur Khoisan-Forschung, 17. Cologne: Köppe.

Khamis, Cornelia 1994. *Mehrsprachigkeit bei den Nubi. Das Sprachverhalten viersprachig aufwachsender Vorschul- und Schulkinder in Bombo/Uganda.* Hamburg: LIT Verlag.

Kidima, Lukowa 1987. Object agreement and topicality hierarchies in Kiyaka. *Studies in African Linguistics* 18.2: 175–209.

Kleinewillinghöfer, Ulrich 1996. Die nordwestlichen Adamawa-Sprachen. *Frankfurter Afrikanistische Blätter* 8: 81–104.

Klieman, Kairn A. 1997. Peoples of the western equatorial rainforest: a history of society and economy, from ca. 3000 BC to 1890. Ph.D. thesis, University of California at Los Angeles.

Klingenheben, August 1927/8. Die Silbenauslautgesetze des Hausa. *Zeitschrift für Eingeborenen-Sprachen* 18: 272–97.

1951. Althamito-semitische nominale Genusexponenten in heutigen Hamitensprachen. *Zeitschrift der Deutschen Morgenländischen Gesellschaft* 101: 78–88.

1956. Die Präfix- und die Suffixkonjugationen des Hamitosemitischen. *Mitteilungen des Instituts für Orientforschung* 4: 211–77.

Koch, Harold 1995. The creation of morphological zeroes. In: Booij and van Marle (eds.) 1995. Pp. 31–71.

Köhler, Oswin 1971. Noun classes and grammatical agreement in !Xũ (ʒû-|ɦoà dialect). *Actes du 8e Congrès de la Société Linguistique de l'Afrique Occidentales. Annales de l'Université d'Abidjan.* Série H: Linguistique, Hors-Série, vol. II: 489–522.

1973/4. Neuere Ergebnisse und Hypothesen der Sprachforschung in ihrer Bedeutung für die Geschichte Afrikas. *Paideuma* 19/20: 162–99.

1975. Geschichte und Probleme der Gliederung der Sprachen Afrikas. Von den Anfängen bis zur Gegenwart. In: Baumann (ed.) 1975. Pp. 135–373.

1981. Les langues khoïsan. In: Perrot (ed.) 1981. Pp. 455–615.

Köhler, Oswin, Peter Ladefoged, Jan W. Snyman, Anthony Traill and Rainer Vossen 1988. The symbols for clicks. *Journal of the International Phonetic Association* 18.2: 140–2.

Koelle, Sigismund Wilhelm 1854. *Polyglotta Africana.* London: Church Missionary House.

Koopman, Hilda 1984. *The Syntax of Verbs.* Dordrecht: Foris.

Kraft, Charles H. and Marguerite G. Kraft 1973. *Introductory Hausa.* Berkeley: University of California Press.

Krause, Gottlieb A. 1885. Die Stellung des Temne innerhalb der Bantusprachen. *Zeitschrift für afrikanische und oceanische Sprachen* 1: 250–67.

Kropp-Dakubu, Mary-Esther (ed.) 1973. *Papers in Ghanaian Linguistics 2.* Legon: University of Ghana, Institute of African Studies.

Kuryłowicz, Jerzy 1964. On the methods of internal reconstruction. In: Lunt (ed.) 1964. Pp. 9–31.

Kutsch Lojenga, Constance 1994. *Ngiti: A Central-Sudanic Language of Zaire.* Cologne: Köppe.

Lackner, Jerome A. and John H. Rowe 1955. Morphological similarity as a criterion of genetic relationship between languages. *American Anthropologist* 57: 126–9.

Ladefoged, Peter 1964. *A Phonetic Study of West African Languages.* Cambridge: Cambridge University Press.

1968. *A Phonetic Study of West African Languages.* 2nd edition. Cambridge: Cambridge University Press.

Ladefoged, Peter and Ian Maddieson 1996. *The Sounds of the World's Languages.* Oxford: Blackwell.

Ladefoged, Peter and Anthony Traill 1994. Clicks and their accompaniments. *Journal of Phonetics* 22: 33–64.

Ladefoged, Peter, Kay Williamson, Ben O. Elugbe and Ann Angela Uwalaka 1976. The stops of Owerri Igbo. *Studies in African Linguistics*, supplement 6: 147–63.

Lamberti, Marcello 1991. Cushitic and its classifications. *Anthropos* 86: 552–61.

1993a. *Die Shinassha-Sprache.* Studia Linguarum Africae Orientalis, 4. Heidelberg: Universitätsverlag C. Winter.

1993b. *Materialien zum Yemsa.* Studia Linguarum Africae Orientalis, 5. Heidelberg: Universitätsverlag C. Winter.

Leben, Will R. 1977. Length and syllable structure in Hausa. *Studies in African Linguistics*, supplement 7: 137–43.

Lepsius, Richard 1880. *Nubische Grammatik*, mit einer Einleitung über die Völker und Sprachen Afrika's. Berlin: Hertz.

Levinsohn, Stephen H. (ed.) 1994. *Discourse Features of Ten Languages of West-Central Africa.* Dallas: Summer Institute of Linguistics and the University of Texas at Arlington.

Leynseele, Helene van 1975. Restrictions on serial verbs in Anyi. *Journal of West African Languages* 10.2: 189–218.

Li, Charles (ed.) 1975. *Word Order and Word Order Change.* Austin: University of Texas Press.

Lindau, Mona 1975. *Features for Vowels.* Working Papers in Phonetics, 30. Los Angeles: University of California at Los Angeles.

1984. Phonetic differences in glottalic consonants. *Journal of Phonetics* 54: 147–55.

Longacre, Robert E. 1990. Storyline concerns and word order typology in East and West Africa. *Studies in African Linguistics,* supplement 10: 1–181.

Loprieno, Antonio 1995. *Ancient Egyptian: A Linguistic Introduction.* Cambridge: Cambridge University Press.

Lord, Carol 1973. Serial verbs in transition. *Studies in African Linguistics* 4.3: 269–96.

1975. Igbo verb compounds and the lexicon. *Studies in African Linguistics* 6.1: 23–48.

1977. How Igbo got from SOV serializing to SVO compounding. *Studies in African Linguistics,* supplement 7: 145–55.

1993. *Historical Change in Serial Verb Constructions.* Typological Studies in Language, 26. Amsterdam, Philadelphia: Benjamins.

Lottner, C. 1860/1. On sister families of languages, especially those connected with the Semitic family. *Transactions of the Philological Society.* Pp. 20–7, 112–32. (Reprinted 1968, Amsterdam: Swets & Zeitlinger N.V.)

Ludolf, Hiob 1702. *Grammatica Aethiopica.* Frankfurt.

Lukas, Johannes (ed.) 1955. *Afrikanistische Studien Diedrich Westermann zum 80. Geburtstag gewidmet.* Deutsche Akademie der Wissenschaften zu Berlin; Institut für Orientforschung, 26. Berlin: Akademie Verlag.

Lunt, Horace (ed.) 1964. *Proceedings of the 9th International Congress of Linguists.* The Hague: Mouton.

Lystad, Robert A. (ed.) 1965. *The African World: A Survey of Social Research.*

Maddieson, Ian 1987. The Margi vowel system and labiocoronals. *Studies in African Linguistics* 18: 327–55.

1990. Shona velarization: complex consonants or complex onsets? *UCLA Working Papers in Phonetics* 74: 16–34.

Maddieson, Ian (with Kristin Precoda) 1992. UPSID and PHONEME, version 1.1 Database and program for the PC. Los Angeles: University of California at Los Angeles.

Maddieson, Ian and Thomas Hinnebusch (eds.) 1998. *Language, History and Linguistic Description in Africa.* Trends in African Linguistics. Lawrenceville, N.J.: Africa World Press.

Madugu, Omen N. 1988. Size and shape ideophones in Nembe: a phonosemantic analysis. *Studies in African Linguistics* 19: 93–113.

Mandelbaum, David (ed.) 1963. *Selected Writings in Language, Culture and Personality.* Chicago: University of Chicago Press.

Manessy, Gabriel 1965–6. Les substantifs à préfixe et suffixe dans les langues voltaïques. *Journal of African Languages* 4: 170–81; 5: 54–61.

1975. *Les langues Oti-Volta.* Paris: Centre National de la Recherche Scientifique.

1978. Les langues voltaïques. In: Barreteau (ed.) 1978. Pp. 71–83.

1979. *Contribution à la classification généalogique des langues voltaïques.* Paris: Centre National de la Recherche Scientifique.

Manfredi, Victor 1989. Igboid. In: Bendor-Samuel (ed.) 1989. Pp. 335–58.

Marchese, Lynell 1983. *Atlas linguistique kru.* Abidjan: Agence de Coopération Culturelle et Technique, Institut de Linguistique Appliquée, Université de'Abidjan.

1986. *Tense/Aspect and the Development of Auxiliaries in Kru Languages.* Dallas: Summer Institute of Linguistics and the University of Texas at Arlington.

1989. Kru. In: Bendor-Samuel (ed.) 1989. Pp. 119–40.

Martin, Phyllis M. and Patrick O'Meara (eds.) 1986. *Africa.* 2nd edition. Bloomington: Indiana University Press.

Masica, Colin P. 1976. *Defining a Linguistic Area: South Asia.* Chicago: University of Chicago Press.

Matthews, Peter H. 1974. *Morphology: An Introduction to the Theory of Word-Structure.* Cambridge: Cambridge University Press.

McCall, Daniel *et al.* (eds.) 1969. *Eastern African History.* Boston University Studies in African History, 3. New York: Praeger.

McCarthy, John J. 1981. A prosodic theory of nonconcatenative morphology. *Linguistic Inquiry* 12.3: 373–418.

1994. The phonetics and phonology of Semitic pharyngeals. In: Keating (ed.) 1994. Pp. 191–233.

Mchombo, Sam A. 1993. A formal analysis of the stative construction in Bantu. *Journal of African Languages and Linguistics* 14: 5–28.

McIntyre, Joseph A. 1995. It's still NAg-ging: compounds in Hausa. *Afrika und Übersee* 78: 239–59.

Meeussen, A. E. 1959. *Essai de grammaire rundi.* Tervuren: Musée Royal du Congo Belge.

1967. Bantu grammatical reconstructions. *Annales du Musée Royale de l'Afrique Centrale* 61: 81–121.

1975. Possible linguistic Africanisms. *Language Sciences* 35: 1–5.

1980. *Bantu Lexical Reconstructions.* Reprint. Tervuren: Musée Royale de l'Afrique Centrale.

Meillet, André and Marcel Cohen (eds.) 1924. *Les langues du monde.* 2 Vols. Paris: H. Champion.

Meinhof, Carl 1903. Das Dahlsche Gesetz. *Zeitschrift der Deutschen Morgenländischen Gesellschaft* 57: 299–304.

1912. *Die Sprachen der Hamiten.* Hamburg: Friederichsen.

Meinhof, Carl (with N. J. van Warmelo) 1932. *Introduction to the Phonology of the Bantu Languages.* Berlin: Reimer.

Mel'čuk, Igor 1996. *Cours de morphologie générale.* 3 Vols. Montréal: Les Presses de l'Université de Montréal.

Middleton, John (ed.) 1997. *Encyclopedia of Africa South of the Sahara.* Vol. II. New York: Charles Scribner's Sons.

Militariev, A. Yu. and V. A. Shnirelman 1984. *K probleme lokalosatzii drevneishikh afraziitsev; opyt lingvoarkheologicheskoi rekonstruktzii.* (*On the Problem of Location of the Early Afrasians. An Essay in Linguo-Archaeological Reconstruction.*) Lingvisticheskaya rekonstruktsiya i drevneyshaya istoria Vostoka. Chast' 2. Moscow.

Miller, Catherine 1996. Nubien, berbère et beja; notes sur trois langues vernacuaires nomades. *Langues en Égypte* 27/8: 411–34.

Mithun, Marianne 1986. On the nature of noun incorporation. *Language* 62: 32–7.

Mkanganwi, K. G. 1975. A description of Shona spelling. *African Languages/Langues Africaines* 1: 225–58.

Moravcsik, Edith A. 1978. Reduplicative constructions. In: Greenberg (ed.) 1978. Pp. 297–334.

Morolong, Malillo and Larry Hyman 1977. Animacy, objects and clitics in Sesotho. *Studies in African Linguistics* 8.3: 199–218.

Mous, Maarten 1994. Ma'a or Mbugu. In: Bakker and Mous (eds.) 1994. Pp. 175–200.

Müller, Friedrich 1877. *Grundriss der Sprachwissenschaft.* I. Band, II. Abteilung: Die Sprachen der wollhaarigen Rassen. Wien: A. Hölder.

Mukarovsky, Hans G. 1976–7. *A Study of Western Nigritic.* 2 Vols. Wien: Institut für Ägyptologie und Afrikanistik, Universität Wien.

1983. Die Nominalklassen im Serer und im Ful. *Afrika und Übersee* 66: 175–90.

Munson, Patrick 1986. Africa's prehistoric past. In: Martin and O'Meara (eds.) 1986. Pp. 43–63.

Murdock, George P. 1959. *Africa: Its People and Their Culture History.* New York: McGraw-Hill.

Mutaka, Ngessimo and Larry M. Hyman 1990. Syllables and morpheme integrity in Kinande reduplication. *Phonology* 7: 73–119.

Muzzolini, A. (ed.) forthcoming. *Proceedings of the 1996 International Rock Art Congress, Turin.*

Myers-Scotton, Carol 1993. *Social Motivations for Code-Switching. Evidence from Africa.* Oxford: Oxford University Press.

Naden, Tony 1989. Gur. In: Bendor-Samuel (ed.) 1989. Pp. 140–68.

Nespoulous, Jean-Luc (ed.) 1993. *Tendances actuelles en linguistique générale.* Neuchâtel: Delachaux et Niestlé.

Newman, Paul 1970. *A Grammar of Tera: Transformational Syntax and Texts.* University of California Publications in Linguistics, 57. Berkeley: University of California Press.

1972. Syllable weight as a phonological variable. *Studies in African Linguistics* 3: 301–23.

1974. *The Kanakuru Language.* West African Language Monographs, 9. Leeds: Institute of Modern English Language Studies, University of Leeds and West African Linguistic Society.

1977. Chadic classification and reconstructions. *Afroasiatic Linguistics* 5.1: 1–42.

1980. *The Classification of Chadic Within Afroasiatic.* Leiden: Universitaire Pers.

1990. *Nominal and Verbal Plurality in Chadic.* Dordrecht: Foris.

1992. Chadic languages. In: Bright (ed.) 1992a. Pp. 251–4.

1995a. Hausa tonology: complexities in an 'easy' tone language. In: Goldsmith (ed.) 1995. Pp. 762–81.

1995b. *On Being Right: Greenberg's African Linguistic Classification and the Methodological Principles Which Underlie It.* Bloomington: Institute for the Study of Nigerian Languages and Cultures and African Studies Program, Indiana University.

1995c. The historical development of double negatives. Paper presented at the 12th International Conference on Historical Linguistics, Manchester.

in press. *The Hausa Language.* New Haven: Yale University Press.

Newman, Paul and Roxana Ma 1966. Comparative Chadic: phonology and lexicon. *Journal of African Languages* 5: 218–51.

Newman, Paul and Roxana Ma (eds.) 1977. *Papers in Chadic Linguistics.* Leiden: Afrika-Studiecentrum.

Newman, Paul and Russel G. Schuh 1974. The Hausa aspect system. *Afroasiatic Linguistics* 1.1: 1–39.

Nichols, Johanna 1986. Head-marking and dependent-marking grammar. *Language* 62: 56–119.

Nicolaï, Robert 1981. *Les dialectes du songhay.* Paris: CNRS.

1990. *Parentés linguistiques (à propos du songhay).* Paris: CNRS.

Nicolaï, Robert and Franz Rottland (eds.) 1995. *Proceedings of the 5th Nilo-Saharan Linguistics Colloquium, Nice 1992.* Nilo-Saharan Linguistic Analyses and Documentation, 10. Cologne: Köppe.

Nida, Eugene 1946. *Morphology: The Descriptive Analysis of Words.* Ann Arbor: University of Michigan Press.

Nketia, J. H. Kwabena 1971. The linguistic aspect of style in African languages. In: Sebeok (ed.) 1971. Pp. 733–57.

Noonan, Michael 1985. Complementation. In: Shopen (ed.) 1985b. Pp. 42–140.

1992. *A Grammar of Lango*. Berlin: Mouton de Gruyter.

Nougayrol, Pierre 1989. *La langue des aiki dits rounga*. Paris: LACITO.

Novelli, Bruno 1985. *A Grammar of the Karimojong Language*. Berlin: Reimer.

Nsuka Nkutsi, François 1982. *Les structures fondamentales du relatif dans les langues bantoues*. Tervuren: Musée Royal de l'Afrique Centrale.

Nurse, Derek 1996. 'Historical' classifications of the Bantu languages. In: Sutton (ed.) 1996. Pp. 65–81.

1997. The contribution of linguistics to the study of history in Africa. *Journal of African History* 38: 359–91.

1999. *Inheritance, Contact, and Change in Two East African Languages*. Cologne: Köppe.

Nurse, Derek and Thomas J. Hinnebusch. 1993. *Swahili and Sabaki: A Linguistic History*. Berkeley: University of California Press.

Nyombe, Bureng G. V. 1993. Book review of Chet A. Creider, *The Syntax of the Nilotic Languages: Themes and Variations. Journal of African Languages and Linguistics* 14: 76–80.

Odden, David 1987. Kimatuumbi phrasal phonology. *Phonology Yearbook* 4: 13–26.

1995. Tone: African languages. In: Goldsmith (ed.) 1995. Pp. 444–75.

1996. *The Phonology and Morphology of Kimatuumbi*. Oxford: Oxford University Press.

Ohiri-Aniche, Chinyere 1999. Language diversification in the Akoko area of Western Nigeria. In: Blench and Spriggs (eds.) 1999.

Orel, Vladimir E. and Olga V. Stolbova 1995. *Hamito-Semitic Etymological Dictionary: Materials for a Reconstruction*. Leiden: Brill.

Pagliuca, William (ed.) 1994. *Perspectives on Grammaticalization*. Amsterdam, Philadelphia: Benjamins.

Painter, Colin 1973. Cineradiographic data on the feature 'covered' in Twi vowel harmony. *Phonetica* 28: 97–120.

Paradis, Carole 1993. Phonologie générative multilinéaire. In: Nespoulous (ed.) 1993. Pp. 11–47.

Pasch, Helma 1985. Possession and possessive classifiers in Dongo-ko. *Afrika und Übersee* 68: 69–85.

Payne, Doris L. 1996. Maasai gender in typological perspective. *Studies in African Linguistics* 27: 159–75.

Payne, John R. 1985. Negation. In: Shopen (ed.) 1985a. Pp. 197–242.

Perrin, Mona J. 1994. Rheme and focus in Mambila. In: Levinsohn (ed.) 1994. Pp. 231–41.

Perrot, Jean (ed.) 1981. *Les langues dans le monde ancien et moderne*. Part I, Les langues de l'Afrique subsaharienne, ed. Gabriel Manessy. Paris: Editions du Centre National de la Recherche Scientifique.

Pike, Kenneth L. 1943. *Tone Languages*. Glendale, Calif.: Summer Institute of Linguistics.

Piron, Pascale 1998. *Classification interne du groupe bantoïde*. 3 Vols. Munich: LINCOM Europa.

Plank, Frans (ed.) 1991. *Paradigms: The Economy of Inflection*. Berlin: Mouton de Gruyter.

1994. *Objects: Towards a Theory of Grammatical Relations*. London: Academic Press.

Polomé, Edgar C. (ed.) 1990. *Research Guide on Language Change*. Trends in Linguistics, Studies and Monographs. Berlin and New York: Mouton de Gruyter.

Postel, Guillaume 1538. *De originibus seu de Hebraicae linguae et gentis antiquitate deque variarum linguarum affinitate liber*. Paris.

Praetorius, Franz 1894. Über die hamitischen Sprachen Ostafrikas. *Beiträge zur Assyrologie* 2: 312–41.

Prost, André 1964. *Contribution à l'Etude des Langues Voltaïques.* Dakar: Institut Français d'Afrique Noire.

1971. *Eléments de Sembla.* Lyon: Afrique et Langage.

Pulleyblank, Douglas 1986. *Tone in Lexical Phonology.* Dordrecht: Reidel.

1989. Nonlinear phonology. *Annual Revue of Anthropology* 18: 203–26.

Pumphrey, M. E. C. 1937. Shilluk 'royal' language conventions. *Sudan Notes and Records* 20: 319–21.

Ranger, Terence O. and Isaria N. Kimambo (eds.) 1972. *The Historical Study of African Religion.* London: Heinemann, and Berkeley: University of California Press.

Renan, Ernest 1855. *Histoire générale et système comparé des langues sémitiques.* Paris: Imprimerie impériale.

Reh, Mechthild 1981. Sprache und Gesellschaft. In: Heine, Schadeberg, and Wolff (eds.) 1981. Pp. 513–57.

1983. Krongo: a VSO language with postpositions. *Journal of African Languages and Linguistics* 5.1: 45–55.

1985. *Die Krongo-Sprache.* Berlin: Reimer.

Rialland, Annie and Mamadou Badjimé 1989. Réanalyse des tons du bambara. *Studies in African Linguistics* 20: 1–28.

Robins, R. H. 1959. In defence of WP. *Transactions of the Philological Society 1959.* Oxford: Blackwell. Pp. 116–44.

Rössler, Otto 1950. Verbalbau und Verbalflexion in den Semito-Hamitischen Sprachen. Vorstudien zu einer vergleichenden Semito-Hamitischen Grammatik. *Zeitschrift der Deutschen Morgenländischen Gesellschaft* 100: 461–514.

Ross, Malcolm D. 1988. *Proto Oceanic and the Austronesian Languages of Western Melanesia. Pacific Linguistics* C–98. Canberra: Australian National University Press.

Rottland, Franz 1982. *Die Südnilotischen Sprachen.* Berlin: Reimer.

Rottland, Franz (ed.) 1986. *Festschrift zum 60. Geburtstag von Carl F. Hoffmann.* Bayreuther Beiträge zur Sprachwissenschaft, 7. Hamburg: Buske.

Ruhlen, Merritt 1987. *A Guide to the World's Languages.* Vol. I, *Classification.* Stanford: Arnold.

1994. *On the Origin of Languages.* Studies in Linguistic Taxonomy. Stanford: Stanford University Press.

Sagey, Elisabeth 1990. *The Representation of Features in Nonlinear Phonology: The Articulator Node Hierarchy.* New York: Garland. (1986 MIT Ph.D. dissertation.)

Samarin, William J. 1971. Adamawa-Eastern. In: Sebeok (ed.) 1971. Pp. 213–44.

Sanders, Edith R. 1969. The Hamitic hypothesis: its origin and function in time perspective. *Journal of African History* 10: 521–32.

Sands, Bonny 1998. *Eastern and Southern African Khoisan.* Evaluating claims of distant linguistic relationships. Quellen zur Khoisan-Forschung, 14. Cologne: Köppe.

Sankoff, David, Shana Poplack and Swathi Vanniarajan 1991. The empirical study of code-switching. *European Science Foundation. Network on Code-Switching and Language Contact. Papers for the Symposium on Code-Switching in Bilingual Studies: Theory, Significance and Perspectives. Barcelona, March 21–23.* Vol. I. Pp. 181–206.

Sapir, Edward 1921. *Language.* New York: Harcourt, Brace & World.

1963. Time perspective in aboriginal American culture. In: Mandelbaum (ed.) 1963. Pp. 432–62.

Sapir, J. David 1965. *A Grammar of Diola-Fogny: A Language Spoken in the Basse-Casamance Region of Senegal.* Cambridge: Cambridge University Press.

1971. West Atlantic. In: Sebeok (ed.) 1971. Pp. 45–112.

Sasse, Hans-Jürgen 1979. The consonant phonemes of Proto-East Cushitic (PEC): a first approximation. *Afroasiatic Linguistics* 7.1: 1–67.

1984. Case in Cushitic, Semitic and Berber. In: Bynon (ed.) 1984. Pp. 111–26.

1994. The pragmatics of noun incorporation in Eastern Cushitic languages. In: Plank (ed.) 1994. Pp. 243–68.

Satzinger, Helmut 1997. Egyptian in the Afroasiatic frame: recent Egyptological issues with an impact on comparative studies. In: Bausi and Tosco (eds.) 1997. Pp. 27–48.

Saxon, Douglas 1982. Linguistic evidence for the eastward spread of Ubangian peoples. In: Ehret and Posnansky (eds.) 1982. Pp. 66–77.

Schachter, Paul 1974. A non-transformational account of serial verbs. *Studies in African Linguistics*, supplement 5: 253–70.

Schadeberg, Thilo C. 1981a. *A Survey of Kordofanian*. Vol. I, *The Heiban Group*. Hamburg: Buske.

1981b. *A Survey of Kordofanian*. Vol. II, *The Talodi Group*. Hamburg: Buske.

1981c. The classification of the Kadugli language group. In: Schadeberg and Bender (eds.) 1981. Pp. 292–306.

1994. Comparative Kadu wordlists. *Afrikanistische Arbeitspapiere* 40: 11–48.

Schadeberg, Thilo C. and M. Lionel Bender (eds.) 1981. *Nilo-Saharan: Proceedings of the 1st Nilo-Saharan Linguistics Colloquium, Leiden, 1980*. Dordrecht: Foris.

Schadeberg, Thilo C. and Philip Elias 1979. *A Description of the Orig Language*. Tervuren: Musée Royale de l'Afrique Centrale.

Schaefer, Ronald P. and Richard Gaines 1997. Toward a typology of directional motion for African languages. *Studies in African Linguistics* 26: 193–220.

Schapera, Isaac 1930. *The Khoisan Peoples of South Africa*. Bushmen and Hottentots. London: Routledge & Kegan Paul.

Schaub, Willi 1985. *Babungo*. London: Croom Helm.

Schladt, Mathias (ed.) 1998. *Language, Identity, and Conceptualization Among the Khoisan*. Quellen zur Khoisan-Forschung, 15. Cologne: Köppe.

Schlözer, Ludwig von 1781. *Repertoire für Biblische und Morgenländische Literatur* VIII:161.

Schneider, Harold K. 1981. *The Africans: An Ethnological Account*. Englewood Cliffs: Prentice-Hall.

Schuh, Russel G. 1976. The Chadic verbal system and its Afroasiatic nature. *Afroasiatic Linguistics* 3.1: 1–14.

Schuh, Russel G. and L. D. Yalwa 1993. Hausa. *Journal of the International Phonetic Association* 23: 77–82.

Schultze, Leonhardt 1928. *Zur Kenntnis des Körpers der Hottentotten und Buschmänner*. Jena: G. Fischer.

Schuring, G. K. 1985. *Kosmopolitiese omgangstale*. Pretoria: Human Science Research Council.

Sebeok, Thomas A. (ed.) 1971. *Linguistics in Sub-Saharan Africa*. Current Trends in Linguistics, 7. The Hague and Paris: Mouton.

Segert, Stanislav and András J. E. Bodrogligeti (eds.) 1983. *Ethiopian Studies: Dedicated to Wolf Leslau*. Wiesbaden: Harrassowicz.

Selkirk, Elisabeth 1986. On derived domains in sentence phonology. *Phonology* 3: 371–405.

Sethe, Kurt 1899–1902. *Das ägyptische Verbum*. Leipzig: Hinrichs.

Shaw, Thurstan 1978/9. Holocene adaptations in West Africa: the late Stone Age. *Early Man News* 3/4.

Shaw, Thurstan, Paul Sinclair, Bassey Andah and Alex Okpoko (eds.) 1993. *Archaeology of Africa: Foods, Metals and Towns*. London and New York: Routledge.

Shimizu, Kiyoshi 1975. A lexicostatistical study of Plateau languages and Jukun. *Anthropological Linguistics* 17: 13–18.

Shopen, Timothy (ed.) 1985a. *Language Typology and Syntactic Description*. Vol. I, *Clause Structure*. Cambridge: Cambridge University Press.

1985b. *Language Typology and Syntactic Description*. Vol. II, *Complex Constructions*. Cambridge: Cambridge University Press.

1985c. *Language Typology and Syntactic Description*. Vol. III, *Grammatical Categories and the Lexicon*. Cambridge: Cambridge University Press.

in press. *Language Typology and Syntactic Description*. Cambridge: Cambridge University Press.

Slabbert, Sarah 1994. A re-evaluation of the sociology of Tsotsitaal. *South African Journal of Linguistics* 12: 31–41.

Smieja, Birgit and Meike Tasch (eds.) 1997. *Human Contact Through Language and Linguistics*. Duisburger Arbeiten zur Sprach- und Kulturwissenschaft, 31. Frankfurt-on-Main: Lang.

Snyman, Jan W. 1970. *An Introduction to the !Xũ (!Kung) Language*. Communications of the School of African Studies, University of Cape Town, 34. Cape Town: A. A. Balkema.

1974. The Bushman and Hottentot languages of southern Africa. *Limi* 2.2: 28–44.

Snyman, Jan W. (ed.) 1980. *Bushman and Hottentot Linguistic Studies*. Miscellanea Congregalia, 16. Pretoria: University of South Africa.

Spencer, Andrew and Arnold M. Zwicky (eds.) 1998. *The Handbook of Morphology*. Oxford: Blackwell.

Spencer, Robert F. (ed.) 1954. *Method and Perspective in Anthropology: Papers in Honor of Wilson D. Wallis*. Minneapolis: University of Minnesota Press.

Staden, P. von (ed.) 1993. *Linguistica – Festschrift E. B. van Wyk*. Pretoria: J. L. van Schaik.

Stahlke, Herbert F. 1970. Serial verbs. *Studies in African Linguistics* 1: 60–99.

1974. Serial verbs as adverbs: a reply to Paul Schachter. *Studies in African Linguistics*, supplement 5: 271–7.

Stallcup, Kenneth L. 1980. Noun classes in Esimbi. In: Hyman (ed.) 1980. Pp. 139–53.

Stevenson, Roland n.d. Kordofanian Comparative Wordlists. Typescript.

Stewart, John M. 1967. Tongue root position in Akan vowel harmony. *Phonetica* 16: 185–204.

1973. The lenis stops of the Potou Lagoon languages and their significance for pre-Bantu reconstruction. In: Kropp-Dakubu (ed.) 1973. Pp. 1–49.

1989. Kwa. In: Bendor-Samuel (ed.) 1989. Pp. 217–45.

1993. The second Tano consonant shift and its likeness to Grimm's Law. *Journal of West African Languages* 23: 3–39.

1994. The comparative phonology of Gbe and its significance for that of Kwa and Volta-Congo. *Journal of African Languages and Linguistics* 15: 175–93.

1998. An explanation of Bantu vowel height harmony in terms of a pre-Bantu nasalized vowel lowering. Paper presented at the 28th Colloquium on African Languages, Leiden.

Sutton, J. E. G. (ed.) 1996. *The Growth of Farming Communities in Africa from the Equator Southwards*. Nairobi: British Institute in Eastern Africa.

Talmy, Leonard 1985. Lexicalization patterns: Semantic structure in lexical forms. In: Shopen (ed.) 1985c. Pp. 57–149.

Tellier, Christine 1989. Head internal relatives and parasitic gaps in Mooré. In: Haïk and Tuller (eds.) 1989. Pp. 298–318.

Thomason, Sarah Grey and Terrence Kaufman 1988. *Language Contact, Creolization, and Genetic Linguistics*. Berkeley: University of California Press.

Thompson, Sandra A. and Robert E. Longacre 1985. Adverbial clauses. In: Shopen (ed.) 1985b. Pp. 171–243.

Thwing, Rhonda and John R. Watters 1987. Focus in Vute. *Journal of African Languages and Linguistics* 9: 95–121.

Todd, Loreto 1974. *Pidgins and Creoles*. London: Routledge & Kegan Paul.

Tosco, Mauro 1993. The historical syntax of East Cushitic: a first sketch. In: Bearth *et al.* (eds.) 1993. Pp. 415–40.

Traill, Anthony 1974a. Agreement systems in !xõ. *Limi* 2.2: 12–27.

1974b. *The Compleat Guide to the Koon*. African Studies Institute Communications, 1. Johannesburg: University of the Witwatersrand.

1975. Phonetic correspondences in the !Xõ dialects: how a Bushman language changes. In: Traill (ed.) 1975. Pp. 77–102.

1980. Phonetic diversity in the Khoisan languages. In: Snyman (ed.) 1980. Pp. 167–89.

1985. *Phonetic and Phonological Studies of !Xóõ Bushman*. Quellen zur Khoisan-Forschung, 1. Hamburg: Buske.

1986. Do the Khoi have a place in the San? New data on Khoisan linguistic relationships. *Sprache und Geschichte in Afrika* 7.1: 407–30.

1993. The feature geometry of clicks. In: von Staden (ed.) 1993. Pp. 134–40.

1994. *A !Xóõ Dictionary*. Quellen zur Khoisan-Forschung, 9. Cologne: Köppe.

1995. Place of articulation features for clicks: anomalies for universals. In: Windsor-Lewis (ed.) 1995. Pp. 121–9.

1997. Linguistic phonetic features for clicks. In: Herbert (ed.) 1997. Pp. 99–117.

Traill, Anthony (ed.) 1975. *Bushman and Hottentot Linguistic Studies*. African Studies Institute Communications, 2. Johannesburg: University of the Witwatersrand.

1977. *Khoisan Linguistic Studies 3*. African Studies Institute Communications, 6. Johannesburg: University of the Witwatersrand.

Traill, Anthony and Rainer Vossen 1997. Sound change in the Khoisan languages: new data on click loss and click replacement. *Journal of African Languages and Linguistics* 18.1: 21–56.

Tucker, A. N. 1940. *The Eastern Sudanic Languages*. Vol. 1, London: Dawsons.

Tucker, A. N. and M. A. Bryan. 1956. *The Non-Bantu Languages of North-Eastern Africa*. Oxford: Oxford University Press.

1966. *Linguistic Analyses: The Non-Bantu Languages of North-Eastern Africa*. London: Oxford University Press.

Tucker, A. N. and J. Tompo ole Mpaayei 1955. *A Maasai Grammar with Vocabulary*. London: Longmans & Green.

Ukoko, Joseph *et al.* 1964. *Proeve van Dho Alur-Woordenboek*. Gent: Rijksuniversiteit Gent.

UNESCO 1997. Working document prepared for the Intergovernmental Conference on Language Policies in Africa, in Harare (17–21 March 1997).

Unseth, Pete 1985. Gumuz dialect survey. *Journal of Ethiopian Studies* 18: 91–114.

1990. *Linguistic Bibliography of the Non-Nilo-Saharan Languages of Ethiopia*. East Lansing: African Studies Center, Michigan State University.

Valdman, Albert (ed.) 1977. *Pidgin and Creole Linguistics*. Bloomington: Indiana University Press.

Vansina, Jan 1990. *Paths in the Rainforests: Toward a History of Political Tradition in Equatorial Africa*. Madison: University of Wisconsin Press.

Vitale, Anthony J. 1981. *Swahili Syntax*. Dordrecht: Foris.

Voeltz, Erhard 1977. Proto-Niger-Congo verb extensions. Mimeograph.

Voogt, Alex J. de 1992. Some phonetic aspects of Hatsa and Sandawe clicks. M.A. thesis, University of Leiden.

Vossen, Rainer 1982. *The Eastern Nilotes: Linguistic and Historical Reconstructions*. Berlin: Reimer.

1985. Encoding the object in the finite verb: the case of ‖Ani (Central Khoisan). *Afrikanistische Arbeitspapiere* 4: 75–84.

1986. Some observations on nominal gender in Naro. In: Rottland (ed.) 1986. Pp. 373–90.

1992. *q* in Khoe: borrowing, substrate or innovation? In: Gowlett (ed.) 1992. Pp. 363–88.

1997a. *Die Khoe-Sprachen. Ein Beitrag zur Erforschung der Sprachgeschichte Afrikas.* Quellen zur Khoisan-Forschung, 12. Cologne: Köppe.

1997b. What click sounds got to do in Bantu. Reconstructing the history of language contacts in southern Africa. In: Smieja and Tasch (eds.) 1997. Pp. 353–66.

Vossen, Rainer (ed.) 1988. *New Perspectives on the Study of Khoisan.* Quellen zur Khoisan-Forschung, 7. Hamburg: Buske.

Wardhaugh, Ronald 1992. *An Introduction to Sociolinguistics.* 2nd edition. Oxford: Blackwell.

Watson, Richard L. 1997. OV word order in Ma'di? *Occasional Papers in Sudanic Linguistics* 7: 103–13. Nairobi: Summer Institute of Linguistics-Sudan.

Watters, John R. 1979. Focus in Aghem: a study of its formal correlates and typology. In: Hyman (ed.) 1979. Pp. 137–97.

1981. A phonology and morphology of Ejagham – with notes on dialect variation. Ph.D. dissertation, University of California at Los Angeles.

Webb, Vic 1998. *Language in South Africa: The Quest for a Future.* Pretoria: University of Pretoria Press.

Wedekind, Klaus 1972. An outline of the grammar of Busa (Nigeria). Roneotyped, Ph.D. dissertation, University of Kiel.

Weinreich, Uriel 1953. *Languages in Contact, Findings and Problems.* The Hague: Mouton.

1958. On the compatibility of genetic relationship and convergent development. *Word* 14: 374–9.

Weinstein, Brian 1980. Language planning in Francophone Africa. *Language Problems and Language Planning* 4.1: 55–77.

Welmers, William E. 1973. *African Language Structures.* Berkeley: University of California Press.

Welmers, William E. and Bee F. Welmers 1968. *Igbo: A Learner's Dictionary.* Los Angeles: University of California, African Studies Center.

Wendorf, Fred and R. Schild 1998. Nabta Playa and its role in northeastern African history. *Anthropological Archaeology* 20: 97–123.

Wendorf, Fred, R. Schild and Angela E. Close 1984. *Cattle Keepers of the Eastern Sahara: The Neolithic of Bir Kiseiba.* Dallas: Southern Methodist University Press.

Werner, Heinrich 1994. *Das Klassensystem in den Jenissej-Sprachen.* Veröffentlichungen der Societas Uralo-Altaica, 40. Wiesbaden: Harrassowitz.

Westermann, Diedrich 1911. *Die Sudansprachen.* Hamburg: Friederichsen.

1927. *Die westlichen Sudansprachen und ihrer Beziehungen zum Bantu.* Hamburg: Reimer.

1930. *A Study of the Ewe Language.* London: Oxford University Press.

Westermann, Diedrich and M. A. Bryan 1952. *The Languages of West Africa.* Handbook of African Languages, part 2. London: Oxford University Press for the International African Institute.

Westermann, Diedrich and Ida C. Ward 1933. *Practical Phonetics for Students of African Languages.* London: Kegan Paul.

Westphal, Ernst O. J. 1962. On classifying Bushman and Hottentot languages. *African Language Studies* 3: 30–48.

1971. The click languages of southern and eastern Africa. In: Sebeok (ed.) 1971. Pp. 367–420.

n.d. Unpublished field notes on Kwadi. African Studies Archive, University of Cape Town.

Wetzels, Leo and Engin Sezer (eds.) 1986. *Studies in Compensatory Lengthening.* Dordrecht: Foris.

Whiteley, W. H. (ed.) 1974. *Language in Kenya.* Nairobi: Oxford University Press.

Wiesemann, Ursula (ed.) 1986. *Pronominal Systems.* Tübingen: Gunter Narr.

Will, Hans-Georg 1998. The Me'en verb system: does Me'en have tenses? In: Dimmendaal and Last (eds.) 1998. Pp. 437–58.

Williamson, Kay 1973. More on nasals and nasalization in Kwa. *Studies in African Linguistics* 4: 115–38.

1989a. Linguistic evidence for the prehistory of the Niger Delta. In: Alagoa *et al.* (eds.) 1989. Pp. 65–119.

1989b. Niger-Congo overview. In: Bendor-Samuel (ed.) 1989. Pp. 1–45.

1993. Linguistic evidence for the use of some tree and tuber food plants in southern Nigeria. In: Shaw *et al.* (eds.) 1993. Pp. 139–53.

in prep. *Comparative Ijoid.*

Wilson, W. A. A. 1989. Atlantic. In: Bendor-Samuel (ed.) 1989. Pp. 81–104.

Windsor-Lewis, Jack (ed.) 1995. *Studies in General and English Phonetics.* Essays in honour of J. D. O'Connor. London: Routledge.

Winter, Jürgen Christoph 1981. Die Khoisan-Familie. In: Heine, Schadeberg and Wolff (eds.) 1981. Pp. 329–74.

Wolff, H. Ekkehard 1977. Patterns in Chadic (and Afroasiatic?) verb base formations. In: Newman and Newman (eds.) 1977. Pp. 199–233.

1979a. Grammatical categories of verb stems and the marking of mood, aktionsart, and aspect in Chadic. *Afroasiatic Linguistics* 6.5: 1–48.

1979b. Sprachkontakt und Ethnizität: Sprachsoziologische Anmerkungen zum Problem der historischen Interpretierbarkeit genetischer Sprachbeziehungen. *Sprache und Geschichte in Afrika* 1: 143–73.

1983. *A Grammar of the Lamang Language (GwàdLàmàŋ).* Glückstadt: J. J. Augustin.

1999. Language and society in Africa. An introduction to African sociolinguistics. Unpublished ms.

Wolff, H. Ekkehard (ed.) in press. *Proceedings of the 2nd World Congress of African Linguistics, Leipzig.*

Wolff, H. Ekkehard and Ousseina Alidou in press. On the non-linear ancestry of Tasawaq (Niger). Or: how 'mixed' can a language be? *Sprache und Geschichte in Afrika,* 16. Special issue: Historical Language Contact in Africa, ed. Derek Nurse.

Wolff, H. Ekkehard and Hilke Meyer-Bahlburg (eds.) 1983. *Studies in Chadic and Afroasiatic Linguistics.* Hamburg: Buske.

Zaborski, Andrzej 1975. *The Verb in Cushitic.* Studies in Hamito-Semitic, 1. Cracow: Nakladem Uniwersytetu Jagiello´nskiego.

1976. The Semitic external plural in an Afroasiatic perspective. *Afroasiatic Linguistics* 3.6: 1–9.

1984. Remarks on the genetic classification and the relative chronology of the Cushitic languages. In: Bynon (ed.) 1984. Pp. 125–38.

1986a. Can Omotic be reclassified as West Cushitic? In: Goldenberg (ed.) 1986. Pp. 525–9.

1986b. *The Morphology of Nominal Plural in the Cushitic Languages.* Beiträge zur Afrikanistik, 28. Wien: Afro-Pub.

1990. Preliminary remarks on case morphemes in Omotic. In: Hayward (ed.) 1990. Pp. 617–29.

1997. The position of Cushitic and Berber within Hamitosemitic dialects. In: Bausi and Tosco (eds.) 1997. Pp. 49–59.

Zima, Petr 1974. Types of standard language development in sub-Saharan Africa. In: Černy *et al.* (eds.) 1974. Pp. 13–44.

INDEX OF AUTHORS

Ahmed, Christine Choi 287
Aikhenvald, Alexandra Y. 169, 171, 186, 187
Albright, William F. 84
Alexandre, Pierre 3
Ali, Mohamed Nuuh 279–81
Alidou, Ousseina 332
Allan, Edward J. 97
Amha, Azeb 185
Ambrose, Stanley 287
Andersen, Torben 72, 144, 147, 176, 177, 180, 191, 197
Anderson, Stephen R. 193, 206
Ansre, Gilbert 336
Anttila, Raimo 72
Applegate, Joseph R. 96
Appleyard, David L. 88, 89, 97
Archangeli, Diana 160, 188
Argyle, John W. 102
Armstrong, Robert G. 294
Aronoff, Mark 193
Arvanites, Linda 85
Austin, J. L. 343
Awobuluyi, Oladele A. 220
Ayre, Malik A. 73

Badjimé, Mamadou 153
Bakker, Peter 332
Baldi, Sergio 270
Bamgboṣe, Ayọ 220, 221, 301, 305, 306, 343, 346
Banti, Giorgio 90
Barnard, Alan 104
Barreteau, Daniel 27
Basset, André 76
Bastin, Yvonne 35, 185

Batibo, Herman M. 104
Beach, Douglas M. 104
Bearth, Thomas 170, 229, 258
Bender, Lionel M. 3, 4, 9, 43, 48, 50, 52, 54, 57, 63, 68, 72, 82, 85, 86, 90, 206, 219, 229, 230, 296
Bendor-Samuel, John 3, 16, 23, 34, 42, 160, 201, 230, 293
Bennett, Patrick R. 16, 17, 27, 28, 30, 34
Bergslund, Knut 296
Berry, Jack 3
Bertho, Jacques 23
Bickerton, Derek 329, 330
Bird, Charles 22
Black, Paul 85
Blanchon, Jean Alain 234
Bleek, Wilhelm Heinrich Immanuel 14, 101, 113
Blench, Roger M. 4, 17, 27, 30, 31, 32, 34, 57, 281, 297
Blevins, Juliet 139, 144
Bliese, Loren 226
Bloomfield, Leonard 271
Bole-Richard, Rémy 29, 30, 132, 133, 159
Booij, Geert 173
Boyd, Raymond 18, 27
Boyeldieu, Pascal 36, 60, 207
Breedveld, Anneke 189, 190
Brenzinger, Matthias 6, 320
Bresnan, Joan 169, 212
Brusciotto, Giacinto 123
Bryan, Margaret A. 53, 56, 58, 61, 64, 72, 198, 199, 261
Bybee, Joan C. 185
Bynon, James 85
Bynon-Polak, Louise 182

Cahill, Mike 229
Callender, John 89
Capo, Hounkpati B. C. 30
Cardinall, A. W. 36
Caron, Bernard 197, 204
Carlson, Robert 198, 199, 204
Carstairs-McCarthy, Andrew 193
Casali, Rod 229
Castellino, Giorgio R. 94
Cave, G. N. 346
Cerulli, Enrico 306
Childs, Tucker 39
Chomsky, Noam 124
Clark, Mary M. 160
Claudi, Ulrike 10, 39, 241, 258, 267
Clements, George N. 4, 7, 124, 126, 136, 138, 144, 160, 166, 188, 192
Cloarec-Heiss, France 168, 202, 203, 208
Cobarrubias, J. 341
Cohen, Marcel 85
Cole, Desmond T. 123
Collins, Chris 112, 113
Comrie, Bernard 176, 193, 229, 230, 258
Connell, Bruce 30, 33, 34, 42, 129
Cook, Thomas 33
Cooper, Robert L. 346
Corbett, Greville 242
Coupez, André 35
Crabb, David W. 33
Crazzolara, J. P. 208
Creider, Chet A. 158, 198, 230
Creissels, Denis 4, 16, 36, 55, 133, 147, 160, 164, 180, 184, 230, 239
Crozier, David H. 27
Crystal, David 326, 328
Cust, Robert N. 84
Cyffer, Norbert 72

Dalgish, Gerard M. 250
Daniels, Peter T. 82
Delafosse, Maurice 27, 85
Dell, François 134
Delplanque, Alain 189, 190
Demolin, Didier 131
Demuth, Katherine 189
Diakonoff, Igor M. 75, 77, 87, 90, 91, 93, 95, 97
Dickens, Patrick 109, 111, 112, 121
Dimmendaal, Gerrit J. 4, 73, 158, 175, 186, 190, 193, 200, 214, 217, 229, 252, 258
Dixon, R. M. W. 4, 186, 187
Dolgopolsky, Aharon B. 85
Donneux, Jean L. 21, 22, 37, 40
Doornbos, Paul 55
Dressler, Wolfgang U. 193

Dubinsky, Stanley 213
Duranti, Alessandro 236
Durie, Mark 185
Dwyer, David J. 18, 20

Edgar, John 72
Egner, Inge 229
Ehret, Christopher 3, 4, 8, 9, 54, 57, 85, 86, 87, 93, 94, 95, 96, 97, 98, 102, 276, 279, 295
Elderkin, Edward D. 118, 119
Elias, Philip 41
Elmedlaoui, Mohamed 134
Elugbe, Ben O. 134
Embleton, Sheila 287, 296
Erman, Adolf 84

Faber, Alice 96
Faraclas, Nicholas 33, 239
Farb, Peter 306
Feinen, Monika 10
Ferguson, Charles A. 79, 322
Finlayson, Rosalie 305
Fivaz, Derek 229
Fleming, Harold C. 85, 86
Frajzyngier, Zygmunt 225, 246, 258, 267

Gaines, Richard 192
Gal, Susan 317
Gensler, Orin 241
Gerhardt, Ludwig 30, 31, 32
George, Isaac 220
Gilley, Leoma G. 134, 143, 144, 229
Givón, Talmy 200, 230, 239, 241, 267
Goodman, Morris 55
Goldsmith, John A. 124, 139, 153, 155, 160
Grandouiller, Christian 211
Greenberg, Joseph H. 3, 5, 7, 9, 15, 16, 17, 18, 24, 27, 28, 29, 30, 31, 33, 34, 39, 43, 50, 55, 56, 58, 59, 64, 72, 74, 85, 86, 91, 92, 94, 98, 99, 101, 123, 130, 177, 193, 230, 244, 260, 271, 294
Gregersen, Edgar 3, 16, 57, 230, 262
Grimes, Barbara F. 1, 4, 11, 27, 28, 31, 43, 50, 51, 71, 79, 76, 96
Grinevald, Colette 258
Gruber, Jeffrey S. 111, 112, 121
Güldemann, Tom 4, 106, 108, 198, 229, 258
Guthrie, Malcom 34, 35, 38, 271
Gutt, Eeva H. M. 198, 203, 211, 219, 224, 229
Gutt, Ernst-August 229

Haacke, Wilfrid H. G. 172, 178
Hagman, Roy S. 115

Halle, Morris 124, 126, 132, 160
Haller, Beat 212
Hayward, K. M. 128
Hayward, Richard J. 4, 89, 90, 94, 97, 128
Heath, Jeffrey 176
Hedinger, Robert 229
Heine, Bernd 3, 10, 13, 30, 40, 42, 58, 59, 72, 76, 85, 108, 159, 189, 192, 197, 222, 229, 230, 241, 248, 250, 251, 258, 267, 270, 308
Heikkinen, Terttu 110
Hérault, Georges 30
Herbert, Robert K. 147
Hetzron, Robert 78, 85, 86, 87, 88, 91, 271
Hinnebusch, Thomas J. 189
Hinton, Leanne 183
Hockett, Charles F. 183
Hodge, Carlton T. 75, 93
Hoenigswald, Henry M. 271
Hoffmann, Carl 137, 188
Hoijer, Harry 271
Honken, Henry 107
Houis, Maurice 231
Hudson, Grover 160
Hünnemeyer, Friederike 10
Huttar, George 229
Hyman, Larry M. 140, 144, 159, 160, 193, 195, 208, 220, 227, 236, 239, 241

Ibriszimow, Dymitr 85
Ikoro, Suanu 178, 190, 241
Isserlin, Benedikt S. J. 95

Jakobi, Angelika 72, 73
Jarvis, Elisabeth 241
Jenewari, Charles E. W. 22
Johnston, Sir Harry 53
Jungraithmayr, Herrmann 85, 91, 93, 97

Kagaya, Ryohai 119
Kastenholz, Raimund 18, 19
Katamba, Francis 188, 193
Kaufman, Terrence 271, 332, 344
Kaye, Jonathan 159
Keenan, Edward L. 210, 225
Kenstowicz, Michael 124, 160
Keyser, S. K. 144
Khamis, Cornelia 318, 345
Kidima, Lukowa 236
Kleinewillinghöfer, Ulrich 27
Klieman, Kairn A. 281, 294
Klingenheben, August 90, 94, 268
Kisseberth, Charles 160
Koch, Harold 175

Köhler, Oswin 53, 111
Koelle, Sigismund Wilhelm 14, 19, 20
Köhler, Oswin 101, 102, 106, 115
Kompaore, Anne 227, 229
Konter-Katani, Maggy 192
Koopman, Hilda 199, 205
Kraft, Charles H. 207
Kraft, Marguerite G. 207
Krause, Gottlieb A. 25, 28, 34
Kümmerle, Tanja 73
Kury ł owicz, Jerzy 271
Kutsch Lojenga, Constance 174, 196

Lackner, Jerome A. 271
Ladefoged, Peter 36, 106, 131, 133, 137, 138, 159, 160
Lafage, Philippe 29, 30
Lamberti, Marcello 86, 89, 90, 97
Last, Marco 73
Leben, Will R. 142
Lepsius, Richard 53, 84, 101
Leynseele, Helene van 220
Lindau, Mona 36, 133, 137
Link, Christa 170
Lloret, Maria-Rosa 213
Lloyd, Lucy C. 113
Longacre, Robert E. 197, 219, 222, 223, 224, 241
Loprieno, Antonio 89, 91, 96
Lord, Carol 185, 241, 248
Lottner, C. 84
Louali, Naima 96
Ludolph, Hiob 83

Ma, Roxana 85
Maddieson, Ian 133, 150, 159, 160
Madugu, Omen N. 183
Manessy, Gabriel 25, 26, 39, 40
Manfredi, Victor 220
Mann, Michael 35
Marchese, Lynelle, 24, 199, 210
Martin, Phyllis M. 72
Masica, Colin P. 184
Mason, Ruth 229
Matthews, Peter H. 178, 193
McCarthy, John J. 129, 178
Mchombo, Sam A. 169, 211, 212
McIntyre, Joseph A. 181
McWhorter, John 9
Meeussen, A. M. 40, 164, 170, 180, 186
Meinhof, Carl 14, 53, 57, 58, 84, 148, 149, 260, 268
Mel'čuk, Igor 193
Militariev, A. Yu. 95
Miller, Catherine 96
Mithun, Marianne 169

Moñino, Yves 27
Moravcsik, Edith 167
Morgan, David 206, 229
Morolong, Malillo 236
Mous, Maarten 96, 332
Mpaayei, J. Tompo ole 172, 187
Mukarovsky, Hans 15, 37, 42, 55, 165
Müller, Friedrich 101
Munson, Patrick 290
Murdock, George Peter 48, 72
Mussa, Hussein Mohammed 198, 203, 211, 219, 224
Mutaka, Ngessimo 193
Myers-Scotton *see* Scotton, Carol

Naden, Tony 26
Newman, Paul 4, 8, 13, 77, 85, 87, 90, 94, 96, 97, 98, 142, 147, 148, 159, 160, 165, 167, 169, 192, 207, 213, 229, 247, 258, 262, 271
Nichols, Johanna 183, 187
Nicolai, Robert 54, 72
Nicole, Jacques 211, 218, 229
Nida, Eugene 193
Nketia, J. H. Kwabena 306
Noonan, Michael 174, 223
Nougayrol, Pierre 198, 200, 218
Novelli, Bruno 174
Nsuka Nkutsi, François 227
Nurse, Derek 34, 42, 159, 181, 189, 192, 229, 258, 271, 332
Nyombe, Bureng G. V. 197, 198, 199

Odden, David 144, 158, 160
Ohala, John J. 183
Ohiri-Aniche, Chinyere 30
Okombo, Okoth 229
Olson, Ken 229
O'Meara, Patrick 72
Orel, Vladimir E. 85, 86, 94, 95, 96, 98

Painter, Colin 137
Paradis, Carole 160
Pasch, Helma 170, 241
Payne, Doris 174
Payne, John P. 208
Perrin, Mona J. 205, 216
Petracek, Karel 55
Pike, Kenneth L. 38
Piron, Pasquale 34, 35
Postel, Guillaume 83
Poplack, Shana 346
Praetorious, Franz 97
Prost, André 26, 39
Pulleyblank, Douglas 160, 188
Pumphrey, M. E. C. 306

Reh, Mechthild 10, 73, 252, 267, 306
Renan, Ernest 84
Rialland, Annie 153, 155, 159
Robert, Stephanie 239
Robins, R. H. 184
Ross, Malcolm D. 17, 42
Rössler, Otto 90
Rottland, Franz 73
Rowe, John H. 271
Ruhlen, Merrit 52, 53, 72, 102

Sagey, Elisabeth 126, 152, 159, 160
Samarin, William 27
Sanders, Edith R. 260
Sands, Bonny 102
Sankoff, David 346
Sapir, Edward 177, 193, 271
Sapir, J. David 21, 135, 165
Sasse, Hansjürgen 85, 88, 169
Satzinger, Helmut 89
Saxon, Douglas 294
Schachter, Paul 220
Schadeberg, Thilo C. 17, 40, 41, 73, 159
Schaefer, Ronald P. 192
Schapera, Isaac 102
Schaub, Willi 196, 210, 213, 222
Schild, R. 285, 288
Schlözer, Ludwig von 83
Schneider, Harold K. 48, 72
Schuh, Russel G. 90, 91, 97
Scotton (Myers-Scotton), Carol 317, 345
Searle, J. R. 343
Selkirk, Elisabeth 139
Sethe, Kurt 84
Shaw, Thurstan 294
Shimizu, Kiyoshi 30
Shnirelman, V. A. 95
Shopen, Timothy 193
Sim, Ronnie 229
Snyman, Jan 107, 111, 159
Soukka, Maria 205, 229
Stahlke, Herbert F. 220
Stallcup, Kenneth L. 39
Sterk, Jan P. 16, 28, 30
Stevenson, Roland C. 41
Stewart, John M. 16, 29, 30, 36, 37, 38, 42, 133, 134, 135, 137, 159
Stolbova, Olga V. 85, 86, 94, 95, 96, 98

Talmy, Leonard 191
Thomason, Sarah Grey 271, 332, 344
Thompson, Sandra A. 219, 222, 223, 224
Thwing, Rhonda 216

Todd, Loreto 329
Tosco, Mauro 241
Traill, Anthony 102, 105, 106, 107, 108,
    111, 112, 139, 150, 151, 159
Treis, Yvonne 10
Tucker, Archibald N. 53, 56, 58, 61, 72,
    73, 172, 187, 198, 199
Tsuge, Yoichi 89

Ukoko, Joseph 183
Unseth, Pete 48, 64, 72, 73, 229

Valette, Rene
Vanniarajan, Swathi 346
Vansina, Jan 281, 294, 295
Vitale, Anthony 197, 212, 226, 227
Voeltz, Erhard 10, 13, 26, 39, 42
Vogt, Hans 296
Voogt, Alex J. de 120
Vossen, Rainer 4, 73, 105, 107, 108, 113,
    114, 115, 159

Ward, Ida C. 160
Wardhaugh, Ronald 329
Watson, Richard L. 197, 229

Watters, John R. 4, 202, 205, 212, 215,
    216, 227, 239
Wedekind, Klaus 216, 229
Weinreich, Uriel 261
Weinstein, Brian 340
Welmers, Bee F. 206
Welmers, William E. 3, 53, 146, 160, 196,
    207, 230
Wendorf, Fred 285, 288
Westermann, Diedrich 14, 15, 16, 25, 37,
    39, 41, 52, 160, 191, 261
Westphal, Ernst O. J. 102, 119
White, Steve 210
Whiteley, W. H. 327
Wiesemann, Ursula 172
Will, Hans-Georg 175, 179
Williamson, Kay 4, 16, 22, 34, 38, 39, 139,
    159, 281, 294, 297
Wilson, W. A. A. 21, 22
Winter, Christoph 101
Wolff, H. Ekkehard 91, 178, 332

Zaborski, Andzrej 86, 89, 92, 98
Zima, Petr 347
Zwicky, Arnold 193

INDEX OF LANGUAGES

Aari 81, 91, 93, 94, 97
Abbey 29, 30
Abidji 29, 30
Abrako 24, 25
Abuan 33
Abure 29
Acoli *see* Acholi
Acholi (Acoli) 46, 51, 71
Adangme *see* Dangme
Adele 29
Adja *see* Aja
Adola 46, 71
Afar 80, 84, 89, 91, 92, 226
Afitti *see* Dinik
Afrikaans 1, 333, 339, 343, 346
Aghem 195, 205, 206, 215, 216
Agoi 33
Agwagwune 33
Ahan 31
Ahlo 29
Aiki 44, 66, 198, 200, 218
Aizi 24
Aja 45
Aja (Adja) 29
Ajukru (Adioukrou, Adjukru) 29, 30
Aka 46
Akaha (Akassa) 22
Akan 11, 29, 136, 137, 138, 146, 147, 221,
    340
Akassa *see* Akaha
Akita (Okordia) 22
Akkadian 78, 89, 90, 91, 92
Akokoid 31
Akpafu-Lolobi 29
Akpes 30, 31

Akposo *see* Kposo
Aku 326
Akuapem 340
Alege 33
Alladian 29
Alur 46, 71, 183
Ama (Nyimang) 45, 48
Amdang 44, 47, 55, 67
Amharic 80, 83, 93, 205, 234, 319, 324
Americo *see* Merico
Anaang 33
Anfillo 82
Angas 77
Animere 29
Anuak *see* Anywa
Anufɔ 29
Anum 29
Anyi 29
Anywa (Anuak) 46
Arabic 1, 76, 78, 79, 83, 90, 130, 158, 177,
    179, 189, 246, 269, 270, 293, 306, 312,
    322, 323, 324, 343, 346
Arabic, Classical 89, 127, 178, 321, 346
Aramaic 78, 79, 83
Arbore 81, 90, 91
Asante 340
Asax 81
Ashuku 158
Asmara Pidgin Italian 327
'Assyrian' 79
Asua 45
Attié 29
Atumfuor 20
Atuot 46
Avatime 29

Avikam 29
Avokaya 45
Awjilah 76
Awngi 80
Awutu 29
Ayere 31
Azer *see* Soninke

Ba (Kwa) 18, 28
Baan (Ogoi) 33
Babungo 196, 210, 213, 222
Bachama-Bata 77
Bade 77
Badha *see* Baledha
Bagirmi (Barma) 45
Baka 45
Bakwe 25
Balanta 21
Balé 45
Balese 45
Baledha (Badha, Lendu) 45, 51
Bambara (*see also* Manding) 11, 20,
    153–7, 158, 226, 248, 255
Bambassi 82
Bamileke 138, 158
Bamum 347
Banda 28, 168
Bandi (Gbande) 20
Baŋeri mɛ 23
Banna 81
Banyun 21
Barea *see* Nera
Bari 46, 59, 64
Barikanci 327
Barma *see* Bagirmi
Barracon 328
Basa 32
Basila 29
Basketto 82
Bassa 25
Bassari 21
Baule 29
Baushi 32
Bayso 81
Bedawi *see* Beja
Bedik 21
Bedjond 45
Bedi 158
Beja (Bedawi) 80, 84, 86, 91, 92, 98, 128,
    285
Beli 47
Bemba 160
Bench 82, 128
Bendi 31, 33, 45
Beng (Gan) 20
Beni Sheko 46

Berber 44, 54, 59, 75, 76–7, 84, 88, 89, 90,
    94, 97, 130, 134, 263, 269, 290, 291,
    292, 346
Bɛrɛ (Pre) 36
Beromic 31, 32
Berta (Wetawit) 45, 47, 51, 52, 53, 54, 55,
    59, 60, 68, 72
Berti 44, 68, 283, 286
Beygo 46
Biafada 21
Bideyat 44
Bijago 21
Bikwin 18, 28
Bilala 45
Bilin 80
Biltiné 64
Binga 45
Biralé *see* Ongota
Birgid 45
Birom 125
Bisa (*see also* Busa) 20
Bobo (Bɔbɔ, Sya) 20, 21, 158
Bodi 45
Boghom 77
Bokyi 33
Bole (Bolanci) 77, 147, 148, 264
Bondum dom 23
Bongo 45, 51, 64
Boni (Awera) 81
Bor 46
Bora-Mabang 44
Boro 81
Bowiri (Bowili) 29
Bua 28
Buduma 77
Buga 102, 103, 114, 115, 116, 117
Buli-Konni 26
Bumaji 33
Bura 77, 265
Bura-Mabang *see* Bora-Mabang
Burji 80
Burmana 32
Burunge 81
Busa (Bisa, Boko) 20, 216
Bwamu 26
B'eli 45

Cameroon Pidgin English 327
Cangin 21
Cape Verde Creole 326
Chaha 80
Chamba Daka 34
Cherepong 29
Chewa (Chichewa) 169, 211, 212
Chichewa *see* Chewa
Chinese 176

Cipu 32
Colo *see* Shilluk
Coptic 78, 98, 347
Crioulo 327

Daasenech (Dasenech) 81
Daba 77
Dagba 45
Dahalo (Sanye) 81, 131, 150, 276
Dair 45
Daisu 332
Daju 46, 51, 285
Damara (*see also* Khoekhoe) 102, 104
Dan (Yakuba, Gio) 20, 158
Dangaleat 78
Dangme (Adangme) 29
Danish 337
Danisi 102, 116
Dasenech *see* Daasenech
Datooga (Tatoga) 46, 59
Day 18, 28
Defaka 18, 22
Degema 133
Demotic 78, 347
Dendi 44, 61
Dengebu 19
Deti 102, 114, 115
Dida 25
Didinga 45, 285
Dillinj 45
Dime 81
Dinik (Afitti) 45, 48
Dinka (Jieng) 46, 51, 137, 144, 176–7, 191
Diola 21, 125, 135, 136, 137
Dizi 81, 97
Dodoth 46
Dogon 16, 23, 24, 25, 37, 39
Dogose 26
Dogul dom 23
Doko 33
Dongola(wi) 45, 61, 63, 283
'Dongo-ko 170, 241
Doni 46
Duleri dom 23
Dullay 80, 81, 169
Duru 28
Dutch 264
Dyan 26
Dyula (*see also* Manding) 11, 20
Dzuun (Samogo-Guan) 20

Ebang (Heiban) 19
Ebrié 29, 38, 132, 133
Ebughu 33
Edo (Edoid) 31, 134
Edoid *see* Edo

Efai 33
Efe 45
Efik 33, 223
Efutu 29
Ega 29, 30
Ẹgẹnẹ *see* Engenni
Eggon 148, 150
Egyptian 75, 76, 84, 88, 90, 96, 97, 252, 263, 290, 291, 347
Ehom 33
Ejagham 196, 201, 202, 204, 213, 215, 219, 223, 230
Ejẹŋge dõ, 23
Ekit 33
Ekoid 35
Eleme 33
Elwana (Ilwana) 181, 332
Endo-Marakwet 46
Engenni (Ẹgẹnẹ) 140
English 1, 168, 178, 209, 229, 263, 264, 270, 312, 319, 321, 322, 343
Enwang 33
Eotilé 29
Erenga 45
Esimbi 39
Etsako 134
Ewe (*see also* Gbe) 14, 29, 127, 160, 167, 175, 191, 334, 335, 336
Ewondo 327
Ewondo Populaire 327

Fali 18, 28
Fanagalo (Fanakalo) 314, 327
Fang 139
Fante (*see also* Akan) 146, 340
Fer (Kara) 45, 207
Fe'fe' (*see also* Bamileke) 158, 219, 220
Fon 10, 29
Fongoro 45
For *see* Fur
French 1, 138, 303, 305, 312, 321, 322, 323, 341, 343
Fula *see* Fulfulde
Fulani *see* Fulfulde
Fulfulde (Fula, Fulani, Peul, Pulaar) 11, 15, 21, 42, 57, 85, 133, 165, 189, 190, 210, 271, 320, 347
Fur (For) 44, 51, 52, 54, 55, 58, 61, 65, 67, 72, 282, 285, 286, 340
Furu 45

Ga 29
Gaam (Ingessana, Tabi) 46, 47, 48, 53, 61
Gafat 80
Galgaliya 327
'Galla' *see* Oromo

Gamo 82, 90, 93, 94
Gan (*see also* Beng) 20
Ganda (Luganda) 11, 141, 143, 144, 145,
    147, 159
Gao *see* Zerma
'Gawwada' 81
Ga'anda 264
Gbande *see* Bandi
Gbaya 28
Gbe (*see also* Ewe) 10, 27, 30, 139, 146,
    147, 149, 158
Gbeya 127
Gen 29
German 263, 305
Ge'ez *see* Gi'iz
Ghotuọ 134
Gidar 77
Gikuyu 11, 158, 268, 278
Gimira 82, 89, 97, 128, 158
Gio *see* Dan
Gi'iz (Ge'ez, Gǝ'ǝz) 80, 83, 92, 319, 321, 347
Glavda 332
Godie 25, 224
Goemai 131
Gofa 82
Gokana 33, 144
Gola 21
Gonga (*see also* Shinasha) 89, 91
Gorowa 81
Grebo 25, 158
Greek 176, 337
Grusi (Tem) 26
Guanche 77
Guang 29, 36
Guere 25
Gula 45
Gulay 45
Gulé 46, 48, 66, 69, 70
Gulfan 45
Gullah 9
Gumuz 46, 47, 48, 51, 54, 55, 56, 60, 72,
    273, 274
Gurage 80, 83
Gurma 26
Guro (Kweni) 20
Gurunsi 26
Gwamhi 32
Gwandara 246
Gwari 129, 159
Gǀui 102, 103, 116, 117
Gǁana 102, 103, 116, 117

Hadiyya 80, 92
Hadrami 79
Hadza 100, 102, 103, 104, 120, 198, 242,
    289, 290

Hainyaxo 20
Haitian 9
Haiǁ'om 102, 103
Hamer (Hamar) 81
Harsusi 80
Hassaniya 79
Hausa 77, 84, 92, 93, 97, 133, 141, 142,
    143, 145, 158, 162–3, 165, 167, 168,
    171, 172, 174, 177, 179, 180, 193, 197,
    204, 207, 223, 247, 251, 264–6, 268–9,
    270, 299, 303, 311, 312, 320, 324, 333,
    335, 338, 340, 344, 347
Heiban (*see also* Ebang) 40, 41
Hebrew 83, 92
Hebrew, Biblical 79
Hieratic 78
Hiecho 103
Hozo 82
Hun 32
Hungarian 250

Ịbạnị 22
Ibibio 33
Ibino 33
Ibuoro 33
Icelandic 193, 337
Idoma 31, 129
Idomoid *see* Idoma
Igede 158
Igbo 11, 31, 130, 131, 132, 133, 137, 138,
    185, 206, 207, 219, 220, 246, 334, 335
Igboid *see* Igbo
Ịjọ 15, 18, 22, 28, 38, 39, 129, 131, 137,
    185, 197, 242, 253
Ijoid *see* Ịjọ
Ik (Teuso) 44, 51, 61, 63, 67, 131, 139
Iko 33
Ikom 33
Ikwere 130, 159
Ilit 61, 66, 69
Ilue 33
Ilwana *see* Elwana
Ingessana *see* Gaam
Inuit 177
Iscamtho 314
Isoko 129
Italian 79
Itsekiri 305
Iyongiyong 3
Iraqw 58
Ịzọn 22

Jamaican creole 329
Jamsay tegu 23
Janjero 306
Jaya 45

Jen 28
Jeri (Jeli) 20
Jibbali 80
Jie 46
Jieng *see* Dinka
Jirru 46
Jɔ (Samogo-Don) 20, 21
Jɔgɔ 20
Jomang (Talodi) 19
Ju *see* Ju|'hoan
Juba Arabic 327
Jukun 32
Jukunoid *see* Jukun
Jur 47
Jur Modo 45
Ju|'hoan (Ju|'hoan si, Ju) 102, 103, 104,
    109, 110, 111, 112, 121
Jyang 282

Kaado 68
Kaba 45
Kaba-Dunjo 45
Kabiye (Kabre) 223
Kabre *see* Kabiye
Kabyle 76, 90, 92, 323
Kadu 46, 48, 51, 54, 55, 56, 58, 60, 73
Kadugli 17, 46
Kaficho 81
Kag 32
Kainji 31, 32
Kakia 102
Kakwa 46
Kalaḅari 22
Kalak (Katla) 19
Kalenjin 45, 51
Kaliko 45
Kam 18, 28
Kamba sɔɔ 23
Kambari 32
Kambata 80
Kamuku 32
Kamwe 77
Kana 33, 178, 190, 241, 255
Kanakuru 147, 267
Kanembu 44, 51
Kanga 46
Kanuri 44, 51, 61, 62, 178, 224, 234, 248,
    253, 254, 270, 282, 283, 286, 324, 340
Kara 45, 65
Kara *see* Fer
Karekare 265–6
Karimojong 46, 174
Karko 45
Karo 81
Kasanga 21
Kasem 28

Katcha (Kaca) 46, 63, 64
Katla *see* Kalak
Kebu 29
Keiga 46
Keiyo 46, 71
Kelo 46
Kemant (Kemantney, Qemant) 80, 89
Kendeje 44
Kenga 45
Kenzi 45
Kera 78
Khoekhoe (Nama/Damara) 104, 106, 113,
    115, 116, 117, 178
Khoekhoe, Cape 102
Kibet 44, 55
Kikongo *see* Kongo
Kikuyu *see* Gikuyu
Kim 28
Kimatuumbi *see* Matuumbi
Kinande *see* Nande
Kinyarwanda *see* Ruanda
Kiong 33
Kipsigis 46, 71
Ḳịrịkẹ (Okrika) 22
Kirma 26
Kirundi *see* Rundi
KiSettla 327
Kituba 327
Klao 25
Ko 19
Koalib 19
Kobiana 21
Kohumono 33
Kokit 64
Koma 131
Koman 48, 51, 52, 55, 56, 72, 273, 274
Komo 46, 61, 62, 65, 69
Kongo (Kikongo) 10, 11, 123
Konni 204
Kɔnɔ 20
Konso 81
Konyagi 21
Koorite 90
Koranko 20
Koring 33
Korop 33
Kouva 25
Kpelle 20, 347
Kposo (Akposo) 29, 238
Kresh 45, 61, 64, 65, 127
Krio 326, 327, 329
Krobu 29
Krongo 46, 65
Kru 18, 24, 28, 170, 189, 199, 208, 210
Kryôl 326
Kua 102, 114, 116

Kugbo 33
Kuka 45
Kukele 33
Kukuya 127
Kulango 26
Kullo 131
Kumam 46, 71
Kunama 45, 51, 52, 54, 62, 72, 273, 274,
    277, 283, 286, 287, 288
Kurumfe 26
Kuteb 148
Kuwaa 24, 25
Kwa 28
Kwadi 100, 102, 103, 119–20, 242
Kwadia 25
Kwama 46, 61, 64, 68
Kwara 80
Kwegu 45
Kweni *see* Guro
Kw'adza 81
Kxoe 102, 103, 104, 114, 115, 116, 117

Laal 36
Lafofa 41
Laka 45
Lamang 77, 178
Lango 46, 47, 71, 173
Lango 46, 47
Larteh 29
Laru 19, 32
Latin 176
Lefana *see* Lelemi
Legbo 33
Leko 28
Lela 32
Lelemi (Lefana) 29, 139
Lendu (*see also* Baledha) 51, 130, 139, 158
Liberian Pidgin English 327
Libyan, Old 77
Libyco-Berber *see* Berber
Ligbi 20
Liguri 46
Likpe 29, 139
Limba 21, 190
Linda (*see also* under Banda) 202, 203, 208
Lingala 11, 327
Lobala 206
Lobi 26
Logba 29
Logbara *see* Lugbara
Logo 45
Logone 92
Loko 20
Lokoya 46
Lolobi *see* Akpafu
Loma 347

Lombi 45
Lomorik (Tima) 19
Longuda 28
Looma 20
Lopa 32
Lopit 46
Loron 26
Lotuko 46
Luba 170
Luba-Kasai 11
Lugbara (Logbara) 45, 51, 208
Luhya *see* Luyia
Luluba 45
Luo 46, 47, 51, 62, 158
Lutos (Ruté) 45
Luyia (Luhya) 11
Lwo *see* Luo

Maa (Maasai, Chamus, Samburu) 46, 51,
    62, 174
Maale 185
Maasai (*see also* Maa) 46, 51, 57, 84, 85,
    172, 187, 198, 234, 286
Maba (Maban) 47, 51, 54, 55, 58, 61, 62,
    71, 72, 128
Mabang *see* Bora-Mabang
Madi (Ma'di) 45, 65, 147, 158, 199
Mafa 77
Majang (Mesengo) 45, 62
Maka *see* San
Malagasy 1, 250, 315
Male 82
Malkan 46
Maltese 79
Mambila 36, 139, 205, 216
Mamvu (Tengo) 45
Mandari 46
Manding (Mandingo, Mandekan) 20, 324
Mandinka 20, 244, 245, 320
Mangbetu 45, 49, 51, 61, 62, 130
Mangbutu 45, 51
Maninka 245
Mano 20
Mao 82
Margi 148, 263, 332
Masa 78, 246
Masakin *see* Ngile
Masalit 44, 61
Masana 78
Mashi *see* Shi
Mäsqan 80
Matuumbi 144, 158, 160
Mauritian French Creole 328
Maxay 279
Maya 20
Ma'a (Mbugu-Ma'a) 81, 332

Mbai 45
Mbatto 29
Mba 28
Mbe 35
Mbembe 33
Mbugu *see* Ma'a
Mbum 28, 127
Mbundu (Lunda) 11
Mebaan 47
Medogo 45
Mehri 80
Mekan *see* Me'en
Mende (Mɛnde) 10, 20, 152, 200, 239
Merarit 45
Merico (Americo) 327
Meroitic 43, 56
Mesengo *see* Majang
Me'en (Mekan) 45, 175, 179
Midob 45, 62
Migama 91, 97
Mikeyir *see* Shabo
Mimi 44, 47, 55, 69, 71
Minaean 79
Miri 46, 61
Miza 62, 65
Moda 45
Modo 45, 47, 51, 62
Mokulu 78
Molo 46
Mongo 46
Moore (Mõõre, Moré) 25, 189, 190, 315, 324
Morisyen 328
Moro 19
Morokodo 45
Moru 45, 51, 158
Mpre 36
Mubi 91, 97
Mudo 46
Muguji 45
Mumuye 28
Mupun 225
Murlé 45, 63, 285
Mursi 45
Musey 78
Musgu 77, 92
Mwa 20

Naath *see* Nuer
Nalu 21
Nama (*see also* Khoekhoe) 84, 102, 103, 104, 114, 115, 116, 172
Nande (Kinande) 193
Nandi 46, 71, 210
Nancere 78
NaNa tegu 23

Nara *see* Nera
Naro 102, 103, 104, 113, 114, 115, 116, 121
Nawdm 26, 210, 211, 218
Nayi 81
Ndebele 300, 340
Nding 19
Ndo 45
Negerhollands 9
Nembe 22, 183
Nera (Nara, Barea) 45, 51, 53, 56, 61, 63, 283
Ngam 45
Ngambai 45, 51
Ngbaka 28, 129
Ngbandi 28
Ngie 204, 216
Ngile (Masakin) 19
Ngiti 45, 139, 174, 196
Ngizim 77, 92, 93, 223, 224, 264
Nguni 300, 335, 340
Ngwe 138
Niaboua 25
Nigerian Pidgin 346
Nimbari 28
Nkọrọ 22
Nobiin 45, 51
Noni 216
Noon 205
Nootka 193
Nouchi 314
Nubian 45, 47, 50, 53, 58, 283, 286
Nubian, Hill 45, 51, 56
Nuer (Naadh) 46, 50, 51, 139
Numu 20
Nupe 31, 219, 220, 221, 306
Nupoid *see* Nupe
Nwa *see* Wan
Nyala 61
Nyala-Lagowa 46
Nyalgulgulé *see* Nyolgé
Nyamusa 45
Nyang 35
Nyangatom 46
Nyangbo-Tafi 29
Nyangi (Nyangiya) 44, 52, 62, 67
Nyima 45, 51
Nyimang (*see also* Ama) 61, 282
Nyolgé (Nyalgulgulé) 46
Nzema-Ahanta 29

Obolo 33
Odual 33
Ogbia 33
Ogoi *see* Baan
Ogoni 33
Oigob *see* Maasai

Okiek-Sogoo 46
Okọ 31
Okobo 33
Okollo 45
Okordia *see* Akịta
Okpẹ 137, 188, 305
Okrika *see* Kịrịkẹ
Ometo 82, 89, 90, 91, 97
Ongamo 46
Ongota (Biralé) 56
Opo (Shita) 46, 47, 48, 62, 68, 282
Orig 41
Orma (*see also* Oromo) 181
Oro 33
Oromo ('Galla') 81, 84, 213, 216, 234, 253, 319
Oru yille 23
Oruma 22

Pajade 21
Päkot (Pokot) 46, 71
Papel 21
Papiamentu 9
Pari 250
Pero 246
Petit Mauresque 326
Petit-Nègre 327
Peul *see* Fulfulde
Phera 29
Phla 29
Phoenician 79
Pokot *see* Päkot
Pongu 32
Portuguese 1, 322, 343
Pre *see* Bɛrɛ
Pulaar *see* Fulfulde
Punic 79

Qatabanian 79

Rashad 41
Rendille 81, 280
Reshe 32
Réunionnais 328
Rif 323
Ron 77
Ron-Daffo 91, 97
Rongé (*see also* Temein) 65
Ruanda (Kinyarwanda) 224, 315
Rundi (Kirundi) 164, 186, 315
Runga 44
Russian 250
Ruté *see* Lutos

Saare 32
Sabaean 79

Saho 80, 84
Sai 61, 63, 67
Samburu (*see also* Maa) 46
Samo, South *see* San
Samogo-Tougan 20
San (South Samo, Maka) 20
Sandawe 100, 102, 103, 104, 118–19, 120, 242, 250, 253, 289, 290
Sane 20
Sango 324, 327
Samogo-Don *see* Jɔ
Samogo-Guan *see* Dzuun
Samogo-Tougan 20
Santrokofi 29
Sapiny 46
Sar 45
Sara 45, 239
Saramaccan 9
Sebei 46
Sembla 20, 21, 39
Sɛmɛ 24, 25
Senufo 18, 25, 26, 28, 39, 197
Sere 28
Sereer (Serer) 15, 21, 130, 165
Sesé 66
Seselwa *see* Seychellois
Sesotho *see* Sotho
Setswana *see* Tswana
Seychellois (Seselwa) 328
Shabo (Mikeyir) 43, 56
Shakacho 81
Shanga 20
Shatt 46
Sheko 81
Shemya (Sinyar) 45
Sheng 314
Sherbro 21
Shi (Mashi) 182
Shilha 89
Shilluk (Colo) 46, 128, 134, 142, 143, 144, 306
Shinasha (*see also* Gonga) 91
Shirumba 19
Shita *see* Opo
Shona 148, 333, 334, 336
Shua 79, 102
Sidamo 80, 93
Sila 46
Sillok 46
Silt'i (Silt'e, Silti) 80, 198, 203, 211, 219, 214
Sinyar *see* Shemya
Soddo 80
Sogoo 46
Sokoro 78
Somali (Soomaali) 57, 158, 216, 234, 253, 279, 280, 315, 333, 335, 338, 339

Somrai 47
Songay (Songhay, Songhai) 17, 44, 47, 51,
  52, 54, 59, 61, 62, 72, 190, 210, 252,
  282, 283, 286, 324, 340, 346
Soninke (Azer) 20, 239
Soo (Tepeth, Tepes) 44, 58, 69
Sooso (Soso, Susu) 20, 239
Sorko *see* Sorogama
Soqotri 80
Sorogama (Sorko) 20
Soso *see* Sooso
Sotho 148, 335, 340
Sotho, Northern 11, 300, 340
Sotho, Southern 138, 150, 300, 315, 340
Spanish 1, 322, 343
Sua 21, 22
Sukuma 11
Sukur 77
Sulaimitian 79
Sungor 45
Supyire 198, 199, 204
Surbakhal 44
Suri 45
Susu *see* Soso
Swahili (Kiswahili) 11, 158, 161–2, 163,
  165, 173, 176, 179, 180, 189, 197, 205,
  212, 223, 226, 227, 270, 278, 315, 320,
  324, 333, 335, 347
Swati (Swazi) 236, 245, 300, 340
Swazi *see* Swati
Sya *see* Bobo

Tabi *see* Gaam
Tadaksahak 44
Tafi *see* Nyangbo-Tafi
Tagoi 19
Tai *see* Tee̩
Talodi (Jomang) 19, 41
Tama 45, 51, 55, 56, 58, 61
Tamazight (Tamajaq) 76, 210, 211
Tarifit 76
Tarok 31, 32
Tasawaq 332
Tashelhit (Tashilhait) 76, 313
Tatoga *see* Datooga
Teda 44, 62, 66
Tee̩ (Tai) 33
Tegali 19
Tegem 19
Teke 127
Tekrur 327
Tem *see* Grusi
Tembisa Mixed Language 314
Temein (Rongé) 46, 51, 56, 282, 285
Temne 21, 128, 158
Tene kã, 23

Tengo *see* Mamvu
Tennet 45
Tepes *see* Soo
Tera 77, 158, 207, 263
Tesé 46
Teso (Ateso) 46, 51, 139, 173
Teuso *see* Ik
Thuri (Turi) 46
Tibu (*see also* Tubu) 286
Tiegba 24, 25
Tieyaxo 20
Tiɛma Cɛwɛ 20
Tigre 80, 234
Tigrinya 80, 91, 128
Tikar 34, 35
Tima (Lomorik) 19
Tirma 45
Tiro 19
Tishena 45
Tocho 19
Tombo kã, 23
Tombo sɔɔ 23
Tonga 158
Topotha 46
Tornasi 46
Toro sɔɔ 23
Toro tegu 23
Toussian *see* Win
Town Bemba 328
Tsamay 81
Tsonga 11, 127
Tsotsitaal 314
Tsua 102
Tswana (Setswana) 11, 117, 237, 243, 255,
  300, 340
Ts'ixa 102, 104, 117
Tuareg 44, 76, 91, 292
Tubu 44, 66
Tugen (Tuken) 46, 71
Tuken *see* Tugen
Tulishi 46, 67, 69
Tumak 78
Tumma 46
Tumtum 17
Tura (Wen) 20
Turi *see* Thuri
Turkana 46, 139, 164, 166, 168, 173,
  186–7, 190, 199, 200, 205, 216,
  280
Turkish 176
Turoyo 79
Twi (*see also* Akan) 10
Tyefo 26
Tyenga 20
Tyurama 26
T'wampa (Uduk) 46, 47, 61, 62

Uda 33
Uduk *see* T'wampa
Ugaritic 79
Ukaan 30, 31
Ukpet 33
Umbundu 11
Ura 32
Usaghade 33
Utoro 19

Vai 20, 347
Valé 45
Venda 150
Viemo 26
Vute 36, 216

Waja 28
Wali 45
Wan (Nwa) 20
Wane 25
Wara-Natioro 26
Warji 77
Warnang 19
Wela 20
Wen *see* Tura
Wes Cos *see* West African Pidgin
West African Pidgin (Wes Cos) 314
Wetawit *see* Berta
Win (Toussian) 26
Wobé 25, 170
Wolaytta 82
Wolof 11, 15, 21, 236, 249
Wuri 32

Xamtanga 80
Xhosa 11, 150, 300, 301, 305, 340

Yaaku 80
Yakoro 33
Yakuba *see* Dan
Yalunka 20
Yanda dom 23
Yaure 20
Yękhee 134

Yemsa 82, 97
Yendang 28
Yeniseian 13
Yeyi 150, 151
Yom 26
Yoruba 10, 11, 27, 31, 158, 196, 221, 306
Yoruboid *see* Yoruba
Yulu 45, 62
Yungur 28
Yupik 176

Zagawa (Zaghawa) 44, 49, 61, 66, 286
Zande 28, 158, 236, 242
Zarma (Zerma, Gao; *see also* Songay) 44,
    62, 66, 68, 69, 70, 238, 303, 340
Zayse 92, 128
Zenaga 77
Zerma *see* Zarma
Zilmamu 45
Zulgo 212
Zulu 11, 150, 245, 300, 305, 340
Zumaya 78

|Xaise 102, 114
|Xam 102, 103, 113
|'Auni 102

!Ora 102, 114, 115, 116, 117
!Xóõ, (!Xõõ), 101, 102, 103, 104, 106, 108,
    110, 111, 112, 121, 139, 148, 150, 151,
    159, 160
!Xũũ (!Xun, !Xũ; *see also* Juǀ'hoan) 103,
    110, 159, 199
!'O-!Xũũ (*see also* !Xũũ) 102

‡Aakhoe 102, 103
‡Haba 102, 115, 116, 117
‡Hoõã 101, 102, 103, 104, 110, 111, 112,
    113, 121
‡Khomani 102

ǁAni 102, 103, 114, 115, 116, 117, 121, 122
ǁXegwi 102, 103
ǁX'auǁ'e 102

INDEX OF SUBJECTS

absolutive 88
accent 303, 311
    social 303
accusative 234
acquisition planning 346
acrolect 329
adjective 195
    adjectival modifier **249–50**, 266–7
    phrase 229
adjunct 214
adposition 195, **247–8**
    adpositional phrase 113, **200–1**
advanced tongue root, *see* distinctive
    feature
adverb 195, 196
affix 12–13
    circumfix 165
    infix 165
    phrasal affix 245, 247, *see also* clitic:
        special clitic
    possessive affix 248, 249
    prefix **38–9**, 165
    suffix 165
    suprafix 165, 174, 263
agreement 201
    agreement morpheme 235, 249
alienable (possession) 249
allophone 165
alphabetic writing 82
ambivalent 137
analogical realignment 310
Ancient Stage 91
anti-edge effect 159
apartheid 301, 335, 341, 302
areal 260–1

areal feature 331
areal grouping (classification) 9, 59, 34,
    57–60
aspect 230
association line 155
Autosegmental Phonology 153
auxiliary **206–8**, **239**
    auxiliary phrase 199
    auxiliary verb 198

basic vocabulary **39–41**, 287, *see also*
    vocabulary
basilect 329
bilingualism, *see* multilingualism, polyglossia
bioprogram 330
bisegmental analysis 144–6
block pattern 58
borrowing 13, 59, 181, 261–2, **269–71**, 312,
    317, *see also* loanwords
    ad hoc borrowing 346
branch 12
branching 16

calque 181
case 214
    case affix **247–8**
    case marker **88–90**, **93**
    case marking typology **233–4**
caste 302
category shift 170
causative 39, 63, 213
chronolect 320
clause 232
    adjectival clause 222, **225–8**
    adverbial clause **222–3**

clause constituent order 250
complement clause 222
consecutive, *see* consecutive construction
dependent clause, *see* secondary clause,
    subordinate clause
embedded clause, *see* secondary clause,
    subordinate clause
main clause 199, 217
nominal clause 222, **223–5**
relative clause 199, 222, 255–6
secondary clause 217, 221–2, *see also*
    subordinate clause
subordinate clause 199, *see also*
    secondary clause
click, *see* consonant
accompaniment, *see* consonant
clitic 180
    cliticisation 249
    enclitic 180
    proclitic 180
    simple 180
    special clitic 180, *see also* affix: phrasal
        affix
cluster **144–52**
    liquid cluster **146–7**
    nasal cluster **147–8**
    obstruent cluster **148–50**
coda 140
code 299
    code-changing, *see* code-mixing
    code-choice, *see* code-mixing
    code-mixing 299, 303, **317–19**, 331
    code-switching, *see* code-mixing
    codification 332, 334, **336–7**
collective 190
command **203**
communicative distance 304
commutation 145
comparative linguistics 260
Comparative Method 60, **265–7**
comparative reconstruction, *see*
    reconstruction
comparison 53–4, 85, 86, 259, **262–4**
complement 195, 200, 229
    complementation 257
    complementiser 223–5
complex construction **255–7**
compositionality 145
compound 113, 167, **167–70**
    appositional compound, *see* co-ordinate
        compound
    compound sentence **217–21**
    co-ordinate compound 168
    endocentric compound 168
    exocentric compound 168
    root compounding 185

serial compound, *see* co-ordinate
    compound
synthetic compound 168
concord 12, 39
conjunction 195, 196
conjunctive meaning 164
consecutive construction **219–20**
consonant **37–8**
    click 107, **150–2**; click accompaniment
        150–2
    cluster 145
    coronal 127–8
    dorsal 128–9
    feature **126–34**
    labial 127
    labial-velar 129, 37
    laryngeal 128–9
    lenis 37
    pharyngeal 128–9
    sonorant 132–3
    stop: ejective 131; implosive 130–1,
        132–3
contour segment 152, 159
converb 219
convergence 5, 17, 310, 331
conversion, *see* derivation: zero derivation
co-ordination **217–18**
copula 62–3
corpus planning 332, 333
creole 299, 322, **325–30**
    creolisation 314, 326, 346
    decreolisation 329
    post-creole continuum 329
cultivation 334, **339**
culture **48–50**, **82–3**, **275–6**, **278–80**

Dahl's Law 268
declarative sentence 203
definiteness **243–6**
deictic pattern 62
demonstrative 115
dependent marking **187–8**
derivation **170–5**
    derivational marker 170
    derivative verbal extension 116
    zero derivation 173
determination **334–6**
determiner 195
dialect 1–3, 76, **299–301**, 311
    dialect chain 31, 301, 313
    dialect cluster 34, 50
    dialect continuum, *see* dialect chain
    dialect geography 311
    dialectology **311–14**
diglossia 79, **322–4**, 331, 346, *see also*
    triglossia

digraph 337
discourse 115
discrimination 301, 302
disjunctive meaning 164
distinctive feature 126
  ATR (advanced tongue root) 36, **135–8**
  fortis **133–4**
  lenis **133–4**
divergence 310
domain **307**, 331
dominance 330
dorsal 127
drift 264, 267, 311

economy, principle of 124, 159
edge effect 146, 159
education 309
efflux 105, 151
elaboration 334, **337–8**, 346
emphasis 130, **214–17**, *see also* focus
endoglossic (language policy) 308, 341,
  342–3
ergative 234
ethnic
  ethnic identity 301
  ethnic language 320, 322
ethnolect 332
euphemism 305
exoglossic (language policy) 341, **342–3**
exponent 163
  cumulative exponence 163
  extended exponence 164
  fused exponence 164
external planning, *see* status planning

factitive 63
family 75
  family tree 260, 273
feature 159
focus 194, 201, 214
free morpheme 238

gender **94**
  gender marker 64, **95**
  gender system 242–3
genetic
  classification 9, 50, 52, **54–7**, 59
  grouping **11–14**, 34, 51
  relationship 273
glottochronology 285, 287, 296
glottophagia 324, 346
grammaticalisation 10, 13, 267, 311

harmonisation 334, **339–40**
head (of a compound) 168
head (of a phrase) 195

head-final 110, 168
head-initial 168
head-marking **187–8**
heterorganic affricate 148
historical linguistics 260
hlonipa 305
homonymy (homophony) 166
horizontal domain, *see* sequential domain
horizontal media 308
hypercorrection 304, 310

iconicity **185–7**
idealised norm 334
identity **301–3**
ideological system 48
ideophone 196
idiolect 299, 303
imbrication 185
imperative (mood) 203
imperfect language learning 309,
  310
imperfect learning theory 329
imperfect participle 91
implementation 334, **338–9**
inalienable (possession) 249
index of agglutination 177
indexation 233
  indexation typology **235–6**
indicative mood 203
indirect object 199
inflection **170–5**
  inflectional marker 170
  nominal inflection 237–8
influx 105, 150
informant 313
innovation 54, 59
  grammatical innovation 56
  lexical innovation 16, 19, 337
  shared innovation 264
instrumental 214
intelligibility
  intercomprehension 312
  mutual intelligibility 1, **312–13**
intensifier 195
interjection 195
interlarded speech 318
interlinear glossing 161, 163
interlocking pattern 58
internal modification 175
internal reconstruction **267–8**
internationalisation 341
interrogative
  clause 199
  formative 65
  mood 203
intimacy 305

isogloss 312, 313
  bundles of isogloss 313
isolex 313
isomorph 313
isophone 313
isoseme 313
item 183
Item and Arrangement 183
Item and Process 183

juncture 116
juxtaposition **218–19**

kinship terminology 173
Klingenheben's Law 268–9
koine 311, 322

labial 127
labialisation 37
language 1–3, 76, **299–301, 301–3**
  African language **1–3,** 13
  agglutinative language 176
  attitude **307–8,** 331
  barrier 308; horizontal language barrier
    308; vertical language barrier 308–9
  birth 326
  change 273–5, 298, **309–14**
  classical language 321
  classification **14–17,** 35, **52–60, 83–6,**
    99–103, 231, **259–65;** *see also* areal
    grouping, genetic classification,
    subclassification, typological
    classification, genetic grouping,
    subgrouping, typological grouping
  click language 99
  community language 320
  contact 346
  cross-border language 320, 340
  death 6, 299, **330–1**
  divergence 273–5
  ethnic language 320, 322
  evolution 273–5
  family 4
  family tree **17**
  first language 321
  foreign language 320, 342
  function **319–32**
  fusional language 176
  head-final language 200
  head-initial language 200
  innovating language **63–5**
  Inter-African language 320
  isolating language 176
  lingua franca 299, 320, **324–30**
  local language 320, 322
  major language (majority language) 321

maintenance 299, **331–2**
  minor language (minority language) 321
  mixed language 53
  mother tongue 299, 320, 321
  name 44–5, 46–8
  national language 1, 308, 320, 321, 322,
    334, 341
  non-standard(ised) language 321
  of African intercommunication 320
  of wider communication 304, 320
  official language 308, 320, 321, 322, 334,
    341
  planning 299, **332–43**
  proto-language 260, 265, 266, 273, 276
  regional language 320
  second language 321
  shift 299, 308, **330–1**
  special-purpose language 320, 321
  standard language 321, 332
  standardisation 299, **332–40**
  subclassification 33, **264–5**
  subgrouping 85–6
  symbolic language 176
  tonal accent language 157
  tribal language 320
  use 298, **305–7**
  variation 298, **299**
  variety 2, 76, 298, 344
  verb-serialising language 109
laryngeal feature **130–1**
lect 303
lenis, *see* consonant
lexical mass comparison, *see* comparison
lexicalisation pattern **191–2**
lexicon **60–3, 65–8, 94–5**
lexicostatistics 16, 19, 34
lingua franca 299, 320, **324–30**
linguicide 324, 346, *see also* language
    death, glottophagia
linguistic
  accommodation **303–4,** 330–1
  assimilation 308, 341
  geography 311
  pluralism 341
  stratigraphy 281–5, **273–5, 276–7**
loanword 87, 278, 280, 310, 312, 346,
    see also borrowing
locative 214
lumper 3, 102

macrophylum 16–17
markedness 126
mass comparison, *see* comparison
meaning 164
medium of instruction 309, 317
mesolect 329

metaphorical code-switching 318
minimal contrast 159
minor articulation 129–30
modernisation 334
modifier 195, 229
  adjectival modifier **249–50**, 266–7
  genitival modifier **248–9**
monogenesis 329
monosegmental analysis 144–6
monovalent 137–8
mora structure **141–4**
morph 162, **165–7**
  empty morph 183
morpheme 161, 165
  agreement morpheme 235, 249
  bound morpheme 165, 247
  content morpheme 165
  functional morpheme 165
  grammatical morpheme **263–4**
  lexeme 120, 179, *see also* content
    morpheme
  portmanteau morpheme 163
  suprasegmental morpheme 164
morphology **60–3**, **188–9**, 261
  morphological typology **175–9**;
    agglutinative 176; analytic 176;
    fusional 176; isolating 176;
    polysynthetic 176; symbolic 176;
    synthetic 176
  non-agglutinative morphology 177
  non-concatenative morphology, *see* non-
    agglutinative morphology
  vertical morphology 176
mother tongue 299, 320, 321
multilateral comparison, *see* comparison
multilingualism 308, **314–32**, 343, *see also*
    polyglossia
  individual multilingualism 314, **316–19**
  institutional multilingualism 314, **319–24**
  unstable multilingualism 346

nasal consonant **132**
nation state profile 314
national harmonisation 339–40
natural class (of sounds) 126
negation 65, 117, **205–8**
  constituent negation 205
  predicate negation 205
  negative particle 207
neologism 305
neutralisation 172, 174
non-verbal predication **254–5**
normalisation 334, 337
noun 195
  class 111–12, 114, 236, **189–91**; class
    affixation 165; class concord system

202–3; class marker 161; class system
    12, 13, 15, 34, **38–9**, 202, 242;
    classification 111–12, 114, **189–91**,
    241–3
  incorporation 169
  phrase 195, **200–4**, 229, 232, **241–50**
  prefix 58
number 62, 64, **246–7**

object 196, **233–7**
oblique 89
obsolescence 174
occupation 309
onset 140

palatalisation 37
pan-Africanism 60
paradigm 161–2, 193
  paradigmatic axis 161
  vertical axis, *see* paradigmatic axis
participant 298
particle 215
passive 116, **208–14**, 236–7
  passive-intransitive 65
  passive sentence 208–9
pattern 167
person marker 162
PGN (person-gender-number) suffix 113
pharyngealisation 159
phonaestheme 183
phoneme 165
  phoneme system 125
  phoneme type 124
  phonemic inventory **124–6**
phonetic transcription 313
phonology **36–8**, **68–70**, **94–5**, **188–9**
  phonological alternation 142
  phonological quantity **139–44**
  phonological system **105–7**
  phonological word **179–82**
phrase 195
  adjective phrase 229
  adpositional phrase 113, **200–1**
  auxiliary phrase 199
  locational phrase 200
  noun phrase 195, **200–4**, 229, 232,
    241–50
  temporal phrase 200
  verb phrase 195, **201–2**, 229; verb phrase
    particle **206–8**
phylum 4, **43**, 75
pidgin 299, 322, **325–30**
  pidginisation 309, 325, 346
place of articulation 105–7, 125, **127–30**
pluractional 13, 267
plural formative **91–2**

points of elicitation 313
politeness 305
political correctness 305
politics 48, 49, 299, **340–3**
polygenesis 329–30
polyglossia 343, 346, *see also*
    multilingualism
polyglot 343
polysemy 166
population 50
possession 170
    alienable 249
    possessive 249
post-creole continuum 329
postposition 195, 247
pragmatic 246, 298
predicative marker 239
Prefix Conjugation 90
preposition 195, 247
present stem 91
productivity 174, 181
proficiency 316
pronoun 195
    anaphoric 202, 203
    logophoric 225
    pattern 60–2
    personal **87–8**
    possessive 249
    subject 235
proposition 194
prosodic structure 193
prosodic system **152–8**
proto-language 260, 265, 266, 273, 276
proto-pidgin 329

question **203–5**
    indirect question 203
    marker 203
    WH-question 204
    yes/no question 203, 204

race 50, 302
reciprocal 39
    sentence 212
reconstruction 11–14, 19–20, **36**, 39–41,
    53, 85, 259, **265–8**, *see also* internal
    reconstruction, syntactic
    reconstruction
reduplication 167, 193
    complete reduplication 167
    partial reduplication 167
    triplication 167
referent 115
    referentiality 305, **243–6**
reflex 276–7
reflexive 237

reflexive sentence 212
register 299, 344
register tone system 38
relatedness of meaning 166
relatedness of morphosyntactic function
    166
relative clause 199, 222, 255–6
    relativisation 255–6
relexification 326, 330
religion 49, *see also* ideological system
reorientation 347
respect 305
retention 54, 264
role 301
rule of transitivity in language relatedness
    261

secondary articulation, *see* minor
    articulation
segmental tier 141
semantic 246–7
    semantic roles: agent 210; benefactive
        199, 210, 221; locative 214; patient
        210
sentence
    complex sentence **217**, **221–8**
    compound sentence **217–21**
    simple sentence 203, **195–217**
separability 145
sequential domain 161
setting 298
sex gender 58
    system 13
simple exponence 164
simplification 346
social
    accent 303
    distance 304
    identity 302
    planning, *see* status planning
    stratification **301–3**
sociolect 300, 311, 314
sociolinguistics **104–5**, 275–6, **303–4**
    sociolinguistic context 298
solidarity 233
sound
    change **107–8**, 268
    correspondence 34, 38, 68–70, **107–8**,
        262; regular sound correspondence
        265, **277–8**; sound-meaning
        correspondence 15, 68, 86
    law **268–9**
    shift 277
    symbolism 261
SOV 197
special purpose function 342

specialisation (semantic unpredictability)
168
specifier 195, 199, 229, 298
speech act 298
Speech Act Theory 343
splitter 3, 102
Sprachbund 331
stage II article 244–5
standard orthogprahy 336
stative 90
status 301
planning 332, 333
strength oscillation 107
stridency 159
subject 196, **233–7**
pronoun 235
substratum theory 329
SVO 197
Swadesh list 287
syllable **139–44**
structure **140–4**
tier 141
weight 142, 159
syncretism (inflectional homonymy) 172
syntactic function 170
syntactic reconstruction 266–7
syntactic typology **184–5**
synthesis 176

taboo 305
tag switching 318
TAM distinction 239
tense 115–16, 162, 230
terminology 333
tier 153
quantity tier 141
skeleton, *see* quantity tier
timing tier, *see* quantity tier
tone **38, 152–8**
contour tone 152, 153; contour tone
system 38
floating tone 153, 155
spreading tone 153
tonal accent language 157
tone case 234, 248
tone class 155
tone level 152
tone melody 153
tone shift 153
topic 194, 201, **208–14**, 298
topicality hierarchy 236
totalisation 180
trade economy 82
transcription 336
transitive 63
transmission 310

transposition 171
tree 14, 17
triglossia 323, 346, *see also* diglossia
trigraph 337
triplication 167
typology **36, 105–7**, 260–1
case marking typology **233–4**
implicational typology, *see* universal
typology
indexation typology **235–6**
morphological typology **175–9**
syntactic typology **184–5**
typological 13; typological classification
57–60; typological grouping **11–14**
universal typology 311
word order typology 58–9, **250–4**

underlying form 162
universal language learning theory 330
Urheimat **95**
Ursprache, *see* proto-language

valence 212, 233
vehicular language, *see* lingua franca
velarisation 37
verb 195, 196, **237–41**
applied verbal extension 39
auxiliary verb 198
complex verb form 239
conjugation **90–1**
consecutive verb form 257
derivation **93**; derivative verbal
extension 116
phrase 195, **201–2**, 229; particle
206–8
serial verb **240**; construction **220–1**;
serialisation 185, 241
sequential verb form, *see* consecutive
verb form
verb-serialising language 109
verbal affix **206**
verbal auxiliary 206
verbal extension **39**
verbal inflection **237–9**
verbal negation 63
verbal root compounding 184
verbal word **206–8**
vernacular 308, 320, 322
vernacularisation 341
vertical media 308–9
vocabulary 261, *see also* basic vocabulary
voice **208–14, 236–7**
applicative voice **236–7**
middle voice 237
quality 139
volitive mood 224

vowel **36–7**
  feature **134–9**
  vowel harmony **134–8**; cross-height
    vowel harmony system 136; dominant
    vowel harmony system 135; root-
    controlled vowel harmony system 135
VSO 197

Wanderwörter 59–60
word 179, *see also* loanword, borrowing
  complex word 121
  grammatical word 167, **179–82**
  order **39**, 194, 197, 266–7; basic word
    order 197; dominant word order 59;
    typology 58–9, **250–4**
  phonological word **179–82**

primary word category **195–6**
  simple word 121
  verbal word **206–8**
word formation 93, 181
  acronym 181
  back formation 182
  blending 182
  clipping 181
  folk etymology 181
  language 320
Word and Paradigm 184
Words and Things Hypothesis 310
Wörter und Sachen, *see* Words and Things
  Hypothesis
writing 78, 82

zone of constriction 129